AFRICAN HISTORICAL DICTIONARIES
Edited by Jon Woronoff

1. *Cameroon*, by Victor T. LeVine and Roger P. Nye. 1974
2. *The Congo (Brazzaville)*, by Virginia Thompson and Richard Adloff. 1974
3. *Swaziland*, by John J. Grotpeter. 1975
4. *The Gambia*, by Harry A. Gailey. 1975
5. *Botswana*, by Richard P. Stevens. 1975
6. *Somalia*, by Margaret F. Castagno. 1975
7. *Dahomey*, by Samuel Decalo. 1975
8. *Burundi*, by Warren Weinstein. 1976
9. *Togo*, by Samuel Decalo. 1976
10. *Lesotho*, by Gordon Haliburton. 1977
11. *Mali*, by Pascal James Imperato. 1977
12. *Sierra Leone*, by Cyril Patrick Foray. 1977
13. *Chad*, by Samuel Decalo. 1977
14. *Upper Volta*, by Daniel Miles McFarland. 1978
15. *Tanzania*, by Laura S. Kurtz. 1978
16. *Guinea*, by Thomas O'Toole. 1978
17. *Sudan*, by John Voll. 1978
18. *Rhodesia/Zimbabwe*, by R. Kent Rasmussen. 1979.
19. *Zambia*, by John J. Grotpeter. 1979.
20. *Niger*, by Samuel Decalo. 1979.

Historical Dictionary
of
RHODESIA/ZIMBABWE

by

R. Kent Rasmussen

African Historical Dictionaries, No. 18

The Scarecrow Press, Inc.
Metuchen, N.J. & London
1979

Library of Congress Cataloging in Publication Data

Rasmussen, R   Kent.
    Historical dictionary of Rhodesia/Zimbabwe.

    (African historical dictionaries ; no. 18)
    Bibliography: p.
    1.   Rhodesia, Southern--History--Dictionaries.
I.   Title.   II.   Series.
DT962. 5. R37   968. 9'1'003   78-23671
ISBN 0-8108-1187-1

To

Zimbabwe's future historians,

whose perspectives on present problems will be much
better than ours

EDITOR'S FOREWORD

No African country has been a hot spot for as long as the country variously known as Rhodesia or Zimbabwe. Its nearly two decade history of almost perpetual crisis has generated a tremendous amount of writing, including the serious, popular, and outright propagandistic. In this atmosphere of controversy and confusion the present dictionary is particularly welcome, for it will help both novice and expert "Africanists" to work their way through the maze of people, places, organizations, and events of Rhodesia's busy recent past. But, no matter what happens to Rhodesia/Zimbabwe in the future, this dictionary makes a further contribution which will continue to make the book an essential part of any Africana library: it sheds considerable light on Rhodesia's more remote past.

All too much of what has been written on southern Africa, or on Africa generally, neglects the deeper background of recent events. The history of Rhodesia itself is too frequently seen as having begun with the occupation of the country by Europeans in the late 19th century. However, much of great importance, and of great interest, occurred well before Cecil Rhodes established his empire. A sound understanding of that past serves as an indispensable foundation for understanding what is going on today, as well as what may happen tomorrow, when the country becomes Zimbabwe. For this reason the author of this dictionary has thoroughly covered the broad sweep of the country's history, and has not limited the book to only the most recent events.

The author of this dictionary, Dr. R. Kent Rasmussen, has visited and studied much of southern Africa, and has written broadly on the continent's history. His particular specialization has been the history of the Ndebele people, on whom he has written two books.

But, while his obvious interests lie in pre-colonial history, he has also done an extraordinary job of attaining objectivity and impartiality in covering the controversial recent period in this dictionary. This in itself is a laudable achievement for both the author and the series, since these dictionaries aim to enhance readers' understanding of Africa, particularly of those regions where authorities all too frequently gloss over or distort facts which do not fit in with their own political views.

Jon Woronoff
Series Editor

TABLE OF CONTENTS

Editor's Foreword (Jon Woronoff)   v

List of Maps   viii

Acknowledgments   ix

Note on the Names "Rhodesia" and "Zimbabwe"   xi

Notes on Use of the Dictionary   xii

Abbreviations   xv

Chronology   xix

Introduction   1

THE DICTIONARY   9

THE BIBLIOGRAPHY [see detailed table of bibliography
    contents beginning on page 369]   372

LIST OF MAPS

1	Rhodesia, showing provinces	2
2	Altitudinal Zones	18
3	Annual Rainfall Distribution	65
4	Minerals	189
5	Transportation System	326

All maps are reprinted from H. D. Nelson, et al.,
Area Handbook for Southern Rhodesia (Washington, D.C.:
U.S. Gov. Printing Office, 1975), with the permission of
the Director of Foreign Area Studies, the American University.

ACKNOWLEDGMENTS

This book is the product of a more solitary effort than I would have preferred, but I have nevertheless been fortunate in having friends who have given generously of their time. I am particularly indebted to Christopher Ehret for encouraging me at every stage of my work, and for reading and commenting on the entire manuscript. Oliver Pollak also read the entire manuscript and contributed valuable suggestions. My wife Nancy helped with the mind-numbing task of proof-reading at each stage, while providing the tangible support which enabled me to get through the entire project.

I am also indebted to James Armstrong, L. W. Bolze, and E. E. Burke for providing information and encouragement over several years. Julian Cobbing kindly gave me a copy of his fine thesis on Ndebele history, enabling me to make that subject one of the strongest sections of this book. Oliver and Karen Pollak gave me a copy of their incredible bibliography, thereby saving me from much legwork.

My own bibliography in the present book lists most of my published sources, but I would nevertheless like to give special thanks to the authors and compilers of the various handbooks, year-books, and encyclopedias which made my task easier. I would also like to call attention to the handful of authorities upon whose writings I have drawn most often. At the risk of omitting a deserving name or two, I offer special thanks to David Beach, L. H. Gann, Peter Garlake, Michael Gelfand, George Kay, T. O. Ranger, Roger Summers, E. C. Tabler, G. H. Tanser, and Lawrence Vambe. Theirs were the books which never seemed to leave my sight.

I would like readers to note that I completed the main text of this dictionary during the first two months of 1978. Much of importance has happened in Rhodesia since then, but I have made only minor additions and corrections to the dictionary entries. However, I have updated the Chronology section (pages xix-xxiv) through late November 1978, the moment the book is being prepared for the printers.

R. Kent Rasmussen
Los Angeles, California

NOTE ON THE NAMES
"RHODESIA" AND "ZIMBABWE"

The titles of all volumes in the African Historical Dictionaries Series have contained the names of countries used by their
respective governments. Rhodesia presents a special case. Since
1964 the white government there has called the country "Rhodesia."
No other country officially recognizes this name, and the United
Nations and Britain officially call the country "Southern Rhodesia."
In the meantime, African nationalists have called the country "Zimbabwe," but this name also is not officially recognized by any government. As this book was being proofread in late 1978, however,
the white government of Rhodesia has moved towards acceptance of
a political transformation which will put the country's African majority in power. When and if this transition is carried out, it appears almost inevitable that the new African government will change
the name of the country to "Zimbabwe." The title of this book,
Historical Dictionary of Rhodesia/Zimbabwe, therefore reflects this
transitional status.

Entries within the dictionary refer to the country as "Rhodesia," except in historical contexts which allow for the use of such
contemporary names as "Southern Rhodesia." The etymologies and
applications of the above and other changing place names are fully
discussed under their respective dictionary entries.

ALPHABETIZATION OF ENTRIES

All entries are alphabetized by individual words, not whole
phrases, as in this simplified sequence:

> RHODESIA RAILWAYS COMPANY
> RHODESIAN AFRICAN RIFLES
> RHODESIANA

Personal names take precedence in any given sequence. Thus,
HARTLEY, HENRY precedes HARTLEY (the town). No distinctions
are made between "first" and "last" names of pre-20th-century Africans with obviously non-Christian names. A name such as MBIGO
MASUKU is therefore entered under MBIGO. Prefixes are dropped
from Bantu proper names; e. g. , for MASHONA see SHONA. Non-
proper Bantu nouns are entered under their singular forms; e. g. ,
IBUTHO (pl. , amabutho). To aid in the understanding of prefixes,
the dictionary contains individual entries on important class prefixes,
such as ABA-, BA-, CHI-, MA-, and many others. Broader discussions of prefixes can be found in the entries on BANTU, CHI-
SHONA, and SINDEBELE.

CROSS-REFERENCES

In the interest of making information as easy to locate as
possible, several forms of cross-referencing are employed throughout the dictionary. Names and terms of special pertinence to the
entries in which they appear are followed by "q. v. " (quod vide,
"which see"; plural, qq. v.). Less pertinent terms, most typically
place names, are simply starred (*). Additional cross-references

are occasionally enclosed in parentheses with the words "see also" or "cf." (confer, "compare").

DATES

Wherever possible exact dates are given. Unqualified dates may be regarded as firm. Dates qualified by "c." (circa, "about") are informed approximations. Dates divided by slash lines, such as "1824/5," represent "either/or" estimates. Rougher estimates of dates are generally given as decades, such as the "1790s." Note that an expression such as "1800s" indicates the first decade of the 19th century, and not the entire century. In biographical entries the abbreviation "fl." (flourit, "flourished") indicates the period in which the person is known to have been alive. In most such cases it can be assumed that the person was actually born several decades earlier than the dates given.

The distribution of firm and approximated dates presented in the Chronology (beginning on page xix) reflects the availability of written documentation for the country's history as a whole. With isolated, and perhaps tenuous, exceptions, the written record begins in the early 16th century, with significant gaps until the 1850s. Dates for earlier archaeological findings are generally derived from radiocarbon tests and other techniques.

GEOGRAPHICAL REFERENCES

Unless otherwise stated, place names used in the dictionary are those current to the periods under discussion. Wherever possible exact longitudinal and latitudinal coordinates are provided. Almost all of these are taken from the United States Board on Geographic Names, Southern Rhodesia: Official Standard Names (Washington, D.C., 1973), a gazetteer containing more than 22,000 entries.

Figures for altitudes are taken from a variety of government yearbooks, travel guides, and other publications. These sources are not always consistent, so altitudes given in the dictionary are generally rounded off to the nearest five meters. Figures for the areas of districts and other regions are also rounded off for this reason.

VARIANT FORMS AND SPELLINGS

Every attempt has been made to enter names and terms under their most widely accepted spellings and forms, but it should be recognized that consistency is impossible. Different authorities often disagree or change their minds on what these forms should be, and orthographies of African languages are far from fully settled. The variant forms given in parentheses in dictionary entry headings often represent only a small sample of the variations which have been used. Two examples illustrate the dimensions of this problem: historians have compiled more than 100 forms of "Munhumutapa" and more than 300 forms of "Mzilikazi" alone.

Some help in spelling Bantu words is offered in the note on alphabetization, above. The dictionary also contains special entries on important letters and combinations of letters which present regular problems. For example, Chishona orthography once rendered the ch sound simply as c. See the entries C, L, Q, SW, TSH, U, and X. Other spelling shifts are too numerous to discuss fully in a book of this nature, but a recurrent problem to watch for is use of the aspirant -h- after consonants, as in MHONDORO and NHOWE. Unfortunately, few authorities agree on when this letter should or should not be used, so one can only be alert to its possible absence from a word.

ABBREVIATIONS

ABC	American Board of Commissioners for Foreign Missions
a. k. a	also known as
alt.	altitude
AMEC	American Methodist Episcopal Church
ANC	African National Congress; African National Council
b.	born
BBP	Bechuanaland Border Police
BSAC	British South Africa Company
BSAP	British South Africa Police
c.	circa (about)
CA	Central Africa
CAF	Central African Federation
CAP	Central African Party
CAS	Capricorn Africa Society
cf.	confer (compare to)
CP	Confederate Party; Centre Party
d.	died
DP	Democratic Party; Dominion Party
DRC	Dutch Reformed Church
fl.	flourit (flourished)
FROLIZI	Front for the Liberation of Zimbabwe
HMC	Historical Monuments Commission
ICU	Industrial and Commercial Workers' Union
IDAF	International Defense and Aid Fund
Legco	Legislative Council
LMS	London Missionary Society
MFF	Mashonaland Field Force
MRF	Matabeleland Relief Force

NAR	National Archives of Rhodesia
NDP	National Democratic Party
NIBMAR	"No independence before majority African rule"
NPU	National Peoples' Union
OAU	Organization of African Unity
PCC	Peoples' Caretaker Council
PEA	Portuguese East Africa (Mozambique)
R$	Rhodesian Dollar
RAP	Rhodesian Action Party
RAR	Rhodesian African Rifles
RBC	Rhodesian Broadcasting Corporation
RBVA	Rhodesian Bantu Voters' Association
RF	Rhodesian Front Party
RH	Rhodesia Herald
RICU	Reformed Industrial & Commercial Workers' Union
RISCO	Rhodesian Iron & Steel Company
RP	Rhodesia(n) Party; Reform Party
SA	South Africa(n)
SLA	Sabi-Limpopo Authority
SPG	Society for Propagation of Gospel
SR	Southern Rhodesia(n)
SRMC	Southern Rhodesian Missionary Conference
Tilcor	Tribal Trust Land Development Corporation
TTL	Tribal Trust Land
UCR(N)	University College of Rhodesia (& Nyasaland)
UDI	Unilateral Declaration of Independence
UFP	United Federal Party
UMC	United Methodist Church
UN	United Nations
UP	United Party
UPP	United Peoples' Party
UR	University of Rhodesia
URP	United Rhodesian Party
WMMS	Wesleyan Methodist Missionary Society
YL	Youth League

Abbreviations

ZANLA   Zimbabwe African National Liberation Army
ZANU   Zimbabwe African National Union
ZAPU   Zimbabwe African Peoples' Union
ZIPA   Zimbabwe Peoples' Army
ZIPRA   Zimbabwe Peoples' Revolutionary Army
ZLA   Zimbabwe Liberation Army
ZNP   Zimbabwe National Party
ZUPO   Zimbabwe United Peoples' Organization

CHRONOLOGY

Headings of relevant dictionary entries are printed in all-
capital letters here.   Within each chronological period,
the least precisely dated entries are given first.

c. 100, 000 BC   Beginning of Early STONE AGE

c. 35, 000 BC   Beginning of Middle Stone Age

c. 9000 BC   Beginning of Late Stone Age

c. 5000 BC   Earliest possible date for extant ROCK PAINTINGS

c. AD 200   Introduction of IRON AGE cultures

c. 600   GOLD mining begins in SINOIA region

c. 900   Rise of LEOPARD'S KOPJE CULTURE

947   al-Masudi chronicles SOFALA gold trade

c. 1100   Substantial stone building initiated at ZIMBABWE
                  RUINS; Sofala founded at present site

c. 1300   Radiocarbon date for MONK'S KOP OSSUARY

1331   Ibn Battuta mentions YUFI

c. 1400   Zimbabwe state at its peak

c. 1450   MUTOTA and MATOPE establish MUNHUMUTAPA
                  state in the north

c. 1494   CHANGAMIRE and TOGWA states separate from
                  Munhumutapa state; CHIKUYO CHISAMARENGU be-
                  comes Munhumutapa

1505   (Sept.   19)   PORTUGUESE occupation of Sofala

1506   (Nov.   20)   Diogo Aleaçova writes to Portuguese king
                  giving first description of Munhumutapa state

c. 1511   Antonio FERNANDES becomes first European to visit
                  present Rhodesia

c. 1530   NESHANGWE becomes Munhumutapa

c. 1547   Neshangwe expels Changamire from Mbire region

c. 1550   CHIVERE NYASORO becomes Munhumutapa

c. 1560   NEGOMO CHIRISAMHURU becomes Munhumutapa

1561   (March 15/16) Goncalo da SILVEIRA killed by Shona

1570   BARRETO/HONEM expedition sent against Munhumu-
               tapa by Portugal

1575   MUTASA Chikanga signs treaty with Honem; numer-
               ous trade FAIRS opened in northeast

c. 1589   GATSI RUSERE becomes Munhumutapa

1597   ZIMBA people enter Shona territory

1607   (Aug. 1) Gatsi Rusere signs treaty with Diogo
               Simões MADEIRA

1623   NYAMBO KAPARIDZE becomes Munhumutapa

1629   (May) MAVURA II becomes Munhumutapa after
               Portuguese help to oust Nyambo; Mavura signs
               treaty with Portuguese

1635   First documentation of MAUNGWE people

1644   BAYĀO expedition into BUTUA

1652   (May) SITI KAZURUKUMUSAPA becomes Munhumu-
               tapa

1663   Siti assassinated; KAMBARAPASU MUKOMBWE be-
               comes Munhumutapa

1693-5   CHANGAMIRE armies under DOMBO drive Portuguese
               out of country; Munhumutapa state goes into decline

c. 1710   Founding of MANGWENDE and SVOSVE dynasties

c. 1714   ZUMBO trading fair founded on Zambezi River

1769   Portuguese fail in effort to reopen DAMBARARE fair

1790s   Birth of MZILIKAZI in Zululand

c. 1816   Mzilikazi succeeds MASHOBANE as KHUMALO ruler

1820s   Beginnings of MFECANE invasions in country

c. 1821   Mzilikazi leads Khumalo out of Zululand, founds
               NDEBELE kingdom in the Transvaal

c. 1828   NGWATO ruler KGARI killed during foray into
               KALANGA territory; SHANGWA drought afflicts
               much of country

1829   Robert MOFFAT among the first Europeans to visit
               Mzilikazi near present Pretoria

1831   KALIPHI commands first Ndebele foray into present
               Rhodesia from central Transvaal

1830s   NGONI of ZWANGENDABA attack Changamire cen-
               ters, killing CHIRISAMHURU

1835   (Nov. 20)   Solar eclipse over country, associated in
               traditions with Zwangendaba's crossing of the Zam-
               bezi into present Zambia

1836   (March 3)   MNCUMBATHE signs treaty with governor
               of the British Cape Colony, in the name of Mzili-
               kazi; A. H. POTGIETER, et al., scout north of
               the Limpopo River; first AFRIKANER clashes with
               Ndebele around the Vaal River

1837   Ndebele centers in western Transvaal attacked by
               Afrikaners, GRIQUA, SOTHO, and ZULU; Ndebele
               begin to migrate north

1838   (c. March)   Ndebele divide into two main migration
               parties in Ngwato territory; Kaliphi's division goes
               directly to present MATABELELAND

1839   (c. June)   Mzilikazi's division of migrants arrives in
               Matabeleland; NKULUMANE and dissident Ndebele
               izinduna executed in political crisis

c. 1840   NXABA MSENE killed in western Zambia

1841   Ndebele begin raiding Sotho/Tswana territories from
               their new base in Matabeleland

1840s   Ndebele-KOLOLO wars along the Zambezi

1847   POTGIETER raids the Ndebele

1851   Kololo king SEBITWANE dies shortly after visit by
               David LIVINGSTONE

1852   Establishment of South African Republic in the
               TRANSVAAL

1853   Ndebele kill NANZWA ruler Lusumbami; (Jan. 8)
            Ndebele sign treaty with Transvaal Afrikaners

1854   Robert Moffat and Samuel EDWARDS visit Mzilikazi,
            opening Ndebele communications with south; Mzili-
            kazi releases TRUEY THE GRIQUA to Moffat

1855   (Nov.) Livingstone visits and names VICTORIA
            FALLS

1857   Moffat revisits Ndebele, arranges for release of
            Ngwato royal heir MACHENG

1859   (Dec.) LONDON MISSIONARY SOCIETY opens
            MATABELE MISSION at INYATI

1860s-1870s Peak of IVORY trade

1862   MZILA becomes GAZA king

1863   (March) MANGWANE leads Ndebele attack on
            Ngwato

1864   LOZI overthrow Kololo rulers, refugees flee south

1866   (c. Oct.) Ndebele capture TOHWECHIPI, ending
            ROZVI resistance

1867   Karl MAUCH begins publicizing discovery of GOLD
            in Mashonaland

1868   (Sept.) Mzilikazi dies; MNCUMBATHE becomes
            Ndebele regent

1869   (July) SOUTH AFRICA GOLD FIELDS EXPLORA-
            TION CO. expedition into Shona territory

1870   "FEVER YEAR"; Cecil RHODES arrives in South
            Africa; (Jan.) LOBENGULA installed as Ndebele
            king; (June) Lobengula suppresses rebels at
            ZWANGENDABA

1871   Mauch visits and describes ZIMBABWE RUINS; es-
            tablishment of first BULAWAYO; raising of IM-
            BIZO ibutho; (Aug. 29) Lobengula signs BAINES
            CONCESSION

1872   (Jan.) Mangwane leads "NKULUMANE" coup attempt
            against Lobengula

1875   Thomas Morgan THOMAS founds independent mission

1876   (Dec.) Alexander BAILIE attempts to recruit mine laborers in Matabeleland

1877	François COILLARD attempts to start mission among Shona; British occupy the Transvaal
1878	(Sept.) Massacre of PATTERSON expedition
1879	(Sept.) Jesuit ZAMBEZI MISSION arrives in Matabeleland; Lobengula marries XWALILE and Gaza princesses; (Oct.) Ndebele kill CHIVI Mazorodze
1880s	Manuel de SOUSA advances into Shona territory from northeast
1880	(April) Execution of Lobengula's sister, MNCE-NGENCE; (Nov. 25) Augustus LAW dies while attempting to open Jesuit mission among Gaza
1881	Bulawayo moved to new location
1883	(April) GAMPU SITHOLE commands Ndebele attack on TAWANA; (May) Ndebele kill CHAMINUKA medium
1884	GUNGUNYANE becomes Gaza king
1885	(March 14) BECHUANALAND PROTECTORATE declared over present BOTSWANA; (April) LOTSHE commands disastrous Ndebele attack on Tawana
1887	(July 30) Lobengula signs treaty with the Transvaal's P. GROBLER
1888	(Feb. 11) Lobengula signs "MOFFAT TREATY"; (Oct. 30) Lobengula signs RUDD CONCESSION
1889	Gungunyane moves Gaza capital to lower Limpopo; PORTUGUESE sign treaties with northern SHONA rulers; (Jan.) Lobengula repudiates Rudd Concession; (March) formation of BRITISH SOUTH AFRICA CO.; (Oct. 29) BSAC incorporated by royal CHARTER
1890	(June 28) BSAC's PIONEER COLUMN enters country; (Sept. 12) Column founds Fort SALISBURY; (Sept. 14) Archibald COLQUHOUN obtains treaty from MUTASA; (Nov. 15) P. W. FORBES arrests Portuguese agents J. C. P. d'ANDRADA and SOUSA at Mutasa's
1891	(Feb. 15) Temporary frontier with Portuguese territory established in MANICALAND; (May 9) British Order-in-Council declares protectorates over

Bechuanaland, Matabeleland, and Mashonaland;
(May 11) British and Portuguese clash at MAÇE-
QUEÇE; (June 11) ANGLO-PORTUGUESE CONVEN-
TION; (June 24) BSAC disperses ADENDORFF
trekkers at Limpopo; (Nov.) Ndebele kill reigning
NEMAKONDE; (Nov. 17) Lobengula signs LIPPERT
CONCESSION

1892   First PASS LAWS issued in Salisbury; (Oct.) first
section of RAILWAY from BEIRA opened

1893   (July 18) Ndebele raid Shona near Ft. Victoria in
"Victoria Incident"; (Sept.) beginning of NDEBELE
WAR; (Oct. 24) Battle of Shangani; (Nov. 1) Battle
of Bembezi; (Nov. 4) British occupy Bulawayo;
(Dec. 4) Ndebele annihilate "SHANGANI PATROL"

1894   (Jan./Feb. ?) Death of Lobengula; British work to
dismantle Ndebele kingdom

1895   (Jan.) Native Department created in Matabeleland;
(May 3) Territory proclaimed "RHODESIA"; (Dec.
29) JAMESON RAID leaves Mafeking

1896   (Jan. 2) JAMESON surrenders in Transvaal; (Feb.)
RINDERPEST breaks out in Matabeleland; (March
20) Ndebele REVOLT begins; (June 14) Shona RE-
VOLT begins; (June 25) NYAMANDA made Ndebele
king; (Aug. 21) first of Rhodes' five INDABAS with
southern Ndebele rebels; Ndebele Revolt ends

1897   (July) Last Ndebele rebel, MPOTSHWANA, captured;
(Oct. 27) Shona Revolt pronounced ended; (Nov.)
railroad to Bulawayo opened

1898   (Feb.) Beira to UMTALI railroad opened; (April 27)
KAGUVI and NEHANDA mediums executed

1899   (May 15) First session of LEGISLATIVE COUNCIL;
(May 22) Beira railroad reaches Salisbury; (Oct.
11) outbreak of SOUTH AFRICAN WAR

1901   MAPONDERA'S revolt begins; administrations of
Matabeleland and Mashonaland combined under W.
H. MILTON; EAST COAST FEVER hits cattle

1902   Death of CHIOKO DAMBAMUPUTE, the last Munhumutapa; (March 26) death of C. J. RHODES; (May)
end of South African War

1903   New CHAMINUKA medium emerges; COAL production
begins at WANKIE

1904   Government eases mining restrictions on SMALL-
            WORKERS; (June 19) railway reaches VICTORIA
            FALLS

1906   Formation of SOUTHERN RHODESIAN MISSIONARY
            CONFERENCE; beginning of commercial COPPER
            production; appearance of new NEHANDA medium;
            publication of RANDALL-MACIVER'S Medieval
            Rhodesia opens ZIMBABWE CONTROVERSY

1907   Beginning of commercial CHROME production; es-
            tablishment of HARARE township

1908   Charles COGHLAN and others attend SOUTH AFRICA's
            National Union Convention

1910   Formation of Union of South Africa

1914   Creation of MATABELE NATIONAL HOME SOCIETY

1915   Matthew ZWIMBA founds Church of the White Bird;
            Clemens KADALIE arrives in country; (March 13)
            BSAC CHARTER extended ten years

1918   INFLUENZA PANDEMIC hits country

1919   Passage of WOMEN'S FRANCHISE ORDINANCE

1920   CAVE COMMISSION recommends cash settlement for
            BSAC assets in country

1921   BUXTON COMMITTEE makes recommendations on
            country's constitutional future

1923   (Jan. 20)   RHODESIAN BANTU VOTERS' ASSOCIA-
            TION launched; (Sept. 12) Great Britain annexes
            Southern Rhodesia as a Crown Colony, with J. R.
            CHANCELLOR as first GOVERNOR; (Oct. 1) RE-
            SPONSIBLE GOVERNMENT established with COGH-
            LAN as first premier

1924   (May 30)   New LEGISLATIVE ASSEMBLY opens

1925   Establishment of Department of Native EDUCATION

1927   INDUSTRIAL & COMMERCIAL UNION founded in
            Bulawayo; (Sept. 2) H. U. MOFFAT succeeds
            Coghlan as premier after latter's death; (Sept. 12-
            17) African miners strike at SHAMVA

1928   First government GAME RESERVE established in
            Wankie

1929 Gertrude CATON-THOMPSON excavates at Zimbabwe; foundation of RUWADZANO Methodist women's organization; (Jan. 24) HILTON YOUNG Report on eastern African closer union; (Aug. 31) BEIT BRIDGE opened on Limpopo

1930 Beginning of STRIP ROAD construction; (Oct. 10) promulgation of LAND APPORTIONMENT ACT

1931 Godfrey HUGGINS founds REFORM PARTY

1932 Johane MARANKE founds independent church

1933 Creation of AFRICAN FARMERS' UNION; (June 29) government buys BSAC's MINERAL rights; (July 6) George MITCHELL replaces Moffat as PRIME MINISTER; (Sept. 6) Huggins' party carries general election

1934 Aaron JACHA founds Bantu Congress, predecessor of AFRICAN NATIONAL CONGRESS; after split in Reform Party, Huggins carries new election at head of new UNITED PARTY; promulgation of IN-DUSTRIAL CONCILIATION ACT

1935 Creation of NATIONAL ARCHIVES

1936 Creation of HISTORICAL MONUMENTS COMMISSION

1939 (March 21) Publication of BLEDISLOE Report respecting AMALGAMATION OF THE RHODESIAS; (April 14) Huggins' party again carries general election

1940 RHODESIAN AFRICAN RIFLES raised

1943 AFRICAN NEWSPAPERS LTD. enters country

1944 (Oct. 18) Establishment of CENTRAL AFRICA COUNCIL

1945 KAROI made center of resettlement scheme for European war veterans; (Oct. 20) African railway workers strike

1946 NATIVE (URBAN AREAS) ACCOMMODATION & REGISTRATION ACT passed; (Feb. 10) REFORMED ICU founded in Salisbury; (April 25) Huggins' party wins general election in which LIBERAL PARTY SHOWS major gains

1947 (July) Benjamin BUROMBO founds African Voice Association

1948   (April 14-22)   African general strike in major urban
            centers; (Sept. 15) Huggins' party again wins
            general election, in which Ian SMITH enters Legis-
            lative Assembly

1949   Foundation of CAPRICORN AFRICA SOCIETY; Doris
            LESSING emigrates to England; creation of RHO-
            DESIA RAILWAYS CO.; (Feb.) first Victoria Falls
            conference on federation; (late) NATIONAL PARK
            Act

1950   Robert TREDGOLD made Chief Justice of country

1951   Formation of ALL-AFRICA CONVENTION; passage
            of NATIVE LAND HUSBANDRY ACT

1953   (April 9)   European voters ratify federation in general
            referendum; (Sept.) inauguration of FEDERATION
            OF RHODESIA AND NYASALAND with Huggins as
            Federal prime minister; Garfield TODD succeeds
            Huggins as Southern Rhodesian prime minister

1954   (Jan.)   First Federal elections put Federal Party in
            power; Todd retained in power in territorial elec-
            tions

1955   Mai CHAZA founds independent church; CHISHONA
            orthography standardized by government; new rail-
            way line to Lourenzo Marques opened; work begun
            on KARIBA DAM; (Aug.) YOUTH LEAGUE founded
            in Harare

1956   Formation of DOMINION PARTY, predecessor of
            RHODESIAN FRONT; (Aug.) Yough League organizes
            Salisbury bus boycott; (Oct. 31) Roy WELENSKY
            succeeds Huggins (now Lord Malvern) as Federal
            prime minister

1957   (March)   UNIVERSITY College of Rhodesia & Nyasa-
            land opened to students in Salisbury; (Sept. 12)
            founding of new AFRICAN NATIONAL CONGRESS

1958   (Feb. 18)   Edgar WHITEHEAD replaces Todd as
            Southern Rhodesian prime minister after cabinet
            revolt; (June 5) Whitehead retained as prime minis-
            ter after UFP barely carries general election.

1959   (Feb. 26)   Government declares state of emergency,
            proscribes ANC; passage of UNLAWFUL ORGANI-
            SATIONS ACT

1960   (Jan. 1)   Formation of NATIONAL DEMOCRATIC
            PARTY; (May 17) Kariba Dam formally opened;

(July 19) arrest of NDP leaders leads to bloody rioting; (Oct.) LAW AND ORDER (MAINTENANCE) ACT introduced; MONCKTON COMMISSION Report issued on future of Federation; (Dec.) Federal Constitutional Review Conference opens in London

1961   COUNCIL OF CHIEFS created; (June) ZIMBABWE NATIONAL PARTY founded; (July 26) public refer- endum approves proposals for new CONSTITUTION, 41,919 to 21,846; (Dec. 9) NDP banned; (Dec. 18) ZIMBABWE AFRICAN PEOPLE'S UNION founded

1962   (March) RHODESIAN FRONT founded; (April-May) first full census of African POPULATION; (April) Federal election boycotted by Africans; (Aug. 14) T. S. PARIRENYATWA dies under mysterious circumstances; (Sept. 20) ZAPU banned; (Dec. 14) Rhodesian Front wins Southern Rhodesian election, Winston FIELD becomes prime minister

1963   Beginning of TANGWENA LAND DISPUTE; (July) ZAPU leaders split in Dar es Salaam; (Aug. 8) ZIMBABWE AFRICAN NATIONAL UNION founded; (Aug. 10) PEOPLE'S CARETAKER COUNCIL formed as ZAPU front; (Dec. 31) Federation of- ficially dissolved

1964   (April 13) Ian SMITH displaces Field as prime minister; (April 16) government details Joshua NKOMO; (Aug. 26) government bans ZANU, PCC, and AFRICAN DAILY NEWS, and declares HIGH- FIELD an emergency area; (Oct. 21-26) "DOMBO- SHAWA INDABA" of chiefs endorses independence; (Oct. 24) Northern Rhodesia becomes independent as ZAMBIA; (Nov. 5) public referendum endorses independence

1965   (Jan.) Creation of SABI-LIMPOPO AUTHORITY; (May 7) Rhodesian Front wins all 50 European seats in general election; (May 31) UNITED PEOPLE'S PARTY founded; (Sept.) British government articu- lates "FIVE PRINCIPLES" respecting Rhodesian in- dependence; (Oct. 26-30) Harold Wilson visits Salis- bury to discuss independence; (Nov. 5) state of emergency declared; (Nov. 11) UNILATERAL DEC- LARATION OF INDEPENDENCE issued; CONSTI- TUTION revised, press CENSORSHIP instituted; Britain applies economic SANCTIONS

1966   (April) ZANU launches first guerrilla attacks from Zambia; (Dec. 2-4) Wilson and Smith meet off Gibraltar in "TIGER TALKS"; (Dec. 16) United Nations vote selected mandatory economic sanctions

1967   (Aug.) ZAPU and South African ANC launch guerrilla campaign in northwest

1968   (May 29) UN votes comprehensive mandatory sanctions; (Aug.) CENTRE PARTY formed by Rhodesian Front opponents; (Aug. 28) Abel MUZOREWA made UMC Bishop of Rhodesia; (Sept. 30) Bechuanaland becomes independent as Republic of BOTSWANA; (Oct. 10-13) Wilson and Smith meet in "FEARLESS TALKS"; (Nov. 11) new Rhodesian FLAG adopted

1969   LAND TENURE ACT passed; (April-May) census of African POPULATION; (June 20) European electorate votes in favor of a REPUBLIC in referendum; (June 24) H. V. GIBBS resigns as governor; (Nov. 29) new CONSTITUTION becomes law

1970   (March 2) Rhodesia declared a republic; (April 10) Rhodesian Front sweeps European seats in general election; (April 16) Clifford DUPONT sworn in as first PRESIDENT; (June 15) Leopold TAKAWIRA dies in prison

1971   (May 8) Death of Lord Malvern (G. HUGGINS); (April) informal British-Rhodesian talks begin in Salisbury; (Oct.) FRONT FOR THE LIBERATION OF ZIMBABWE (FROLIZI) formed; (Nov. 17) United States President Richard Nixon signs bill containing "BYRD AMENDMENT"; (Nov. 24) Ian Smith and Sir Alec Douglas Home sign Anglo-Rhodesian Settlement Proposals; (Dec. 16) AFRICAN NATIONAL COUNCIL formed

1972   (Jan. 11-March 11) PEARCE COMMISSION in Rhodesia; (May 23) Commission's Report published in London; (June 6) 427 miners killed in WANKIE colliery explosion; (Dec.) large-scale guerrilla war begins in northeast

1973   (Jan. 9) Rhodesia closes border with ZAMBIA; (Feb.) Rhodesia reopens border, but Zambia keeps its side closed; (July) MUZOREWA and Smith begin talks which last almost a year

1974   "PROTECTED VILLAGE" program begun by government; government launches "Settler 74" campaign to attract EUROPEAN immigrants; (April 25) PORTUGUESE government falls in coup d'état; new government pledges independence for African colonies; (May) GONAKUDZINGWA detention camp closed; (July) Rhodesian Front sweeps general elections; (Sept. 15) direct RAILWAY link to SOUTH AFRICA opened through BEITBRIDGE; (Dec.) Organization

of African Unity Liberation Committee creates
"FRONTLINE PRESIDENTS" group; (Dec. 8)
leaders of ZANU, ZAPU, and FROLIZI announce
acceptance of ANC as "umbrella" organization with
Muzorewa as head; (Dec. 11) Ian Smith announces
agreement with nationalists for cease-fire in civil
war, release of political prisoners, and plan for
new constitutional conference

1975   (Feb.) Smith meets with NKOMO, MUZOREWA,
                Ndabaningi SITHOLE, and others to set up formal
                constitutional conference; (March 4) Sithole arrested
                on conspiracy charge; (March 18) Herbert CHITEPO
                assassinated in Lusaka; (April 5) Sithole released;
                (June 1) police kill about a dozen Africans in Salis-
                bury townships; (June 25) MOZAMBIQUE becomes
                independent with Samora Machel as president; (July
                8) Rhodesian government announces step-up of anti-
                guerrilla campaign after failure of cease-fire; (Aug.)
                SOUTH AFRICA announces pull-out of its military
                forces from Rhodesia; (Aug. 25-26) abortive VIC-
                TORIA FALLS CONFERENCE; (Oct.) Edson SI-
                THOLE disappears from streets of Salisbury; (Dec.
                10) J. J. WRATHALL succeeds Dupont as PRESI-
                DENT; (Dec. 15) Smith and Nkomo begin weekly
                talks in Salisbury

1976   (Feb.) Rhodesian forces begin making "hot pursuit"
                forays into Mozambique; (March 3) Mozambique
                closes its border to Rhodesia; (March 19) Smith-
                Nkomo talks break down; (April 27) Smith announces
                addition of government chiefs to his cabinet; (June)
                beginning of massive black urban protests in South
                Africa; (Sept. 19) Smith and U.S. Secretary of State
                Henry Kissinger meet in Pretoria; (Sept. 24) Smith
                announces willingness to bring about African ma-
                jority rule within two years; (Oct. 9) Nkomo and
                Robert MUGABE announce formation of "PATRIOTIC
                FRONT"; (Oct. 28) GENEVA CONFERENCE opens;
                (Dec. 9) conference adjourns for holidays, never to
                reopen; (Dec. 29) government chiefs found ZIM-
                BABWE UNITED PEOPLE'S ORGANISATION

1977   (Jan.) "FRONTLINE PRESIDENTS" pledge support for
                "Patriotic Front"; (Jan. 22) letter bomb kills Jason
                MOYO in Lusaka; (March) Donal LAMONT deported;
                (March 18) U.S. President Jimmy Carter signs re-
                peal of "BYRD AMENDMENT"; (April 1) amend-
                ments to LAND TENURE ACT lift some color bar
                laws; (April 13) British Foreign Secretary David
                Owen presents new Anglo-American constitutional
                proposals to Ian Smith in Cape Town; (April 16)
                Owen consults with Smith in Salisbury, becoming

first British cabinet-level official to visit country
in six years; (April 18) emergency RHODESIAN
FRONT convention endorses principle of eventual
majority rule; (April 29) SOUTH AFRICA reportedly
threatens to cut off Rhodesia's oil supply if constitutional settlement is not soon reached; (May 16)
President Kaunda announces that ZAMBIA is "in a
state of war" with Rhodesia; (May 27) UN Security
Council tightens mandatory sanctions; (July 4) right-
wing members of Parliament form RHODESIAN
ACTION PARTY; (July 5) general meeting of OAU
endorses Patriotic Front as sole representative of
people of Zimbabwe; (July 18) Smith dissolves
Parliament, calls for new elections; (Aug. 6) bomb
blast in Salisbury store kills eleven, opening new
phase of civil war; (Aug. 31) Rhodesian Front
sweeps European seats in general election; (Sept.
1) David Owen and American UN Ambassador
Andrew Young meet with Smith and local nationalist
leaders in Salisbury to discuss new Anglo-American
proposals; (Sept. 24) Frontline Presidents group
endorses Anglo-American plan; (Sept. 25) Smith and
two ministers fly secretly to Lusaka to confer with
Kaunda; (Sept. 28) Britain presents Anglo-American
plan to UN Security Council; (Nov. 23-28) Rhodesia
mounts major raids into Mozambique, killing large
numbers of guerrillas and Mozambican civilians;
(Nov. 24) Smith announces conditional acceptance of
principle of "one man, one vote" for country; (Dec.
2) Smith opens new round of internal negotiations
with MUZOREWA, N. SITHOLE, and Jeremiah
Chirau of ZUPO; (Dec. 7) Zambia announces withdrawal of support for Anglo-American plan

1978   (Jan. 7) Government issues strictest CENSORSHIP
laws since UDI to control reportage on civil war;
(Feb. 6) N. Sithole, Muzorewa, and Chirau reject
Anglo-American proposals; (Feb. 15) After 37th
session of internal settlement talks, Smith and nationalist participants announce agreement on an
eight-point plan calling for universal adult suffrage
and a 100 member parliament with 28 seats reserved for whites; (Feb. 16) Smith announces conditional acceptance of plan to allow anti-government
guerrillas to join government armed forces; Patriotic Front rejects both internal settlement and
Anglo-American plan; (March 3) Smith, Sithole,
Chirau, and Muzorewa formally sign agreement for
transition to majority-ruled Zimbabwe by end of
1978; these men, known as the "Salisbury Four,"
are to form ruling Executive Council; (March 6)
Rhodesian forces raid guerrilla bases near Luangwa
River in first acknowledged foray into Zambian

territory; government claims 38 guerrillas killed; Zambia claims 22 Zambian troops killed; (March 14) UN Security Council votes 10-0 to condemn Rhodesian settlement; U. S. , U.K. , France, Canada, and West Germany abstain on vote; (March 21) Smith designated first chairman of new Executive Council after members draw lots; other members to follow as chairmen on rotating basis; (March 29) Guerrillas abduct c.440 students and staff members from British Methodist school at Tegwani, taking them to Botswana; all but 37 abductees return to school within a few days; (March 30) Multi-racial government formally assumes full powers; (April 2) U. S. President Jimmy Carter calls for all-faction Rhodesian talks while visiting Nigeria; (April 5) Executive Council announces consolidation of 18 cabinet ministries into 9 ministries, with black and white co-ministers; (April 14-15) U. S. Sec. of State Cyrus Vance, U.K. Foreign Sec. David Owen, Mugabe, and Nkomo meet in Dar es Salaam; no agreement on new settlement strategy reached; (April 17) Vance and Owen met with Executive Council in Salisbury; (April 28) Executive Council dismisses Muzorewa-nominee Bryon Hove from his new post of black co-minister of Justice, Law and Order because of his public criticism of government; (May 2) Rhodesian government lifts ban on ZAPU and ZANU political activity within country and calls for guerrillas to agree to cease-fire; (May 14) More than 50 black civilians in Gutu TTL killed in cross-fire between guerrillas and government troops; (May 18) Zambian President Kaunda calls for increased U. S. pressure on Rhodesia during visit to Washington, D. C.; (June 23) Guerrillas kill 12 British Pentacostal missionary family members at school near Vumba; Mugabe attributes murders to government's SELOUS SCOUTS; (July 1) Guerrillas kill 14 black farm workers near Rusape; (c.July 9) Guerrillas kill 39 black civilians in Wedza TTL, according to delayed government report; government also later claims to have killed 106 guerrillas in retaliation; (July 15) Guerrillas kill 17 black civilians at Makanza village in Zwimba TTL; (July 21-22) First-reported clashes with guerrillas inside Salisbury; (July 26) U. S. Senate votes twice to continue SANCTIONS against Rhodesia at least until majority government is elected; Rhodesian government sets Dec. 4-6 as dates for national election; (August) 8000 PATRIOTIC FRONT guerrillas estimated to be operating inside Rhodesia; (Aug. 2) U. S. House of Representatives votes 229-180 to end trade boycott of Rhodesia on Jan. 1, 1979, if free elections are held, as promised; (Aug. 6) Abel

(1978 cont.)   MUZOREWA returns from trip to U.S. and U.K.
and demands immediate end to racial discrimina-
tion in Rhodesia; (Aug. 8) Executive Council re-
peals some minor discriminatory laws; (Aug. 10)
Geneva office of the World Council of Churches announces it is granting $85,000 to the Patriotic Front
for non-military purposes; (Aug. 12) Muzorewa
causes stir by visiting camp of mysterious pro-
government guerrillas near Salisbury; the camp's
Soviet-armed guerrillas are thought to be defectors
from the Patriotic Front; (Aug. 14-15) African mine
workers strike at MANGULA; government police kill
4 miners; (Aug. 14) Ian SMITH and Joshua NKOMO
meet secretly in Lusaka, along with Nigerian Foreign Minister Joseph Garba; (Aug. 17-Sept. 2) speculation increases that an all-party conference will
soon be convened to discuss Anglo-American constitutional proposals; (Aug. 20) Smith denies rumors
that he has purchased a farm in South Africa and
driven cattle there in preparation for his flight from
Rhodesia; (Aug. 27) London's Sunday Times breaks
story of massive and systematic SANCTIONS-busting
by government-controlled British Petroleum (BP)
and Shell Oil from 1966 to 1975; investigation initiated 18 months earlier by Foreign Minister David
Owen reveals several British governments tacitly
approved of supplying oil to Rhodesia while simultaneously spending several hundred million dollars
to blockade shipments by way of the sea; (Aug. 31)
J. J. WRATHALL, state president, dies of heart
attack; (Sept. 3) AIR RHODESIA Viscount airliner
shot down by guerrillas near KARIBA; 38 civilians
die in crash; 10 others apparently killed by guerrillas; Joshua Nkomo claims credit for downing the
aircraft, but denies massacre of survivors, while
charging that the aircraft was engaged in a military
mission; incident ends speculation about all-party
conference; (Sept. 8) government begins dismantling
of unpopular PROTECTED VILLAGE program in
MTOKO DISTRICT; (Sept. 10) Smith announces imposition of limited martial law over fifth of the
country and warns of crack-down against supporters
of Patriotic Front; (Sept. 10-13) government arrests
more than 300 PF supporters within the country, but
Josiah CHINAMANO and other important leaders
leave the country without hindrance; (Sept. 16) government announces first plan to draft previously
exempt black Africans into military service; (Sept.
20-23) Rhodesian forces raid guerrilla bases deep
inside of MOZAMBIQUE, claiming about 300 guerrillas killed; (Oct. 2) government bans 18-month-old
Zimbabwe Times, the country's own daily black newspaper, for publishing material favorable to the Pa-

(1978 cont.)   triotic Front; (Oct. 4) after two weeks of debate,
U. S. Department of State grants entry visas to
Rhodesian government leaders invited to visit the
U. S. by 27 conservative senators headed by S. I.
Hayakawa (Rep. -Calif.); (Oct. 6) ZAMBIA reopens
border with Rhodesia in order to expedite delivery
of large fertilizer shipment stalled in Mozambique;
(Oct. 7-20) Ian Smith and Ndabaningi SITHOLE
visit the United States unofficially; they are joined
by Muzorewa and Chirau on Oct. 13; (Oct. 10)
Rhodesian government announces plans to end all
remaining discriminatory laws, including LAND
TENURE ACT; (Oct. 18) Rhodesian forces begin
major raids deep into Mozambique; (Oct. 19) Rhodesian forces begin bombing and occupying guerrilla forces deep inside of Zambia, killing--ac-
cording to various estimates--up to 1500 people;
Nkomo and Zambian government claim that the
destroyed camps contained only unarmed refugees;
(Oct. 21) Rhodesia reports all its forces withdrawn
from Zambia and Mozambique; (Oct. 27) Britain
begins airlifting advanced anti-aircraft and other
defensive weapons to assist Zambia against Rhodesian raids; (Oct. 31) Rhodesian government extends martial law over more than half of country;
(Nov. 16) after prolonged debate, Rhodesia's bi-
racial government announces postponement of
scheduled election from Dec. 13, 1978, to April
20, 1979; new constitution is promised for Dec.
22, subject to referendum among white electorate
on Jan. 30, 1979; transition to black majority
government is expected to occur shortly after April
20 elections, if they take place as scheduled.

INTRODUCTION

Rhodesia, or Zimbabwe as it should soon be called, is a completely landlocked country, tucked between the Zambezi and Limpopo rivers in southern Africa. It shares its borders with four larger neighbors: Botswana, Zambia, Mozambique, and South Africa. Its area of 389,370 square kilometers, or 150,333 square miles, is roughly the same as that of Japan, Paraguay, or California. Its compact shape resembles that of Poland, which is a fifth smaller. Its population of around six and a half million people is about average among African nations, but its comparatively developed and diversified economy makes it one of the continent's most prosperous countries.

Since Rhodesia's white minority government declared itself independent of Britain just over a dozen years ago, the country has occupied a center stage in world news. Scores of books have analyzed the country's political problems, and there has been endless speculation as to how long the minority regime would last. Often overlooked, however, is the country's deeper historical past. This is a pity, for Rhodesia contains abundant historical riches. The region is an archaeological treasure trove for both Stone Age and Iron Age scholars. Its thousands of openly visible rock painting sites and megalithic ruins are a delight to both students and tourists. A succession of large-scale state systems and wholesale population movements left behind a fascinating body of oral traditions, and these are often richly supplemented by written records dating back to the early 16th century. The 19th century was a particularly interesting period of new struggles for mastery of the country, culminating in a revolt against European occupation with few parallels in Africa. Nor is the early 20th century without special interest,

1

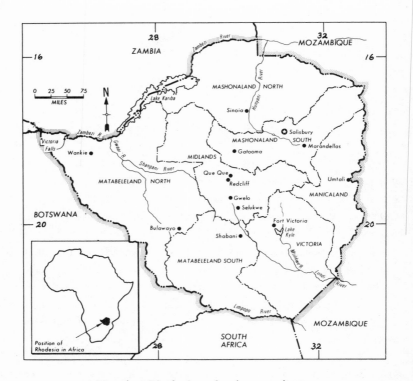

Map 1. Rhodesia, showing provinces.

for the country was the scene of an unusual experiment in administration by a private company, followed by four decades of local
parliamentary self-government and African attempts to mobilize politically, and a decade-long attempt to join the country with its two
northern neighbors. All of these developments, and many others,
took place before the world ever heard of "UDI."

Modern man has occupied Rhodesia for at least 100,000
years, and his hominid antecedents go back perhaps a further million years. The country possesses a wealth of Stone Age remains,
the most striking of which are the nearly 1500 rock painting sites
of the Late Stone Age, which commenced around 9000 BC. In the
early centuries of the modern era intrusive Iron Age cultures began
absorbing and displacing the Stone Age peoples, giving rise to the
first metal and ceramic industries and to agriculture. These earliest Iron Age peoples were most probably Bantu-speaking immigrants

from the north. By around AD 1000, the ancestors of the modern
Shona-speaking peoples were clearly in the ascendant throughout the
country. Cattle-keeping was becoming important, and a trade in
gold and ivory was being initiated with Indian Ocean ports.

The early centuries of the second millenium saw the rise of
a purely indigenous stone-building tradition, originating in the southeastern part of the country at the place now known as "Great Zimbabwe. " Great Zimbabwe also became the center of a large state
system which flourished until the mid-15th century, when the impressive center at Great Zimbabwe itself was abandoned. The center of
the stone-building tradition then shifted west to focus on a site now
known as "Khami, " near present Bulawayo. The apparent political
heirs of the Zimbabwe state moved north, however, founding the
famous Munhumutapa kingdom in the Zambezi Valley.

By the 16th century the Munhumutapa state dominated the
northern part of present Rhodesia and parts of Mozambique. There
it controlled the trade routes to the Muslim ports of the east coast.
During this same period Portuguese forces displaced the Muslim
rulers and traders of the coast, and they began attempting to control
the inland sources of gold. Contacts between the Shona and the
Portuguese were alternately cooperative and hostile. In the 17th
century the Portuguese made increasingly aggressive attempts to
control Munhumutapa commerce directly. Their efforts brought
them little success, but nevertheless contributed to the weakening
of the Munhumutapa state. The resulting disorder allowed already
independent and breakaway Shona dynasties to increase their autonomy
at Munhumutapa's expense.

In the late 17th century a southwestern Shona state known to
historians both as "Changamire" after its rulers and as "Rozvi"
after a nickname for its peoples, rapidly developed into a major
power. Changamire forces drove the Portuguese out of the country
in the northeast, reduced the Munhumutapa and many other Shona
states to tributary status, and then settled down to become the
country's dominant political and military power through the 18th
century.

By the early 19th century the Changamire empire was in disarray. Before internal political problems could be resolved, the
country was invaded by a succession of more militaristic Nguni-
speaking bands from South Africa. These bands were spawned by
the upheavals known as the Mfecane. During the 1830s several different bands known as Ngoni passed through the country. Before
crossing the Zambezi River to the north, some of these Ngoni killed
the reigning Changamire ruler, sacked population centers, disrupted
trade patterns, and generally left the country in political and commercial chaos. These transient invaders were soon followed by
other Nguni who established permanent homes in present Rhodesia.
The Ndebele (or "Matabele") of Mzilikazi occupied the center of the
former Changamire state where they eventually made Bulawayo their
capital. Meanwhile, the Gaza (or "Shangane") of Soshangane settled
in the border region east of the Sabi River. These two intrusive
groups prevented the vastly more numerous Shona peoples from reorganizing large-scale polities by raiding their communities, disrupting trade, and meddling in local politics. In no sense did the
Ndebele and Gaza "conquer" the entire country, but throughout the
rest of the 19th century these new invaders--particularly the Nde-
bele--dominated the country's politics and commerce.

The mid-19th century saw a resurgence of European interest
in the country. This time Europeans entered from the south. They
came in search of elephant hunting grounds, Christian converts, and
gold mining concessions. The Ndebele rulers monopolized European
access to the country, giving outsiders an exaggerated impression of
their control over the Shona. Thus, when Rhodesia began attracting
the attention of European imperial powers in the late 1880s, the
Ndebele kingdom became the focus of diplomatic rivalries.

In 1888 agents of the South African financier and politician
Cecil Rhodes obtained from the Ndebele king Lobengula a mining
concession. This "Rudd Concession" provided the legal basis for
the new British South Africa Company to obtain a British Royal
Charter the next year. In 1890 the BSAC sent a small occupying
force into "Mashonaland, " the eastern part of the country, establishing

its headquarters at Salisbury.   European settlement developed rapidly, extending into the western half of the country ("Matabeleland")
in 1894, after a brief war was fought against the Ndebele.

By 1896 few Africans recognized British sovereignty in the
country, despite the Company's gains.   Most Africans bitterly resented cattle seizures, land alienations, forced labor recruitment,
and other abuses.   In early 1896 most subjects of the then dormant
Ndebele kingdom rose in revolt.   They were soon followed by many
Shona in the central and northeastern parts of the country.   The
British finally suppressed these risings only in late 1897.   Though
badly shaken, the BSAC retained its Royal Charter.   It reorganized
its administration, giving Africans some relief from prior abuses,
but Africans were virtually excluded from the legislative representation granted to European settlers in 1898.

Over the next twenty-five years European mining interests
were paramount in the country's economic development.   In 1923
the BSAC turned over responsibility for the country to the British
Imperial Government, but the settlers were granted effective self-
government under a constitution which remained in effect until 1961.
Although Britain retained reserve powers over African affairs in
the country, in practice the local government arrogated to itself
increasing authority for all local matters.   The settler-dominated
government was thus able to enact discriminatory laws affecting
land allocation, labor rights, and other important matters, with
little regard for either British Imperial oversight or local African
opinion, though the latter grew increasingly outspoken.   The country
was a British "colony" only in name.

From 1953 through 1963 Southern Rhodesia (as it was then
called), Northern Rhodesia, and Nyasaland (now Zambia and Malawi,
respectively) joined together to form the Federation of Rhodesia and
Nyasaland.   Southern Rhodesia dominated the Federation politically
and economically, reaping the largest share of economic benefits
which the Federation generated.   Many Southern Rhodesian settlers
hoped to transform the Federation into a white-controlled dominion
within the British Commonwealth, but Africans protested vigorously,

particularly in the northern territories. African opposition eventually doomed the Federation, forcing a reevaluation of Rhodesia's
own constitutional future.

Negotiations between Britain, the Rhodesian government, and
African nationalists produced a new constitution in 1961. This document granted Africans limited parliamentary representation in a
complex double-roll voting system, and it theoretically recognized
the eventuality of majority rule in the country. Britain refused to
grant Rhodesia full independence, however, until the settler government provided satisfactory guarantees that majority rule would in
fact be attained. This issue created a constitutional impasse which
remained unresolved in 1978.

In November 1965 Prime Minister Ian Smith issued Rhodesia's
Unilateral Declaration of Independence ("UDI") in an effort to overcome the impasse by asserting his government's de facto independence from Britain. World criticism of UDI was immediate and
harsh. The United Nations soon began voting increasingly strong
economic sanctions against Rhodesia, and to date not a single foreign
government has officially recognized Rhodesia's independence. Nevertheless, Smith's government has remained firmly in power. The
regime has always held the overwhelming support of its minority
electorate, while internal African opposition has remained generally
fragmented and ineffective. The country's economy is comparatively
highly diversified, and thus able to respond flexibly to shifting trade
situations. UN sanctions, while taking their toll of certain export
commodities such as tobacco, have been ignored by many foreign
markets, and South Africa has always been very cooperative in
channeling Rhodesian trade in and out of Africa. By mid-1977 it
was generally recognized that sanctions against Rhodesia were futile
without South African cooperation.

Since 1959 the Rhodesian government has increasingly used
its legislative, judicial, and police apparatus to stifle African dissent within the country. The government has persistently banned
African political organizations and has regularly imprisoned leaders.
The effect has been to drive political opponents into exile, and to

transform legitimate opposition parties into armed guerrilla forces. Since the mid-1960s Zambia has provided limited support for guerrilla bases, while its government has worked to bring rival Zimbabwean nationalist factions together. The liberation of Mozambique by its own armed nationalists in the early 1970s opened new sectors to the Zimbabwean nationalists on the eastern frontier, thereby helping to intensify the armed conflict greatly after 1972. After Mozambique became independent in 1975, the entire Mozambican border was opened to anti-Rhodesian guerrilla forces, but little progress was made towards unification of the rival factions.

The mid-1970s saw a renewal of serious diplomatic efforts to resolve the constitutional impasse through negotiations, but every international effort failed. By late 1977 Smith's government had made major verbal concessions to nationalist aspirations, but the external guerrilla forces grew even more intransigent as they became more confident of their ability eventually to dictate a settlement by force of arms. What may yet prove a decisive breakthrough in the impasse finally occurred in February 1978, when Smith and several locally-based nationalist leaders jointly announced agreement on the principles of universal adult suffrage, with special political representation for whites to last for ten years. However, externally-based nationalist leaders remained opposed to any negotiated settlement, and world leaders were hesitant to embrace the new settlement. As this book goes to press, the country's future remains very much in doubt.

THE DICTIONARY

ABA-. Sindebele* class prefix for the plural forms of many nouns and names for people (sing., um-, or umu-). In accordance with modern English usage, such prefixes are dropped from proper names in this dictionary. Thus, e. g., for Abananzwa, see NANZWA. Note that before stems with the initial letter e, aba- becomes abe-. Thus, for abenhla, see ENHLA. (Cf. AMA-.)

ABERCORN. James Hamilton, the 2nd Duke of Abercorn (1838-1913) was the first president of the BSAC (1889-1913). The present town of Shamwa (q. v.) was originally named after him.

ABRAHAM, DONALD P. British historian. He came to the country in 1950 to work for the Native Department, later becoming a research fellow at the University College* (1960-67). During this period he collected an immense body of Shona oral traditions and did archival research on Shona history in Portugal. His scattered articles on Shona history, though full of contradictions, remain seminal works on early Shona history (see BIBLIOGRAPHY). At the University of North Carolina since 1969.

ABUTUA see BUTUA

"ACROPOLIS." Popular, but perhaps misleading, name for the Hill complex in the Zimbabwe Ruins (q. v.). The term was first used by J. T. Bent* in 1891.

ADENDORFF TREK (a. k. a. Banyailand Trek). In August 1890 Louis Adendorff and several other Transvaal Afrikaners* obtained a written land concession* from two Karanga* chiefs, each claiming to be the Chivi (q. v.) of the Mari people. These chiefs, Chivasa (Sebasa) and Nyajena Musavi (Mazobi), wished to enlist Afrikaner mercenaries to help defend the Mari against Ndebele raids. When Cecil Rhodes* later visited the Transvaal, he met Adendorff, who tried to sell him the concession. Rhodes rejected the offer as worthless, on the grounds that because the Chivi was a vassal of the Ndebele, his territory was covered by the BSAC's Rudd Concession (q. v.), which the Company was using as a legal pretext for occupying Mashonaland*. Adendorff then advertised widely in South African newspapers for Afrikaners to form a 2000-man trek to create a "republic" in "Banyai-

9

land" (see NYAI). The BSAC regarded this venture as a serious threat to British predominance north of the Limpopo River
and persuaded the Transvaal's (q. v.) president Paul Kruger to
oppose the trek. On June 24, 1891, about 100 trekkers appeared
at the Limpopo. A heavily-armed detachment of the BSAP prevented their crossing and L. S. Jameson* persuaded them to
disperse. Some of the trekkers, including their commander, a
Col. Ignateus Ferreira, accepted the BSAC's offer to settle in
Mashonaland as individuals. (Cf. MOODIE TREK.)

ADMINISTRATORS OF BSAC GOVERNMENT (1890-1923). During the
33 years that the BSAC ruled the country, the senior official in
the government was the Administrator. Organization of the government was rather haphazard until 1898, when the British government issued an Order-in-Council. This edict created an
Executive Council and a Legislative Council (qq. v.), with the
Administrator presiding over both. The Administrator also
served as Secretary for Native Affairs, appointing magistrates
and Native Commissioners. Although ultimate authority lay
with the British government and the BSAC board of directors,
in practice the Administrators exercised considerable local
power.
       Administrators of Mashonaland, 1890-1901: 1890-91
A. R. Colquhoun; 1891-94 L. S. Jameson; 1898-1901 W. H.
Milton. Administrator of Matabeleland, 1898-1901: 1898-1901
A. Lawley (subordinate to Milton). Administrators of Southern
Rhodesia: 1894-96 L. S. Jameson; 1896-97 A. H. G. (Earl)
Grey; 1897-98 W. H. Milton (acting); 1901-14 W. H. Milton;
1914-23 F. P. D. Chaplin. (See individual entries for each ad-
ministrator; see also GOVERNORS; PRIME MINISTERS.)

AFRICAN COAST FEVER. Variant name for East Coast Fever
(q. v.).

AFRICAN DAILY NEWS (ADN). Perhaps the most important newspaper yet published in the country for African readers, ADN
was issued from Salisbury between 1956 and 1964. African
Newspapers, Ltd. (q. v.) founded the paper in response to urg-
ing by Garfield Todd*, who was anxious for a propaganda vehicle to help counter a developing African miners' strike. The
government initially subsidized and helped to distribute ADN,
giving the paper a pro-government stigma which lasted until
1962. In that year the new management of African Newspapers
changed the ADN's editorial policy to a strongly pro-African
stance. ADN then became the only non-party paper in the country which voiced African nationalist opinions. It relentlessly
criticized the new Rhodesian Front government, calling attention
to a wide variety of issues ignored by the rest of the country's
press (q. v.). By 1964, when the paper's circulation had reached
c. 15, 000, ADN was giving coverage to Joshua Nkomo and ZAPU.
On August 26, 1964 Ian Smith banned ADN, terminating its publication. (See CENSORSHIP.)

AFRICAN FARMERS' UNION.　Organization representing the interests of private farmers in Purchase Areas (q. v.); formed
around 1933 under the leadership of Aaron Jacha (q. v.).　By
1972 the Union had c. 9000 members.

AFRICAN LAND HUSBANDRY ACT.　Name by which the Native Land
Husbandry Act (q. v.) is retrospectively known.

AFRICAN METHODIST EPISCOPAL CHURCH (AMEC).　American-
based black church with world-wide mission program.　Richard
Allen, a freed slave, founded the church in Philadelphia in 1816
because of racial discrimination in the established Methodist
Church.　AMEC leaders and missionaries came to South Africa
in the late 1890s in response to interest by African independent
church leaders, many of whom quickly affiliated with AMEC.
American AMEC officials tried to enter Southern Rhodesia, but
were kept out by the administration.　South African AMEC missionaries then entered the country.　The most important of these
pioneers was Moses Makgatho, a Sotho who bought a farm outside of Bulawayo.　Makgatho's farm remained the center of
AMEC operations in the country for the next 25 years.　In 1927
Zephaniah Cam Mtshwelo, a South African Thembu, was appointed head of the AMEC Southern Rhodesian church.　Under
his leadership the church expanded rapidly, building missions
and schools throughout the country.　The government prohibited
AMEC from working in reserves*, so it operated mainly in urban areas and in African mine compounds.　The church's purely
black leadership and urban emphases contrasted sharply with the
rural emphasis of white-dominated missions.　By 1959 AMEC
claimed more than 32, 000 members in the country, and it had
expanded its field of operations to north of the Zambezi.　(See
METHODIST MISSIONS.)

AFRICAN NATIONAL CONGRESS (ANC).　The country's modern congress movement started in 1934, when Aaron Jacha (q. v.)
founded the Bantu Congress.　Though this organization had been
inspired by the large ANC of South Africa, it attracted a small
membership through the 1930s.　Its political goals were modest,
featuring mainly appeals for exemption of educated Africans
from discriminatory laws.　Its leaders protested the Industrial
Conciliation Act (q. v.), but registered approval of the Land Apportionment Act before the Bledisloe Commission (qq. v.).
　　　Under the leadership of T. D. Samkange (q. v.) the movement experienced a minor resurgence after the Second World
War, by which time it was known as the Southern Rhodesian
African National Congress.　The ANC failed to catch on as national mass movement, however, and was moribund by the early
1950s.　Only the Bulawayo branch of the ANC survived the de-
fection of leaders to multi-racial, Federation-oriented parties
and societies, and that branch operated mainly as a social organization.　This early phase of ANC later became known, retrospectively, as the "old African National Congress. "
　　　On September 12, 1957--a date chosen because of its

significance to settlers as "Occupation Day" (now "Pioneer Day"*)
--the ANC was reformed by the leaders of the Youth League
(q. v.), which it effectively replaced. Joshua Nkomo (q. v.) was
made president, and James Chikerema, vice president (q. v.).
Other early leaders included Jason Moyo and George Nyandoro
(qq. v.). The new ANC quickly attracted mass support in both
urban and rural areas throughout the country. Employing
strictly constitutional means of seeking redress, ANC protested
the pass laws, Native Land Husbandry Act (qq. v.), and other
discriminatory laws, and it demanded universal adult suffrage.
Its leaders wrote letters and petitions to the government and
organized large public demonstrations. By 1959 the government
estimated ANC membership at 6000 to 7000 people, while ANC
supporters claimed a membership 30 to 40 times greater. Non-
racial in orientation, ANC attracted more than a hundred European members, including Guy Clutton-Brock who later became
the only European arrested because of ANC activities.

Alarmed by civil disturbances north of the Zambezi, and
by the supposed subversive influence of ANC--particularly in
rural areas--Edgar Whitehead's government declared a state of
emergency and arrested nearly 500 ANC leaders in a sudden
morning sweep on February 26, 1959. The government banned
ANC, later passing the Unlawful Organizations Act (q. v.) further
to restrict ANC leaders. The government's ruthless and largely
unexpected action demoralized nationalists during the remainder
of the year and caused a further revulsion against the concept
of "partnership" (q. v.). The National Democratic Party (q. v.)
was founded as a successor organization on the first day of 1960.

AFRICAN NATIONAL COUNCIL (ANC). The country's leading inter-
nal African political body since late 1971, ANC was founded on
December 16, 1971, as a temporary pressure group opposing the
Anglo-Rhodesian Settlement proposals signed three weeks earlier.
Two Methodist ministers without prior political reputations, Abel
Muzorewa and Canaan Banana (qq. v.), headed the Council. Other
leaders, mostly veterans of ZAPU and ZANU, included Edson
Sithole, Josiah Chinamano, and Michael Mawema (qq. v.). The
name of the Council was consciously chosen to recall the "ANC"
acronym of the older and highly respected African National Congress (q. v.).

ANC branches arose spontaneously throughout the country.
By the time the Pearce Commission (q. v.) arrived in early
1972, ANC was well represented in both urban and rural areas,
and its central executive served mainly to disseminate information. Legal aid was provided by IDAF lawyers (q. v.). Efforts
to persuade the Pearce Commission of the country's rejection of
the settlement proposals were a complete success. ANC then
formally reconstituted itself as a permanent political organization on March 10th and began a membership drive. Muzorewa
was retained as president.

The government never moved to proscribe ANC, but
severely hindered its organizing efforts by banning the sale of
membership cards, prohibiting acceptance of foreign funds, and

arresting and generally harassing leaders. Nevertheless, ANC remained officially committed to non-violent change, calling upon the government to participate in a national constitutional conference in order to bring about majority rule. By late 1972 Muzorewa was rumored to be holding secret negotiations with Ian Smith. Further meetings in 1973 were more openly acknowledged.

In late 1974 the changing international situation made the government more amenable to serious constitutional negotiations. Talks were held between government officials and ANC leaders in Lusaka in December. On December 8th ANC leaders there announced that formerly-rival nationalist parties, ZAPU, ZANU, and FROLIZI (qq. v.), had merged under ANC's "umbrella." The merger was encouraged by President Kenneth Kaunda of Zambia and the emerging "Frontline Presidents" group (q. v.). The agreed-upon constitutional negotiations finally began at the Victoria Falls Conference (q. v.) in August 1975. After the Conference's speedy collapse, old rifts in the nationalist leadership resurfaced, with Nkomo publicly denouncing James Chikerema and Ndabaningi Sithole (qq. v.). Nkomo himself returned to Salisbury under the ANC banner and held private talks with Ian Smith in early 1976. Muzorewa and the other leaders remained outside the country.

Although the old party labels increasingly came back into use, the name "ANC" was retained by the rival factions. Muzorewa's group, no longer committed to non-violence, adopted the name "United African National Council" to avoid confusion with Nkomo's ANC inside Rhodesia. When the Geneva Conference (q. v.) convened in late 1976, Nkomo, Muzorewa, Sithole, and Robert Mugabe (q. v.) all headed separate delegations.

AFRICAN NATIONAL YOUTH LEAGUE   see   YOUTH LEAGUE

AFRICAN NEWSPAPERS, LTD. (ANL). White-owned and managed group of newspapers published between 1943 and 1964 (see PRESS). Publication of newspapers for African readers had begun with the Bantu Mirror (q. v.) in the 1930s. In 1943 ANL was started in Southern Rhodesia by B. G. and C. A. G. Paver, South African brothers who managed Bantu Press in Johannesburg. With the encouragement of the Southern Rhodesian government, ANL acquired control of the Bantu Mirror in Bulawayo, and started African Weekly (q. v.) in Salisbury. Publications later added included The Harvester for African farmers and The Recorder for teachers. In 1956 African Daily News (q. v.) was begun. Although the management of ANL co-operated closely with the government to make its publications politically innocuous, the mainly African editorial and writing staffs were allowed considerable freedom through the 1950s.

The ANL group was owned by a consortium comprising the Anglo-American Corporation, Rhodesian Selection Trust, Imperial Tobacco, and the BSAC, but these companies are said to have interfered less in editorial policy than did the government. In 1962 the consortium sold ANL to Lord Thomson, the

owner of London's Sunday Times and other papers. Under the
new ownership African Daily News began developing a strongly
pro-African nationalist editorial policy. This change increasingly
irritated the Rhodesian Front government, which had come in
about the same time. In August 1964 the government banned
Daily News. It and the other ANL publications then ceased publication.

    Among the ANL's editors-in-chief were J. Z. Savanhu,
Lawrence Vambe, and Nathan Shamuyarira (qq. v.). (See also
ARGUS GROUP; CENSORSHIP.)

AFRICAN PURCHASE AREAS (APA) see PURCHASE AREAS

THE AFRICAN TIMES. Biweekly government-published newspaper,
    distributed free to Africans by the Ministry of Information. The
Rhodesian Front government started the paper in 1965, after it
had effectively suppressed the African Newspapers, Ltd. group
(q. v.). By the mid-1970s the government was circulating
c. 500,000 copies of the propaganda sheet, which it claimed
were being read by two million Africans. A parallel publication, Rhodesian Commentary, was also being published for recent settlers in six different European languages. (N. B.: an
independent commercial newspaper named The African Times
was briefly published in Fort Victoria* in 1963.)

AFRICAN WEEKLY. An African Newspapers, Ltd. (q. v.) publica-
    tion started in Salisbury in 1943 as a Mashonaland counterpart
of the older Bantu Mirror, published in Bulawayo. In 1962 it
and the Mirror were merged into the Daily News (q. v.) weekend
edition.

AFRICAN WORKERS' VOICE ASSOCIATION see under BUROMBO,
    BENJAMIN

AFRIKAANS (old variant: "Cape Dutch"). The language of the
    Afrikaner people (q. v.), Afrikaans is an off-shoot of Dutch,
whose grammar it simplified, and to whose vocabulary it added
many non-Germanic words. Afrikaans is reckoned to have
emerged as a distinct language in South Africa at least as early
as 1800. In 1918 it was recognized as an official language in
the Union of South Africa. Afrikaner settlers in Southern Rhodesia then lobbied unsuccessfully for similar recognition there.

AFRIKANER PEOPLE (a. k. a. Boers*; South African or Cape Dutch).
    South African people of Dutch, French, and other non-English
European descent who speak Afrikaans (q. v.) as their first language have been known as Afrikaners since the early 19th century. The Afrikaners originated in the Cape Colony (now South
Africa's Cape Province) in the 17th century, spreading throughout the South African interior only since the 1830s. Afrikaner
migrants of the 1830s, known as Voortrekkers, clashed with the
Ndebele kingdom (q. v.) then in the Transvaal (q. v.), helping to
drive the Ndebele into present Rhodesia (see POTGIETER, A. H.).

Afterwards the Voortrekkers established many small republics
and two big ones: the Transvaal and the Orange Free State.
    Transvalers began hunting and trading in Matabeleland
during the 1860s (see, e.g., VILJOEN, J.). By the 1880s the
possibility of Afrikaner expansion north of the Limpopo River
was a real threat, providing Cecil Rhodes with one of his main
incentives for acquiring Mashonaland and Matabeleland (qq.v.)
for Britain (see ADENDORFF TREK). Nevertheless, during the
1890s hundreds of Afrikaner families migrated into Mashonaland,
where they became the majority white populations in many rural
districts (see, e.g., MOODIE TREK). Between the 1920s and
the 1950s Afrikaner settlers constituted roughly one-sixth to one-
fifth of the country's whole white population, making them the
most important white ethnic group aside from British-derived
settlers. Their language, their religion (see DUTCH REFORMED
CHURCH), and their feelings of identity with South Africa made
them a cohesive political faction favoring the Unionist Movement
(q.v.) and opposing all measures designed to advance Africans
politically.

AGRICULTURE. Despite rapid development of the country's indus-
    trial and mining sectors, agriculture remains the primary eco-
    nomic activity of the vast majority of the people. The govern-
    ment has never kept detailed statistics on African subsistence
    agriculture--which typifies the Tribal Trust Lands (q.v.)--and
    since UDI it has been reticent to publish figures on European-
    dominated cash agriculture. Nevertheless, it is clear that the
    country is virtually self-sufficient in food production, and that
    it earns considerable revenue from agricultural exports. It is
    also clear that modern agricultural techniques and marketing
    advances have had little impact on the farmers of the TTL's,
    which are physically isolated from cheap transport facilities,
    and which suffer from rapidly increasing populations (q.v.) on
    limited land.
        Agricultural activity apparently began with the arrival of
    Iron Age (q.v.) peoples early in the first millenium A.D. By
    the 19th century the Shona peoples were primarily farmers, with
    some cattle (q.v.) and smaller livestock. The main Shona crops
    were millets (q.v.), maize (q.v.), and sorghums--all of which
    were also grown extensively by the Ndebele after their arrival
    in the country. Other crops included groundnuts, yams, pump-
    kins, beans, rice, and citrus fruits, as well as cotton and to-
    bacco (qq.v.). The Ndebele kept more cattle than did the Shona,
    but these were used largely for social rather than purely eco-
    nomic functions. No draft animals were used, and plowing was
    done by hand. Production figures for the pre-colonial era are
    not obtainable, but the Ndebele are known to have produced suf-
    ficient grain surpluses to export sizeable quantities outside the
    country. When Europeans began occupying the country in the
    1890s, they found African food production capable of meeting
    most of their own needs as they concentrated on mining (q.v.)
    and other activities.
        Twentieth-century European agriculture developed slowly

until the Second World War, with maize ranking as the primary crop. Direct participation of farmers in politics from the early 1930s began an era of government support for European agriculture, while African farmers were largely left to their own devices in the less fertile and more poorly watered lands to which most of them were restricted (see LAND APPORTIONMENT ACT). An American agriculturalist, E. D. Alvord (q. v.), stimulated government assistance to African farmers, but as late as 1970 it was estimated that half the country's African farmers remained unbenefitted by the changes.

The Second World War revolutionized European agriculture by greatly expanding markets within the British Empire. After the war a rapid influx of new immigrants increased the numbers of European farmers, stimulating more efficient organization of commercial farming, increased mechanization, and scientific research which led to higher-yielding strains of many crops. The most intensive development occurred in the two Mashonaland* provinces, where tobacco production boomed, while the drier remaining provinces developed ranching and extensive maize cultivation.

Post-UDI sanctions (q. v.) affected agriculture more severely than any other economic sector, but their main impact was to encourage diversification rather than to reduce the total value of production. Between 1965 and 1971 the gross value of agricultural production is estimated to have risen more than half, accounting for about one-sixth of gross domestic product. The southeastern low veld region (see ALTITUDINAL ZONES) has benefitted especially from the irrigation schemes of the Sabi-Limpopo Authority (q. v.). By 1972 outside authorities estimated that farm exports had regained pre-UDI levels, accounting for more than half of total non-subsistence agricultural production. Outstanding export products include beef, maize, cotton, and tobacco (see also FORESTRY; DAMS AND WATER SUPPLY; LOCUSTS).

AIR TRANSPORT/AIR RHODESIA. Air transportation began in the country when a South African plane landed in Bulawayo in 1920. It crashed on take-off the next day. In 1932 Imperial Airways (the predecessor of BOAC) extended its services to Cape Town, with stops in Southern Rhodesia. The next year this airline and the Beit Trust (q. v.) helped to found Rhodesia and Nyasaland Airways, or "Rana" (q. v.), which the government took over in 1940 and renamed Southern Rhodesian Air Services. In 1946 the airline was reorganized as Central African Airways Corporation (CAA), under the control of the three territorial governments (see CENTRAL AFRICAN COUNCIL). CAA operated as an international airline through the years of Federation (q. v.), and then divided into separate national airlines: Air Zambia, Air Malawi, and Air Rhodesia. The last was officially formed in 1968. With a small fleet of DC-3s, Viscount propjets, and Boeing 720s, Air Rhodesia provided internal air services and international flights to South Africa and, until recently, Malawi and Mozambique (q. v.). More distant flights have been provided

by South African Airlines, TAP, Lufthansa, and Air Malawi.
There are major airports at Salisbury, Bulawayo, and Victoria
Falls, and smaller airports at Fort Victoria, Gwelo, Kariba,
Buffalo Range, and Wankie National Park (qq. v.). A few small
charter companies also operate in the country (see TRANSPORT
AND COMMUNICATIONS).

ALASKA MINE. One of the largest copper (q. v.) mines in the
country; located west of Sinoia* on the branch railway* line (at
17° 24'S, 30° 1'E). In 1959 production began on the site of pre-
colonial African mine workings. Population in 1969 was 4410
(92% Africans).

ALDERSON, EDWIN ALFRED HARVEY (April 8, 1859-Dec. 22,
1927). British army officer with experience in South Africa
and Egypt before coming to Rhodesia. As a Lt.-Colonel in
1896, Alderson was made commander of four companies of
Mounted Infantry, with which he was sent by way of Beira* to
relieve Salisbury during the Shona Revolt (q. v.). He engaged
in several actions while entering the country, most notably
capturing Makoni's* town. He arrived at Salisbury in August
and was made responsible for all British forces in Mashonaland,
answering only to the supreme British commander, F. Carrington (q. v.) in Matabeleland. Alderson combined his imperial
troops with local forces to form the Mashonaland Field Force
(q. v.), which operated through November. He left the country
when the force was disbanded, later writing a book about the
campaign. During the First World War he commanded Canadian
troops in France.

ALL-AFRICAN CONVENTION. Short-lived political organization
formed in 1951 to cooperate with Northern Rhodesian and Nyasa-
lander groups opposing Federation (q. v.). The Convention joined
together representatives of older organizations, such as the African National Congress, Reformed Industrial and Commercial
Union (qq. v.), and trade unions. Charles Mzingeli (q. v.) was
made interim president. Other leaders included George Nyandoro, Joshua Nkomo, Benjamin Burombo, and Stanlake Samkange (qq. v.). The body faded quickly after the creation of the
Federation in 1953.

ALTITUDINAL ZONES. Most of the country lies more than 1000
meters (m.) above sea level. Its lowest point, where the Sabi
River* exits the country in the southeast, is 168 m. Its highest
point, Mount Inyangani*, is 2594 m. The country as a whole is
generally seen as dividing into three altitudinal zones, which
occasionally meet in escarpments.
        The High Veld includes land over 1220 m. (4000 ft.),
comprising about a fifth of the country. Most of this land
forms the Central Plateau, a ridge which runs approximately
southwest to northeast, with important extensions northwest
and east of Salisbury. Although the term "high veld" is sometimes treated as synonymous with "central plateau," it also

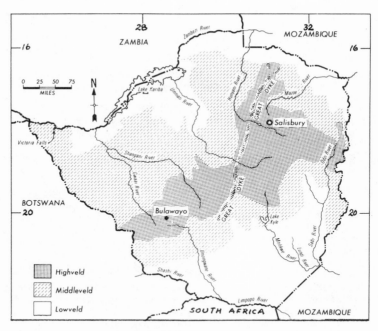

Map 2. Altitudinal Zones

properly applies to the Eastern Highlands (q.v.), which include
the country's highest points. The high veld areas contain the
country's most developed regions, most of its important towns
(see URBANIZATION), and most of its European population (q.v.).
The Middle Veld is variously defined as land over 2000
or 2500 ft. (600 to 760 m.), but below 4000 ft. This land forms
a penumbra around the high veld regions, except in parts of the
west, where it rises alone.
The Low Veld makes up the remaining, lower parts of
the country. It is separated into two distinct regions by the
central plateau: the Zambezi Valley (q.v.) in the north, and
the southeastern corner of the country (see SABI-LIMPOPO
AUTHORITY). The term "low veld" is applied most frequently
to the latter region. The low veld regions are hot, they receive mostly light and unreliable rainfall (see CLIMATE), and
they harbor the country's most troublesome human and animal
diseases (see HEALTH). Hence, they are the least populated
and least developed parts of the country.

ALVORD, EMORY DELMONT (March 25, 1889-May 6, 1959).
Pioneering agriculturalist. Born in Utah, Alvord obtained a
B.S. degree in agriculture (q.v.) from Washington State College (1915). Though raised as a Mormon, he joined the Congregationalist Mount Silinda Mission (q.v.) in Chipinga District in
1919. His success in teaching agricultural techniques to Africans

caught the attention of the government, which appointed him
"Agriculturalist for Instruction of Natives" in 1926. Despite
limited staff and funds, he initiated a small revolution in the
country's agriculture which earned him the esteem of both
Africans and Europeans. His basic system emphasized cen-
tralization of arable lands and their isolation from grazing
animals, heavy use of steer for manure, crop rotation, and
soil conservation. The system was well suited for small plots
and was easily taught with the use of demonstration farms.
Greatly increased crop yields encouraged many African farmers
to follow the system, but these gains have been offset by the
rapidly growing populations (q.v.) in the Tribal Trust Lands
(q.v.). Alvord retired from the government in 1950 and returned to mission work. The next year the government passed
the Native Land Husbandry Act (q.v.) in an effort to enforce
many of his ideas.

AMA- . Common Nguni* and Sindebele* prefix (Class 3) for plural
   forms of nouns or names of people (sing., i[li]-*). In accordance with modern English usage, such prefixes are dropped
   from proper nouns in this dictionary. For example, for
   Amandebele, see NDEBELE. For ordinary nouns, see under
   i-. For example, for amadlozi, see IDLOZI. Note that the
   ama- prefix is frequently shortened to ma-, as in Mandebele,
   and that ma- also happens to be a Chishona* prefix (q.v.).
   (Cf. ABA-.)

AMALGAMATION MOVEMENT. Thirty-five years before the creation of the Federation of Rhodesia and Nyasaland (q.v.), a movement arose to amalgamate Southern and Northern Rhodesia (the
   latter is now Zambia*) integrally. The initial proponents of
   this movement were mainly officials of the BSAC who hoped to
   achieve some administrative economies and to strengthen the
   economic position of the BSAC's central African territories in
   relation to South Africa*. At first most Southern Rhodesian
   settlers opposed the plan, for fear that amalgamation would de-
   lay achievement of Responsible Government (q.v.). The British
   government acquiesced to settler pressures, so the idea temporarily died. Amalgamation again became an issue in the mid-
   1920s, when new mineral discoveries on Northern Rhodesia's
   Copperbelt offered the prospect of much-needed economic stimu-
   lation to Southern Rhodesia's government. Northern Rhodesian
   settlers also began pushing for amalgamation, in the hope of
   breaking free from Colonial Office control. Britain responded
   to settler pressures in 1927 and in 1938 by setting up the Hilton
   Young and Bledisloe Commissions (qq.v.) to investigate the issue. By then some attention was being paid to African opinion,
   which in Northern Rhodesia strongly opposed any form of merger
   with Southern Rhodesia. The commissions' negative reports
   killed the amalgamation idea, but a new movement, this time
   for federation, arose after the Second World War. (Cf.
   UNIONIST MOVEMENT.)

AMANDAS.   Village located c. 55 km. north of Salisbury, on the
    Shamva* railway* line (at 17° 22'S, 30° 57'E).   In 1969 the
    population of Amandas and its immediate southern neighbor,
    Concession (q. v.), was 3120 (93% Africans).

AMERICAN BOARD OF COMMISSIONERS FOR FOREIGN MISSIONS
    (ABC).   Based in Boston, the Congregationalist (q. v.) ABC is
    the oldest foreign mission body in the United States.   It began
    work in Southern Africa in 1835, when it sent mission parties
    to labor among the Zulu* of Natal and the Ndebele of Mzilikazi
    (qq. v.), then living in the western Transvaal*.   The American
    Zulu Mission eventually prospered, but the Ndebele mission,
    known as the "Inland Zulu Mission," was abandoned when Afri-
    kaners* attacked the Ndebele in early 1837.
        In 1893 representatives of the Zulu mission were granted
    large tracts of land in Gazaland (q. v.) by the BSAC.   That year
    they founded the Mount Silinda Mission (q. v.) in Ndau* terri-
    tory.   They soon expanded their operations around the Sabi
    River* and southern Mozambique.   During the present century
    they have made a major contribution to African education (q. v.)
    in the southeastern part of the country through the creation of
    numerous primary schools and an industrial school at Mt.
    Silinda.   The organization is now known locally as the Rho-
    desian Mission American Board.

AMNESTY INTERNATIONAL (AI).   Non-political voluntary organiza-
    tion, founded in London in 1961.   Its member groups bring
    pressure on both leftist and rightist national governments to
    adhere to the United Nation's Universal Declaration of Human
    Rights.   Since UDI in 1965, AI groups have publicized alleged
    Rhodesian government use of preventive detention, secret trials,
    capital punishment, torture of prisoners, military atrocities,
    and forced resettlement of Africans in "protected villages" (q. v.).
    AI groups have taken up the cases of more than a thousand indi-
    vidual political prisoners in Rhodesia.   (See LAW AND ORDER
    [MAINTENANCE] ACT.)

"ANCIENT."   Chronological term frequently applied by archaeolo-
    gists and antiquarians to virtually all pre-colonial sites and
    artifacts in the country.   The Southern Rhodesian Monuments
    and Relics Act of 1936 formally defined as "ancient" all historic
    sites existing prior to 1890.   (See HISTORICAL MONUMENT
    COMMISSION.)

ANCIENT PARK NATIONAL MONUMENT   see   MONK'S KOP

ANCIENT RUINS COMPANY   see   RHODESIA ANCIENT RUINS

ANDRADA, JOAQUIM CARLOS PAIVA DE (Nov. 29, 1846-April
    1928).   Sometimes described as a would-be imitator of C. J.
    Rhodes (q. v.), d'Andrada used both private companies and his
    official posts in an attempt to extend Portuguese (q. v.) im-
    perialism inland from Mozambique (q. v.).   In 1878 he obtained

a vast "paper" mineral concession to the area between Zumbo
and Tete (qq.v.), but he never got sufficient financial backing
to exploit it. During the 1880s he allied with M. A. de Sousa
(q.v.) in an attempt to extend Portuguese influence through
Sousa's African conquests. In 1888 he helped to form the
Mozambique Company to realize Portuguese domination over
Mashonaland and Manicaland (qq.v.). Meanwhile, Rhodes'
BSAC was advancing its own claims north of the Limpopo
River*. In November 1890 d'Andrada and Sousa were at Mutasa's (q.v.) town trying to secure that chief's cooperation. A
BSAC force under P. W. Forbes (q.v.) "arrested" them both
there. They were sent off to the Cape. When they were later
released, they found that most of Manicaland had been secured
by the British (see ANGLO-PORTUGUESE CONVENTION).
D'Andrada resumed his military career, later dying in Paris.

ANGLICAN MISSIONS. The Church of England entered the country
mainly through the efforts of its semi-autonomous Province of
South Africa, but its own Society for the Propagation of the
Gospel (SPG) supported mission work from the start. In 1876
a South African priest, W. Greenstock, visited Lobengula (q.v.)
in the hope of starting a mission, but the effort came to nothing.
Twelve years later G. W. H. Knight-Bruce (q.v.), the Bishop
of Bloemfontein, visited Lobengula and traveled extensively
throughout Mashonaland*. When the British occupied Mashonaland in 1890, Canon F. R. T. Balfour (1846-1924) accompanied
the Pioneer Column* and established the first Anglican church
in Salisbury. Meanwhile, the Province of South Africa created
the Diocese of Mashonaland, making Knight-Bruce its first Bishop
(January 1891). The new diocese included all of present Rhodesia and parts of Botswana and Mozambique. Knight-Bruce returned to the country with Bernard Mizeki (q.v.) and other African catechists and opened mission stations at Penhalonga* and
elsewhere in Mashonaland.
        Progress was slow until after the 1896-7 Shona Revolt
(q.v.), when Knight-Bruce's successors put mission work on a
firmer footing. Mission stations, schools, and parishes were
gradually extended throughout the entire country. The first local
African priest was ordained in 1923. Two years later E. F.
Paget (q.v.) began three decades of service as bishop. By the
late 1950s the church claimed 29,500 African members--the
second largest number of any Christian church in the country.
(See MISSIONS.)
        The Mashonaland Diocese was renamed Diocese of Southern
Rhodesia in 1915. In 1953 separate dioceses of Matabeleland and
Mashonaland were created. Two years later these dioceses fell
under the newly-created Province of Central Africa, which included present Zambia and Malawi. (See also A. S. CRIPPS.)

ANGLO-NDEBELE WAR (1893) see NDEBELE WAR

ANGLO-PORTUGUESE CONVENTION (1891). Portuguese (q.v.) claims
    to parts of present Rhodesia go back to the time of their earliest

explorations there, but only became concerted in the late 1880s, when it was clear that the British were beginning to regard the region as falling within their own "sphere of interest." The Portuguese government reluctantly conceded that the Moffat Treaty of February 1888 (q. v.) gave the British priority over Matabeleland*, but it then acted to make good its long-standing claims over Mashonaland and Manicaland (qq. v.; see also ANDRADA). Meanwhile, the government negotiated with the British in an effort to preserve the old Portuguese-British alliance in the face of mounting competition in Africa. On August 20, 1890, a Portuguese envoy signed a draft convention in London. This document defined the British-Portuguese borders in southern Africa, guaranteeing British railway* access from Mashonaland to the Indian Ocean, and promising to keep the Zambezi River (q. v.) open to foreign navigation. The agreement was so unpopular in Portugal that it contributed to the fall of the government in Lisbon and the document was not ratified.

The BSAC occupied Mashonaland a few months later (see PIONEER COLUMN), and then obtained a grant to Manicaland from chief Mutasa (q. v.) and made efforts to secure an Indian Ocean port in Gaza (q. v.) territory. Anti-British feeling mounted in Portugal and Mozambique. Incidents at Mutasa's in November (see P. W. FORBES) and at Maçequeçe (q. v.) the following May brought tensions to a peak. Nevertheless, continuing negotiations in Europe led to the signing of a somewhat modified Anglo-Portuguese Convention in Lisbon on June 11, 1891. This document was ratified by the Portuguese Cortes. It fixed the approximate modern borders (q. v.) of Mozambique, forever ending Portuguese ambitions of linking that territory with Angola, and it effectively ended Portuguese-British rivalry in southern Africa.

ANGLO-RHODESIAN SETTLEMENT PROPOSALS (1971)   see   PEARCE COMMISSION

ANGONI   see   NGONI

ANGWA RIVER.   Rises just southwest of Sinoia*, whence it flows north, then northeast, before joining the Hunyani* in Mozambique. The Angwa separates the Urungwe and Lomagundi districts (qq. v.).

ANTELOPE MINE.   Village c. 100 km. south of Bulawayo, on the Shashani River* (at 21° 3'S, 28° 27'E). It is named after a gold mine which operated there between 1913 and 1919 on the site of earlier African workings.

APARTHEID.   An Afrikaans* word meaning, literally, "apartness," apartheid is the official name of the South African government's policy of territorial segregation. The term is not officially used in Rhodesia, but similarities between its government's policies and those of South Africa have caused the term to be popularly used by outsiders. The roots of the country's segregation policies lie in the Morris Carter Commission Report of 1925 (q.v.; see also LAND APPORTIONMENT and LAND TENURE ACTS; TWO-PYRAMID POLICY).

ARABS see MUSLIMS

ARCHAEOLOGY see STONE AGE; IRON AGE

ARCHIVES see NATIONAL ARCHIVES OF RHODESIA

ARCTURUS. Gold mining center in the Goromanzi District* (at 17°47'S, 31°19'E). Population in 1969 was 1770 (95% Africans).

ARGUS GROUP OF NEWSPAPERS. Unofficial name for publications of the present Rhodesian Printing and Publishing Company, which controls most of the country's European press. The Argus Printing and Publishing Company was founded in South Africa in 1889, 32 years after the Cape Argus commenced publication. Cecil Rhodes (q.v.), a share-holder in the company, invited Argus to start a newspaper in Mashonaland* shortly after his BSAC had occupied the region. In 1891 Argus sent W. E. Fairbridge (q.v.) to Salisbury, where he immediately started the forerunner of the Rhodesia Herald (q.v.). In 1894 Argus entered Matabeleland* and started the Bulawayo Chronicle (q.v.), the only daily paper to survive there.
      The editorial policies of these papers reflected those of their South African counterparts. During the early 1920s the Rhodesia Herald and Bulawayo Chronicle ran strongly counter to settler opinion by supporting the Unionist Movement (q.v.). Settler resentment against South African control of the press led to formation of the Rhodesian Printing and Publishing Company, Ltd. in 1927. Majority control of the new company was vested in Southern Rhodesians, but the Argus company sold its papers to the company while retaining a nearly 50% interest. For this reason the local company's papers are still known as the "Argus Group." The company also controls the Umtali Post and the Sunday Mail (qq.v.), as well as many minor publications. (See PRESS.)

ARMY see MILITARY

ASBESTOS. The rather unglamorous fibrous silicate mineral known as asbestos displaced gold (q.v.) as the country's leading mineral (q.v.) product in value in 1952. Production began near Mashaba* in 1907, and asbestos soon became one of the country's leading export items. Since the Second World War the country has been one of the world's leading asbestos producers, and it is said to rank first in production of high grade fibers (chrysotile). Before UDI more than 95% of production was exported to 50 countries. Since then asbestos has fallen behind copper (q.v.) and gold in export value because of the increased emphasis on shipping high value/low bulk commodities (see SANCTIONS). Shabani (q.v.) is the main asbestos mining center, followed by the region between Gwanda* and Mashaba.

ASIANS.   During the 1890s a small but steady stream of Asians
began immigrating into the country.   Most were Hindus from
British India.   By the mid-1920s, when the government began
discouraging Asian immigration, there were about 1500 Asians
in the country.   Since then the population has increased at an
accelerating rate, mainly through natural increase.   By 1975
there were about 10,000 Asians in the country, living mostly
in the main towns.   The white government has defined Asians
as a separate "race," subject to discriminatory laws which
place them and Coloureds (q.v.) in an intermediate position
between Europeans and Africans.   (See MUSLIMS; POPULA-
TION.)

ASSEGAI.   Widely-used European term for African spears.   Introduced into southern African usage by the Portuguese, "assegai"
had, ironically, been introduced into western Europe much
earlier from north Africa.   Of the many different kinds of
spears used in pre-colonial Rhodesia, the long-shafted throwing
spears might most appropriately be called "assegais," but the
term is also frequently applied to the short-handled, broad-
bladed stabbing spears used by the Ndebele (q.v.).   Assegai is
now the name of a Rhodesian army publication.

AYRSHIRE.   European farming region c.15 km. north of Banket*,
taking its name from the former Ayrshire Mine.   The mine
was opened in 1900 to exploit a major gold (q.v.) working previously abandoned by the Shona.   A narrow gauge railway* line
was extended from Banket in 1902, but it was closed down in
1911 after the mine had been worked out.   Thereafter the center
of development in the Lomagundi District (q.v.) shifted to Eldorado and Sinoia (qq.v.) to the southwest.

- B -

BA- .   Common Bantu* prefix for the plural forms of names of
people.   English usage normally drops such prefixes, e.g.,
for Banyai, see NYAI.   (Cf. ABA-; AMA-; MA-.)

BABA.   Common Bantu* word for "father"; used as a polite form
of address when speaking to any older man.   (Cf. MAMA.)

BABAYANE (variant: Babyaan) (fl. 1880s-1890s).   A senior Ndebele
induna* by the late 1880s, when he was estimated to be about
65 years old.   In late 1888 Lobengula (q.v.) named Babayane
and Mshete (q.v.) as emissaries to London, where they met
with Queen Victoria the next year.   Although the British made
a particular effort to impress the Ndebele emissaries with
armaments and military installations, Babayane was an active
leader in the anti-British Revolt (q.v.) of 1896.   He fought
mainly in the central Matopo Hills* in association with Mlugulu

(q. v.), and he was one of the izinduna who supported the installation of Nyamanda (q. v.) as king. In the negotiations with
Cecil Rhodes which ended the Matopos fighting, Babayane
emerged as a leading spokesman of Ndebele grievances.

BADEN-POWELL, ROBERT STEPHENSON SMYTH (Feb. 22, 1857-
   Jan. 8, 1941). British army officer of twenty years' experience but with little reputation before serving in the 1896 Ndebele
   Revolt (q. v.). Then a colonel, Baden-Powell arrived in Matabeleland* with General Carrington (q. v.) in June 1896. As staff
   officer he and Col. Plumer (q. v.) planned most military operations. Baden-Powell was particularly fond of scouting work,
   and he later applied some of the ideas he developed during the
   Revolt in the Boy Scout movement which he founded in 1910.
   As the Ndebele campaign wound down, he and Carrington went
   to Mashonaland* to assist E. A. H. Alderson (q. v.) against the
   Shona rebels. By December all imperial forces were out of
   the country. Afterwards Baden-Powell wrote a breezy book
   about the Revolts which made him a popular hero in England.
   His fame increased during the South African War (q. v.), when
   he commanded British forces at Mafeking during its seven-
   month siege. He was created a peer in 1929, dying in Kenya
   12 years later.

BAILIE, ALEXANDER CUMMING (1850-1903). A surveyor in South
   Africa, Bailie was sent by the government to Matabeleland* in
   1876 to map the region, to recruit laborers for the Kimberley
   diamond mines, and to arrange passage for migrant laborers.
   Between December 1876 and February 1877 he visited Lobengula
   (q. v.) at Bulawayo*, but managed to collect only 50 Ndebele
   men as laborers. On his return trip he was accompanied for
   part of the way by an Ndebele embassy sent by Lobengula to
   Letsie, the king of Lesotho.

BAINES, THOMAS (Nov. 27, 1820-May 8, 1875). English painter
   and explorer. Born in Norfolk, Baines went to South Africa
   in 1842 and began a long and productive career as a painter.
   In 1858 he joined David Livingstone's (q. v.) Zambezi expedition,
   but was soon dismissed by the latter because of personal differences. He returned to the Zambezi in 1863 and painted the
   first full-color pictures of the Victoria Falls (q. v.).
        After a sojourn in England, Baines returned to southern
   Africa in 1869 in the employ of the recently-formed South African Gold Fields Exploration Company (q. v.). He negotiated
   several times with Lobengula (q. v.) and traveled and painted
   extensively in northern Mashonaland*. In late 1871 he obtained
   Lobengula's first written concession* to mine for gold* in Shona
   territory. He then returned to South Africa to paint, but died
   before he was able to exploit his mining concession personally.

BALFOUR, F. R. T. see under ANGLICAN MISSIONS

BALLA BALLA. Village located c. 55 km. due southeast of Bulawayo

on the West Nicholson* railway* line (at 20°27'S, 29°3'E; alt.
1098 m.).   The village serves as the railhead for the Filabusi
(q.v.) mining region and as a military training center.

BAMANGWATO   see   NGWATO

BAMBATA CAVE.   Major archaeological site located in the Matopo
   Hills* (at 20°30'S, 28°24'E).   Although the granite cave was
   known to the Ndebele in the 19th century, it was not discovered
   by Europeans until 1918.   Neville Jones (q.v.) and others investigated it in the first systematic excavation of any such cave
   in the country.   Archaeologists have turned up important artifacts representing the middle and late Stone Age (q.v.) and the
   earliest local Iron Age (q.v.).   The cave also contains fine
   examples of rock paintings (q.v.) representing an unusually
   broad range of styles.   The cave's name has been given to a
   major phase of the middle Stone Age Stillbay (q.v.) industries.

BANANA, CANAAN SODINDO (b. March 5, 1936).   Born near Bulawayo
   and educated at Methodist* mission schools, Banana was ordained
   a Methodist minister at Epworth* in 1966.   He broke from the
   church in early 1971, but reached a reconciliation by the end of
   the year, by which time he had joined Abel Muzorewa (q.v.) to
   form the African National Council (q.v.).   In early 1972 he
   played a major role in organizing vocal opposition to the Anglo-
   Rhodesian Settlement Proposals during the visit of the Pearce
   Commission (q.v.).   His passport was withdrawn by the government in August 1972, but he nevertheless went to the United
   States the following May to study theology.   He rejoined Muzorewa's branch of the ANC on his return, but was soon imprisoned
   by the government.   When he was briefly released to confer with
   British Foreign Secretary David Owen in April 1977, he was
   described by the press as a supporter of the "Patriotic Front"
   (q.v.).

BANKET (formerly Banket Junction).   Town located c. 25 km. east
   of Sinoia* on the main road and railway line to Salisbury in
   eastern Lomagundi District* (at 17°23'S, 30°24'E; alt. 1300 m.).
   Banket is the center of a prosperous European farming area,
   featuring grains and cotton*.   Population in 1969 was 3480 (93%
   Africans).

BANNINGS   see   CENSORSHIP; UNLAWFUL ORGANIZATIONS ACT;
   LAW AND ORDER (MAINTENANCE) ACT

BANNOCKBURN.   Small village at the junction of the Vila Salazar*
   railway line and the Shabani* branch line (at 20°17'S, 29°52'E).

BANTU.   Although this term is commonly used in southern Africa
   as an ethnic or racial identification, it is properly only a linguistic term.   Bantu languages occupy a unique place in Africa.
   Though they constitute only a sub-subgroup of the Niger-Congo
   family of languages (which also extend through West Africa), they

are spoken by almost all the peoples south of a line between Cameroon and central Kenya. The historical spread of Bantu languages remains controversial, but it is generally agreed by historical linguists that proto-Bantu originated in southeastern Nigeria more than 3000 years ago, and then spread comparatively rapidly throughout central, eastern, and southern Africa. Bantu-speakers appear to have first entered present Rhodesia sometime early in the first millenium A. D. Their arrival in southern Africa appears also to have coincided with the start of the Iron Age (q. v.).

Among the characteristics shared by the 250 or so classified Bantu languages are the division of nouns into classes, and the use of prefixes to inflect nouns and verbs (see, e.g., AMA-, ISI-, MA-, etc.). The name "Bantu" itself derives from a word for person which appears in many of the languages. The stem of the word is -ntu. The addition of prefixes creates such forms as muntu ("person"), bantu ("people"), kintu ("thing"), etc. These prefixes vary from language to language. Since variations create obvious problems in alphabetizing Bantu words, language dictionaries typically list the words by their stems, and the prefixes are normally dropped altogether in European use of proper names (see note on alphabetizing in this dictionary, on page xii).

Bantu languages spoken south of the Zambezi River* are usually called "southeast African Bantu." Their exact interrelationships have not been fully worked out, but certain broad patterns have been recognized. One cluster includes the various Shona, or Chishona (q. v.) dialects, which are spoken throughout Rhodesia and central Mozambique. A second, broader group of less closely related languages includes Nguni, Sotho, Tsonga, Venda (qq. v.), and Chopi. Dialects of all but Chopi are spoken in Rhodesia. Shona languages predominate in Rhodesia, accounting for about 75% of the population. In the mid-19th century a second major Bantu language was introduced from the south by the intrusive Ndebele people, whose Nguni tongue is known as Sindebele (q. v.).

BANTU CONGRESS. Original name of the "old" African National Congress (q. v.).

BANTU MIRROR. Started as a mission quarterly called Chiringiro ("The Mirror"), this publication became the country's first African newspaper, The Native Mirror, in 1931. In 1943 the paper was taken over by African Newspapers, Ltd. (q. v.) and was used by the government to disseminate wartime propaganda. Through the 1950s, by which time it was known as the Bantu Mirror, the weekly paper published considerable general interest news, but it failed to develop into a significant African political voice. (See PRESS; AFRICAN WEEKLY.)

BANTU VOTERS' ASSOCIATION see RHODESIAN BANTU VOTERS' ASSOCIATION

BANYAILAND TREK   see   ADENDORFF TREK; NYAI

BAOBAB (Chishona*: muuyu; Sindebele*: umkhomo).   Large tree
    native to tropical Africa, characterized by enormous girth,
    moderate height, smooth bark, and few leaves.   The tree
    stores considerable water, which can be tapped during drought,
    and it bears edible fruit.   Baobabs are found mostly in low-
    lying savanna* and grassland regions, particularly in the Lim-
    popo and Zambezi valleys.   (See FORESTS.)

BARING, EVELYN (Sept. 29, 1903-March 10, 1973).   Fourth gover-
    nor (q.v.) of Southern Rhodesia (1942-44).   During his brief
    tenure of office, Baring gained the respect of the African popu-
    lation because of his close attention to conditions in the reserves.
    Afterwards he served as British High Commissioner to South
    Africa (1944-51), and as Governor of Kenya Colony (1952-9).
    He was later created Baron Howick of Glendale.

BARRETO, FRANCISCO (1520-June 1573).   Portuguese (q.v.) mili-
    tary commander.   After serving as governor of Portuguese India
    (1555-8), Barreto returned to Lisbon, where he became influen-
    tial at the royal court.   In the late 1560s he persuaded the young
    king Sebastian to appoint him head of a punitive expedition against
    Munhumutapa* Negomo (q.v.) to avenge the murder of Gonçalo da
    Silveira (q.v.).   His expedition attracted numerous volunteers,
    anxious to pillage the wealth of the supposed "Ophir" (q.v.).
    Barreto set sail in 1569 with three ships and a thousand men.
    He reached Mozambique* in May 1570, but then dallied along the
    eastern coast for almost a year.   Pressured by Jesuit members
    of the expedition, he finally selected the Zambezi Valley (q.v.)
    as his route to the interior.   The choice proved disastrous.
    Most of his men and his horses* succumbed to malaria and try-
    panosomiasis (qq.v.).   He suffered further losses in major cam-
    paigns against Africans in the valley, turning back before he
    himself reached present Rhodesia.   He died at Sena (q.v.) and
    was replaced as commander by Vasco Honem (q.v.).

BARWE (variant: Barue).   People living along the border areas of
    the Mtoko and Inyanga districts (qq.v.) and, mostly, in Mozam-
    bique*.   The Barwe are frequently described as Shona (q.v.),
    but they speak a non-Shona Bantu (q.v.) language belonging to
    the Nyanja (or Cewa) group spoken mainly north of the Zambezi
    River.   Since about the 15th century the Barwe have lived under
    the Makombe dynasty (q.v.), which was imposed by an off-shoot
    of the Shona Munhumutapa state (q.v.).

BATOKA GORGE.   Located c.48 km. below the Victoria Falls*, this
    gorge severely contracts the flow of the Zambezi River (q.v.)
    into a narrow defile about 90 km. long which now meets the
    southeastern end of Lake Kariba (q.v.).   The name "Batoka"
    derives from the Sotho (q.v.) pronunciation of "Batonga" (see
    TONGA).

BATTLE CRY. Zimbabwe African National Union (ZANU, q.v.)
   party newspaper, issued in Salisbury during 1963-4.

BATTLEFIELDS. Village in the Gatooma District (q.v.) located on
   the railway* line between Gatooma* and Que Que* (at 18° 36'S,
   29° 50'E; alt. 1115 m.). It is frequently incorrectly written
   that the village takes its name from the sites of local battles
   fought in the Ndebele War (q.v.), but the name "Battlefields"
   actually derives from the many local mines named after famous
   European battles.

BAYÃO, SISANDO DIAS (variant: Baião) (fl.1640s). Portuguese
   (q.v.) trader. As a youth Bayão settled at Sena (q.v.), where
   he became the leading trader, land-owner, and military commander. During the 1640s he was appointed to command Portuguese forces in Manicaland (q.v.). There he is said to have
   met a deposed Changamire (q.v.) ruler who requested Portuguese
   military aid to regain his power. In 1644 Bayão led a large
   force deep into "Butua" (q.v.). His exact route is unknown, but
   he may have reached the present Bulawayo (q.v.) region. He
   seems to have died around 1645.

BAYETE (variant: Hayete). Ndebele salutation used when addressing
   the king.

BEADLE, THOMAS HUGH WILLIAM (b. Feb. 6, 1905). Born in
   Salisbury, Beadle studied law in England and returned to practice in Bulawayo. Godfrey Huggins (q.v.) made him parliamentary secretary in 1940 and Minister of Justice and Internal Affairs in 1946. In 1961 Beadle succeeded Robert Tredgold (q.v.)
   as Chief Justice. He initially resisted UDI in 1965, but later
   passed down a series of court decisions legalizing the independence of the regime within the context of Rhodesian law.

BEATRICE. Town located 50 km. south of Salisbury, where the
   road to Enkeldoorn* crosses the Umfuli River* (at 18° 16'S,
   30° 52'E). The town arose by the Beatrice Gold Mine, which
   was started in 1894. The mine was once a leading gold (q.v.)
   producer in the country, but has since been closed down. Beatrice is now a small center for European agriculture. Population in 1969 was 810 (84% Africans).

BECHUANA see TSWANA

BECHUANALAND BORDER POLICE (BBP). Para-military force
   organized by the British Imperial government shortly after
   present Botswana (q.v.) was made into the Bechuanaland Protectorate (q.v.) in 1885. Col. F. Carrington (q.v.) was the
   first BBP commander, with his headquarters at Mafeking in
   South Africa. Some members of the BBP served in the Pioneer
   Column (q.v.) which occupied Mashonaland in 1890. In May
   1893 Lt.-Col. H. Goold-Adams (q.v.) became BBP Commander,
   with his headquarters on the Macloutsie River, just southwest

of present Rhodesia. Later the same year Goold-Adams led a
BBP contingent against Bulawayo (q.v.) in the Ndebele War
(q.v.). At the end of 1895 the BBP was disbanded. Many of
its members then served in the Jameson Raid (q.v.), the Matabeleland Relief Force (q.v.), and then the BSAP.

BECHUANALAND PROTECTORATE. In March 1885 a British military expedition under Charles Warren (q.v.) declared most of
present Botswana (q.v.) to be a British protectorate. The
British had acted in response to appeals for protection issued
by the Ngwato (q.v.) and other peoples, and in order to block
Afrikaner (q.v.) expansion from the Transvaal (q.v.). An immediate effect of the declaration was the circumscription of
Ndebele (q.v.) raiding activity in the west and increased Ndebele
willingness to negotiate with the Transvalers (see GROBLER, P.).
The gradual demarcation of the protectorate's northeastern
boundary essentially defined what was to become the western
border (q.v.) of present Rhodesia.
     During the mid-1890s the British government considered
turning over the protectorate's administration to the BSAC,
which by then was attempting to administer Rhodesia. In 1895
the Ngwato chief Khama III (q.v.) and two other Tswana* rulers
successfully protested the plan in London. The British instead
ceded to the BSAC a narrow strip of protectorate land for construction of the main railway (q.v.) line to Bulawayo. On September 30, 1968, the protectorate became the independent
Botswana Republic. (See also TATI CONCESSION.)

BEIRA. Now the second largest city in Mozambique (q.v.) with a
population of c.120,000, Beira arose in the early 1890s as a
railway (q.v.) line was being built from the Indian Ocean to
Umtali (q.v.). The line reached Umtali in 1898, and was extended to Salisbury the next year. Until the closing of the
Mozambique-Rhodesia border in 1976, Beira handled much of
Rhodesia's export traffic. The town is located on the northern
shore of the Pungwe River's (q.v.) estuary, across the inlet
from old Sofala* (at 19° 51'S, 34° 52'E).

BEIT, ALFRED (Feb. 15, 1853-July 16, 1906). Financial partner
of Cecil Rhodes (q.v.). Born in Germany, Beit came to South
Africa in 1875 as a representative of a Dutch diamond company.
He soon went to the Kimberley diamond fields, established his
own company, and became a British subject. There he joined
with Rhodes to form the De Beers Consolidated Mines and he
built a vast fortune with diamond and gold mining interests in
South Africa. He supported Rhodes' efforts to expand British
power north of the Limpopo River*, concentrating on the financial aspects, while Rhodes worked in politics. In 1889 he became a founding member of the BSAC board of directors, later
using his private wealth to help see the company through occasional difficulties. Because of his close association with
Rhodes, he resigned from the BSAC board in the aftermath of
the Jameson Raid (q.v.). He rejoined the board in 1903 and

became the company's vice president.

Although Beit is closely associated with the founding of British rule in Rhodesia, he only visited the country briefly, in 1891 and in 1903. Beit was one of the trustees of Rhodes' will. On his own death, he bequeathed much of his fortune to the Beit Trust (q.v.).

BEIT TRUST. Philanthropic trust fund created with a £1,200,000 bequest made by Alfred Beit (q.v.) on his death in 1906. Since then its trustees have multiplied the size of the fund several times, while dispersing money over a wide variety of projects throughout central Africa. Through the 1920s the money was used mainly to improve transport (q.v.) facilities, most notably bridges (see BEITBRIDGE; OTTO BEIT BRIDGE; BIRCHENOUGH BRIDGE). After 1927 an increasing share of the money was used for education (q.v.), particularly private schools in Southern Rhodesia. More recently, funds have been channelled through mission schools for Africans. Other contributions have gone to hospitals, museums, charities, and sports facilities.

BEITBRIDGE. Town (at 22° 13'S, 30° E; alt. 500 m.) serving as the main port of entry into the country from South Africa, and the headquarters of the district of the same name. It was founded in 1929 with the opening of Beit Bridge (a.k.a. Alfred Beit Bridge; cf. OTTO BEIT BRIDGE) over the Limpopo River (q.v.). In 1974 a new railway (q.v.) line between Beitbridge and Rutenga* was opened, giving the country its first direct rail link to South Africa.

BEITBRIDGE DISTRICT. A relatively new region of 12,920 sq. km. separated from the southeastern portion of the old Gwanda District (q.v.) in Matabeleland South Province (q.v.). The district is divided roughly evenly between European and Tribal Trust Lands (see LAND TENURE ACT) and is used mainly for ranching. Other district centers include Tuli and Mazunga (qq.v.).

BELINGWE. Administrative center for the district of the same name in Matabeleland South Province* (at 20° 29'S, 29° 55'E; alt. 1065 m.). Founded as a mining town in the 1890s, Belingwe is now the center of a varied mineral (q.v.) industry, including important asbestos, gemstone, and chrome mines (qq.v.).

BELINGWE DISTRICT. Now covering 6020 sq. km., it formerly included part of the present Shabani District (q.v.), which borders it on the north. Belingwe District also borders the districts of Insiza on the west, Gwanda and Nuanetsi on the south, and a small section of Chibi (qq.v.) on the east. The northern part of the district is reserved for Europeans. Most of the rest comprises Tribal Trust Lands* (see LAND TENURE ACT).

BEMBEZI RIVER (variants: Imbembesi; Bembesi). Rises c.40 km. northeast of Bulawayo, whence it flows northwest to join the

Gwai (q.v.) near Lupane*. The British and the Ndebele fought
the "Battle of Bembezi" near the river's headwaters during the
1893 Ndebele War (q.v.).

BENT, JAMES THEODORE (March 30, 1852-May 5, 1897). English
antiquarian and traveler. After doing archaeological fieldwork in
the Middle East, Bent was invited by Cecil Rhodes to investigate the Zimbabwe Ruins (q.v.). In 1891 he, his wife, and
R. M. W. Swan undertook the first systematic survey and excavations of the ruins. Bent's expedition cleared away much of
the plant overgrowth, produced the first accurate plans of the
ruins, and collected artifacts--notably the Zimbabwe "Birds"
(q.v.). Publication of Bent's book, The Ruined Cities of Mashonaland (1892), aroused worldwide interest in Zimbabwe. The
book is a mine of information on artifacts, the layout of the
ruins, and contemporary Shona life, but it lacks the kind of
rigorous analysis of fieldwork demanded by modern archaeology,
and it propounded the untenable hypothesis that the ruins were
of ancient Semitic origin (see ZIMBABWE CONTROVERSY).
Bent unfortunately kept poor records of his digs, which destroyed much irrecoverable stratigraphical evidence on the site.
(See also RHODESIA ANCIENT RUINS, LTD.; HALL, R. N.)

BERLIN MISSIONARY SOCIETY (a.k.a. Berlin Society). Founded
in 1824, this Lutheran organization began work in South Africa
in 1834. By 1860 it was operating in the Transvaal*, where
Alex Merensky (1837-1918) labored among the Pedi people.
Merensky was one of the first Europeans to learn about the
Zimbabwe Ruins (q.v.; see also RENDERS, A.). He passed
much of what he learned on to Karl Mauch (q.v.) and others,
stimulating European interest in the "Ophir" (q.v.) myth.
During the 1880s BMS agents made tentative ventures in
to Shona territory north of the Limpopo River. In 1892 the
Society founded a mission station in the Gutu chiefdom (q.v.).
Various problems impaired the Society's work in Mashonaland,
so it abandoned its stations there in 1907, turning over its
interests to the Dutch Reformed Church (q.v.).

BIKITA. Administrative center of the district of the same name in
Victoria Province* (at 20° 5'S, 31° 38'E; alt. 1065 m.).

BIKITA DISTRICT. Originally the northeastern part of the old
Ndanga District (q.v.), from which it was separated in 1920.
It now covers 6925 sq. km. in the southeastern low veld. The
Sabi River (q.v.) separates it from the Chipinga District (q.v.)
in the east. It also borders the districts of Chiredzi on the
south, Ndanga and Victoria on the west, and Gutu and Buhera
on the north (qq.v.). The eastern part of the district is reserved for Europeans, who are mostly cattle ranchers, while
the western part comprises Tribal Trust Lands (q.v.) containing mostly African subsistence farmers (see LAND TENURE
ACT). Bikita mine is the largest lithium (q.v.) producer in the
country.

BILHARZIA (a. k. a. schistosomiasis). Infectious disease transmitted
by waterborne parasites which enter mammalian bodies through
unbroken skin. One variety of the disease damages the bladder,
kidneys, and genital organs; another damages the large intestine,
liver, and sometimes the lungs. Both prevention and treatment
are difficult, making the disease a particularly dangerous one in
rural areas, where small snails carry the parasites. Although
the disease is believed to have entered the country only during
the 20th century, it now ranks as one of the most serious endemic health (q. v.) problems.

BILTONG. Strips of sun-dried, or smoked meat; similar to American "beef jerky." Used extensively by European hunters and
travelers during the 19th century, biltong is now commercially
prepared in Rhodesia. The name is from an Afrikaans* term
equivalent to "bull tongue."

BINDURA. Mining town in the Mazoe Valley*, serving as the administrative center of the district of the same name in Mashonaland North Province* (at 17° 18'S, 31° 20'E; alt. 1510 m.). Formerly known as Kimberley Reefs, Bindura has in recent decades
expanded rapidly along with nickel (q. v.) production at the nearby Trojan Mine. Estimated population at the end of 1974 was
15,000 (91% Africans).

BINDURA DISTRICT. Containing 2140 sq. km., this area was
carved out of the eastern part of the Mazoe District (q. v.) relatively recently. A rich mixed farming region, the district is
reserved entirely for Europeans (see LAND TENURE ACT). It
borders the districts of Mazoe on the west, Darwin on the
north, Shamva on the east, and Goromanzi (qq. v.) on the south.

BINGA. Fishing (q. v.) and resort village on the southeastern end
of Lake Kariba* (at 17° 37'S, 27° 20'E), and headquarters for the
district of the same name. Located in an otherwise sparsely
inhabited region, Binga had a fixed population of 610 (90%
Africans) in 1969.

BINGA DISTRICT. Covering 15,070 sq. km., it is carved out of
the former Sebungwe District (q. v.), in Matabeleland North
Province (q. v.). Except for a single strip of Purchase Land
(q. v.) along the lake, and some game reserves (q. v.) classified as "national land," the district comprises only Tribal Trust
Lands (q. v.; see LAND TENURE ACT). It borders the districts
of Wankie on the west, Lupane on the south, Gokwe on the east,
and Kariba on the northeast (qq. v.).

BINGAGURU. Prominent 1800-meter peak north of Umtali*, near
the Mozambique border (at 18° 46'S, 32° 37'E). Until 1902 the
Manyika* rulers of the Mutasa dynasty (q. v.) maintained their
headquarters atop Bingaguru. In 1891 Portugal and Britain
were nearly brought to war when P. W. Forbes (q. v.) arrested
two important Portuguese officials on the mountain.

BIRCHENOUGH BRIDGE. Large, single-span suspension bridge
    built over the Sabi River (q.v.) on the Umtali to Fort Victoria
    road (qq.v.) in 1935 (at 19° 58'S, 32° 20'E). Financed by the
    Beit Trust (q.v.), the bridge was named after Henry Birche-
    nough (1853-1937), who was president of the BSAC from 1925
    to 1937.

BIRWA. Section of Sotho*-speaking people living around the Tuli
    River* in the southwestern part of the country.

BISSET, MURRAY (April 14, 1876-Oct. 24, 1931). A South African
    lawyer and legislator, Bisset was made Chief Justice of the
    Southern Rhodesian High Court in 1926. He died in office.

BLANKET MINE. Gold (q.v.) mining village, just north of Gwanda*
    (at 20° 51'S, 28° 55'E). Population in 1969 was 1100 (94% Afri-
    cans.

BLEDISLOE COMMISSION (1938-39). In response to renewed settler
    demands for amalgamation (q.v.) of Southern and Northern Rho-
    desia, the British government created an investigatory commis-
    sion under Charles Bathurst Bledisloe (1st Viscount Bledisloe),
    a former governor-general of New Zealand. The Commission,
    which comprised representatives of three different British parlia-
    mentary parties, also considered inclusion of Nyasaland (now
    Malawi), collecting evidence in all three territories during 1938
    and 1939. It found settlers generally in support of amalgama-
    tion, with Africans strongly opposed. Africans north of the
    Zambezi River feared extension of Southern Rhodesia's land and
    tax laws, its pass laws (q.v.), and its political emasculation of
    traditional chiefs (see COUNCIL OF CHIEFS). By contrast,
    Southern Rhodesian Africans feared increased competition from
    northern migrant laborers and a weakening of the country's
    comparatively good educational system (q.v.). The report of
    the Commission, issued in 1939 (Cmd 5949), concluded that
    closer union was a worthwhile goal, but that it was not politi-
    cally acceptable at that moment, largely because of the restric-
    tive nature of Southern Rhodesia's labor laws, notably the In-
    dustrial Conciliation Act (q.v.). The report recommended crea-
    tion of an interterritorial council and further investigation of the
    issue. These plans were interrupted by the Second World War,
    but a Central Africa Council (q.v.) was created in 1944, be-
    coming the first tangible step in the movement towards actual
    Federation (q.v.).

BOARD OF CENSORS see CENSORSHIP

BOER. Dutch word for farmer; used to describe the people who
    now generally prefer to be called Afrikaners (q.v.). In many
    Bantu* languages "Boer" is rendered bunu.

BOER WAR (1899-1902) see SOUTH AFRICAN WAR

BONDA (d. 1897).   Shona Revolt (q. v.) leader.   Originally a headman in a Rozvi* chiefdom in the Charter District*, Bonda is
said to have become a "priest" in the Mwari cult (q. v.).   In
May 1896 he and emissaries of chief Mashayamombe (q. v.) consulted with Mkwati (q. v.) at Ntabazikamambo (q. v.) in Matabeleland*.   Bonda is said then to have returned to Mashayamombe's
country and to have helped organize the Revolt there and to the
south.   Throughout the rest of 1896 and early 1897 he moved
about rebel territories constantly, attracting the pursuit of
British forces.   In July or August 1897 he was shot to death
in the Hartley District*.

BOOKS OF RHODESIA.   Bulawayo publishing house specializing in
high quality facsimile reprints of Rhodesiana since its establishment in 1968.   The firm's list has included major documents
on African life and history, including works by F. C. Selous,
R. N. Hall, T. M. Thomas (qq. v.), et al.   It has also printed
combined volumes of Rhodesiana and Nada (qq. v.).   Most of the
firm's sales have been to subscription book club members, including many American libraries.   (See BIBLIOGRAPHY.)

BORDERS.   The present shape of Rhodesia reflects, somewhat,
European interpretations of the extent of Ndebele (q. v.) rule
during the late 19th century.   King Lobengula (q. v.) claimed
all territory between the Shashi and Zambezi rivers (qq. v.),
as well as hegemony over the Shona peoples to the east.   The
Ndebele actually controlled only the southwestern part of the
present country.   In any case, the notion of fixed boundaries
was alien to most African societies, whose spheres of sovereignty often overlapped physically.   Nevertheless, the BSAC
used concessions (q. v.) wrested from Lobengula as its main
legal basis for carving out the entire country.
         In 1890 the British reached accords with Germany and
the Transvaal (q. v.) acknowledging the purported Ndebele domain as falling within the British sphere of interest.   The
agreement with the Transvaal effectively fixed the Limpopo
River (q. v.) as the future border between South Africa and
Rhodesia.   In September 1890 the BSAC occupied and claimed
Mashonaland (q. v.) by virtue of its own generous interpretation
of the Rudd Concession (q. v.) granted by Lobengula.   In October
BSAC agents got the Manyika chief Mutasa (q. v.) to sign a
treaty, giving the company a claim to Manicaland (q. v.).   Meanwhile, the British Bechuanaland Protectorate (q. v.) was being
extended north to the Chobe River, thereby creating the future
border between Rhodesia and Botswana.
         The BSAC then attempted to extend its domain east to
the Indian Ocean by treating with the Gaza ruler Gungunyane
(q. v.).   The Portuguese successfully resisted this British intrusion, and a temporary frontier between Portuguese Mozambique and British Mashonaland was created through Manicaland
in February 1891.   The Anglo-Portuguese Convention (q. v.) of
the following June detailed the complete border, and further ad-
justments were made in 1897.

After L. S. Jameson (q. v.), the administrator* of
Mashonaland, decreed an arbitrary border between British
Mashonaland and Ndebele territory, the BSAC used Ndebele
violations of the border as provocation for the Ndebele War
(q. v.) in 1893. The British won the war, occupying Matabeleland (q. v.) and thereby rounding out colonial claims to the entire territory of present Rhodesia. The Zambezi River (q. v.)
seems always to have been regarded as the natural northern
boundary of the colony.
          Rhodesia is now separated from Zambia (q. v.) by a
c. 715 km. stretch of the Zambezi. The South Africa (q. v.)
border extends along c. 217 km. of the Limpopo River. The
c. 790 km. border with Botswana (q. v.) follows an arbitrary
line running nearly straight from Kazungula to Plumtree
(qq. v.), whence it follows the Ramaquabane River south to the
Shashi (qq. v.), and from there to the Limpopo, except for the
Tuli Circle (q. v.). The c. 1165 km. border with Mozambique
(q. v.) is the longest and most arbitrary. Except for a few
short stretches of rivers, the Eastern Highlands (q. v.) provide the only natural features forming this border.
          Clockwise, from Beitbridge on the Limpopo River, im-
portant border posts are located at, or near, Plumtree, Pandamatenga, Kazungula, Victoria Falls, Kariba, Chirundu, Umtali,
and Vila Salazar (qq. v.).

BORROW, HENRY JOHN (March 17, 1865-Dec. 4, 1893). Born in
    Cornwall, Borrow came to South Africa in 1882, serving in
    Charles Warren's Bechuanaland expedition (qq. v.) two years
    later. Afterwards he joined the Bechuanaland Border Police
    (q. v.), in which he met M. Henry and F. Johnson (qq. v.), with
    whom he formed the Northern Goldfields Exploring syndicate.
    In 1890 he served in the Pioneer Column (q. v.). Afterwards
    he farmed at Borrowdale, which is now a northeastern suburb
    of Salisbury (q. v.). During the Ndebele War (q. v.) he com-
    manded a cavalry troop, the Salisbury Horse. He was killed
    while attempting to relieve the Shangani Patrol (q. v.).

BOTSWANA. Nearly 50% larger than Rhodesia, but containing only
    about a ninth of the latter's population, Botswana shares a
    c. 790 km. border (q. v.) with Rhodesia, stretching from the
    Zambezi to the Limpopo. Except for a few moderate-sized
    rivers in the southeast, no natural features separate the two
    countries, and the border region has long been a zone of free
    movement for San, Sotho-Tswana, and Kalanga peoples (qq. v.).
    In the 19th century Botswana served as the main approach route
    for visitors to Rhodesia from the south. In the late 1830s the
    Ndebele (q. v.) entered Matabeleland* by way of Botswana.
    Later, Sotho, Griqua*, and European hunters, traders, and
    missionaries passed through eastern Botswana to Rhodesia,
    mostly by way of the Ngwato (q. v.) capital of Shoshong (see
    HUNTERS' ROAD). The Ndebele regularly raided the predomi-
    nantly Tswana peoples of Botswana, reaching as far west as
    Lake Ngami, where the Tawana (q. v.) lived. Ndebele and

Ngwato sovereignty overlapped around the present southeastern part of the border, producing conflicting territorial claims, particularly after the discovery of gold at Tati (q.v.) in the 1860s.

Declaration of the Bechuanaland Protectorate (q.v.) in 1885 began the formation of Botswana, which became an independent republic in 1968. In the meantime, the external economy of Botswana became inextricably tied to Rhodesia and South Africa when a railway (q.v.) line was constructed through the eastern part of the country linking Mafeking and Bulawayo in 1897. Ownership and control of the railway remained in Rhodesian hands, leaving the present government of Botswana little option to enforce sanctions (q.v.) against the white minority government. Nevertheless, the Botswana government has been openly committed to supporting majority rule in Rhodesia, and its president, Seretse Khama, is a member of the "Frontline Presidents" (q.v.). In the 1970s Botswana has become an important refuge for Zimbabwe nationalists. Anti-Rhodesian guerrilla bases are said to exist in Botswana, but by 1977 the full extent of their activities was unknown. (See FRANCISTOWN.)

BRITISH SOUTH AFRICA COMPANY (BSAC; a.k.a. "the Chartered Company"). London-based commercial organization which colonized the country and administered from 1890 to 1923. In 1888 Cecil Rhodes, C. D. Rudd, and F. R. Thompson (qq.v.) formed a syndicate, the Central Search Association, which obtained the Rudd Concession (q.v.) from the Ndebele king Lobengula (q.v.). This group then amalgamated with a similar body, the Exploring Company, Ltd., to form the BSAC in March 1889. Rhodes became the Company's managing director in Africa and was its guiding force through the remainder of his life.

In London Rhodes and his financial partner Alfred Beit (q.v.) got five prominent British financiers and politicians, including A. H. G. Grey (q.v.), to join them in forming the Company's first board of directors. The Duke of Abercorn* served as the first BSAC president (see list below). The prestige of this body of men, as well as an exaggerated interpretation of the rights conferred by the Rudd Concession, enabled the BSAC to obtain a Royal Charter (q.v.) of incorporation on October 29, 1889. The Charter conferred upon the BSAC sweeping rights over a vast, but undefined, territory north of the Limpopo River*, and west of present Malawi and Mozambique*, excluding the Tati Concession area (q.v.). The company eventually carved out the colonies which became present Rhodesia and Zambia*.

Through its Charter the company was empowered to make treaties with African rulers, to form banks, to own and distribute land, and to create its own police (see BRITISH SOUTH AFRICA POLICE). In return it promised to develop its territories economically, to respect existing African law, to allow free trade, and to tolerate all religions. The British Secretary of State for Colonies retained supervisory powers over administration, and the Charter was set to run for 25 years.

To avoid competing with other imperialist powers, notably the Portuguese (see ANGLO-PORTUGUESE CONVENTION)
and Transvaal Afrikaners* (see ADENDORFF TREK), the BSAC
claimed that the Ndebele ruled all the Shona, and that the Rudd
Concession therefore conferred upon it the right to occupy
Mashonaland*. This the company's Pioneer Column (q.v.) did
in mid-1890. Once in Mashonaland, the company proceeded to
distribute land and mining claims to settlers and missionaries,
and to establish an administration (see ADMINISTRATORS).
With the notable except of Mutasa (q.v.), few Shona were consulted.

In 1893 the BSAC Administrator L. S. Jameson (q.v.)
provoked the Ndebele War (q.v.), which the British quickly won.
Afterwards the company began occupying Matabeleland*, laying
the basis for the country's modern borders (q.v.). Up to this
point few Africans recognized company rule. Nevertheless, the
BSAC appropriated land and livestock, and attempted to assess
taxes. Administrative abuses were a prime contributor to the
large-scale Ndebele and Shona Revolts (q.v.) which erupted in
1896. After the Revolts were suppressed, the company reorganized its administration and brought the whole country under
more systematic government, but Africans were granted very
little additional participation. In 1898 European settlers gained
a voice in the government through the establishment of a Legislative Council (q.v.). Meanwhile, the company established
separate administrations over the territories north of the Zambezi.

In 1915 the British Crown granted the BSAC a supplemental charter to run an additional ten years. By then, however,
settlers were growing tired of the company administration. They
formed the Responsible Government Movement (q.v.) to demand
self-government. Anticipating a change of administrations, the
British government created the Cave Commission (q.v.) in 1919
to determine the amount of compensation to be paid to the company for its administrative assets in the country.

In 1922 the company's shareholders accepted a cash offer
from the government of South Africa* to assume control of
Southern Rhodesia, but the settlers rejected this proposal in a
referendum in October of that year (see UNIONIST MOVEMENT).
A year later administration was turned over to the settlers (see
C. P. J. COGHLAN) and the country became a British Crown
Colony. At the same time the company surrendered its adminis-
tration of Northern Rhodesia to the British Colonial Office.
Thereafter the company's interests in central Africa were only
financial.

The BSAC had been incorporated in 1889 with a capitali-
zation of only £1 million. Unlike other chartered companies, it
did not engage directly in trading or mining operations, but
concentrated on investments and financial operations. Heavy
expenses incurred during the 1890s wars and the costs of administrative and economic development prevented the company
from paying any dividends to shareholders until 1924. By then
its worth was estimated at £9 million. In 1933 the company

sold its mineral (q.v.) rights in Southern Rhodesia to the settler government for £2 million, while retaining its more valuable mineral rights in Northern Rhodesia. Over the ensuing decades the company flourished, while developing a network of subsidiary companies controlling vast interests in mining, railways, agriculture, real estate, forestry, and various secondary industries. The company received a setback in 1964 when it was forced to relinquish its mineral rights in Zambia to that country's newly independent government. The next year the BSAC merged with two other companies to form Charter Consolidated, Ltd., which has since been closely associated with the Anglo-American Corporation, also based in London.

BSAC Presidents, 1889-1937: 1889-1913 Second Duke of Abercorn*; 1913-17 L. S. Jameson*; 1917-20 (vacancy); 1920-23 Philip Lyttelton Gell; 1923-25 J. R. Maguire*; 1925-37 Henry Birchenough. (See also list of ADMINISTRATORS.)

BRITISH SOUTH AFRICA POLICE (BSAP, or BSA Police). Official name of the country's para-military police force. The force was first organized as the "British South Africa Company Police" when the BSAC received its Charter* in 1889. The police served in the Pioneer Column (q.v.) the following year, and then went through a succession of reorganizations under such names as Mashonaland Mounted Police, Matabeleland Mounted Police, and Southern Rhodesian Constabulary. An African contingent was organized as the Native Police Force in 1893. After the Ndebele Revolt (q.v.) in 1896 these forces were combined under a single command as the British South Africa Police, a name retained after the BSAC relinquished authority for the force to the British government in 1909.

Until the creation of the Federation* in 1953, the BSAP was the country's only standing security force (see MILITARY). Since UDI it has continued to serve as a para-military force, working closely with the regular army, while retaining its primary responsibility for crime and internal security. By 1973 the BSAP had expanded to c.8000 regulars and c.35,000 partially-trained reserves. All officers were Europeans, but about two-thirds of the total manpower were Africans.

BROADCASTING see RHODESIAN BROADCASTING COMPANY

BROWN, WILLIAM HARVEY "CURIO" (Aug. 22, 1862-April 5, 1913). American settler. Born in Iowa, Brown took a B.S. degree at the University of Kansas and then worked for the Natural History Department of the Smithsonian Institution. He later went to South Africa, where he joined the Pioneer Column (q.v.) as a scout. Afterwards he remained in Mashonaland* to farm. He served on the Salisbury town council for nine years, including two as the town's mayor (1909-10). He also became a British subject in order to serve on the Legislative Council* (1908-11).

BUBI DISTRICT. A 6960 sq. km. section of Matabeleland North Province (q.v.). Most of the district is reserved for Europeans

and is given over to extensive ranching (see LAND TENURE
ACT). Inyati is the administrative center. The district borders the districts of Bulawayo and Nyamandhlovu on the west,
Lupane and Nkai on the north, Que Que and Gwelo on the east,
and Insiza and Umzingwane (qq. v.) on the south.

BUBI RIVER. Rises in the Mchawacha Hills, near Inyati (q. v.),
flowing generally northwest before meeting the Gwai River near
Lupane (qq. v.). The river cuts through the northern part of
the district of the same name.

BUBYE RIVER. Rising about 40 km. northeast of West Nicholson
(q. v.), the Bubye flows southeast before joining the Limpopo
River c. 25 km. west of the Mozambique border. It has several
large dams* which collect irrigation water for the region. Part
of its course separates the Belingwe and Nuanetsi districts
(qq. v.).

BUDJGA (variants: Budga, Budja, Budya). Major Shona groups
speaking a dialect of Korekore (q. v.) in the present Mtoko
District (q. v.). Budjga settlement there goes back at least
several centuries. In more recent times the paramount chiefs
have taken the hereditary title of Mutoko (or Mtoko). During
the 19th century the Budjga frequently had to fight to maintain
their independence, particularly against Portuguese-African incursions led by Manuel de Sousa (q. v.) in the 1880s. In 1890
the Mutoko signed a concession* for the newly-arrived BSAC,
but thereafter resisted paying taxes. In early 1895 the British
mounted a major punitive expedition against the Budjga, but the
Budjga did not join in the general Shona Revolt (q. v.) which
erupted the next year.

BUFFALO RANGE. Village with an airport serving the southeastern
low veld region, located near Chiredzi* (at 21° 1'S, 31° 32'E).
The airport was opened on a ranch of the same name in 1965.
In 1977 its landing facilities were expanded to accommodate mili-
tary aircraft used against guerrillas based in Mozambique. (See
AIR TRANSPORT; MILITARY.)

BUHERA. Village serving as the administrative center for the
district of the same name in Manicaland Province* (at 19° 20'S,
31° 26'E).

BUHERA DISTRICT. Originally the southeastern section of Charter
District (q. v.), the entire district is now Tribal Trust Land
(q. v.). It is separated from the Umtali District (q. v.) on the
east by the Sabi River*. It also borders the districts of Melsetter on the southeast, Bikita on the south, Gutu on the west,
and Wedza (qq. v.) on the north. Most of the inhabitants are
Hera people (q. v.).

"BUILD A NATION." Name of a campaign launched by the government of Edgar Whitehead (q. v.) in order to increase the number

of registered African voters. Whitehead hoped to enhance the
electoral strength of his United (Federal) Party (q. v.) against
that of the more right-wing European parties, and to lure Africans away from the growing nationalist movement (see AFRICAN
NATIONAL CONGRESS; NATIONAL DEMOCRATIC PARTY).
Less than a quarter of the anticipated 50,000 new African voters
registered, and most of these boycotted the 1962 election, thereby helping the Rhodesian Front (q. v.) to win.

BULALIMA-MANGWE DISTRICT. West-central border district in
Matabeleland North Province (q. v.), roughly bisected by the
railway (q. v.) line between Francistown and Bulawayo (qq. v.).
The district covers 12, 205 sq. km. It is separated from the
Nyamandhlovu District (q. v.) in the north by the Nata River
(q. v.). It touches Bulawayo District on the east, and shares
a long north-south border with the Matobo District on its southeast. Plumtree (q. v.) is its administrative center. Other
centers include Mphoengs, Figtree, and Mangwe (qq. v.). The
central part of the district is reserved for Europeans, while
the end parts are mostly Tribal Trust Lands (q. v.). Animal
husbandry is the dominant commercial industry.
    Bulilima is a locative form for "country of the Lilima, "
a branch of the Kalanga-speaking people (q. v.). The district
also contains many Ndebele.

BULAWAYO (Sindebele* locative: Gubulawayo). Historically, there
have been three distinct Bulawayos.
    (1) In 1871 the Ndebele king Lobengula (q. v.) raised the
Bulawayo ibutho*, making its town his chief headquarters in
place of Gibixhegu (q. v.). This town--later known as "Old
Bulawayo"--was located c. 5 km. southwest of present Hope
Fountain (q. v.). It is said that Lobengula chose the name
Bulawayo, "place of killing, " to commemorate casualties in the
battle of Zwangendaba (q. v.) fought in June 1870. "Bulawayo"
had also been the name of two of the Zulu king Shaka's (q. v.)
chief towns in the early 19th century. (Note that the belief that
Mzilikazi [q. v.] founded Bulawayo is incorrect.)
    (2) In 1881 Lobengula relocated Bulawayo farther north,
at a site in the northern part of the modern city (20° 9'S,
28° 35'E; alt. 1350 m.). Over the next 13 years Bulawayo was
the chief gathering place for the Ndebele during religious festivals (see INXWALA) and military reviews, and it was the main
center for European and other non-Ndebele hunters and traders.
It was not a "capital" in the Western sense, however. Lobengula moved about the kingdom frequently, holding court where
he happened to be (see e. g., UMVUTSHA). During this period
Bulawayo had a fixed population of several thousand people.
    (3) Towards the end of the 1893 Ndebele War (q. v.)
Lobengula set fire to Bulawayo and fled north. On November
4, 1893, British forces under L. S. Jameson (q. v.) occupied
the site. European settlement began immediately. Occupation
of the town was the most striking British achievement during
the war. To symbolize British conquest, Government House

was erected on the site of Lobengula's former home.   The new
European town grew rapidly.   It soon displaced Fort Victoria
(q. v.) as the major transport link between South Africa and
Salisbury (q. v.).   The outbreak of the Ndebele Revolt (q. v.) in
1896 gravely threatened British occupation of the region.   For
several months rebels besieged the Europeans concentrated in
Bulawayo, until British imperial troops put the Ndebele on the
defensive.   After the Revolt Bulawayo's growth resumed, accelerating even further when the railway (q. v.) line to Mafeking
was opened in 1897.

     During the present century Bulawayo has grown into the
country's second largest city (see URBANIZATION).   Its population in early 1975 was estimated at 329,000 (79% Africans; 18%
Europeans).   The city is the country's leading commercial
center, largely because it stands at the junction of railway links
with Salisbury, Victoria Falls, Mafeking, and Beitbridge.   This
commercial advantage has in turn made Bulawayo the country's
leading industrial center, with more than 600 factories of many
types.   The city is also administrative center for Bulawayo
District and for both Matabeleland provinces (qq. v.).

BULAWAYO CHRONICLE (a. k. a. The Chronicle).   Second biggest of
     the country's two daily newspapers (see PRESS), with about half
     the circulation of the Rhodesia Herald (q. v.), the Chronicle was
     started by the Argus Group (q. v.) as a weekly in October 1894.
     It became a daily in 1897.   Circulation in 1973 was over 26,500.
     (American libraries receiving the Chronicle include Howard Uni-
     versity; UCLA; Library of Congress.)

BULAWAYO DISTRICT.   Surrounding the city of the same name,
     Bulawayo District is the country's smallest, with an area of
     only 1675 sq. km. (it was formerly more than twice as large).
     Virtually all its land is reserved for European farmers and
     ranchers, who specialize in intensive ranching, dairying, and
     maize and cotton growing.

BULAWAYO FIELD FORCE (BFF).   Volunteer military force raised
     in April 1896, at the start of the Ndebele Revolt (q. v.).   It
     comprised about 850 Europeans and South African non-whites.
     The BFF was reinforced by the Matabeleland Relief Force (q.v.)
     in May, and was itself abandoned on July 4th.

BULLOCK, CHARLES (1880-1952).   Amateur ethnographer and Afri-
     can administrator.   Bullock began his career in the Southern
     Rhodesian Native Department in 1904, serving in many of the
     country's districts before retiring as Chief Native Commissioner
     in 1940.   He wrote several standard books on the Shona and
     Ndebele peoples; edited the journal Nada* (1944-5); and wrote
     Rina (1949), a novel dealing with local miscegenation.

BUMBUZI RUINS (variant: Bumboosie).   Group of megalithic ruins
     in the Wankie District (q. v.).   Similar to, but widely separated
     from the Zimbabwe and Khami-type ruins (qq. v.) of the rest of

the country.   The origin of the Bumbuzi ruins is in doubt, but
they are generally attributed to Rozvi* offshoots from the Changamire state (q.v.) who may have entered the region in the late
18th or early 19th century.   Nanzwa (q.v.) traditions hold that
the main ruin, Bumbuzi proper (at 18° 30'S, 26° 11'E) was built
and occupied by their first Zanke (ruler) around the early 19th
century.   Nearby is an unrelated cave filled with sandstone
petroglyphs (q.v.) of animal spoor* believed to have been
fashioned by Stone Age* hunters.   Sandstone is also the main
building material of the ruins.   Other complexes in the group
of ruins include Halfway House Ruin (18° 44'S, 27° 21'E), and
Mtoa Ruin (18° 42'S, 26° 41'E).

BUMI RIVER (a.k.a. Ume; Omay).   One of the Zambezi River's
    (q.v.) main southern tributaries in the country, the Bumi rises
    c. 30 km. north of Gokwe (q.v.), flowing roughly north.   It now
    enters Lake Kariba (q.v.) just east of the Bumi Hills.

BUNDU.   Term for wild bush country.   Possibly introduced into
    southern African usage from the Philippines' Tagalog language,
    in which bundok means "mountain."   The same word gave
    American slang "boondocks."   Bundu may also be related to such
    Bantu words as Chishona's* bundo, for "grazing grass."

BUNGA FOREST.   Evergreen forest, now part of Vumba National
    Park (q.v.).

BUNU (variants: Bhunu, Vabunu, Amabunu, etc.).   Widely used
    Bantu* form of Boer (q.v.).

BURANDAYA (pl., Maburandaya).   Chishona* term for a person from
    Malawi; derives from the name "Blantyre," the former capital
    of Malawi.

BURMA VALLEY.   Located just south of the Vumba Mountains (q.v.),
    Burma Valley is the center of year-round intensive agricultural
    production on European farms.   The valley's Nyamataka River
    flows east into Mozambique.

BURNHAM, FREDERICK RUSSELL (1860-Sept. 5, 1947).   American
    scout, born in Minnesota, where he is said to have acquired his
    skills from Indians.   He came to southern Africa in 1893 and
    quickly became involved in the Ndebele war (q.v.), during which
    he was one of two white survivors of the Shangani Patrol (q.v.;
    see also DHLO DHLO).   He also scouted for the Bulawayo
    Field Force during the Ndebele Revolt (qq.v.).   In June 1896 he
    and another man gained fame by claiming to have killed the
    "Mlimo" (q.v.), i.e., the supposed religious leader of the Re-
    volt (cf. MKWATI).   It was later learned that the murdered man
    was the Kalanga* priest of a southwestern Mwari cult center
    which had previously been neutral during the Revolt.   Burnham
    later served as a scout in the South African War (q.v.) before
    returning to the United States, where he helped to establish the
    Boy Scout movement (cf. BADEN-POWELL, R. S. S.).

BUROMBO, BENJAMIN B. (c. 1909-1959). Variously said to have
  been born in the Buhera or Selukwe districts (qq. v.), Burombo
  came to Bulawayo during the early 1940s after having worked in
  Johannesburg, South Africa. There he ran a small store and
  began assisting farmers to resist government destocking measures. Around July 1947 he organized the (British) African
  Workers' Voice Association--an organization now regarded as
  an important forerunner of modern nationalism. He played an
  active role in organizing and in negotiating the general strike of
  1948 in Bulawayo. Afterwards he used his organization to con-
  centrate on rural issues. He attained notable successes in opposing implementation of the Land Apportionment Act and the
  Native Land Husbandry Act (qq. v.), but the government merely
  responded by amending the laws to overcome the loopholes which
  he found. In 1952 his Voice Association was banned under the
  terms of the Subversive Activities Act of 1950. Burombo was
  a dynamic and charismatic leader, but his health was always
  poor and he succumbed to cancer.

"BUSHMAN." Popular, but somewhat pejorative name for the San
  people (q. v.) in southern Africa. From the Dutch word boschjes-
  man.

BUTUA (variants: Abutua, Butwa). Portuguese (q. v.) name for the
  southwestern part of the country which lay just beyond their
  penetration (cf. BAYÃO, S.). The same part of the country is
  known in Shona tradition as Guruhuswa (q. v.). The word
  "Butua" is apparently a Portuguese contraction of "Gunuvutwa,"
  the Tavara (q. v.) pronunciation of Guruhuswa.

BUXTON COMMITTEE (1921). Once it was certain that the BSAC
  would be ending its administration of Southern Rhodesia, the
  question of the colony's future constitutional status arose. In
  March 1921 Winston Churchill, then Secretary of State for
  Colonies, set up a committee to investigate the feasibility of
  the settlers' assuming power in a Responsible Government (q.v.).
  The Committee was headed by a former Governor-General and
  High Commissioner of South Africa, Lord Buxton (1853-1934).
  The Committee's Report, dated April 12, 1921 (Cmd 1273),
  recommended an immediate referendum on the issue among the
  settlers, and it outlined a constitution (q. v.) based on that of
  the former colony of Natal. An important further recommendation was that the British government retain the same reserve
  powers over legislation affecting African rights that it held over
  the BSAC regime.

"BYRD AMENDMENT." Popular name for Section 503 of the Armed
  Forces Procurement Appropriations Authorization Act, passed by
  the United States Congress in November 1971. Senator Harry F.
  Byrd (Independent, Virginia) introduced the section to prevent the
  President of the United States from prohibiting importation of
  designated strategic materials from any non-Communist country
  so long as such materials were being imported from a Communist

country. The law, signed by President Nixon on November 17,
1971, therefore allowed the United States openly to import
chrome (q. v.) from Rhodesia in violation of United Nations
sanctions (q. v.) because the country was already importing
chrome from the Soviet Union.

The United States had imported $5 million worth of Rho-
desian chrome in 1965, but it ceased all imports the next year.
In 1972 the U. S. imported $13. 3 million worth of Rhodesian
chrome, nickel, and asbestos (qq. v.), even though large domestic stockpiles of chrome were reported as available. Rhodesian chrome imports rose to $45 million in 1975, and by the
next year Rhodesia was estimated to be supplying 17% of U. S.
imports of the metal. Other major American suppliers included
the Soviet Union, South Africa, and Turkey.

Implementation of the Byrd Amendment caused the United
States to be repeatedly condemned at home and abroad for
flouting the sanctions policy which it had previously endorsed.
Under the pressure of newly elected President Jimmy Carter,
Congress repealed the Amendment on March 14-15, 1977. The
Rhodesian government then announced that loss of the American
market would have little impact on the country's economy, but it
is clear that the change of American policy was a blow to Rhodesian morale.

- C -

-C-. In Sindebele (q. v.) orthography the letter c represents the
    dental click sound (q. v.), as in Mncumbathe*. In Chishona
    (q. v.) orthography c occurs only in the ch digraph, which was
    formerly often written simply as c, as in "Cishona."

CAM AND MOTOR MINE   see   EIFFEL FLATS

CAMELS.   At the beginning of the 20th century much of the country's
    goods transport was still dependent upon animal carriage.   In
    1901 East Coast Fever (q. v.) hit the country, killing many oxen
    and threatening the transportation industry.   Two years later 34
    camels and Sikh drivers were imported from India as an experi-
    mental alternative.   The camels enjoyed a brief success car-
    rying goods between Salisbury and Mazoe (qq. v.), but most of
    them soon succumbed to local diseases and the experiment was
    abandoned.   (See CATTLE; HEALTH.)

CAMPBELL, ARCHIBALD ANDREW (Oct. 11, 1863-1946).   Early
    African administrator and amateur historian.   Born and educated
    in Natal, Campbell came to Mashonaland* in the early 1890s to
    prospect.   He joined the Matabeleland* Native Department in
    1896, serving for 23 years before becoming manager of the
    labor compound at Shabani*.   During his Matabeleland service
    he pioneered the collection of Ndebele traditions, which he used
    to write a book in 1911.   He later published the volume under
    the pen-name "Mziki" (reedbuck) as Mlimo: The Rise and Fall

of the Matabele (1926). Campbell's book was not the pure compilation of authentic traditions it purported to be, but it has had
a major impact on later writings on Ndebele history. An early
draft of his work was used by D. F. Ellenberger in the latter's
account of Ndebele history in The History of the Basuto (London,
1912). A. T. Bryant in turn borrowed from Ellenberger in his
own monumental Nguni* history, Olden Times in Zululand and
Natal (London, 1929).

CAPRICORN AFRICA SOCIETY. Multi-racial organization founded in
1949 by Col. David Stirling (b. 1915), a post-war immigrant who
had been a British commando leader in the North African campaign. The Society's main goal was to foster a sense of non-
racial African identity throughout central and east Africa. After
several years of formulating principles, the Society issued a
manifesto and attempted to recruit members of all races. A
handbook issued in 1955 pronounced a doctrine of racial equality,
calling for an end to all racial discrimination, as well as an
abandonment of black African nationalism. It further proposed
a franchise system in which multiple votes would be awarded
to citizens on the basis of civic contributions--a system recog-
nizing the ideal of universal suffrage, while assuring that whites
would retain political dominance. Unique multiracial study groups
were formed throughout the country, but the Society's identification with the "partnership" principles of Federation (qq. v.) made
"Capricornist" a dirty word among Africans north of the Zambezi. In 1956 the Society held a large conference in Nyasaland
(now Malawi), but failed to develop into a significant mass movement. Leading African members, such as Leopold Takawira
(q. v.), drifted into more militant African organizations. In 1957
European members of the Society launched the Constitution Party
in Northern Rhodesia, but the party won no elections. The same
year Society branches began folding up throughout Southern Rhodesia. In 1965 the Society's Salisbury headquarters ceased
operations, turning over its records to the National Archives*.

"CAPTAIN OF THE GATES" see MASAPA

CARNEGIE, DAVID (Nov. 26, 1855-Jan. 1910). A Scottish-born
agent of the LMS, Carnegie joined C. D. Helm at Hope Fountain
(qq. v.) in 1882. During the Ndebele Revolt (q. v.) of 1896 he
worked as an interpreter to help bring about the negotiations
which ended the Matopos fighting. In 1898 he founded Centenary
Mission at Figtree (qq. v.) with the financial aid of Cecil Rhodes.
During an earlier leave in England he wrote Among the Matabele
(1894). His wife, a Matabeleland-born daughter of William
Sykes (q. v.), translated Pilgrim's Progress into Sindebele*.

CARRINGTON, FREDERICK (Aug. 23, 1844-March 22, 1913). British
army officer of considerable experience in minor South African
campaigns after 1875. Between 1885 and 1893 Carrington commanded the Bechuanaland Border Police (q. v.), and then served
as military advisor to H. B. Loch, High Commissioner of South

Africa, during the Ndebele War (q.v.). After the 1896 Ndebele Revolt (q.v.) erupted, Carrington was named supreme commander of British forces in Matabeleland*, where he arrived on June 2nd. There he commanded about 2000 white and 600 black troops, including H. C. O. Plumer's MRF (qq.v.). His subordinates, Plumer and Baden-Powell (q.v.), pursued an active campaign of using mounted patrols to keep the rebels in motion, building forts, seizing cattle, and burning crops to disrupt Ndebele supplies. By August they had succeeded in neutralizing most rebels north of the Matopo Hills (q.v.), but they could not dislodge the remaining rebels in the Hills themselves. That theater of the war was ended by negotiation when Cecil Rhodes met Matopos leaders in the famous "indabas" (q.v.). After the outbreak of the Shona Revolt in late June, Carrington was designated supreme commander for the whole country, with E. A. H. Alderson (q.v.) directing the Mashonaland campaign. During the South African War (q.v.) Carrington commanded the Rhodesia Field Force (q.v.).

CARTER COMMISSION see MORRIS CARTER COMMISSION

CATON-THOMPSON, GERTRUDE (b. 1888). British archaeologist commissioned in 1929 to investigate the dispute over the origins and dating of the country's stone ruins (q.v.) begun a generation earlier by D. Randall-MacIver and R. N. Hall (qq.v.). Only the second professional archaeologist to work in the country, Caton-Thompson conducted digs at Zimbabwe, Dhlo Dhlo (qq.v.), and other ruins, undertaking her most thorough investigation in the Maund Ruin at Great Zimbabwe. She published her findings in The Zimbabwe Culture: Ruins and Reactions (London, 1931), which contains one of the most detailed inventories of artifacts yet presented. She unequivocally supported Randall-MacIver's conclusion that the country's ruins were strictly African in origin, but departed from her predecessor in pushing the date for Great Zimbabwe's beginnings back to the 8th or 9th century. Except for her early Zimbabwe dating, her work has stood up well against more recent investigations, but it failed to settle the Zimbabwe Controversy (q.v.) among the lay public.

CATTLE. Animal husbandry, like plant cultivation, is reckoned to have begun in the country in the early Iron Age (q.v.), though cattle-keeping apparently did not become a significant economic activity until late in the first millenium A.D. Comparatively large-scale cattle-keeping was introduced by the Ndebele (q.v.) who arrived around 1839. The Ndebele brought South African breeds with them, acquired local animals, raided outside the country for additional cattle, and bred ever-larger herds by restricting their slaughter for beef. By the late 19th century the Ndebele alone appear to have owned more than 150,000 head of cattle.
     European occupation of Matabeleland after the Ndebele War (q.v.) of 1893-4 was accompanied by a vigorous effort to

confiscate Ndebele herds on the pretext that all cattle had belonged to the king, and were therefore the property of the
BSAC by right of conquest.   Confiscation was followed by
rinderpest (q. v.) and enforced destocking throughout the country, and further confiscations and losses during the 1896-7
Revolts (q. v.).   By the turn of the century it was estimated
that only c. 55,000 head were still in the hands of the entire
African population.   Recovery was rapid, however, aided by
European importation of fresh breeding stock from outside the
country.   By 1913 African-owned cattle had risen to nearly
400,000 head, a figure which rose to over 1.8 million in 1949,
and c. 2.5 million in 1972.   Meanwhile, European farmers were
developing a commercial beef and dairy industry with their own
animals.
        African participation in the commercial cattle industry
has always been slight.   To the difficulties of reaching cash
markets inherent in the separation of African and European
agricultural sectors, is added the traditional regard for cattle
as wealth, rather than as a commodity for attaining other forms
of wealth.   As in many African societies, cattle have long
played an important social role among the Shona and, especially,
among the Ndebele as an index of prestige and as a currency for
important social transactions, such as marriage (see LOBOLO).
Rapid population growth in Tribal Trust Lands (q. v.) and govern-
ment-enforced destocking measures have limited the numbers of
cattle owned by individual families, enhancing their reluctance
to sell stock for cash.
        Cattle have become an increasingly important part of the
European agricultural sector, particularly since UDI, when many
farmers began putting tobacco (q. v.) land into beef cattle production (see SANCTIONS).   Between 1965 and 1972 European cattle
herds rose by about two-thirds, to c. 2.6 million head, just ex-
ceeding the number owned by Africans.   The annual off-take for
slaughter is estimated at 10% of the country's total herds, but
most of this comes from European owned animals.   Beef has
proven a particularly successful sanctions-busting commodity.
About 60% of the 1972 production was exported, much of it to
neighboring African countries hostile to the Ian Smith regime.
(See AGRICULTURE; TSETSE FLY; EAST COAST FEVER; LUNG
SICKNESS.)

CAVE COMMISSION (1919-20).   When it appeared likely that the
    British Imperial government would take over responsibility for
    Southern Rhodesia from the BSAC, the question of compensating
    the company for its local assets arose.   The company claimed
    assets worth £8 million, but members of the Legislative Council
    (q. v.) protested the amount.   To resolve the dispute the British
    government appointed a cabinet minister, George Cave (1856-
    1928) to head a commission of investigation.   The commission
    held hearings in London and Salisbury in 1919, issuing its re-
    port on January 15, 1920.   The report suggested a compensa-
    tion of £4,435,225--somewhat more than the company actually

received four years later. (See BUXTON COMMITTEE; RE-
SPONSIBLE GOVERNMENT.)

CAVE OF HANDS   see   MCHELA CAVE

CENSORSHIP. The various European governments of the country
    have been sensitive to criticism since the establishment of the
    BSAC administration in Mashonaland* in 1890.   It is said that
    Cecil Rhodes threatened W. E. Fairbridge (q.v.) with deporta-
    tion shortly after the latter had started the forerunner of the
    Rhodesia Herald (q.v.) in 1891.   Fairbridge then toned down
    his editorial criticisms of the administration.   Until the Rho-
    desian Front (q.v.) came to power in 1962, the European press
    (q.v.) tended to identify closely with the interests of the govern-
    ment, so overt censorship was rarely a problem.   By contrast,
    the majority African population--whose interests have almost al-
    ways conflicted with those of the government--have never es-
    tablished anything like an independent press (see AFRICAN
    NEWSPAPERS, LTD.).   Papers such as the African Daily News,
    Chapupu, the Zimbabwe Sun (qq.v.), and others were quickly
    suppressed when they expressed overtly African nationalist sen-
    timents.
        Shortly before UDI in 1965, Ian Smith's government pro-
    mulgated emergency regulations allowing for wide press censor-
    ship.   One month after UDI the government officially instituted
    censorship, arguing that the country was virtually at war.
    Censorship was directed mainly against the Argus group of
    newspapers (q.v.), which editorially opposed UDI.   Government
    censors inspected newspaper galley proofs and stopped publica-
    tion of considerable material.   The newspapers responded by
    leaving large blank columns and printing notices calling atten-
    tion to the fact of censorship.   In February 1966 new regula-
    tions forbade these practices, but were generally ignored.   The
    government overlooked these offenses, apparently because it
    feared having UDI challenged in the courts.   In April 1968 cen-
    sorship restrictions were formally lifted.   It is said that the
    government worked out a secret accommodation with the news-
    papers calling for self-censorship.   Whatever, press criticism
    of the government was subsequently muted.
        In December 1967 the government established a permanent
    Board of Censorship to examine publications and films of all
    kinds.   It has frequently banned importation of foreign materials
    for political or moral reasons.   Among the banned authors are
    James Baldwin, Norman Mailer, Henry Miller, Frank Harris,
    and Kenneth Kaunda.   Banned publications are listed in the
    Government Gazette.
        In the absence of a significant pro-Rhodesian Front press,
    many party leaders have called for nationalization of the news-
    papers, but this has not yet been seriously considered.   As an
    alternative the government has issued propaganda through its
    Ministry of Information (see AFRICAN TIMES) and has dominated
    the Rhodesian Broadcasting Corporation (q.v.).

CENSUSES see POPULATION

CENTENARY. (1) LMS mission station founded near Figtree (q.v.) in 1898 by David Carnegie (q.v.). The station was closed in 1913 because encroaching European farmlands cut it off from African settlements.
(2) Village in the Darwin District (q.v.) 132 km. north of Salisbury, named in 1953 to commemorate Cecil Rhodes' (q.v.) birth. A center of a European farming region, Centenary has become one of the most beleaguered European towns since the escalation of African nationalist guerrilla incursions in the mid-1970s.

"CENTRAL AFRICA." At one time or another this term has been applied to almost every part of Africa between the Western Sudanic region and present Rhodesia. During the 1890s Malawi has briefly been known as "British Central Africa." Later "Central Africa" was increasingly used to refer to present Malawi, Zambia, and Rhodesia. Perhaps the best claimant to the term, however, is the former French Equatorial African territory renamed Central African Republic in 1960. (Cf. "SOUTHERN AFRICA.")

CENTRAL AFRICA COUNCIL. Advisory and consultative body created by the British government in October 1944 for the purpose of stimulating inter-territorial cooperation among Southern Rhodesia, Northern Rhodesia, and Nyasaland (see BLEDISLOE COMMISSION). The governor (q.v.) of Southern Rhodesia was made chairman. The governors of the other territories and the Southern Rhodesian prime minister (q.v.) were made ex officio members. Each territory also supplied three common members. The Council met twice yearly, beginning in June 1945. Although it had no powers of enforcement, its recommendations to the territorial legislative bodies led to the mergers of air transport (q.v.), meteorological, statistical, and archival services (see NATIONAL ARCHIVES) and to formation of a commission to investigate building the Kariba Dam (q.v.). The Council provided an institutional framework which facilitated establishment of the Federation (q.v.) in 1953.

CENTRAL AFRICAN AIRWAYS see AIR RHODESIA

CENTRAL AFRICAN EXAMINER. Monthly newspaper published in Salisbury from 1957 to 1965, when government pressure shut it down. (See PRESS.)

CENTRAL AFRICAN FEDERATION (CAF). Popular but unofficial name of the Federation of Rhodesia and Nyasaland (q.v.).

CENTRAL AFRICAN PARTY (CAP). Short-lived multi-racial party formed by Garfield Todd (q.v.) in 1959. The party attracted such African leaders as Leopold Takawira, Stanlake Samkange, and Ndabaningi Sithole (qq.v.) but lost many African supporters to the new National Democratic Party (q.v.) the next year. Todd himself resigned his leadership in July 1960. The remaining party leaders supported the proposals for the 1961 constitution (q.v.), but failed ever to score an electoral victory within Southern Rhodesia.

CENTRAL AFRICAN POWER CORPORATION see ELECTRICAL POWER

CENTRAL PLATEAU. The main watershed of the country, the Central Plateau runs southwest to northeast, separating the Zambezi and Limpopo basins (qq.v.). It is also known as the "high veld," but this term also appropriately applies to any land over 1220 m. (4000 ft.). (See ALTITUDINAL ZONES; RIVERS.)

CENTRE PARTY (CP). Moderate multi-racial political party formed in August 1968 by opponents of the Rhodesian Front government, such as T. H. Patrick Bashford (b.1915). The CP favored gradual African political advancement along the lines of the "Tiger Talks" (q.v.) proposals, and it attracted some middle class African support. In the 1970 election the party won 7 of the 8 African parliamentary seats it contested (cf. NATIONAL PEOPLES' UNION), but all its white candidates were badly defeated despite support from the Argus Group (q.v.) newspapers. In early 1972 the CP reluctantly advocated acceptance of the Anglo-Rhodesian Settlement terms in the absence of any apparent alternatives (see PEARCE COMMISSION).

CHAKAIPA, PATRICK F. (b.1932). One of the most popular novelists writing in Chishona*, Chakaipa is a Roman Catholic archbishop and a former teacher. Born in the Mondoro TTL of the eastern Hartley District*, Chakaipa has used his own homeland as the main setting in all his books. His first two books, Karikoga Gumiremiseve ("Karikoga and the ten arrows," 1958) and Pfumo Reropa ("The spear of blood," 1961) are historical romances based on traditional stories. Three later novels (1961 to 1967) have modern settings and are moralistic tales dealing with the problem of reconciling Western notions of individual liberty with traditional African community values. (See LITERATURE.)

CHAKARI. Town in the Hartley District* located c.25 km. northwest of the main road between Gatooma and Salisbury (qq.v.) (at 18° 4'S, 29° 51'E; alt. 1160 m.). The town arose to support the Dalny Mine, begun in 1908. This mine is now the country's leading producer of gold (q.v.). Population in 1969 was 5100 (95% Africans).

CHAMINUKA. Name of the most famous Shona "lion spirit," or mhondoro (q.v.). The identity of the historical Chaminuka personage is uncertain, but is believed to go back several hundred years. The Chaminuka spirit appears first to have

entered a medium during the early 19th century--possibly after
the arrival of the Ndebele (q.v.) in the country. According to
a recent Chaminuka medium, the spirit entered a Korekore*
man named Mutota at Great Zimbabwe*, and then abandoned him
to reside near Bulawayo*. It then followed a Zezuru* man named
Kachinda to Mashyamombe's* chiefdom, where it possessed him.
From Kachinda the spirit switched to Pasipamire (a.k.a. Tsuro),
the son of the Zezuru chief Rwizi.

Pasipamire used his personal charisma to develop Chaminuka, his alter ego, into a famous rainmaker and the center
of Shona resistance to the Ndebele. Operating from a group of
villages known as Situngwiza (Chitungwiza) between the Umfuli
and Hunyani rivers (qq.v.), Pasipamire developed a wealthy and
influential cult associated with that of Nehanda (q.v.). During
the 1870s the Ndebele king Lobengula (q.v.) paid tribute to him
and exempted his region from raids. By the early 1880s
"Chaminuka" was behaving so independently that he was seen
as a challenge to Ndebele authority throughout central Shona
country. In May 1883 an Ndebele impi* (in which the Imbizo*
ibutho* participated) attacked the Chaminuka headquarters and
had Pasipamire killed. The medium's death later became the
subject of many popular legends, some of which include the
apocryphal claim that Chaminuka personally confronted Lobengula before being tried and executed. More likely, he was
killed near the Shangani River* while being brought to Bulawayo.

The Chaminuka spirit is not known to have possessed
another medium until 1903, so it did not figure into the 1896-7
Revolt (q.v.). A female medium emerged in 1903, but she soon
committed suicide while being held in a British jail. Later 20th-
century mediums have revived the Chaminuka cult and restored
the spirit's reputation as a rainmaker in Zezuru country.

The 19th-century medium, Pasipamire, is now regarded
as a major symbol of African resistance and is venerated by
many modern nationalists. Ironically, a recent medium, Muchetera, has been an outspoken opponent of African nationalism.
In the early 1960s Muchetera proposed to Edgar Whitehead
(q.v.) that a national convocation of all the country's leaders
be called, so that he--"Chaminuka"--could instruct them on the
future of the country.

CHANCELLOR, JOHN ROBERT (Oct. 20, 1870-July 31, 1952). A
Scot, Chancellor had a military background before entering the
colonial service as governor of Mauritius (1911-16) and then of
Trinidad and Tobago (1916-21). In 1923 he became the first
Governor (q.v.) of Southern Rhodesia. He is said to have
exercised considerable influence over the inexperienced government of Charles Coghlan (q.v.) and somewhat less influence
over H. U. Moffat (q.v.). He was succeeded by C. H. Rodwell (q.v.) in 1928. He later served as British High Commissioner in Palestine.

CHANGA (fl. late 15th cent.). The son, or perhaps son-in-law, of
Munhumutapa* Matope (qq.v.), Changa was made a district chief

over an area around present Sipolilo* when the Munhumutapa
state was established in the Dande (q. v.). In the 1480s Changa
rebelled against his relative Mukombera (q. v.), killing him in
a battle in c. 1490. For about four years Changa held the Munhumutapa-ship himself. By this time he had adopted the name
"Changamire" (q. v.), apparently bestowed upon him by Muslims
(q. v.), who called him amir. Changa was in turn killed by a
son of Mukombero, Chikuyo Chisamarengu (q. v.), who reclaimed
the kingship (c. 1494). Changa's son (name unknown) then
adopted "Changamire" as a title and moved south, where he
allied with Togwa (q. v.) in defiance of the Munhumutapa state.

CHANGAMIRE. Dynastic title of the rulers of the Shona state
variously known to historians as the Changamire Kingdom or
the Rozvi Empire. Its rulers were also known by the generic
Shona title mambo (q. v.).
   The Changamire state dominated most of the country
from the late 17th century to the early 19th century, but its
history is poorly known, in contrast to that of the older Munhumutapa state (q. v.). Changamire history divides into at
least two distinct periods, separated by a long gap about which
little is known. The first person to hold the title "Changamire"
was Changa (q. v.), who briefly usurped the Munhumutapa-ship
in the early 1490s. After his death, his son adopted the name
Changamire as a dynastic title and, apparently, retreated south.
In c. 1547 Munhumutapa Neshangwe (q. v.) is said to have expelled the reigning Changamire from the Mbire region (q. v.).
This may have been the time the dynasty moved farther southwest, into the Guruhuswa region (q. v.), where the formerly
allied Togwa dynasty (q. v.) ruled. Some authorities, however,
suggest a 17th-century Changamire intrusion into Guruhuswa.
Whichever, it is fairly clear that the Changamire state was
established in Guruhuswa by the mid-17th century, and that its
main centers were at Dhlo Dhlo and Ntabazikamambo (Manyanga)
(qq. v.). There the Changamires ruled mainly Kalanga-speaking
peoples (q. v.).
   The second phase of Changamire history began in the
1680s, when Changamire military campaigns began attracting
the notice of Portuguese (q. v.) traders and missionaries in
the northeast. In the early 1690s Changamire forces under
Dombo (q. v.) swiftly advanced into Munhumutapa, Manyika*,
and other territories. It was apparently then that the people
earned the nickname Rozvi, "the destroyers." From then until
the Mfecane era (q. v.) the Changamire state ruled most of the
country directly, or through tributary chiefdoms. Rozvi officials sanctioned chiefly succession in many societies--a practice
which persists today.
   The 18th century is the country's "dark age" in modern
historiography. Dombo's campaigns expelled most of the
Portuguese from the country, thereby isolating the state from
literate observers. Traditional evidence has been collected,
but has not yet been fully worked out. Consequently, there is
not yet even a satisfactory list of 18th-century Changamires.

By the early 19th century the state appears to have been in disarray. Internal succession disputes, wars with Karanga and Ngwato (qq.v., see KGARI), and droughts were breaking down central authority. In the early 1830s the Mfecane brought a succession of South African invaders to the country. The most important of these were the Ngoni of Zwangendaba and Nyamazana (qq.v.), who killed the reigning Changamire, Chirisamhuru (q.v.) at Ntabazikamambo.

An attempt at recovery was made, and Chirisamhuru's son Tohwechipi (q.v.) was made king at Dhlo Dhlo after the Ngoni had left. Soon, however, Mzilikazi's Ndebele (qq.v.) invaded the country. The Ndebele invasion was initially less violent, but most of the Rozvi leaders fled. A section under Mutinhima, a rival claimant to the Changamire title, resisted the Ndebele in the nearby Mulungwane Hills (q.v.), but he was driven further east. Tohwechipi resisted the Ndebele successfully from a place near Great Zimbabwe* into the 1850s, but was captured farther east in 1866. His capture effectively ended any pretensions the Rozvi had to be sustaining the Changamire state. It did not, however, end the succession. The titular mambo-ship has remained a lively focus of political contention into the 20th century.

CHANGANA. Variant of Shangane (q.v.).

CHAPLIN, FRANCIS PERCY DRUMMOND (Aug. 10, 1866-Nov. 16, 1933). Last BSAC Administrator (q.v.) of the country. Chaplin left England for Southern Rhodesia in 1897, but decided not to enter the country because of the Revolts (q.v.) then active. Instead, he became a correspondent for the London Times in South Africa. In 1898 he briefly visited Southern Rhodesia, but disliked what he saw there. After a stint as a correspondent in Russia, he returned to the Transvaal* and became a manager of Consolidated Gold Fields of South Africa, Ltd. He soon became one of the most influential people in the mining industry, and was elected to the Transvaal Legislative Assembly (1907) and then to the Union House of Assembly (1910). In late 1914 he succeeded W. H. Milton (q.v.) as Administrator of Southern Rhodesia.

Fearful of Afrikaner* domination in southern Africa (see UNIONIST MOVEMENT), Chaplin advocated amalgamation (q.v.) of Southern and Northern Rhodesia to strengthen their economies. In the face of strong settler opposition, he abandoned this goal, but, ironically, later assumed the additional responsibility of administering Northern Rhodesia in 1921. His appointments ended in September 1923, when the BSAC turned administration of the country over to the settlers (see RESPONSIBLE GOVERNMENT). Chaplin retained extensive mining interests in central Africa. He returned to South Africa, where he re-entered national politics. In 1925 he was made a director of the BSAC.

CHAPUPU ("The Witness"). African newspaper started in Salisbury by the Youth League and African National Congress (qq.v.) in

1957. One of the few attempts at a truly independent African
press (q.v.), the paper was banned by the government in 1958,
and in 1962, when a revival was attempted. (See CENSOR-
SHIP.)

CHARTER, ROYAL (1889). Document signed on October 29, 1889
by Queen Victoria, officially incorporating the BSAC and granting
it wide rights over the territories of present Rhodesia and
Zambia for a period of 25 years. In 1915 a supplemental
charter extended these rights an additional ten years.
    During the 1880s the British Crown granted similar
charters to the Imperial British East Africa Company, which
operated mainly in Kenya; the Royal Niger Company, operating
in Nigeria; and the British North Borneo Company.

CHARTER DISTRICT. Easternmost district in Midlands Province
(q.v.), Charter covers 6670 sq. km. Its original headquarters
were established at Ft. Charter (18° 36'S, 31° 4'E), but that
site declined rapidly after the railway (q.v.) was extended from
Bulawayo to Salisbury, and the administrative center was shifted
to Enkeldoorn (q.v.). The original southeastern section of the
district was separated to form the Buhera District (q.v.). The
remaining parts of the district are now roughly equally divided
between European area, Purchase Land, and Tribal Trust Land
(qq.v.; see LAND TENURE ACT). Most of the whites are
Afrikaners (q.v.). The Africans are mostly Zezuru-speaking
Shona (q.v.). The district borders Mashonaland South Province
on the north, Manicaland and Victoria provinces on the south,
and the district of Chilimanzi (qq.v.) on the west.

CHARTERED COMPANY (a.k.a. "the Charter"). Popular name for
the British South Africa Company (q.v.).

"CHARTERLAND." One of the unofficial names by which the country
was known in the early 1890s. (See "RHODESIA.")

CHATSWORTH. Village in the western Gutu District (q.v.) on the
Fort Victoria railway line (at 19° 38'S, 30° 50'E).

CHAZA, MAI (d. 1960). A famous faith-healer, Mai ("Mother")
Chaza began her brief but spectacular religious career as a
member of the Methodist Church. Around 1953-4 she became
ill and was believed mentally deranged. When she fell into a
coma, she was thought to have died. Her recovery was thus
interpreted as a return from the dead--an idea she corroborated
with her announcement that she had had a vision in which God
instructed her to become a faith-healer. In this capacity her
fame grew rapidly; she was particularly successful in curing
barren women. She found a refuge in the Seke Reserve, just
south of Salisbury, calling it Guta ra Jehova, "City of God."
In 1955 she broke from the Methodists, forming her own independent church, variously known to her followers as Guta ra
Jehova, or the Mai Chaza Church. She received thousands of

supplicants at Seke, including many from outside the country.
Additional refuges were established throughout the country.
Little is known about the membership of her church, except
that it apparently numbered in the tens of thousands at her
death in 1960, and that most of her followers had little education.   The next year a Malawian, Bandal Mapaulos, assumed
leadership of the Mai Chaza Church.   Thereafter membership
is believed to have declined.

CHI- (former variant: ci-).   Chishona (q.v.) noun prefix (Class 7)
for things (pl. zvi-).   The chi- prefix is also used for nouns
denoting language, culture, or style, as in Chishona itself.   Except for the Chishona entry, below, prefixes for languages are
dropped in this dictionary, unless they are used as locatives in
proper place names, as in Chishawasha.   (Cf. SINDEBELE.)

CHIBAMBAMU (variant: Sibambamu) see TOHWECHIPI

CHIBERO COLLEGE OF AGRICULTURE.   Government agricultural
training center for Africans, located in a rural area c.50 km.
southwest of Salisbury (at 18°4'S, 30°39'E).   The college was
opened in 1961 to provide a three-year practical training course,
leading to the Diploma in Agriculture, for up to 80 students.
(Cf. GWEBI AGRICULTURAL COLLEGE; EDUCATION.)

CHIBI.   Village serving as the administrative center for the district
of the same name.   The village was originally the center of
the Chivi (q.v.) chiefdom of the Mari people (located at 20°19'S,
30°31'E).

CHIBI DISTRICT.   Originally covering more than 27,000 sq. km.,
it lost most of its area to the later Nuanetsi District (q.v.).
Still later, the southern wedge of Chibi was separated to help
form the new Chiredzi District (q.v.).   By the 1970s the
district covered just 3775 sq. km. within Victoria Province
(q.v.).   Virtually the entire district is now Tribal Trust Land
(q.v.).   Its longest borders are with the districts of Victoria
on the east, and Shabani (qq.v.) on the west.

"CHICKEN RUN."   White settler expression for emigration undertaken to avoid having to live under majority rule.   Popularized
since the 1976 Geneva Conference (q.v.).

CHIDZERO, BERNARD THOMAS GIBSON (b.July 1, 1927).   United
Nations official.   Born in Salisbury to a Shona mother and a
Malawian father, Chidzero was educated in Salisbury, South
Africa, and Basutoland (now Lesotho) before attending graduate
schools in Canada.   There he obtained a doctorate in political
science from McGill University in 1958 and married a French-
Canadian.   His only direct involvement in Southern Rhodesian
politics came when he joined the London branch of the National
Democratic Party (q.v.) in 1960.   Denied a teaching post at
the University College (q.v.) in Salisbury because of his "mixed"

marriage, he joined the staff of the UN in Addis Ababa the same year. He worked for the UN in Kenya from 1963 to 1968, when he was appointed Director of Commodities Division of the UN Conference on Trade and Development (UNCTAD) in Geneva.

CHIEFS, AFRICAN   see   COUNCIL OF CHIEFS; see also under specific dynastic titles, e.g., MAKONI or MANGWENDE; and under the generic titles, INDUNA; INKOSI; MAMBO.

CHIKEREMA, JAMES ROBERT DAMBAZA (b. May 1925).   Nationalist leader.   Born at Kutama (q.v.), where his father was a teacher, Chikerema began his education there, and later attended the University of Cape Town in South Africa.   At Cape Town he became active in student protest movements and joined the Communist Party.   After the Nationalist Party came to power in South Africa in 1948, Chikerema returned to Southern Rhodesia to avoid arrest.   In 1955 he helped to found the Youth League (q.v.) and became its first president, as well as editor of Chapupu (q.v.).   Two years later he became vice president of the revived African National Congress (q.v.) and was among those arrested in a government sweep in February 1959.   Imprisoned without trial, he was finally released by Winston Field's (q.v.) government in 1963.   He then traveled to eastern Europe and China, returning to Dar es Salaam, and then to Lusaka, to help Joshua Nkomo lead ZAPU (qq.v.), beginning 13 years of self-exile.   He helped to form FROLIZI in Lusaka in 1971, assuming its presidency the following year.   In August 1975 he briefly allied with Ndabaningi Sithole (q.v.) in order to participate in the abortive Victoria Falls Conference (q.v.). He was subsequently described as head of the "Zimbabwe Liberation Front."   In September 1977 he returned to Salisbury to join Abel Muzorewa's (q.v.) faction.

CHIKUNDA (Bachikunda).   People speaking an Nsenga, or Sena, branch of Bantu*.   Most Chikunda are in Mozambique (q.v.), but several thousand live in the extreme northern part of present Rhodesia, around the Hunyani River (q.v.).   Chikunda society appears to have coalesced from diverse Bantu groups during the 19th century, when the Chikunda played an active role in Zambezi River trade with the Portuguese (q.v.).

CHIKUYO CHISAMARENGU (a.k.a. Kakuyo Komunyaka) (c. 1475-c. 1530).   Early Munhumutapa (q.v.) ruler.   While he was still a youth in c. 1490, his father Mukombero (q.v.) was killed and displaced as Munhumutapa by Changa (q.v.).   After Chikuyo himself became an adult, he organized a counter-coup and regained the Munhumutapa-ship for himself (c. 1494).   Thereafter his reign was troubled by intermittent wars with the rebellious Togwa and Changamire (qq.v.) dynasties to the south.   Meanwhile, the Portuguese (q.v.) occupied Sofala* (1505) and began penetrating the interior.   In c. 1511 Chikuyo was visited by António Fernandes (q.v.), the first European known to enter the country.   The meeting was a mutual success, beginning an era of Portuguese-Shona trade. On his death in c.1530 Chikuyo was succeeded by a nephew, Neshangwe Munembire (q.v.). Later, his own son, Chivere Nyasoro (q.v.), became Munhumu-tapa.

CHILIMANZI. Village, named after chief Chirumanzi (q.v.), serving as an agricultural center (at 19°35'S, 30°45'E) for the district of the same name.

CHILIMANZI DISTRICT. Covering 5305 sq. km. near the center of the country in the eastern part of Midlands Province (q.v.), its administrative center is Umvuma (q.v.). The northern three-quarters of the district is reserved for Europeans, who are mainly cattle* ranchers and tobacco* farmers. The south-ern quarter is Tribal Trust Land (q.v.). The district borders the districts of Charter and Gutu on the east, Victoria on the south, Selukwe, Gwelo, and Que Que on the west, and Gatooma on the north (qq.v.). Population of the district in 1969 was 54,400, of whom only 320 were Europeans.

CHIMANIMANI MOUNTAINS (a.k.a. Mawenje Mountains). Southern-most part of the Eastern Highlands (q.v.), the Chimanimani Mts. straddle the Mozambique* border just east of Melsetter (q.v.). An 8180 hectare section of the range along the border was set aside in 1950 as the Chimanimani National Park, featuring dense flora, trout fishing (q.v.), and mountain climb-ing. The park's tourist trade, never great because of the region's relative inaccessibility, was severely hurt by African nationalist guerrilla activities in the mid-1970s. (See NA-TIONAL PARKS.)

CHIMURENGA (pl. zvimurenga). Chishona* word for resistance or rebellion, used especially to refer to the Revolts (q.v.) of 1896-7 and the modern liberation struggle. (Cf. MURENGA; CHINDUNDUMA.)

CHINAMANO, JOSIAH MUSHORE (b.Oct. 29, 1922). Educator and nationalist leader. Born at Epworth Mission (q.v.), Chinamano was educated in Methodist* missionary schools and he briefly taught at Waddilove (q.v.). In 1953 he returned to the country after a teaching stint in London and became headmaster of a mission school. Later he founded the country's largest non-government school in Highfields (q.v.). In 1960 he and his wife Ruth (b.1925) were among the founders of the National Democratic Party (q.v.). Later they stayed with Joshua Nkomo in ZAPU (qq.v.). Constantly harassed by the government be-cause of their political activities, the Chinamanos were ar-rested in the government sweep of April 26, 1964, and their school was closed down. They both spent most of the next eight years in detention or prison. Chinamano became trea-surer of the African National Council (q.v.) in December 1971, and was vice president of Nkomo's branch of ANC in Salisbury through 1976.

CHINAMORA.   Dynastic title of the rulers of the most important
Shavasha (q. v.) chiefdom.   The dynasty was established just
northeast of present Salisbury in the mid-18th century.   The
Chinamoras remained independent through most of the 19th
century, despite invasion by the Ngoni (q. v.) in the 1830s and
occasional later Ndebele (q. v.) raids.   In c. 1888 Kuvimadzama
became Chinamora and was visited by the Portuguese agent
Manuel de Sousa (q. v.).   The British established Salisbury in
1890, and then granted part of Shavasha land at Chishawasha
(q. v.) to Jesuit missionaries two years later.   The Shavasha
participated in the Revolt (q. v.) of 1896-7.   The Chinamora
himself surrendered in September 1897, but was retained in
office.   He later converted to Catholicism.   After his death
in 1907, Shambare (d. 1916) became the first of the government-
appointed Chinamoras.

CHINDUNDUMA.   Chishona* term for uprising, or riot; one of the
names by which the Revolt (q. v.) of 1896-7 is known.   (Cf.
CHIMURENGA.)

CHIOKO DAMBAMUPUTE (d. 1902).   Last titular Munhumutapa (q.v.).
The son of Munhumutapa Kataruza (d. 1860s?), Chioko became
Munhumutapa in c. 1887.   He ruled only a small branch of the
Tavara (q. v.) along the present Rhodesia-Mozambique border
near the Mazoe River*, but his title still carried considerable
prestige among other Shona.   During the 1890s he refused to
acknowledge Portuguese (q. v.) sovereignty and also encouraged
Shona in Southern Rhodesia to defy the British administration.
From 1900 to 1902 he was the focus of a small revolt, in which
he was aided by Mapondera (q. v.).   After his death in 1902
the Portuguese defeated his people, finally bringing to an end
more than 400 years of Munhumutapa independence.

CHIPINGA.   Town at the southern end of the Eastern Highlands
(q. v.) founded by members of the Moodie Trek (q. v.) in 1893,
and now serving as administrative center (at 20° 12'S, 32° 37'E;
alt. 1135 m.) of the district of the same name.   The village
was first called Melsetter (q. v.), but that name was soon
transferred to another settlement 65 km. to the north.   Population in 1969 was 2350 (87% Africans).

CHIPINGA DISTRICT.   Originally the southern part of the Melsetter
District, it now covers 5260 sq. km. between the Sabi River and
the Mozambique border (qq. v.).   A well-watered region, the
district is reserved mostly for Europeans in the north, and for
Tribal Trust Land in the south.   It is a center of tea, coffee,
mixed farming, and timber production.   Population of the
district in 1969 was 114,170 Africans, and 790 Europeans.
(See also SILINDA, MOUNT.)

CHIPURIRO (variant: Sipolilo).   Dynastic title of the rulers of a
small Korekore (q. v.) chiefdom in the Sipolilo District (q. v.).

The Chipuriros maintained their independence through the 19th century, until British occupation in the 1890s.

CHIRAU, J. S.   see under   ZIMBABWE UNITED PEOPLE'S OR-
GANISATION

CHIREDZI.   Town founded in 1961 about 15 km. west of the Chiredzi River (q. v.) on the railway (q. v.) line which connects low veld farms to the main railway line (at 21° 3'S, 31° 40'E).   The town now serves as the administrative center of the new district of the same name.

CHIREDZI DISTRICT.   Carved out of the southern parts of the old districts of Chibi, Victoria, Ndanga, and Bikita (qq. v.), the Lundi River (q. v.) separates it from the Nuanetsi District (q.v.) on the south.   The above districts, plus Gutu, constitute Victoria Province (q. v.).   On the east Chiredzi is separated from Chipinga District by the Sabi River (qq. v.).   Except for small Tribal Trust Lands (q. v.) on the district's eastern and western borders, the entire area is reserved for European farmers, who have prospered as a consequence of the Sabi-Limpopo Authority (q. v.) development schemes.   (See also BUFFALO RANGE.)

CHIREDZI RIVER.   Rising c. 50 km. east of Fort Victoria (q. v.), the Chiredzi River flows southeast to join the Lundi about midway between the latter's connections with the Mtilikwe and Sabi rivers (qq. v.).   In 1966 Manjirenji Dam was built at about the mid-point of the Chiredzi, creating Lake MacDougall.

CHIREMBA (pl. zviremba).   Chishona* word for doctor, or healer; title by which nganga healers (q. v.) are addressed.   Zviremba are usually specialized herbalists, in contrast to most nganga, who specialize in divining.

CHIRINDA FOREST (variant: Silinda Forest).   Located on the slopes of Mount Silinda in Gazaland (qq. v.), the 640 hectare Chirinda Forest is an unusual remnant of a prehistoric tropical forest.   It contains over a hundred species of trees, including ironwoods and mahoganies, as well as a large variety of birds. The smaller Bunga Forest in the Vumba Mountains (q. v.) is the only other significant stand of trees like it in the country (see FORESTS).   During the mid-1970s African nationalist guerrilla fighters began using the forest's dense vegetation as cover while infiltrating the country from bases in neighboring Mozambique (q. v.).

CHIRINGIRO.   Original name of Bantu Mirror (q. v.).

CHIRISAMHURU (a. k. a. Rupengo; Dhlembewu) (d. 1830s).   The reigning Changamire (q. v.) ruler at the time of the Mfecane (q. v.) invasions, Chirisamhuru was killed by the followers of Zwangendaba and Nyamazana (qq. v.), then traveling together,

at Ntabazikamambo (q.v.). One line of tradition holds that
Chirisamhuru died when he hurled himself from a precipice
overlooking the invading throng of Ngoni*. Another tradition
claims that he was captured and skinned alive. Chirisamhuru
is usually described as the last Changamire ruler in the Matabeleland* region, but traditional evidence indicates that his son,
Tohwechipi (q.v.), was installed as his successor at Dhlo Dhlo
(q.v.) before the arrival of the Ndebele in 1838 drove the
Changamire leaders east. (For Chirisamhuru Negomo, see
NEGOMO CHIRISAMHURU.)

CHIRUMANZU (variant: Chilimanzi [q.v.]). Dynastic title of
the Govera branch of the Karanga-speaking Shona (qq.v.), now
living in a Tribal Trust Land* in the Chilimanzi District. The
dynasty appears to have been established in the mid-18th century
by a man named Mhepo, connected with the Mutasa dynasty of
the Manyika (qq.v.). Mhepo is said to have been nicknamed
Chizimuhanzu--later contracted to "Chirumanzu"--because he
wore a hanzu robe obtained from Muslim (q.v.) traders. During
the 19th century the Govera responded to the Ndebele occupation
of Matabeleland (qq.v.) by aggressively raiding Ndebele cattle.
The Ndebele successfully retaliated in the mid-1850s, making
the Chirumanzu chiefs their tributaries for the next 35 years.
Chirumanzu Chatikobo briefly revolted against the Ndebele in
1889, but was overthrown by Chinyama with the aid of the
Ndebele two years later. Chirumanzu Chinyama nevertheless
lent men to the British in the Ndebele War (q.v.) of 1893.
He also collaborated with the British against the Ndebele in the
Revolt (q.v.) three years later.

CHIRUNDU. Northern port of entry into the country from Zambia*,
on the main road between Lusaka and Salisbury. The town
stands on the south bank of the Zambezi River (q.v.), just
above the river's confluence with the Kafue River. The crossing
is made on the Otto Beit Bridge (q.v.) (location: 16°2'S,
28°51'E).

CHISAMHURU NOGOMO see NEGOMO CHIRISAMHURU

CHISHAWASHA MISSION. Roman Catholic mission station just east
of Salisbury (at 17°47'S, 31°14'E). The station was founded
in 1892 on a 5665 hectare tract of Shavasha (q.v.) land granted
to the Jesuits by the BSAC. Andrew Hartmann and Peter
Prestage (qq.v.) organized the station before returning to
Matabeleland* in 1896. The station subsequently developed an
agricultural and industrial training center dominated by the
strict supervision of the Jesuit priests.

CHISHONA. By far the most widely spoken language in the country,
Chishona is the language of the Shona peoples (q.v.) and stands
apart as a major cluster of southeastern Bantu (q.v.). The
above equation might be more appropriately reversed, as it is
primarily commonality of language which has given the Shona

their collective identity. Six main dialects of Chishona are
generally recognized as distinct. These are, in order of the
numbers of speakers within the country: Karanga, Zezuru,
Korekore, Manyika, Ndau, and Kalanga (qq. v.). Zezuru is the
dialect around which "standard Shona" has been built since the
1930s. A unified orthography was fixed by the government in
1955. Kalanga is the most distinct of the dialects, and is sometimes described as a separate language. The unifying features
of Chishona dialects are considerable shared vocabulary; similar phonology, including tonal vowels and "whistling fricatives";
and common grammar, which features monosyllabic noun prefixes such as chi-, ma-, mi-, mu-, u-, and va- (qq. v.). (See
also SINDEBELE; LITERATURE.)

CHITEPO, HERBERT WILTSHIRE TFUMAINDINI (June 5, 1923-
March 18, 1975). The country's first African lawyer, Chitepo
was born in the Inyanga District* and educated at local mission
schools and in Natal before taking his B.A. degree from Ft.
Hare University College in South Africa in 1949. Afterwards
he worked at the School of Oriental and African Studies in London while qualifying as a lawyer. When he returned home in
1954, the government had to amend the Land Apportionment Act
(q. v.) to allow him to open a law office in Salisbury. He entered politics in 1957 by joining the new African National Congress (q. v.). He later served as Joshua Nkomo's legal counsel
in the National Democratic Party (qq. v.). In May 1962 he went
to Tanganyika, where he became that country's first African
public prosecutor.
        After the split between ZANU and ZAPU in 1963, Chitepo
sided with Ndabaningi Sithole's (q. v.) faction and became chairman of ZANU, moving to Lusaka in early 1966. There he is
said to have organized ZANU military operations against Rhodesia. Often at the center of party factional disputes, he was
killed in Lusaka when his car was blown up. ZANU leaders
blamed the Rhodesian government, but an international commission concluded that he had been assassinated by political rivals.

CHITUPA (pl. zvitupa). Chishona* form of situpa (q. v.), a term
for registration certificate (see PASS LAWS).

CHIVERO NYASORO (d. c.1560). Early Munhumutapa (q. v.) ruler.
The son of Munhumutapa Chikuyo Chisamarengu (q. v.), Chivero
succeeded his cousin Neshangwe Mumembire (q. v.) as Munhumutapa in c.1550. He established his headquarters just west
of the Musengezi River in the Dande (qq. v.) and devoted much
of his reign to driving local Tonga people (q. v.) out of the
northeastern part of the country to make room for his own
people. He was succeeded by his son Negomo (q. v.).

CHIVI (variants: Chibi [q. v.]; Tschibi). Title of the paramount
chiefs of the Mari (or Mhari) chiefdom. The Mari are a
branch of the Karanga (q. v.) cluster of Shona, and were often
called "Banyai" (see NYAI) during the 19th century. The Chivi

paramountcy seems to have originated in Manyika (q.v.) country in the early 18th century, and to have been established between the Tokwe and Lundi rivers (qq.v.) of the present Chibi District (q.v.) in the early 19th century, when it was loosely associated with the Changamire state (q.v.).

Chivi Tavengerweyi was in power when Zwangendaba (q.v.) swept through the country during the 1830s. Matsweru then became Chivi just before the arrival of the Ndebele (q.v.), to whom he paid tribute. Matsweru died in c.1865--possibly killed in an Ndebele raid--and was succeeded by Chivi Mazorodze after a succession dispute. In 1877 a large Ndebele impi* commanded by Lotshe (q.v.) was repelled by the Mari, but Mazorodze was later captured and returned to Bulawayo*, where he is said to have been skinned alive by the Mfengu* "witch doctor" William Mzizi (q.v.) in October 1879. During this period the Mari increasingly asserted their independence from the Ndebele, defending themselves in kopjes (q.v.) with firearms obtained largely from the Venda (q.v.). In 1890 Madhlangove (d.1907) was the Chivi, but rival claimants to the title signed the Adendorff Concession (q.v.) in the hope of obtaining Afrikaner (q.v.) mercenaries to fight with them against the Ndebele. The question of the real Chivi's independence from the Ndebele then became an issue in the BSAC's claims to Mashonaland*, which the Pioneer Column (q.v.) was then occupying. The Mari assisted the British in the Ndebele War (q.v.) of 1893, and also collaborated with the Europeans during the Revolt (q.v.) three years later.

CHRISTMAS PASS. Entrance to the Penhalonga Valley from Umtali (qq.v.), which is just to the southeast (at 18° 55'S, 32° 38'E). So named by European road builders who camped there on Christmas Day, 1890.

CHROME. The country is said to have the world's largest known reserves of high-grade chrome ore. Production began in 1907 but became significant only after the Second World War. Chrome is found all along the Great Dyke (q.v.), but the most important areas of current production are around Selukwe, Belingwe, and Mashaba (qq.v.). About two-thirds of production is mined in the Selukwe District (q.v.), where subsidiaries of the Union Carbide Company and the Vanadium Corporation of America have major interests. By 1965 chrome accounted for only about 8% of the value of the country's mineral (q.v.) production. The government has since claimed enormous increases in both production and exports, despite international sanctions (q.v.; see also BYRD AMENDMENT).

CHURCH OF ENGLAND. The major religion of the country's settler population. (See ANGLICAN MISSIONS for information on African membership.)

CITY YOUTH LEAGUE   see   YOUTH LEAGUE

CLAN-NAMES   see ISIBONGO (Ndebele); MUTUPO (Shona)

"CLICKS." Explosive consonant sounds made by suddenly drawing
air across the tongue while it is pressed against the inside of
the mouth.   The three basic clicking sounds are (1) dental,
represented by the letter c; (2) palatal, represented by the
letter g; and (3) lateral, represented by the letter x.   Spelling
variations in African words frequently derive from shifting or
misunderstood clicks, as in the name Nxaba (q.v.), variously
spelled "Ncaba," "Ngaba," or "Nxaba."
        Clicking consonants are the most outstanding characteris-
tic of the Khoisan languages (q.v.), from which they have been
introduced into all Nguni dialects, including Sindebele (qq.v.).
Chishona (q.v.) languages do not have clicks.

CLIMATE.   (1) General overview.   Although the country lies entirely within the southern tropics, most of it enjoys an equable
climate comparable to the temperate regions because of the
ameliorating influence of the country's inland location and
generally high altitudes (q.v.).   The most temperate regions
are the Central Plateau and the Eastern Highlands (qq.v.).
These are also the most densely populated parts of the country,
and they accommodate most of the European population.
        (2) Rainfall.   A dominant climatic feature is concentra-
tion of almost all rainfall within a five-month "wet season" between November and March.   Less than 3% of the annual rainfall occurs outside this period, except in the Eastern Highlands,
which sometimes receive up to 10% of their precipitation during
other months.   The rains are brought by the Inter-Tropical
Convergence Zone, which sends moist air inland from the Indian
Ocean.   Precipitation is thus greatest in the eastern parts of
the country, diminishing as the moist air moves west.
        The Eastern Highlands and the northeastern section of
the Central Plateau receive more than 750 millimeters (mm.)
of rain per annum.   Stations recording more than 1250 mm.
of rain are rare.   More than two-thirds of the country receives
less than 750 mm. of rain per annum, with the Limpopo basin
receiving the least.   Also important is the erratic and unreliable rainfall in many areas.   Further, loss of water to evaporation and rapid runoff is great, so conservation of surface water
is critical to development.   (See RIVERS; DAMS AND WATER
SUPPLY).
        (3) Temperature.   The sun passes directly over the
entire country twice between late September and late March,
but heat is severe only in the Zambezi Valley and in the southeastern lowveld during these months.   The highest recorded
temperature was 45.6°C (about 114° Fahrenheit), set at Kariba
(q.v.) in 1955.   As a general rule, each 300 meter rise in
altitude reduces temperatures by 2°C.   Temperatures are
further ameliorated by the correspondence between the months
of most intense solar radiation and the rainy season, during
which rainfall and cloud cover greatly cool the air.   The lowest
temperature on record was -9.5°C (about +14.9° F) set at

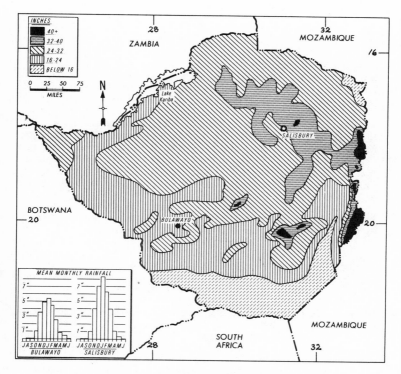

Map 3. Annual Rainfall Distribution

Matopos (q.v.) in 1968. Such cold is highly unusual, as freezing temperatures rarely occur anywhere in the country. Groundfrosts develop occasionally, but snowfall has never been recorded.

(4) _Seasons_. The distinction between "summer" and "winter" seasons means little in the country, as its seasons are reckoned around the dominant rainy season. Outside that important period, however, climatic changes are not sharply divided, and wide fluctuations can occur from year to year. A typical year follows this pattern, however: November--hot, beginning of rains with storms; December-February--warm, steady rainfall; March--warm, rains begin to abate; April-May--cooler, occasional showers; June-July--cool and dry; August-September--warmer, but dry; October--hot and dry, with storms sometimes beginning late in the month.

COAL. The country's coal reserves are so vast that they have been described as virtually inexhaustible. Major coalfields have been found in the Limpopo basin and in the southeastern lowveld, but commercial exploitation has been undertaken only at Wankie (q.v.), which lies at the western tip of a vast coalfield stretching as far east as Copper Queen (17°31'S, 29°20'E).

The Wankie coalfield was discovered in 1894 by a German prospector, Albert Giese (1865-1938). Rights to the field were

obtained by a company now known as Wankie Colliery, Ltd.,
which has close financial ties with the BSAC and Rhodesian
Railways (qq. v.). Production began at No. 1 Colliery in 1903.
Second and third collieries were opened nearby in 1927 and
1953. Each has operated independently, maintaining its own
African labor compound. Total production first topped a million tons per annum in 1927. After a brief slump, production
rose to two million tons in 1949, and then to four million tons
in 1957. The No. 1 Colliery was closed in 1958, and production leveled off during the 1960s. In June 1972 No. 2 Colliery
was shut down for a year after an underground explosion killed
427 miners.

Wankie's bituminous coal is ideal for steam raising.
Until activation of the hydroelectric facilities at Kariba Dam
(q. v.) in 1961, coal-burning thermal plants generated virtually
all the country's electrical power (q. v.). Coal also fueled the
country's railways (q. v.), as well as much of those of Botswana,
Zambia, and parts of Mozambique and Zaïre.

Coal is so bulky it can be transported economically only
by rail. The decision to route the main northern railway line
through Victoria Falls (q. v.) was reached in order to make
Wankie accessible to rail transport. Since then Wankie's productive capacity has consistently outstripped the country's capacity to carry its coal by rail. Until the opening of Kariba,
as much as a third of the country's railway capacity was used
to move coal to thermal plants. Kariba's hydroelectric output
allowed most thermal plants to be shut down, freeing considerable rail capacity and obviating the need for further expansion
of coal production. Increased electrical consumption since the
early 1960s has, however, revived thermal power generation,
and the government has in recent years begun studying the feasibility of converting coal to liquid petroleum, which the country
lacks. (See MINERALS.)

COFFEE. Production of coffee began in the Melsetter District (q.v.)
around 1900. Since the 1950s the region between Vumba and
Mount Silinda (qq. v.) has developed into a major center of Ara-
bica coffee production, well over half of which was being exported by the early 1970s.

COGHLAN, CHARLES PATRICK JOHN (June 24, 1863-Aug. 28, 1927).
First Prime Minister (q. v.) of Southern Rhodesia (1923-7). Born
in King William's Town, South Africa, Coghlan came to Bulawayo
in 1900 after having practiced law in Kimberley. He soon established a reputation as a vigorous defender of the rights of
settlers, especially miners, against the unpopular BSAC administration. In 1908 he was elected to the Legislative Council (q.v.),
in which he quickly rose to leadership of the unofficial members.
The same year he attended the national union convention in South
Africa (see UNIONIST MOVEMENT).

Back home, the Legislative Council wrung enough concessions from the BSAC for Coghlan to support renewal of the Company's Charter (q. v.) in 1914, but he soon found himself clashing

with the administration again--particularly over the issue of
amalgamation (q. v.), which he vigorously opposed. Coghlan
lost his initial enthusiasm for union with South Africa and
joined the Responsible Government Movement (q. v.) in 1919.
Over the next several years he put increasing pressure on the
British government to grant the settlers self-government. In
1921 he led a delegation to London to negotiate the question.
When self-government was achieved in September 1923, the new
governor, J. R. Chancellor (q. v.), invited him to form a government as premier. He was sworn in on October 1st, when
he also assumed the "Native Affairs" portfolio. He then reorganized his party as the Rhodesian Party (q. v.), leading it
to victory in a general election the next year.
    Favorable world prices for the country's exports made
Coghlan's term of office a relatively prosperous and undramatic
era within the context of settler politics. His main concerns
were fiscal problems. The Morris Carter Commission (q. v.)
recommended discriminatory land tenure laws during Coghlan's
administration (1925), but he died in office, leaving the problem
for his successor, H. U. Moffat (q. v.).

COILLARD, FRANÇOIS (July 17, 1834-May 27, 1904). French mis-
    sionary. After two decades of mission work for the Paris
    Evangelical Missionary Society, Coillard crossed the Limpopo
    River in 1877 in an attempt to start a mission among the people
    of Chivi (q. v.). There his party was arrested by Ndebele scouts
    and taken to King Lobengula (q. v.). After his release in 1878
    he visited the Lozi (q. v.) people north of the Zambezi. There
    he later founded a successful and influential mission station.
    His book, On the Threshold of Central Africa (London, 1897),
    contains one of the rare written accounts of the Shona during
    the 1870s.

COLENBRANDER, JOHANNES WILHELM (Nov. 1, 1855-Feb. 10,
    1918). Born in Natal, where he later served with the colonial
    army against the Zulu*, Colenbrander was fluent in the Zulu
    language (closely akin to Sindebele*) and very knowledgeable
    about northern Nguni* culture. He came to Bulawayo in 1888
    and made a favorable impression on Lobengula (q. v.). Later
    that year he acted as interpreter for Babayane and Mshete
    (qq. v.), Lobengula's emissaries to Queen Victoria. He re-
    turned to Matabeleland* as official representative of the BSAC.
        Despite his intimacy with the Ndebele, Colenbrander ad-
    vocated British conquest of Lobengula. He himself got out of
    the country just before the Ndebele War (q. v.), returning later
    as a Native Commissioner in the BSAC administration. He
    then played a leading role in the collection and redistribution
    of loot cattle (q. v.). During the 1896 Revolt (q. v.) he raised
    and led a corps of South Africans to fight the Ndebele. He
    also served as Cecil Rhodes' interpreter during the "Indaba"
    (q. v.) peace negotiations. Two decades later he accidentally
    drowned while playing the role of Lord Chelmsford in a film
    about the Zulu War, which he had earlier survived.

COLLEEN BAWN.   Village on the railway (q.v.) line between
    Gwanda and West Nicholson (qq.v.) (at 21° S, 29° 13'E; alt.
    90 m.).   The local Colleen Bawn gold (q.v.) mine was es-
    tablished atop early African workings in 1905.   The village's
    main modern industry is cement, with one factory supplying
    most of the country.

COLOURED PEOPLE.   Since the beginning of the 20th century the
    white government of Southern Rhodesia has followed South Afri-
    can precedent in designating as a separate "race" people of
    mixed African and European or Asian descent, whom they clas-
    sify as "Coloured."   Many of these people immigrated from
    South Africa, where the Coloured population was originally
    largely Khoi and Afrikaner (qq.v.) in descent.   Another large
    segment of this community originated in early local relation-
    ships between white males and African women.   By 1911 more
    than 2000 people were classified as Coloured.   Since the 1920s
    the population has had a relatively high rate of natural increase,
    reaching 6000 in 1951, and about 20,000 in 1975.   These people
    legally stand in an ambiguous position between the European and
    African populations, and are subject to discriminatory laws
    which are said to place them somewhat below Asians (q.v.) in
    legal rights.   (See also GRIQUA.)

COLQUHOUN, ARCHIBALD ROSS (March 1848-Dec. 18, 1914).   Early
    administrator.   After a varied career in Asia, Colquhoun came
    to South Africa in 1889 and met Cecil Rhodes.   Rhodes made him
    civil administrator of the Pioneer Column (q.v.) which occupied
    Mashonaland* the next year.   During the Column's advance,
    Colquhoun and F. C. Selous (q.v.) went to Manicaland*, where
    they obtained chief Mutasa's (q.v.) signature to a mining conces-
    sion.   Colquhoun finally arrived at Salisbury (q.v.) in October
    1890, when he took up office as the first BSAC resident com-
    missioner for Mashonaland.   Frustrated with the rough and ready
    exigencies of frontier administration, he resigned on the pretext
    of ill health, and was replaced by L. S. Jameson (q.v.) in Sep-
    tember 1891.   Colquhoun later wrote his autobiography and
    several books on British imperialism in southern Africa.   His
    wife was the later Ethel Tawse-Jollie (q.v.).

CONCESSION.   Village immediately south of Amandas (q.v.) on the
    Shamva* railway* line (at 17° 23'S, 30° 57'E).   It is the com-
    mercial center for a mainly agricultural region.

CONCESSIONS.   During the late 19th century European entrepreneurs
    and adventurers known as "concessionaires" beleaguered African
    rulers throughout southern Africa for concessionary rights to
    mine, to monopolize trade, to cut timber, etc.   Concession-
    gathering was the technique used by the BSAC to gain control
    of present Rhodesia.   (For examples, see RUDD CONCESSION;
    LIPPERT CONCESSION; ADENDORFF TREK; TATI CONCES-
    SION.)

CONFEDERATE PARTY (CP). Successor to the Democratic Party
(q. v.), the CP was formed in 1953 to oppose Federation (q. v.).
It was the only party to oppose the United (Federal) Party
(q. v.) in both territorial and federal elections that year, but it
won no seats in either assembly. The party broke up the next
year when English-speaking members quit to protest Afrikaner*
domination.

CONGREGATIONALIST MISSIONS   see   LONDON MISSIONARY SO-
CIETY; AMERICAN BOARD OF COMMISSIONERS FOR FOREIGN
MISSIONS

CONICAL TOWER. Descriptive name for the imposing ten-meter
high structure in the southern end of the Elliptical Building in
the Zimbabwe Ruins (q. v.). Built with an even-coursed stone
facing over a solid core, it was apparently erected when the
nearly adjacent outer wall was constructed. Similar, but much
smaller, towers are found in some of the nearby valley ruins
and elsewhere. The tower, like the "Zimbabwe Birds" (q. v.),
has come to symbolize the ruins. Its superficial resemblance
to ancient Near Eastern structures has fueled arguments for
non-African origins of the ruins (see ZIMBABWE CONTRO-
VERSY). The tower has been popularly interpreted as a phallic
symbol associated with some unknown "fertility rites. " A more
plausible interpretation suggests that it and similar towers simply
symbolized Shona grain bins, and that they were used as tribute
collection centers.

"CONSOLIDATED VILLAGES"   see   "PROTECTED VILLAGES"

CONSTITUTION PARTY   see under   CAPRICORN AFRICA SOCIETY

CONSTITUTIONS. Formal constitutions were promulgated in 1923,
1961, 1965, and 1969, with African demands for sweeping constitutional changes mounting steadily since 1960.
    Constitution of 1923. In September 1923 Britain annexed
Southern Rhodesia as a Crown Colony, replacing the BSAC
government (q. v.), while granting Responsible Government (q.v.)
to settlers under a loosely outlined constitution (see BUXTON
COMMITTEE). This constitution created a Legislative Assembly
(q. v.) elected by a non-racial franchise effectively limited to
Europeans because of high property and income qualifications.
A British Governor (q. v.) was placed at the head of the government. Britain retained important reserve powers over entrenched
portions of the constitution; it could, theoretically, legislate for
African affairs itself, as these were seen as falling outside the
jurisdiction of the local Assembly. In practice, however, the
Assembly and its Prime Ministers (q.v.) arrogated increasing
powers to themselves, legislating for African as well as settler
affairs. The British government neither legislated for Southern
Rhodesian affairs, nor did it overrule Assembly decisions affecting Africans. It instead amended its own reserve powers
while permitting the settler government greater autonomy. This

constitution was maintained, with certain modifications, through
1961. In 1953 many local government offices were transferred
to the Federation (q.v.) government, which had its own constitution.

Constitution of 1961. This document was drafted by a
convention held in London and Salisbury in 1960 and 1961.
Settler representatives sought to safeguard their control of the
government, while African representatives (see NDP) fought unsuccessfully for ultimate majority rule. The result was a
compromise constitution which created separate voter rolls
giving Africans their first seats in the Assembly. It also contained complex provisions for attainment of majority rule in the
remote future. Britain retained ultimate sovereignty, but relinquished its reserved powers over local legislation. In place
of British oversight, the constitution contained a bill of rights
and created a Constitutional Council meant to safeguard African
rights. Existing legislation which contradicted the new bill of
rights was unaffected, and the settler-dominated Assembly effectively nullified the Constitutional Council, which it was empowered to overrule with a two-thirds majority vote on any
challenge. The British Privy Council remained the ultimate
court of appeals. Britain and other outside nations still regard
this constitution as valid in Rhodesia.

Constitution of 1965. Promulgated shortly after UDI
(q.v.), this constitution was essentially a modification of the
1961 constitution. It still recognized Queen Elizabeth as the
country's sovereign, but replaced the British governor with an
"Officer Administering the Government" (q.v.). It also eliminated all vestigial British reserve powers. The new constitution and subsequent legislation gave the government wide discretionary powers to declare states of emergency, to arrest
and detain opponents without trial, and to censor (q.v.) publications.

Constitution of 1969. Approved by public referendum in
June 1969 and passed by Parliament in November, this constitution renounced British sovereignty altogether and made the
country a republic, effective March 1970. It created the office
of President (q.v.), divided Parliament (q.v.) into two chambers,
and instituted loyalty oaths for government officials. For the
first time voter rolls were defined on an explicitly racial basis,
and the possibility of eventual majority rule was denied. The
government was granted still wide powers to restrict civil
rights, and the power of the judiciary to rule on the constitu-
tionality of legislation was given to the legislature itself.

Since UDI the white government, the British government,
African nationalists, and other national governments, including
the United States, have held numerous consultations and conferences to create a new constitution based on the principle of
eventual majority rule enshrined in the 1961 constitution. (See,
e.g., PEARCE COMMISSION; VICTORIA FALLS CONFERENCE;
GENEVA CONFERENCE.)

COPPER. Archaeological evidence indicates that copper has been

mined in the country almost as long as iron (q.v.), i.e., from
about the A.D. 100s.   Almost all modern copper mines are
sited over old African workings, more than 150 of which have
been identified.   There is also evidence of early bronze casting,
but it is believed that the tin (q.v.) employed in this alloy was
imported--probably from present Zambia.   Modern copper production began in the Gwanda District (q.v.) in 1906.   The industry developed rapidly after 1954 and is now believed to rank
first among the country's minerals (q.v.) in both total production and export values.   The largest current mine is at Mangula
(q.v.).   Other major mining centers are Alaska, Headlands,
Shangani, and the Wankie region (qq.v.).

COSGRAVE, MARY ANN (Mother Patrick) (May 22, 1863-July 31,
     1900).   Pioneer Roman Catholic nun.   Born in Ireland, Cos-
     grave came to South Africa as a youth and entered the Domini-
     can Order in King William's Town, South Africa.   In 1890 she
     volunteered to accompany the Pioneer Column into Mashonaland
     (qq.v.).   The BSAC would allow no European women in the
     country, so she and four other nuns ran a nursing station for
     the Column just southwest of Ft. Tuli (q.v.).   In July 1891 she
     accompanied Father Peter Prestage (q.v.) to Salisbury, where
     she helped to establish the first hospital, a school, and a con-
     vent.   In 1899 she was made Dominican Prioress for the whole
     country.

COTTON.   The Shona people have long grown cotton, and weaving
     is one of the crafts associated with the development of the Zim-
     babwe culture (q.v.) before the 15th century.   Demand for cloth
     outstripped local production, however, making Indian cotton cloth
     a major import item during the period of the Munhumutapa
     state (q.v.).
         During the 20th century, cotton has ranked as a major
     secondary agricultural (q.v.) product among both African and
     European farmers, especially since UDI, when tobacco (q.v.)
     production began to give way to other crops.   Precise statistics
     are not available, but it is believed that an enormous increase
     in cotton production since 1965 has greatly contributed to the
     government's efforts to get around the difficulties imposed by
     international sanctions (q.v.).   Production in 1971 is estimated
     to have been nearly 150 million kg.   Although the domestic tex-
     tile industry absorbs considerable cotton, an estimated 90% of
     the crop was being exported in 1972.

COUNCIL OF CHIEFS.   Since the suppression of the 1896-7 Revolts
     (q.v.) the white governments have largely controlled the nomina-
     tion and installation of African chiefs, whom they have used as
     paid government servants to administer rural areas.   Traditional
     ethnic boundaries have frequently been realigned in order to con-
     solidate and to rearrange chiefdoms.   The chiefs were originally
     stripped of most of their traditional political and judicial powers;
     however, since the 1920s there has been a consistent trend of
     increasing the range of the chiefs' functions, while further

co-opting them into the white power structure.   In 1961 the Council of Chiefs was created to represent African concerns in the Tribal Trust Lands* (formerly "reserves") within the government's Ministry of Interior Affairs.   The Council normally comprises 26 chiefs, ten of whom have been selected to sit in the Senate (q. v.) since 1965.   Since the Rhodesian Front assumed power, the government has frequently turned to the Council to elicit manifestations of African support for its actions (see, e. g., DOMBOSHAWA INDABA).   In April 1976 Ian Smith named several chiefs to undefined posts in his cabinet.   In late December 1976 many of these people founded the Zimbabwe United People's Organisation (q. v.).

CRIPPS, ARTHUR SHEARLY (June 18, 1869-Aug. 1, 1952).   English missionary and poet.   After studying at Oxford, Cripps trained for the Anglican (q. v.) clergy and served as a vicar in Sussex. In 1901 he came to Mashonaland* as a missionary for the Society for the Propagation of the Gospel.   He was stationed at Wreningham, just northeast of Enkeldoorn (q. v.).   During the First World War he served as a chaplain to British forces in East Africa, returning to Wreningham in 1916.   Through this period he acquired grants of land closer to Enkeldoorn on which he built Maronda Mashanu (q. v.) as a mission sub-station.   In 1926 he returned to England because of homesickness and mounting disagreements with mission authorities.   He particularly opposed the mission's policy of accepting government financial support.   After doing parish work in east London slums, he returned to Maronda Mashanu permanently in 1931.   There he set himself up as an independent missionary, selling some of the mission's land to support its work.   Under the terms of the new Land Apportionment Act (q. v.) the government could have expelled him from the site, but left him alone to avoid trouble with his many supporters. During the late 1930s Cripps' health deteriorated and his sight began failing.   By 1941 he was completely blind.   Thereafter he resided mostly at Enkeldoorn, while his unpaid secretary, Leonard Mamvura, supervised the mission's operation.

    Cripps' impact on African attitudes was profound.   In contrast to other missionaries, he shunned Western materialism and lived much as an average African.   He championed African rights, relentlessly criticizing European settlers and the government. An admirer of Clements Kadalie, he supported the latter's ICU (qq. v.).   He was a prolific writer and correspondent, using his pen to condemn every government policy inimical to African interests, from the hut tax raise in 1903, to the establishment of Federation (q. v.), which came a year after his death.   Often described as a "Utopian socialist," Cripps' apparent goal was to see a merger of true Christian ideals and the traditional African way of life.   He expressed his philosophy in pastoral poetry, fiction, and pamphlets.   (See also WHITE, J.)

CRIPPS, LIONEL (Oct. 11, 1863-Feb. 3, 1950).   First speaker of the Southern Rhodesian Legislative Assembly (q. v.).   Born in India and educated in England, Cripps came to South Africa in

1879.   In 1890 he participated in the Pioneer Column (q.v.) as
a trooper.   He then prospected in the Mazoe* area, eventually
settling near Umtali*, where he was a pioneer tobacco* farmer.
In 1914 he was elected to the Legislative Council (q.v.).   On
the achievement of Responsible Government (q.v.) in 1923 he
was elected speaker of the new Assembly.   He retired from
politics in 1935 and then helped to establish the National Archives (q.v.).

CROONENBERGHS, CHARLES (1843-1899).   Belgian Jesuit priest.
As a member of the Zambezi Mission (q.v.), Croonenberghs
ran the Jesuits' Matabeleland* stations from 1879 to 1884.
Afterwards he spent a year in the Transvaal* before returning
to Belgium.   (See EMPANDENI; DEPELCHIN, H.)

CURRENCY.   During the early years of the BSAC administration,
the country officially adopted the Cape Colony's currency.   After
1910 both British and South African currency were used in the
country.   Southern Rhodesia began issuing its own coinage in
1932, dropping South African coins the next year.   Commercial
banks issued Southern Rhodesian paper currency until 1940,
when the government took over.   The previous year both British
and South African currency ceased to be legal tender in the
country.   Southern Rhodesian currency was based upon British
sterling, and was similarly divided into pounds, shillings, and
pence.   Between 1955 and 1965 currency issued by the Federation government (q.v.) was also used locally.   After UDI in
1965, the Rhodesian pound was disassociated from the British
pound and placed on its own gold standard.   In 1970 the government decimalized the currency, making the "Rhodesian dollar"
(R$) equivalent to one half a former Rhodesian pound, or ten
shillings.   The dollar is divided into 100 cents, with coins of
various denominations between a half cent and 25 cents.   Despite
the pressures of international economic sanctions (q.v.), the
Rhodesian dollar has a high rate of exchange, with its price
generally hovering around $1.40 (American) and 75 new pence
(British).

CWALILI   see   XWALILE

- D -

DAGA (variant: daka).   Translated literally as "mud," daga is a
common Bantu* word for plastering and building material made
with powder from termite hills.   Mixed with water and various
other ingredients, the resulting compound dries to varying degrees of hardness.   Daga has long been one of the most important building materials used in the country, even in the construction of stone ruins (q.v.).   An unrelated word, dagga, for hemp
or marijuana, derives from a Khoi* language.

DAILY NEWS   see   AFRICAN DAILY PRESS

DAISYFIELD. Small trading center in the Gwelo District (q.v.),
  located on the main road between Bulawayo and Gwelo (at
  19°43'S, 29°30'E; alt. 1405 m.).

DALHOUSIE, SIMON RAMSAY (Lord Dalhousie from 1950) (b.Oct.
  17, 1914). Second and last Governor-General of the Federation
  (q.v.), Dalhousie succeeded J. J. Llewellin (q.v.) in 1957.
  Like his predecessor, he had little real power. He left the
  country when the Federation was dissolved in 1963.

DALNY MINE see under CHAKARI

DAMBARARE. Portuguese trading fair (q.v.) located near the
  present Jumbo Mine (q.v.), c.32 km. north-northwest of Salisbury. Dambarare appears to have been established around
  1580, and to have become the dominant Portuguese center in the
  Munhumutapa state (q.v.) during the 17th century. It was apparently destroyed by a Changamire (q.v.) army in 1693. Portuguese attempts to reestablish the fair in 1769 failed. The site
  now consists only of ditches and foundation structures.

DAMS AND WATER SUPPLY. An enormous number of dams and
  weirs have been built throughout the country to enable the development of intensive agriculture (q.v.) and industry in the face
  of an endemic water shortage situation (see CLIMATE). Most
  parts of the country receive only sparse, irregular, and short-
  term rainfall. And much of the rain which falls comes in brief,
  heavy storms, resulting in rapid runoff (see RIVERS). Considerable water is lost to evaporation and to seepage into underground reserves. Some underground water can easily be retrieved from vleis (q.v.), but to obtain large quantities thousands
  of expensive bore-holes have been drilled. Only more efficient
  retention of surface water is economical on a large scale.
      Construction of dams, weirs, and irrigation ditches was
  begun at least several centuries ago by the builders of the Inyanga Ruins (q.v.), where some water furrows still function.
  Elsewhere, African agriculturalists seem not to have employed
  irrigation systems. When Europeans began settling the country
  in the 1890s, dam-building began in earnest. Private farmers
  and government agencies built thousands of small weirs and dams,
  but large projects were restricted mostly to the rivers around
  major urban centers. The uneven distribution of water supplies
  has influenced the distribution of industries, favoring the larger
  centers such as Salisbury, Gwelo, Bulawayo, and Umtali (qq.v.).
  Since the mid-1960s the government has shifted emphasis from
  small dam building to large-scale regional projects, such as the
  vast Sabi-Limpopo Authority (q.v.) in the southeastern low veld
  (see KARIBA DAM; individual dams are discussed mostly under
  the names of their rivers; see also LAKES).

DANANGOMBI. Rozvi* name for the ruins site now known as Dhlo
  Dhlo (q.v.).

DANCING   see   MUSIC; INXWALA [Ndebele "Great Dance"]

DANDE.   Traditional Shona name for the region circumscribed by the Zambezi River on the north, the Zambezi Escarpment on the south, and the Angwa and Muzengezi rivers on the west and east, respectively (qq. v.).   Originally the home of the Tande (Vatande) branch of Korekore-speaking people (q. v.), the Dande was occupied by the early Munhumutapa (q. v.) kings from the mid-15th to 17th centuries.   (Cf. GURUHUSWA; MBIRE.)

DARWENDALE.   Village c. 60 km. west of Salisbury on the Zawi* railway* line (at 17° 43'S, 30° 33'E).   It is the center of tobacco, cattle, and chrome production (qq. v.).   Population in 1969 was 910 (91% Africans).

DARWIN DISTRICT.   Northeastern border district in Mashonaland North Province (q. v.), covering 11, 310 sq. km.   It borders the districts of Sipolilo on the west; Mazoe, Bindura, Shamva, Mrewa, and Mtoko (qq. v.) on the south.   The southwestern part of the district is reserved for European farmers; most of the rest is Tribal Trust Land (q. v.).   The district administrative center is the village of Mount Darwin (16° 47'S, 31° 35'E), which is just northwest of Mount Pfura (renamed "Mount Darwin" by F. C. Selous*).

DAWSON, JAMES (Nov. 1852-Oct. 7, 1921).   A Scottish trader, Dawson came to Matabeleland* in the 1870s.   On the eve of the Ndebele War (q. v.) Lobengula (q. v.) asked Dawson to take three chiefs to Cape Town to meet with the British High Commissioner in the hope of averting war.   On the way south the party met British soldiers at the Shashi River* and two of the Ndebele men were killed in a misunderstanding because of Dawson's negligence.   Dawson returned to Matabeleland after the war, and then commanded a troop of the Bulawayo Field Force (q. v.) during the Ndebele Revolt (q. v.) of 1896.   Thereafter he farmed around Essexvale* until 1905, when he went to western Zambia to trade.   Accumulated financial difficulties were the apparent cause of his suicide years later.

DEMOCRATIC PARTY (DP).   Of the many political parties with this name, the following stand out: (1) Strongly pro-Afrikaner (q.v.) nationalist party founded in 1948 by members of the country's Association of Afrikaners (Afrikaner Genootskap).   In 1953 it became the Confederate Party (q. v.), with DP dissidents forming a new "Rhodesian Party," which was soon absorbed by the United Party (q. v.).
        (2)   African political party which broke away from the United Peoples' Party (q. v.) in August 1968.   Chad Chipunza was the party's only member of parliament.   In June 1969 the DP reunited with the UPP to form the National Peoples' Union (q. v.).
        (3)   Right-wing European political party founded in 1972

by C. W. Phillips, a defector from the Rhodesian Front (q.v.). (See also NATIONAL DEMOCRATIC PARTY.)

DEPELCHIN, HENRI (1822-1900). Belgian Jesuit priest. After 17 years of missionary work in India, Depelchin was placed in charge of the Jesuits' Zambezi Mission (q.v.) to central Africa. Between 1879 and 1882 he traveled extensively between the Limpopo and Zambezi rivers, attempting to set up mission stations. With C. Croonenberghs (q.v.) he wrote Trois Ans dans l'Afrique australe (2 vols., Brussels, 1882-3), describing the peoples of the region.

DE SADELEER, FRANS (Dec. 8, 1844-Jan. 20, 1922). A Belgian Jesuit missionary, De Sadeleer joined the Zambezi Mission (q.v.) to Bulawayo* in 1879. The next year he accompanied A. H. Law (q.v.) and two other missionaries to Gazaland (q.v.) in an abortive attempt to open a new mission. After Law died there, De Sadeleer and the others walked to Sofala*, where a second man died. De Sadeleer and the remaining lay missionary, Joseph Hedley, then returned to Bulawayo on foot. During the next several years De Sadeleer participated in further unsuccessful attempts to launch fresh missions at Pandamatenga and in Barotseland (qq.v.). He later did mission work in the Cape Colony (1886-91) and in present Zaïre (1893-1906).

DETT. Village on the Bulawayo to Victoria Falls railway* line (at 18°37'S, 26°52'E; alt. 1080 m.). A center for mining and tourism, it is the headquarters for Wankie National Park (q.v.). Population in 1969 was 2470 (83% Africans).

DHLISO MATHEMA (variant: Hliso) (fl.1890s). Ndebele induna* associated with the Nqama ibutho*, quartered just north of the Matopo Hills (q.v.). During the 1896 Revolt (q.v.) Dhliso was a major rebel leader in the Matopos fighting, and was one of those who installed Nyamanda (q.v.) as king. He participated in the peace negotiations with Cecil Rhodes, and was then made a salaried chief in the Matobo District (q.v.).

DHLO DHLO (a.k.a. Danangombi). Important Khami culture (q.v.) ruins located in the northern Insiza District* (at 19°57'S, 29°20'E). The complex comprises a number of buildings, the most important of which is built around two platforms containing an estimated 10,000 tons of rubble fill. The enclosure's well-built retaining walls are noted for their varied and colorful decoration.

     Known to the Rozvi (q.v.) as Danangombi, Dhlo Dhlo was one of the main Changamire (q.v.) administrative centers until it was sacked by the Ngoni (q.v.) in the early 1830s. Rebuilding then began, and Tohwechipi (q.v.) was apparently installed there as the new Changamire. The subsequent Ndebele (q.v.) invasion of the late 1830s caused the Rozvi to abandon the site. Europeans first discovered the ruins during the 1893 Ndebele War (q.v.). The following year F. R. Burnham (q.v.)

and another American scout ransacked the ruins for gold, carrying off nearly 18 kg. in ornaments. W. G. Neal and others
(see RHODESIA ANCIENT RUINS, LTD.) took an additional four
kg. of gold ornaments in 1895. Virtually all these artifacts
soon disappeared without record. Also found by early pillagers
were two Portuguese (q.v.) bronze cannons and a number of
Roman Catholic relics. These items have been interpreted as
indicating a Portuguese presence in the area during the 16th
and 17th centuries, but they more likely were obtained through
trade or from raids into the northeast.
        The Ndebele knew the ruins as Imithangala ka Mambo,
"the Mambo's* Stone Walls," giving rise to the early 20th century name "Mambo Ruins." This name was, however, soon
dropped to avoid confusion with the Ntabazikamambo ruins (q.v.).
The site was renamed "Dhlo Dhlo" after a local 19th-century
Ndebele settlement which had nothing to do with the original
ruins builders. Archaeological digs at Dhlo Dhlo have been
undertaken by D. Randall-MacIver (1905), G. Caton-Thompson
(1929), and R. Summers (1959) (qq.v.).

DIAMONDS see GEMSTONES

DIANA'S VOW CAVE. Located c.30 km. from Rusape* (at 18°21'S,
    21°18'E), this cave contains some of the finest and most un-
    usual rock paintings (q.v.) in the country. A complex frieze
    features a large reclining human figure believed to be the center
    of a burial ceremony. Detailed smaller figures which surround
    it represent many cultural features. associated only with Iron
    Age (q.v.) peoples, such as baskets, cattle*, and a leashed dog.
    The paintings are now interpreted as an outstanding example of
    a Stone Age (q.v.) artist's depiction of Bantu* culture.

DISTRICTS. The basic territorial unit through which the country
    has been administered during the 20th century has been the
    district. The BSAC administration began creating "Native
    Districts" for the purpose of African administration during the
    mid-1890s. Each district was headed by a Native Commissioner
    (more recently called "District Commissioners") with responsi-
    bility for implementation of virtually all laws and policies af-
    fecting Africans. By 1923 there were 32 such districts. The
    number has steadily increased as established districts have been
    divided and as completely new districts have been created from
    sections of older districts. By 1970 there were 50 districts,
    virtually all of which had undergone at least slight boundary
    changes in previous decades. The districts retain their primary
    function as African administrative units, now within the Ministry
    of Internal Affairs. They are also used for other government
    functions, notably the collection of census and other statistical
    data.
        All present and former official districts are entered in
    this dictionary, largely because their names are used constantly
    as geographical referents in almost everything written about the
    country. Complete lists of their names will be found under the

entries for the individual provinces (q. v.) which they define.
(See also LAND APPORTIONMENT and LAND TENURE ACTS.)

DOMBO (a. k. a. Dombolakonachingwano) (d. 1695).   Outstanding
    Changamire (q. v.) ruler.   Although Portuguese (q. v.) records
    show that the Changamire dynasty was established in the late
    15th century, Dombo is one of the earliest Changamires re-
    membered in traditions, which credit him as the "founder" of
    the state.   Dombo emerged suddenly in Portuguese records of
    the 1680s, when he began a wave of conquests from his base
    in Guruhuswa (q. v.).   In the early 1690s he was apparently in-
    vited by the reigning Munhumutapa (q. v.) to ally against the
    Portuguese.   Between 1693 and 1695--when he died--Dombo
    directed campaigns against Portuguese fairs (q. v.) in the north-
    east, and against the Manyika (q. v.) and other previously au-
    tonomous Shona states.   The full extent of his conquests remains
    controversial, but he clearly initiated a major expansion of
    Changamire authority which made his "Rozvi" (q. v.) empire the
    single greatest power in the country in the early 18th century.
    He was apparently succeeded by a son, Negomo, who died be-
    tween 1704 and 1710.

DOMBO (pl. madombo).   Chishona* word for large stone or rock,
    such as a kopje* (cf. DWALA).   The word appears in many
    place names, such as Dombo ro Mambo, "Mambo's Hill"
    (Ntabazinduna*).

DOMBOSHAWA.   Chishona* for "red kopje, " this place name occurs
    in at least six places in Mashonaland*.   The most important of
    these is located c. 30 km. north of Salisbury in the present
    Chinamora TTL (at 17° 36'S, 31° 8'E).   This hill is a massive
    granite dome containing several shelters with notable rock
    paintings (q. v.).   These include fine animal and human depic-
    tions of several different styles.   Some of the human figures
    are believed to be San (q. v.) representations of Bantu-speaking
    peoples (q. v.).   Another of the many important rock painting
    sites in the area is Makumbe Cave (q. v.) to the north.   The
    nearby town of Domboshawa contains an industrial school for
    Africans established by the government in 1920.

"DOMBOSHAWA INDABA" (1964).   In order to convince Britain that
    Africans supported its plans for UDI, Ian Smith's government
    assembled 600 government chiefs and headmen at Domboshawa
    school to discuss the issue "according to tribal custom and tra-
    dition" (see INDABA).   The convocation was not publicly an-
    nounced until it opened on October 21, 1964, when the area was
    sealed off by military forces to avoid interference from African
    nationalists.   On the last day, October 26th, the chiefs announced
    unanimous acceptance of government plans to declare indepen-
    dence.   (Cf. COUNCIL OF CHIEFS.)

DOMINION PARTY (DP).   (1) Short-lived political party which unsuc-
    cessfully contested two Legislative Assembly (q. v.) seats in the

1948 election.

(2)   Forerunner of the Rhodesian Front Party (q.v.), founded in 1956 out of disparate opponents of the United (Federal) Party (q.v.).   Drawing upon the growing European reaction to African nationalism and European dissatisfaction with government policies, the DP built a strong grassroots organization and rapidly developed into the strongest opposition party.   It won 13 of 30 legislative seats in the 1958 election, which the UFP won only because of complex vote-counting technicalities.   William Harper (q.v.) became leader of the opposition in the Assembly, and a Federal DP was formed with the support of Northern Rhodesian settler politicians.   The Federal DP sought to create a white-dominated dominion comprising Southern Rhodesia and the most developed parts of Northern Rhodesia.   The two DP branches split in 1960, with the southern branch concentrating on achieving dominion status for Southern Rhodesia alone.   In March 1962 the DP merged with other right-wing groups to form the Rhodesian Front, which won the next election under the leadership of Winston Field (q.v.).

DONGA.   Widely used southern African term for a ravine or gully cut by running water, though dry most of the year.   Introduced into English usage from Zulu*, the word is also found in Sindebele*.

"DOUBLE PYRAMID POLICY"   see   "TWO PYRAMID POLICY"

DRUMS.   The Shona people use a wide variety of drums (ngoma) in their music (q.v.).   Most are carved from solid blocks of wood, with one or both ends covered with stretched hide.   The Ndebele people, like their Zulu* relatives, have historically made little use of drums.   They have, however, introduced to the country the earthenware "pot drum" (ingungu).

DUMA (Vaduma).   Branch of the Karanga (q.v.) cluster of Shona, with unclear connections with the Rozvi (q.v.).   A belt of Duma communities has occupied the region between present Fort Victoria and Chipinga (qq.v.) since at least the mid-19th century.

DUMBUSEYA.   Shona group of obscure, but apparently recent, origins.   The Dumbuseya appear to have coalesced from various refugee Shona groups after the Ngoni (q.v.) invasions of the 1830s.   The original Dumbuseya may have included some Ngoni people, for Dumbuseya culture is said to have many Nguni (q.v.) elements.   By the mid-19th century the Dumbuseya were settled near present Shabani (q.v.), where they were harassed by Ndebele raids.   During the 1870s two of their chiefs, Wedza and Mazeteze, allied with the Ndebele in raids against other Shona.   In 1896 the same chiefs joined the Ndebele in the anti-British Revolt (q.v.).

DUPONT, CLIFFORD WALTER (b. Dec. 6, 1905).   President (q.v.) of Rhodesia (1970-5).   Born in London, where he practiced law,

Dupont came to Southern Rhodesia in 1948. Despite his previous inexperience in agriculture, he became wealthy as a tobacco* farmer. In 1958 he entered politics and was elected to the Federal Assembly from Fort Victoria*. In 1962 he helped to organize the Rhodesian Front Party (q.v.), becoming its first party chairman. The same year he was elected to the Southern Rhodesian Legislative Assembly (q.v.), and was made Minister of Justice, Law and Order by Winston Field (q.v.). In his new capacity he quickly had Joshua Nkomo (q.v.) detained. Ill-health subsequently interfered with Dupont's work, so he changed ministerial posts several times. In August 1964 he resigned his parliamentary seat in order to challenge Roy Welensky (q.v.) in a Salisbury by-election. The main issue was independence, which Welensky opposed. Dupont's easy electoral victory over Welensky retired the latter and strengthened the Rhodesian Front's position on UDI.

Dupont is credited with having been the legal expert behind the following year's UDI. Because of this contribution and because of his fragile health, he was given the post of "Officer Administering the Government" (q.v.) on November 17, 1965. In this office he effectively replaced H. V. Gibbs (q.v.) in the role of governor (q.v.). An avowed anti-African nationalist, Dupont created an international stir in September 1967 by signing death warrants for three Africans convicted of offenses before UDI. On April 16, 1970, he was sworn in as President of the country under the terms of the 1969 republican constitution (q.v.). In December 1975 he retired from public life and was succeeded as president by J. J. Wrathall (q.v.).

DUTCH REFORMED CHURCH (DRC; a.k.a. Nederduits Gereformeerde Kerk). Calvinist Protestant sect which has been the dominant church in South Africa since the 17th century, and is also the main church of Rhodesia's Afrikaner (q.v.) population. The DRC became the second Protestant denomination to field missionaries in the country in 1872, when European and African evangelists based in the Transvaal* began making tentative forays into southern Shona territory. A more formal start was made in 1891, when the Rev. A. A. Louw (1862-1956) founded Morgenster Mission (q.v.) near Great Zimbabwe*. Under Louw's direction seven other missions, as well as schools, and medical facilities were established around the country. By 1959 DRC missions--by then known locally as the African Reformed Church in Southern Rhodesia--claimed nearly 28,000 African members. By then the mission ranked first in mission school attendance (see EDUCATION) and out-patient medical treatments (see HEALTH), but the DRC's popularity among Africans has suffered because of the church's austere liturgy and its identification with South Africa's ruling minority. DRC missions are consequently said to have lost considerable numbers of their members to African independent churches.

DUTCHMAN'S POOL DAM. Built in 1954 on the Sebakwe River, just north of Que Que (qq.v.).

DWALA. Term from Sindebele* for a large, dome-shaped granite
  kopje (q. v.), such as World's View (q. v.) in the Matopos. Also
  known locally as "whaleback kopjes. " (Cf. DOMBO.)

DZIMBABWE   see   ZIMBABWE

DZIVAGURU. Shona spirit medium, or mhondoro (q. v.), in the
  Korekore* area of the northeastern part of the country. The
  Dzivaguru spirit is said to antedate the arrival of the Korekore
  people. During the early 20th century the medium representing
  Dzivaguru traveled extensively in the northeast, establishing a
  wide reputation as a rainmaker, and playing an active role in the
  revolts of Mapondera (q. v.). Dzivaguru, "the Great Pool," is
  also a praise-name for the high god, Mwari (q. v.), among some
  Shona groups.

DZVITI (pl. Madzviti; variants: Mazwiti; Madviti; etc.). Shona
  name for Mfecane (q. v.) invaders, including the Ndebele, Gaza,
  and Ngoni (qq. v.). The name derives either from the Chishona*
  verb -dzvita, "to disturb," or from the name of the Ndwandwe
  king Zwide (q. v.), whose wars helped to set the Mfecane in motion. (Cf. LANDEEN; MATABELE; ROZVI.)

                              - E -

EAST COAST FEVER (a. k. a. African coast fever). Cattle (q. v.)
  disease transmitted by ticks; endemic to the eastern coast. In
  1901 infected animals from present Tanzania were brought into
  the country by way of Beira*. Within a year the disease spread
  through the entire country and entered the Transvaal*. The
  epidemic posed a major threat to the country's already much reduced cattle herds, and killed enough oxen to retard the incipient
  transport industry (see CAMELS). Localizing of herds and
  dipping animals were employed to combat the epidemic. By the
  1950s the disease was virtually eradicated, but vigorous counter-
  measures have been continued to prevent a recurrence. (See
  HEALTH.)

EASTERN HIGHLANDS. Series of mountain ranges running along
  the eastern border with Mozambique (q. v.), from the Inyanga
  District in the north, to the Mount Silinda area in the south
  (qq. v.). Among the constituent ranges are Inyanga, Vumba, and
  Chimanimani (qq. v.). (See ALTITUDINAL ZONES.)

EDUCATION. While the country's educational facilities are well developed in comparison to many African countries, its educational
  system has long had several characteristics bitterly resented by
  Africans. Schools are, for the most part, racially segregated,
  with an enormously disproportionate share (about 95%) of expenditures going to the minority of non-African students. African
  education is neither free nor compulsory, while that of non-
  Africans (Europeans, Asians, and Coloureds, qq. v.) is both free

and compulsory. Further, African education is characterized by a continuing emphasis on agricultural and industrial training, while most academically-oriented students are channeled into teaching careers.

The origins of the system lie in the early BSAC administration's reliance on Christian missions (q.v.) to provide African education. From the early 1890s the BSAC encouraged missionary societies to come to the country by providing generous grants of land. After 1899 it began subsidizing mission schools, while encouraging their industrial orientation, and discouraging integration. By the early 1920s African school attendance was well over 40,000 pupils, but total expenditures in 1923 amounted to only £70,000, of which the BSAC contributed only 28%.

The first government schools were opened in the 1920s and a Department of Native Education was finally established in 1925. This agency was shifted around frequently, finally emerging as the Department of African Education within the racially divided Ministry of Education in 1964. Since then the government has gradually assumed control of most mission schools, and has promulgated a policy of pegging African educational expenditures at 2% of gross national product, despite the disproportional rate of African population increase relative to economic development.

Except for occasional slack periods, such as the 1930s, African school enrollments have steadily risen since 1900, reaching c.100,000 in 1929, c.165,000 in 1945, and over 700,000 in 1972. The emphasis, especially in the early decades, has always been on primary education. Even as late as 1972 secondary school attendance accounted for only 4% of total African enrollments. By the 1970s an estimated 30% of the total African population was functionally literate. Throughout the 20th century Africans have striven to overcome the limitations imposed by the system by establishing their own schools, or by continuing their education outside the country. Before the first government African secondary schools were opened in the mid-1940s, many Africans got their secondary education in South African mission schools or elsewhere. This tradition has also more recently characterized higher education. Although several thousand Africans have graduated from the multi-racial University of Rhodesia (q.v.) since its opening as a University College in 1957, thousands more have completed university educations in Europe and America. It is now believed that the country has one of the highest ratios of African college graduates to population of any country on the continent.

EDWARDS, SAMUEL HOWARD (Nov. 27, 1827-June 21, 1922). South African hunter, trader, and concessionaire. Edwards began his interior career at Mabotsa, a mission station his father and David Livingstone (q.v.) had founded in former Ndebele territory in the western Transvaal* in 1843. After several hunting and trading expeditions into Botswana*, he accompanied Robert Moffat (q.v.) to Matabeleland* in 1854. During this trip he conducted a profitable trade in ivory (q.v.) and became the

first European trader to enter the new Ndebele domain.   In 1869
Edwards returned to Matabeleland as guide for the London and
Limpopo Mining Company (q.v.) expedition.   After this company
lost its mining concession*, Lobengula (q.v.) awarded it to Edwards and several associates in 1881.   Edwards then resided
mostly at what became the Tati Concession (q.v.) until his retirement to Port Elizabeth in 1892.   Edwards also is credited
with having assisted Cecil Rhodes' party in the negotiations which
led to the Rudd Concession (q.v.) in 1888.

EIFFEL FLATS.   Mining town located c.7 km. northeast of Gatooma
(q.v.) on the main road to Salisbury (at 18° 19'S, 29° 59'E).
Most working residents have been employed by the nearby Cam
and Motor Mine.   This mine, formed out of an amalgam of
small mines in 1909, was the largest gold (q.v.) producer in
the country until the late 1960s (cf. CHAKARI).   Since then it
has increasingly processed nickel (q.v.) and other minerals.
Population of the town in 1969 was 4040 (89% Africans).

ELDORADO.   Village just east of Sinoia (q.v.) on the site of the
former Eldorado gold (q.v.) mine (at 17° 21'S, 30° 14'E).   The
site was one of the last major gold mines worked by the Shona
up to the late 19th century.   Shona production apparently ceased
after 1892, when the local ruler, Nemakonde (q.v.), was killed
by the Ndebele.   The mine was reopened by Europeans in 1904,
causing a minor gold rush.   The next year a narrow-gauge railway* line was extended from Salisbury, further accelerating local
development.   The mine itself shut down in 1928.

ELECTIONS, GENERAL.   Since the granting of Responsible Government (q.v.) in 1923, general political elections have been held
in 1924, 1928, 1933, 1934, 1939, 1946, 1948, 1954, 1958, 1962,
1965, 1970, 1974 and August 31, 1977.   (See CONSTITUTIONS;
LEGISLATIVE ASSEMBLY; PRIME MINISTERS.)

ELECTRICAL POWER.   Generation of electricity was first begun by
a private firm in Bulawayo in 1897.   Two years later the operation was taken over by the municipality, setting the pattern for
other towns.   Salisbury got its first municipal power station in
1913.   In 1936 the government created the Electrical Supply Commission, which erected transmission lines and built new power
stations to extend services over a wider area.   Virtually all
electrical power in the country was generated in thermal plants
burning Wankie's coal (qq.v.).   Through the 1940s inability to
transmit power over long distances required coal to be shipped
to many separate power stations.   By the 1950s coal shipments
were creating a serious bottleneck in the country's railways
(q.v.).   Rapid industrialization made development of major new
sources of power imperative.   By this time technological advances made possible much longer-distance power transmission,
making feasible the development of a major hydroelectrical project which would serve both Southern and Northern Rhodesia.
Some industrialists favored expanding thermal power capacity

because of abundant coal and cheap mine labor resources, and because of the smaller initial capital investments needed. However, long-term costs of hydroelectric energy were seen to be cheaper, and the railways were urgently needed for other tasks. Under the aegis of the new Federation (q. v.) government, Kariba Dam (q. v.) was built during the late 1950s. It began generating power in 1960, with a 705 megawatt capacity. This was initially sufficient to supply both Zambia's Copperbelt and all of Rhodesia's needs through a new network of transmission lines, but further industrial demands for energy required the reopening of many thermal plants by 1969.

The hydroelectric facilities at Kariba are owned by the Central African Power Corporation, which divides the output between Rhodesia and Zambia. In the mid-1970s Zambia began building a second hydroelectric facility on its side of the dam in order to protect its own electrical supply in the face of increasing hostility between the two nations.

ELEPHANTS. Although elephant populations were greatly reduced by 19th-century ivory hunters (qq. v.), remnant herds are still found throughout the country's rural regions, notably in Wankie National Park (q. v.).

ELLIOTT, WILLIAM ALLAN (b. 1851). London Missionary Society (q. v.) agent sent to Matabeleland* to replace J. B. Thomson (q. v.) in 1877. Frustrated by the mission's lack of progress among the Ndebele, Elliott left the country in 1892, resigning from the LMS two years later. Drawing upon vocabulary data he had collected in the country, he later published the first Sindebele and Chishona (qq. v.) dictionaries, and he wrote a useful book on the Ndebele, Gold from the Quartz (London, 1910).

ELTON, JAMES FREDERICK (1840-1877). Indian-born British military officer; first came to South Africa in 1868. In 1870 he conducted the first survey of the middle Limpopo River (q. v.) for the London and Limpopo Company (q. v.). He later worked for the British consular service in east Africa, where he died.

EMERALDS see GEMSTONES

EMPANDENI MISSION. Jesuit mission station founded in 1887 near the site of present Plumtree (q. v.) on the site of the Impande ibutho* of the Ndebele (20° 45'S, 27° 58'E). Under the leadership of Peter Prestage and Andrew Hartmann (qq. v.), the mission labored with little success and was closed in 1889. Prestage reopened the mission in 1895, however. (See ZAMBEZI MISSION.)

EMPRESS MINE. Of the several mines with this name, the most important is that located c. 30 km. west of Gatooma* in the northern Que Que District* (18° 27'S, 29° 26'E). Nickel (q. v.) has been mined extensively there since 1955. Population of the settlement in 1969 was 2640 (92% Africans).

ENHLA (pl. abenhla). Sindebele* term meaning, literally, "north,"
or "upcountry." Within the context of Ndebele (q.v.) society,
the term was applied during the 1820s to people from the north,
or South African highveld, to distinguish them from the zansi
(q.v.)--the people from the south, or Zululand*. By the time
the Ndebele migrated from the Transvaal* to Matabeleland* in
the late 1830s, enhla outnumbered zansi roughly two to one.
This ratio remained similar over the next century. Popular
views of Ndebele society hold that the people were rigidly divided into three "castes," and that the enhla occupied a middle
position between the zansi and the holi (q.v.)--the latter being
mainly Shona. Regardless of the accuracy of such views, it is
clear that the enhla were, and are, Ndebele who trace their
ancestry to the mainly Sotho-speaking peoples (q.v.) of the
South African highveld.

ENKELDOORN. Main commercial and administrative center of the
Charter District (q.v.), Enkeldoorn stands between the headwaters of the Umniati and Sebakwe rivers (qq.v.) (at 19° 1'S,
30° 54'E; alt. 1480 m.). Afrikaners (q.v.) founded the town in
1897 and have remained its predominant European community.
Population in 1969 was 1670 (85% Africans). Nearby is the
Maronda Mashanu (q.v.) mission.

EPWORTH MISSION. Wesleyan Methodist (q.v.) mission station and
theological college, located just east of Salisbury (at 17° 52'S,
31° 8'E). Isaac Shimmin (q.v.) and another South African missionary founded the station in 1892 on land granted by the BSAC.
The station has since developed into one of the country's most
important missions and training centers, and has had particular
success in attracting South African labor immigrants. Many
Africans have resided on the mission's farms, which are now
in the midst of Salisbury's expanding European settlements.
Since the promulgation of the Land Tenure Act (q.v.) in 1969,
the government has attempted to use the law's segregation provisions to evict these African residents.
        Near the mission are many fine examples of rock paintings
(q.v.) in natural granite shelters. Also nearby are the "Epworth
Balancing Rocks," a spectacular natural formation created by
wind and erosion.

ESPUNGABERA. Mozambique (q.v.) town just across the border
from Mount Silinda (q.v.).

ESSEXVALE. Village just southeast of Bulawayo on the main road
to Beitbridge* (at 20° 18'S, 28° 56'E; alt. 1165 m.). Established
in 1894 as the center of now depleted mining area, Essexvale
is now a minor commercial center within Umzingwane District
(q.v.). Population in 1969 was 1350 (92% Africans).

EUROPEANS. According to Rhodesian law, as well as southern
African custom, a "European" is any person of purely European
descent, regardless of place of birth. Although Europeans

constituted only 4% of the country's population (q.v.) by 1977,
they have for nearly 90 years held a virtual monopoly of political power (see CONSTITUTIONS), controlled the monetary
economy, and enjoyed a share of land equal in size--but superior in quality--to that of the entire African population (see
LAND APPORTIONMENT and LAND TENURE ACTS). Despite
the reservation of the best rural lands for Europeans, most of
them live in urban centers (q.v.), particularly in Salisbury
(q.v.).

The Portuguese (q.v.) were the first Europeans to enter
the country. During the 16th and 17th centuries they played
active commercial and military roles in the northeastern parts
of the country from their bases in Mozambique (q.v.), but by
the early 18th century they were largely gone. The next
Europeans to arrive entered from the south, mainly by way
of Botswana (q.v.), during the 1850s. From that point increasing numbers of missionaries (q.v.), hunters (q.v.), and
traders entered the country. Few settled permanently, however, and significant European settlement began only in the
1890s, when the BSAC occupied the country and established a
European administration.

There were an estimated 1500 European residents in
1891. This figure rose to 11,000 in 1901; 23,600 in 1911;
33,600 in 1921; 49,900 in 1931; and 69,000 in 1941. The
Second World War created a boom in European immigration,
particularly from Britain, raising the number of Europeans to
82,400 in 1946, and to 136,000 in 1951. The figure topped
200,000 in 1959, and then diminished slightly in the early
1960s, as fear of an African political takeover stimulated emigration. Net immigration gains again rose in 1966. The 1969
census recorded 228,300 Europeans, 41% of whom were native-
born; another 22% were born in South Africa; 23% in Britain;
and the rest elsewhere. By the end of 1975 the European population was 278,000--a figure probably near the peak number of
settlers. Since then net emigration has steadily increased--
again in response to white fears of a black takeover (see VIC-
TORIA FALLS and GENEVA CONFERENCES). In mid-1977 the
net loss of Europeans to emigration was estimated at 50 people
a day.

EWANRIGG ALOE GARDENS NATIONAL PARK. Botanical gardens
located c. 35 km. northeast of Salisbury (at 17° 41'S, 31° 20'E).
The 24 hectare national park (q.v.) features aloes and cycads.

EXECUTIVE COUNCIL. In 1894 the British Secretary of State for
Colonies issued an Order-in-Council creating an advisory council for the BSAC's administration in Southern Rhodesia. The
council included a high court judge, three BSAC appointees,
and the BSAC Administrator (q.v.), who presided. The council
as a whole was responsible for the routine governing of the
country. Another Order-in-Council in 1898 recreated the body
as an Executive Council, and added a Legislative Council (q.v.)
with elected settler members. A non-voting British Resident

Commissioner sat on both councils, reporting on their actions
to the British High Commissioner for Southern Africa.

When Responsible Government (q.v.) was achieved in
1923, the Executive Council became the government's cabinet,
and was formally presided over by the British Governor (q.v.).
Membership comprised the Prime Minister (q.v.) and the heads
of the various ministries. Over time the influence of the
governors diminished and the Executive Council evolved into a
cabinet in the more truly parliamentary sense. Under the
terms of the 1969 republican constitution (q.v.), ministers are
appointed to the Council by the President (q.v.) on the advice
of the Prime Minister.

- F -

FAIRBAIRN, JAMES (1853-April 11, 1894). A Scottish trader, Fairbairn first came to Matabeleland* in the 1870s. There he formed
a trading partnership with James Dawson (q.v.) and also formed
a concessionary company with Thomas Leask, George Westbeech,
and G. A. Phillips (qq.v.) in 1881. Three years later Lobengula (q.v.) awarded this company a mining concession (q.v.) between the Gwelo and Hunyani rivers (qq.v.) which they sold to
the BSAC for a large sum in 1889. Fairbairn and W. Usher
(q.v.) remained unharmed in Bulawayo* through the 1893 Ndebele
War (q.v.), but Fairbairn died from dysentery at Inyati* a few
months later.

FAIRBRIDGE, KINGSLEY (May 5, 1885-July 19, 1924). Fairbridge's
direct role in the country's history is slight, but he is revered
by Europeans as a folk hero because of the youthful exploits in
eastern Rhodesia he described in his posthumously published
autobiography. Born in Grahamstown, South Africa, he went to
Umtali* with his family in 1896. He later won a Rhodes Scholarship to Oxford, where he wrote poetry about Rhodesia and
worked out a scheme for training English orphans to be farmers
in Commonwealth countries. He launched such a scheme in
western Australia, where he died, but the idea was never applied in Rhodesia.

FAIRBRIDGE, WILLIAM ERNEST (Nov. 2, 1863-Oct. 5, 1943).
South African journalist. In 1891 the Argus group (q.v.) of
newspapers sent Fairbridge to Salisbury, where he almost immediately started the Mashonaland Herald & Zambesian Times,
the forerunner of the Rhodesian Herald (q.v.). Argus then
made him their manager in the country, until his return to
South Africa around 1904. Between December 1897 and July
1898 he also served as the first mayor of Salisbury (q.v.).
(See also CENSORSHIP.)

FAIRS (Portuguese: Feiras). Markets, or trading centers, established in Shona territory and the Zambezi Valley by coastal-
based Muslims (q.v.), at least as early as the 14th century.

The fairs were set up in the interior to buy gold dust, ivory,
and iron goods (qq.v.) from African producers who had insufficient quantities to merit transport to coastal ports, such as
Sofala (q.v.). After the Portuguese (q.v.) occupied Muslim
ports in the early 16th century, they gradually recognized the
necessity of establishing their own network of fairs. By the
early 17th century they had opened at least a dozen fairs in
Shona territory--mostly in the Munhumutapa and Manyika regions
(qq.v.). Each fair typically contained a market center, small
fort, Dominican mission church, and a few Portuguese houses.
Among the most important fairs in the country were Dambarare,
Luanze, Maramuca, and Masapa (qq.v.). In the early 1690s
the Changamire state (q.v.) expanded into the northeast and
destroyed most of the fairs. Thereafter Portuguese traders
were largely kept out of the country, and they had to work indirectly through African employees or slaves, known as mussambazes. The Portuguese retained their bases at Tete and
Sena (qq.v.) on the Zambezi River, and opened a fair at Zumbo
(q.v.) in c.1714 in order to have a closer link with the Changamire state.

FAKU NDIWENI (fl.1870s-90s). Ndebele induna*. In 1872 Faku is
said to have informed on a brother who supported the abortive
coup attempt of "Nkulumane" and Mangwane (qq.v.). After his
brother was executed in early 1875, Faku became regent of the
Ndiweni chieftaincy, centered by the headwaters of the Gwai and
Khami rivers (qq.v.). When his nephew, the rightful chief,
came of age in the early 1890s, Faku refused to give up his
position. Lobengula (q.v.) was about to intervene in the dispute, but the Ndebele War (q.v.) interrupted him, bringing the
British to power. The new BSAC administration recognized
Faku as Ndiweni chief, and he became one of its strongest supporters in Matabeleland*. His collaboration with the company
seriously divided his people during the 1896 Revolt (q.v.), in
which he was regarded as a leading British "loyalist." Afterwards he was made a salaried chief. Later his own descendants
were confirmed as heirs to the Ndiweni chieftaincy in the Kezi
area, south of the Matopo Hills*.

FALCON MINE see UMVUMA

FANAKALO (variant: Fanagalo; a.k.a. Chilololo; Chilapalapa;
"Kitchen Kaffir"). A pidgin language, Fanakalo is an amalgam
of Afrikaans, Sindebele, Chishona (qq.v.), English, and other
African languages. It is widely used throughout the country as
a simplified mode of European-African communication. The
name derives from a similar lingua franca developed in the
South African mines. (See also LANGUAGE; "KAFFIR.")

"FEARLESS TALKS" (1968). Two years after the abortive agreement produced by their "Tiger Talks" (q.v.), Ian Smith and
British Prime Minister Harold Wilson met again (October 9-13,
1968) off Gilbraltar, aboard the warship HMS Fearless. Although

Britain dropped the demand for a return to "legality," no agreement was reached.   The next Anglo-Rhodesian settlement agreement was reached in November 1971 (see PEARCE COMMIS-
SION).

FEDERAL PARTY   see   UNITED PARTY

FEDERATION OF RHODESIA AND NYASALAND (a.k.a. Central
   African Federation [CAF]).   From 1953 through 1963 Southern
   Rhodesia, Northern Rhodesia (now Zambia), and Nyasaland
   (Malawi) were linked together by a self-governing federation
   dominated by white Southern Rhodesian politicians.
      (1) Creation of the Federation.   Amalgamation (q.v.) of
   the two Rhodesias was first proposed during the First World
   War as an alternative to Unionist Movement (q.v.) proposals to
   link Southern Rhodesia to South Africa.   The idea was opposed
   by Southern Rhodesian settlers until after the achievement of
   Responsible Government (q.v.) in 1923.   Then the British
   government's Hilton Young Commission (1929) and Bledisloe
   Commission (1939) (qq.v.) issued reports rejecting the idea.
   The latter report did, however, pave the way for creation of
   the Central African Council (q.v.) in 1944 to stimulate inter-
   territorial cooperation.   After the Second World War Godfrey
   Huggins' (q.v.) government abandoned the goal of amalgamation
   in favor of federation--a looser form of union.   Roy Welensky
   (q.v.) became the leading advocate of federation in Northern
   Rhodesia.
      Settler motives for creating a federation were primarily
   economic.   They wished to tap the wealth generated by Northern
   Rhodesia's Copperbelt, to create a larger and more diversified
   national economy, and to attract foreign investments away from
   South Africa.   Federation was also seen as a more promising
   vehicle to attain autonomous dominion status, although many settlers feared being politically overwhelmed by the larger African
   majorities north of the Zambezi River.   This risk was enhanced
   by the need to persuade the British government that federation
   would not retard African political advancement.   Huggins and his
   supporters met this challenge by articulating the concept of
   federal "partnership" (q.v.).
      The CAF was planned in a series of conferences between
   territorial representatives and British government officials from
   1948 to 1953.   The British government committed itself to the
   scheme only after 1951, when the Conservative Party took power.
   At British insistence Nyasaland was included in federation plans,
   though that country had little to contribute but migrant laborers.
   Africans north of the Zambezi strongly opposed federation, for
   fear of falling under the domination of white Southern Rhodesians.
   African opinion in Southern Rhodesia was divided.   Most Africans
   there recognized that federation meant enhanced white power, but
   many saw closer union with South Africa as an even more un-
   pleasant alternative (see ALL-AFRICAN CONVENTION).   In any
   case, African objections were largely ignored, and the British
   Parliament approved a federal constitution in March 1953.   On

April 9th a Southern Rhodesian referendum ruled in favor of
federation by a vote of 25,580 to 14,929.   Only a few hundred
Africans were able to vote on the issue.   A British Order-in-
Council created the CAF on August 1st.   By October the Federation was in full operation.
      (2) Federal structure.   The federal constitution created
a Federal Assembly with 35 seats (later raised to 60), including
six reserved for Africans.   Southern Rhodesia had 14 seats
open to all races, but in practice these were held only by
whites.   A fifteenth European was elected to represent African
interests.   The two initial African seats were won by M. M.
Hove and J. Z. Savanhu (qq.v.), who were elected by predominantly European constituencies.   After the first general election
in December 1953 Huggins became Prime Minister.   His new
Federal Party, an offshoot of the United Party (q.v.), was never
seriously challenged during the life of the Federation.   After
Huggins' retirement in 1956, Welensky became the second and
last Prime Minister.
      A British governor-general became head of state (see
J. J. LLEWELLYN and S. R. DALHOUSIE).   He signed all
federal legislation, but exercised almost no discretionary powers.
      A special body, the African Affairs Board, was created
within the Assembly to guard against discriminatory legislation.
This Board was to report to the British government, which had
reserve veto powers.   The Board's ineffectiveness was proven
when Britain refused to block discriminatory federal franchise
legislation in 1957.
      Existing territorial institutions, including Southern Rho-
desia's Legislative Assembly and Governor (qq.v.), were retained.   The federal government assumed jurisdiction only over
specified government functions, including external affairs, customs and immigration, non-African and general higher education,
and public health.   Southern Rhodesia's government retained sole
responsibility for its African affairs, local government, police,
and various internal economic sectors.   Revenues were shared
among the three territorial and the federal governments, with
Southern Rhodesia generally expending more than it contributed.
      (3) Developments and dissolution, 1953-63.   It is gener-
ally recognized that the period of Federation was one of increased economic prosperity, but authorities disagree on the
contribution the Federation itself made to this state of affairs.
The Federation's economy was built largely around Northern
Rhodesian copper exports, and copper happened to enjoy a world-
wide price boom in the mid-1950s, thereby stimulating the entire
Federation economy.   The most obvious economic benefits which
the Federation itself produced were those arising from construction of the huge Kariba Dam (q.v.) hydroelectric scheme.   Southern Rhodesia was the clearest beneficiary of Federation.   It received a disproportionate share of Federal revenues; it contained
the Federal capital, Salisbury (q.v.); and it experienced a rapid
rate of industrial expansion.   In 1955 the Federation extended a
new railway (q.v.) line through Southern Rhodesia to provide a
connection with Lourenzo Marques (now Maputo).   In 1957 the

federally-sponsored University (q.v.) was opened in Salisbury.
On the dissolution of Federation, Southern Rhodesia inherited
these facilities and others, including most of the federal army
equipment (see MILITARY).

Although the Federation government was dominated by
Southern Rhodesian settlers who hoped to make it an independent
dominion (see DOMINION PARTY), its eventual dissolution was
almost foreordained by its inherent structure. The Federal
government had no control over constitutional advances within
its constituent territories, and Britain was already committed
to bringing African majority rule to the two northern territories. It was only the speed with which this happened that
was unexpected. In 1959 Britain set up the Monckton Commission (q.v.) to make proposals respecting constitutional changes.
This Commission found opposition to Federation so well organized among the Africans north of the Zambezi that it technically
exceeded its own instructions by recommending that the individual territories be given the right of secession. When the
ensuing Federal Review Conference, which met in London in
late 1960, became deadlocked, it deferred decision-making until
the attainment of responsible government in Northern Rhodesia
and Nyasaland. When this was achieved, Britain granted both
territories the right to secede from the Federation (December
1962-). Both territories did so quickly, and the CAF was
formally terminated on the last day of 1963.

Welensky's ruling party regarded Britain's condoning of
territorial secession as a betrayal, but by then the government
of Southern Rhodesia itself was in the hands of the Rhodesian
Front Party (q.v.), which opposed Federation for reasons of
its own.

FEIRAS. Portuguese term for trading fairs (q.v.). For Feira
town, see ZUMBO.

FERNANDES, ANTÓNIO (fl.1506-1520s). The first European known
to have entered the country, Fernandes is an elusive character
in Portuguese (q.v.) records, partly because his name was a
common one. He apparently came to Sofala (q.v.) in 1506 as
a degredado (perhaps an exiled criminal) after seeing service in
the Kongo kingdom of west-central Africa. Though described as
a carpenter, he was commissioned by the commander at Sofala
to discover the gold (q.v.) fields in the interior. He apparently
made his first journey in 1511, traveling inland from Sofala to
Manyika (q.v.). By mid-1513 he had made a second and longer
journey, this time meeting Munhumutapa* Chikuyo Chisamarengu
(q.v.) and traveling widely in the northeastern section of present
Rhodesia. The reports of his trips were recorded by a clerk
in Sofala. His later activities are unknown, but Fernandes was
reported as dead by 1525.

"FEVER YEAR" (1870). Year in which unusually long rains greatly
increased incidence of malaria (q.v.) throughout the country.

FIELD, WINSTON (June 6, 1904-March 1969). Seventh Prime
Minister (q.v.) of Southern Rhodesia. Born in England, Field
came to the country in 1921. He became successful as a tobacco* farmer in the Marandellas District* and served as the
president of the Rhodesian Tobacco Association from 1938 to
1940. During the Second World War he served in the British
army. Afterwards he returned to the country and initiated an
unsuccessful scheme to settle Italian peasant farmers (1952).
He entered politics in 1956 as the leader of the new Dominion
Party (q.v.). The following year he was elected to the Federation (q.v.) Assembly in an Mrewa* by-election. As the leader
of the opposition to the United (Federal) Party (q.v.) government, Field advocated dissolution of the Federation and creation
of a white-dominated dominion which would include the main
European areas of Northern Rhodesia, as well as all of Southern
Rhodesia. In 1962 he became leader of the DP's successor
party, the Rhodesian Front (q.v.), leading it to victory in the
December election. As new Prime Minister he surprised Africans by releasing political detainees in January 1963, but he
then quickly toughened the Law and Order (Maintenance) Act
(q.v.). RF hardliners became impatient with his leadership because of his failure to press the British government sufficiently
hard on the independence issue (see UDI). In April 1964 a
party congress forced him to resign in favor of his deputy, Ian
Smith (q.v.). Field then retired from politics.

FIGTREE. Village 38 km. southwest of Bulawayo on the main road
to Plumtree* in the Bulalima-Mangwe District* (at 20°22'S,
28°20'E; alt. 1380 m.). Figtree is a commercial center in a
mainly cattle-keeping region.

FILABUSI. Mining village and headquarters for the Insiza District
(q.v.), of which "Filabusi District" was formerly a separate
part (at 20°32'S, 29°17'E on the Insiza River*). Filabusi experienced a brief boom during the Second World War when military demand for tungsten increased local scheelite production.
Population in 1969 was 550 (85% Africans).

FINAUGHTY, WILLIAM (1843-1917). South African ivory hunter
(qq.v.) and trader. Between 1864 and 1874 he claimed to have
killed more than 500 elephants (q.v.) in Matabeleland* and
Mashonaland*, retiring because of the increasing difficulty of
pursuing the dwindling herds into tsetse fly (q.v.) areas. In
1876 he sold Lobengula (q.v.) two useless ship's cannons for
ivory. Two decades later he became a farmer near Bulawayo*.

FINGO LOCATION. Special area granted to Mfengu (q.v.) immigrants who entered the country between 1898 and 1902. Now
designated as a Purchase Area (q.v.), the Location is near
the junction of the Bembezi River (q.v.) and the Bulawayo to
Salisbury Road (at 19°56'S, 28°55'E).

FINGOS   see   MFENGU

"FIRST FRUITS FESTIVAL" see INXWALA

FISHING.   More than 100 varieties of fish are native to the country.
   The most important of these are members of the carp family
   (Cyprinidae), Bream (Cichlidae), and catfish (Siluridae).   The
   Shona, Tonga, and other peoples--excepting many South African-
   derived Ndebele--have long caught fish to supplement their diets.
   The development of modern dams (q. v.) has greatly enlarged
   the country's fishing waters, particularly in Lake Kariba (q. v.),
   which has the country's only commercial fishing industry.   Many
   dams on European farms are stocked with fish to feed African
   workers, and the government has a program of introducing
   fishing dams to African areas.   Sport fishing is an important
   feature of the tourist industry.   Exotic fish such as black bass
   and trout are bred locally and stocked in national parks (q. v.).
   Rainbow, Brown, and American Brook Trout thrive in the rivers
   of the Eastern Highlands (q. v.).   An unusual native variety, the
   Tiger Fish (Characidae) is regarded as the most exciting sport
   fish, and is found in the larger lakes.   It grows up to 15 kg.,
   and is noted for its long, razor sharp teeth, which can destroy
   ordinary fishing gear.

"FIVE PRINCIPLES."   Conditions cited by the British government
   as essential to any Anglo-Rhodesian constitutional settlement.
   The five principles were first expressed in a letter from the
   British Secretary of State for Commonwealth Relations to Ian
   Smith in September 1965.   They were (1) unimpeded progress
   towards majority rule, (2) guarantees against retrogressive
   constitutional changes, (3) immediate improvements in the political status of Africans, (4) progress towards ending racial
   discrimination, and (5) acceptance of any Anglo-Rhodesian settlement terms by the people of Rhodesia as a whole.   Shortly after
   UDI a sixth principle was added to ensure that there was no
   oppression of the majority by a minority, or of a minority by
   the majority.   These principles formed the basis of British-
   Rhodesian negotiations after late 1965, but critics have disputed
   Britain's faith in securing Rhodesian compliance.   (See, e. g.,
   PEARCE COMMISSION.)

FLAGS.   The BSAC and Southern Rhodesian governments flew the
   British Union Jack with their respective coats of arms added
   in the center.   The Federation (q. v.) government used a flag
   combining symbols of each of its constituent territories.   In
   April 1964 the Rhodesian government adopted a light blue British
   ensign with the Union Jack in the canton, and the shield from
   its own coat of arms on the fly.   The government symbolically
   asserted its independence from Britain on the third anniversary
   of UDI in 1968 by dropping the Union Jack altogether.   It introduced a completely new flag, made up of three equal-sized
   vertical stripes.   Two outside green stripes surround a central
   white stripe dominated by the national coat of arms.   The most
   prominent features of these arms are a shield with a gold

pickaxe, two standing sable antelopes, and a somewhat fanciful
representation of a "Zimbabwe Bird" (q.v.).

FLEMING, ANDREW MILROY (Jan. 28, 1871-1954). Early health
(q.v.) officer. A Scottish physician, Fleming came to the
country in 1894. During the 1896 Revolts (q.v.) he was made
principal Medical Officer to BSAC forces. Afterwards he became the country's first Director of the Public Health Department (1898-1931). His early researches into malaria (q.v.)
made a major contribution in combating this disease around the
world. He retired to Scotland.

FORBES, PATRICK WILLIAM (Aug. 31, 1861-May 27, 1923).
British army officer with service in South Africa during the
1880s. In 1889 he joined the forerunner of the British South
Africa Police (q.v.), with which he served in the 1890 Pioneer
Column (q.v.). In November he was sent by Archibald Colqu-
houn (q.v.) to chief Mutasa (q.v.) in Manicaland* to prevent
Portuguese* infiltration into BSAC-claimed territory. Although
Forbes commanded only 15 troopers, he boldly arrested two im-
portant Portuguese officials there, J. C. P. d'Andrada and
M. A. de Sousa (qq.v.), whom he sent to Salisbury (November
15, 1890). He then began a push to open a route to the Indian
Ocean, but was recalled by the government.
    In July 1893 L. S. Jameson (q.v.) named Forbes com-
mander of BSAC forces while preparing for the Ndebele War
(q.v.), which began in October. Forbes commanded the Salisbury Column through two major battles and the occupation of
Bulawayo*. He then led a column north in pursuit of Lobengula (q.v.). In an incident which has since become famous as
the "Shangani Patrol," a detached force under Major Allan Wilson (qq.v.) was annihilated. Forbes then fought Ndebele skir-
mishers while retreating to Bulawayo, with his own military
reputation thereafter tarnished. In 1895 he became BSAC Administrator of North-Eastern Rhodesia (now eastern Zambia).
Poor health caused him to retire to Southern Rhodesia in 1898,
but he later became staff officer for the Southern Rhodesian
Volunteers in the South African War (q.v.). He returned to
England in 1902 and later served in the First World War.

FORESTS/FORESTRY. The country's indigenous woodlands are of
limited economic potential, except in the dry region of Matabeleland North Province (q.v.), where Rhodesian teak and other native
hardwoods are profitably exploited (see SAWMILLS). Most hardwood production is exported. The Eastern Highlands (q.v.) are
ideally suited for rapid tree growth, but indigenous trees of commercial potential are concentrated in a few small areas which
are now protected as reserves (see CHIRINDA FOREST; VUMBA).
A commercial forestry industry began in the early 20th century
with the importation of pines and Australian wattles to the
Eastern Highlands. More than 800 sq. km. of land are given
over to intensive plantation cultivation, supplying most of the

country's internal demand for softwood and paper products.
(See also BAOBAB; MOPANE; SAVANNA.)

FORT CHARTER see under CHARTER DISTRICT

FORT SALISBURY see SALISBURY

FORT VICTORIA. Administrative and commercial center for both
the Victoria District and Victoria Province (qq.v.), Ft. Victoria
is located just north of the Zimbabwe Ruins (q.v.) on the
Mtilikwe River* (at 20° 5'S, 30° 50'E; alt. 1065 m.). The site
was chosen by the Pioneer Column (q.v.) in 1890, and a fort
was built the following year to guard the main transport route
to Salisbury (q.v.). European settlement grew fairly rapidly,
encouraged by local mining and by the town's favorable position
in the transportation network. Conditions for Europeans remained unsettled, however, as the Ndebele (q.v.) continued to
wage punitive military raids in the area. In July 1893 an
Ndebele impi* raided particularly near the town, arousing European residents to demand BSAC retaliation (this was the "Victoria Incident"). The result was the Ndebele War (q.v.), which
had the ironic effect of initiating European settlement at Bulawayo (q.v.) and causing Ft. Victoria's own development to suffer
as most northern commerce passed through Matabeleland*. By
the end of 1974 the town's population was estimated at only
16,000 (81% Africans; 18% Europeans). Construction in 1961
of the Kyle Dam (q.v.), just southeast of Ft. Victoria, gave the
town's tourist industry a boost by adding major recreational
facilities to the already important attractions of Zimbabwe National Park.

FOUNDERS DAY. In 1903 the 6th of July was made into a public
holiday (q.v.) to commemorate the Pioneer Column's (q.v.)
crossing of the Shashi River* into present Rhodesia in 1890.
Seven years later the holiday was shifted to the second Tuesday
of July in order to follow Rhodes Day (q.v.) every year.

FRANCISTOWN. Botswana (q.v.) town on the Mafeking to Bulawayo
railway (q.v.) line in the former Tati Concession (q.v.) area
(at 21° 13'S, 27° 31'E). In the mid-1970s Francistown became
an important base for anti-Rhodesian nationalists, who used
local broadcasting facilities to communicate propaganda to southwestern Rhodesia.

FRONT FOR THE LIBERATION OF ZIMBABWE (FROLIZI). In
October 1971 nationalist leaders resident in Lusaka, Zambia announced the formation of FROLIZI as a merger of ZAPU and
ZANU (qq.v.). It appears, however, that FROLIZI was simply
a new organization formed by dissident leaders from the two
rival parties. Skilkom Siwela and Godfrey Savanhu, the titular
leaders of the new organization, were ousted early in 1972 by
James Chikerema, George Nyandoro, and Nathan Shamuyarira

(qq. v.).   FROLIZI never established itself within Rhodesia, but
instead attempted to ally with the African National Council (q. v.).
The party gained considerable outside support in 1972, but early
in 1973 it was officially ignored by the Liberation Committee of
the OAU.   Thereafter it faded in importance.

"FRONTLINE PRESIDENTS."   In December 1974 the Liberation Committee of the OAU created a "Front-line President's Committee"
to coordinate external support and strategy for the African liberation of Rhodesia.   The original members of the group were
Kenneth Kaunda of Zambia*, Seretse Khama of Botswana*, Samora Machel of Mozambique*, and Julius Nyerere of Tanzania.
President Augustinho Neto of Angola joined later.   These presidents initially supported Abel Muzorewa's (q. v.) nationalist movement, but later denounced him and threw their support behind
the "Patriotic Front" of Joshua Nkomo and Robert Mugabe (qq.v.).
After the failure of the Geneva Conference (q. v.) in late 1976,
British and American government leaders regarded support of the
"Frontline Presidents" as crucial to any negotiated settlement in
Rhodesia.

FRY, IVON (c. 1864-1941).   A South African, Fry visited Lobengula
(q. v.) in 1887, returning the next year as Cecil Rhodes' agent
to seek a concession*.   Superseded in this task by C. D. Rudd
(q. v.), Fry later entered into an acrimonious dispute with BSAC
officials.   Nevertheless, he became a member of the BSAC's
Pioneer Column (q. v.) in 1890, and he fought with the BSAC
against the Ndebele in the 1893 war.

FYNN, PERCIVAL DONAL LESLIE (Aug. 16, 1872-April 25, 1940).
Born in the Transkei, Fynn joined the Cape civil service in
1889.   In 1897 he followed W. H. Milton (q. v.) to Southern Rhodesia, where he held a series of important posts in the BSAC
government.   He joined Charles Coghlan's (q. v.) government in
1923, and thereafter dominated finance for a decade.   He initially
opposed Godfrey Huggins (q. v.) in 1933, but then led the opposition members who helped to form the United Party (q. v.).   He
retired from the cabinet the year before his death.

- G -

GAIREZI RIVER.   Flows north from the eastern slopes of the Inyanga Mountains (q. v.) to form an 80 km. stretch of the Mozambique border (q. v.) before joining the Ruenya River (q. v.).

GAME RESERVES.   Conservation of the country's vast wildlife resources was initiated by European landowners in the Wankie
District (q. v.), part of which became the first government-
designated game reserve in 1928.   Efforts to protect game were
intensified after the creation of the Natural Resources Board in
1942.   This led to the National Parks Act in 1949 and the Wildlife Conservation Act of 1960.   Some reserves, such as Wankie,

became national parks (q.v.), which differ from non-park reserves in that they are developed to accommodate vacationers
and tourists. By the early 1970s fourteen game reserves proper
had been designated, including six open to the public on a limited
basis. Sites are selected only if they have poor agricultural potential. The largest reserves are Chete, Chizarira, and Matu-
sadona--all near Lake Kariba (q.v.); Mana Pools (q.v.) and
Chewore, north of the Zambezi Escarpment (q.v.); and Gona-re-
Zhou (q.v.) in the southeastern lowveld. (See also HUNTING.)

GAMPU SITHOLE (variant: Gambo Sitole) (c.1840s-1916). Ndebele
induna*, whose father, Magekeni (d.1870), was one of Mzilikazi's original followers in Zululand*. Gampu inherited his
father's leadership of the Igapa ibutho* in the southwestern section of the kingdom after having supported Lobengula's accession to the kingship in 1870. His influence became great, but
in 1887 he was charged with seducing one of Lobengula's daughters and had to flee to the Transvaal* (apparently with P. D.
Grobler*) to avoid punishment. He returned home the next year,
but his position remained insecure. During the 1893 Ndebele
War (q.v.) he commanded the force guarding the southern approaches to the kingdom. His standing among the Ndebele was
further compromised when his force was easily pushed aside by
Goold-Adams' (q.v.) invasion column.
    The next year Gampu became one of the most prominent
Ndebele leaders openly to support British occupation of the country. The British rewarded him with land and cattle* which
eventually made him wealthy. Over the next two years he opposed attempts to make Nyamanda (q.v.) king, and then sided
with the British in the 1896 Revolt (q.v.; see also FAKU). He
fought rebel forces in several engagements which gave the Revolt
the character of a civil war, and helped to keep open the British
supply route in southwestern Matabeleland. After the Revolt he
was one of the first izinduna whom Rhodes made a salaried chief.
He settled down to become the British ideal of a "loyal" and
progressive African leader.

GANN, LEWIS H. (b.Jan. 28, 1924). A German-born, English-edu-
cated historian, Gann began his productive career in central
African history in Northern Rhodesia (now Zambia) after the
Second World War. He came to Salisbury in 1954 and became
publications editor in the National Archives (q.v.). A firm supporter of the Federation (q.v.), he used his immense skills as
a professional historian to defend the role of Europeans in building a multiracial society by writing the first thoroughly scholarly
histories of the region. He was commissioned by the Federation to write major histories of each territory, but completed
only the volumes on Northern and Southern Rhodesia before the
Federation collapsed. His History of Southern Rhodesia (1965)
still stands as the most nearly balanced synthetic history of the
country, though its emphasis is Eurocentric. Disenchanted with
Rhodesia's retreat to territorial nationalism in the mid-1960s,
Gann joined his frequent coauthor, Peter Duignan, at the Hoover

Institution in Stanford, California. He subsequently expanded
his inquiries to examine the impact of Western imperialism on
Africa as a whole. (See BIBLIOGRAPHY.)

GATHS MINE.   Major asbestos (q.v.) mine just north of Mashaba
(q.v.) in the Victoria District* (at 20° 1'S, 30° 31'E).   Population in 1969 was 6180 (89% Africans).

GATOOMA.   Administrative and commercial center of district of the
same name in the extreme western portion of Mashonaland South
Province* (at 18° 21'S, 29° 55'E; alt. 1165 m.).   The town arose
on the main road between Bulawayo and Salisbury amid a cluster
of small European gold (q.v.) mines in the late 19th century,
and was formally organized as a town in 1907.   The population
has grown at an increasingly rapid rate, reaching an estimated
33, 000 (91% Africans; 8% Europeans) in early 1975.

GATOOMA DISTRICT.   Covering 6864 sq. km., it originally formed
the southwestern part of Hartley District (q.v.).   The banana-
shaped district is roughly bisected by the main road and railway
line, and is mostly reserved for Europeans (see LAND TENURE
ACT), except for some Purchase Land (q.v.) in the northwestern
corner, and some Tribal Trust Land (q.v.) in the southeastern
corner.   It borders the districts of Gokwe on the west; Que Que
on the south; Chilimanzi, Charter, and Salisbury on the east;
Hartley on the northeast; and Lomagundi (qq.v.) on the north.

GATSI RUSERE (variant: Gassi Lusere) (c. 1560-1623).   Perhaps the
best-documented of the early Munhumutapas (q.v.), Gatsi Rusere
unintentionally initiated a major era of Portuguese (q.v.) influence
in the country.   The grandson of Munhumutapa Neshangwe (q.v.),
Gatsi Rusere succeeded Negomo (q.v.) as ruler in c. 1589 as the
result of an earlier agreement with the latter's rival ruling house.
Beset with rebellions in his eastern provinces, he achieved order
with the help of Portuguese forces.   On August 1, 1607, he
signed a treaty with Diogo Simões Madeira (q.v.), theoretically
ceding all his country's mines to the Portuguese.   Conflict over
implementation of these cessions led to a war with the Portuguese
after his own passing.   He and some of his sons (see Dom
MIGUEL) accepted Christian baptism.   On his death in 1623 he
was succeeded as Munhumutapa by his son Nyambo Kapararidze
(q.v.).

GAZA KINGDOM (a.k.a. Shangane*; Landeen*; Vatua; etc.).   One of
the most important of the Mfecane era (q.v.) states, the Gaza
kingdom was created in southern Mozambique* in the early 1820s
by Soshangane (q.v.) and Nguni* refugees from Zululand*.   In the
1830s the Gaza (who took their name from Soshangane's grandfather) established their headquarters by Mount Silinda (q.v.), in
the southeastern part of present Rhodesia.   Soshangane moved
back to the lower Limpopo basin after a few years, but his son
Mzila (q.v.) returned to Mount Silinda in the early 1860s.   In
1889 Mzila's son Gungunyane (q.v.) made the final move back to

southern Mozambique (see MANHLAGAZI). Throughout this entire period the Gaza raided African communities and Portuguese
(q. v.) posts between the Zambezi and Limpopo rivers.   They
raided the Ndau (q. v.) especially intensively, but their impact
on other Shona-speaking peoples of the country was much less
disruptive than that of the similar Ndebele kingdom (q. v.) in the
west.
        The Gaza state was brought to an end by Portuguese con-
quest in 1895, when Gungunyane was sent into exile.   An unsuccessful revolt two years later brought down strong reprisals.
Although the Gaza paralleled the Ndebele in many ways, they
did not have the latters' success in imprinting Nguni culture on
their subject peoples.
        Gaza kings, c. 1820-95: c. 1820-c. 1859 Soshangane*;
c. 1859-62 Mawewe (usurper); 1862-84 Mzila*; 1884-95 Gungunyane*.

"GAZA QUEENS" see under XWALILE

GAZALAND.   European term for the area dominated by the Gaza
        kingdom (q. v.) during the late 19th century.   The region roughly
        encompasses the territory east of the Sabi River* and south of
        present Melsetter* in eastern Rhodesia and southern Mozam-
        bique*.   Gazaland was effectively partitioned between Britain
        and Portugal by the 1891 Anglo-Portuguese Convention (q. v.).
        Within present Rhodesia "Gazaland" has since been applied
        loosely to refer to the Melsetter and Chipinga districts (qq. v.).
        The Portuguese made "Gaza" the official name of an adminis-
        trative district south of the Sabi (Save) River.   (Cf. MATA-
        BELELAND; MASHONALAND; MANICALAND.)

GEMSTONES.   Although the country is a major producer of precious
        gems, production accounts for only a minor part of the total
        value of mineral (q. v.) production, and is undertaken mostly by
        "small-workers" (q. v.).   Nearly all varieties of gemstones are
        found in the country.   Most occur in alluvial deposits in the
        Somabula Forest area (q. v.).   Diamond production began there
        in 1906, and accounted for the largest part of gemstone produc-
        tion until the late 1950s, when production virtually ceased.
        Ruby, sapphire, and other gem deposits have been found mainly
        in association with diamonds.   In 1965 emeralds were first dis-
        covered in the Belingwe District (q. v.).   These now account for
        the bulk of gemstone production, much of which goes into local
        jewelry markets.   (See also MTOROLITE.)

GENEVA CONFERENCE (1976).   The first major attempt at a ne-
        gotiated constitutional settlement after the abortive August 1975
        Victoria Falls Conference (q. v.), and the first settlement at-
        tempt in which Britain was directly involved after the 1972
        Pearce Commission (q. v.), the late 1976 Geneva Conference
        was the product of a direct American diplomatic initiative.   On
        September 19, 1976, U. S. Secretary of State Henry Kissinger
        met with Ian Smith in Pretoria, outlining to him a settlement

proposal which the Rhodesian government accepted under apparent pressure from the South African government. On September 24th Smith publicly announced his government's willingness to negotiate a settlement leading to African majority rule within a two year period. This was a major retreat from his 1964 vow never to permit majority rule within his lifetime, but the announcement was greeted skeptically by nationalist leaders, and it appeared that there were some discrepancies between the plan Kissinger presented to Smith and the proposals he communicated to the "Frontline Presidents" group (q. v.).

Despite African reservations, a conference to discuss the settlement proposals was convened at Geneva on October 28th under the chairmanship of British UN Ambassador Ivor Richards. Five official delegations attended: Smith's government; Ndabaningi Sithole's branch of ZANU; Abel Muzorewa's branch of the African National Council; Joshua Nkomo's wing of ANC; and Robert Mugabe's branch of ZANU (qq. v.). The last two men announced formation of a "Patriotic Front" (q. v.) on the eve of the conference.

The conference quickly became deadlocked over the issue of a timetable for transition to majority rule. The African nationalists agreed on a one-year deadline, but Smith demanded at least 23 months. Richards got the nationalists to compromise on a March 1, 1978, deadline, but the Smith government demurred and the issue was deferred. The next dispute centered on the composition of office-holders in any transition government. The Smith government insisted on adherence to the Kissinger proposals, which called for a complex two-tiered, multiracial council system, but the nationalists rejected the Kissinger proposals altogether, citing special objections to control of the police and military by Europeans.

In the second week of December the conference adjourned for the Christmas holidays without having achieved any substantive accords among the white and black delegations. Smith's increasing intransigence was attributed to his government's apparent successes in the current anti-guerrilla campaigns. In January 1977 the British government attempted to reopen the conference, but the Smith government refused to participate. A new British initiative was made by Foreign Secretary David Owen in April, but through July this came to nothing. Smith meanwhile dissolved Parliament and announced his intention to achieve an internal settlement on the basis of the original Kissinger proposals.

GIBBS, HUMPHREY VICARY (b. Nov. 22, 1902). Eighth and last Governor (q. v.) of Southern Rhodesia (1959-69). Born in London, Gibbs came to Southern Rhodesia in 1928 and started a farm near Bulawayo. He became prominent in national farming organizations and briefly represented Wankie* in the Legislative Assembly* in the late 1940s. In 1959 Edgar Whitehead (q. v.) nominated Gibbs to replace P. William-Powlett (q. v.) as Governor. Gibbs accepted the post on the assumption that his duties would be mostly ceremonial. In late 1963 he also served briefly as acting governor-general of the Federation* as it was being dissolved.

After the Rhodesian Front government proclaimed UDI in 1965, Gibbs attempted to dismiss Ian Smith from office, calling upon the population not to support the regime because UDI had made it illegal. Smith in turn tried to force Gibbs from the Government House residence by cutting off its utilities, but Gibbs held firm for more than three years. Meanwhile, the government disregarded his office, creating its own "Officer Administering the Government" (q.v.) with all the functions and perquisites of the governorship. Britain cited Gibbs' continued residence in Salisbury as evidence of its authority in the country, and had him attend both the "Tiger" and "Fearless" talks (qq.v.) as an "intermediary." After settlers voted to create a republic (q.v.) in June 1969, Gibbs resigned his post and returned to Britain, where he was feted. He then retired to his Rhodesian farm.

GIBIXHEGU. Once the name of Shaka's* chief town in Zululand, this name was briefly used for two Ndebele towns in Matabele-land* in the 19th century. When Kaliphi's (q.v.) division of migrants reached the Mulungwane Mountains (q.v.), they established a town of Gibixhegu as their center. This site was abandoned in favor of Mahlokohloko (q.v.) after Mzilikazi's arrival in mid-1839. When Lobengula became Ndebele king in early 1870, he established a new Gibixhegu at the headwaters of the Umzingwani River (q.v.). A year later he either abandoned this town, or changed its name to "Bulawayo" (q.v.), which he located a little to the north.

GLOBE AND PHOENIX MINE. Third largest gold (q.v.) mine in the country, ranking after mines at Chakari and Eiffel Flats (qq.v.). The mine is contiguous with the town of Que Que (q.v.), which has essentially arisen around it. Its gold-bearing ore is particularly rich. It is estimated that in pre-colonial times Africans extracted more than 1400 kg. of gold there. The modern mine has been in continuous production since 1902, producing over 100,000 kg. of gold.

GOKOMERE. Term for an early Iron Age (q.v.) culture, or industry, named after a site found near Fort Victoria* in the 1920s. Many Gokomere culture sites have since been found throughout Mashonaland and southern Matabeleland. The culture featured cultivation, livestock-raising (but without cattle*), metal-working, and "stamped ware" pottery. It flourished from c.A.D. 200 to about the tenth century, when it was displaced by the Leopard's Kopje culture (q.v.). The latter half of the Gokomere period has recently been divided into separate Zhizo and Malapati cultures. (Cf. ZIWA.)

GOKWE. Administrative center for the district of the same name, Gokwe stands on the northern edge of the Mafungabusi Plateau* (at 18° 13'S, 28° 56'E; alt. 1285 m.). Population in 1969 was 590 (96% Africans).

GOKWE DISTRICT.   Covers 23,030 sq. km. making up the northwestern section of Midlands Province (q.v.).   It previously was
the largest chunk of the former Sebungwe District (q.v.).   Except for some Purchase Land (q.v.) in the northeast, and some
national land and European land in the southeast, the entire district is made up of Tribal Trust Land (q.v.).   Population in
1969 was nearly 135,000.   The district borders the provinces
of Matabeleland North on the west and south; Mashonaland North
on the north; and Mashonaland South on the east (qq.v.).   It is
connected to the rest of Midlands Province by Que Que District
(q.v.) on the southeast.

GOLD.   It would be difficult to exaggerate the role gold has played
in the country's history.   It appears first to have been mined
in the northern areas around the 7th century.   By about the 11th
century mines were operating throughout most of the presently-
known gold-bearing areas, which correspond, very roughly, to
the Central Plateau (q.v.).   The identity of these "ancient" (q.v.)
miners is often treated as a mystery, but they were almost
certainly Shona-speaking peoples.   Trade with Muslim (q.v.)
settlements on the east coast may have started as early as the
10th century.   It clearly was flourishing by the 12th century,
when monumental stone-building commenced at Zimbabwe (q.v.).
    By the late 15th century the Munhumutapa state (q.v.) in
the northeast was controlling most of the coastal trade for the
country.   Rulers taxed production heavily and most of the output
was traded for cloth and luxury goods.   Muslim traders entered
the country from Sofala (q.v.) in order to facilitate the trade,
but production remained firmly in Shona hands.   Portuguese
(q.v.) penetration into the country from the early 16th century
was motivated largely by desire to monopolize the gold trade.
    Although Shona miners occasionally worked in shafts more
than 30 m. deep, most extraction was limited to surface deposits.
It appears that these were largely worked out by the 18th century.
The Mfecane (q.v.) invasions of the early 19th century greatly
disrupted mining, and most remaining workings were then abandoned.   The newly-arrived Ndebele (q.v.) were not gold miners.
Further, they actively inhibited Shona trade and vigorously attempted to prevent Europeans from prospecting in the country.
Despite their efforts, Henry Hartley and Karl Mauch (qq.v.)
identified old gold workings during the 1860s.   After Mauch
publicized his findings, a minor European gold rush began.
Concession-hunters flocked to Lobengula's (q.v.) court in the
1870s and 1880s.   Lobengula reluctantly awarded concessions to
the Tati and Northern Goldfields regions (qq.v.), but no significant production was achieved before the 1890s.
    Exaggerated descriptions of the country's gold prospects
and romantic notions about "King Solomon's Mines" and "Ophir"
(q.v.) greatly stimulated fresh European interest in the country,
especially after the major gold discoveries in the Transvaal's*
Rand in the mid-1880s.   Cecil Rhodes' BSAC gained entry to the
country with Ndebele concessions, and recruited settlers and
mercenaries through promises of generous mining claims.

European prospectors swarmed over the country in the 1890s, mostly simply looking for signs of abandoned Shona gold workings.   More than 150,000 claims were registered before 1900, but only 2258 kg. of gold were extracted, and only a fraction of the early miners made any profits.   (See also RHODESIA ANCIENT RUINS, LTD.)

From the 1890s to the 1930s gold mining was the country's single most important industry.   Production generally rose until 1940, when it peaked at 23,533 kg., then worth £6,900,000. Most of this gold was exported, accounting for nearly 60% of the country's export trade.   Thereafter gold production gradually declined.   In 1952 it was displaced by asbestos (q.v.) as the leading mineral (q.v.) product.   Some recovery was effected when the government began subsidizing mining in late 1963. Production was further boosted by the rising free market price of gold in the early 1970s.

Thousands of "small-workers" (q.v.) dominated gold production during the early decades of European occupation, but they were gradually replaced by larger operations which could afford the capital equipment necessary to work increasingly deep deposits.   By 1930 two-thirds of production was achieved by large mines.   By 1958 there were only 256 mines in the country.   Recent expansion has led to the reopening of many old mines, but these are mainly extensions of existing large-scale operations.   The presently leading mining centers are at Chakari, Que Que, Arcturus, Gwanda, and elsewhere (qq.v.). Eiffel Flats (q.v.) was also once a leading center.

GOLDEN VALLEY.   Mining town located 20 km. northwest of Gatooma* (at 18°13'S, 29°48'E).   Golden Valley gold (q.v.) mine was opened there in 1899.   Tungsten is also produced locally. Population in 1969 was 3310 (98% Africans).

GOMBWE (pl. makombwe).   Shona name for a type of "lion spirit" medium, similar to, and sometimes synonymous with, the more important mhondoro (q.v.).   Like mhondoro, the word gombwe refers both to the spirit and to its medium (see SVIKIRO).   Unlike most mhondoro mediums, however, the makombwe tend to lack territorial bases, and to work more frequently as professional healers and diviners.   The mediums represent the spirits of long-dead ancestors, but usually their own personal reputations are more important to their success.   (See RELIGION-- SHONA.)

GONAKUDZINGWA.   Former government detention camp for political prisoners, located in the extreme southeastern corner of the country near the Limpopo River*.   Through the 1960s the camp was used primarily to hold ZAPU supporters, including Joshua Nkomo (q.v.).   It was closed in May 1974 in anticipation of difficulties with the new regime in neighboring Mozambique (q.v.).

GONA-RE-ZHOU.   Kentucky-shaped game reserve (q.v.) covering 1370 sq. km. along the southeastern border with Mozambique

(q. v.). It stretches between the Sabi River on the northeast and
the Nuanetsi River (qq. v.) on the southwest. This undeveloped
reserve became an area of nationalist guerrilla incursions in the
mid-1970s.

GOOLD-ADAMS, HAMILTON JOHN (June 27, 1858-April 12, 1920).
Irish-born British army officer. After military experience
around the world, Goold-Adams served in the Warren Expedition
which made Botswana the Bechuanaland Protectorate in 1885
(qq. v.). Afterwards he was transferred to the new Bechuanaland Border Police (q. v.), succeeding Frederick Carrington
(q. v.) as commander in May 1883. Later that year he commanded the southern British invasion column in the Ndebele
War (q. v.; see also GAMPU SITHOLE). He resigned from the
BBP in March 1895, and later held administrative posts in South
Africa and Cyprus.

GOROMANZI. Administrative center of the district of the same
name, located directly east of Salisbury (at 17° 51'S, 31° 23'E).

GOROMANZI DISTRICT. An area of 2805 sq. km. which formerly
was part of the Salisbury District (q. v.), which now forms its
western border. It is a well-watered region, with important
agricultural and mining industries. Except for some Tribal
Trust Land (q. v.) territory on the east, the district is reserved
for Europeans. In 1969 the population included 92,900 Africans
and 1770 Europeans. The district lies at the center of the
Mashonaland South Province (q. v.), bordering the districts of
Mrewa on the east; Marandellas on the south; and Mazoe, Bindura, and Shamva (qq. v.) on the north.

GOULDSBURY, HENRY CULLEN (May 9, 1881-Aug. 27, 1916). A
popular writer within the country's European community, Gouldsbury came to the country from Britain in 1902 as a civil servant.
He wrote stories and verse about European life in Mashonaland,
even after he was transferred to Northern Rhodesia in 1908. He
was killed in East Africa during the First World War. He left
ten published novels and volumes of poems, including a posthu-
mous collection of his best verse, Rhodesian Rhymes (1932).
(See LITERATURE.)

GOUVEIA (variant: Guveya). African nickname for M. A. de Sousa
(q. v.).

GOVA. Several otherwise unrelated Shona groups share this name.
The Gova branch of Korekore (q. v.) live in the Zambezi Valley*
near Kariba*. The Gova branch of Zezuru (q. v.) live in Mazoe
District*, north of Salisbury. The Karanga (q. v.) Gova live in
the Selukwe District*.

GOVERA. A branch of the Karanga (q. v.) cluster of Shona. (See
GUTU.)

GOVERNORS OF SOUTHERN RHODESIA (1923-1969).   When the British government took over responsibility for the country from the
BSAC in 1923, the colony's new constitution (q.v.) established
the office of Governor as local head of state and representative
of the British Crown.   The British government had sole right to
select the governors, but in practice it consulted with the leaders
of the local settler government.   In 1942 such consultation was
formalized, and by the 1950s the local Prime Ministers (q.v.)
were nominating the governors themselves.
        As head of state, the Governor appointed prime ministers,
authorized legislation, and had other executive functions.   Under
the original constitution the Governor was vested with enormous
reserve powers over the local government, but these were almost never exercised.   Nevertheless, the governors wielded significant influence over government policies and ministerial appointments, particularly in the early days of Responsible Government (q.v.) when the local office-holders were inexperienced.
Until UDI in 1965 the governors were noted for working closely
with the prime ministers, and no significant conflicts ever developed, a state of affairs made more possible by the gradual
curtailment of the governors' reserve powers.   By the late
1950s the governors' duties were mostly perfunctory and ceremonial.   After UDI the Rhodesian Front government replaced
the governor with its own "Officer Administering the Government" (q.v.), who assumed the former's duties and perquisites.
Britain nevertheless retained its governor in Salisbury until
June 1969, when the settlers voted to create a republic (q.v.).
        Governors, 1923-69:   1923-8 J. R. Chancellor; 1928-34
C. H. Rodwell; 1935-42 H. J. Stanley; 1942-4 E. Baring; 1945-
6 E. C. Tait; 1947-54 J. N. Kennedy; 1954-9 P. B. R. W.
William-Powlett; 1959-69 H. V. Gibbs (qq.v.).

GREAT DYKE.   Natural geological formation, so named because of
its distinctive appearance on geological maps.   Not a true "dike"
in the geological sense, the Great Dyke is a narrow mass of
ultra-basic and basic rocks, stretching in a nearly straight line
c. 515 km. long, from Belingwe in the south, to Sipolilo (qq.v.)
in the north.   Chrome and other minerals (qq.v.) are mined
from it at many points.

GREAT ZIMBABWE   see   ZIMBABWE RUINS

GREY, ALBERT HENRY GEORGE (4th Earl Grey from 1894) (Nov.
28, 1851-Aug. 29, 1917).   After serving in the British Parliament (1880-86), Grey was asked by Cecil Rhodes to become a
founder-director of the BSAC (q.v.) when it got its Charter* in
1889.   Grey visited Southern Rhodesia in 1894, and then returned
there in April 1896 to replace L. S. Jameson (q.v.) as Administrator (q.v.).   His arrival coincided with the outbreak of
the Ndebele Revolt (q.v.), and Grey later participated in Rhodes'
negotiations with rebel leaders in the Matopo Hills (see "IN-
DABA").   From Bulawayo, Grey went to Salisbury to assist in
putting down the still active Shona Revolt.   He resigned his

administrative post in June 1897, leaving the country for good. He retained his seat on the BSAC board until 1903, and then began a seven year stint as governor-general of Canada.

GRIQUA.   South African Coloured people (q.v.), of mainly Khoi (q.v.) and Afrikaner (q.v.) descent.   The original Griqua migrated out of the Cape Colony at the end of the 18th century, settling around the Orange River.   During the first half of the 19th century they hunted and traded extensively in the deeper interior.   Mzilikazi's Ndebele clashed with Griqua raiding parties several times in the Transvaal* in the 1820s and 1830s, but other Griqua later became successful hunters (q.v.) and traders in Matabeleland*.   (See WILLIAM THE GRIQUA.)

GROBLER, PIETER D. C. J. (variant: Grobelaar) (May 2, 1855-1888).   Afrikaner* hunter, trader, and diplomatic agent for the South African Republic of the Transvaal (q.v.).   After several commercial trips to Matabeleland* during the 1880s, Grobler was sent back there by the Transvaal government to negotiate a treaty with Lobengula (q.v.).   On July 30, 1887 he got his Ndebele king to sign what became known as the "Grobler Treaty," a rather one-sided document reaffirming the treaty A. H. Potgieter (q.v.) was said to have made with Mzilikazi in 1853.   Although the treaty acknowledged Ndebele independence, it called Lobengula a Transvaal ally, binding him to assist the Republic militarily.   It also required the Ndebele to extend considerable rights to Transvalers in Matabeleland, as well as to accept a consul at Bulawayo.   The existence of the treaty was not announced until after the signing of the Rudd Concession (q.v.) the next year.   Lobengula denied having signed the treaty, and the British government discounted its authenticity.   Grobler himself was shot by an Ngwato* patrol while traveling to take up the post of consul; he later died from his wound.   The whole episode helped to quicken the pace of British involvement north of the Limpopo.

GROOTBOOM, JOHN (fl. 1890s).   South African scout.   An enigmatic figure, Grootboom was evidently a Southern Nguni* man, for he was variously described as either a Xhosa, a Thembu, or an Mfengu (q.v.).   He came to Matabeleland* in the 1880s as a wagon-driver for Charles Helm (q.v.).   During the 1893 Ndebele War (q.v.) he served as a scout for BSAC forces.   At the end of the war he carried a message from L. S. Jameson (q.v.) to the fleeing Lobengula (q.v.) asking for the latter's surrender.   During the 1896 Revolt (q.v.) he was the best-known African scout working for the British.   He helped to arrange the first "indaba" (q.v.), which he attended.   Afterwards he accepted only a horse from Cecil Rhodes as payment and then disappeared from historical record.

GUBULAWAYO (variant: Kubulawayo).   Sindebele* locative form for Bulawayo (q.v.).

GUERRILLAS, AFRICAN NATIONALIST see MILITARY FORCES

GUEST, ERNEST LUCAS (Aug. 20, 1882-Sept. 21, 1972). Born
and educated in South Africa, Guest came to Southern Rhodesia
as a high court solicitor in 1910. He was elected to the Legislative Assembly* in 1928, rising to cabinet rank under Godfrey
Huggins (q.v.) in 1938. During his last years in the Assembly
(1944-48) he served as leader of the house and as Huggins'
leading parliamentary spokesman. A representative of the conservative wing of the United Party (q.v.), he opposed Huggins'
pet project, Federation (q.v.).

GULUBAHWE CAVE (variant: Gulabahwa). Located just east of the
Matopo Hills National Park (q.v.), Gulubahwe contains rock
paintings (q.v.) which feature an unusual picture of a snake 4.5
meters long, with small human figures on its back.

GUNDWANE NDIWENI see KALIPHI

GUNGUNYANE (variants: Gungunhana; Ngungunyana) (c.1850-1906).
Last king of the Gaza (q.v.), Gungunyane illegally seized power
on the death of his father Mzila (q.v.) in 1884. In many ways
his reign parallels that of his contemporary, the Ndebele king
Lobengula (q.v.), whose daughter he married. The two Nguni*
rulers found themselves the last major independent African
rulers in southern Africa during the era of rapid European takeover. Further, Gungunyane also found his military position
relative to his African neighbors deteriorating. His armies
could not overcome the Manyika of Mutasa (q.v.) to his north,
and his Chopi tributaries in the south were successfully defying
him. In 1889 he shifted his capital Manhlagazi (q.v.) from
Mount Silinda (q.v.) in the present Chipinga District (q.v.) to
the lower Limpopo Basin in southern Mozambique (q.v.). As
the Gaza were still the major power in the region, the BSAC
negotiated with him in the hope of obtaining a seaport for future
Rhodesia. On October 4, 1890, Gungunyane signed a concession* with a BSAC agent very similar to the Rudd Concession
(q.v.), which Lobengula had signed two years earlier. The
Company's efforts to carry through with the deal collapsed, however, when the British and Portuguese governments partitioned
their southern African spheres of interest in such a way as to
leave Gungunyane in the Portuguese domain (see ANGLO-PORTU-
GUESE CONVENTION). In 1895 the Portuguese finally conquered
the Gaza kingdom, effectively destroying it. Gungunyane was
exiled to the Azores Islands, where he died a decade later.

GUNUVUTWA see GURUHUSWA; BUTUA

GURUHUSWA (variants: Guruuswa; Gunuuswa; Gunuvutwa; etc.).
Traditional Shona name for the southwestern part of the coun-
try--the same region known to the early Portuguese (q.v.) as
"Butua" (q.v.). Guruhuswa was the center of the Togwa and

Changamire states (qq.v.), and is believed to have corresponded roughly with the region known as Matabeleland (q.v.) in the 19th century. (Cf. DANDE; MBIRE.)

GUSU. Ndebele name for the sandy-soiled country northwest of central Matabeleland (q.v.).

GUTI. Widely-used Chishona* word (pl. makuti) for misty or drizzly weather of the kind especially common during the "winter" months of maritime wind invasions from the east. The Sindebele* equivalent term is umkhiso. (See CLIMATE.)

GUTU (variant: Mukutu). Dynastic title of the rulers of the Govera (q.v.) branch of Karanga (q.v.) in the present Gutu District (q.v.). During the 19th century the Govera were caught between Ndebele and Gaza (qq.v.) raids. They managed to expel the Gaza in 1880, but afterwards they became reluctant tributaries to the Ndebele. Although the Ndebele assisted Gutu Makuvaza to attain his position in 1892, they raided him the same year. The next year Gutu allied with the British in the Ndebele War (q.v.).

GUTU DISTRICT. Originally the northeastern part of Victoria District (q.v.), Gutu District became a separate district in 1906. It now covers 5780 sq. km. in the extreme northern part of the Victoria Province (q.v.). It borders Midlands Province on the northwest; Manicalands Province on the northeast; and Victoria and Bikita (qq.v.) districts on the south. The district contains large sections of Purchase Land and Tribal Trust Land (qq.v.) in its eastern parts, while its upland western section is reserved for Europeans. District population in 1969 was 152,000, including only 450 Europeans, who were mostly Afrikaners*. District headquarters are at the village of Gutu (19° 39'S, 31° 10'E). Another district center is Chatsworth (q.v.).

GWABALANDA MATHE (variant: Kabalonte) (fl. 1830s-1860s). Ndebele induna*, said to have been one of Mzilikazi's most influential chiefs during the 1830s. When the Ndebele migrated to Matabeleland in 1838-9, Gwabalanda traveled with Mzilikazi's division. In the political crisis which ensued (see NKULUMANE and KALIPHI) he is said to have saved the young Lobengula (q.v.) from execution. Thereafter his influence in the kingdom seems to have declined, though he was the induna of the important Mhlahlandhlela ibutho (q.v.) during the last years of Mzilikazi's life in the 1860s. His position was inherited by his son Luthuli, who became one of Lobengula's top advisers during the late 1880s.

GWAI RIVER (variant: Gwaai). One of the Zambezi River's (q.v.) main southern affluents, the Gwai rises near Figtree (q.v.), flowing northwest to join the Zambezi c.130 km. below the Victoria Falls (q.v.). The Gwai's chief tributaries are the Umguza, Bembezi, Bubi, and Shangani (qq.v.), all of which enter it from the east.

GWANDA.   Administrative center for the district of the same name
(at 20° 56'S, 29° E; alt. 985 m.).   Founded as a mining center
at the beginning of this century, Gwanda developed into an important livestock shipping depot as well after a railway (q.v.)
line was extended to it from Heany (q.v.) in 1905.   In 1969 its
population was 2050 (80% Africans).

GWANDA DISTRICT.   A Y-shaped region covering 10,875 sq. km.
in the central part of Matabeleland South Province (q.v.).   The
district was formerly more than twice as large, but it gave up
its southeastern section to form a new Beitbridge District (q.v.).
It now borders Botswana on the south; and the districts of Matobo on the west; Umzingwane, Insiza, and Belingwe on the
north; and Nuanetsi (qq.v.) on the northeast.   A poorly-watered
region, the district's main industries are cattle and mining
(qq.v.).   Its land is divided roughly equally between Tribal
Trust Land and European ranches.   Its population in 1969 included 78,920 Africans and 1095 Europeans.   Other district
centers include West Nicholson and Colleen Bawn (qq.v.).

GWEBI AGRICULTURAL COLLEGE.   Government agricultural school
for Europeans; located on a large farm just west of Salisbury,
astride the road to Sinoia* (at 17° 41'S, 30° 50'E).   The site
was established as a government demonstration, experimental,
and training farm between 1909 and 1915.   In 1950 it was transformed into an agricultural college.   (Cf. CHIBERO COLLEGE
OF AGRICULTURE.)

GWELO.   One of the largest towns in the country (see URBANIZA-
TION), Gwelo is located near the intersection of the Gwelo
River (q.v.) and the main road between Bulawayo and Salisbury
(at 19° 27'S, 29° 48'E; alt. 1415 m.).   It was founded in 1894
amidst a thriving gold mining area, but it eventually developed
into one of the country's most important commercial and industrial centers.   It enjoys the advantages of good water and electricity supplies, and a location at the junction of many roads
and railway lines in the very center of the country.   It now has
both light and heavy industries, and is one of the most important
stock and dairying centers of the country.   In 1971 it was granted
"city" status.   Estimated population at the beginning of 1975 was
62,000 (82% Africans; 15% Europeans).   Gwelo is also administrative center of the Gwelo District.

GWELO DISTRICT.   Located in the center of the country in Midlands
Province (q.v.), Gwelo District covers 6795 sq. km. between the
upper Shangani and Umniati rivers (qq.v.).   It was formerly more
than twice as large, but the northern section was separated to
help form the newer Que Que District (q.v.).   Other neighboring
districts are Chilimanzi on the east; Selukwe on the southeast;
Insiza on the south; and Bubi on the west (qq.v.).   The district
is rich in gold, chrome and other minerals (qq.v.).   With the
exception of some small Tribal Trust Land (q.v.) territory, the
entire district is reserved for Europeans (see LAND TENURE

ACT). Population in 1969 included 92,120 Africans and 9970
Europeans.

GWELO RIVER. Rises just south of Gwelo (q.v.), flowing northwest to join the Shangani River (q.v.) southwest of the Mafungabusi Plateau (q.v.). The name derives from the Sindebele* description of the river's steep banks.

GWELO TIMES. Independent weekly Gwelo (q.v.) newspaper; founded
in August 1897, when its owners bought out the Northern Optimist, which had started three years earlier. (See PRESS.)

GWINDINGWI HILL. Site of the chief town of the Shona ruler Makoni (q.v.) during the 19th century. The hill, which is honey-
combed with deep caves, served as the Makoni's stronghold
during the 1896-7 Revolt (q.v.) until British forces used dynamite to blast out resisters (at 18°55'S, 32°26'E).

                         - H -

HAGGARD, HENRY RIDER (June 22, 1856-May 14, 1925). English
novelist. Haggard did not visit present Rhodesia until 1914, but
he worked for the British colonial government in South Africa
between 1875 and 1879 and gathered vague information on Rhodesia which he later used in some of his romantic adventure
novels. King Solomon's Mines (1885), for example, is clearly
inspired by the Zimbabwe Ruins (q.v.) and the stories of "Ophir"
(q.v.) which were circulating in South Africa in the 1870s. His
character Allan Quartermain is said to have been modeled on
the famous hunter F. C. Selous (q.v.). Most interesting is the
character in Mines called "Umbopa," who appears to have been
based upon the Ndebele royal pretender "Nkulumane" (q.v.)--
who, like Haggard, had worked for Theophilus Shepstone (q.v.).

HAKATA. Shona divining "dice." Of several types used, the most
important are carved wooden, ivory, or bone pieces. Each
piece is typically inscribed with a special symbol, and the di-
viner--usually an nganga (q.v.)--throws them in multiples of
four. The diviner interprets the throws according to established
formulae similar in principle to Tarot card reading.

HALFWAY HOUSE RUIN. Ruin site in the Bumbuzi group (q.v.),
named after a local hotel.

HALL, RICHARD NICKLIN (1853-Nov. 18, 1914). Pioneer archaeologist and journalist. An English lawyer, Hall came to the country
around 1897 to work for a farmers' association and the Bulawayo
chamber of commerce. He edited some local newspapers (see
PRESS) and helped to publicize the country in London, but he
somehow ran afoul of the BSAC administration. Around 1900,
W. G. Neal, a director of Rhodesia Ancient Ruins, Ltd. (q.v.),
turned over to Hall his company's descriptive records of the

many Iron Age ruins (q.v.) its prospectors had ransacked. The
two men used this and other data to write Ancient Ruins of Rhodesia (London, 1902), a massive compendium which immediately
attracted considerable popular attention. With his reputation
somewhat restored, Hall was made "Curator of Great Zimbabwe," a post he held for most of 1902 to 1904. Although he
was assigned merely to prepare the ruins for tourists, he undertook large scale excavations of the site. A completely untrained
archaeologist, he destroyed deep stratigraphical layers in order
to remove evidence of what he regarded as "degenerate" African
occupation over presumably alien ancient deposits. In 1905 he
published Great Zimbabwe, using his new findings to elaborate
on the theories of ancient Near Eastern builders he had presented in his first book. He was removed from his curator
post, and the administration brought in D. Randall-MacIver
(q.v.), a trained archaeologist, to conduct proper investigations.
Randall-MacIver condemned Hall's techniques and completely
overturned his interpretations by conclusively demonstrating that
the country's megalithic ruins had purely African origins. An
acrimonious debate ensued in which the embarrassed Hall was
supported by his fellow settlers.
    In 1909 Hall published an emotional rebuttal to Randall-
MacIver, Prehistoric Rhodesia, in which he introduced the explicitly racialist argument that Africans were incapable of sustaining a non-degenerate culture. Though Hall is damned by
modern archaeologists for his destructive digs and unfounded
interpretations, his books remain valuable for their generally
reliable descriptive material--especially of structures which no
longer stand. Further, his conclusions about non-African origins
of the ruins have remained popular among the lay settler community, and are still an active component in the Zimbabwe Controversy (q.v.).

HAMPDEN, MOUNT (Shona name: Musitikwe). Located 16 km.
    northwest of Salisbury, Mount Hampden rises 1600 meters. It
    is adjacent to a small town which shares its name. The moun-
    tain was designated as the destination of the Pioneer Column
    (q.v.) when the BSAC occupied Mashonaland* in 1890.

HARARE (variant: Harari). Salisbury's (q.v.) oldest and largest
    African township; located immediately south of the city center
    between two industrial areas. Since its establishment as a
    township in 1907, Harare has developed into one of the country's
    most important urban African centers. Roughly two-thirds of
    its residents are single men, and almost all of its occupants are
    renters. In 1973 its population density was estimated to be 15
    times greater than that of Salisbury as a whole. Population in
    the 1969 census was 58,010.

HARPER, WILLIAM JOHN ("Wild Bill") (b. July 22, 1916). Born in
    Calcutta, India, Harper came to Southern Rhodesia in 1949 after
    service in the Royal Air Force. In 1958 he was elected to the
    Legislative Assembly (q.v.) for Gatooma* on the Dominion Party

(q.v.) ticket.   The next year he became president of the DP
and emerged as a leading spokesman for white supremacy.   He
joined Winston Field's (q.v.) cabinet in 1962, and was made
Minister of Internal Affairs by Ian Smith (q.v.) in 1964.   Ada-
mantly opposed to any kind of direct African parliamentary representation, he split with Smith in July 1968 over the terms of
the new draft constitution (q.v.), resigning from both the cabinet and the ruling Rhodesian Front Party (q.v.).   During the
Pearce Commission (q.v.) investigation in early 1972 he briefly
re-emerged to criticize Smith and to help found the ultraright
wing United Front Party.

HARTLEY, HENRY (1815-Feb. 1876).   An English-born hunter
    (q.v.), Hartley first came to South Africa in 1820.   In 1859
    he began hunting north of the Limpopo River*.   Six years later
    he became one of the first Europeans permitted by Mzilikazi
    (q.v.) to hunt in Mashonaland*, where he observed old Shona
    gold (q.v.) workings near the Umfuli River (q.v.).   In 1866 and
    1867 he returned to Mashonaland with Karl Mauch (q.v.), who
    confirmed the presence of gold and publicized the findings to the
    world.   Hartley himself retired from hunting in 1870, while
    European prospectors flooded into the country.

HARTLEY.   Town in the Hartley Hills (18° 12'S, 30° 23'E) about 100
    km. southwest of Salisbury on the main road and railway to
    Bulawayo.   The hills were named after Henry Hartley (q.v.),
    who frequently camped there.   The present town was founded in
    1901--relocated from a site founded c. 29 km. further east a
    decade earlier.   Hartley is a commercial and administrative
    center for the Hartley District (q.v.).   Population in 1969 was
    8630 (92% Africans).

HARTLEY DISTRICT.   Located in the western part of Mashonaland
    South Province (q.v.), Hartley District covers 7345 sq. km. in
    a region rich in gold, nickel and other minerals (qq.v.), as
    well as maize, cotton, and cattle (qq.v.).   The district was
    originally almost twice as large, but it gave up its southwestern
    sector to form the new Gatooma District (q.v.).   Most of the
    district is reserved for Europeans (see LAND TENURE ACT).
    In addition to Gatooma, the district borders Lomagundi District
    on the north, where the boundary is defined by the Umfuli River;
    and Salisbury District (qq.v.) on the east.   The population in
    1969 included 120,750 Africans and 2930 Europeans.

HARTMANN, ANDREW (1851-Dec. 27, 1928).   An Austrian Jesuit
    missionary, Hartmann came to Bulawayo in 1888 as a priest in
    the Zambezi Mission (q.v.).   He spent two years with Peter
    Prestage at Empandeni (qq.v.), and then served as Roman Catho-
    lic chaplain with the BSAC Pioneer Column (q.v.).   On behalf of
    the Jesuits, he accepted from the BSAC a tract of land near
    Salisbury on which he and Prestage founded the Chishawasha
    Mission (q.v.).   After the Revolts (q.v.) he returned to Empan-
    deni, where he remained until 1924.

HAYETE.   Spelling variation of <u>Bayete</u>, the Ndebele royal salute.

HEADLANDS.   Railroad siding village roughly midway between Salisbury and Umtali (qq. v.) in the Makoni District* (at 18° 17'S,
32° 3'E; alt. 1570 m.).   Nearby is the Inyati Mine, one of the
country's major copper (q. v.) producers.

HEADRINGS.   (Sindebele*: sing. <u>isidlodlo</u>; pl. <u>izidlodlo</u>).   Mixture
of natural, growing hair and <u>gum</u>, sewn into tight rings on the
heads of Ndebele and other northern Nguni* men during the 19th
century.   (See IJAHA; INDODA.)

HEALTH.   (1) <u>Human health</u>.   Although the country lies completely
within the tropics, its population enjoys one of the highest
standards of health in Africa.   Prior to the 20th century the
country was relatively free of many endemic diseases widespread in areas north of the Zambezi River.   Malaria (q. v.)
has historically afflicted people in regions below 1000 meters,
and it remains a major health problem.   Other maladies, such
as sleeping sickness, bilharzia, typhoid (qq. v.), and tuberculosis, became local threats only with the development of modern
international labor migration.   Epidemic diseases, such as
smallpox and influenza (qq. v.), have invaded the country at
various times in recorded history.   (See also LEPROSY;   TRA
CHOMA; RABIES.)
     Prior to the advent of European settlement in the 1890s
medical treatment was largely in the hands of healers and diviners who treated patients with herbal medicines and psychosomatic cures closely tied to traditional religious beliefs (see
RELIGION--SHONA).   These were often efficacious against mental illness and mild physical ailments, but mortality rates were
high and life expectancies short.   Christian missionaries (q. v.)
began offering Western medical treatments to Africans during
the 1860s, but such services had a negligible impact, except
among a small Ndebele elite.
     Since the country was colonized in the 1890s, the European governments have played a leading role in providing preventative and curative medical services.   The BSAC administration established a civil medical department in 1897, with A. M.
Fleming (q. v.) as the first director.   In 1923 this agency became the Public Health Department.   In 1948 the department
was made into a separate Health Ministry, which fell under the
aegis of the Federation (q. v.) government between 1953 and
1963.   The government has operated most of the country's
hospitals, whose facilities have been mostly segregated along
racial lines, and it has also supported mission hospitals.   Other
hospitals have been run by the larger mines.   By the early
1970s there were 112 government hospitals, as well as numerous rural clinics.   In 1975 there were about 333 inhabitants per
hospital bed, and c. 9300 people per physician.   A medical
school was opened at the University (q. v.) in 1963.   Life expectancy is estimated at c. 64 years at birth, and the population
(q. v.) growth rate among Africans is among the highest in the
world.

(2) <u>Animal health</u>. Disease has also played a major role
in the breeding of domestic animals in both the agricultural
(q. v.) and transportation industries. The country's indigenous
and imported cattle (q. v.) have been periodically devastated by
epidemics of lung-sickness, rinderpest, East Coast Fever (qq.v.),
and hoof-and-mouth disease--the last particularly in the 1930s.
An endemic disease, nagana (q. v.), has long inhibited the raising of livestock in the country's tsetse fly (q. v.) areas. These
diseases and horsesickness (q. v.) have also made horses (q. v.)
particularly difficult animals to raise in the country.

HEANY, MAURICE (1856-June 25, 1927). Born in Virginia, Heany
served in the United States army before going to South Africa
in the 1870s. In 1884-5 he served in the Warren Expedition
which made Botswana into the Bechuanaland Protectorate, and
then joined the Bechuanaland Border Police (qq. v.), where he
met Frank Johnson and H. J. Borrow (qq. v.), with whom he
formed a concession-seeking company. In 1890 he was a member of the Pioneer Column (q. v.) which occupied Mashonaland*,
and in 1893 he fought in the Ndebele War (q. v.). In 1895 he
participated in the Jameson Raid (q. v.), but managed to evade
capture. He spent his last years in Bulawayo, where he died.

HEANY JUNCTION. Village 25 km. east of Bulawayo on the main
railway (q. v.) line and road to Gwelo* (at 20° 5'S, 28° 47'E;
alt. 1360 m.). In 1905 a branch railway line was extended
south from Heany Junction to West Nicholson (q. v.) to serve
mines in the Gwanda Valley. Since World War II Heany has
been an important military training center.

HELM, CHARLES DANIEL (1844-Jan. 1915). A South African-born
agent of the London Missionary Society (q. v.), Helm joined
J. B. Thomson at Hope Fountain (qq. v.) in 1875. In 1888 he
acted as interpreter and intermediary during Lobengula's (q. v.)
negotiations with Cecil Rhodes' representatives. Helm is said
to have advised Lobengula to sign one sweeping concession*
rather than many small ones, and he himself signed the resulting Rudd Concession (q. v.) as a witness. He retired from mission work in 1914, and was replaced at Hope Fountain by Neville
Jones (q. v.).

HERA (Vahera). Shona-speaking group, usually classified as a
branch of the Zezuru (q. v.), though some Hera regard themselves as Karanga (q. v.). By the 19th century there were
several autonomous Hera chiefdoms. One has been ruled by
the Hwata dynasty (q. v.) in the southern Mazoe District (q. v.).
Branches under the Mutekedzi and Nyashanu dynasties are in
the Buhera District (q. v.), which is named after the Hera.
These chiefdoms apparently split off from the Munhumutapa
state (q. v.) about 300 years ago. Living near Mount Wedza
(q. v.), the Hera and their neighbors, the Njanja (q. v.), became famous as iron-workers.

HIGH VELD. Land over 1220 meters, including the Central Plateau
and the Eastern Highlands (qq.v.; see ALTITUDINAL ZONES).

HIGHFIELD. Second largest of Salisbury's (q.v.) African townships;
located 8 km. southwest of the city center, just west of the
main road to Fort Victoria*. In 1969 the population was 52,560.
(N.B.: the similarly named "Highfields" is a railroad siding
located 58 km. northwest of Bulawayo.)

HILTON YOUNG COMMISSION (1927-8). British Imperial commission created to investigate the possibilities of closer union between the British territories of east and central Africa. Sir
Edward Hilton Young chaired the body. After collecting evidence
in the various territories, the Commission issued its report in
1929 (Cmd. 3234). The report recommended against immediate
amalgamation (q.v.) of Southern and Northern Rhodesia, but the
Commission members differed on future recommendations.
While the chairman suggested later partitioning Northern Rhodesia to enlarge Southern Rhodesia, the majority rejected adding
any territory to Southern Rhodesia. The majority opinion was
upheld by the British government and was reiterated in the report of the Bledisloe Commission (q.v.) a decade later.

HIPPO VALLEY. Center of a major sugar (q.v.) estate in the
southeastern low veld, near the confluence of the Mtilikwe and
Lundi rivers (qq.v.) (at 21°10'S, 31°33'E). Hippo Valley Estate was established by local Europeans in 1956. With the help
of government-assisted irrigation schemes, Hippo Valley and
neighboring Triangle (q.v.) developed into the country's foremost sugar producers by the early 1960s. The loss of export
markets after UDI hit the industry hard (see SANCTIONS). The
estate has since diversified its crops, but sugar remains predominant.

HIPPOPOTAMUSES. Once common throughout the country, these
amphibious pachyderms were extensively hunted during the late
19th century for their edible flesh, hides (see SJAMBOK), and
teeth (see IVORY). The animals are now largely restricted to
the Zambezi and Limpopo valleys, and are hunted on a very
limited basis (see HUNTING). Early Europeans often called
hippos "sea cows," an ironic name in view of the literal translation of the Greek word hippopotamus as "river horse."

HISTORICAL MONUMENTS COMMISSION (HMC). In 1936 the Southern Rhodesian Legislative Assembly* established the HMC, en-
trusting it with the tasks of designating, controlling, repairing,
restoring, and investigating pre-1890 African sites and pre-1910
European edifices (see "ANCIENT"; RUINS). Belated creation
of the HMC helped to preserve what was left of the many bat-
tered megalithic ruins, which had suffered in the well-meaning
but ignorant hands of the Public Works Department previously
(see RHODESIA ANCIENT RUINS, LTD; HALL, R. N.). By
1975 the HMC had designated 140 National Monuments on both

public and private lands.   The most important of these are
Stone Age sites (q.v.); rock paintings (q.v.); Iron Age sites
and ruins (qq.v.); early Portuguese sites, including fairs (q.v.);
1890s-era "pioneer" and Revolt sites (qq.v.); and graves, such
as World's View (q.v.).
    The HMC exercises exclusive control over all archaeo-
logical digs, and it employs the only resident professional archaeologists in the country. The scientific integrity of the
HMC has not been questioned, but its position as a government
agency with monopolistic control over archaeological research
has compromised its independence. Occasionally its work has
been threatened by hostile members of the government who dispute its findings (see ZIMBABWE CONTROVERSY). In 1973
the HMC was incorporated into the National Museums and Monuments Administration.

HLENGWE (Bahlengwe).   Bantu-speaking people of the Tsonga (or
    Thonga) group (q.v.), who occupy the southeastern districts of
    the country and most of southern Mozambique* and parts of the
    northern Transvaal*.   Only a small part of the nearly two mil-
    lion Tsonga live in present Rhodesia.   Tsonga is sometimes
    described as an Nguni language, but it occupies an independent,
    intermediary position between Nguni, Sotho and Venda (qq.v.),
    and is more distantly related to Shona.   During the early 19th
    century Hlengwe country was occupied by the Gaza state (q.v.),
    to which Hlengwe chiefdoms paid tribute.   The Hlengwe absorbed
    some Nguni vocabulary and cultural features from the Gaza, and
    have since also been called "Shangane" (q.v.), like other south-
    eastern peoples.   (Note that the Tsonga--sometimes written
    "Tonga"--have no connection with other Tonga (q.v.) groups.)

HOLE, HUGH MARSHALL (1865-1941).   Early BSAC official and
    amateur historian.   Born in England and trained in law at Ox-
    ford, Hole came to South Africa in 1889.   He went to work for
    Cecil Rhodes just as the BSAC was obtaining its Charter, and
    then commenced a long career in the Company's administration,
    holding posts in Salisbury, Bulawayo, and London.   He had con-
    siderable experience in African administration, and he fought in
    the 1896-7 Revolt (q.v.).   In 1926 Hole published the first
    standard history of the country, The Making of Rhodesia.   Two
    years later he retired from the administration and devoted his
    energies to writing, turning out personal reminiscences, histo-
    ries, and even a fictionalized biography of Lobengula (q.v.).
    His books set a high standard for the developing tradition of
    amateur historical scholarship in the country, but his bias was
    overwhelmingly pro-imperialist.   (See BIBLIOGRAPHY.)

HOLI (variants: Maholi; Roli; etc.).   Poorly understood Sindebele*
    term used to refer to local peoples of neither Nguni* nor Sotho*
    origin (sing., iholi; pl., amaholi).   The Ndebele tended to call
    all neighboring Shona, Venda, and other Bantu-speaking peoples,
    as well as local peoples incorporated into Ndebele society, ama-
    holi.   Derivation of the term is controversial, but it appears

not to have been used before the 1840s or 1850s.

According to 19th century European observers, the Ndebele people (q.v.) were rigidly divided into three "castes," with
the amaholi at the bottom, below the zansi and enhla (qq.v.).
Europeans no doubt exaggerated the degree of holi degradation
in describing them as "slaves," but it is clear that the term
carried pejorative connotations which the people themselves
wished to shake off (cf. SWINA).   Whatever their precise status, the amaholi formed a strong majority within the Ndebele
kingdom by the 1890s.

Use of the term holi has persisted into the 20th century,
but the people themselves prefer such terms as lozwi, or abantu
ba ka mambo ("people of the mambo"), which stress pre-Nde-
bele roots in the Rozvi (q.v.) state system.

HOLIDAYS, PUBLIC.   The Rhodesian government recognizes five
official holidays, in addition to the standard Western holidays
of Christmas, Easter, and New Year's day.   The local holidays
commemorate events honored only within the country's European
community (q.v.).   They are: Rhodes Day and Founders' Day
(second Monday and Tuesday of July); Pioneer Day (September
12); Republic Day (penultimate Monday of October); and Independence Day (November 11) (qq.v.).   Prior to 1970 the government recognized Victoria Day (May 24), the birthdays of reigning British monarchs, and Armistice Day, which now coincides
with Independence Day.

HONDE RIVER.   A tributary of the Pungwe (q.v.), the Honde River
rises just north of the Odzani Falls (q.v.), flowing north, then
northeast into Mozambique*.   The river drops off the Eastern
Highlands (q.v.) quickly, flowing through the broad Honde Valley,
where tea and tropical fruits are grown intensively.   During the
mid-1970s the valley became a major area of armed clashes between African nationalist and government forces.

HONEM, VASCO FERNANDES (fl. 1560s-1570s).   Portuguese (q.v.)
military commander.   In 1569 Honem was made a sub-com-
mander of Francisco Barreto's (q.v.) expedition against Munhumutapa* Negomo (q.v.).   He took command of the expedition
in early June 1573, when Barreto died at Sena (q.v.).   By then
only 180 men were still alive, and Honem himself had just recovered from a near-fatal illness.   He retreated to the coast to
recuperate.   There he received fresh Portuguese reinforcements.
In early 1875 he launched a new expedition, this time taking the
healthier route from Sofala to Manyika (qq.v.).   After surveying
the local goldfields, he retreated to the coast.   The Barreto/
Honem expeditions achieved tacit recognition of Portuguese
privileges from the Munhumutapa state, but they were the last
concerted Portuguese efforts to gain a military foothold in present Rhodesia until the 1880s.

HOPE FOUNTAIN.   London Missionary Society (q.v.) station, located 16 km. southeast of modern Bulawayo (at 20° 16'S,

28° 39'E). It was founded in late 1870 by J. B. Thomson (q.v.),
who was anxious to conduct mission work at a site closer to
Lobengula's new Bulawayo (q.v.) center than the existing LMS
station at Inyati (q.v.). C. D. Helm and David Carnegie (qq.v.)
later joined the station. As at Inyati, the work of converting
the Ndebele to Christianity moved slowly until after the Ndebele
Revolt (q.v.) of 1896. In 1912 Shishi Moyo (d.1938) became the
first African ordained minister by the LMS in Matabeleland at
the station. Mtompe Kumalo (q.v.) followed suit in 1917. Under
the direction of Neville Jones (q.v.), an African girls' institution was opened at Hope Fountain in 1916.

HORSES. The only equine animals indigenous to southern Africa are
zebra, which are not amenable to domestication. Horses were
first introduced to the country, on a small scale, by hunters
(q.v.) and traders during the mid-19th century. Their high
susceptibility to endemic diseases, such as horsesickness and
nagana (qq.v.), made local breeding almost impossible until
well into the 20th century. Even now the country contains relatively few horses. Donkeys, however, are much hardier and
many are owned by Africans.

Although horses have never been particularly numerous,
they have affected the country's history in several ways. During
the 19th century their speed and agility gave riders many advantages in hunting and in fighting. The country would probably
not have been opened up to European occupation quite so soon,
had not hunters had horses with which to pursue elephants.
Hunter penetration of the country led to the discovery of gold
(q.v.), drawing into more intensive European activities. Further,
it was largely horses which gave Afrikaners and Griqua (qq.v.)
military advantages over unmounted African spearmen in early
encounters. Ndebele (q.v.) setbacks at the hands of mounted
enemies in the Transvaal greatly contributed to their migration
to present Rhodesia in the late 1830s. The Ndebele themselves
acquired some horses as early as the 1830s, but they had little
success in keeping them alive. During the late 19th century
Lobengula (q.v.) acquired about a hundred horses from hunters
and traders, but the Ndebele did not use them for military purposes. By contrast, the British combined horses and advanced
firearms to good advantage in both the 1893 Ndebele War and
the 1896-7 Revolts (qq.v.).

HORSESICKNESS (Oedema mycosis). Serious infectious equine fever,
unique to Africa. It is usually fatal to domesticated horses
(q.v.), but only affects mules and zebras mildly, and has little
effect on donkeys. The disease's mode of transmission is
poorly understood, but it is endemic to the country's warmer
regions, particularly during the wet season (see CLIMATE).
Horsesickness has inhibited the use of horses in eastern and
southern Africa since it was recognized by Arabs in East Africa
in the 14th century. Hunters and traders who entered the
country during the 19th century lost most of their horses to
the disease very quickly. Animals which survived infection

carried an uncertain immunity for several years and were known as "salted horses" (q.v.). Since the 1920s increasingly effective anti-toxins have greatly reduced mortality of horses locally. (See also HEALTH.)

"HOTTENTOT." European term for Khoi people (q.v.); coined in South Africa by the Dutch in the 17th century. The name is now regarded as pejorative.

HOUSE OF ASSEMBLY. Formal name of the lower chamber of the Parliament (q.v.), established in 1970 by the Constitution (q.v.) of the previous year. As the successor to the Legislative Assembly (q.v.), the House is the main law-making body of the Rhodesian government, which is headed by the Prime Minister (q.v.). The 1969 Constitution provided for 66 Assembly members, including 50 Europeans elected by a European voters' roll; eight Africans elected by an African voters' roll; and eight Africans elected through special electoral colleges made up of government chiefs.

HOVE, MICHAEL MASOTSHA. One of the first two Africans to represent Southern Rhodesia in the Federation (q.v.) Assembly (cf. SAVANHU, J. Z.), Hove entered politics after having been a teacher and the editor of Bantu Mirror (q.v.). He won his seat in the Assembly by defeating Joshua Nkomo (q.v.) in a 1953 election. A faithful supporter of the ruling United (Federal) Party (q.v.), Hove was rewarded with the post of Federation High Commissioner in Nigeria in 1962. After the break-up of Federation in late 1963, he entered the African administration in the city of Bulawayo.

HUGGINS, GODFREY MARTIN (Viscount Malvern of Rhodesia from 1955) (July 6, 1883-May 8, 1971). Fourth Prime Minister (q.v.) of Southern Rhodesia (1933-53), and first Prime Minister of the Federation of Rhodesia & Nyasaland* (1953-6). Born in England, where he qualified as a medical doctor, Huggins came to Southern Rhodesia in 1911 to practice medicine temporarily. He liked the country and found that his profession placed him in an elite group, so he stayed. In 1924 he entered politics and was elected to the Legislative Assembly (q.v.) from Salisbury as a member of the ruling Rhodesian Party (q.v.). By the late 1920s he stood out as a strong advocate of racial segregation as the best means of securing the settlers' future in the country. After pushing H. U. Moffat's (q.v.) government on the issue, he broke from the ruling party to form the Reform Party (q.v.) in 1931. Increasing economic difficulties brought on by the world depression added fuel to his criticisms of the government, bringing his party to power in the 1933 election. Within a year of taking office as Prime Minister, he enlisted the aid of P. D. L. Fynn (q.v.) to merge the main leaders of the Rhodesian and Reform parties into the new United Party (q.v.), which he led to victory in a fresh general election in 1934. He retained his premiership without interruption for more than 21 years--a period said to be a record within British Commonwealth countries.

Although Huggins had been an early supporter of the Unionist Movement (q. v.), he became a strong advocate of amalgamation (q. v.) of Southern and Northern Rhodesia during the mid-1930s. Frustrated in this ambition by the report of the Bledisloe Commission (q. v.) in 1939, he later became the leading advocate of Federation (q. v.). Meanwhile, he articulated his segregationalist ideas in which he called the "Two Pyramids" policy (q. v.) and promoted passage of the Industrial Conciliation Act (q. v.) in 1934.

During the 1940s Huggins retained control of the government against strong challenges from the Labour and Liberal parties (qq. v.), even though he emerged from the 1946 election with only a plurality of Assembly seats. The same year he introduced the Native (Urban Areas) Accommodation and Registration Act (q. v.) which extended the principles of the Land Apportionment Act (q. v.) to the towns. The 1948 election restored his strong Assembly majority, giving him the opportunity to push plans for Federation. With the support of Roy Welensky (q. v.) from Northern Rhodesia, he began Federation discussions with the British government in 1950. In 1952 he obtained the British agreement to his Federation plans, despite the opposition of Joshua Nkomo and J. Z. Savanhu (qq. v.), who had participated in London talks with him.

By the 1950s Huggins had abandoned the "Two Pyramids" concept in favor of "Partnership" (q. v.), an equally hazy concept expressed in order to satisfy the British that Federation would not benefit merely settlers. He obtained settler support for Federation by promising that prosperity would ensue without the possibility of Africans ever achieving political power. When the Federation was created, he resigned his Southern Rhodesian premiership in favor of Garfield Todd (q. v.) and took up the leadership of the new Federal government. After his pet project, the Kariba Dam (q. v.), was launched in 1956, he retired from active politics and was succeeded as Federation Prime Minister by Welensky.

"HUMBUG CONCESSION" (1891). Nickname for the Lippert Concession (q. v.).

HUNGWE (Bahungwe; Wahungwe). Variant of Maungwe, the name of a Shona group ruled by the Makoni dynasty (q. v.).

HUNTERS/HUNTING. During the Stone Age (q. v.) hunting was the principal means people had of obtaining meat, but techniques and human needs were too limited to have a significant impact on the country's vast game populations. Later Iron Age (q. v.) herders and cultivators, such as the Shona and Ndebele peoples, supplemented their diets with feral animal flesh and hunted elephants for ivory (qq. v.) to trade. Large-scale hunting began only in the 1860s, when European hunters and traders began entering the country in increasing numbers (see, e.g., EDWARDS, S. H.; HARTLEY, H.; FINAUGHTY, W.; VILJOEN, J.; SELOUS, F. C.).

Europeans hunted primarily to obtain ivory.   Using firearms and
horses (q. v.), they turned hunting into systematic slaughter.
The Ndebele kings attempted to control hunting throughout the
country, mainly to protect their monopoly over the ivory trade.
Nevertheless, increased African acquisitions of firearms by the
1880s greatly reduced the populations of large animals, such as
elephants, hippopotamuses, rhinoceroses, and ostriches (qq. v.).
     During the 20th century the country's white governments
have exercised increasingly strict controls over hunting, while
protecting remaining animal herds in game reserves and national
parks (qq. v.).   Hunting is now tightly regulated through licensing
laws.   Hunting for "sport" is restricted mainly to private farms
and Controlled Hunting Areas in the Tuli Bloc (q. v.) and in the
Zambezi Valley.   (See also FISHING.)

HUNTERS' ROAD.   Europeans and other South Africans who visited
     Matabeleland (q. v.) after the early 1860s entered the country al-
     most exclusively from the southwest.   The Ndebele kings care-
     fully controlled foreign access to their country, and the south-
     western approach route had the further advantage of circumventing
     the tsetse fly (q. v.) regions around the Limpopo River* to the
     east.   Soon a clear wagon track known as the "Hunters' Road"
     was established between the Ngwato* town Shoshong in Botswana*,
     and the mission station at Inyati (q. v.).   Later the Road was ex-
     tended northeast to the Hunyani River (q. v.) in Mashonaland*.
     A modern village named Hunters' Road now stands midway be-
     tween Gwelo and Que Que (qq. v.) on the main road.

HUNYANI RIVER (a. k. a. Manyami or Mhanyami River).   Rises just
     west of Marandellas (q. v.), flowing generally northwest before
     turning north near Sinoia* to join the Zambezi River in Mozam-
     bique.   The Hunyani is well fed by many tributaries, including
     the Angwa (q. v.).   Its main dams, Prince Edward (built in 1928)
     and Hunyani Poort (1952), supply Salisbury and other towns with
     water.   The latter dam forms Lake McIlwaine, which is sur-
     rounded by the 57 sq. km. Robert McIlwaine National Park and
     a small game reserve, just west of Salisbury.   The national
     park also contains several important rock painting (q. v.) sites.

HWANGE.   Variant of Zanke, the title of the Nanzwa (q. v.) rulers.

HWATA (variant: Wata).   Dynastic title of the rulers of an inde-
     pendent Hera (q. v.) chiefdom, located at the headwaters of the
     Mazoe River*, just north of present Salisbury.   By the early
     19th century the Hwata chiefdom held a dominant position in
     regional trade.   Apparently for this reason, the Ndebele strove
     to subjugate the Hwatas from the middle of the century.   In
     1864 an Ndebele impi* captured Hwata Gwindi and brought him
     to Mhlahlandlela*, where he was kept prisoner for six months.
     Gwindi was released on the promise of paying tribute regularly,
     but he was soon behaving independently.   In 1868 another Nde-
     bele impi--in which Lobengula (q. v.) personally participated--
     again raided the Hera.   Afterwards the Hwatas were nominally

tributary to the Ndebele until 1889, when the reigning Hwata
signed a treaty with Portuguese* agents in return for firearms.
In 1896 the Hwata--who is said to have had a special relationship with the Nehanda (q.v.) medium--was one of the first Shona
chiefs to rise against the British in the Revolt (q.v.). The
Hwata himself was eventually captured and hanged. Subsequent
Hwatas were government-appointed chiefs.

- I -

I- (variant: ili-). Sindebele (q.v.) prefix (Class 3) for singular
forms of nouns and proper names, mainly pertaining to words
for people (pl., ama-). The prefix is dropped for Ndebele
personal names in this dictionary, but is retained for ordinary
nouns, e.g., idlozi. (Cf. U-.)

IBUTHO (variant: ilibutho; pl., amabutho). Sindebele* term for
a group of men of roughly the same age organized into a unit
which was given an individual name, e.g., Mhlahlandlela*.
During the 19th century the Ndebele kings periodically raised
new amabutho, which were given an older leader (induna*),
cattle* to tend, and a town in which to live. The amabutho
could be mustered for military or police work, and were periodically moved to new locations within the kingdom. Since the
early 19th century Europeans have consistently described the
amabutho as "regiments," but this description is appropriate in
only the loosest sense. The Ndebele did not possess a true
standing army. The towns which arose around the amabutho
carried the amabutho's names, but were essentially non-military
in character. Between the early 1820s and 1893 roughly 70
amabutho were formed, each containing from 50 to several hundred men. Amabutho with as many as a thousand men were
rare. (See also IMBIZO; ZWANGENDABA; etc.)

IDLOZI (variants: ilidlozi; idhlozi; pl., amadlozi). Ndebele name
for ancestor spirit. The amadlozi are said to stay near their
descendants, whose welfare they watch over. They act as intermediaries between individual mortals and the high god Nkulunkulu (q.v.). Typically, these spirits reside in the bodies of
living animals. They require prayers and propitiation. During
the period of the 19th-century Ndebele kingdom (q.v.), the royal
(Khumalo*) spirits were thought to look over the welfare of the
whole nation, and they played a special role in the annual
inxwala festivals (q.v.). (See RELIGION--NDEBELE.)

IJAHA (variant: ilijaha; pl., amajaha; variants: majaha; machaka).
Sindebele* term for young man. Under the military system of
the 19th century Ndebele kingdom (q.v.), an ijaha could join an
ibutho (q.v.), but he normally had to see active service before
gaining the status of an adult (indoda*). The amajaha thus constituted a naturally militaristic faction within the kingdom, particularly during the reign of Lobengula (q.v.).

IMBIZO (variants: Mbizo; Imbezu; etc.). Most prestigious of Lobengula's amabutho (see IBUTHO), the Imbizo was raised in
1871, and its manpower was constantly renewed over the next
two decades. Lobengula groomed the Imbizo as an elite unit,
and occasionally used it as his bodyguard. Through the 1870s
the Imbizo saw action in most major military campaigns, including the 1879 siege of Chivi (q.v.). At an apparently early
date Lobengula made his cousin Mtshani Khumalo (q.v.) the
induna* of the Imbizo, but by the early 1890s Mtshani was assuming much wider command responsibilities as well. During
the 1893 Ndebele War (q.v.) Lobengula held back the Imbizo
and two other amabutho as a reserve until the battle at Bembezi, in which the Imbizo suffered the largest Ndebele losses.
Some Imbizo members accompanied Lobengula on his flight north
and saw action against Wilson's "Shangani Patrol" (q.v.). Afterwards the unit broke up. Many members joined the BSAC administration's Native Police (see BSAP), but then went over to
the Ndebele rebels during the 1896 Revolt (q.v.).

IMPI (pl., izimpi). Sindebele* term for a military force, or expedition. It is frequently used incorrectly to refer to standing
military units (see IBUTHO).

IN- (variant: im-). Sindebele* prefix (Class 5) for the singular
forms of many kinds of nouns (pl., izin-, or izim-). The initial
i- is frequently dropped in English usage, but is retained in this
dictionary for the sake of consistency. (Cf. I-; U-.)

INDABA (pl., izindaba). Widely-used Nguni* word for "meeting" or
"discussion," also carrying the more general meanings of "affair," "news," or "story." A tree under which the Ndebele king
Lobengula (q.v.) frequently held meetings became known as the
"Indaba Tree." It is now protected as a National Monument.
      The word "indaba" has found its way into southern African
English usage. The name "Great Indaba" has been popularly applied to the peace negotiations held between Cecil Rhodes and a
number of Ndebele Revolt (q.v.) leaders in the Matopo Hills
(q.v.). There were actually four such meetings in 1896, on
August 21st and 28th, September 9th, and October 13th. Although these negotiations clearly helped to end the Revolt, it should
be realized that most rebel leaders, including Nyamanda (q.v.),
did not participate.

INDEPENDENCE DAY. Prior to 1965 the country recognized Armistice Day, November 11th, as a public holiday. After UDI on
that date, the holiday was redesignated "Independence Day" (see
HOLIDAYS).

INDEPENDENT INDUSTRIAL AND COMMERCIAL WORKERS UNION
   OF RHODESIA   see   INDUSTRIAL AND COMMERCIAL WORKERS
   UNION (ICU)

INDIANS   see   ASIANS

INDODA (pl., amadoda; variant: madoda). Sindebele* term for
adult man, or husband. During the period of the 19th century
Ndebele kingdom (q.v.) the amadoda were entitled to wear headrings (q.v.), to marry, and to serve as izinduna (see INDUNA).
A younger man was known as an ijaha (q.v.).

INDUNA (pl., izinduna). Nguni* term of such widespread usage in
southern Africa that it has virtually become an English synonym
for "chief." In literature pertaining to the 19th-century Ndebele
kingdom (q.v.), and similar Northern Nguni-derived states, the
term induna is frequently used in the sense of military commander, or head of a "regiment" (see IBUTHO). In actual
Sindebele* usage, however, the term induna was applied to a
wide variety of office-holders who had mainly non-military
functions.

INDUSTRIAL AND COMMERCIAL WORKERS UNION (ICU). Now regarded as perhaps the most important forerunner of modern
mass nationalism in the country (cf. AFRICAN NATIONAL CON-
GRESS), ICU was founded as the Independent Industrial and Commercial Workers Union of Rhodesia in 1927. In response to
Southern Rhodesian African appeals for assistance in organizing
a trade union movement, Clemens Kadalie (q.v.), the head of
the then enormously powerful South African ICU, sent Robert
Sambo and Mansell Mphamba, two fellow Nyasalanders, to Bulawayo to start the movement there. Sambo was soon deported
and Mphamba left on his own account, but ICU leadership was
quickly taken up by local workers. The first chairman was
Thomas Sikaleni Mazula, but S. Masotsha Ndlovu, Charles Mzingeli (q.v.), and Job Dumbutshena were the most assertive and
powerful leaders by 1929.
        ICU attracted a mass following in Bulawayo by holding
frequent public meetings in which speakers boldly denounced the
white government, missionaries, African elitist organizations,
and ethnically-based social and welfare groups. Despite its
name, ICU never developed into a true trade union organization,
but instead grew as a quasi-political movement, calling for
united African resistance to white oppression, and demanding
higher wages and better working conditions generally. In late
1929 Mzingeli founded a Salisbury branch of ICU. By the next
year ICU was active in the main urban centers throughout the
country. Efforts to recruit agricultural workers were abandoned
early, however, and ICU achieved no success in reaching workers
in the tightly-controlled mining compounds, despite Dumbutshena's
earnest efforts.
        ICU grew rapidly for several years, but soon withered
under the combined pressures of government harassment, missionary opposition (only A. S. Cripps* supported ICU), and the
conservatism of workers unprepared to commit themselves.
Finances were also a chronic problem, and the organization's
image was badly damaged by destructive splits in the South African ICU leadership. Several ICU leaders were imprisoned in
the mid-1930s. By 1936 ICU had vanished in Southern Rhodesia.

A decade later, however, Mzingeli revived the movement as the Reformed ICU (q. v.).

INDUSTRIAL CONCILIATION ACT (1934).   Law passed early in Godfrey Huggins' (q. v.) administration to provide conciliation ma-
chinery for European labor disputes, particularly in the building
and printing trades.   In response to pressures from both European employers and employees, the law specifically excluded
"natives," i. e., Africans, from its definition of "employees."
This exclusion effectively barred Africans from forming their
own trade unions, from striking, and from obtaining apprentice-
ships in skilled trades.   A 1937 amendment required that the
government set minimum African wages at no lower a level than
those of their European counterparts in order to prevent cheaper
African labor from competing with European labor.   The law
thus severely restricted African entry into skilled labor.   Its
harshly discriminatory nature was cited by the 1939 Bledisloe
Commission Report (q. v.) as a particularly objectionable feature
of the country's African policy.
    While the law stimulated European trade unionism, it left
African workers with little opportunity to voice grievances.   An
African railway workers' strike in 1945 and a general African
strike in 1948 led to some improvements in working conditions,
but Africans were not granted the right to organize unions until
the Industrial Conciliation Act was completely rewritten in 1959.
A 1971 amendment to this Act reimposed government restrictions
on striking, and gave the government's President (q. v.) power to
declare any strike illegal.

INFLUENZA PANDEMIC OF 1918 (a. k. a. furuwenza).   The "Spanish
Flu" pandemic, which is believed to have killed as many as 10
million people worldwide in late 1918, entered Southern Rhodesia
from South Africa in early October 1918.   The viral disease
raged locally for about five weeks, virtually bringing commerce
to a halt.   Africans living in crowded urban areas and mining
compounds were especially hard hit.   An estimated 2% to 3% of
the rural population died.   Afterwards measures were taken to
relieve overcrowding and to improve government health services.
(See HEALTH.)

INGEZI   see   NGEZI

INKOSI (pl., amakosi).   Sindebele* term for "king" or "ruler"; also
widely used in other Nguni* languages.   The locative form is
enkosini, "at the king's place."   During the 19th century the
Ndebele (q. v.) had two reigning amakosi: Mzilikazi and Lobengula (qq. v.).   In modern usage the term inkosi is used as a
respectful form of address to an important man, and is the title
by which Christ is known.   (Cf. MAMBO.)

INKOSIKAZI (pl., amakosikazi).   Female equivalent of inkosi (q. v.),
meaning "queen" or woman of high rank (Chishona* form: hosi-
kadzi).   The term "queen" is misleading in the context of the

19th-century Ndebele kingdom (q. v.), as the many wives of the king had no formal political powers. For examples of "royal wives," see XWALILE; LOZIGEYI. Lobengula's sister Mncengence (q. v.) was also known as an inkosikazi.

INKUNABULA. Neologism for Sindebele* books printed before 1900.

INSIZA DISTRICT. Northernmost district in Matabeleland South Province (q. v.), covering 8700 sq. km. Most of the northern part of this district, which lies on the Central Plateau (q. v.), is reserved for European ranchers. The southern, lower part of the district is mostly Tribal Trust Land (q. v.). On the northwest the district border is almost congruent with the main road between Bulawayo and Gwelo. The village of Insiza stands on the road where it is intersected by the Insiza River (q. v.). Filabusi (q. v.) is the administrative center. The district borders the districts of Gwanda on the southwest; Umzingwane on the west; Bubi and Gwelo on the north; and Shabani and Belingwe (qq. v.) on the east. Population in 1969 included 51,110 Africans and 640 Europeans.

INSIZA RIVER. Rises by the village of Insiza (at 19° 47'S, 29° 12'E; alt. 1413 m.) and flows almost due south within the Insiza District (q. v.), joining the Umzingwane River (q. v.) just north of West Nicholson (q. v.).

INTABA (pl., izintaba; variant: thaba). Sindebele* word for hill. Note that many place-names are spelled without the initial i-, as in Ntabazikamambo and Ntabazinduna (qq. v.).

"INTERIOR." Term used in 19th-century southern Africa (q. v.) to designate territory north of European settlement. The "far interior" was usually regarded as territory north of the Limpopo River (q. v.).

INTERNATIONAL DEFENCE AND AID FUND (IDAF). British organization founded to provide legal aid for South Africans. After 1958 it extended its services to Southern Rhodesia. In 1972 an IDAF legal team followed the Pearce Commission (q. v.) to Rhodesia to assist Africans in presenting evidence, to press the government to clarify its definition of acceptable "normal political activity," and to reveal the activities of the security police. Since then the IDAF has provided legal assistance to nationalist organizations.

INXWALA (pl., izinxwala). Annual Ndebele religious festival celebrated during the 19th century. Variations of the inxwala have long been celebrated by most Nguni-speaking peoples (q. v.). The Ndebele began observing the inxwala as soon as Mzilikazi founded their kingdom. The festival quickly became one of the kingdom's most important unifying forces, as it regularly brought most of the people together in one place. After the start of the long rains, usually around January, the Ndebele gathered for a

complex series of rites which lasted several weeks.   The
inxwala proper, known as the "great dance," lasted about five
days during the middle of the sequence, and was the most important part.   The personal participation of the kings was crucial.   They led the dancing and some prayers, and symbolically
ate from the first harvested crops--hence the popular name
"first fruits festival."   The most significant rites included ceremonies of national thanks giving, reaffirmation of allegiance to
the king, and honoring of the royal ancestors, whose spirits
(see IDLOZI) were thought to be contained in black oxen which
were paraded (see, e.g., MASHOBANE).

    After the Ndebele left the Transvaal* in late 1837, they
celebrated an inxwala in eastern Botswana*.   Afterwards they
were separated in two main parties for over a year.   Mzilikazi's party celebrated the next inxwala north of present Matabeleland*.   The other migrants apparently made Mzilikazi's son
Nkulumane (q.v.) acting king in order to celebrate their inxwala
in Matabeleland, where they arrived first.   In 1870 Lobengula's
installation as king was incorporated into the regular inxwala.
Two years later his half-brother Mangwane (q.v.) attempted to
invade the kingdom in January, hoping to catch Lobengula off
guard during the inxwala.   The death of Lobengula in 1894 effectively ended inxwala celebrations, but an abortive attempt to
revive them was made in 1896 during the Revolt (q.v.).

INYANGA.   Town on the western edge of the Inyanga Mountains (at
    18°13'S, 32°45'E; alt. 1860 m.), serving as administrative
    center for Inyanga District (q.v.) and as the commercial center
    for the region's stock and fruit producing industries.   Popula-
    tion in 1969 was 730 (86% Africans).

INYANGA DISTRICT.   Eastern border district in the extreme north
    of Manicalands Province (q.v.), covering 6635 sq. km.   The
    northern part of the district is Tribal Trust Land (q.v.); most
    of the southern part is national land and land reserved for Euro-
    pean farmers.   Population in 1969 included 97,520 Africans and
    780 Europeans.   Inyanga is separated from the Mtoko District on
    the north by the Ruenya River (qq.v.).   It also borders the dis-
    tricts of Makoni on the west and Umtali (qq.v.) on the south.
    The Gairezi River (q.v.) forms the north part of its boundary
    with Mozambique (q.v.).

INYANGA MOUNTAINS.   The highest range in the country, the In-
    yangas form the northernmost part of the Eastern Highlands
    (q.v.).   The range runs from Mount Nyangui (17°53'S, 32°44'E;
    alt. 2228 m.) in the north, to Mount Inyangani (q.v.) in the
    south.   The southern part of the range falls within the 35,225
    hectare Rhodes Inyanga and Mtarazi National Park.

INYANGA RUINS.   Covering most of present Inyanga District, and
    extending into Makoni and Umtali districts and a small part of
    Mozambique (qq.v.), the Inyanga Ruins are the largest single
    concentration of stone ruins (q.v.) in the country.   They appear

to have developed independently of the Zimbabwe and Khami-type ruins (qq. v.) characteristic of the rest of the country. Al-though they were occupied by Shona-speaking peoples from about the mid-15th century, their origins have been attributed to Nsenga, or other non-Shona, immigrants from the north.

The ruins fall into two main complexes: an early "up-land" (above 1500 m.) group in the southeast, and a later "low-land" group towards the northwest. The Van Niekerk Ruins (q. v.) are the largest complex of the latter group.

The Inyanga Ruins are characterized by a number of fea-tures rarely found elsewhere in the country. The most out-standing feature is an extensive system of cultivation terraces and irrigation ditches (see DAMS). The lines of terraces, many of which have stone retaining walls, extend over several thousand kilometers. Their only southern African parallels are found in the Transvaal*. Stone-lined pits (q. v.) are another characteristic. Less common, but equally characteristic of the group, are massive "forts, " of which Nyangwe (q. v.) is the best known example.

In contrast to the stone ruins associated with ruling mi-norities elsewhere in the country, the Inyanga Ruins are mostly remains of ordinary peoples' buildings. Inyanga is not a mining region, and the ruins have produced few metal artifacts or im-ported luxury goods. Even midden dumps are rare. Pottery finds have been plentiful, but ceramic workmanship is considered inferior to that of the earlier Ziwa culture (q. v.). Most of the sites appear to have been abandoned by the early 19th century--perhaps in response to the Mfecane invasions (q. v.).

INYANGANI MOUNTAIN. The highest peak in the country, rising to 2595 meters; located at the southern tip of the Inyanga Mountains (at 18° 18'S, 32° 51'E).

INYATI. The first permanent mission station and European settle-ment in the country, located 80 km. northeast of Bulawayo (at 19° 41'S, 28° 51'E), Inyati was founded as an LMS station by Robert Moffat (q. v.) in late 1859. The station took its name from the nearby Inyathi ("buffalo") ibutho*, in which the Ndebele king Mzilikazi was then living.

The Matabele Mission (q. v.), as it was called, became the center of European activities in the country for several decades, but its agents had little success in gaining converts. After Mzilikazi moved to Mhlahlandhlela* in 1861, the mission's links with the king were weakened, and six years later the In-yathi ibutho itself moved to another site. The increased isola-tion of the station from the Ndebele people gave J. B. Thomson the incentive to found a second station at Hope Fountain (qq. v.) in 1870.

After British occupation of Matabeleland* in the mid-1890s, Inyati became the administrative center of the Bubi District (q.v.), as well as the commercial center of a developing gold mining region. More recently the area's importance has been enhanced by the development of nickel (q. v.) mining. LMS work at the

station has continued, and an African secondary school was
founded there in 1953. (For Inyati copper mine, see HEAD-
LANDS.)

INYAZURA.   Southern Makoni District (q.v.) village, located c.73
km. northwest of Umtali* on the railway* line to Salisbury (at
18° 43'S, 32° 10'E; alt. 1220 m.). The village is the center
for a predominantly Afrikaner (q.v.) farming region.

IRON.   This important metal is the earliest mineral (q.v.) known to
have been mined in the country (see IRON AGE), and is widely
distributed. Pre-colonial workings are numerous, but almost
all were small. While iron smelting and smithery were highly
esteemed skills in local African societies, production was
generally limited to weapons and tools. No significant long-
distance trade in iron goods seems to have developed, in contrast to that for gold and copper (qq.v.). Local trade was,
however, important, and by the 19th century the Hera and
Njanja peoples (qq.v.) were particularly famous as iron workers.
        Modern iron production has been important but unspec-
tacular. Most iron ore is now mined at Redcliff (q.v.) and is
used in local industries. Iron pyrite (FeS_2), mined mainly north
of Salisbury, makes an important contribution to the country's
chemical industry.

IRON AGE.   The first Iron Age culture was introduced into the
country by at least the end of the A.D. 100s. The arrival of
iron-using peoples also heralded the beginnings of agriculture
(q.v.), livestock raising (see CATTLE), and pottery. The connection is not proven, but it is highly likely that the Iron Age
was introduced by Bantu-speaking (q.v.) immigrants, who gradually absorbed or displaced the earlier Stone Age peoples (q.v.).
        Both classification and periodization of Iron Age cultures
within the country are far from settled. New archaeological
finds and radiocarbon dates have regularly inspired reclassifi-
cations and new periodizations. The terminology applied within
the field is thus ever-changing. The most important historical
problem to be resolved is determining whether the appearance
of major cultural innovations--which archaeologists typically associate with pottery styles--represent local changes or intrusions
of new societies. Generally, archaeologists have attributed in-
novations to new peoples from the north, but such peoples are
rarely identified.
        The earliest known Iron Age culture has been called
Gokomere (q.v.). Ziwa (q.v.) was once regarded as an independent contemporary culture, but is now treated as a Gokomere
variation. Gokomere flourished from about A.D.200 to c.900.
Its latter phases are now called Zhizo and Malapati. The 10th
century introduced the "late" Iron Age, represented by Leopard's
Kopje culture (q.v.). The culture which developed stone building
techniques at the Zimbabwe Ruins (q.v.) has been regarded as
either an offshoot of Leopard's Kopje, or a separate tradition.
In the west the early and later phases of Leopard's Kopje are

now called Mambo and Woolandale, respectively. Monumental
building in stone (see RUINS) began around the 12th century,
during the latter Zimbabwe periods. The late 15th century
heralded the beginnings of the Khami culture (q.v.) throughout
the southern parts of the country. Around the same period a
major independent stone-building culture arose in the Inyanga
Ruins (q.v.) region to the northeast. (See also MONK'S KOP.)
        The 19th century is regarded as an era of sweeping Iron
Age culture convergences, brought about by the disruptions and
population movements caused by the Mfecane invasions (q.v.).
Occupation of the country by Europeans in the 1890s terminated
many traditional Iron Age industries by introducing the Western
industrial Iron Age.

IRON MINE HILL (a.k.a. Chimhanguru; Ntaba Insimbi). Located
on the Gwelo to Fort Victoria railway line (at 19°19'S, 30°23'E),
this 1495 meter hill is named after its many old iron workings.
During the 1893 Ndebele War (q.v.) it was the site where the
BSAC forces combined before marching on Bulawayo.

ISI-. Sindebele (q.v.) prefix (Class 4) for many kinds of nouns
(pl., izi-). The initial i- is frequently dropped in English usage, as in "Sindebele" itself. (Cf. CHI-.)

ISIBONGO. Term whose meaning varies somewhat among Nguni
languages (q.v.). In Ndebele usage it means family surname,
or clan name. In its plural form, izibongo, it also means
praises, or praise-name (the latter being distinct from a "surname"). An imbongi (pl., izimbongi) is a poet, or praise-
singer--someone who is well versed in traditional history. The
Ndebele term for "clan" is usendo (pl., izinsendo). Ndebele
clans are patrilineal. Among the zansi and enhla (qq.v.) members of Ndebele society possession of a common isibongo implies
descent from a common ancestor, precluding intermarriage.
        The Ndebele consider it rude to address an adult by other
than his surname. If this is unknown, then the honorifics baba
or mama (qq.v.) should be used. During the 19th century all
subjects addressed the Ndebele kings by the latters' royal clan
name, Khumalo*. (Cf. Shona MUTUPO.)

ISIGODLO (pl., izigodlo). Sindebele* term for the enclosure in
which the king's wives (see INKOSIKAZI) maintained their quarters. The isigodlo was usually situated at the center of a town,
and was the spot where the king held court while in residence.

IVORY. Until the late 19th century vast herds of elephants (q.v.)
roamed the country, particularly in the western regions. From
early times ivory ranked only behind gold (q.v.) as a Shona export item to Muslims (q.v.) on the east coast. The Portuguese
(q.v.) continued the trade from the 16th century, but allowed it
gradually to taper off until the early 19th century. In the mid-
19th century renewed European (q.v.) interest in ivory products
brought British and Afrikaner (q.v.) hunters (q.v.) and traders

to the country from the south.   This time traders dealt primarily with the Ndebele rulers.   In 1854 S. H. Edwards (q. v.)
bought a large amount of ivory from Mzilikazi, who thereafter
maintained a formal, but loose, monopoly over Ndebele trade.
Mzilikazi also controlled the entry of hunters into the country,
charging irregular fees for hunting licenses.   His successor
Lobengula exercised more systematic controls over hunting and
preferred to have his own men hunt so he could sell the ivory
directly.   Statistics on the ivory trade are imprecise and irregular, but it is clear that the 1860s and 1870s were the peak years.
Thousands of elephants were killed annually.   Each animal bore
about 35 to 55 kg. of ivory, fetching 8 to 11 shillings a kg. in
South Africa.   On top of this, a smaller trade in hippopotamus
(q. v.) teeth was also conducted.   By the 1880s the surviving
elephant herds had been driven into tsetse fly (q. v.) regions,
beyond the reach of professional hunters using horses (q. v.),
and the ivory trade largely ended.

IZI-.   Sindebele (q. v.) prefix for plural forms of Class 4 nouns
whose singular prefix is isi- (q. v.).   Izim- and izin- are variants of the plural prefix for Class 5 nouns with im- or in-
(q. v.) as singular prefixes, and for plurals of Class 6 nouns
with u(lu)- (q. v.) as the singular prefix.

- J -

JACHA, AARON RUSIKE (b. Oct. 1899.)   Raised and educated at Epworth (q. v.), Jacha taught in Methodist* mission schools before
turning to political activism in the 1930s.   He was inspired by
the congress movement in South Africa, and was, apparently, in
touch with its leader J. T. Jabavu.   In 1934 Jacha organized the
Bantu Congress in Southern Rhodesia.   The Congress remained
an essentially elitist organization through the 1930s (cf. ICU).
By the early 1940s the movement was being led by T. D. Samkange (q. v.) and was becoming known as the African National
Congress (q. v.).   Jacha himself later became the leader of the
African Farmers' Union (q. v.).   In 1952 he became the first
African in the country appointed to an official government policy-
making body when he accepted a post on the Native Land Board.
The following year he was defeated in a bid for a seat in the
new Federation assembly.

JAMESON, LEANDER STARR (Feb. 9, 1853-Nov. 26, 1917).   Cecil
Rhodes' confidant and agent in Rhodesia.   Born in Scotland and
trained as a doctor in London, Jameson came to the Kimberley
diamond fields in South Africa in 1878--a year after taking his
M. D.   There he became a trusted friend of Rhodes.   After Lobengula (q. v.) repudiated the Rudd Concession (q. v.) in 1889,
Jameson went to Bulawayo* as Rhodes' agent to persuade the
Ndebele king to reconsider.   During three visits to Matabeleland*
in 1889 and 1890, he got Lobengula to concede a few minor points
in the dispute.   These Jameson exaggerated in his reports, giving

the false impression that Lobengula had reconfirmed the Rudd
Concession and that he had become amenable to the passage of
a British occupation force into Mashonaland*. Armed with
Jameson's reports, Rhodes obtained British government permission to organize the Pioneer Column (q.v.). Jameson then accompanied the Column as Rhodes' personal representative. Afterwards, he and Frank Johnson (q.v.) made a dramatic trip down
the Pungwe River (q.v.) in an attempt to find a practical route
to the sea.

The following year, 1891, Jameson succeeded A. Colquhoun
(q.v.) as the BSAC administrator of Mashonaland. He exercised
much firmer control over the incipient administration than had
his predecessor, and he worked to find excuses for invading
Matabeleland (see LIPPERT CONCESSION). In 1893 he arbitrarily designated a "boundary" line between Matabeleland (q.v.)
and Mashonaland. He then charged the Ndebele with having vio-
lated the boundary when they raided Shona villages near Fort
Victoria (q.v.) in mid-July. He organized and led the ensuing
Ndebele War (q.v.). With the addition of Matabeleland to its
territories, the BSAC made Jameson the first Administrator
(q.v.) of the whole country. Jameson lost this position to A. H.
G. Grey (q.v.) in early 1896, after leading the abortive "Jameson Raid" (q.v.). Jameson surrendered to Transvaal* authorities during the raid; they turned him over to Britain for trial and
imprisonment.

Jameson was released from prison in December 1896, returning to South Africa to begin a new career in Cape politics.
There he inherited Rhodes' party leadership and became Prime
Minister of the Cape Colony (1904-8). He retired to England in
1912, and was elected president of the BSAC early the next year.
He was particularly interested in the question of joining Southern
Rhodesia either with South Africa (see UNIONIST MOVEMENT) or
with Northern Rhodesia (see AMALGAMATION MOVEMENT), and
he made several trips to Southern Africa before his death from
accumulated tropical ailments. His body was interred at World's
View (q.v.) in the Matopos in 1920.

"JAMESON RAID" (1895). In the hope of overthrowing the Transvaal's (q.v.) Afrikaner government, Cecil Rhodes--then Prime
Minister of the Cape Colony--secretly commissioned L. S. Jameson (q.v.) to organize an invasion force in eastern Botswana*.
Jameson took most of the European police out of Southern Rhodesia for this purpose (see BRITISH SOUTH AFRICA POLICE;
BECHUANALAND BORDER POLICE). On December 29, 1895,
he advanced into the Transvaal with just over 500 men. The expected uprising of expatriate Transvaal miners (uitlanders) did
not materialize and the raid was a fiasco. Disgraced, Rhodes
resigned his premiership and his seat on the BSAC Board of Directors. Jameson was tried and imprisoned in England, and he
too resigned all his official positions. The removal of most of
the police from Southern Rhodesia contributed to the timing of the
Shona and Ndebele Revolts (q.v.), and the Raid itself helped to
bring about the South African War (q.v.) four years later.

JESUIT MISSIONARIES see   SILVEIRA, G. DA; ZAMBEZI MISSION

JOHNSON, FRANK WILLIAM FREDERICK (1866-Sept. 6, 1943).
    Born in England, Johnson came to South Africa when he was 16.
    In 1884 he joined the British army and served in Warren's Ex-
    pedition into Bechuanaland (qq.v.). Afterwards he joined the
    BBP. In 1887 he, H. J. Borrow and M. Heany (qq.v.) formed
    a syndicate to seek mining concessions* in Matabeleland*. John-
    son met Rhodes at Kimberley in 1889, and obtained from him a
    contract to command the "Pioneer Corps" section of the Pioneer
    Column (q.v.) which occupied Mashonaland* the next year. After
    arriving at Salisbury in September 1890 he joined L. S. Jameson
    (q.v.) in an expedition down the Pungwe River (q.v.). He then
    returned to Mashonaland to consolidate mining interests and other
    commercial activities. He left the country before the outbreak
    of the Ndebele War* in 1893, but retained active control over his
    financial interests there. After the First World War he returned
    to Southern Rhodesia, and was elected to the Legislative Assem-
    bly (q.v.) in 1927. In that body he led the opposition against
    C. P. Coghlan's (q.v.) government, but was turned out of office
    the very next year. He returned to Britain permanently in 1930
    and later published his autobiography, Great Days (1940).

JOLLIE, ETHEL MAUDE see   TAWSE-JOLLIE, E. M.

JONES, NEVILLE (1880-1954). English missionary and archaeolo-
    gist. In 1912 Jones came to the LMS Hope Fountain (q.v.) sta-
    tion in Matabeleland*, where he worked for the remainder of his
    life. Meanwhile, he trained himself in archaeology and investi-
    gated traces of Stone Age (q.v.) occupation, particularly in the
    Matopo Hills (q.v.). His fieldwork led to several books and
    numerous articles in which he developed the basic sequences of
    Stone Age cultures in the country. From 1936 to 1951 he served
    as secretary of the Historical Monuments Commission (q.v.), be-
    coming its chairman in 1951. Jones also wrote several books
    on modern African life. Most notable was My Friend Kumalo
    (published under the pen-name "Mhlagazanhlansi"), recording
    Mtompe Kumalo's (q.v.) views of Ndebele life and history.

JUMBO MINE. Gold (q.v.) mine and town, located just west of Ma-
    zoe District* (at 17° 28'S, 30° 55'E). Pegged in October 1890,
    the mine is said to have been named after the famous elephant
    in the London Zoo. Nearby is the site of the old Portuguese
    trading fair Dambarare (q.v.).

- K -

KABALONTA see   GWABALANDA

KADALIE, CLEMENS (c.1896-1951). Malawi-born labor leader whose
    Industrial and Commercial Workers Union (ICU) became the largest
    African organization in South Africa during the late 1920s. After

a brief stint as a teacher in Nyasaland (now Malawi), Kadalie
started for South Africa in 1915, unexpectedly remaining in
Southern Rhodesia for three years along the way. There he
held clerking jobs in many different places, including Bulawayo
and the Shamva* mining compound. His experiences in the
country sensitized him to racial discrimination and European
mistreatment of African workers--evils he vowed to correct in
South Africa. Later, during his meteoric rise to prominence
in South Africa, he remained concerned with Southern Rhodesian
problems. He corresponded with the missionary A. S. Cripps
(q.v.), and in 1927 he responded to an appeal for assistance
from Southern Rhodesian workers by sending Robert Sambo and
other fellow Nyasalanders north to help organize the Southern
Rhodesian ICU (q.v.).

"KAFFIR." Term for African widely used by white southern Africans; it is today regarded as highly pejorative. The term derives from Arabic kafir, for "infidel" or "non-believer." Portuguese (q.v.) explorers adopted the word from east African
Muslims (q.v.) in the early 16th century, thinking it meant
simply, "black African." However, it was from 19th-century
South Africa that the word found its way into modern Rhodesian
usage. The Portuguese, as the first Europeans to encounter the
Nguni-speaking* peoples of the southeastern coast, called these
peoples "Caffres." The term was later adopted by Dutch and
English-speaking settlers. By the late 19th century whites tended
to call all Bantu-speaking* peoples "Kaffirs," and it was in this
sense that the word was introduced into present Rhodesia.

"KAFFIR BEER." European term for fermented African beverages,
usually made from eleusine (finger millet).

"KAFFIR CORN." European term for sorghum, an important African
grain crop (see AGRICULTURE). Sometimes also applied to millet (q.v.).

"KAFFIR-FARMING." Term used during the period of BSAC rule
to refer to a system of tenant farming in which Africans paid
rents to work and to live on European-owned land. The practice
was abolished by the Land Apportionment Act (q.v.).

KAGUVI (variant: Kagubi). Shona "lion spirit," or mhondoro (q.v.),
whose medium, Gumporeshumba, was a leader during the 1896-7
Shona Revolt (q.v.). Unlike other famous mhondoro, Kaguvi has
had no known mediums (see SVIKIRO) other than Gumporeshumba,
who rose to fame suddenly as "Kaguvi" during the Revolt. Gumporeshumba is believed to have been a member of a Zezuru
(q.v.) chiefly family, and possibly to have been the brother of
Pasipamire--the most famous Chaminuka (q.v.) medium. Gumporeshumba's prominence as a Revolt leader appears to have
rested on his own charisma, not on the prior reputation of the
Kaguvi spirit.

Early in 1896 "Kaguvi" joined chief Mashayamombe (q.v.), making the latter's town his Revolt headquarters.   From April to October he sent out messengers to surrounding chiefs, issuing instructions, collecting loot, and distributing captured firearms (cf. NEHANDA). The extent of his actual authority over other rebels is now being debated, but his reputation was clearly great. Europeans called him the "Lion God," but he titled himself simply Murenga (q.v.), "The Resister." After Alderson's (q.v.) forces began blowing up Mashayamombe's shelters, "Kaguvi" began a long period of moving about the country. At this time he was joined by Mkwati (q.v.) from Ndebele country, and the two exhorted Shona chiefs to continue their resistance against Europeans. By early 1897 Europeans concluded that killing "Kaguvi" would end the Shona Revolt, so they began a concerted effort to get him. His prolonged success in evading capture increased his fame, but the Revolt was meanwhile breaking down as other leaders either surrendered or were killed.   Finally, in late October 1897 "Kaguvi" himself surrendered in the Sipolilo District*. The following March he and the Nehanda medium were tried for murder. On April 27, 1898, "Kaguvi," "Nehanda," and chief Mashanganyika were hanged in Salisbury. Under the pressure of a Roman Catholic priest and one of his daughters-- who, remarkably, attended the Chishawasha Mission* school-- "Kaguvi" accepted baptism while "Nehanda" was being hanged. Christened Dismas, "The Good Thief," he thus became one of the first Shona converted to Catholicism since the early days of Portuguese missionaries (q.v.).

KAKUYO KOMUNYAKA   see   CHIKUYO CHISAMARENGU

KALANGA (variant: Kalaka). One of the six main clusters of Shona (q.v.) languages, Kalanga--or "Western Shona"--stands apart as both the most isolated and the most different form of Chishona (q.v.). Some authorities have even classified Kalanga as a non-Shona language.
Kalanga-speakers (called Va-, or Makalanga) have inhabited the western and southwestern parts of the country, as well as eastern Botswana*, for at least a millenium (see LEOPARD'S KOPJE CULTURE). They have seen a succession of Shona and non-Shona invaders, many of whom have adopted the Kalanga form of Chishona. These invaders have included Karanga (q.v.) from the Zimbabwe (q.v.) culture in the 15th or 16th century, and the Ndebele (q.v.) in the early 19th century. Ndebele occupation of present Matabeleland (q.v.), which corresponds roughly with Kalanga territory, further isolated the Kalanga from other Shona and resulted in many Kalanga adopting the Sindebele* language.   Today about 5% to 6% of the country's Shona-speakers speak Kalanga. Among the surviving distinct Kalanga groups are the Nanzwa (q.v.) and Lilima (see BULALIMA-MANGWE DISTRICT).

KALIPHI (variants: Mkaliphi; Nkaliphi; a.k.a. Gundwane) (c.1800s-1839?). Ndebele induna*. Described as one of Mzilikazi's top

military commanders during the 1830s, Kaliphi led an impi* in
pursuit of fleeing Sotho* subjects from the central Transvaal*--
where the Ndebele then lived--to Kalanga (q.v.) country, in what
was probably the first Ndebele penetration of present Rhodesia,
in 1831.   He also commanded many other campaigns, including
a force which fought Afrikaner (q.v.) Voortrekkers at the Battle
of Vegkop in October 1836.   After the Ndebele left the western
Transvaal at the end of 1837, Kaliphi commanded the division
of migrants who marched directly to Matabeleland*.   When Mzilikazi arrived there in mid-1839, Kaliphi appears to have been
executed for having allowed Nkulumane (q.v.) to be made acting
king.

    (Recent research indicates that the man known by the
praise name [see ISIBONGO] "Kaliphi" was the same man re-
membered in Ndebele tradition as "Gundwane Ndiweni.")

KAMATIVI.   Mining town east of Wankie (q.v.), on the lower Gwai
River* (at 18° 19'S, 27° 4'E).   Since the mid-1950s Kamativi's
tin (q.v.) mine has become the country's largest.   Mining and
smelting operations occupy most of the adult population.   Total
population in 1969 was 3590 (94% Africans).   Lobengula's (q.v.)
grave is nearby.

KAMHARAPASU MUKOMBWE (variant: Kambarapasu; a.k.a. Affonso)
(d. 1690s).   The son of Mavura II (q.v.), Kamharapasu was described as a "young man" when he succeeded his brother Siti
Kazurukumusapa (q.v.) as Munhumutapa (q.v.) in 1663.   The last
Munhumutapa to rule from the Dande region (q.v.), he was perhaps also the last truly effective ruler of the kingdom.   Although
he was baptized "Affonso," he worked to turn back Portuguese
influence in the country.   In this he was aided by tropical diseases which greatly reduced the number of resident Portuguese
(q.v.) in the late 17th century.   He resecured the homage of
Manyika, Barwe (qq.v.), and other former provinces, but was
defeated in a war against the Changamire state (q.v.) in 1684.
He died some time the next decade.   He was succeeded by an
uncle, Nyakunembire, who called in Changamire aid against the
Portuguese.   A rapid succession of new Munhumutapas then followed, and the state was reduced to tributary status by Changamire Dombo (q.v.).

KANDA.   Real name of an Ndebele royal pretender who called himself "Nkulumane" (q.v.) in the 1870s.

KAPARARIDZE   see   NYAMBO KAPARARIDZE

KARANGA (a.k.a. "Southern Shona").   According to linguistic classifications, the Karanga (or Chikaranga) dialect of Chishona (q.v.)
is spoken by about one-third of all Shona people (q.v.) in the
country.   Its speakers are concentrated in a compact area between, roughly, Gwelo in the northwest, Bikita in the northeast,
Chiredzi in the southeast, and West Nicholson in the southwest
(qq.v.).

Karanga (or Ma-, or Vakaranga) is also used as an ethnic identification which includes not only the Karanga-speakers,
but also other Shona, notably some of the Kalanga-speakers
(q. v.) of the west.   Some authorities use "Karanga" as a synonym for "Shona" itself, arguing that the term is the original
name of the Shona-speaking peoples.   Within the Karanga dialect
cluster are included such important chiefdoms as the Mari of
Chivi, the Govera of Chirumanzu, the Duma, Gova (qq. v.),
Jena, Nyubi, and others.

KARIBA.   Town serving as the administrative center of the district
of the same name; located on the promontory (at 16° 31'S, 28° 48'E)
which separates Kariba Gorge (q. v.) from the eastern bulge of
Lake Kariba (q. v.) very near the dam.   The town arose after
construction began on Kariba Dam (q. v.) in 1956.   The population peaked at 7000 people the next year.   By 1969 the population had leveled off to 3940 (87% Africans).   Now a major tourist
center for lakeside recreation, the town has its own international
airport (see AIR TRANSPORT).   Its border (q. v.) post by the
dam is one of three major crossing points into Zambia (q. v.).

KARIBA, LAKE.   One of the largest artificial bodies of water in the
world, Lake Kariba began to form in 1959 when the retaining
wall of Kariba Dam (q. v.) was completed.   By the early 1960s
it stretched more than 280 km.:   from the Kariba Gorge (q. v.)
in the northeast; up the Zambezi River (q. v.) to near the Batoka
Gorge (q. v.) in the southwest.   As wide as 40 km in places, the
lake covers c. 5200 sq. km.   At its completion, Kariba ranked
as the world's largest man-made lake, with a volume of c. 160, 400
cubic meters (130, 100 acre-feet), but it has since been slightly
surpassed by new lakes in Egypt and Russia.   The area along the
southern shore of the lake is relatively wild and inaccessible (see
GAME RESERVES), but the eastern part of the lake has developed
into a major tourist area, centering on Kariba township (q. v.).
The government has stocked the lake with several varieties of fish
(q. v.), and the country's only commercial fisheries have developed
at both ends of the lake.   Easily navigable, the lake offers cheap
water transport, but the areas surrounding the lake are insufficiently developed to promote significant shipping.   (See also districts of BINGA and KARIBA.)

KARIBA DAM.   Interrupting the flow of the Zambezi River (q. v.) at
Kariba Gorge (q. v.), Kariba Dam is a massive concrete arch
structure 128 m. high, and 579 m. wide (at 16° 32'S, 28° 46'E).
It is the product of the single biggest construction project in
which the country has ever participated.   After World War II it
was generally recognized that the greatly increasing electrical
power (q. v.) needs of both Southern and Northern Rhodesia would
best be met by the development of a cooperative, large-scale,
hydroelectric scheme.   Indeed, the need for such a project was
an incentive for creating the political Federation (q. v.) which
eventually undertook the project.

The first problem faced was choosing between the Zam-

bezi River and Northern Rhodesia's Kafue River for a dam site.
At first Federal Premier Huggins (q. v.) favored the Kafue, but
Southern Rhodesian Premier Todd (q. v.) and other politicians
pushed for a site on Kariba Gorge. The Southern Rhodesians
prevailed, causing considerable resentment among Northern Rhodesian politicians. A French consulting firm reported on the
advantages of Kariba, which offered a much greater hydroelectrical energy potential than Kafue. The topography of the Zambezi Valley and the river's proven low siltage were factors which
bode well for the longterm operation of a dam at Kariba. After
the Federal Assembly voted 25 to 7 in favor of Kariba in 1955,
the next problem was the major one of financing the huge project
with the relatively small resources of the Federation. Huggins
quickly committed Federation funds to undertake preliminary construction work, and was personally vindicated when the World
Bank announced it would underwrite part of the project. Northern
Rhodesian copper companies, the BSAC (q. v.), and British banks
also invested. Of the estimated £78 million which the project
eventually cost, about 59% originated outside of Central Africa.
By 1956 French, Italian, and British firms were at work on the
dam.

Placement of the underground power generating facilities

The relative remoteness of the dam site from established
population centers required building new access roads, airstrips,
and the town of Kariba (q. v.). Salisbury served as the administrative center for the whole project. Brush had to be cleared
away where the new lake was to rise, and more than 20,000
Tonga people (q. v.) living on the southern banks of the river had
to be relocated. In 1958 nearly disastrous floods did considerable damage to the dam site, but the main retaining wall was
nevertheless finished the next year. As lake waters rose, thousands of animals were ferried to the main shores in "Operation
Noah" (q. v.). In May 1960 the dam's hydroelectric generators
began supplying power. A large road atop the dam created a
new link across the river.

Placement of the underground power generating facilities
on the southern side of the dam caused considerable resentment
in Northern Rhodesia, although the siting was defended on purely
technical grounds. The issue later became an important sore
point in Zambian-Rhodesian relations. At the time Rhodesia declared UDI in 1965, Zambia was receiving 68% of its electrical
power (including 90% of Copperbelt power) from Kariba Dam.
Shortly after UDI President Kaunda unsuccessfully appealed to
the British government to protect the dam with ground troops,
but Zambia's electrical services from the dam have never been
interrupted. Since 1965 Zambia has developed its own coal
(q. v.) resources for emergency thermal power generation, and
has undertaken to build a second hydroelectric facility on its
side of the dam.

KARIBA DISTRICT. The westernmost part of Mashonaland North
    Province (q. v.), covering 3220 sq. km. The district was cre-
    ated out of the northern part of the former Sebungwe District,
    and a section of the western part of Urungwe District (qq. v.).
    It now borders the districts of Urungwe on the east, Gokwe on

the south, and Binga (qq. v.) on the west.   Except for a small
area north of Kariba township, the district is separated from
Zambia by the lake.   Its land east of the lake is reserved for
Europeans.   The land south of the lake is divided between Purchase Areas, Tribal Trust Lands (qq. v.), and the Matusadona
Game Reserve.   Population in 1969 included 12, 600 Africans
and 700 Europeans.

KARIBA GORGE.   A c. 26 km. stretch of the Zambezi River (q. v.)
in which the river originally narrowed from a width of 640 m.
to less than 90 meters at a point where it turns sharply to the
north.   Cutting through hard basement rocks, the Gorge provided an ideal site for construction of Kariba Dam (q. v.).

KAROI.   Town serving as commercial center for Urungwe District
(q. v.); located c. 90 km. northwest of Sinoia*, on the main road
to Chirundu* (at 16° 49'S, 29° 41'E; alt. 1310 m.).   The town
was founded in 1945 as the center of a government resettlement
scheme for European war veterans.   Over the next two decades
the region developed into one of the country's most profitable
tobacco (q. v.) areas.   Since, UDI local farmers have diversified
their crops and have increased cattle (q. v.) production.   Also
important to the local economy are nearby mica (q. v.) mines.
Population in 1969 was 5380 (91% Africans).   (N. B.:   another,
smaller Karoi village is located just south of the Mavuradonha
Mountains*.)

KAROSS.   A blanket made of animal skins; from a South African
Khoi* word.

KAYA   see   KIA

KAZUNGULA.   Botswana (q. v.) border post at the disputed junction
between Botswana, Rhodesia, Zambia, and South West Africa
(Namibia).   Since Zambia (q. v.) closed its borders to Rhodesia
in 1973, travelers between the two countries have tended to use
the Kazungula ferry to cross the Zambezi River, instead of the
Victoria Falls Bridge (q. v.), located 80 km. downstream.

KENNEDY, JOHN NOBLE (Aug. 31, 1893-June 1970).   Sixth Governor
(q. v.) of Southern Rhodesia (1947-54).   A Scot, Kennedy spent
30 years in the British army and navy before succeeding W. E.
C. Tait (q. v.) as Southern Rhodesian Governor in 1947.   He is
regarded as one of the country's more open-minded governors,
and is noted for his attempts to mix socially with Africans.
After Kennedy left office, Edgar Whitehead (q. v.) invited him to
chair a national convention to discuss the country's future in
1960.   Although the convention was unofficial, many of its proposals were developed in the subsequent constitutional conference.
(See CONSTITUTIONS.)

KGARI I (variant: Khari) (d. c. 1828).   Ngwato (q. v.) ruler credited
with greatly expanding Ngwato power during the 1820s. Kgari was

killed in the Matopo Hills* while leading a raid against the
Kalanga (q.v.). His widow bore a son, Macheng (q.v.), who
was regarded as Kgari's rightful heir because he had been
sired by an official "ghost husband." One of Kgari's natural
sons, Sekgoma I, succeeded first, however. (See also KHAMA
III.)

KHAMA III (variant: Kgama) (c.1837-1923). Ngwato (q.v.) ruler.
Khama was the son of Sekgoma I (c.1810s-1883), who ruled the
Ngwato from the mid-1830s until 1857, and then intermittently
until 1875 (see MACHENG). Khama early fell under the influence of LMS agents, including John Mackenzie (q.v.), and
was later regarded as a model Christian ruler in Africa. A
capable military leader, he led a successful defense against the
Ndebele during an attack on Shoshong in 1863. Over the next
30 years he was regarded as an Ndebele nemesis, whose strategic importance was enhanced by the location of the Ngwato
state astride the Hunters' Road (q.v.) to Matabeleland*. After
he became Ngwato ruler in 1875, he conciliated the Ndebele king
Lobengula (q.v.) by renouncing the Ndebele pretender "Nkulumane" (q.v.), whom his predecessors had supported. Thereafter he and Lobengula made protestations of friendship, but the
two rulers never met and Ndebele-Ngwato relations were always
touchy. In the mid-1880s Khama was a leading Botswana spokesman for creation of the Bechuanaland Protectorate (q.v.) and in
1895 he helped to prevent the new Protectorate from falling under
the administration of the BSAC (q.v.).

KHAMI CULTURE. Term for stone-building culture which displaced
the earlier Leopard's Kopje culture (q.v.) in the southwestern
part of the country. Khami culture is believed to have derived
directly from the Zimbabwe culture (q.v.), which went into a
decline around the early 15th century. The most outstanding
ruins of the Khami tradition are Khami, Dhlo Dhlo, and Nalatale (qq.v.).

KHAMI RIVER (former variant: Khumalo* River). A minor tributary of the Gwai River (q.v.), the Khami rises south of Bulawayo and flows northwest to meet the Gwai c.50 km. above the
latter's confluence with the Umgusa (q.v.). Though small, the
river fills three dams, including Khami Dam (built in 1928),
which supplies water to Bulawayo. The lake formed by this
dam reaches part of the Khami Ruins (q.v.).

KHAMI RUINS. One of the most important complexes of stone ruins
(q.v.) in the country; located by the upper Khami River (q.v.),
after which it is named, c.21 km. west of Bulawayo (at 20°9'S,
28°25'E; alt. 1300 m.). The complex comprises ten distinct
ruins spread over a large area, 40 hectares of which were declared a National Monument in 1938. The structures display a
fine standard of workmanship, featuring extensive checker pattern wall decorations. The main structure in the complex,
known simply as the Hill Ruin, is atop a rise surrounded by

tiered retaining walls.   The nearby Cross Ruin contains a
"Maltese" cross made of stones laid flat.   This structure has
long been popularly attributed to early Portuguese (q. v.) missionaries, but no historical evidence supports such theories
(cf. BAYAO, S.).   Partly submerged by the waters of Khami
Dam is the Precipice Ruin--the largest decorated retaining wall
in the country.

The Khami Ruins are the largest and probably the oldest
of the Khami culture (q. v.) buildings in the southwest.   They
have been dated to the 17th century, and their last occupants
were clearly associated with the Changamire state (q. v.).   However, the site was apparently not an important Changamire administrative center.   It is possible that Khami was originally
the center of the Togwa state (q. v.), which the Changamire
state seems peacefully to have displaced.   If so, building may
have commenced at Khami in the 16th century.   Khami was
abandoned as a Changamire center after the Ndebele (q. v.) occupation of the region in 1838-9.   The Ndebele kept outsiders
away from the ruins during the 19th century, and it is said that
King Lobengula (q. v.) used the site as a private rain-making
center.   After Europeans occupied Matabeleland*, the ruins
were ransacked for gold ornaments by Rhodesia Ancient Ruins,
Ltd. (q. v.).   R. N. Hall (q. v.) undertook some crude excavations there between 1900 and 1910, while David Randall-MacIver
(q. v.) conducted the first scientific excavations in 1905.   More
thorough professional excavations were begun by K. R. Robinson
in 1947.

The original name of the ruins site is not known.   The
local Ndebele still call the ruins Ntaba zi ka Madhladhla, named
after a mambo* who is said to have ruled there.   Nearby is
Leopard's Kopje (q. v.).

KHOI (variant: Khoikhoi).   Name preferred by the Khoisan (q. v.)
people known to Europeans as "Hottentots."   Khoi are known to
have migrated south through present Rhodesia thousands of years
ago (see e. g., RUCHERO CAVE), but the length of their occupation in the country is uncertain.   (See also GRIQUA.)

KHOISAN.   Collective term for the ancient and complex family of
languages containing Khoi (q. v.) and San (q. v.) languages, all
of which are characterized by "click" sounds (q. v.).   The name
Khoisan properly applies only to cultural, not physical groupings
of people, but most Khoisan peoples share certain distinct characteristics, including small stature, light-colored skin, and
steatopygia.   (See LANGUAGES.)

KHONZA (variant: konza).   Sindebele* verb meaning "to serve."
Adapted into limited English usage to express tributary relationships, as in the expression, "The Kaa chief konza'd Lobengula."

KHUMALO (variant: Kumalo).   Common Ndebele clan name (see
ISIBONGO).   Khumalo clan members constituted most of Mzilikazi's original following when he left Zululand in c. 1821.   The

royal branch of the clan provided the Ndebele kings and many
other leading officials in the kingdom. (See, e.g., MNCUM-
BATHE; MTSHANI; MLUGULU.)

KIA (variants: kiai; kaya). One room hut, such as African servants
live in behind European houses.

KILDONAN. Village serving as the terminus of the branch railway*
line built in 1930 to connect the Salisbury to Sinoia line with
the chrome (q.v.) mines just west of the Umvukwe Hills* at
17° 21'S, 30° 37'E).

KIMBERLEY REEFS. Former name of Bindura (q.v.).

"KING SOLOMON'S MINES" see OPHIR; GOLD; HAGGARD, H. R.

KISSINGER, HENRY see under GENEVA CONFERENCE

"KITCHEN KAFFIR" see FANAKALO

KNIGHT-BRUCE, GEORGE WYNDHAM HAMILTON (March 23, 1852-
Dec. 16, 1896). Anglican (q.v.) missionary. After beginning
his career as a cleric in the London slums, Knight-Bruce accepted the unpopular post of Bishop of Bloemfontein in the heart
of Calvinist Afrikaner (q.v.) territory. Anxious to extend mission work to the Shona people, he visited Lobengula (q.v.) in
1888 and got his permission to travel widely in Mashonaland*.
Three years later he returned with Bernard Mizeki (q.v.) and
two other African catechists to open mission stations in British-
occupied Mashonaland. In January 1891 he was made Bishop of
the newly-established Diocese of Mashonaland. He opened his
first station at Penhalonga (q.v.), on land granted by Mutasa
(q.v.). He then attempted to extend Anglican influence throughout the country with African teachers. Ill-health forced his
resignation in late 1894 and he died two years later from malaria*.

KNOBKERRIE (variant: kierrie). Stick with a heavy knob at the
end; used as a bashing or throwing weapon by many southern
African peoples. From Afrikaans* kierie, for "walking stick."

KOLOLO (Makololo). Members of a Sotho (q.v.) kingdom founded
by Sebitwane (d.1851) in the southern Transvaal* during the
early 1820s. After clashing with the Ndebele (q.v.) and other
peoples in the western Transvaal, Sebitwane led the Kololo
through Botswana* into southern Zambia*, occupying the upper
Zambezi flood plains of the Lozi people (q.v.) by the early
1840s. During the late 1840s the Ndebele launched several
large campaigns against the Kololo there, but each met with
disaster. During the 1850s David Livingstone (q.v.) became
an ally of the Kololo, and attempted to plant an LMS mission
among them (see MATABELE MISSION). When the Kololo were
overthrown by the Lozi in 1864, many Kololo men sought refuge
among the Ndebele in Matabeleland*.

KOPJE (variant: koppie). Afrikaans* term for a small hill; used widely throughout Southern Africa to refer to granite outcroppings which assume various shapes and formations. Such outcroppings occur throughout much of Rhodesia, where they have played many historical roles. Early San (q.v.) left many of their rock paintings (q.v.) in kopje caves. Later Shona communities frequently erected their dwellings atop rugged clusters of rocks for defensive purposes. This practice served them well during the late 19th century, when they used firearms effectively to ward off Ndebele and Gaza raiders. The kopjes also served as effective strongholds early in the 1896-7 Shona Revolt (q.v.). Later, however, the British ruthlessly dislodged rebels from their kopje caves and crevices with dynamite. Some kopjes were also used for religious shrines and stone edifices. (See also DWALA; DOMBO; MATOPO HILLS.)

KOREKORE (a.k.a. "Northern Shona"). Linguistic and ethnic classification for the northernmost cluster of Shona-speaking peoples (q.v.). The Korekore dialect (or Chikorekore) is spoken south of the Zambezi River, from, roughly, the middle of Lake Kariba in the west, to the point where the Mazoe River exits the country in the east (qq.v.). To the south Korekore country merges into Zezuru (q.v.) territory. About one-sixth of the country's Shona speak a dialect of Korekore. Among the main Korekore subgroups are Tavara, Budjga, Shangwe, Gova (qq.v.), Nyungwe, Pfungwe, and Tande.

KRAAL. Widely used southern African term for a cluster of African dwellings, usually incorporating a livestock enclosure. The term may refer either to the enclosure itself, or to the social unit which occupies it. Kraal is the Afrikaans* form of Portuguese curral, for "cattle pen." The latter is closely related to Spanish corral, as used in North America.

KUMALO, MTOMPE (variant: Khumalo) (c. 1875-1949). Born into the Ndebele royal Khumalo (q.v.) family, Kumalo (as he spelled his name) was in line to become an adviser to the king, had the kingdom not fallen in the 1890s. After the 1896 Revolt (q.v.) his family settled near the LMS Hope Fountain (q.v.) mission station, where he attended school. In 1914 he went to Tiger Kloof Institution in South Africa to train for the ministry, into which he was ordained in 1917. He worked closely with Neville Jones (q.v.) at Hope Fountain the remainder of his life. In the 1940s Jones recorded Kumalo's life story and his views on Ndebele society and history in My Friend Kumalo.

KUNZWI-NYANDORO see NYANDORO

KURUMAN. LMS mission station founded in 1821 by Robert Moffat (q.v.); located in the north of South Africa's present Cape Province. Mzilikazi is said to have named his heir "Nkulumane" (q.v.) in honor of the station.

KUTAMA. Village in the southern Lomagundi District* (at 17° 48'S, 30° 23'E). Kutama mission school is a Roman Catholic institution founded at the beginning of the First World War. By the 1930s the school had been developed into a major African teacher training and technical school, attracting students from all over the country and surrounding territories.

KWE KWE RIVER (variant: Hwe Hwe). Rises c. 20 km. east of Gwelo*, flowing northwest to join the Sebakwe River* just northeast of the town of Que Que (q.v.). The river's name is believed to be an onomatopoeic rendering of some animal sound. (N.B.: the different spellings of "Kwe Kwe" and "Que Que" are formalized in modern usage, although both forms have the same origin.)

KYLE, LAKE. Located between Fort Victoria and the Zimbabwe Ruins (qq.v.), man-made Lake Kyle is by far the largest body of water lying entirely within the country (at 20° 12'S, 31° E). Kyle Dam, completed in 1961, traps the waters of the Mtilikwe River (q.v.) and some of its tributaries to irrigate sugar* and citrus estates in the southeastern low veld region (see SABI-LIMPOPO AUTHORITY). The 92-sq. km. lake and a somewhat smaller game reserve on its northern shores together form Kyle National Park, a major European recreational area and tourist center. (See LAKES.)

- L -

-L-. The letter l is not used in standardized Chishona (q.v.)--which ignores the Kalanga (q.v.) dialect. Instead Chishona uses only the rolled alveolar consonant r. By contrast, Sindebele (q.v.) almost always uses l where Chishona would use r. Hence, Chishona Mwari becomes Sindebele Mwali, etc.

LAAGER. Afrikaans* term for fortified camp; usually formed by lashing ox wagons (q.v.) together in a tight circle, reinforcing gaps with thorny branches. The technique was developed by Afrikaners (q.v.) during their wars with the Ndebele and other African peoples in South Africa in 1830s. The same technique was later employed by the Pioneer Column (q.v.) and other British forces in present Rhodesia during the 1890s. The term laager was also used in the broader sense of any fortified position, such as the towns besieged during the 1896-7 Revolts (q.v.).

LABOUR PARTY. European political party which became the official opposition in the Legislative Assembly (q.v.) in 1934, when it won five of 30 seats against the United Party (q.v.). Its representation increased to seven seats in the 1939 election, after its leaders achieved some success in widening its political base beyond the labor movement. The party later split into "Rhodesian" and "Southern Rhodesian" Labour parties, which won a total of five seats in 1946. Thereafter both parties greatly declined in support. (See MZINGELI, C.)

LAKES. Although the country has many rivers (q.v.), it has virtually no natural lakes. Construction of dams (q.v.) has, however, created many artificial lakes used for water conservation and recreation. The largest lakes, in order of surface areas, are: Kariba* (510,000 hectares [ha.]); Kyle* (9105 ha.); MacDougall, on the Chiredzi River* (2025 ha.); McIlwaine, on the Hunyani River *(2630 ha.); Sebakwe* (1520 ha.); and Bangala, on the Mtilikwe River* (1135 ha.). (See also NATIONAL PARKS; FISHING.)

LAMONT, DONAL RAYMOND (b. July 27, 1911). An Irish-born Roman Catholic cleric, Lamont came to Southern Rhodesia as a missionary in 1946. In 1957 he was made bishop of Umtali*. Long noted as an outspoken critic of the white government's racial policies, Lamont became the center of international attention in 1976 as the first European convicted under the Law and Order (Maintenance) Act (q.v.), for failure to report the presence of nationalist guerrillas in his diocese. On October 1, 1976, he was sentenced to ten years at labor. An enormous international protest, including an appeal by Pope Paul VI, led to a significant reduction of the sentence the following February. The government then decided to unburden themselves of a potential martyr, so they stripped him of his local citizenship and deported him in March 1977.

LAND APPORTIONMENT ACT (1930). Introduced into the Legislative Assembly (q.v.) in 1929, passed in 1930, and put into effect in April 1931, the Land Apportionment Act adopted the recommendations of the Morris Carter Commission (q.v.) by introducing the principle of racial segregation into land allocation throughout the country. Prior to this Act the only racial element of official land allocation had been the creation of "Native Reserves" (see TRIBAL TRUST LAND) restricted to communal African occupation. Outside the reserves there were no restrictions on land ownership. In practice, however, few Africans could afford to buy land, and by 1925 Africans had acquired only 18,210 hectares of non-reserve land. By contrast, Europeans (q.v.) had acquired c. 12.5 million hectares of land, including virtually all high veld land surrounding the railway (q.v.) lines, and all major urban centers (see URBANIZATION). The Morris Carter Commission was set up in 1925 to investigate the question of allocating land outside the reserves, partly because of concern that Africans would be virtually excluded from further private land acquisitions, and partly because of European pressure to separate European and African farmlands.

The Land Apportionment Act defined six separate categories of land, of which the most important were Native Reserves (accounting for 22.4% of the whole country); Native Purchase Areas (7.7%); European areas (50.8%); and "unassigned areas" (18.4%). With minor exceptions, Africans could buy or lease individual plots only in the Purchase Areas (q.v.), while Europeans could buy land anywhere within the much larger, and generally superior, European areas. Over the next three decades the Act was frequently amended and revised to adjust the proportions of land and to designate new categories.

The revised Land Apportionment Act of 1941 extended the Act to urban areas by acknowledging the existence of African townships in the midst of European areas. The Act allowed Africans to live in, but not to own land in, the towns. See also NATIVE (URBAN AREAS) ACCOMMODATION ACT. After the Second World War major amendments to the Act recognized the increasing inadequacy of the amount of reserve land by creating "Special Native Areas" to increase communal African holdings. Later these areas were consolidated with the reserves in newly-designated "Tribal Trust Lands." By 1964 TTL accounted for 41.6% of total land; Purchase Areas, 4.4%; European area, 37%; "unreserved area" (which both Africans and Europeans could buy), 6.1%; and "national land" (including game reserves and national parks, qq.v.), 10.9%.

In the early 1960s the United (Federal) Party (q.v.) was moving towards repeal of the Land Apportionment Act by breaking down segregated categories of land, but this trend was reversed by the Rhodesian Front (q.v.) after it came to power. The RF simply halted the trend during the mid-1960s, so as not to imperil its attempts to reach a constitutional settlement with Britain. However, when the Republican Constitution (q.v.) was promulgated in 1969, the Land Apportionment Act was superseded by the more rigidly segregationist Land Tenure Act (q.v.).

Although the Land Apportionment Act was clearly the most significant element of the country's many discriminatory laws, it had the ironic effect of making impossible the kind of total racial segregation envisioned in South Africa's policy of "separate development" (cf. "TWO PYRAMID" POLICY). The Act formalized the haphazard allocation of European and African areas which had arisen before 1925, thereby fragmenting the country into sections mostly too small to provide economically or politically autonomous units. Nevertheless, the Act and its successor have been the focus of most African rural protest since the 1930s, as they have limited the rapidly growing African rural population (q.v.) to the agriculturally poorer and more isolated parts of the country, while causing considerable human suffering through periodic forced resettlement schemes. (See also AGRICULTURE.)

LAND HUSBANDRY ACT   see   NATIVE LAND HUSBANDRY ACT

LAND TENURE ACT (1969). Land allocation law which replaced the Land Apportionment Act (q.v.) when the Constitution (q.v.) of 1969 was promulgated. By the mid-1960s virtually all land already reserved for Europeans was privately owned or controlled, thereby limiting the expansion of European commercial agriculture (q.v.). Despite the fact that most European farms were clearly under-utilized, the Rhodesian Front government sought a

solution to the European agricultural problem by expanding the
amount of land available to white farmers, while more rigidly
segregating African and European areas. The resulting Land
Tenure Act converted most existing "unreserved land" into European areas, but otherwise made only minor changes in designated boundaries. The Act divided the country into three basic
categories of land: European, African, and "national"--the last
comprising most of the national parks and game reserves (qq.v.).
European and African areas were equalized, each with 46.6% of
the total country. Forest (q.v.), park, and game reserve lands
were also included in parts of the European and African areas,
leaving 40% of the country available to European farms and settlements; 41.4% to Tribal Trust Lands (q.v.); and 3.8% to Purchase Areas (q.v.).

Promulgation of the law was followed by more vigorous
government efforts to evict African "squatters" from European
areas, and by tightened controls over European entry into African areas. In March 1977 the House of Assembly (q.v.) amended
the Land Tenure Act to allow Africans some access to formerly
reserved European areas. The move was initiated by Prime
Minister Ian Smith as a step towards an internal constitutional
settlement after the failure of the Geneva Conference (q.v.).
(See also "PROTECTED VILLAGES.")

LANDEEN. Term used in the 19th century--particularly around the
lower Zambezi Valley--to refer to the various Mfecane bands,
especially the Ngoni (qq.v.). The word is believed to derive
from l'Indien, though the reason this name was applied to Africans is unclear. (Cf. MATABELE; DZVITI.)

LANGUAGES. With the exception of a few tiny San-speaking (q.v.)
bands in the west, the African peoples of the country all speak
Bantu languages (q.v.). Chishona (q.v.) is the first language
of c.75% of the population and is an important second language
among most of the rest. The most important minority languages
are Sindebele (q.v.) and English. The latter is also an important second language among most Africans, as well as the only
official government language. Afrikaans (q.v.) is the most
widely spoken minority European language. Fanakalo (q.v.),
or "Kitchen Kaffir," serves as a lingua franca throughout the
country.

LAW, AUGUSTUS HENRY (Oct. 21, 1833-Nov. 25, 1880). A Jesuit
missionary born into an English Anglican family, Law abandoned
his naval career in 1853 to follow his father into the Roman
Catholic Church. The next year he entered the Society of Jesus.
In 1875 he came to South Africa to teach at the Jesuit College
in Grahamstown. He soon volunteered to join the Jesuits' Zambezi Mission (q.v.), arriving in Bulawayo* in time to witness
Lobengula's marriage to the Gaza princess Xwalile (q.v.) in
1879. Encouraged by Xwalile's reports of Gazaland (q.v.), Law,
F. De Sadeleer (q.v.), and two other missionaries walked across
the country with Ndebele guides in mid-1880. They were hospi-

tably received by King Mzila (q.v.) in Gazaland, but were in-
adequately fed and without medical supplies. Law died there
from fever and dysentery.

LAW AND ORDER (MAINTENANCE) ACT (1960). Exceptionally tough
security law introduced by Edgar Whitehead's (q.v.) government
in October 1960, shortly after government arrests of National
Democratic Party (q.v.) leaders provoked bloody urban rioting.
According to Chief Justice Robert Tredgold (q.v.), who resigned
his post to protest the law, the measure "outrages every basic
human right." The Act enabled the police (see BSAP) to declare
any group of three or more people an unlawful assembly. It imposed heavy prison sentences for participation in proscribed
gatherings, and it generally provided for the suppression of political dissent. The Dominion Party (q.v.) also supported the
Act in 1960, and its successor, the Rhodesian Front (q.v.), repeatedly amended and toughened the law after coming to power in
late 1962, making it the primary tool for suppressing African
nationalist political activity. (Cf. UNLAWFUL ORGANIZATIONS
ACT.)

LAWLEY, ARTHUR (later Baron Wenlock) (Nov. 12, 1860-June 14,
1932). Early BSAC official. A former British military officer,
Lawley became secretary to A. H. G. Grey (q.v.) at Bulawayo*
in 1896. When Grey shifted his headquarters from Bulawayo to
Salisbury later that year, Lawley was unofficially left in charge
of Matabeleland* just as the Ndebele Revolt (q.v.) was ending.
His official status there remained unclear until 1898, when he
was formally designated Administrator (q.v.) of Matabeleland.
He resigned in 1901 to become governor of Western Australia,
but returned to southern Africa the next year as Lt. Governor
of the Transvaal*. He later served as governor of Madras
(1905-11).

LEASK, THOMAS SMITH (Oct. 12, 1839-Feb. 7, 1912). A Scottish
hunter (q.v.), trader, and concessionaire, Leask came to South
Africa in 1862. Two years later he made the first of five annual trips into Matabeleland* and Mashonaland* to hunt and trade.
He settled in the Transvaal* in 1871, but a decade later he
formed a partnership with J. Fairbairn, G. Westbeech, and G.
Phillips (qq.v.) which secured a concession* from Lobengula to
prospect for minerals. His posthumously published diaries are
an important record of the country in the 1860s.

LEE, JOHN (b. July 10, 1827). South African hunter (q.v.) and
trader who became the first European other than missionaries
(q.v.) to settle in present Rhodesia. In 1866 Mzilikazi granted
Lee a large tract of land west of the upper Shashani River (q.v.)
where his house (now a National Monument) became an important
station along the Hunters' Road (q.v.). Lee served both Mzilikazi and Lobengula as an adviser, and played a particularly important role in their dealings with other Europeans (see SOUTH
AFRICAN GOLD FIELDS EXPLORATION CO.). He retired to

the Transvaal* in 1891.   Two years later the BSAC confiscated
his Matabeleland farm because of his refusal to fight against
the Ndebele in the Ndebele War (q.v.).   His subsequent fate is
unknown.

LEGION MINE.   Village named after a group of local gold* mines
located on the lower Shashani River* c.135 km. south of Bulawayo in the Matobo District* (at 21° 55'S, 28° 32'E).   The mines
were all opened over pre-colonial African workings.

LEGISLATIVE ASSEMBLY.   Formal name for the country's main
governing body from 1924 to 1965, when it was redesignated
"Parliament."   The 1969 Constitution (q.v.) reconstituted the
body as the House of Assembly (q.v.), the lower chamber of a
new bicameral Parliament (q.v.).
    The "Responsible Government" (q.v.) Constitution of 1923
modelled the Assembly after the British House of Commons, but
placed sharp limitations on its powers of legislation.   The British
Crown recognized the Assembly as Southern Rhodesia's primary
law making body, but reserved the right to block any legislation
it disapproved (see GOVERNORS).   It further limited the Assembly's competence to purely internal matters, while excluding
certain reserved constitutional clauses pertaining to African affairs.   In practice, however, the Assembly and its Prime Ministers (q.v.) gradually broadened their range of competence and
never had any legislation vetoed by the British government.
When faced with local legislation such as the Land Apportionment and Industrial Conciliation Acts (qq.v.), Britain tended to
amend the Letters Patent upon which its reserve powers were
based, thereby legitimizing the Assembly's actions.
    From 1924 to 1961 the Assembly comprised 30 seats.
Creation of the Federation (q.v.) in 1953 headed off a planned
expansion, but the Constitution of 1961 anticipated the dismantling
of the Federation by increasing the number of Assembly seats to
65.   Throughout this whole period the Assembly held at least one
session each year and was reformed by general elections (q.v.)
an average of about every fourth year.
    Assembly members were elected by a technically color-
blind franchise, but high property qualifications for voters left
the settler community with an overwhelming majority through
1957.   In that year new franchise qualifications created a special
voters' roll for Africans.   This dualism was refined by the 1961
constitution, which instituted a complex voting system with "A"
and "B" rolls.   "A" roll voters had higher educational, property,
and income qualifications than "B" roll voters.   The "A" roll
elected 50 European Assembly members from 50 "constituencies."
The "B" roll voters elected African members from 15 "electoral
districts."   By mid-1965 Europeans constituted 95% of the 97,284
"A" roll voters, while Africans constituted 92% of the 11,577
"B" roll voters.   The impact of African voters was further di-
luted by an effective nationalist boycott of the general elections
in 1962 and 1965.   (See also POLITICAL PARTIES.)

LEGISLATIVE COUNCIL (Legco). By the Southern Rhodesia Order-in-Council of October 20, 1898, the British government introduced representative government into the territory with the creation of a Legislative Council similar to those introduced in other British colonies. The Council had its first session in May of the next year, with four elected "unofficial" members, and five "official" members nominated by the BSAC. As with the Executive Council (q.v.), the BSAC Administrator (q.v.) presided. A British Resident Commissioner sat on the Council as a non-voting member and was responsible for reporting on Legco decisions to the High Commissioner for Southern Africa. The BSAC responded to persistent settler demands for increased representation by periodically adding new unofficial seats to Legco. By 1908 elected members held a majority, and by 1920 there were 13 such members. Over time Legco played an increasingly important role in law-making, but the elected members' majority was held in check by built-in restrictions on Legco's range of powers and by the Administrator's power to veto legislation relating to revenue generation or to BSAC land and rights. Nevertheless, Legco became the first formal arena of settler politics, particularly after Charles Coghlan (q.v.) was elected in 1908. By the late 1910s the dominant issues the Council faced pertained to the constitutional status of the country following the planned termination of BSAC rule (see AMALGAMATION; RESPONSIBLE GOVERNMENT; UNIONIST MOVEMENTS). When Responsible Government was achieved in 1923, Legco was replaced by the Legislative Assembly (q.v.).

LEMBA (Valemba; variants: Remba; Baremba; etc.). Small but historically prominent community living mainly in the Belingwe (q.v.) area. The Lemba are closely associated with the Venda (q.v.) but, unlike the latter, speak a dialect of Shona. By the 19th century the Lemba were noted as traders, metal-workers, potters, and weavers. They tended to live as endogamous groups within other societies. Many Lemba fell under the Ndebele tributary state during the 19th century and fought with the Ndebele in the 1896 Revolt. Though they are not Muslims (q.v.), the Lemba exhibit many Islamic cultural traits and are said to be "Semitic" in appearance. According to popular, but unsupported theories, the Lemba are descendants of early non-African immigrants. (See ZIMBABWE CONTROVERSY.)

LENGWE see HLENGWE

LEOPARD'S KOPJE CULTURE. Term for a late Iron Age (q.v.) culture, or industry, which extended over the southwestern parts of the country and into neighboring Botswana* and the Transvaal* from the end of the first millenium A.D. to about the 15th century, when it was displaced by the intrusive Khami culture (q.v.). The culture is named after a site less than a kilometer north of the Khami Ruins (q.v.). The Leopard's Kopje culture complex featured mixed farming and limited cattle* raising, and is archaeologically identified by characteristic shouldered pottery.

The culture is believed either to have been introduced among
the local Kalanga (q. v.) by northern immigrants, or to have
been a local development of the prior Gokomere Culture (q. v.).

LEPROSY (a. k. a. Hansen's disease). Infectious bacterial disease
found throughout the country, particularly in the Sabi and Zambezi valleys. Leprosariums were established near Fort Victoria in 1926 and Mtoko in 1932. Willingness of sufferers to
accept medical treatment has gradually improved, giving hope
of eradicating the disease from the country. (See HEALTH.)

LESSING, DORIS [née Taylor] (b. Oct. 22, 1919). The best-known
and most distinguished writer associated with the country, Lessing was born to British parents in Kermanshah, Persia (now
Iran), where her father was a bank manager. In the mid-1920s
her family immigrated to Southern Rhodesia, taking up maize
farming near Banket (q. v.). Around 1937 Lessing went to Salisbury to work as a secretary and as a telephone operator. In
the early 1940s she helped to organize a local Communist Party,
but it had no impact on the country's politics. She left the
country for England in 1949 after two unsuccessful marriages,
retaining the name of her second husband, Gottfried Lessing.
    Although Lessing started writing early, she published
nothing of importance until she reached England. Her first
published novel, The Grass Is Singing (1950) had an implicitly
Southern Rhodesian setting, and depicted the psychological deterioration of a settler couple struggling on an isolated farm.
A volume of short stories, This Was the Old Chief's Country
followed in 1951. Some of these and other stories were later
published in a major collection, African Stories (1965). With
the exception of her "Children of Violence" pentalogy (1952-69),
most of her later fiction is set outside of Africa. Her African
fiction contains strong condemnations of settler society and
colonialism, but she is most noted for her intensely personal
treatment of the more general themes of individual alienation,
madness, paranormal psychology, aging, and the fate of mankind. Her work is said to have had a particularly strong influence on feminist writers, and she is regarded as a prospective candidate for a Nobel Prize in literature. (Cf. LUTHULI,
A.)
    Lessing returned to central Africa just once, in 1956.
After traveling extensively throughout the region she was declared a proscribed immigrant because of her earlier political
activities. She described her trip in Going Home (1957). Be-
sides fiction, she has also written poetry, essays, reviews, and
dramatic scripts. (See LITERATURE.)

LEWANIKA   see under   LOZI

LIBERAL PARTY. European political party formed in 1943 by a
former Huggins cabinet minister, Jacob Hendrik Smit (1881-
1959), who attempted to combine non-Labour Party (q. v.) opposition against the ruling United Party (q. v.). Despite its name,

the Liberal Party represented strongly conservative interests
which opposed government economic regulation and African political advancement. The party won 12 of 30 Legislative Assembly (q.v.) seats in 1946, but declined rapidly after 1948,
when it won only five seats.

LILFORD, D. C. "BOSS" (b. July 30, 1908). Rhodesian Front
(q.v.) leader. Born in South Africa, Lilford was brought to
Southern Rhodesia as an infant by his poor farming family.
He eventually built up a prosperous 13,350 hectare farm, "Lil-
fordia," near Salisbury. Described as the wealthiest farmer--
if not the wealthiest person--in the country, he has been regarded as one of the most powerful backers of the Rhodesian
Front Party since its formation in 1962. He helped Ian Smith
to oust Winston Field (qq.v.) as premier in 1964, and has since
opposed every constitutional settlement proposal which would
surrender real political power to Africans.

LIMBO. Term used by European traders in the 19th century for a
kind of coarse calico which is an important African trade item
in the country. Derives from the Nguni* word ubulembu, for
"web."

LIMPOPO RIVER. Although it is the second largest river on the
African continent to empty into the Indian Ocean, the Limpopo
carries only a fraction of the volume of water in the Zambezi
River (q.v.). During the dry season the Limpopo is usually
little more than a stream, and as such has never impeded human movements. The river rises in South Africa near Pretoria,
whence it cuts about a 1400-km. curve, first to the northwest,
and then east and southeast to the sea. Its upper reaches are
known as the Crocodile, or Oori, River, a name sometimes applied to its entire length. After forming a stretch of the Bots-
wana/South Africa border, the Limpopo is fed by the Shashi
River (q.v.). From that point it flows east c.220 km., defining the Rhodesia/South Africa border (q.v.) before entering
Mozambique. Beitbridge (q.v.) is the main crossing point into
Rhodesia.
        Along with the Sabi River (q.v.) system, the Limpopo
system drains the eastern side of the Central Plateau (q.v.).
The Shashi is its major Rhodesian affluent. Others include--
from west to east--the Umzingwane, Bubye, and Nuanetsi (qq.v.).
J. F. Elton (q.v.) was the first person to map the central Limpopo in 1870. (See RIVERS.)

LIONS (Sindebele*: isilwana; Chishona*: shumba; mhondoro). These
animals are still fairly numerous in the country, though they are
now found mainly in national parks and game reserves (qq.v.).
Outside such preserves they are classified as "vermin" and can
be hunted* with few restrictions. (On Shona "lion spirits," see
MHONDORO; GOMBWE.)

LIPPERT CONCESSION (a.k.a. "Humbug Concession"). After the

BSAC had used the Rudd Concession (q.v.) to legitimize its occupation of Mashonaland in 1890, the Ndebele king Lobengula
still hoped to improve his position by playing off European powers against each other.   To this end he granted sole rights to
issue European land titles within BSAC-claimed territory to the
German speculator Edward Amandus Lippert (1853-1925)--a cousin
of Alfred Beit*--and his agent Edward R. Renny-Tailyour (1851-
1894).   This document, which he signed at Umvutsha* on November 17, 1891, became known as the "Lippert Concession." BSAC
officials reportedly called the concession a "humbug," but they
nevertheless bought it from Lippert a few months later for Company shares and a large sum of money (some authorities argue
that Lippert arranged in advance to sell the concession to the
BSAC).   Lobengula was outraged to learn the concession had
fallen into BSAC hands.   L. S. Jameson (q.v.) nevertheless
argued that through the document Lobengula acknowledged European law in Mashonaland, thereby strengthening his Company's
pretexts for starting the Ndebele War (q.v.) in 1893.   Thereafter the Lippert Concession was regarded by Europeans as a
mainstay of BSAC land rights in the country.

LITERATURE.   There is no pre-20th-century tradition of writing in
the country, but most African societies have rich traditions of
oral literature in the forms of myths, tales, poems, songs, and
histories.   Many of these have been translated and published,
notably in the antiquarian journal Nada (q.v.).   Publication of
modern forms of written literature is a relatively late development, owing a great deal to the government's creation of the
African Literature Bureau in 1953.   This Bureau was established
to encourage vernacular writing for use in schools.   The year
1957 saw publication of the first "novel" in Chishona*:   Feso, by
S. M. Mutswairo (q.v.).   Since then more than 40 short novels
have been published by about 30 writers.   About 75% of these
books are in Chishona, the rest in Sindebele*.   Most of these
works are apolitical in nature, and many are highly moralistic
in tone.   In common with African fiction elsewhere, the conflict
between Western and African cultures is a dominant theme.   One
of the most popular vernacular writers has been Patrick Chakaipa
(q.v.), who is credited with helping to bridge the gap between
traditional oral literature and modern Western prose forms.
     Few African writers have yet published fiction in English.
Ndabaningi Sithole and Stanlake Samkange (qq.v.) have published
a few novels.   More recently, Charles Mungoshi (b.1948) has
published Waiting for the Rain (1975).
     European literature relating to the country is very diverse.
Some of H. R. Haggard's (q.v.) fantastic romances were inspired
by Rhodesian settings, but Olive Schreiner's (q.v.) Trooper Peter
Halket of Mashonaland (1897) is probably the earliest novel explicitly set in the country.   Gertrude Page (q.v.) was the first
settler novelist to use local settings.   Many more novels have
since been written by settlers, but few have achieved any distinction.   Kingsley Fairbridge and Cullen Gouldsbury (qq.v.) were
poets highly regarded by the settler community, but A. S. Cripps

(q. v.) is the only poet writing on local themes to achieve much attention outside the country. The most distinguished writer associated with the country to date is Doris Lessing (q. v.), a former settler, but all her major work has been published since she emigrated to England in 1949. (See BIBLIOGRAPHY.)

LITHIUM. The country has some of the richest lithium ore deposits in the world. Production of this light metal was of little economic importance before the Second World War, but new technologies relating to jet aircraft, rocketry, and atomic power have since transformed lithium into one of the country's major minerals (q. v.). World demand for lithium boomed during the 1950s. Major production was undertaken at Bikita (q. v.), with minor mines in northeastern Mashonaland. After prices dropped in the early 1960s, only the Bikita Mine remained open, producing an average annual output valued at £349,000 between 1961 and 1964. Total value of lithium ore production through 1964 was over £4 million.

LIVINGSTONE, DAVID (March 19, 1813-c. May 1, 1873). Livingstone's name is strongly associated with Rhodesian history, but his direct ties to the country were limited. He began his career as an LMS missionary in former Ndebele territory in the western Transvaal* in 1841, but he soon grew restless to travel farther north. By 1851 he had reached the upper Zambezi headquarters of the Kololo people (q. v.), with whom he explored the Zambezi River between 1853 and 1856. During this journey he visited and named the Victoria Falls (q. v.). In 1858 he returned to the Zambezi in charge of expedition concerned primarily with exploring the river's northern affluents. Through this whole period he was also encouraging the LMS to establish missions among the Kololo and Ndebele. His father-in-law Robert Moffat (q. v.) helped to plant such a mission among the Ndebele in 1859, but the Kololo mission was a disaster. One of the "Matabele Mission's" (q. v.) pioneer agents was Livingstone's brother-in-law, John Smith Moffat (q. v.), whose work Livingstone personally financed for several years with the royalties from his successful book, Travels and Researches in South Africa. Although Livingstone himself barely penetrated what is now Rhodesia, his voluminous books and posthumously published letters and diaries contain valuable chronological details and allusions to events inside the country during the 1840s and 1850s--an otherwise poorly documented period.

LLEWELLIN, JOHN JESTYN (Baron Llewellin from 1945) (Feb. 6, 1893-Jan. 1957). After a long political career in England, Llewellin became the first Governor-General of the Federation of Rhodesia and Nyasaland (q. v.) in 1953. He died in office and was succeeded by S. R. Dalhousie (q. v.).

LOBENGULA KHUMALO (variants: Lo Bengula; Nombengula; Ulopengula; Upengula; etc.) (c. 1836-early 1894). Ndebele king (1870-94). Born in the western Transvaal*, Lobengula was the

son of Mzilikazi by a wife described as a "Swazi" (q.v.). Little
is known about his early life, but he appears to have narrowly
escaped execution in the political crisis which occurred on his
father's arrival in Matabeleland* in c.1839. By the 1850s he
was a member of the Mahlokohloko ibutho (q.v.).

When Mzilikazi died in 1868, his other son Nkulumane
(q.v.) was universally recognized as rightful heir to the kingship, but Nkulumane's whereabouts were unknown. Many Ndebele believed Nkulumane had been killed in the 1839 political
crisis. An embassy to Natal failed to turn up the missing heir,
so Mncumbathe, Mhlaba, Lotshe, Gampu (qq.v.) and other leading izinduna designated Lobengula as successor. Lobengula's
candidacy for the kingship caught resident European observers
by surprise. Up till then he had enjoyed no special status, and
was known for his adoption of European clothes and his close
associations with European residents. Many Ndebele dismissed
Lobengula's candidacy because of his mother's allegedly inferior
social rank. Lobengula himself appears to have been unwilling
to become king until the question of Nkulumane's fate was resolved. Further attempts to find Nkulumane in Natal produced
no new information, so Lobengula was formally installed as king
during the January 1870 inxwala (q.v.).

Lobengula's authority as king was immediately challenged
by pro-Nkulumane amabutho (see IBUTHO). In June Lobengula
personally led a successful assault against the rebels at the
Zwangendaba (q.v.) ibutho town. Several hundred opponents, including their leader Mbigo (q.v.), were killed. Many survivors
fled to the Transvaal, where they schemed against Lobengula
through the remainder of his reign. Lobengula was lenient to
the rebels who remained within the kingdom, but these people
continued to oppose him and he never gained complete control
of the kingdom. One known attempt to overthrow him forcibly
occurred in January 1872, when an "Nkulumane" pretender and
another half-brother, Mangwane (q.v.), tried to invade the country. In 1878 a semi-official British delegation led by R. R.
Patterson (q.v.) was wiped out--apparently after Patterson tact-
lessly hinted that the British might support "Nkulumane's" claims
to the Ndebele kingship.

Shortly after becoming king, Lobengula made the new
Gibixhegu (q.v.) town his headquarters. About a year later he
either relocated this town and changed its name, or created a
totally new Bulawayo (q.v.) as his headquarters. Thereafter
Bulawayo--which was again moved in 1881--served as Lobengula's headquarters, but the king also spent much of his time
in private villages such as Umvutsha (q.v.). And, like his
father, Lobengula also traveled about the kingdom frequently
while living out of an ox wagon (q.v.).

The local LMS missionaries had hoped that Lobengula
would support their work, but he soon disappointed them. He
stopped wearing European clothes, and maintained a policy of
merely tolerating the missionaries' presence. Nevertheless,
he allowed Jesuits of the Zambezi Mission (q.v.) to open a
Bulawayo station in 1879. The general failure of missionaries

to win converts made them outspoken critics of both Lobengula
and the Ndebele way of life.   They increasingly lobbied for
European conquest of the kingdom.

Although Lobengula allowed missionaries and many European traders to work inside the Ndebele kingdom, he strictly
forbade them to enter Mashonaland (q.v.; see COILLARD, F.).
He also exercised a near-monopoly over the movements of explorers and hunters (q.v.).   He personally conducted most
Ndebele trade with outsiders, from whom he obtained a considerable volume of such goods as firearms, horses*, tools,
and luxury items.   These he used mostly to reward his supporters.

Mzilikazi had died just as Europeans were discovering
gold (q.v.) at Tati and Northern Gold Fields (qq.v.).   An influx
of prospectors was thus one of the first problems with which
Lobengula had to deal as king.   European pressure for mineral
concessions (q.v.) grew intense after he awarded his first formal concession to Thomas Baines (q.v.) in 1871.   During the
mid-1880s European imperial powers began competing for influence north of the Limpopo in an effort to head off Afrikaner
(q.v.) expansion from the Transvaal.   Lobengula signed a treaty
with the Transvaal agent P. Grobler (q.v.) in 1887, and then a
similar treaty with Britain's agent J. S. Moffat (q.v.) the next
year.

In October 1888 Lobengula awarded the Rudd Concession
(q.v.) to agents of Cecil Rhodes, thinking he had signed a
limited mineral concession.   Rivals of Rhodes pointed out to
Lobengula that the document had been seriously misrepresented,
so he attempted publicly to repudiate it the next year.   Rhodes
sent his associate L. S. Jameson (q.v.) to Bulawayo to renegotiate the concession, while at the same time he obtained a
royal Charter* for his newly-formed BSAC (q.v.).   As Lobengula made fresh, minor concessions to Jameson, Rhodes and
the BSAC assembled an occupation force known as the Pioneer
Column (q.v.).   In mid-1890 the Column advanced into Mashonaland, establishing a beachhead for further British expansion.
Whether Lobengula willingly permitted the Column to enter
Mashonaland remains controversial, but he clearly made no
serious attempt to stop it.   Through all these proceedings he
also tried to deal directly with the British government through
Mshete (q.v.) and other emissaries.   In 1891 he awarded the
Lippert Concession (q.v.) to men he thought were rivals of
Rhodes and the BSAC, but Rhodes himself acquired the document and used it further to validate BSAC occupation of Ma-
shonaland.

Throughout his reign Lobengula oversaw frequent Ndebele
military campaigns against neighbors.   By the 1880s his relations with his neighbors were largely stabilized.   Most campaigns by then were little more than tribute-collecting expeditions or "police actions" against recalcitrant subordinates.
There were, however, notable military reverses against the
distant Tawana (q.v.) and some peoples north of the Zambezi
River.   British occupation of Mashonaland provided Shona rulers

with a new ally against resented Ndebele exactions, thereby increasing Lobengula's need to mount punitive expeditions.   In
mid-1893 Jameson--by then administrator of Mashonaland--used
an Ndebele foray into the Fort Victoria* area as an excuse for
declaring war on Lobengula.

Lobengula attempted to negotiate a peaceful settlement
through the ensuing Ndebele War (q.v.), but the British were
intent on outright conquest.   Ndebele resistance was half-hearted,
and the British quickly advanced on Bulawayo.   In early November 1893 Lobengula had the town burned as he fled north with a
large entourage.   It is believed that he sought asylum with the
Ngoni ruler Mpezeni (q.v.) in what is now eastern Zambia.
What actually happened to him has been the subject of considerable myth-making, but it is clear that he died of some illness
without even reaching the Zambezi River--probably around February 1894.   The location of his grave remained generally secret
until its rediscovery near Kamativi (q.v.) in 1943, when it was
declared a National Monument.   Another myth, that Lobengula
hid a vast "treasure," inspired fortune-hunters well into the 20th
century.

Like his father, Lobengula died without leaving a clear
successor.   He had many wives, but his "royal wife" Xwalile
(q.v.) bore him no children, and his favorite wife Lozigeyi
(q.v.) produced no sons.   When the British occupied Matabeleland, they did everything they could to abolish the Ndebele kingdom.   At Rhodes' instigation three of Lobengula's sons, Mpezeni,
Njube, and Nguboyenja (qq.v.), were sent to South Africa to be
educated and to be kept out of the way.   Meanwhile, another
son, Nyamanda (q.v.), asserted his own claim to the kingship,
and restoration of the kingship became one of the major issues
during the ensuing Revolt (q.v.).

LOBOLO (Sindebele*: ilobolo; Chishona*: roworo).   Bantu* term
widely used in southern Africa for payments made by husbands
to the families of their brides.   In what is now Rhodesia the
pre-colonial lobolo systems of different peoples were broadly
similar, and have since been codified and elaborated in African
law by the government.   Lobolo has never been a system where-
by husbands "bought" wives, but rather one in which the husbands made payments to their in-laws for guarantees that their
wives would prove both fertile and faithful.   In the 20th century
laws respecting lobolo have been increasingly concerned with
defining parents' rights to children.   Traditionally, lobolo payments were made in livestock--cattle (q.v.) when available;
otherwise, sheep, goats, or iron hoes.   Cattle are still used
for lobolo payments, but cash payments have also become common.   (For an example of royal lobolo, see XWALILE.)

LOCUSTS.   Though the country contains no "outbreak areas" of
these orthopteric insects, it has historically suffered periodic
plagues of invading swarms.   Red locusts (Nomadacris septem-
fasciata) are widespread throughout eastern and southern Africa,
and have usually entered the country from the north.   Brown

locusts (Locustana pardalina) are restricted to southern Africa
and have entered the country mainly from outbreak areas in
Botswana*. A particularly devastating locust invasion hit the
country in the early 1890s, adding to the suffering which contributed to the 1896 Revolts (q. v.). Other major invasions occurred in 1910, 1924, and 1934. Increasingly efficient retalia-
tory measures have lessened the amounts of crop damage, and
international cooperative organizations have worked to destroy
breeding grounds.

LOMAGUNDI (Shona chief)   see   NEMAKONDE

LOMAGUNDI DISTRICT (former variant: Lo Magundi).   Originally
    a huge district covering the northernmost wedge of the country,
    Lomagundi District lost its western section to form Urungwe
    District (q. v.) in the 1940s, and later lost its remaining north-
    ern border portion to create the Sipolilo District (q. v.).   The
    district now covers 13,170 sq. km. in Mashonaland North Prov-
    ince (q. v.).   Except for the southern fringe of the district, the
    entire territory is reserved for Europeans (see LAND TENURE
    ACT).   Population in 1969 included 213,490 Africans and 5590
    Europeans.   Administrative center for the district is Sinoia
    (q. v.).   Other important centers include Banket, Mangula,
    Alaska Mine, Darwendale, and Mtoroshanga (qq. v.).   The econ-
    omy of the district is based on mixing agriculture and diverse
    mineral production.
        Lomagundi is separated from Urungwe District by the
    Angwa River (q. v.).   It also borders the districts of Sipolilo on
    the north; Mazoe and Salisbury on the east; and Hartley and Ga-
    tooma (qq. v.) on the south.

LONDON AND LIMPOPO MINING COMPANY (LLMC).   Prospecting
    company formed in London in 1868 to exploit the gold (q. v.)
    fields found by Henry Hartley (q. v.).   In 1869 John Swinburne
    (q. v.) led a well-equipped expedition to the Tati River (q. v.),
    where a small European settlement was founded.   The LLMC's
    real objective, however, was the Northern Goldfields (q. v.), so
    Swinburne went to Inyati*, where he obtained T. M. Thomas's
    (q. v.) aid in persuading the Ndebele regent Mncumbathe (q. v.)
    to permit his party to prospect in Mashonaland*.   In return the
    LLMC provided an escort for the Ndebele embassy sent to Natal
    to interview the royal pretender "Nkulumane" (q. v.).   Swinburne
    and S. H. Edwards (q. v.) prospected around the Hartley Hills
    (q. v.) in Mashonaland, but the next year the new Ndebele king
    awarded the northern concession to the rival South African Gold
    Fields Exploration Co. (q. v.).   The LLMC men then retreated
    to the Tati area, where they began crushing quartz with the first
    mechanical crushing machines ever used in southern Africa.   In
    1870 the LLMC hired J. F. Elton (q. v.) to explore the Limpopo
    River* in search of a route to the sea.   Late the next month
    Lobengula awarded the LLMC an exclusive mining concession to
    Tati, where the LLMC outlasted all its smaller competitors.
    By 1871 the company was the sole proprietor of the Tati fields,

but it was taking out little gold. By 1875 the company had abandoned the district. (See TATI CONCESSION.)

LONDON MISSIONARY SOCIETY (LMS). Founded as a non-denominational evangelical society in 1795, the LMS soon fell under the aegis of the Congregational Churches. It began opening missions in South Africa before the turn of the century, and thereafter made the region one of its most intense foreign mission fields. Agents such as Robert Moffat and David Livingstone (qq.v.) helped to make the LMS a pioneer in advancing Christianity into the interior regions. During the 1830s the LMS encouraged its Boston counterpart, the American Board of Commissioners (q.v.), to open a mission among the Ndebele, then living in the Transvaal. In 1859 Moffat himself led an LMS party into the new Ndebele home in Matabeleland*, where the Matabele Mission (q.v.) was permanently established. The LMS enjoyed little success in proselytizing among the Ndebele until after the Ndebele Revolt (q.v.) of 1896, but its agents played a crucial role in Ndebele affairs as the forerunners of European occupation. After the Revolt the BSAC confirmed the LMS in possession of its stations and granted it additional sites in Matabeleland. During the 20th century the LMS enjoyed considerably more progress than it had seen in the country during the previous century, but its work was still limited by lack of staff and funds. By the time the LMS celebrated its centenary in 1959, it could claim 2915 African church members, but this figure ranked only 12th among the country's missions (q.v.), and accounted for less than 1% of the country's total avowed African Christians. In 1966 the LMS amalgamated with another body to become the Congregational Council for World Missions. (See MISSIONS.)

LONELY MINE. Mining community located c.85 km. north of Bulawayo, near the headwaters of the Bubi River* in central Bubi District* (at 19°30'S, 28°45'E). Lonely Mine began operations in 1906, exploiting a rich gold (q.v.) vein previously untouched by earlier Shona miners. Nickel (q.v.) and tungsten are also mined locally.

LOTSHE HLABANGANA (variant: Lotje) (d. Sept. 1889). An Ndebele induna* of considerable seniority by the mid-1860s, Lotshe was leader of the Induba ibutho*. After the death of Mzilikazi, Lotshe supported the candidacy of Lobengula and participated in an embassy to Natal in 1869 to investigate the disappearance of the preferred heir, Nkulumane (q.v.). After Lobengula's installation as king, Lotshe's influence increased further. In 1879 he and Xukutwayo (q.v.) led the Ndebele delegation to Gazaland to fetch the royal bride Xwalile (q.v.). His prestige dipped badly after 1885, however, when he commanded a disastrous impi* against the Tawana (q.v.) in central Botswana. Over the next several years he emerged as the most outspoken Ndebele advocate of peaceful accommodation with the Europeans then pressing in on the Ndebele kingdom. He favored Lobengula's

signing of the Rudd Concession (q.v.) in 1888, but then became
the national scapegoat when Lobengula realized that the concession had been badly misrepresented. In early September 1889
Lotshe and many of his relatives were killed on Lobengula's
authority.

LOTTERIES. In 1934 the white electorate voted overwhelmingly in
favor of establishing a state-operated lottery. The Southern
Rhodesian government then created a State Lottery Trust to administer the first drawings the following year. Ticket purchases
were restricted to non-Africans until 1959. Revenues not paid
out in prizes or expenses have been distributed to service projects and charities. Prize amounts and frequency of drawings
have steadily increased over time. By the mid-1970s the top
prizes were R$80,000 to R$100,000, awarded 12 times a year.

LOUW, A. A.   see under MORGENSTER

LOW VELD   see ALTITUDINAL ZONES; SABI-LIMPOPO AUTHORITY

LOZI (Balozi; variant: Barotse).   Large Bantu-speaking society
living in the Zambezi floodplains of western Zambia*--a region
known as Barotseland.   The Lozi kingdom was occupied by the
Kololo (q.v.) from the early 1840s to 1864.   After the expulsion
of the Kololo rulers, the Lozi themselves were unsettled by
political strife until Lewanika (c.1845-1916) settled into power
firmly in 1885.   Lewanika's assumption of power coincided with
renewed Ndebele military activity north of the Zambezi River,
and the two states fought several times until 1893.   The Lozi
were the most formidable Ndebele enemy north of the Zambezi,
and competed with the latter for control of such riverine peoples
as the Nanzwa and Tonga (qq.v.).   (See also COILLARD, F.)

LOZIGEYI DHLODHLO (d. Feb. 23, 1919).   One of Lobengula's first
wives, Lozigeyi lacked the official status of Lobengula's "great
wife" (or "royal wife") Xwalile (q.v.), but she was unusually
outspoken and was regarded as the king's most influential wife.
In view of Xwalile's barrenness, Lozigeyi might have produced
a royal heir herself, but she bore the king only daughters.
Lacking a son of her own, she championed the kingship claims
of a co-wife's son, Nyamanda (q.v.), with whom she worked
closely during the 1896 Revolt (q.v.).   Afterwards she retired
to "Queens' Location" (q.v.) on the middle Bembezi River*,
where she became wealthy.   She subsequently broke with Nyamanda.   In 1906 she wrote her will to leave everything she
owned to another of Lobengula's sons, Njube (q.v.).   (See
INKOSIKAZI.)

LOZWI (ABALOZWI)   see HOLI

LUANZE (variant: Ruhanje).   Portuguese trading fair (q.v.); located just south of the Mazoe River* and west of the Mozambique border (at 16° 55'S, 32° 30'E).   The fair operated from

c. 1580 to c. 1680.   Its ruins, now a national monument, are among the most extensive of early Portuguese sites.

LUNDI RIVER.   A major internal river, the Lundi rises just south of Gwelo (q. v.), whose water it supplies from the Gwenoro Dam, built 30 km. from the town in 1958.   The Lundi flows generally southeast before joining the Sabi (q. v.) where the latter enters Mozambique.   The Lundi's own major tributaries are the Tokwe, Mtilikwe, and Chiredzi (qq. v.).

LUNGSICKNESS (pleuro-pneumonia).   Non-indigenous, contagious bovine disease.   Long-known in Europe, lungsickness was introduced into both South Africa and the United States in 1854. Seven years later South African traders brought oxen infected with the disease into Matabeleland*.   The Ndebele then lost thousands of cattle (q. v.) to the disease, though the local LMS agents helped to reduce losses by inoculating uninfected animals and assisting in quarantining others.   The last local outbreaks of the disease occurred between 1902 and 1904.   (See HEALTH.)

LUPANE.   Administrative center of the district of the same name; located on the main road between Bulawayo and Victoria Falls, at a point near the confluences of the Gwai, Bembezi, Bubi (qq. v.), Gwampa, and Lupane rivers (at 18° 56'S, 27° 46'E). The Lupane River itself originates about 125 km. due east.

LUPANE DISTRICT.   A relatively recent creation, comprising mostly the western part of the former Shangani District (q. v.). The present district covers 8670 sq. km. in the center of Matabeleland North Province (q. v.).   Except for some national forest land in the south, and some European land in the northwestern corner, most of the district is Tribal Trust Land (q.v.). Population in 1969 included 53, 570 Africans and only 190 Europeans.   The district borders the districts of Binga and Gokwe on the north; Nkai on the east; Bubi and Nyamandhlovu on the south; and Wankie (qq. v.) on the west.

LUTHULI, ALBERT JOHN (c. 1898-July 21, 1967).   Southern Rhodesian-born South African political leader.   Luthuli's parents were Zulu* who had joined the Congregational Church in Natal (see ABC).   In 1896 his father accompanied a group of Europeans to Southern Rhodesia to assist in putting down the Ndebele Revolt (q. v.).   Afterwards he joined the staff of a Seventh Day Adventist Mission near Bulawayo.   His wife joined them there, and Albert was born in c. 1898.   Although the father soon died, the Luthulis remained at Solusi until c. 1908.   At that time Albert and his brother returned to Natal.   Albert was educated there and later was appointed a government chief.   He rose to prominence during the 1950s as the President-General of the African National Congress.   For his advocacy of passive resistance against white repression he was awarded the Nobel Peace Prize in 1961, thus becoming the only Rhodesian-born person ever to receive a Nobel Prize.

- M -

MA-. Chishona* prefix (Class 6) for plural forms of unprefixed
    Class 5 nouns, e.g., shave/mashave. The ma- prefix is also
    used for things or people usually thought of as numerous or as
    a group, e.g., Mashona, "the Shona people." In the case of
    proper names, such prefixes are dropped in this dictionary.
    (Cf. VA-.)
        Note that the Sindebele* prefix ama- (q.v.) is frequently
    shortened to ma-, as in madoda and majaha (see INDODA and
    IJAHA).

MacDOUGALL, THOMAS MURRAY see under TRIANGLE

MAÇEQUEÇE INCIDENT (1891) (variant: Massi Kessi). After an
    abortive attempt by the British and Portuguese governments to
    delimit their respective spheres of influence in 1890, the village
    of Maçequeçe (just east of present Umtali*) became the arena
    of physical rivalry. Major P. W. Forbes (q.v.) secured the
    nearby town of Mutasa (q.v.) in November 1890 and the BSAC
    then occupied Maçequeçe. At the end of the following April the
    British abandoned their fort there, and camped a few kilometers
    to the west. A much larger Portuguese force then occupied the
    fort. On May 11th the Portuguese advanced on the British camp
    and a brief armed skirmish took place. The Portuguese then
    withdrew, allowing the British to retake the fort. Meanwhile,
    negotiations in Europe resulted in the signing of the Anglo-Por-
    tuguese Convention (q.v.) the next month. This agreement ended
    hostilities and placed Maçequeçe (now known as Villa de Manica)
    in Portuguese territory. (See MOZAMBIQUE.)

MACHEKE. Town c.35 km. east of Marandellas* on the main road
    and railway line to Umtali* (at 18° 9'S, 31° 51'E; alt. 1535 m.).
    Nearby are the headwaters of the Macheke River, which flows
    south to feed the Sabi River*. Founded in 1906, Macheke de-
    veloped into a center for a major tobacco (q.v.) producing area.
    Population in 1969 was 1110 (84% Africans).

MACHENG (variant: Matsheng) (c.1828-1873?). Ngwato (q.v.) ruler.
    Captured as a child by the Ndebele, Macheng was taken to Mata-
    beleland* in 1842 and raised as an Ndebele. In 1857 Robert
    Moffat (q.v.) interceded in his behalf, obtaining his release from
    King Mzilikazi. With the aid of the Kwena ruler Sechele, Ma-
    cheng made good his claim to the Ngwato chiefship, based upon
    his status as the official--though not physical--offspring of Kgari
    (q.v.). After Mzilikazi's death in 1868 Macheng gave material
    support to the Ndebele royal pretender "Nkulumane" (q.v.) in
    order to improve the Ngwato position in the boundary dispute
    with the Ndebele over the Tati gold fields (q.v.). Macheng him-
    self had meanwhile been in and out of power among the Ngwato,
    and was finally ousted by Khama III (q.v.) in 1872.

MACHILA (variant: machilla). Rig similar to a litter, or palanquin,

usually consisting of a hammock slung below one or two poles
carried by porters.   Portuguese (q.v.) traders used machilas
in the Zambezi Valley from the 16th century, and British immigrants occasionally used them in the 1890s.

McILWAINE, LAKE   see under   HUNYANI RIVER

MacIVER, DAVID RANDALL   see   RANDALL-MacIVER, D.

MACKENZIE, JOHN (Aug. 30, 1835-March 23, 1899).   A Scot, Mackenzie came to southern Africa as an LMS agent.   He was working among the Ngwato (q.v.) at Shoshong when the Ndebele attacked the town in 1863.   His account of the raid is one of the
   best descriptions of an Ndebele foray extant.   This account,
   along with Mackenzie's description of his six-month stay in
   Matabeleland later in 1863, is published in his book, Ten Years
   North of the Orange River (1871).   Mackenzie also paid a second,
   briefer visit to the Ndebele in 1873.   During the rest of his life
   he campaigned vigorously for the extension of British rule over
   Southern Africa.

MADEIRA, DIOGO SIMÕES (fl. 1590-1620s).   A Portuguese (q.v.)
   trader, Madeira was granted land in the Zambezi Valley by the
   governor of Mozambique town in 1590.   By the early 1600s he
   was the most powerful military leader in the region of Tete
   (q.v.).   In 1607 he responded to Munhumutapa* Gatsi Rusere's
   (q.v.) appeal for Portuguese help by raising an army for the
   Shona king.   On August 1, 1607, he met Gatsi Rusere by the
   Mazoe River* and obtained the latter's mark on a treaty ceding
   all the country's mines in return for military protection.   (Cf.
   RUDD CONCESSION OF 1888).   Over the next several years
   Madeira waged successful campaigns in the Munhumutapa's be-
   half, but the locations of the ceded mines were not revealed.
   Madeira later lost and regained his Portuguese offices in purely
   European intrigues.

MADZIWA MINE.   Major nickel (q.v.) mine, located 35 km. north
   of Shamva* (at 16° 55'S, 31° 32'E).   Population in 1969 was
   2280 (97% Africans).

MAFUNGABUSI PLATEAU (variant: Mapfungavutsi).   Isolated high
   veld area in the southern Gokwe District (q.v.), separated from
   the Central Plateau (q.v.) by the Gwelo River Valley* (at 18° 25'S,
   29° E).   Infested with tsetse fly (q.v.) in the 19th century and only
   sparsely inhabited, the area is now designated a national forest
   reserve.   The village of Gokwe (q.v.) is on the Plateau's northern slopes.

MAGOSIAN CULTURE (a.k.a. Shangula Culture).   Stone Age (q.v.)
   culture period, taking its name from a site in Uganda.   The
   Magosian is associated with the last phase of the Middle Stone
   Age, or the Second Intermediate Period.   It maintains features
   reminiscent of earlier Middle Stone Age tool complexes, but

shows trends that are characteristic of Late Stone Age industries.

MAGUIRE, JAMES ROCHFORT (Oct. 4, 1855-April 18, 1925). Born in Ireland and trained as a lawyer in England, Maguire came to the South African diamond fields in the 1880s and met Cecil Rhodes there. In 1888 he was a member of the Rudd Concession (q.v.) party to Matabeleland. He later returned to Britain and was elected to Parliament from Ulster. In London he represented Rhodes before the BSAC Board of Directors, on which he himself obtained a seat in 1898. He served as vice president of the BSAC from 1906 to 1913, and was president from 1923 until his death. During the whole of this period he was one of the leading forces behind the expansion of Southern Rhodesia's railways (q.v.).

MAHLOKOHLOKO (variants: Amahlokohloko; Amahlogohlogo; Matlokotloko). Ndebele ibutho (q.v.) raised by Mzilikazi in c.1850. The ibutho's town stood on the watershed between the Bembezi and Umgusa rivers (qq.v.), near the latter's confluence with the Koce. Mzilikazi lived mostly in this town until the late 1850s, when he moved to Inyati*. His successor Lobengula also lived with the Mahlokohloko until becoming king in 1870.

MAHUKU (a.k.a. Makobe; Nopelume) (d.1863). Talowta (q.v.) chief whose people lived by the upper Inkwezi (Ingwesi) River, where it was intersected by the Hunters' Road (q.v.). Mahuku switched his allegiance from the Ngwato (q.v.) to the Ndebele after the latter settled in Matabeleland in the early 1840s, but it is unknown whether he did so voluntarily or by force. In any case, by 1854 his town was being used as the southern port of entry into the Ndebele kingdom, and Mahuku was under the direct supervision of the Ndebele induna* Manyami (q.v.). When the Ndebele attacked the Ngwato town Shoshong in 1863 (see MANGWANE; KHAMA III), Mahuku and his brother Kirelkiwe were accused of aiding the Ngwato and were killed by the Ndebele.

MAI CHAZA CHURCH see CHAZA, MAI

MAIZE (American Indian "corn"; a.k.a. mealies). Now clearly the country's most important food crop among both African and European farmers (see AGRICULTURE), maize was introduced into the country some time before the 19th century. It is grown throughout the country, but flourishes best only in the well watered districts of the northeast. By the 20th century maize seems to have displaced millet (q.v.) and sorghums as the primary African food crop. It ranked as the country's most valuable agricultural crop until the Second World War, when it was overtaken by tobacco (q.v.). Since then improved strains and expanded acreage have rapidly increased yields, which exceeded 350 million kg. in 1956. Maize production received an additional spurt after UDI, when sanctions (q.v.) forced many tobacco farmers to turn to other crops. Despite government

encouragement to diversify farms as broadly as possible, most
abandoned tobacco land went into maize production because of
the similar soil and climatic needs of the two crops. By 1971
roughly 1.2 to 1.5 billion kg. were being produced annually,
and about 80% of production was being exported.

MAKGATHO, MOSES D.   see under AFRICAN METHODIST EPIS-
    COPAL CHURCH

MAKOBE (variant: Makhobi) see MAHUKU

MAKOLOLO see KOLOLO; and see under MATABELE MISSION

MAKOMBE (variant: Macombe).   Dynastic title of the rulers of the
    Barwe kingdom (q.v.) of the Honde Valley*.   The dynasty was
    established by Korekore (q.v.) from the Munhumutapa state
    (q.v.) in about the 15th century, and first documented by the
    Portuguese (q.v.) in 1506.   Although their realm lay chiefly
    within what is now Mozambique (q.v.), the Makombes played
    an important role in present Rhodesia's history as intermedi-
    aries between the Shona states and the Portuguese.   The Ma-
    kombes finally lost their independence to the Portuguese in 1902
    (see MAPONDERA).

MAKOMBWE.   Plural of gombwe (q.v.).

MAKONI.   Dynastic title of the rulers of the Maungwe, whose
    Manyika-speaking (q.v.) people are known as Hungwe, or
    Maungwe.   The extent of Maungwe territory over the past
    several centuries has roughly coincided with the area of the
    present Makoni District (q.v.), which is named after the dy-
    nasty.   The Makoni dynasty appears to have been established
    by a man named Muswere early in the 17th century.   The
    name "Maungwe" first appeared in a Portuguese (q.v.) docu-
    ment of 1635.   The paramountcy was originally tributary to the
    Munhumutapa state (q.v.), but became independent after the
    latter's late 17th-century disintegration.
        Makoni IX Muswati died just as Zwangendaba's Ngoni
    (q.v.) invaded the country in the 1830s.   Maungwe was hit hard
    by both the Ngoni invasion and the shangwa (q.v.) drought, as
    well as by internal political disputes.   Under the reign of Ma-
    koni XI Nyamanhindi (c.1840-65) comparative peace and pros-
    perity were restored, but disorder returned just before his
    death when the Gaza (q.v.) invaded Maungwe.   The next Makoni,
    Muruko, reigned through an era of intermittent warfare with the
    neighboring Mutasa paramountcy (c.1865-89).   In the mid-1880s
    the Makoni obtained military aid from the Portuguese adventurer
    Manuel de Sousa (q.v.).   Soon after Mutota (a.k.a. Chingaira)
    became the next Makoni, peace was restored with the Mutasa,
    but then the BSAC occupied the country in 1890 (see PIONEER
    COLUMN).
        In 1894 the British established an administrative post at
    Rusape (q.v.).   Two years later Makoni Mutota became one of

the most active leaders of the Shona Revolt (q.v.). In August
1896 the British retaliated especially hard against his headquarters, dynamiting his people out of Gwindingwi Hill (q.v.).
Mutota surrendered, only to be tried and shot on September 4,
1896. One of his sons, Ndapfunya (d.1921), who had not participated in the Revolt, was made the first government-appointed
Makoni.

MAKONI DISTRICT. Covering 8020 sq. km. of the northern part
of Manicaland Province (q.v.), Makoni District is divided by
the main road and railway line between Salisbury and Umtali
(qq.v.). The central parts of the well watered district are reserved for European farmers, who grow mostly tobacco and
maize (qq.v.). Population of the district in 1969 included
158,420 Africans and 2090 Europeans. Rusape (q.v.) is district
administrative center. Other major centers include Inyazura and
Headlands (qq.v.). Makoni borders the districts of Mtoko on the
north; Inyanga on the east; Umtali on the south; and Wedza, Marandellas, and Mrewa (qq.v.) on the west.

MAKUMBE CAVE (variants: Mkumbe; Nkumbe). A large cave north
of Domboshawa (q.v.) in the Mwanga Hills (at 17° 38'S, 31° 22'E),
Makumbe contains naturalistic polychrome rock paintings (q.v.)
representing an exceptionally wide variety of animals, as well
as "matchstick" human figures.

MALARIA. Infectious parasitic disease transmitted by several varieties of anopheline mosquitoes. The most widespread disease
in the country (see HEALTH), malaria is endemic to the low
veld areas (see ALTITUDINAL ZONES). The disease is most
active around April, after mosquitoes have bred through the long
rainy season. In its most serious forms malaria can damage
the brain (cerebral malaria) or the kidneys (blackwater fever).
The Shona and other longstanding residents of the country are
largely immune to the worst effects of the disease. Immigrant
peoples and visitors are most susceptible to serious attacks.
The Ndebele, for example, coming from a largely malaria-free
area in the late 1830s, suffered many malarial deaths during
their first decades in the country. In 1870, the "fever year,"
particularly long rains greatly increased mortality throughout
the country. Mortality was also exceptionally high among construction workers building the Beira to Umtali railway (q.v.)
line during the 1890s, when the causes of the disease were still
unknown. By 1898 the connection between the disease and mosquitoes was recognized, and more efficacious preventive measures
were undertaken. A local doctor, A. M. Fleming (q.v.), made a
major contribution to world-wide malarial research.

MALINDIDZIMU. African name for World's View (q.v.) in the Matopo Hills.

MALVERN, LORD. Title of Godfrey Huggins (q.v.) from 1955.

MALVERNIA.   Mozambique (q.v.) border post opposite Vila Salazar
   (q.v.).

MAMA.   Common Bantu* word for mother; often used as a term of
   respect in addressing a woman.   (Cf. BABA.)

MAMBA.   Large and deadly poisonous, but usually unaggressive
   snake occurring in two main varieties.   The Black Mamba
   (Dendroaspis polylepis) is the larger and more deadly.   Despite
   its name, its color tends towards olive-brown.   It is common
   in the country's low veld areas.   The Green Mamba (Dendroaspis angusticeps) is a rarer, tree-dwelling variety, occurring
   in the eastern parts of the country.   "Mamba" derives from the
   Nguni* name appearing in Sindebele* as imamba (pl., izimamba).

MAMBO (pl., vamambo, or vadzimambo).   Generic Shona term for
   king or paramount chief.   The title is associated particularly
   with the rulers of the Changamire state (q.v.), but was also
   used by the Munhumutapas (q.v.) and other dynastic title holders
   in Shona-speaking states.   "Mambo" is now often used as a polite form of address.   (Cf. INKOSI.)

MAMBO HILLS   see   NTABAZIKAMAMBO

MANA POOLS.   A 2810-sq. km. game reserve (q.v.) covering the
   mopane* savanna* land between the Zambezi River and the Zambezi Escarpment (qq.v.) 50 km. east of Chirundu (q.v.).   The
   riverine plain is dotted with deep holes which trap the flood
   waters, attracting numerous large animals.   Mana Pools is one
   of the few game reserves in the country which was easily accessible to tourists, but it was closed to visitors in 1974 because of African nationalist guerrilla incursions into the region.
   (Cf. DANDE.)

MANCHESTER GARDENS.   Former name of Vumba National Park
   (q.v.).

MANGULA.   Town located 45 km. north of Zawi* in the Lomagundi
   District* (at 16° 54'S, 30° 9'E; alt. 1370 m.).   Mangula has developed rapidly since 1959, when the Mangula copper (q.v.) mine
   opened.   The mine is now the country's leading copper producer,
   and is one of the few major modern copper mines not established
   over pre-colonial African workings.   Population in 1969 was 7750
   (92% Africans).

MANGWANE KHUMALO (c.1825-c.1890s).   Born in the Transvaal*,
   Mangwane was the eldest son of the Ndebele king Mzilikazi.
   During the 1850s he was regarded as his father's heir apparent,
   but he did not get along well with his father.   His political position deteriorated rapidly after 1862, when his confidant Manxeba
   Khumalo (q.v.) was executed.   In March 1863 Mangwane commanded an unsuccessful impi* against the Ngwato (q.v.) capital

Shoshong in eastern Botswana*. By the late 1860s it appeared
that Lobengula (q.v.) was destined to become Ndebele king.
Mangwane and other dissidents therefore fled the country when
Mzilikazi died in 1868. In 1870 he and a contingent of the dispersed Zwangendaba ibutho (q.v.) met the pretender "Nkulumane"
(q.v.) in Natal, where they planned a coup d'état against Lobengula. By late 1871 both men were in Shoshong, where the
Ngwato ruler Macheng (q.v.) joined in their plot. The following
January Mangwane directed an invasion of Matabeleland under
"Nkulumane's" banner, but he seems to have sought the Ndebele
kingship for himself. The invasion was easily repelled by Lobengula. Afterwards Mangwane and a few followers settled at
Rustenburg in the Transvaal, where he was reported still to be
living in 1890. A largely Sotho-ized community of his descendants still reside there.

MANGWE. Mangwe Pass is a defile in the Matopo Hills (q.v.)
through which the old Hunters' Road (q.v.) ran in the 19th century (at 20°41'S, 28°4'E). South from the Pass the small
Mangwe River flows into the Shashi River (q.v.). John Lee
(q.v.) established the first non-missionary European settlement
in the country near the Pass in 1866, when entrance to the Ndebele kingdom was guarded nearby under the direction of Manyami (q.v.). In 1893 the BSAC built Mangwe Fort there to protect British supply movements. The Fort was made into a
laager (q.v.) during the Ndebele Revolt (q.v.) of 1896, but it
was never assaulted. Mangwe village is now a small center in
a mainly cattle-producing region.

MANGWENDE. Dynastic title of the Nhowe (q.v.) rulers in the
Mrewa District (q.v.). The Mangwende dynasty was founded
around 1710 by Mangwende Sakuvunza. During the 19th century
the chiefdom was briefly occupied by the Ngoni (q.v.) during
the 1830s, and was attacked by the Gaza (q.v.), but was relatively free of Ndebele raids. Mungati (or Mgati) became the
last independent Mangwende in c.1880. He was shortly thereafter visited by Manuel de Sousa (q.v.), who tried to bring the
Nhowe into the Portuguese (q.v.) sphere, while getting the Mangwende to support him in a war against the Budjga (q.v.) in 1887.
The Mangwende signed a treaty with Sousa afterwards, but then
renounced the Portuguese when the BSAC occupied the country
in 1890 (see PIONEER COLUMN). Over the next several years
the Nhowe grew increasingly resentful of British occupation, but
the Mangwende reluctantly tolerated their presence. In March
1892 a headman named Nogomo was killed in a dispute with a
British official. The Mangwende's son, Mchemwa (q.v.), then
became the most outspoken opponent of the British. In June
1896 Mchemwa led the Nhowe into the Revolt (q.v.), while the
Mangwende himself played a passively supportive role. The
Mangwende surrendered on September 3, 1897, and soon found
that his prestige among the Nhowe was largely lost. The Nhowe
were forced to resettle near Mrewa, in what is now the Mangwende TTL. Mangwende Mungati died in May 1924. Two years

later the government appointed Chibanda, a member of another family, as Mangwende.

MANHLAGAZI.   Chief town of the Gaza kingdom (q. v.) in the late 19th century; originally located just west of the Mozambique border near the slopes of Mount Silinda (q. v.).   Some authorities state that the town was founded by king Soshangane (q. v.) in the 1830s, but he appears actually to have resided by the middle Sabi River (q. v.) only briefly before settling near the Limpopo River to the south.   Mzila (q. v.) re-established Gaza headquarters by Mount Silinda in the early 1860s.   The town was known as Manhlagazi at least by the time Gungunyane (q.v.) became king in 1884.   Five years later Gungunyane shifted the town c.475 km. south to a location in Mozambique near the mouth of the Limpopo River.   There the town was known to the Portuguese as Manjacaze.   About 60,000 people are said to have undertaken this last Gaza migration, enduring great hardships.

MANICALAND PROVINCE.   "Manica" is a variant form of Manyika (q. v.), the name of a major cluster of Shona-speaking peoples who live in the Eastern Highlands (q. v.).   In its broadest sense, "Manicaland" encompasses Manyika territory in both the eastern parts of the country and in Mozambique*.   Officially, however, Manicaland is the name of one of seven provinces (q. v.), stretching along the eastern border, from the Ruenya River in the north, to the Sabi River in the south (qq. v.).   It now encompasses, from north to south, the districts of Inyanga, Makoni, Umtali, Buhera, Melsetter, and Chipinga (qq. v.).   (Cf. "GAZALAND.")

MANIKUSA.   Alternate name of the Gaza king Soshangane (q. v.).

MANXEBA KHUMALO (variant: Monyebe) (d. Aug. 1862).   An Ndebele induna*, Manxeba was the son of Kaliphi (q. v.).   During the 1850s Manxeba was said to have been one of Mzilikazi's most influential advisers and confidants.   In 1862, however, political rivals accused him of witchcraft, and he and his family were wiped out.   (See also MANGWANE.)

MANYAMI (fl. 1850s-70s).   The Ndebele induna* who oversaw the southwestern gateway to the kingdom,   Manyami detained travelers along the Hunters' Road (q. v.) until the kings conveyed permission for them to proceed.   By 1854 Manyami was stationed at the town of Mahuku (q. v.) by the upper Inkwezi River, which flows between the Ramaquabane and Mangwe rivers (qq. v.).   After Mahuku's town was razed in 1863, Manyami's station was shifted northeast to the Mangwe Pass (q. v.).   In 1873 he was restationed at the first site.   He seems to have retired or died in 1874.

MANYAMI RIVER (variant: Mhanyami).   Original Shona name for the Hunyani River (q. v.).

MANYANGA.   Original Rozvi name for Ntabazikamambo (q.v.).

MANYANO   see   RUWADZANO

MANYIKA (variant: Manica*).   One of the main ethnic and linguistic clusters of the Shona-speaking peoples (q.v.).   The Manyika
dialect (or Chimanyika) of Shona is spoken east of the Zezuru
(q.v.) region, and north of the Ndau (q.v.) region, mainly in
the districts of Makoni, Inyanga, and Umtali (qq.v.), and in
Mozambique* south of the Pungwe River*.   About 75% of the
Manyika people (the Vamanyika) live in present Rhodesia; the
rest are in Mozambique.   The Rhodesian Manyika constitute
about one-ninth of the country's total Shona-speaking population.
Among the local subdialects of Manyika are Manyika proper,
spoken by the people of the Mutasa kingdom (q.v.), and Maungwe
(or Hungwe), spoken in the Makoni kingdom (q.v.).

MANZAMNYAMA RIVER.   Variant name of the Nata River (q.v.).

MAPONDERA (a.k.a. Kadungure Mapondera) (d.1904).   Shona chief
and independent revolt leader.   By the late 1880s Mapondera
was the ruler of an important Korekore (q.v.) chiefdom between
the Umvukwe Hills and the Mazoe River (qq.v.).   Noted for his
military leadership, he is said to have repelled several Ndebele
raiding parties.   In 1889 Mapondera and his brother Temaringa
granted a mineral concession* to F. C. Selous (q.v.), but Mapondera was bitterly opposed to the subsequent BSAC occupation
of the region (see PIONEER COLUMN).   When the BSAC administration attempted to impose a hut tax in 1894, Mapondera
took his immediate family with him to the Makombe state (q.v.)
in Mozambique.
     Mapondera did not personally participate in the 1896-7
Shona Revolt (q.v.) in Southern Rhodesia, but was instead busy
helping the Makombe to fight the Portuguese.   Meanwhile, his
old chiefdom fared badly in the Mashonaland Revolt.   When he
learned that his son had been killed and his cattle had been
looted by the British, he returned home in early 1900 in a futile attempt to raise a new rebellion among the Korekore.
After his followers were dispersed, he went north and allied
with the last Munhumutapa*, Chioko (q.v.).   With the aid of
Chioko's soldiers Mapondera re-entered Mashonaland in early
1901 and attacked the administrative post at Mount Darwin*.
Again defeated, he returned to Mozambique to help the Makobe
against the Portuguese again.   The death of Chioko and the defeat of the Makombe the following year seem to have broken
Mapondera's spirit to resist further.   In August 1903 he returned
to Mashonaland and surrendered to British authorities.   Early
the next year he was convicted of sedition and sentenced to seven
years at hard labor.   He died in prison during a hunger strike.
(Cf. MCHEMWA.)

MARAMUCA (variant: Murimuka).   Portuguese name for a trading
fair (q.v.) and its surrounding district, located just southwest

of the Umfuli River, near present Hartley (qq. v.). This fair seems to have been the southwestern-most Portuguese settlement in the country, and was under the jurisdiction of the Changamire state (q. v.) during the 17th century. Maramuca was the center of a still-productive gold mining region, and was unique in that it was inhabited by an isolated Zambezi Tonga (q. v.) community. The fair appears to have closed down around 1680.

MARANDELLAS. One of the dozen largest towns in the country (see URBANIZATION), Marandellas is an important beef, dairy, and tobacco*-producing center. It is developing as a major industrial center, and it serves as administrative headquarters for the Marandellas District* (at 18° 11'S, 31° 33'E; alt. 1660 m.). The town's cool climate has attracted a concentration of private European schools, and nearby is the Waddilove Institution (q. v.). Estimated population of the town in late 1974 was 14, 000 (c. 85% Africans). The town takes its name from a local Zezuru* chief's town known as "Marondera's."

MARANDELLAS DISTRICT. Covering 4220 sq. km. in the central part of Mashonaland South Province (q. v.), Marandellas District was created in 1899, a year after the Salisbury to Umtali railway (q. v.) line was built through the region. The district was originally about 50% larger, but recently lost its southeastern wedge to create the new Wedza District (q. v.). Except for some Tribal Trust Land and Purchase Area (qq. v.) in the west, most of the district is reserved for Europeans. Marandellas and Macheke (qq. v.) are the main centers. In addition to Wedza, the district borders the districts of Goromanzi and Mrewa on the north; Makoni on the east; Charter on the southwest; and Salisbury (qq. v.). on the west. Population in 1969 included 74, 910 Africans and 4105 Europeans.

MARANKE, JOHANE MOMBERUME (1912-1963). Founder of the largest independent church in the country: the African Apostolic Church of Johane Maranke. Maranke was born in the southwestern part of Umtali District (q. v.). There he was partly educated and baptized by the American Episcopal Methodist Church (now United Methodist Church, q. v.). He forsook a possible career in the Methodist clergy to become an ordinary laborer in Umtali.

Maranke had many visions from an early age. While in Umtali he claimed to have been told by God that he was the African John the Baptist and that he should form a church. This was 1932, when he returned to his homeland to begin his religious work. He quickly became nationally famous as a healer, exorcist, prophet, and teacher. He formed his own church, with his relatives filling most leadership posts, and he and his apostles began itinerating about the country. By 1940 there were more than a hundred branches of his church. The church spread over an even wider area in the 1940s and 1950s as Maranke visited South Africa and countries north of the Zambezi.

A leadership schism split his church on his death in 1963, but the main branch has continued to grow. By the mid-1960s an estimated 50,000 people within Rhodesia were members, with tens of thousands of other members in South Africa, Botswana, Mozambique, Zambia, Malawi, and Zaïre. (See also CHAZA, MAI; ZWIMBA, M.)

MARI (Vamari; variant: Mhari). Branch of the Karanga (q.v.) cluster of Shona, part of whom were under the Chivi dynasty (q.v.).

MARIMBA PARK. African township located c.16 km. west-southwest of Salisbury's (q.v.) city center (at 17° 53'S, 30° 57'E). It was established by the government in 1961 to provide low density housing for wealthy Africans, whose homes are comparable to those in European suburbs. Population in 1969 was 370. (Cf. HARARE.)

MARONDA MASHANU ("Five Wounds"). Independent mission founded by A. S. Cripps (q.v.); located c.9 km. northeast of Enkeldoorn* (at 18° 55'S, 30° 58'E). Between 1916 and 1926 Cripps operated the station as a branch of the nearby Anglican* Wreningham Mission to the northeast. From 1930 till his death in 1952 he ran the mission independently of any organized body. The mission has since been sustained by its African members.

MARONDERA. Dynastic title of a minor Zezuru (q.v.) chiefdom after which Marandellas (q.v.) was named.

MARSHALL-HOLE, HUGH   see   HOLE, H. M.

MASAPA (variant: Massapa). Portuguese trading fair (q.v.); located at the base of Mount Pfura (16° 52'S, 31° 37'E; see DARWIN DISTRICT). Established around 1575, Masapa quickly became the most important Portuguese center in the country because of its proximity to the headquarters of the Munhumutapa (q.v.). The resident Portuguese elected a leader to serve as Capitão das portas ("Captain of the gates")--a post confirmed by the reigning Munhumutapa and formalized by the Portuguese government. All traders entering or leaving the country had to pass through Masapa, where the Capitão das portas exacted taxes for the Munhumutapa and acted as local magistrate. Masapa lost its preeminent position to Dambarare (q.v.) in the early 17th century and was destroyed by a Changamire (q.v.) invasion in 1693.

MASEKO NGONI. First Mfecane (q.v.) band to enter the country in the early 19th century. Originally under the leadership of a man named Ngwane Maseko, this band appears to have migrated out of South Africa in the 1820s, passing through Venda (q.v.) territory, the present Fort Victoria (q.v.) area, and finally the Salisbury region. There they appear to have been joined by the Ngoni of Nxaba (qq.v.), with whom they defeated

Zwangendaba's (q.v.) Ngoni. After c.1835 the Maseko Ngoni
left the country through the Mazoe Valley*. They traveled as
far north as southern Tanzania, eventually turning south and
settling in southern Malawi, where their state became known
as the Gomani kingdom.

MASHABA (variant: Mashava). Of the many places in the country
with this name, two are most important. (1) The Mashaba
Mountains form a range running along the western edge of the
Central Plateau, between the Umfuli and Sebakwe rivers (qq.v.).
These mountains reach heights just over 1400 m. Important
dams have been built on the Sebakwe and Ngezi* rivers in gaps
in the Mashabas.
        (2) Mashaba village is an important asbestos (q.v.)
mining center, located c.37 km. west of Fort Victoria* (at
20° 3'S, 30° 29'E).

MASHAVE (variants: mashawe; mashabi; mashavi). Plural form of
shave (q.v.).

MASHAYAMOMBE SINYENKUNDU (variant: Mashiangombi) (d. July
1897). Shona ruler and Revolt (q.v.) leader in 1896-7. During
the mid-19th century Sinyenkundu--whose dynastic title was
Mashayamombe--led his branch of the Zezuru (q.v.) out of the
present Marandellas District to an area by the upper Umfuli
River in the eastern Hartley District (qq.v.). There he managed
to maintain his independence, despite Ndebele attacks in the
1860s. After the BSAC occupied the country in the early 1890s,
his town was made a British administrative center. Despite the
proximity of a British official, his town became one of the main
planning centers for the Revolt which began in early 1896.
There is some controversy about the degree to which Mashayamombe was influenced by religious leaders during the Revolt,
but he clearly paid a visit to Mkwati (q.v.) in April, and then
was frequently visited by the Kaguvi medium, Bonda (qq.v.),
and other religious officials during the following months.
        On June 14, 1896, Mashayamombe's people killed the
local district commissioner, opening the Shona Revolt. Thereafter his fortified hill was one of the most active Revolt centers
and was the Kaguvi medium's headquarters. The British made
a special effort to defeat Mashayamombe, but he survived three
major assaults in 1896, and then was left alone until early 1897.
After E. A. Alderson's (q.v.) final assault in October 1896,
Mashayamombe and "Kaguvi" were joined by Mkwati from Matabeleland. On July 23, 1897, Mashayamombe was killed when
British forces overwhelmed his hill and dynamited his cave
refuges.

MASHOBANE (variants: Machobane; Matshobana) (fl. 1810s). Father
of the future Ndebele king Mzilikazi (q.v.) and ruler of a small
branch of Khumalo (q.v.) people in Zululand (q.v.). In c.1816
Mashobane was executed by his father-in-law, Zwide (q.v.), on
suspicion of having aided the Zulu against the latter's Ndwandwe

people. Mashobane's name later took a prominent place in the pantheon of Ndebele ancestors (see DLOZI; INXWALA). His name was also given to one of Bulawayo's African townships, Matshobana, during the 20th century.

MASHONALAND. During the mid-19th century Europeans gave this name to the Shona (q.v.) territories east of Matabeleland (q.v.), although many Shona did, and still do, live in both regions. Furthermore, many non-Shona peoples, including the Tonga, Hlengwe, and Venda (qq.v.), also live in parts of what has been called "Mashonaland."
       In 1890 the BSAC established an occupation beachhead in Mashonaland and formalized use of the name as a territorial designation. Later in the 1890s the Company divided all of what is now Rhodesia into two roughly equal-sized provinces. The eastern, and somewhat larger, province was designated "Mashonaland," even though it included parts also known as Manicaland and Gazaland (qq.v.). Later Manicaland and Midlands (qq.v.) were made into separate provinces, and Mashonaland was divided into northern and southern provinces. Still later, Victoria Province (q.v.) was separated. The present provincial borders were fixed in 1962 (see PROVINCES). In colloquial usage the name "Mashonaland" is still frequently applied in the same sense it was used in the 19th century.
       Mashonaland North Province comprises, from west to east, the districts of Kariba, Urungwe, Lomagundi, Sipolilo, Mazoe, Darwin, Bindura, and Shamva (qq.v.).
       Mashonaland South Province includes, from west to east, the districts of Gatooma, Hartley, Salisbury, Goromanzi, Marandellas, Wedza, Mrewa, and Mtoko (qq.v.).

MASHONALAND FIELD FORCE (MFF). Name for the collection of British military units which fought against the Shona in the 1896 Revolt (q.v.). The MFF was formed in August 1896, when Lt. Col. E. A. H. Alderson (q.v.) arrived in Salisbury with four companies of Imperial Mounted Infantry, which he combined with local BSAC and volunteer forces. The combined MFF force contained c.1500 Europeans. The MFF operated successfully around Salisbury until the BSAC complained about paying its bills. By December 1896 it was out of the country and disbanded. Its place was taken by BSAC police (see BSAP).

MASHONALAND HERALD & ZAMBESIAN TIMES. Original name of the Rhodesia Herald (q.v.).

MASSI KESSI see MAÇEQUEÇE INCIDENT (1891)

MATABELE (variants: Matebele; Tebele). Name given to Mzilikazi's (q.v.) followers by South African Sotho peoples (q.v.) during the 1820s. Many meanings of the name have been suggested, but it is clear only that the Sotho had been calling Nguni (q.v.) immigrants from the east coast Matabele for centuries before Mzilikazi arrived in their country (see TRANSVAAL NDEBELE).

Mzilikazi's following was but one of many Mfecane (q.v.) era
bands called Matabele by the Sotho, but the name soon became
primarily associated with his own people. Eventually, they
adopted the name, giving it the Nguni form, Amandebele, which
modern English renders as "Ndebele" (q.v.).

Even after the Ndebele had left Sotho territory in 1838,
most outsiders continued to call them "Matabele." This was
largely because most visitors approached Ndebele country from
the south, passing through Sotho territory and adopting Sotho
forms of names. "Ndebele" is now the preferred name for the
people, but "Matabeleland" (q.v.) has become fixed as a place
name, and many people--particularly white southern Africans--
continue to use the name "Matabele."

MATABELE [National] HOME SOCIETY. Ndebele irredentist movement originally begun during the First World War by Nyamanda
(q.v.). The movement sought a national homeland for the Ndebele people, as well as restoration of the Ndebele kingship (see
REVOLT). The movement almost died out in the early 1920s,
but was revived in the late 1920s, when a formal "Matabele
Home Society" constitution was drawn up and officers were
elected. The Society drew some Ndebele supporters away from
the RBVA and ICU, but its appeal was narrowly ethnic and back-
ward-looking, and the organization failed to have any impact on
government policy during the 1930s.

MATABELE MISSION. LMS name for the mission it sent under
Robert Moffat (q.v.) to Matabeleland in 1859. The LMS simultaneously sent a "Makololo Mission" to the Kololo (q.v.) of
western Zambia in the hope that establishment of the two missions would help to mitigate hostilities between the Kololo and
Ndebele peoples. The Makololo Mission party was, however,
devastated by fever, and that effort was abandoned. (See also
LMS; INYATI; HOPE FOUNTAIN; LIVINGSTONE, DAVID.)

MATABELE WAR (1893) see NDEBELE WAR

MATABELELAND. During the mid-19th century Europeans gave
this name to the region around Bulawayo (q.v.) in which Ndebele (q.v.) settlements were concentrated (see "MATABELE").
Gradually the name was applied to a much larger area, including many non-Ndebele territories. In 1893, after the BSAC
had occupied neighboring Mashonaland (q.v.) for several years,
L. S. Jameson (q.v.) arbitrarily designated a border which
separated the new colony from Matabeleland. This border
started at the Zambezi River, following the Umniati River to
the Central Plateau, then continuing down the Shashe, Tokwe,
and Lundi rivers (q.v.). Later, when the whole of present
Rhodesia was under BSAC administration, Matabeleland and
Mashonaland were designated as separate administrative provinces. Matabeleland covered 47% of the country; Mashonaland
the rest. Matabeleland was later divided into northern and
southern provinces, which were fixed in 1962. Part of the

original "Matabeleland" helped to form Midlands Province (q.v.).
Matabeleland North Province comprises, from north to
south, the districts of Binga, Wankie, Lupane, Nkai, Nyamandhlovu, Bubi, Bulawayo, and Bulalima-Mangwe (qq.v.).
Matabeleland South Province comprises, from west to
east, the districts of Matobo, Umzingwane, Insiza, Gwanda,
Beitbridge, Belingwe, and Shabani (qq.v.).

MATABELELAND RELIEF FORCE (MRF). First unit of British Imperial troops to fight against the Ndebele during the 1896 Revolt
(q.v.). H. C. O. Plumer (q.v.) raised the MRF mainly among
the mining communities between Kimberley and Mafeking in
South Africa. About half of the MRF's c.800 men were former
soldiers, including many who had served in the BBP and in the
Jameson Raid (qq.v.). Under Plumer's command the MRF
reached Bulawayo on May 14, 1896, clearing away the rebels
around the town by the end of the month. MRF operations
played a major role in turning the tide of the war against the
Ndebele north of the Matopo Hills*. (See also CARRINGTON,
F.; BULAWAYO FIELD FORCE.)

MATENDERE RUINS. Zimbabwe-type stone ruin in the Buhera
District* (at 19° 32'S, 31° 48'E). The main structure is an
open-ended elliptical enclosure with a large decorated wall
168 m. in length. The ruins have not been definitely dated,
but were estimated by G. Caton-Thompson (q.v.) to have been
contemporary with Dhlo Dhlo (q.v.).

MATETSI. Village standing at the intersection of the Matetsi River
and the Bulawayo to Victoria Falls railway line (at 18° 5'S,
26° 7'E; alt. 910 m.). The Matetsi River rises in Botswana*
near Pandamatenga (q.v.), flowing northeast till it meets the
Zambezi below the Batoka Gorge (q.v.).

MATIBI. Title of a chief of the Pfumbi branch of Karanga (q.v.)
people living by the middle Nuanetsi River (q.v.). By 1871
the Matibi was paying tribute to the Ndebele. He attempted
to throw off Ndebele influence in the 1880s and was consequently attacked by them as late as 1892. The next year his
people assisted the British in the Ndebele War (q.v.). In the
1896 Revolt (q.v.) the Pfumbi also fought with the British
against the Ndebele and their allies.

MATLOKOTLOKO (variant: Amatlokotloko) see MAHLOKOHLOKO

MATOBO DISTRICT. The westernmost district of Matabeleland
South Province (q.v.), Matobo covers a narrow 7230-sq. km.
area running directly south from Bulawayo to the Botswana
border. The northern part of the district is reserved for
European farmers and ranchers and includes Matopos National
Park, part of the Matopo Hills (q.v.). The southern part of
the district, which is bisected by the Shashani River (q.v.),
is Tribal Trust Land (q.v.). Population in 1969 included

55,680 Africans and 555 Europeans. The district borders the
districts of Bulalima-Mangwe on the west; Bulawayo on the
north; and Umzingwane and Gwanda (qq.v.) on the east. Matopos (q.v.) is the administrative center.

MATOJENI (a.k.a. Wirirani). Oracular shrine of the Mwari cult
(q.v.); located c.40 km. southeast of Bulawayo on the northern
fringe of the Matopo Hills (q.v.). The shrine was founded at
least as early as the mid-19th century, when it was one of four
main Mwari cult centers. It still operates as the most influential and famous Mwari center in the country. Local priests
send messengers (vanyai) over the southeastern parts of the
country and the extreme northern part of the Transvaal*, and
they receive supplicants from the same region. (See also
NJELELE.)

MATOPE NYANHEHWE (a.k.a. Ndebedza; Mutavara) (fl. c.mid-15th
century). Second ruler of the Munhumutapa state (q.v.). After
the death of his father Mutota Nyatsimba (q.v.) sometime before c.1450, Matope acceded to the Munhumutapaship by engaging
in an act of ritual intercourse with his half-sister, Nehanda
(q.v.), who became his consort. He then proceeded to extend
his father's military conquests, subjugating the Barwe, Manyika
(qq.v.), and other peoples as far east as the Indian Ocean.
Matope's successors could not, however, hold his "empire" together. On his death in c.1480, he was succeeded by a son,
Mavura Maombwe. Mavura was killed in a campaign within
about a month. Another of Matope's sons, Mukombero Nyahuma
(q.v.), then became ruler.

MATOPO HILLS (variant: the Matopos). One of the country's most
notable scenic and historic regions, the Matopos cover more
than 3000 sq. km. just below the Figtree to Bulawayo road. The
hills are a spectacular assortment of granite kopjes (q.v.), including large dwalas (q.v.) and bizarrely fractured "castle kopjes." Golati Mountain, at 1550 m., is the highest point in the
hills (at 20° 29'S, 28° 36'E).
    Human occupation of the Matopos is estimated to go back
40,000 years. Among the innumerable Stone Age (q.v.) sites
which pervade the hills, the most visually impressive are caves
with rock paintings (q.v.; see, e.g., BAMBATA; NSWATUGI;
POMONGWE; etc.). By the mid-19th century the hills became
the center of Matojeni (q.v.) and several other major Mwari
cult (q.v.) shrines. In 1847 the Matopos were the focus of the
first modern European foray into the country when A. H. Potgieter (q.v.) attacked the Ndebele there. In 1896 the Matopos
became a major theater of war in the Ndebele Revolt (q.v.).
    In 1953 the Southern Rhodesian government set aside a
457-sq. km. section of the hills in northern Matobo District
(q.v.) as the Rhodes Matopos National Park, which includes a
100-sq. km. game reserve. A popular tourist attraction in the
park is the World's View dwala (q.v.), in which Cecil Rhodes
and other European figures are interred. Less accessible is the

grave of Mzilikazi in Nthumbane Hill (q.v.), c.15 km. to the
northeast of World's View, just outside of the park.

MATOPOS. Village on the northern fringe of Matopos National
Park, serving as administrative center of Matobo District* (at
20°25'S, 28°29'E).

MAUCH, KARL (May 7, 1837-April 1875). A German geologist
and explorer, Mauch came to South Africa in 1864. In 1866
and 1867 he traveled in Matabeleland and Mashonaland and confirmed the presence of gold (q.v.) at both Tati and the Hartley
Hills (qq.v.). Publication of his discoveries set off the first
minor gold rush into the country, and brought the first wave
of concession*-hunters to the Ndebele court. In 1871 Mauch
learned about the Zimbabwe Ruins (q.v.) from the Transvaal
missionary Alex Merensky (q.v.), and set off in search of them.
With the aid of Adam Render (q.v.) he reached the ruins, but
became stranded there for almost a year. During this time he
compiled the first maps and descriptions of the ruins. Publication of his reports further stimulated European prospectors,
also giving rise to the romantic myth that Great Zimbabwe was
the center of "King Solomon's Mines" (see OPHIR). R. N. Hall
(q.v.) later named the "Mauch Ruin" at Zimbabwe after him.

MAUND, EDWARD ARTHUR (1851-March 17, 1932). A British army
officer, Maund served on Charles Warren's (q.v.) expedition in
1885. Afterwards he was delegated to announce the creation of
the Bechuanaland Protectorate (q.v.) to Lobengula in neighboring
Matabeleland. In late 1888 he returned to Matabeleland as a
civilian, hoping to gain a mining concession* for the company
he had formed with George Cawston. He arrived at Bulawayo
after the signing of the Rudd Concession (q.v.), which he then
tried to discredit with Lobengula. Partly on his initiative, he
accompanied Lobengula's emissaries Babayane and Mshete (qq.v.)
to London. He returned to Matabeleland armed with arguments
against Cecil Rhodes' party, but before he arrived there, he
learned that his partner had joined Rhodes' group--a move he
quickly emulated. He later became a businessman in Salisbury.
    Although Maund had never traveled east of Bulawayo,
R. N. Hall (q.v.) named one of the ruins groups at Zimbabwe
(q.v.) after him.

MAUNGWE. Name of the country and of the people ruled by the
Makoni dynasty (q.v.).

MAVURA II MHANDE (a.k.a. Felipe) (c.1580s-May 25, 1652). The
first Munhumutapa (q.v.) said to have been a "puppet" of the
Portuguese (q.v.), Mavura II acceded to the kingship in May
1629 after a combined African-Portuguese army helped him to
oust Nyambo Kapararidze (q.v.), a member of a rival ruling
house. On May 24, 1629, Mavura signed a major treaty with
the Portuguese which virtually made him a vassal of the Portuguese crown. Portuguese residents in the country became

exempt from local law, and final authority and powers of taxation were given over to the "Captain of the Gates" at Masapa (q.v.). More Portuguese entered the country and many were granted landed estates (prazos). Meanwhile, Mavura had to contend with Nyambo's continued resistance. Mavura died from an accidental gunshot wound in 1652 and was succeeded as Munhumutapa by his son Siti Kazurukumusapa (q.v.). (For Mavura I, see under MATOPE.)

MAVURADONHA MOUNTAINS. A 1200- to 1500-meter-high range forming the northern edge of the Zambezi Escarpment (q.v.) in the Darwin District (q.v.).

MAWEMA, MICHAEL ANDREW (b. July 13, 1928). Nationalist leader. Active in the Railway African Workers' Union in the early 1950s, Mawema later became a leader in the African National Congress (q.v.). He was abroad in early 1959 when the government arrested most of the ANC leadership. After his return he became acting president of the new National Democratic Party (q.v.), formed on January 1, 1960. In April he led a delegation to London to head off Edgar Whitehead's (q.v.) attempts to gain greater autonomy for the white government. In July Mawema and other NDP leaders were arrested under the terms of the Unlawful Organisations Act (q.v.), touching off mass demonstrations throughout the country. In September he resigned his NDP presidency under pressure from other party leaders. The following year he helped to form the Zimbabwe National Party (q.v.) to oppose the NDP. He was later a member of ZANU and the organizing secretary of the African National Council (qq.v.).

MAZOE DISTRICT. Located directly north of Salisbury, Mazoe District covers 3980 sq. km. in Mashonaland North Province (q.v.). It was originally almost twice as large, but lost its eastern area to form the Bindura and Shamva districts (qq.v.). Except for Tribal Trust Land in the northeast, most of the district is reserved for Europeans (see LAND TENURE ACT). The district began as a mainly gold (q.v.) mining region, but has since developed into a rich mixed farming and citrus producing region. Administrative headquarters for the district are at Mazoe village near the southern boundary (at 17° 31'S, 30° 58'E). Other centers include Concession, Jumbo Mine, Amandas, and Umvukwes (qq.v.). Population in 1969 included 95,810 Africans and 1990 Europeans. Mazoe borders the districts of Salisbury on the south; Lomagundi and Sipolilo on the west; Darwin on the north; and Bindura and Goromanzi (qq.v.) on the east.

"MAZOE PATROL." Incident in the Shona Revolt (q.v.), when a relief party from Salisbury rescued several Europeans besieged at Alice Mine, near Mazoe, on June 20, 1896.

MAZOE RIVER (variant: Mazowe). Rises just north of Salisbury, whence it flows north and then northeast, forming a brief stretch of the border* with Mozambique, in which it enters the Zambezi River. Mazoe Dam, built in 1920, plugs a gap in the Iron Mask Hills c. 40 km. north of Salisbury. The dam serves to irrigate citrus farms in one of the country's most prosperous agricultural regions.

MAZUNGA. Village in Gwanda District (q. v.); located c. 28 km. north of Beitbridge* on the main road to Bulawayo (at 21° 44'S, 29° 52'E).

MBIGO MASUKU (c. 1800s-June 1870). An Ndebele induna*, Mbigo was apparently one of Mzilikazi's original followers out of Zululand. He achieved immense prestige in 1847, when his Zwangendaba ibutho (q. v.) rebuffed A. H. Potgieter's (q. v.) Afrikaner raiding party into the Matopo Hills*. By the 1860s Mbigo was connected to Mzilikazi's family by marriage, and was the head of an elite group of amabutho. After Mzilikazi died in 1868, Mbigo steadfastly supported the Nkulumane (q. v.) faction in the succession dispute. When Lobengula (q. v.) was installed as king in early 1870, Mbigo and his men refused to recognize him. Troops loyal to Lobengula crushed the rebels in a single battle at the Zwangendaba town in June 1870. Mbigo himself was killed. Lobengula pardoned the rebel survivors, but many fled the country and later joined another dissident, Mangwane (q. v.).

MBIRA. Shona musical instrument of a type popularly known throughout southern Africa as "African pianos" or "thumb pianos." Mbiras contain 25 to 30 iron rods fixed to resonant wooden bases of various shapes. The instruments are held between the hands so that the player's thumbs can pluck the rods, which cover several octaves. The mbira is one of the most melodious Shona instruments, and has long been played by professional performers at social and ritual gatherings. (See MUSIC.)

MBIRE. Traditional Shona name for a region between the Dande and Guruhuswa (qq. v.) which apparently encompassed the area around the present Hartley and Marandellas districts (qq. v.). The name Mbire was also applied to a section of the Zezuru (q. v.) people ruled by the Svosve dynasty (q. v.).

MBULALE (variants: Bulali; Umbulali) see MZIZI, WILLIAM

MCHELA CAVE (a. k. a. Cave of Hands). Located near West Nicholson (q. v.) in the Gwanda District* (at 21° 8'S, 29° 2'E), Mchela Cave contains very fine polychrome rock paintings (q. v.) of elephants and giraffes. It is most noted, however, for its unique collection of hundreds of human handprints painted on the walls. Human remains have rarely been found in such cave sites, but Mchela contained a walled-up female mummy devoid of artifacts.

MCHEMWA (d. Aug. 1909). Shona Revolt (q. v.) leader. A son of the Nhowe ruler Mangwende (q. v.), Mchemwa was a vociferous

opponent of British occupation during the early 1890s.   In June
1896 he led the Nhowe into rebellion, starting with the killing
of the missionary Bernard Mizeki (q.v.).   After a few months
of active fighting, he and his father retreated to the Bogoto
Hills (17° 18'S, 31° 52'E).   In September 1897 he reluctantly
joined his father in surrender, but only after having failed to
persuade the Nhowe to migrate with him to Barwe (q.v.) country.   A year later he assembled other recalcitrant rebels, collected previously cached arms, and went east.   For four and a
half years his outlaw band roamed the eastern part of Mashonaland in a rare demonstration of residual violent resistance (cf.
MAPONDERA).   He surrendered in April 1903, and was killed
six years later by a fellow Nhowe in revenge for a murder he
had allegedly committed during his outlaw period.

MEALIE.   Widely used southern African term for maize (q.v.).
The word derives from Portuguese milho for a European variety
of millet, and has sometimes been loosely applied to other kinds
of grain.

MELSETTER.   Village near the Chimanimani Mountains (q.v.) serving as the administrative headquarters for Melsetter District*
(at 19° 48'S, 32° 52'E; alt. 1555 m.).   A settlement with the
same name was first established by members of the Moodie
Trek (q.v.) near Chipinga (q.v.), 64 km. to the south, and
was moved to its present site in 1895.   The name is taken
from an Orkney Islands village which was the Moodie family's
ancestral home.   Population in 1969 was 670 (82% Africans).

MELSETTER DISTRICT.   Eastern border district, covering 3345
sq. km. in Manicaland Province (q.v.).   The district was originally more than twice as large, but lost its southern part to
form Chipinga District (q.v.).   The western part of Melsetter
is Tribal Trust Land, while the eastern part is reserved for
Europeans and Chimanimani National Park (q.v.).   Population
in 1969 included 58,160 Africans and only 635 Europeans.   In
addition to Chipinga, the district borders Buhera on the west
and Umtali District (qq.v.) on the north.

MERENSKY, ALEX   see under   BERLIN MISSIONARY SOCIETY

METHODIST MISSIONS.   The first Methodist missionaries to work
in the country were agents of the London-based Wesleyan Methodist Missionary Society (q.v.), who started at Salisbury in 1891.
The Wesleyan Church is now known as The Methodist Church in
Rhodesia.   The American Methodist Episcopal Church followed
in 1897, starting its work at Umtali* (see UNITED METHODIST
CHURCH).   Black South African missionaries of the American-
based African Methodist Episcopal Church (q.v.) started at
Bulawayo in 1900.   Another American-based society, the Free
Methodist Church, began work in the southeastern low veld in
1939.   (See MISSIONS.)

METRICATION.   In 1972 the Rhodesian government officially
switched the country from the Imperial System of Weights and
Measurements to the International System of Metric Weights
and Measures.   (On decimalization, see CURRENCY.)

MFECANE (Sotho* variant: Difaqane).   Nguni* term literally meaning "the crushing," applied to the era of Zulu* wars in the
1820s and 1830s when African societies in South Africa were
thrown into violent disorder.   More broadly, Mfecane also refers to the diaspora of South African conquest states north of
the Limpopo River during the late 1820s and 1830s.   Most of
these states passed directly through what is now Rhodesia,
breaking up the Changamire state (q.v.) and having an enormous impact on the peoples of the entire country.   The Ndebele kingdom of Mzilikazi (q.v.) was a product of the Mfecane.
Other Mfecane-derived states included those of the Ngoni, Gaza,
and Kololo (qq.v.).

MFENGU (variant: Fingo).   Somewhat amorphous Nguni-speaking
(q.v.) society living in the eastern Cape Province of South
Africa.   The first Mfengu were refugees from Natal, driven
south in the 1820s by the Zulu* wars of the Mfecane (q.v.).
Nicknamed Mfengu, "beggars," these refugees became alienated
from their new Xhosa and other southern Nguni neighbors and
they sought to ally with the British colonial government by
adopting Christianity and Western education rapidly.   Individual
Mfengu and families, such as William Mzizi (q.v.), began entering Matabeleland in the mid-19th century.   Others entered
with the British as employees and soldiers during the 1890s
(see, e.g., GROOTBOOM, J.).   Cecil Rhodes thought the
Mfengu would make useful African allies in Southern Rhodesia,
so he sent F. R. Thompson (q.v.) to the Transkei in 1898 to
recruit settlers.   Hundreds of Mfengu responded to the scheme,
and most became farmers around Fingo Location (q.v.).
      At first the Mfengu identified their interests with those
of the BSAC government who sought exemption from discriminatory laws affecting Africans (see, e.g., PASS LAWS).   Gradually, however, they became disillusioned as the BSAC reneged
on promises to allocate more land and generally treated the
Mfengu indifferently.   Many Mfengu, such as the Hlazo and Sojini
families, then allied with local Africans and played leading roles
in such movements as the Matabele [National] Home Society and
the RBVA (qq.v.).   One of the most outstanding of these leaders
was Martha Ngano (q.v.).

MFUNDISI (pl., abafundisi).   Sindebele* term for teacher or minister,
usually synonymous with "the reverend."   In Chishona* the term
is rendered mufundisi.

MHLABA KHUMALO (variant: Umhlaba) (d. June 1892).   Ndebele
induna*.   During the interregnum following Mzilikazi's death,
Mhlaba's father Mncumbathe (q.v.) served as regent, and Mhlaba
himself participated in one of the embassies to Natal which

searched for the missing heir Nkulumane (q.v.). When his
father died a few years later, Mhlaba inherited his office as
hereditary regent. By the late 1870s he was regarded as one
of the four most influential izinduna in the kingdom. During
the troubled period leading up to the 1893 Ndebele War (q.v.),
Mhlaba's political enemies accused him of having supported
Nkulumane's claims to the kingship against those of Lobengula
(q.v.). In June 1892 he and most of his family were wiped out
by the Imbizo ibutho (q.v.). However, his brother Mnyenyezi
and his son Ntenende escaped the purge. The next year they
acted as guides for P. W. Forbes' (q.v.) northern invasion
column which occupied Bulawayo*.

MHLAHLANDLELA.   Ndebele ibutho (q.v.) first raised by Mzilikazi
in the Transvaal* in the 1820s. Gwabalanda (q.v.) appears to
have been the ibutho's first induna*. By 1863 Mhlahlandlela was
posted by the upper Khami River (q.v.) in Matabeleland. From
that date Mzilikazi made the ibutho's town his chief residence.
In 1941 European residents of the country erected the "Mzilikazi
Memorial" at the spot where the town had stood at the time of
Mzilikazi's death (at 20°20'S, 28°34'E).

MHONDORO (variant: mondoro).   Chishona* word for lion (q.v.),
and for tutelary spirits, popularly called "lion spirits." Mhondoro spirits typically communicate through living mediums, whom
they possess after residing in the bodies of young lions. Such
mediums, or svikiro (q.v.), assume the personalities of their
spirits, and are themselves often called mhondoro. Most mhondoro are believed to be spirits of important ancestors--typically
political rulers--and are closely associated with the welfare of
whole communities, in contrast to the spirits of ordinary midzimu
(see MUDZIMU), who look after only individual or family interests (see also GOMBWE). Mhondoro are attributed with powers
of rain-making, prophecy, divination, and healing, and they also
function as intermediaries with the high god Mwari (q.v.). In
contrast to other healers, such as nganga (q.v.), the mhondoro
eschew the use of medicines in their work. Mhondoro mediums
collect followings of acolytes, maintain shrines, and receive
propitiary gifts. These organized activities have been described
as "cults."
        Mhondoro cults have been a major part of Shona religion
(q.v.) since at least the 16th century. The mediums have also
played an important role in the processes of political succession. Succession disputes were, and are, generally turned over
to mhondoro for resolution, but the mediums rarely made recommendations which ran counter to popular sentiment. Their political role can thus be seen as the articulation of consensus
within communities.
        During the 19th century one of the famous mhondoro,
Chaminuka (q.v.), became a center of central Shona resistance
to Ndebele domination. In the 1896-7 Revolt (q.v.) a number
of mhondoro played key roles in organizing resistance to British
occupation. The most notable of these, Kaguvi and Nehanda

(qq. v.), have been described as instigators of the Shona Revolt, and as representatives of a new kind of millenarian leadership which anticipated modern African nationalism. This view, developed mainly by T. O. Ranger (q. v.), has been challenged by historians who argue that while the mhondoro clearly played an important part in the Revolt, they did so merely in their traditional role as articulators of majority opinion. (See also DZIVAGURU.)

Despite the failure of the 1896-7 Revolt, the influence of mhondoro has remained great in the eastern parts of the country, where their mediums have carried on their traditional functions. Since the mid-1960s many mhondoro have become closely associated with the antigovernment nationalist movement. Unlike secular political leaders, these mhondoro mediums have rarely been suppressed by the white government, and many are said to have actively supported guerrilla forces.

MI-. Chishona (q. v.) prefix (Class 4), normally used for plural forms of nouns starting with mu- (q. v.). Thus, for a term such as midzimu, see MUDZĪMU.

MIAMI (variant: Mhwami). Village located c. 190 km. northwest of Salisbury, serving as the administrative center for Urungwe District* (at 16° 40'S, 29° 46'E). Miami is surrounded by tobacco* farms, cattle* ranches, and various mines, the most important of which produce mica (q. v.).

MICA. One of the most important non-metallic minerals (q. v.) produced in the country, with the notable exception of coal (q. v.). Significant mica production began at Miami (q. v.) in 1919. A second major production center opened at Rusape (q. v.) in 1927. Through the 1920s production was valued at around £20,000 per year, reaching a peak of £52,000 in 1930. Production almost ceased during the 1930s, but was revived by the Second World War's new demands. Between 1944 and 1948 production varied between £106,000 and £153,000 per year. Afterwards production tapered off to £22,000 in 1964. Total production between 1919 and 1964 was valued at £1,697,000.

MIDLANDS PROVINCE. One of seven provinces (q. v.) in the country, Midlands is the only one not to touch an international border*. Midlands presently comprises the districts of Gokwe, Que Que, Gwelo, Chilimanzi, Charter, and Selukwe (qq. v.). It formerly included Buhera (q. v.), which is now in Manicaland Province (q. v.), and Shabani and Belingwe, which are now in Matabeleland South (qq. v.). Prior to the creation of Gokwe District, Midlands included the former Sebungwe District (q. v.).

MIGUEL, DOM (fl. 1600-1670). The first black southern African ordained a Christian minister, Dom Miguel's original African name is not known. He is known only to have been a son of Munhumutapa* Gatsi Rusere (q. v.). It appears that Dom Miguel joined an order of Portuguese Dominicans when his father signed a treaty with Diogo Simões Madeira (q. v.) in 1607. He was then taken to Goa in India, where he is said to have later been made a Doctor of Divinity and the vicar of a Goanese church. He never returned to Shona country, and appears to have died by 1670.

MILITARY FORCES. Despite the overriding importance of the military situation in the continuing struggle for control of Rhodesia, very little is known by outsiders about either the Rhodesian government or the nationalist military forces. Both sides are highly secretive. The Rhodesian government itself provides most of the available information on the ongoing war, and its information is naturally biased. A balanced historical treatment of the military struggle must be left for the future. Here only outline sketches of the military forces are presented.

Government military forces. As a possible indication of the difficulties future historians may have in untangling the current military situation, it should be noted that even the very early history of the government's military organization is still poorly understood. The only security force with anything like a continuous organizational tradition has been the paramilitary British South Africa Police (q. v.), formed in the 1890s. During international wars the BSAP was partly blended into regular military forces, and since the escalation of guerrilla warfare in the early 1970s the BSAP has worked closely with the regular Rhodesian army.

The Southern Rhodesian government had no standing army, as such, before 1951. The forces used during the 1890s in the Pioneer Column, Ndebele War, and Revolts (qq. v.) were a combination of British Imperial troops, BSAP, and local volunteer forces. In 1898 the various volunteer bodies were combined into a reserve known as the Southern Rhodesian Volunteers (q. v.). This unit formed the nucleus for such wartime units as the Rhodesian Regiments (q. v.) organized during the South African War (q. v.) and the First World War. The Second World War saw a great enlargement and reorganization of the security forces for foreign campaigns, but the Rhodesian African Rifles (q. v.) was the only unit to survive post-war disbandments and still function today. In 1951 the government began organizing a standing army, while making its air force an autonomous service. Two years later these forces were absorbed into the new Féderation (q. v.) army and air force, which were dominated by Southern Rhodesian officers.

After the break-up of Federation in 1963, Federal forces in Southern Rhodesia reverted to the territorial government, with Southern Rhodesia obtaining most military equipment. In 1964 the army had only 3400 men on active duty, and this figure remained nearly constant for a decade. Dramatic expansion began only after 1973, by which time the liberation of central Mozambique regions by Frelimo had opened a major new front in the previously small-scale guerrilla war. In 1974 the government began allocating increasingly larger shares of its budget to security, and began increasing manpower rapidly. Since then the

general pattern has been a broadening of age groups subject to
military draft, a tightening of deferments, longer tours of duty
for regular army personnel, and more frequent call ups of the
reservists in the Territorial Force (q.v.). New units have been
formed, including one to guard the "Protected Villages" (q.v.).
By mid-1976 an estimated 4500 men were in the regular army,
1200 in the air force, and 8000 in the BSAP, with an additional
10,000 reservists in both the army and the air force, and
35,000 reservists in the BSAP. The total number of men under
arms at any given moment have steadily increased, reaching
totals variously estimated at 15,000 to 20,000.

Government security forces have faced growing shortages
of European manpower and equipment. The white government
has been reluctant to draw upon African volunteers for the army,
though many are said to be available, because of the unspoken
fear of mutiny. Involuntary drafts have been limited to non-
Africans, who are mainly Europeans, and these have produced
enormous strains on the limited pool of non-African manpower
available in the country. Removal of Europeans from civilian
occupations has created economic dislocations, and has enhanced
emigration, while discouraging potential immigrants.

Mandatory UN economic sanctions (q.v.) have curtailed
armaments imports perhaps more than any other important commodities. With no internal armaments industries of its own,
Rhodesia has been largely dependent on imports from South
Africa (q.v.), which has a highly developed armaments industry,
and which surreptitiously passes on to Rhodesia equipment imported from elsewhere. Virtually all military aircraft and other
heavy equipment used by Rhodesian forces were in the country
before UDI, and acquisition of replacement parts has evidently
been a critical problem. The opposing nationalist forces possess no aircraft, but they have reportedly used antiaircraft mis-
siles to down irreplaceable airplanes.

Despite these problems, the Rhodesian security forces
were able to check significant guerrilla infiltration into the
country through 1975, when Mozambique (q.v.) became independent. Mozambique's independence opened the entire eastern
border (q.v.) to guerrilla incursions. By mid-1977 the military
situation had significantly worsened for the government, but the
nationalists had still failed to establish any liberated zones within the country, and most of their raids were apparently directed
against unarmed civilian communities and isolated European outposts. In mid-1977 the guerrilla war apparently penetrated the
major cities, when bombing attacks were made in buildings. By
then, however, the government still maintained the major advantages of having a unified command structure, control of the
main lines of transport and communications (q.v.), apparently
high morale among its forces, and a monopoly of air power.

Nationalist forces. So little is presently known about the
manpower, command structure, equipment, training, deployment,
and achievements of the nationalist guerrilla forces that few confident generalizations can yet be made. There was a hiatus of
violent African resistance to the white governments from the time

of the 1890s Revolts (q.v.) to the modern nationalist guerrilla
movements.   Some nationalists are known to have begun military training abroad during the early 1960s, but the first organized attacks on Rhodesian positions were made only in April
1966, when ZANU forces entered the country from Zambia
(q.v.).   ZAPU attacks followed in 1967, but all these efforts
had little impact through 1968.   The next year saw a lull in
guerrilla activities, as leaders reconsidered their strategies
and foreign African leaders tried to get the divided nationalist
forces to unite (see, e.g., FROLIZI).
      Guerrilla incursions resumed in 1970, and became intense
in December 1972--the date the current "war" is reckoned formally to have begun.   The main new development was the liberation of Mozambique's Tete (q.v.) province by Frelimo forces,
with which ZANU forces then began working.   Since then the
entire eastern Rhodesian border has been opened to Zimbabwe
nationalist forces, and the guerrillas have adopted the more effective tactics of "hit and run."   Meanwhile, some guerrilla incursions and mortar attacks have been resumed from north of
the Zambezi River, particularly against the towns of Kariba and
Victoria Falls (qq.v.).   Guerrilla bases have also been established in Botswana (q.v.), but thus far few attacks have been
mounted from that direction.   By late 1976 an estimated 15,000
to 20,000 nationalist guerrillas were estimated to be either under
arms, or in training, and most of these were believed to be
based in Mozambique.   Estimates of the numbers of guerrillas
operating within Rhodesia have varied wildly, but by late 1976
even the Rhodesian government was admitting that as many as
3000 guerrillas were in the country, mostly in the northeastern
districts.
      Since the early 1970s there has been a bewildering pro-
liferation of names of guerrilla armies.   It has not always been
clear to what extent these names have reflected military reali-
ties, as opposed to transient alliances and internal fissions.   It
is generally recognized that rifts between political and military
leaders, as well as active hostilities among separate guerrilla
units have hindered effective combination against the unified
Rhodesian forces.   The military force connected with ZANU
was originally known as the Zimbabwe African National Liberation Army (ZANLA), while that allied with ZAPU was called the
Zimbabwe People's Revolutionary Army (ZPRA) (qq.v.).   The
ZANU forces, based mainly in Mozambique, are generally agreed
to be much the larger and the more active in Rhodesia.   ZAPU
forces have been concentrated in Zambia.   Unified commands
have occasionally been reported, and since mid-1976 the names
"Zimbabwe Liberation Army" (ZLA) and "Zimbabwe People's
Army" (ZIPA) (qq.v.) have dominated reportage.   Robert Mugabe
(q.v.) has generally been credited with having political command
over the largest forces.   Connections of such leaders as Joshua
Nkomo, Ndabaningi Sithole, and Abel Muzorewa (qq.v.) with individual forces are less clear.

MILLET.   Important African cereal crop, several varieties of which have been grown throughout southern Africa for many centuries. In the last hundred years, or so, millet has tended to give way to maize (q. v.) as the primary African grain. (See AGRICUL-TURE.)

MILTON, WILLIAM HENRY (Dec. 3, 1854-March 6, 1930). Early BSAC official. An Englishman, Milton came to South Africa in 1878 and entered the Cape civil service. By 1891 he had risen to the post of private secretary to the Prime Minister, Cecil Rhodes, whose confidence and friendship he won. In August 1896 Milton was transferred to Southern Rhodesia to assist in reorganizing the administration after the Jameson Raid and Revolts (qq. v.) had revealed how chaotically the BSAC government was being run. Milton was soon also made Chief Secretary for Native Affairs. In July 1897 he became acting Administrator (q. v.), replacing A. H. Grey (q. v.). In December 1898 his position was formalized when he designated Administrator of Mashonaland and Senior Administrator of Southern Rhodesia. In the latter capacity Milton oversaw Arthur Lawley's (q. v.) administration of Matabeleland until 1901, when he himself became sole Administrator for all of Southern Rhodesia. During his tenure of office Milton rebuilt the administration, following South African colonial precedents, and brought in many experienced South African civil servants, such as P. D. L. Fynn (q. v.). On his retirement in 1914 he was succeeded by F. P. D. Chaplin (q. v.).

MINERALS/MINING. Rhodesia is said to have been the only British colony occupied solely because of its mineral wealth. True or not, it is clear that the BSAC and its supporters were lured to the country by the prospect of finding goldfields as rich as those discovered in the Transvaal's* Rand in the 1880s. Although the country's gold reserves proved ultimately disappointing, mineral production long dominated the country's economic development and it remains very important today. Diversity is now the most outstanding characteristic of the mining sector, with more than 50 kinds of minerals in commercial production.

Iron (q. v.) is perhaps the most widespread commercial mineral in the country, and has been mined since at least A. D. 200. Production now meets local industrial needs, but its total value does not place the ore among the top mineral products. Copper (q. v.) has also long been mined in the country. Its exploitation in the 20th century was initially slow, but production increased rapidly after 1954. The government has not released precise figures, but copper is now believed to rank as the most important mineral product in both production and export values.

Gold (q. v.) has also been mined since the first millenium. Its role in international trade and Shona state formation was especially great from about the 12th to the 18th centuries. Production virtually ceased during the 19th century, until old workings were discovered by Europeans. Exaggerated estimates of the country's gold reserves helped the BSAC to obtain capital investors in Europe, and promises of mining rights lured early

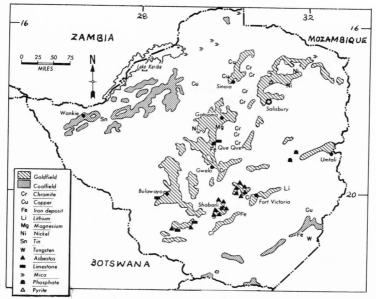

Map 4.   Minerals

settlers and mercenaries.   Although production fell short of ex-
pectations, gold ranked as the leading mineral produced and exported until after the Second World War.   It now ranks fourth.
    Asbestos (q.v.) displaced gold as the most valuable
mineral product in the early 1950s.   It now appears to rank
just behind copper in both production and exports.   Chrome
(q.v.) became about the third most valuable mineral during
this same period.   Nickel (q.v.) production increased rapidly
during the 1960s, and is expected to increase further in relative importance.   Coal (q.v.) production has been important
throughout this century, but relatively little of it has been exported, especially since UDI (see SANCTIONS).   Other important
minerals include gemstones, lithium, mica, silver, and tin
(qq.v.).   Sufficient limestone is quarried at Colleen Bawn (q.v.)
to meet national cement needs.
    Emphasis on mineral development during the early 20th
century greatly influenced the patterns of urbanization (q.v.)
and largely dictated the routes of the main railway lines (q.v.).
The diversity of minerals available has facilitated local industrialization by meeting almost every major need with the notable
exception of petroleum, which the country lacks completely.
Until UDI mineral exports ranked only behind those of agricultural products.   Since then mineral production and exports have
increased, largely because of their relatively high ratios of
value to bulk, and the ease of finding foreign markets in the
face of international sanctions.   The government claimed that
production and exports had doubled between 1965 and 1973, by
which time total mineral production was estimated at well over
R$100 million per annum.   Production is now thought to account
for about 6% of gross domestic product, and for about a third

of export value.

Mineral production was initially characterized by a vast number of small-scale producers known as "small-workers" (q.v.), but the historical trend has been towards concentration of production among large mines. Increased mechanization of the industry since the Second World War has gradually reduced the size of the African mine labor force, while simultaneously providing more skilled employment for Europeans.

MISSIONS, CHRISTIAN. Missionaries have played an important role in the history of the country during every era of European (q.v.) involvement. The first missionary to enter the country was Gonçalo da Silveira (q.v.), a Portuguese (q.v.) Jesuit who succeeded in baptizing the reigning Munhumutapa (q.v.) in 1561. Silveira's murder at the hands of the Shona produced a Portuguese reaction which brought more intense European penetration of the country in the late 16th century. Over the next century Dominicans established missions throughout the northeastern part of the country (see FAIRS). Their success in proselytizing is unknown, however, and by the 1690s they were all out of the country.

The next missionaries to work among the country's peoples were Congregationalists. Agents of the American Board of Commissioners for Foreign Missions (q.v.) spent a fruitless year among the Ndebele, when the latter were living in the western Transvaal* in the 1830s. ABC agents later worked among the southeastern Shona in the 1890s. Meanwhile, their British counterparts of the LMS established the first permanent mission among the Ndebele in Matabeleland in 1859. Jesuits of the Zambezi Mission (q.v.) followed there in 1879. The Ndebele rulers discouraged European contact with Shona peoples, but agents of the Dutch Reformed Church, Berlin Missionary Society, and Anglican bodies (qq.v.) made tentative efforts in Mashonaland in the 1880s. (See also COILLARD, F.) None of these missions had any real success in gaining converts through this period, and the missionaries relentlessly criticized Ndebele society and called for British conquest. After the BSAC occupied Mashonaland in 1890, Cecil Rhodes personally encouraged missionary work by allocating generous tracts of land to 13 different societies during the 1890s. The already established bodies expanded their fields of operation, while Methodist (q.v.), and many other missionary societies entered the country. The BSAC government did not want the bother and expense of establishing an educational system for Africans, so they encouraged the missions to assume this responsibility by providing financial subsidies. (See EDUCATION.) By the 1920s there were 15 recognized mission bodies in the country, and these had formed a powerful lobbying organization, the Southern Rhodesian Missionary Conference (q.v.).

In more recent years the role of foreign missionaries has become increasingly anomalous. Many missionaries have persistently criticized the government's policies affecting Africans (see, e.g., LAMONT, D.), but they have nevertheless

become increasingly alienated from African peoples. Since the
1950s there has been a strong African drift away from established mission churches into independent, African-run churches
(see, e.g., CHAZA, M.; MARANKE, J.; ZWIMBA, M.). Some
African clerics in the established churches have become prominent leaders in the nationalist movement, but in very recent
times European missionaries themselves have frequently been
the victims of violent guerrilla attacks.

MITCHELL, GEORGE (April 1, 1867-July 4, 1937). Third Prime
Minister (q.v.) of Southern Rhodesia (1933). Mitchell came to
the country as a bank manager in 1895 and eventually rose to
a prominent position in the mining industry. He meanwhile
entered electoral politics. In 1930 he joined H. U. Moffat's
(q.v.) cabinet, and then replaced the latter as prime minister
after Rhodesian Party (q.v.) leaders asked Moffat to resign in
1933. Already 66 years old when he assumed the office,
Mitchell overburdened himself by taking on three additional
ministerial portfolios. After less than three months in office
he lost Assembly seat in the September 1933 general election
and was replaced as prime minister by Godfrey Huggins (q.v.).

MIZEKI, BERNARD (a.k.a. Mamiyeri Mizeka Gwambe) (c.1860-
June 18, 1896). Famed Christian martyr. Born in Mozambique near Inhambane--apparently of Tsonga (q.v.) parents--
Mizeki went to Cape Town with other boys to look for work in
the early 1870s. There he attended a small mission school and
was baptized an Anglican in 1886. He trained at a divinity college until 1891, when he accompanied Bishop Knight-Bruce
(q.v.) to Mashonaland*. Mizeki himself opened a small mission station near Mangwende's (q.v.) town in central Mashonaland. He soon became fluent in Chishona*, and established a
good rapport with the local people. Early in 1896 he married
one of the Mangwende's granddaughters. When the Shona Revolt
(q.v.) broke out the following June, Mizeki ignored advice to
leave the country. On June 18th he was one of the first people
killed by rebels led by Mchemwa (q.v.). A shrine built to his
memory has become the focus of periodic pilgrimages.

MJAAN   see   MTSHANI

MKALIPHI   see   KALIPHI

MKUMBE CAVE   see   MAKUMBE CAVE

MKWATI (variant: Umkwati) (d.1897). Born a Leya in western
Zambia, Mkwati was captured by the Ndebele and raised in
Matabeleland. While serving at the Ujinga ibutho* town near
Ntabazikamambo (q.v.), he apparently became a messenger of
the Mwari cult (q.v.). His exact position in this cult, and his
role in the 1896 Ndebele Revolt (q.v.) are controversial. During
the Revolt British officers, such as R. S. S. Baden-Powell
(q.v.), described Mkwati as the "Mlimo" (q.v.)--a figure of

godlike powers.   According to T. O. Ranger's (q.v.) influential
writings, Mkwati was a prime leader in the Ndebele Revolt
who gave it a strongly millenarian character.   This view is
now being challenged, as it appears that Mkwati had little or
no influence over what was essentially a politically-motivated
war.   It is clear, however, that in late 1896 Mkwati went from
Ndebele territory to Shona territory.   There he assisted the
Shona Revolt leader "Kaguvi" (q.v.) until he was killed by disillusioned Shona in September or October of 1897.   (See also
TENKELA; BONDA.)

MLIMO (variants: Umlimo; Molimo; Modimo; Morimo).   Generic
    Sindebele* term for god.   In traditional Sotho (q.v.) religion
    Modimo is the name of a remote high god, regarded as the
    creator and controller of natural phenomena.   These concepts
    are similar to Ndebele beliefs about the Nguni God Nkulunkulu
    (q.v.).   When the Ndebele kingdom (q.v.) started absorbing
    Sotho-speaking peoples during the 1820s, the Ndebele fused the
    concepts of Nkulunkulu and Modimo, naturalizing the latter name
    to Molimo, or Mlimo.   Christian missionaries have adopted
    "Mlimo" for "Jehovah," thereby further widening usage of the
    term to encompass almost any high god.   Europeans have also
    frequently interchanged "Mlimo" with Mwari (q.v.), the name
    of the central Shona high god.   It should be noted that, in
    former times at least, Africans made a clear distinction be-
    tween the concepts of Mlimo and Mwari and that the two names
    are not properly interchangeable.   (See RELIGION.)

MLUGULU KHUMALO (variant: Umlugulu) (fl.1870s-1900s).   An im-
    portant Ndebele induna*, Mlugulu was accused by Europeans of
    having killed R. R. Patterson (q.v.) in 1878.   About the same
    time he succeeded his father Mlota as head of the Eyengo
    cluster of towns, situated just northeast of the Matopo Hills*.
    As a member of the royal Khumalo (q.v.) family, Mlugulu, his
    brother Nungu, and another relative, Bozongwana (d.1894) were
    officiating as "dance doctors" at the annual inxwala (q.v.) festi-
    vals by the late 1880s.   These duties gave rise to the mistaken
    notion that Mlugulu was the "high priest" of the Ndebele nation--
    a misconception reinforced by recent religiously-oriented inter-
    pretations of the 1896 Ndebele Revolt (q.v.) in which he played
    a major part.   (Cf. MWARI; MKWATI.)   After King Lobengula's
    death in 1894 Mlugulu became a leading advocate of restoration
    of the kingship.   After the Revolt began, Mlugulu, Sikombo,
    and Dhliso (qq.v.) were the main leaders in the eastern Mato-
    pos fighting, and they helped to install Nyamanda (q.v.) as king.
    In August 1896 Mlugulu was one of the izinduna who negotiated
    a truce with Cecil Rhodes in the famous "indabas" (q.v.).
    Though he narrowly escaped execution by the British afterwards,
    he was made a salaried chief.   Mlugulu continued to agitate for
    restoration of the Ndebele monarchy, calling for Lobengula's
    son Njube (q.v.) to return from South Africa in 1898.

MNCENGENCE KHUMALO (variants: Mncene; Ningi; Nini; etc.)

(d. April 1880).   Sister of Lobengula (q. v.).   During the first
decade of her brother's reign as Ndebele king, Mncengence was
probably the most powerful woman in the kingdom.   Lobengula
then had no "royal wife" (see INKOSIKAZI) so he allowed the
unmarried Mncengence to exercise considerable influence in his
court.   Unfortunately, her privileged position and close friend-
ships with European traders earned her many enemies.   Her
position was directly challenged when Lobengula married the
Gaza princess Xwalile (q. v.) in 1879.   When Xwalile failed to
become pregnant within a suitable period of time, Mncengence
was accused by enemies of having bewitched the new royal wife.
The following year Lobengula reluctantly assented to Mncengence's
execution on these charges.

MNCUMBATHE KHUMALO (variants: Ncombate; Nombati; Umkum-
    baze; Uncombata; etc.) (c. 1780s-c. 1872/3).   Hereditary regent
    and top adviser in the Ndebele kingdom (q. v.).   One of Mzili-
    kazi's original followers out of Zululand*, Mncumbathe inherited
    his rank as Ndebele regent from his Khumalo (q. v.) forebears.
    In 1829 he went to Kuruman (q. v.) to invite Robert Moffat (q. v.)
    to visit Mzilikazi in the central Transvaal*.   Six years later he
    went to Cape Town as Mzilikazi's ambassador and signed a
    treaty of friendship with the British governor, Benjamin D'Urban.
    Though apparently somewhat older than Mzilikazi, Mncumbathe
    assumed active rule over the Ndebele kingdom after the latter's
    death in 1868.   For 18 months he maintained firm control over
    the kingdom, while working to have Lobengula (q. v.) recognized
    as the legitimate successor.   He opposed the Nkulumane (q. v.)
    faction by insisting that he had personally supervised the young
    prince's execution 30 years before.   He was succeeded in his
    offices by his son Mhlaba (q. v.).

MNYANDA, BRADFIELD JACOB MABHASO (1906-July 29, 1970).
    Born and raised in South Africa's eastern Cape Province,
    Mnyanda came to Southern Rhodesia to work as a Methodist
    teacher and lay evangelist in 1925.   During his long residence
    there he also worked as a government interpreter and trans-
    lator and as a journalist, editing African Weekly (q. v.).   In
    1952 he returned to Port Elizabeth, where he worked in local
    government.   Two years later he published In Search of Truth,
    a book describing African life in Southern Rhodesia.   Probably
    because the book was published in Bombay it is little known;
    however, it is significant both as an insightful account and as
    perhaps the first book on the country written by an African.
    In 1956 Mnyanda visited the United States, Canada and western
    Europe in a Moral Rearmament tour.

MOFFAT, HOWARD UNWIN (Jan. 13, 1869-Jan. 19, 1951).   Second
    Prime Minister (q. v.) of Southern Rhodesia (1927-33).   The
    son of John Smith Moffat (q. v.), H. U. Moffat was born at
    Kuruman (q. v.).   Through most of his early adult life he
    worked for the Bechuanaland Exploration Company, which had
    extensive mining interests in central Africa.   He settled in

Southern Rhodesia after having served as a member of the BBP
in the 1893 Ndebele War (q.v.). He also served in the 1896
Revolts (q.v.) and in the South African War (q.v.).

In 1920 Moffat was elected to the Legislative Council
(q.v.). Though he thought union with South Africa inevitable
(see UNIONIST MOVEMENT), he joined Charles Coghlan's Responsible Government Party (qq.v.). He later became the
latter's first Minister of Mines and Works on the achievement
of Responsible Government in October 1923. On Coghlan's
death in 1927, Moffat was made "premier"--a title he later
had changed to "prime minister." Within two weeks he confronted an African miners' strike at Shamva (q.v.).

Moffat inherited the increasingly pressing problem of
territorial segregation, which had been articulated by the Morris
Carter Commission (q.v.). A liberal by the standards of his
time, he resisted the calls for total segregation made by ex-
tremists such as Godfrey Huggins (q.v.), but nevertheless
personally introduced the bill which led to the Land Apportionment Act (q.v.) in October 1930. Moffat then faced an economic
crisis, as the world depression hit the country's export trade
hard. In common with government leaders around the world at
that time, Moffat's handling of the economic situation provoked
strong political opposition. Particularly unpopular was his
purchase of the BSAC's mineral rights for £2 million in June
1933. Leaders of his own Rhodesian Party (q.v.) called for
his resignation to strengthen their position in the 1933 general
election. Citing ill health, Moffat stepped down in favor of
George Mitchell (q.v.) on July 6, 1933. He later reentered
the Legislative Assembly (q.v.) in an attempt to revive the
Rhodesian Party, but was badly defeated in the 1939 election.

MOFFAT, JOHN SMITH (March 10, 1835-Dec. 25, 1918). Born at
Kuruman (q.v.), Moffat was the son of Robert Moffat (q.v.).
The younger Moffat trained for a mission career, but when the
LMS dallied over his appointment in 1859, his brother-in-law
David Livingstone (q.v.) paid his expenses to work as an inde-
pendent agent. In this capacity he joined T. M. Thomas and
William Sykes (qq.v.) in founding the Inyati (q.v.) mission in
Matabeleland. In 1864 Moffat obtained a regular appointment
within the LMS, but his wife Emily's health forced him to leave
the country the next year.

Moffat returned south to work among the Tswana* until
1879, when he resigned from the LMS because of friction with
other missionaries. Thereafter he held a variety of government
positions in South Africa. In 1887 he returned to Matabeleland
as a British agent. The following year he obtained Lobengula's
signature on a treaty of friendship known as the "Moffat Treaty"
(q.v.), paving the way for British occupation of the entire
country. He served as British resident in Matabeleland from
1890 to 1892, and then returned south for the last time. One
of his sons, H. U. Moffat (q.v.), later became prime minister
of Southern Rhodesia.

MOFFAT, ROBERT (Sindebele* form: Mshete) (Dec. 21, 1795-Aug.
9, 1883). A Scottish-born agent of the LMS, Moffat founded and
managed the mission at Kuruman (q.v.) for 45 years (1824-70).
During this period he made five extended visits to the Ndebele
and became Mzilikazi's (q.v.) most intimate European friend.
His first visit was in 1829, when the Ndebele king was living
near the site of present Pretoria in the Transvaal*. He re-
visited Mzilikazi in the western Transvaal in 1835. Mzilikazi
developed a great trust in Moffat, and tried to use him as his
main intermediary in Ndebele dealings with Europeans. After
the Ndebele migrated to Matabeleland*, Moffat visited Mzilikazi
there in 1854 in the company of the trader S. H. Edwards
(q.v.). This visit reopened Ndebele communication with Europeans and it made Moffat the only literate observer to document
Ndebele society both south and north of the Limpopo River*.

   Moffat returned to Matabeleland in 1857 to negotiate with
Mzilikazi for the opening of a mission station. During this
visit he obtained the release of the Ngwato* captive Macheng
(q.v.). Two years later he led the first permanent mission
party into what is now Rhodesia, helping the LMS to found a
station at Inyati (q.v.) early in 1860. Moffat's son, J. S.
Moffat (q.v.), was among the pioneer missionaries.

   Moffat's influence on Mzilikazi is heavily stressed in
most accounts written about the Ndebele king. One would sus-
pect that this is due to the one-sided perspective of Moffat's
own writings upon which historians of the Ndebele have had
largely to rely. However, Ndebele traditions corroborate
Moffat's role in their history, as manifest in the "Moffat Myth"
(q.v.).

"MOFFAT MYTH." Term for a historical misconception which
pervades nearly all literature on the Ndebele migration from
the Transvaal to present Matabeleland during the late 1830s.
Variations of the Myth occur in most Ndebele traditions of the
migration, but independent documentary evidence demonstrates
their impossibility. The main elements of the Myth are that
Robert Moffat (q.v.) foresaw the coming of Afrikaner (q.v.)
Voortrekkers to the Transvaal* before their "Great Trek" even
began; that he advised Mzilikazi (q.v.) to lead the Ndebele
north of the Limpopo River to avoid war with the Afrikaners;
that he gave Mzilikazi specific instructions on how to reach
Ntabazinduna (q.v.); and--according to one popular variation--
that he met the Ndebele in Botswana during their migration.

   The Moffat Myth serves as a valuable case study in the
use of oral traditions in reconstructing African history, as it
is a clear example of fabrication which can be checked against
contemporary records.

MOFFAT TREATY. On February 11, 1888, J. S. Moffat (q.v.)
obtained from the Ndebele king Lobengula (q.v.) signature to
a document reaffirming the terms of the Mzilikazi's 1836 treaty
of friendship with the British government (see MNCUMBATHE).

Lobengula thereby pledged eternal Ndebele amity with the British, and promised not to sign treaties or land grants with any foreign power without first obtaining permission of the British High Commissioner for South Africa. Lobengula's most likely motive for signing this one-sided document was the hope of staving off the mounting pressure different Europeans were placing on his kingdom. The British government used the treaty to declare the territory north of the Limpopo to be within its "sphere of influence," paving the way for Cecil Rhodes' agents to obtain the Rudd Concession (q. v.). (See also GROBLER, P.)

MOLIMO (variants: Modimo; Morimo) see MLIMO

MONCKTON COMMISSION (1959-60). Investigatory body formed by the British government to assess attitudes towards the Federation (q. v.) and to advise on constitutional changes. The Commission contained 26 members from various Commonwealth territories and was headed by Lord Monckton. After hearing evidence from hundreds of witnesses throughout central Africa, the Commission released its report (Cmd 1148) in October 1960. The report emphasized the strong opposition of Africans north of the Zambezi to Federation, while pointing out that many Southern Rhodesian Africans saw continued Federation as preferable to purely territorial government by Europeans. The Commission called for a general loosening of the federal structure to allow for greater African political power at the territorial level, and for wholesale reform of Southern Rhodesia's discriminatory racial laws and industrial hiring practices if the Federation, in any form, were to continue. Southern Rhodesia's pass laws (q. v.) were cited as particularly unacceptable. These recommendations had little effect in Southern Rhodesia, whose territorial and federal leaders rejected the commission's findings, but a more important Commission proposal was beyond their control. The Commission's recommendation that individual territories be permitted to secede from the Federation was adopted by the British government, resulting in the dissolution of the Federation when Nyasaland and Northern Rhodesia (now Malawi and Zambia) exercised the new option.

MONDORO see MHONDORO

MONK'S KOP. Hill in the southern Sipolilo District* (at 17° 2'45"S, 30° 35'15"E) containing a large cave ossuary filled with human skeletons and artifacts. Excavation of the site in the mid-1960s showed the artifacts to have cultural affinities with non-Shona peoples to the north--possibly riverine Tonga (q. v.; cf. MARAMUCA). Radiocarbon dates indicate that the site was used during the late 13th or early 14th centuries. The finds therefore represent a much later manifestation of an indigenous non-Shona Iron Age (q. v.) culture than had previously been recognized in the region. The site falls within the "Ancient Park" National Monument, which also includes a number of rock paintings (q. v.).

MONOMOTAPA. Popular English variant of Munhumutapa (q.v.).

MONUMENTS, NATIONAL   see   HISTORICAL MONUMENTS COM-
MISSION

MONYEBE   see   MANXEBA KHUMALO

MOODIE TREK. First European effort to settle in Gazaland (q.v.).
In 1892 Dunbar Moodie (1861-1897), a South African of Scottish
descent, got Cecil Rhodes' permission to settle Orange Free
State families in the fertile southern reaches of the Eastern
Highlands (q.v.) section of Gazaland. His cousin Thomas
Moodie (1839-1894) organized and led about 30 Free State families on a grueling trek* which lasted from May 1892 until January 1893. Twenty people completed the trip, establishing Melsetter (q.v.) near present Chipinga (q.v.). Their example
soon inspired many similar treks of South Africans, mainly
Afrikaners (q.v.), into the region.

MOODIE'S PASS. Pass blasted and cut through granite in the Mu-
kuriro Hills (at 19° 57'S, 31° 44'E) by members of the Moodie
Trek (q.v.) in 1892. The main road between Fort Victoria and
Birchenough Bridge (qq.v.) now goes through the pass.

MOPANE TREE (a.k.a. balsam; Rhodesian ironwood; turpentine
tree). Characteristic tree of the dry low veld regions, particularly around the Limpopo and Zambezi valleys. The Mopane grows as high as 13 meters, but its wood has no commercial value. The tree is leguminous and produces edible
seeds. (See FORESTS.)

MORGEN. Unit of land area introduced into southern African usage
by early Dutch settlers. One morgen equals 0.85655 hectares,
or 2.11654 acres. One sq. km. equals 116.75 morgen. One
sq. mile equals 302.38 morgen.

MORGENSTER. Dutch Reformed Church (q.v.) mission station now
serving as DRC headquarters in the country; located 6.5 km.
south of the Zimbabwe Ruins (q.v.). The South African missionary A. A. Louw (1862-1956) founded Morgenster in September 1891, working there until his retirement in 1937.

MORRIS CARTER COMMISSION (1925-6). British Imperial commission headed by Morris Carter, a former Tanganyika chief
justice, to investigate the question of allocating the nearly 45%
of Southern Rhodesian land which was unassigned up to 1925.
The Commission collected evidence from more than 200 Europeans and more than 1700 Africans. It found European farmers
to be anxious for the introduction of segregation laws which
would separate them from African farmers. Africans were
found to be universally eager to get more land, and most were
willing to accept the principle of segregation to get it. (See
RBVA.) The Commission's report, issued in 1926, proved a

bitter disappointment to Africans. It recommended segregation
of land on racial lines, but proposed only slight additions to
African lands. These recommendations formed the basis of the
Land Apportionment Act (q.v.) introduced by H. U. Moffat (q.v.)
into the Legislative Assembly (q.v.) in 1929.

MOSEGA (variant: Mosika). A center of Ndebele (q.v.) settlement
on the upper Marico River of the western Transvaal (near what
is now Zeerust) from 1832 to 1837. Prior to Ndebele occupation Mosega had been a Hurutshe town.

MOSELEKATSE (many spelling variations). Widely used Sotho (q.v.)
form of Mzilikazi (q.v.), who began his career in the Sotho-
speaking regions of South Africa. (Cf. "MATABELE.")

MOSI-OA-TUNYA see MUSI O TUNYA

MOTO. Weekly newspaper published by the Roman Catholic Mambo
Press in Gwelo*. Founded as a monthly in 1959, Moto is
printed in Sindebele, Chishona (qq.v.), and English for African
readers. With a circulation of 35,000 in 1973, it is one of the
most widely-read publications in the country. The paper has
tended to avoid politically sensitive issues, but has nevertheless
occasionally been harassed by government censorship (q.v.), as
in mid-1972 when it published an allegedly subversive article
by Donal Lamont (q.v.). In 1974 the government banned Moto.

MOUNT PLEASANT (a.k.a. Mutekedzi). European residential suburb
of north Salisbury (q.v.) in which the University of Rhodesia
(q.v.) is located.

MOUNTAINS. For most place names beginning with "Mount," see
under proper names, e.g., HAMPDEN, DARWIN, SILINDA.
For general description of topographical regions, see ALTITUDI-
NAL ZONES. See also KOPJE; DOMBO; DWALA; NTABA.

MOYO, JASON (c.1924-Jan. 22, 1977). Nationalist leader. Originally a union leader among railway employees, Moyo helped to
form the new African National Congress (q.v.) in 1957. He became a close ally of Joshua Nkomo (q.v.), holding leadership
positions in ZAPU from its inception. In late 1976 Moyo was
a member of Nkomo's delegation to the Geneva Conference
(q.v.), when he was described as head of ZAPU guerrillas
based in Botswana and Zambia. In January 1977 he was killed
in Lusaka, Zambia by a letter bomb.

MOZAMBIQUE (variant: Moçambique). Rhodesia shares its longest
and most irregular border (q.v.) with this former Portuguese
(q.v.) colony. Southern Mozambique, particularly the region
between the Zambezi and Sabi (or Save) rivers, has long had
close ties with the peoples of present Rhodesia. The Eastern
Highlands (q.v.) are a natural, but far from formidable, barrier between the two countries, and the Zambezi Valley

has historically served as a corridor from the Indian Ocean to the interior. Most of the eastern Shona peoples (q.v.) live in both countries. The entire region between the Pungwe* and Sabi rivers is a Shona-speaking area, containing the majority of the Ndau (q.v.). Other peoples who live in both countries include the Chikunda, Barwe, Tonga, and Hlengwe (qq.v.). The early Munhumutapa state (q.v.) extended into what is now Mozambique, and an important trade in ivory and gold through that country connected the Shona states with the coast.

Portuguese occupation of Sofala (q.v.) and other coastal towns began early in the 16th century, disrupting the existing trade patterns, and beginning a gradual extension of Portuguese influence inland, particularly up the Zambezi Valley. (See also SENA; TETE; ZUMBO.) Although the Portuguese claimed to control vast areas from an early date, their occupation of the interior regions was not effective until the end of the 19th century. As late as the 1870s Portuguese posts paid tribute to the Gaza (q.v.) kings. Around that time, however, the Portuguese began to assert more effective control of the interior. In the 1880s Portuguese and Afro-Portuguese forces pushed the Gaza out of the Zambezi region and began conquering north-eastern Shona chiefdoms (see M. de SOUSA). British occupation of Mashonaland* in 1890 made present eastern Rhodesia and southern Mozambique the arena for Portuguese-British rivalry, nearly bringing the two European countries to war (see MAÇEQUEÇE INCIDENT). The BSAC sought a seaport, and made a nearly successful effort to acquire Delagoa Bay from the Gaza king Gungunyane (q.v.). Meanwhile, the rivalry was settled through European diplomacy, and the present borders were tentatively laid down by the Anglo-Portuguese Convention of 1891 (q.v.).

Thereafter Portuguese relations with the British in Southern Rhodesia were increasingly harmonious. In 1892 a railway (q.v.) was commenced at Beira (q.v.), reaching Umtali (q.v.) in 1898. During the 20th century ties between Southern Rhodesia and colonial Mozambique (a.k.a. Portuguese East Africa) were based largely on mutually profitable rail transport connections. In 1955 a second major railway line connected Southern Rhodesia to Lourenzo Marques (now Maputo) by way of Vila Salazar (q.v.).

As European colonies north of the Zambezi became independent under African rule in the 1960s, Rhodesian-Portuguese relations were strengthened by mutual interest in preserving white rule in southern Africa. After the Rhodesian government declared UDI in 1965, Portugal largely ignored UN sanctions (q.v.), thereby increasing the level of Rhodesian trade through Mozambique. Meanwhile, a Mozambique nationalist movement known as Frelimo began extending its control over northern Mozambique. The fall of the Portuguese right-wing government in Lisbon in 1974 accelerated the liberation of Mozambique, which became independent on June 25, 1975, under President Samora Machel. (See "FRONTLINE PRESIDENTS.")

Rhodesia's rail connections through Mozambique were

initially uninterrupted, but in March 1976 Machel closed the
border. Mozambique's losses in transport revenues are estimated at $57 million a year, but some of this has been made
up by a special UN fund to which the United States has contributed. Rhodesia diverted its trade through South Africa (q.v.),
aided by a new, direct rail link through Beitbridge (q.v.).
        During the 1970s Zimbabwe nationalist forces established
training centers and camps throughout Mozambique (see MILI-
TARY FORCES). After the border closure the guerrillas intensified raids and mortar attacks on Rhodesian centers near the
border. Rhodesian forces responded with airborne counter-at-
tacks and "hot pursuit" forays into Mozambique (see SELOUS
SCOUTS). In August 1976 a major Rhodesian raid into the
Honde Valley (q.v.) killed more than 300 people, including Mozambique soldiers and civilians. In late May 1977 Rhodesians
captured the town of Mapai, c.80 km. southeast of Vila Salazar.
Despite the increasingly bloody border incidents and Machel's
declaration that a "state of war" existed, no hostilities had
erupted between Rhodesia and the regular Mozambique army by
mid-1978.

MPEZENI JERE (c.1832-1900). Ngoni (q.v.) ruler. A son of Zwan-
    gendaba (q.v.), Mpezeni was born in Mashonaland during the
    Ngoni migration north. After Zwangendaba died in c.1845, the
    Ngoni broke into several groups in southern Tanzania. Mpezeni
    became the ruler of the group which settled at Chipata (formerly
    Ft. Jameson) in eastern Zambia. His successors were also
    named Mpezeni.
        The Mpezeni Hills, just northeast of Macheke (q.v.), are
    said to be named after the Ngoni ruler.

MPEZENI KHUMALO (c.1880-1898). Son of the Ndebele king Loben-
    gula. After his father's death in 1894, Mpezeni and his half-
    brothers Njube and Nguboyenja (qq.v.) were sent to South Africa
    for education by the BSAC. Mpezeni died at Zonnebloem College
    in Cape Town.

MPHOENGS (variant: M'phoengs). The center of a Tribal Trust
    Land* of the same name, Mphoengs is a village in the southern
    Bulalima-Mangwe District (q.v.) near the Botswana border,
    where the Ingwezi River enters the Ramaquabane* (at 21° 12'S,
    27° 51'E). Since a dam was built on the Ingwezi in 1967, a
    government irrigation scheme has brought relief to the normally
    arid farms.

MPOTSHWANA NDIWENI (d.Oct. 1897). Ndebele induna*. Mpo-
    tshwana and his brother Manyeu were leaders of the Nyamandhlovu
    ibutho*, which was situated on the middle Khami River (q.v.).
    Both men were noted supporters of Lobengula and were among
    the main military leaders in the 1896 Revolt (q.v.). They
    operated in the northern theater of the war in close association
    with Nyamanda (q.v.), whose candidacy for kingship they sup-
    ported. After the Ndebele suffered some major setbacks in July

1896, Mpotshwana was said to have made an abortive attempt to
lead his own followers across the Zambezi River--an effort
halted by illness among his troops. He then vigorously opposed
efforts at negotiated settlement and became the last major rebel
in the field after all other major leaders had surrendered. He
was finally captured near the Zambezi in July 1897. He died
several months later in jail.

MREWA. Administrative center for both the Mangwende TTL and
the Mrewa District; located on the northeastern edge of the
Central Plateau* (at 17° 39'S, 31° 47'E). The nearby Mrewa
Cave contains rock paintings (q.v.) noted for their depiction of
an unusually wide variety of subjects and styles. The name
Mrewa derives from Murehwa, a local Zezuru* ruler.

MREWA DISTRICT. Covers 5730 sq. km. in the eastern part of
Mashonaland South Province (q.v.). Except for some European
tobacco* farms in the southern high veld area, most of the
district comprises Tribal Trust Land (q.v.). On the east it
borders the district of Mtoko; Makoni on the southeast; Marandellas on the south; Goromanzi and Shamba on the west; and
Darwin (qq.v.) on the north. Population in 1969 included
137,940 Africans and only 330 Europeans.

MSANE (variant: Msene). Clan name of the Ngoni ruler Nxaba
(q.v.).

MSHETE. Ndebele form of Moffat (q.v.).

MSHETE (variants: Moshete; Umshete) (c.1820s-1893?). Senior
Ndebele induna* and emissary. In 1889 King Lobengula sent
Mshete and Babayane (q.v.) to London, along with J. W. Colenbrander and E. A. Maund (qq.v.), to get Queen Victoria's advice on the Rudd Concession (q.v.) which he had just signed.
Mshete and Babayane were lionized by London society. They
met with the queen, and were taken on inspection tours of military installations. They returned to Lobengula with a note from
the colonial secretary advising him to beware of signing away
sweeping rights to a single concessionaire, thereby adding to
the tension in Bulawayo. In July 1890 Mshete went to Cape
Town on Lobengula's behalf to confer with the British High Commissioner, Henry Loch, in an attempt to head off the Pioneer
Column's (q.v.) imminent occupation of Mashonaland. In Sep-
tember-October 1893, Mshete again visited the High Commissioner, this time in an unsuccessful effort to avert the impending Ndebele War (q.v.). Mshete seems to have died without
reaching home.

MTARAZI FALLS. At 762 meters the highest waterfall in the country, Mtarazi deposits its water into the Honde River Valley
(q.v.) in the southern Inyanga Mountains (q.v.). Mtarazi National Park is a wild scenic area of 6000 hectares which abuts
the southern tip of Rhodes Inyanga National Park.

MTILIKWE RIVER (variant: Mutirikwi). Rises just northeast of
Gutu (q. v.), flowing south through Lake Kyle (q. v.), then southeast to join the Lundi River between its confluences with the
Tokwe and Chiredzi rivers (qq. v.). In 1963 Bangala Dam was
built on the Mtilikwe, about halfway between Lake Kyle and the
Lundi River. The Mtilikwe's waters make a major contribution
to the irrigation schemes of the Sabi-Limpopo Authority (q. v.)
in the southeastern low veld.

MTJAAN see MTSHANI

MTOA RUIN. Iron Age site in the Bumbuzi ruins group (q. v.).

MTOKO. Administrative center of the district and Tribal Trust
Land of the same name; located on the middle veld area just
northeast of the Central Plateau* (at 17° 24'S, 32° 13'E). The
name is derived from Mutoko, the title of the ruler of the local
Budjga (q. v.) people. Population of the village in 1969 was
1190 (93% Africans). Nearby is Ruchero Cave (q. v.).

MTOKO DISTRICT. Covers a 8200-sq. km. area bordering Mozambique on the northeastern section of Mashonaland South Province
(q. v.). The district is separated from Darwin District on the
north by the Mazoe River; on the southeast the Ruenya River
separates it from Inyanga District (qq. v.). It also borders
Makoni District on the south, and Mrewa District (qq. v.) on
the west. Except for reserved European land and Purchase
Area in its south, most of the district is Tribal Trust Land
(see LAND TENURE ACT). District population in 1969 included 125, 160 Africans and 490 Europeans.

MTOROLITE. A previously unknown gemstone (q. v.) first discovered
in the Great Dyke (q. v.) in the 1960s, Mtorolite is a green
crypto-crystalline quartz.

MTOROSHANGA. The center of an important chrome (q. v.) producing region, Mtoroshanga is a village in the eastern Lomagundi District* (at 17° 9'S, 30° 40'E). Just to the east, the road
to Mazoe* cuts through the Umvukwe Mountains (q. v.) in the
Mtoroshanga Pass. Nearby is Monk's Kop ossuary (q. v.). Village population in 1969 was 2700 (98% Africans).

MTSHANI KHUMALO (variants: Mjaan; Mtjaan) (c. 1830s-1907). High
ranking Ndebele induna*. A cousin of King Lobengula, Mtshani
was made commander of the elite Imbizo ibutho (q. v.) during the
1870s. The prestige of this ibutho grew enormously, but by 1890
Mtshani's authority over it was threatened. He supported Lobengula's policy of military non-aggression against the BSAC, while
many Imbizo members agitated for action. Nevertheless, Mtshani played a leading role as a military commander in the 1893
Ndebele War (q. v.). He commanded Ndebele troops at the Battle of Shangani, assisted at the Battle of Bembezi, and then accompanied Lobengula on his flight north. After the war Mtshani

appears to have retired from active leadership because of his
advancing age. He collaborated with the Europeans during the
1896 Revolt (q. v.), but apparently did not actively fight against
the rebels. (Cf. FAKU; GAMPU.) Afterwards he was among
the first izinduna to be made a salaried chief by the BSAC.

MTSHWELO, Z. C.   see under AFRICAN METHODIST EPISCOPAL
    CHURCH

MU-.   Chishona (q. v.) prefix for the singular forms of two classes
    of nouns. As a Class 1 prefix it is used with nouns for indi-
    vidual persons, such as a member of an ethnic or national
    group, e.g., Mushona. The normal plural for such nouns is
    va-. In the case of proper names, such prefixes are dropped
    in this dictionary.
          As a Class 3 prefix mu- is used with names of trees and
    other objects, and its normal plural is mi-.

MUDZIMU (variant plural forms: midzimu; vadzimu). Shona term
    for ancestor spirit. Midzimu are the most important kinds of
    spirits in everyday Shona life. In contrast to the "lion spirits, "
    mhondoro and gombwe (qq. v.), which look after public welfare,
    the midzimu are primarily concerned with individual or family
    matters. They cannot harm their own families, but if they are
    offended, they can withdraw their protection. (See RELIGION--
    SHONA; cf. Ndebele DLOZI.)

MUFAKOSE.   Third largest of Salisbury's (q. v.) African townships;
    located 12 km. west-southwest of the city center. Population
    in 1969 was 20, 620. (Cf. HARARE.)

MUGABE, ROBERT GABRIEL (b. c.1928). Nationalist leader. Born
    at Kutama (q. v.), Mugabe was educated at Roman Catholic mis-
    sion schools, including Empandeni (q. v.), and he graduated from
    Ft. Hare College in South Africa. He began a teaching career
    in local mission schools in 1952, and then taught in Northern
    Rhodesia (Zambia) in 1955, and in Ghana from 1956 to 1960.
    He returned to Southern Rhodesia in 1960 and began his political
    career as an officer in the National Democratic Party (q. v.).
    After the NDP was banned, he served as Joshua Nkomo's deputy
    secretary-general in ZAPU (qq. v.). Mugabe was arrested by the
    government in both 1962 and 1963, but managed to escape to
    Tanzania. By then he had broken with Nkomo, so he joined
    Ndabaningi Sithole's newly-formed ZANU (qq. v.) and became its
    secretary-general. When Mugabe returned to Southern Rhodesia
    in August 1963, he was rearrested by the government. He was
    let out on bail, only to be arrested again a year later. This
    time he remained in jail or detention camps for a decade. In
    the meantime he completed additional college degrees by corres-
    pondence.
          In December 1974 Mugabe was among the political pris-
    oners released in Ian Smith's general amnesty. He was not
    then regarded as a major nationalist leader, but he went into

exile and apparently challenged Sithole successfully for control of
ZANU. By mid-1976 he was in Mozambique, claiming to speak
for the main guerrilla forces there (see MILITARY FORCES).
By August 1976 he was generally recognized by outside sources
as the political head of the Zimbabwe Liberation Army (q. v.),
and was being regarded as a serious contender for top leadership within the divided nationalist movement. Shortly before the
Geneva Conference (q.v.) opened in October, Mugabe and Nkomo
reached a reconciliation of some sort, and announced formation
of the "Patriotic Front" (q.v.). During the Conference both men
pushed hard for the earliest possible date for majority rule, and
Mugabe himself was especially outspoken in condemnation of the
Rhodesian government representatives, such as P. van der Byl
(q.v.). Afterwards he repeatedly stressed his belief in the need
for a purely military solution to the contitutional impasse. He
returned to Mozambique, where he was still believed to command
most of the guerrillas.

MUKOMBAHASHA (pl. vakombahasha). Title of hereditary military
commander in the Munhumutapa state (q.v.).

MUKOMBERO NYAHUMA (fl. late 15th century). Early Munhumutapa
(q.v.) ruler. The son of Munhumutapa Matope Nyanhehwe (q.v.),
Mukombero is said to have become Munhumutapa after having
abandoned his brother Mavura I to die in a battle in c.1480.
Over the next decade he struggled to put down the rebellion of
another relative, Changa (q.v.), who killed him and usurped the
kingship in c.1490. His son Chikuyo Chisamarengu (q.v.) later
regained the kingship.

MUKOMBWE see KAMHARAPASU MUKOMBWE

MULUNGWANE HILLS. Small mountain range running north-south
along the 29th line of east longitude, just southeast of Bulawayo.

MUNHUMUTAPA (variants: Monomotapa; Mwanamutapa; Mwene
Mutapa*; etc.). Dynastic title of the rulers of a Shona state
now known by the same name. Long known to outsiders as
"Monomotapa, " the Munhumutapa state is one of the most famous African kingdoms in southern African history. Though
the kingdom played a major role in the country's history, its
importance has probably been somewhat exaggerated because it
was much better documented than other early state systems (see
SHONA HISTORY). The Portuguese (q.v.) arrived in the region
just after the Munhumutapa state had reached its peak power in
the late 15th century. Portuguese traders and missionaries
dealt mostly with the Munhumutapa people during the 16th and
17th centuries. They tended to exaggerate the state's importance
with respect to other Shona states about which they knew less.
    The origins of the Munhumutapa state are not fully under-
stood. It was established in the Dande region (q.v.) of the
northern part of present Rhodesia in the early 15th century by
Mutota Nyatsimba (q.v.), the son of a Shona ruler from the

southern, Guruhuswa (q.v.) region. It remains unclear whether
Mutota simply shifted his father's already established kingdom
from the south, or he created an entirely new state in the north.
It is also unclear what connections, if any, the Munhumutapa
state had with the rulers of Great Zimbabwe (q.v.). It is possible that the shift of Mutota's court to the north occasioned the
decline of Zimbabwe as a political center. Whatever, Mutota's
conquests in the north earned him the praise name munhu mutapa, "one who explores," or "one who pillages," and this name
was adopted as a dynastic title by his successors. Mutota's son
Matope Nyanhehwe (q.v.) extended the kingdom's influence as far
east as the Indian Ocean, thus earning the state the modern description of "empire."

Munhumutapa control over outlying provinces was never
complete. Matope's successors quickly lost territories to rebellious local rulers, giving rise to new dynasties in Manyika,
Maungwe, Barwe (qq.v.) and elsewhere. Two of Matope's provincial administrators, Togwa and Changa (qq.v.), threw off
Munhumutapa control in the south, laying the basis for the state's
most powerful rivals.

During the 17th-century Portuguese intervention became a
paramount problem. Gatsi Rusere and Mavura II (qq.v.) made
major concessions to the Portuguese, leaving their successors to
struggle to regain Munhumutapa autonomy. In the 1680s the
Changamire state (q.v.) to the south began an era of rapid expansion. Munhumutapa Kambarapasu's (q.v.) attempts to ally
with Changamire Dombo (q.v.) against the Portuguese backfired.
Changamire armies were turned against the Munhumutapa state,
apparently reducing it to tributary status. Thereafter the state
ranked as merely one of many unexceptional Shona polities.
Some 18th-century rulers attempted to reassert the state's
former power, but their successes were short-lived. The last
titular Munhumutapa was Chioko Dambamupute (q.v.), who died
in 1902.

The following list of Munhumutapa rulers stops in the
early 18th century for several reasons. After 1695 the state
was only a minor power, and its center was shifting into what
is now Mozambique. Furthermore, genealogical evidence on
18th and 19th century rulers is poorly worked out at present.

Munhumutapa rulers: early 15th century Mutota Nyatsimba*; mid-15th century Matope Nyanhehwe*; c.1480 Mavura I
Maombwe; c.1480-c.90 Mukombero Nyahuma*; c.1490-c.94
Changa*; c.1494-c.1530 Chikuyo Chisamarengu*; c.1530-c.50
Neshangwe Munembire*; c.1550-c.60 Chivere Nyasoro*; c.1560-
c.89 Negomo Chirisamhuru*; c.1589-1623 Gatsi Rusere*; 1623-
29 Nyambo Kaparidze*; 1629-52 Mavura II Mhande*; 1652-63
Siti Kazurukumusapa*; 1663-c.92 Kambarapasu Mukombwe*;
c.1692-c.94 Nyakunembire; c.1694-c.96 Nyamaende Mhande;
c.1696-c.99 Chirimba (?); c.1699-c.1702 Nyadenga (?); c.1702-
c.7 Dehwe Samutumbu; c.1707-c.11 Nyenyedzi Zenda; c.1711-
c.19 Buruma Dangwarangwa; c.1719-c.40 Samatambira Nyamhandu.

"MUNT." Pejorative term for black Africans. Derives from

(u)muntu, the singular form of (a)bantu, the term for "people"
in many Bantu languages (q. v.).

MURENGA (pl. mirenga; variant: mulenga). Chishona* word for
warlike spirit, or for rebellion (see CHIMURENGA); also a war
cry.   The Sindebele* equivalent is umvuleka (pl. imivuleka).
The Shona form appears also to have been used to describe a
manifestation of the high god Mwari (q. v.); as such it was a
title taken by the Revolt leader "Kaguvi" (q. v.).

MURUNGU (pl. varungu). Chishona* term for European. Synonyms
include murumbi and mukiwa (plurals, both va-). Sindebele*
equivalents are ikhiwa (pl. amakhiwa) and umlungu (pl. abelungu).

MUSENGEZI RIVER. Rises in the Umvukwe Mountains (q. v.), flowing generally north.   It is joined by the Kadsi and Mkumvura
rivers by the Mozambique border, and it enters the Zambezi
River at 31° 15'E Long.   (See DANDE.)

MUSHANDIKE DAM (former variant: Umshandige).   Built in 1938
on the Mushandike River, a short tributary of the Tokwe (q. v.),
just west of Fort Victoria.   The dam's lake supplies irrigation
water, and offers fishing (q. v.) and recreational facilities for
the 13,000-hectare Mushandike Dam and Lake National Park
which surrounds it.

MUSI O TUNYA (variant: Mosi-Oa-Tunya).   Tonga (q. v.) name for
the Victoria Falls (q. v.); variously translated as "smoke that
rises" or "smoke that thunders," in reference to the smoke-like
appearance of the falls' mist.   This name was heard by Europeans
in South Africa at least as early as 1840.   David Livingstone
(q. v.) himself recorded the name before he coined the name "Victoria Falls" in 1855.

MUSIC.   Dances and songs of many varieties have long played an important role in Shona life.   Most songs are accompanied by in-
strumental music, produced mostly by drums (q. v.) and the
mbira (q. v.), a melodious plucking instrument.   Other Shona instruments include flutes (sing., chigufe; pl., zvigufe); mouth-
bows (sing., chipendani; pl., zvipendani); and reed instruments
known as panpipes (sing. & pl., nyere).   Songs and instruments
were less important in 19th-century Ndebele culture, and dances
were mostly related to martial ceremonies, notably the inxwala
(q. v.).

MUSLIMS (variants: Moslems; Mohammedans; Moors).   Although
the country is landlocked, its commercial contacts with the
eastern coast go back at least a thousand years.   In A.D. 947
the Arab geographer al-Masudi wrote about the gold (q. v.) trade
through Sofala (q. v.).   This trade likely originated in what is
now Rhodesia, and it is possible that Muslim traders were visiting the country by the tenth century.   These traders are often
described as "Arabs" but they included Muslim Arabs, Persians,

east Africans (mostly Swahili), and perhaps some Indians.
By the 15th century the Muslims had established a network of trading fairs (q.v.) in the country, and used these to
funnel trade goods through Sofala. While their commercial influence was clearly great, their political and cultural impact
was apparently small. (Cf. "CHANGAMIRE"; LEMBA.) A
figure of 10,000+ Muslims resident in the country by 1500 is
frequently quoted, but a more realistic figure was around 200
people, including family members. Muslim commercial dominance ended during the 16th century, after the Portuguese (q.v.)
occupied Sofala and began establishing their own trade centers
in the interior. The few Muslims in the country today are
mainly Indian immigrants (see ASIANS).

MUSSAMBAZES. Professional African traders who operated in
Shona territory for Portuguese (q.v.) based on the Zambezi
River. (See FAIRS.)

MUTAPA. Short form of Munhumutapa (q.v.).

MUTASA (variant: Umtasa). Dynastic title of the rulers of an important Manyika (q.v.) kingdom centered at Bingaguru (q.v.),
near present Umtali*. The dynasty was established in the early
16th century as an offshoot of the Makombe dynasty of the Barwe
(qq.v.). In 1575 Mutasa Chikanga signed a treaty of friendship
with the explorer V. F. Honem (q.v.). Manyika territory subsequently became an important area of local Portuguese (q.v.)
trading activity.
During the 19th century the Mutasas struggled to maintain
their independence against the Gaza (q.v.), only to see their
kingdom become the focus of Portuguese-British rivalry. Mutasa
Chifambausiku (or Tendayi) was pressured to accept Portuguese
sovereignty during the 1870s. In the late 1880s British prospectors entered the country, establishing mines at Penhalonga (q.v.)
in 1889. In September 1890 the Mutasa signed a treaty with the
BSAC official Archibald Colquhoun (q.v.). Portuguese agents
then moved in to reassert their influence, but were arrested by
P. W. Forbes (q.v.) at Bingaguru in November. The Anglo-
Portuguese Convention of 1891 (q.v.) resolved these European
differences, and Manyika was partitioned between Southern Rhodesia and Mozambique (q.v.), with the center of the kingdom
lying in the British side. Mutasa Chifambausiku died in 1902
and was succeeded by Chakanyuka.

MUTEKEDZI. Dynastic title of the rulers of a Hera (q.v.) chiefdom
in the present Buhera District*.

MUTOKO (variant: Mtoko*). Hereditary title of the paramount chiefs
of the Budjga people (q.v.).

MUTORWA (pl., vatorwa). Chishona* term for stranger, or foreigner,
living within a community. Such a person might later give rise
to a shave spirit medium (q.v.).

MUTOTA NYATSIMBA (fl. early 15th century). Founder of the
Munhumutapa state (q. v.). According to tradition, Mutota was
the son of a Karanga (q. v.) ruler in Guruhuswa (q. v.). On the
death of his father, he acceded to the chiefship, and then shifted
his court to the Dande region (q. v.) in the north, leaving
Guruhuswa under a relative named Togwa (q. v.). Mutota
established his first headquarters just north of present Sipolilo
(q. v.), then moved to Chitako Hill, by the Musengezi River
(q. v.). His conquests of the local Tavara people (q. v.) earned
him the nickname Munhumutapa, "the pillager"--a name his successors adopted as a dynastic title. Establishment of the new
state near the Zambezi River led to greatly increased trade with
coastal-based Muslims (q. v.). On his death, some time before
c.1450, Mutota was succeeded by his son, Matope Nyanhehwe
(q. v.).

MUTSWAIRO, SOLOMON MANGWIRO (b. April 16, 1924). Author
of the first novel published in Chishona*. Born of Christian
missionary parents, Mutswairo grew up in present Zambia and
was graduated from the University College of Ft. Hare in South
Africa in 1953. He then returned to Southern Rhodesia to teach
in mission schools. In 1957 he published Feso (trans. into
English, 1974), a short novel set vaguely in 17th-century Munhumutapa (q. v.) territory. The book was adopted by government
schools and it became a local best-seller. Although the story
of Feso--the name of a character--was ostensibly a simple historical romance, it became regarded by African nationalists as
an allegorical protest against European rule. This interpretation enhanced the book's popularity, but caused it to be suppressed by the government. Mutswairo has since written in
both Chishona and English, and has continued his education in
North America. (See LITERATURE.)

MUTUPO (pl., mitupo). Chishona* term for "totem" or clan name.
Shona clans are patrilineal. They are divided into sub-clans
known as zvidao (sing., chidao, or chidawo). Rules of exogamy
permit marriage between holders of the same mutupo, but not
of the same chidao.
    Mutupo and chidao are also sometimes translated as
"praise name." Mitupo are typically named after animals, with
which certain taboos are associated. For example, members
of the Soko clan are not allowed to harm vervet monkeys (soko).
(Cf. Ndebele ISIBONGO.)

MUZOREWA, ABEL TENDEKAYI (April 14, 1925-). Nationalist
leader and head of the United Methodist Church (q. v.). Muzorewa
was born in Umtali* and educated at the American Methodist
School at Old Umtali (q. v.). During the 1940s he taught at mission schools in the Mrewa and Mtoko districts, returning to Old
Umtali in 1949 to study theology. He was ordained a minister
in 1953, later serving as a pastor in Rusape*. From 1958 to
1963 he studied theology in Missouri and Tennessee, returning
home to become a pastor at Old Umtali. On August 28, 1968,

he was made Bishop of Rhodesia--the top post in the UMC.
Although Muzorewa had no prior reputation as a political
activist, he was made chairman of the African National Council
(q.v.) on its formation in December 1971.   ANC's dramatic
success in convincing the Pearce Commission (q.v.) of the
country's overwhelming rejection of the Anglo-Rhodesian Settlement Proposals early the next year suddenly made Muzorewa a
national political figure with an international reputation.   His
adamant rejection of violence made the Rhodesian government
willing to negotiate with him over the next two years, and his
detachment from the previous decade of bitter and fragmented
nationalist politics left him in a promising position to succeed
to overall leadership of the nationalist movement.   This prospect
appeared to have been realized when the other nationalist leaders
placed their organizations under his ANC banner at Lusaka in
December 1974.   The new ANC "umbrella" organization received
the blessing of the "Frontline Presidents" (q.v.), but its unity
was short-lived.   Muzorewa was acknowledged as head of the
African delegation at the abortive Victoria Falls Conference
(q.v.) in August 1975, but afterwards the ANC began fragmenting
into its original components, though each retained the name
"ANC."   Joshua Nkomo (q.v.) returned to Salisbury claiming to
head the "internal wing" of the ANC, while Muzorewa remained
outside the country as head of the "external" ANC.
        In early 1976 Muzorewa stayed mainly in Mozambique*
and denounced Nkomo's negotiations with Ian Smith.   Muzorewa
had by this time abandoned non-violence in the liberation struggle, and was reported as the head of a large section of guerrillas.   However, his actual connection with the military forces
remained unclear, and Robert Mugabe (q.v.) was apparently
emerging as the leader with the closest ties with the guerrilla
movement (see MILITARY FORCES).   By September 1976 Muzorewa was in Zambia with no apparent guerrilla following.   In
October he returned to Salisbury before participating in the
Geneva Conference (q.v.).   Nkomo and Mugabe's announcement
of a "Patriotic Front" (q.v.) attracted OAU and "Frontline
Presidents" (q.v.) support, leaving Muzorewa and Ndabaningi
Sithole (q.v.) without significant external allies.   In early 1977
Muzorewa denounced the Patriotic Front's supporters for ignoring
what he believed to be the majority of Zimbabweans who backed
him.   In April 1977 he visited London in an unsuccessful bid to
get the British government to call for a popular referendum in
Rhodesia.   In early 1978 he joined Ian Smith's "internal settlement" government in Rhodesia.

MUZUNGU (pl., vazungu).   Early Chishona* term for Portuguese
    (q.v.).   (See also MURUNGU.)

MWARI.   Name of the Shona High God.   There is considerable con-
    troversy and confusion over the origins and meaning of the name
    "Mwari," Mwari's role in different varieties of Shona religion
    (q.v.), and the nature of Mwari belief.   The name "Mwari" is
    used in at least three distinct contexts: (1) Mwari is universally

used among the Shona for the concept of high god, or god of
the sky, although various sub-groups also use such other names
as Dzivaguru and Wedenga (qq. v.). (2) A highly organized and
influential cult system based in the Matopo Hills (q. v.) worships
Mwari and communicates with him directly through oracular
shrines maintained by a hierarchy of consecrated priests and
messengers (see, e.g., NJELELE; MATONJENI). This cult
system is recognized mainly in the southern half of the country
among the Venda (q. v.) and southern Shona--mainly the Kalanga
and Karanga (qq. v.). According to some authorities, this cult
system (sometimes called "Mwarism") has nothing to do with
Mwari belief among the northern Shona--the Zezuru and Korekore (qq. v.). (3) Many Christian missionaries have translated
"God" as "Mwari," thereby giving the name a loose, generic
meaning. Further confusion has been caused by Europeans who
frequently treat "Mwari" and the Sotho-Ndebele term Mlimo
(q. v.) as synonyms in all three contexts.

Although there are numerous studies of Shona religion,
there are significant disagreements about the role of Mwari. On
some fundamental points, however, there seems to be general
agreement. All Shona regard Mwari as a remote high god. To
many he is the creator of mankind, the provider of both good
and evil, and the bringer of rain. Mwari stands above the ancestral spirits (see MUDZIMU; MHONDORO), and unlike them
he never had an earthly existence. Mwari is not interested in
personal affairs of mankind, but only in community or national
matters.

There are two ways people approach Mwari: directly,
through the oracular shrines in the Matopos; or indirectly,
through intermediary ancestor spirits. The latter manifest themselves in such mediums as the mhondoro. These two modes of
approach represent a basic split between southern and northern
Shona religious systems; however, the two systems are not mutually exclusive, as some communities worship Mwari both ways.

Many theories about the origin of Mwari belief have been
advanced, but a more immediate historical problem is the question of connections between the southern cult system and local
political systems. Historians have formerly argued that the cult
originated at Great Zimbabwe (q. v.) in the southeast, moving
west to the Matopos with the Rozvi Changamire state (q. v.).
The notion that Great Zimbabwe was connected with either the
Mwari cult or the Rozvi is now increasingly discredited. It appears instead that the cult originated among the Kalanga in the
southwest, where the Rozvi found it in full operation on their
own arrival. The relationship between the Rozvi rulers and the
Mwari priests is also controversial. Recently it has even been
argued that the Rozvi had nothing to do with the cult, which may
have been introduced to the region by Venda priests from the
northern Transvaal* after the break-up of the Changamire state
in the early 19th century.

Yet another controversy surrounds the relationship between the 19th-century Ndebele rulers and the Matopos Mwari
shrines. The Ndebele are known to have consulted the oracles.

From this bare evidence it has been argued that the Ndebele as-
similated Shona Mwari belief into their own system of beliefs,
truly merging their concepts of Mlimo with those of Mwari. It
has further been argued that Mwari cult officials, notably Mkwati
(q. v.), inspired, organized, and directed the 1896 Ndebele Revolt (q. v.) until a split developed between Mwari and Ndebele
leaders. More recently it has been demonstrated that the Mwari
cult had little influence on Ndebele life in the 19th century, and
that its priests played a limited role in the Ndebele Revolt.
(See also the role of mhondoro in the Shona Revolt.)
   Both the Mwari cult and more generalized Mwari belief
have continued to flourish in the 20th century, and must still be
regarded as the country's dominant religion.

"MWENE MUTAPA" (variant: Mwanamutapa). Recently popular, but
   apparently meaningless variant of Munhumutapa (q. v.). "Mwene
   Mutapa" is usually translated by historians as "Master Pillager,"
   but the Chishona* word mwene, meaning "owner," has incorrectly been substituted for munhu, "person."

MWENYE (pl., vamwenye). Chishona* term for Muslim (q. v.); also
   used by other Bantu-speaking peoples in the Zambezi Valley.
   The term is apparently a variation of Chishona mweni, "stranger."
   The term mwenye is also occasionally applied to the Lemba people (q. v.).

MZILA (variants: Umzila; Muzila) (d. 1884). The eldest son of
   Soshangane (q. v.), Mzila became ruler of the Gaza kingdom
   (q. v.) in 1862 after ousting his brother Mawewe, who had
   usurped power on Soshangane's death. Mzila obtained his rightful kingship with the help of the Portuguese (q. v.), who afterwards plagued him with claims of sovereignty over the Gaza.
   Mzila then shifted Gaza headquarters from the lower Limpopo
   River to Mt. Silinda (q. v.), just west of the present Mozambique
   border (see MANHLAGAZI). There he continued his predecessor's policy of raiding surrounding Shona communities, but
   he failed in his attempts to conquer the Manyika of Mutasa (q. v.).
   Portuguese pressure on his kingdom mounted, and the Portuguese
   ally Manuel de Sousa (q. v.) pushed the Gaza back from their outposts in the Zambezi Valley. In 1870 Mzila began a fruitless
   quest to seek British assistance against the Portuguese. He
   meanwhile established cordial relations with the Ndebele kingdom
   (q. v.) to the west, culminating in an exchange of royal wives with
   Lobengula (see XWALILE). After his death, Mzila was succeeded
   by his son Gungunyane (q. v.) (see also LAW, A.).

MZILIKAZI KHUMALO (variants: Moselekatse*; Silkaats; Umziligazi;
   etc.) (c. 1790s-Sept. 1868). Founder and first ruler of the Ndebele kingdom (q. v.). Mzilikazi was born in Zululand*, the son
   of Mashobane (q. v.), a minor Khumalo clan (q. v.) chief. He
   was raised at the court of his maternal grandfather Zwide (q. v.),
   the ruler of the Ndwandwe, during an era of rapid northern
   Nguni* political expansion and militarization. A year or so after

Mzilikazi succeeded his father as Khumalo chief, he and his people shifted allegiance to the new Zulu king Shaka (q.v.) in c.1819. After serving Shaka as an apparently unexceptional frontier administrator, Mzilikazi defied the Zulu king's authority and led perhaps 500 people--mostly men--into the eastern Transvaal* in c.1821. There he founded the Ndebele kingdom and began a two-decade career as a migratory military leader.

Mzilikazi entertained his first European visitors in 1829, while he was living near the site of present Pretoria. One of these visitors was the missionary Robert Moffat (q.v.), for whom Mzilikazi developed a life-long affection. Moffat and other Europeans also visited Mzilikazi in the western Transvaal in 1835, by which time Mzilikazi was living mainly in an ox wagon*, in which he moved about his kingdom almost constantly. Another 1835 visitor was Dr. Andrew Smith, who was head of a scientific exploration expedition. When Smith returned to Cape Town, Mzilikazi sent along his adviser Mncumbathe (q.v.), who signed a treaty in his name with the British governor Benjamin D'Urban in March 1836.

When the Ndebele left the Transvaal for present Matabeleland (q.v.) in 1838, they separated into two main migratory parties in eastern Botswana*. One party followed Kaliphi (q.v.; a.k.a. Gundwane) almost directly to the new homeland. Mzilikazi himself led the second party deeper into Botswana. He appears to have traveled no farther north than the Makarikari Pan, where he turned east, following the Nata River* into Matabeleland in c. mid-1839. When he rejoined the rest of his people, he found they had installed his son Nkulumane (q.v.) as acting king in his place. In what became famous as the Ntabazinduna (q.v.) affair, Mzilikazi eliminated the dissident izinduna (chiefs) and thereafter experienced no further serious challenges to his authority. The fate of Nkulumane during this affair remained a mystery during the rest of Mzilikazi's lifetime, creating serious problems for his successor Lobengula (q.v.), another son.

Over the next 14 years Mzilikazi appears to have played a less active role in Ndebele warfare than previously. His communications with the European world were reopened in 1854 when Robert Moffat paid him a visit. Moffat found him badly overweight and suffering from various ailments of the joints which left him immobile, but the missionary administered some medicinal relief. Mzilikazi accompanied Moffat on a leisurely wagon journey to the north, and then returned to central Matabeleland to trade ivory (q.v.) with S. H. Edwards (q.v.). Many more European traders and hunters soon entered the country, but Mzilikazi retained a monopoly over Ndebele commerce. Moffat visited again in 1857, obtaining permission to bring Christian missionaries into the country. Two years later Moffat brought in an LMS party which established a permanent, but long unsuccessful, mission station at Inyati*.

Mzilikazi's health continued to deteriorate badly during his last years. Meanwhile, European interest in the country increased greatly because of gold (q.v.) discoveries. After his death in early September 1868, Mzilikazi was interred at

Nthumbane (q.v.). Mncumbathe acted as regent until the installation of Lobengula in early 1870.

MZILIKAZI MEMORIAL. National Monument on the 1860s site of the Ndebele ibutho* town Mhlahlandlela (q.v.; see also NTHUMBANE).

MZINGELI, CHARLES (b.1905). Perhaps the country's single most powerful African protest leader before the rise of mass nationalism in the late 1950s, Mzingeli was born into an Ndebele family near Plumtree (q.v.). He was raised a Roman Catholic and received some education at Empandeni (q.v.) before leaving home to become a railway worker at age 14. He worked in Bulawayo, Northern Rhodesia, and, apparently, South Africa, before returning to Bulawayo in the late 1920s. There he joined the newly-formed ICU (q.v.). In late 1929 he was made ICU's organizing secretary and was sent to Salisbury, which he then made his permanent home. In Salisbury he gave speeches before large crowds, denouncing the white establishment and calling for an end to interethnic African rivalries. As an Ndebele in a Shona region, he was notably successful in enrolling members in the ICU. His radicalism brought down constant government harassment--resulting in his brief imprisonment--and forced his reluctant break from the Roman Catholic Church. After the collapse of the ICU in the mid-1930s he made his living by working as a musician in dance bands.

In 1941 Mzingeli turned away from purely African trade unionism by joining the once exclusively European Labour Party (q.v.), for which he formed an African branch in Harare (q.v.). The expulsion of African members from the Labour Party in 1944 dispelled his hopes of working with progressive Europeans. In early 1946 he joined with other African labor leaders to form the RICU (q.v.) in Salisbury and was made its leader. During the late 1940s he led the African fight against the Native (Urban Areas) Accommodation Act (q.v.) and other discriminatory laws and was a leading spokesman before the government during the general strike of 1948. He was also elected to the Advisory Board in Harare, dominating this body for 10 years as the township's "unofficial mayor." He meanwhile maintained himself by running a small grocery store.

Mzingeli's continuing prestige was recognized in 1952 when he was named acting president of the All-African Convention (q.v.). However, this organization was short-lived, and Mzingeli was accused by his fellow officers of being too difficult a person to work with. The Youth League (q.v.) which formed in 1955 made Mzingeli its first target, denouncing him as an outmoded reformist. By 1957 he had lost his Advisory Board seat and his days as a radical were over. Now disillusioned with African nationalists, he turned to multi-racial organizations and joined the ruling UFP (q.v.). During the 1961 constitutional conference he personally presented the UFP's proposals for the double-roll "A" and "B" franchise (see CONSTITUTION OF 1961).

MZIZI, WILLIAM (a. k. a. Mbulale) (fl. 1830s-1890s). Mfengu (q. v.)
"war doctor" among the Ndebele. Mzizi appears to have been
born in Zululand* around 1830, and to have fled with his family
to the eastern Cape during Dingane's reign. He lived near
Peddie until c. 1859, and then went to Lesotho to work for King
Moshweshwe, finally settling among Waterboer's Griqua (q. v.)
near Kimberley. In the late 1860s his son--also named William
Mzizi (or Hlegizana)--went to Matabeleland* as a hunter*. There
he told Mncumbathe (q. v.) and other izinduna of his father's skill
as a war doctor. Ndebele officials then sent for the elder Mzizi
to assist in resolving the current succession dispute--apparently
because Mzizi claimed a connection with the ancestral Khumalo
(q. v.). Mzizi is said to have "consecrated" the new King Lobengula after his arrival in Matabeleland.

Mzizi's family and other Mfengu were given land to live
on near Bulawayo, where they were known as the Amazizi.
During Lobengula's reign Mzizi became famous as a "war doctor," administering medicines to impis* before and after raids
(his son may have shared in this work). He married a daughter
of Lobengula and was granted many special privileges, such as
owning horses* and an ox wagon*. By the late 1880s he was
blind. He later blamed his handicap for his failure to confer
success on Ndebele forces during the 1893 Ndebele War (q. v.).

- N -

NADA (Native Affairs Department Annual). Published continuously
since 1923, this annual journal has served as a forum for the
writings of African administration officers and other amateur
researchers into African affairs. Its articles have dealt mostly
with African history, contemporary life, and customs. Though
many of Nada's contributions suffer from poor scholarship or
narrow antiquarian perspectives, the journal has published many
others of seminal importance--notably those pertaining to regional histories. In 1964 the journal was officially retitled The
Ministry of Internal Affairs Annual, but the familiar acronym
"Nada" was retained as the lead title. A series of reprints of
early Nada volumes was commenced by Books of Rhodesia (q. v.)
in 1972.

NAGANA (Animal trypanosomiasis). Endemic parasitic disease transmitted among animals by tsetse fly (q. v.). The name "nagana,"
now used widely in Africa, derives from the Zulu* word nakane.
Feral animals are largely immune to nagana, but the disease is
usually fatal to the larger domestic animals. The role of nagana
in African history can hardly be exaggerated. It has determined
human migration routes, influenced settlement patterns, and prevented some peoples from breeding livestock. During the Ndebele (q. v.) migration from Zululand to Matabeleland during the
1820s and 1830s, the threat of nagana to cattle (q. v.) may have
altered the direction of their route as many as three different
times. After the Ndebele settled in Matabeleland, the presence

of tsetse fly restricted their settlements to the region south of the Somabula Forest (q.v.). Other peoples in the country--mostly the Shona--lived in more dangerous nagana areas and consequently kept fewer cattle than they otherwise might have. The reduction of the disease during the 20th century has been due mainly to the reclamation of tsetse-infested areas. (Cf. SLEEPING SICKNESS; see HEALTH.)

NALATALE RUINS (variants: Naletali; Nanatali; N'natali). Small but famous stone ruin complex of the Khami culture (q.v.) period; built on a large granite dome in the southern Gwelo District* (at 19° 53'S, 29° 32'E). The ruins comprise a single, isolated building complex, noted for its long and complexly decorated wall, and for its commanding view of the surrounding countryside. The building, which may not have been completed by the 19th century, is believed to have been intended as only a temporary dwelling--perhaps for the Changamire rulers (q.v.). The only recorded excavation of the site was a brief one undertaken by D. Randall-MacIver (q.v.). in 1905.

NAMBYZYA   see   NANZWA

NANATALI (variant: N'natali)   see   NALATALE RUINS

NANDI. Village on the Chiredzi River (q.v.) serving as the terminus of a branch southeastern railway (q.v.) line completed in 1964-5 (at 20° 58'S, 31° 44'E).

N'ANGA. Variant of nganga (q.v.).

NANZWA (Abananzwa; variants: Nambya; Nambzya; etc.). Cluster of peoples living mostly in the Wankie District (q.v.), which takes its name from Zanke (or Hwange), the title of the most important Nanzwa rulers. The origin of these peoples is controversial. They are often classified as a branch of the Kalanga (q.v.) cluster of Shona-speakers, but many now speak Sindebele (q.v.). It is generally believed that the first Zanke was a Rozvi (q.v.) immigrant from the Changamire state (q.v.) who imposed his rule over local Tonga (q.v.). It is not clear, however, whether this conquest took place before or just after the Changamire state itself was broken up by the Ngoni (q.v.) invasions of the early 1830s. The early Zankes are also said to have built and resided in the Bumbuzi Ruins (q.v.).

From the 1840s to the 1890s the Nanzwa were heavily pressured by both the Ndebele in the southwest, and the Kololo and then the Lozi (qq.v.) north of the Zambezi River. In 1853 the Ndebele raided the Nanzwa, killing Zanke Lusumbami (or Rusumbami), and making Silisa the new Zanke. Silisa proved a reluctant vassal, however, and was driven across the Zambezi by the Ndebele in 1862. By the 1870s the Nanzwa were paying tribute to both the Ndebele and the Lozi, and were living on both sides of the Zambezi. The Ndebele helped to make Nekatembe the next Zanke in the 1880s, but their raids continued into

the 1890s. In 1893 Nanzwa chiefs brought the Wankie coalfields
to the attention of Europeans at Tati*, and Wankie was subsequently developed into one of Africa's major coal (q.v.) producing
centers. The Zankes are now government-paid chiefs.

NATA RIVER (a.k.a. Manzamnyama). Draining one of the country's
driest regions, the Nata is the largest stream to flow from
Rhodesia into Botswana*. It rises near Figtree (q.v.), whence
it flows northwest and then west into Botswana, where it enters
the Makarikari Pan. Part of the river separates the districts
of Nyamandhlovu and Bulalima-Mangwe (qq.v.).

NATIONAL ARCHIVES OF RHODESIA (NAR). During the period of
BSAC administration, public records were not centrally housed,
with storage left to individual government departments. After
1923 interest in preserving records grew, culminating in the
Southern Rhodesian Legislative Assembly's creation of the national archives in 1935. Under the direction of Chief Archivist
V. W. Hiller the new archives surveyed and collected surviving
public records, and sought to acquire privately-held documents.
As these records were assembled in Salisbury, Hiller attempted
to retrieve the large body of records stored in the BSAC's long-
closed London offices. Unfortunately, these records were destroyed when the offices were bombed during a German air raid
in 1941. After the war Northern Rhodesia and Nyasaland added
their official records to the Salisbury repository, which became
known as the Central African Archives (see CENTRAL AFRICA
COUNCIL). In 1958 the Federal Archives Act designated the
institution the National Archives of Rhodesia and Nyasaland.
Plans were soon begun for the building of a large, modern facility just outside of Salisbury. The new archives building was
opened in 1961, and it quickly ranked as one of the largest,
best-housed and organized historical archives in tropical Africa.
When the Federation (q.v.) broke up two years later, Zambia
and Malawi withdrew their respective territorial records, while
retaining access to the purely Federal records left in Salisbury.
      Through a vigorous acquisitions policy, which has in-
cluded extensive photocopying and microfilming of overseas documents, the NAR has developed into an unrivaled center for local
historical research. It has generally been open to both African
and European researchers, but some important files pertaining
to early African political activity are known to have been removed from public access since the early 1960s.
      The main divisions of the NAR are: (1) Public Archives,
housing official government records, most of which are protected
by a 30-year rule. (2) Historical Manuscripts Collection, containing private papers of individuals, families, churches, and
other non-official bodies. Notable are papers of David Livingstone and the Moffat family (qq.v.). (3) Library, which houses
more than 35,000 volumes of Africana. The NAR library is
also the official depository for all books and periodicals published
in the country. (4) Records Management. Storage of less than
30-year-old government documents not open to public inspection.

About 10% of these are eventually placed in the Public Archives.
(5) <u>Federal Records</u>. Government documents from the period
of Federation. (6) Pictorial Collection. Notable are the paintings of Thomas Baines (q. v.). (7) Map Collection.
     In addition to the above sections, the NAR building con-
tains a public gallery displaying various artifacts and documents,
including a signed copy of the UDI. (See BIBLIOGRAPHY for
published archival guides and other NAR publications.)

NATIONAL DEMOCRATIC PARTY (NDP). Predominantly African
     political party founded on January 1, 1960, as the successor to
     the banned African National Congress (q. v.). With most of the
     ANC leadership under government arrest, the NDP introduced
     such new leaders as J. M. Chinamano, Herbert Chitepo, Michael
     Mawema, Robert Mugabe, S. T. Parirenyatwa, Leopold Taka-
     wira (qq. v.), and Reuben Jamela, a trade union leader. In
     April Mawema, the acting president, led an NDP delegation to
     the London conference on Federal constitutional review and
     managed to head off Edgar Whitehead's (q. v.) efforts to secure
     greater independence for Southern Rhodesia's white electorate.
     In July Mawema and other NDP leaders were arrested under the
     terms of the Unlawful Organisations Act (q. v.) for their supposed
     membership in the banned ANC. The NDP mounted large-scale
     demonstrations in the main urban centers to protest these ar-
     rests, and violence erupted when the government responded with
     police repression. The government then passed the Law and
     Order (Maintenance) Act (q. v.).
     A leadership dispute in the NDP was resolved later that
     year in favor of a compromise candidate, Joshua Nkomo (q. v.),
     who was recalled from his voluntary exile in November to be-
     come president. In February 1961 Nkomo headed an NDP dele-
     gation at the Salisbury constitutional conference, where the party
     eventually rejected proposals for the 1961 Constitution (q. v.).
     The party later called for an African boycott of the elections
     (see "BUILD A NATION"). On December 9, 1961, Whitehead's
     government banned the NDP. Shortly thereafter the party's
     leaders formed the Zimbabwe African People's Union (q. v.).
     The NDP differed from its predecessor, the ANC, in
     making a more direct attack on the constitutional basis of mi-
     nority rule. Although it succeeded in having the Native Land
     Husbandry Act (q. v.) abolished, it concentrated more on de-
     manding majority rule than on seeking reforms for specific
     grievances. The largely intellectual leadership of the party is
     said to have been less in touch with the rural masses than that
     of the ANC, but this was due in part to government restrictions
     on NDP activities in rural areas. Nevertheless, the NDP is
     generally regarded as the country's first effective mass African
     political movement.

NATIONAL MONUMENTS see HISTORICAL MONUMENTS COM-
     MISSION

NATIONAL PARKS. There are 15 national parks in the country,

ranging in size from tiny Ewanrigg to Connecticut-size Wankie
(qq.v.). The parks, and a similar number of separately-ad-
ministered game reserves (q.v.), cover almost an eighth of the
country on land mostly designated as "national" (see LAND
TENURE ACT). Since the Legislative Assembly* passed the
National Park Act in 1949, parks have been developed to meet
three kinds of needs. Like the game reserves, some parks
protect wildlife resources; unlike the reserves, however, the
parks are designed for public access. Wankie is the most important game reserve. Other parks have been developed primarily to protect naturally scenic or historic attractions (see
also HISTORICAL MONUMENTS COMMISSION). Foremost in
this category are Victoria Falls, Matopos, Sinoia Caves, Inyanga, and Zimbabwe (qq.v.). The third category comprises
a number of small parks developed mostly around artificial
lakes for recreational fishing (q.v.) and camping. These parks
have been created largely in order to encourage the European
community to spend their holidays within the country. Many
of these parks are near urban centers. Lake McIlwaine and
Ewanrigg are close to Salisbury; Ngezi and Sebakwe are near
Que Que and Gatooma; Mushandike and Kyle are near Fort Victoria; and Vumba is near Umtali (qq.v.). Other parks are
Chimanimani and Mtarazi (qq.v.). Foreign tourism has also
been an important factor in the development of the parks, but
in contrast to the resort situation in most tropical African
countries, local tourism has generated most of the parks'
revenue--particularly since the intensification of African nationalist guerrilla operations during the mid-1970s.

NATIONAL PEOPLE'S UNION (NPU). Successor political party to
the United People's Party (q.v.), formed in June 1969. The
NPU started with most of the African members of Parliament,
but only Josiah Gondo (d.Oct. 1972) retained his seat after the
1970 election. In March 1972 NPU leaders dissolved the party
and encouraged its members to support the African National
Council (q.v.). (See also CENTRE PARTY.)

NATIVE ACCOMMODATION AND REGISTRATION ACT   see   NATIVE
(URBAN AREAS) ACCOMMODATION AND REGISTRATION ACT

NATIVE AFFAIRS DEPARTMENT ANNUAL   see   NADA

NATIVE CHRISTIAN CONFERENCE   see under   SOUTHERN RHO-
DESIAN MISSIONARY CONFERENCE

NATIVE LAND HUSBANDRY ACT (LHA; a.k.a. African LHA) (1951).
One of the white Southern Rhodesian government's most ambitious
schemes to transform African life, the LHA was passed in mid-
1951, three years after it had been published as the "Native Reserves Land Utilization and Good Husbandry Bill." The goal of
the law was to improve conservation measures, to regulate the
size of livestock herds, and, most importantly, to divide communal land holdings within the Native Reserves into individual

family plots in order to make cash-earning peasants out of traditional farmers. The law combined the earlier Natural Resources Act of 1941 with many of E. D. Alvord's (q.v.) agricultural programs, with the intention of making individual African
farmers responsible to the government for the efficient operation
of their holdings.

A key element of the LHA was transference of authority
to allocate land from the government chiefs to the Native Commissioners (see DISTRICTS). The sheer magnitude of the task
of surveying, dividing, and allocating plots was ultimately beyond
the means of the government. Most of the reserve lands (see
TRIBAL TRUST LANDS) were left unaffected by the time the
scheme was abandoned in the early 1960s. More important was
the widespread African resistance to the law. Though economically rational, destocking schemes were always unpopular, as
were any schemes for massive change imposed from above.
Further, while the law was naturally resisted by the traditional
African authorities whom it undermined, it was also attacked by
educated and urban Africans. An assumption of the law was
that increased industrialization of the towns would absorb the
Reserves' surplus populations, obviating the need to provide
rural land to all the country's Africans--a principle theoretically
enshrined in the Constitution of 1923 (q.v.). The passage of
time proved the invalidity of this assumption, while giving urbanized Africans opportunity to voice their fears of being left
without security in either the Reserves or in the towns, where
they could not own land (see ANC; RICU; NDP; BUROMBO, B.).
In practice the Africans affected by the LHA in the Reserves
tended to ignore its provisions, carrying on much as before,
and the government finally let the law lapse because of its unen-
forcibility.

In 1965 the Rhodesian Front government passed the Tribal
Trust Land Act, reversing objectives of the LHA. The TTL Act
reinstated the authority of the chiefs to allocate land on communal principles, and it expressed the goal of having the TTL's
absorb surplus African urban populations. (See AGRICULTURE;
LAND APPORTIONMENT AND TENURE ACTS; URBANIZATION.)

NATIVE MIRROR. Early name of the Bantu Mirror (q.v.).

NATIVE REGISTRATION ACT (1936) see under PASS LAWS

NATIVE RESERVES see TRIBAL TRUST LANDS

NATIVE (URBAN AREAS) ACCOMMODATION AND REGISTRATION
ACT (1946). Law introduced by Godfrey Huggins (q.v.) to enforce provisions of the Land Apportionment Act (q.v.) pertaining
to segregation of towns. The law compelled municipal authorities to set aside land for African residences away from white
residential and business areas, and to provide housing units
whose rents were to be paid by employers. An innovative feature of the law stipulated that rents for bachelors and married
couples were to be the same, thereby promoting the stabilization

of families in the towns, in anticipation of a gradual shift of
Africans away from the rural areas (see NATIVE LAND HUS-
BANDRY ACT). Although implementation of the law led to improved housing conditions, particularly in Salisbury (q.v.), Africans vigorously protested the discriminatory principles upon
which it was based, as well as the law's failure to provide security of tenure to Africans. (See URBANIZATION.)

NDALEKA. Sindebele* form of "Hendrik." See POTGIETER, A. H.

NDANGA DISTRICT (former variant: N'danga). After having had its
boundaries completely redrawn several times, Ndanga District
now covers 8754 sq. km. in the center of Victoria Province
(q.v.). On the west the Mtilikwe River* separates it from Victoria District (q.v.), out of which it was carved in 1899. On
the east Ndanga borders Bikita District (q.v.), which was separated from it in 1920. On the south Ndanga borders Chiredzi
District (q.v.), the central part of which was formerly part of
Ndanga. The remainder of Ndanga is now all Tribal Trust Land
(q.v.), with a population of 111,950 Africans in 1969. Zaka
(q.v.) is the district administrative center. The only other significant center is the village of Ndanga (at 20° 11'S, 31° 20'E).

NDAU. Ethnic and linguistic term for one of the main clusters of
Shona-speaking peoples (q.v.). The Ndau (or Vandau) live
mainly in the southeastern part of the country and in Mozambique (q.v.), from just west of the Sabi River* to the Indian
Ocean, and between the Sabi (or Save) River in the south, to
c.19° 30'S Lat. in the north. About two-thirds of the Ndau live
in Mozambique. Those who live in present Rhodesia constitute
about 6% of the country's Shona. During the 19th century Ndau
territory was occupied by the Nguni-speaking Gaza (q.v.), who
left a strong Nguni cultural imprint on the local people. For
this reason the Ndau are also known as "Shangane" (q.v.)--a
variant name of the Gaza--and their country is still called
"Gazaland" (q.v.).

NDEBELE KINGDOM. (1) History. The Ndebele state was founded
in South Africa in c.1821, when Mzilikazi (q.v.) left Zululand*
with c.500 kinsmen. During the state's first few years it was
highly mobile, moving north from base to base in the eastern
part of the Transvaal (q.v.). By combining comparatively well-
developed fighting techniques, efficient discipline, and a strong
impulse for collective survival, the Ndebele conquered and absorbed many of the mainly Sotho-speaking communities they encountered during their migrations. Their numbers were further
augmented by voluntary submissions of other Mfecane-derived
Nguni bands (qq.v.). The Ndebele occupied Pedi territory about
a year, and then turned southwest, settling along the middle Vaal
River between c.1823 and c.1827. Their attempts to establish
permanent settlements there were hindered by frequent raids by
Sotho, Griqua (qq.v.), and other peoples. The Ndebele then
sought greater security along the northern slopes of the Magalies-

berg Mountains, in the area around present Pretoria (c. 1827-32). Through these years the Ndebele continued to mount their own raids, reaching into eastern Botswana*, and, on one occasion, even into present Rhodesia (see KALIPHI). Both the Ndebele population (see NDEBELE PEOPLE) and cattle (q. v.) herds continued to grow.

Although the Ndebele repelled most major attacks on their own cattle posts, continued harassment by enemies threatened their long-term security. After a large-scale assault by the Zulu of Dingane in 1832, the Ndebele moved farther west. From 1832 to 1837 they lived along the upper Marico River in the western Transvaal. By then the military strength of the kingdom was unrivaled by its African neighbors. The situation changed after 1835, when Afrikaner (q. v.) families began migrating inland from the British-ruled Cape Colony in the exodus known as the "Great Trek." Clashes with advance Afrikaner parties in 1836 led to very effective Afrikaner retaliation against Ndebele towns early the next year (see POTGIETER, A. H.). Independent Griqua campaigns and a second major Zulu attack made the Ndebele situation critical by the end of 1837. The Ndebele then moved into eastern Botswana, where they subsequently divided into two migrant parties. Under the leadership of Kaliphi, one party advanced almost directly into present Matabeleland (q. v.), where they established the permanent Ndebele base. Mzilikazi's party continued north, finally rejoining the other Ndebele in Matabeleland in about mid-1839. There Mzilikazi had to deal with a political crisis which ultimately left permanent scars in the kingdom's fabric (see NKULUMANE; NTABAZINDUNA).

Ndebele occupation of the new, mainly Shona-speaking region was made easier by the political disruption of the Changamire state (q. v.) in the wake of Ngoni (q. v.) invasions. During the 1840s raiding parties extended Ndebele influence over neighboring Shona communities, cattle were retrieved from former Sotho tributaries in the south, and several abortive campaigns were waged against the Kololo (q. v.) north of the Zambezi River. The next decade was a period of relative tranquility, marked by the re-establishment of contacts with European missionaries (see MOFFAT, R.; LONDON MISSIONARY SOCIETY), traders (see EDWARDS, S. H.), and hunters (q. v.). By the early 1860s the main challenge to Ndebele dominance of the region came from the Ngwato (q. v.) to the southwest. The Ndebele never completely subdued all the neighboring Shona peoples, but these never seriously threatened the security of the kingdom itself. (See TOHWECHIPI.)

A third phase in the kingdom's history began in 1868. Mzilikazi's death inaugurated a divisive interregnum (see MNCUMBATHE; "NKULUMANE"), and rediscovery of Shona gold (q. v.) workings initiated an era of increasingly intense European pressure for concessions (see HARTLEY, H.; MAUCH, K.; TATI; NORTHERN GOLDFIELDS). Lobengula (q. v.) was made king early in 1870, but he soon had to put down a rebellion (see ZWANGENDABA; MBIGO). Afterwards his reign was never free

of internal challenges. By the late 1880s the expansion of
European imperial pressure--then affecting all of tropical Africa
--clearly threatened the kingdom's independence. One of the
last major states in southern Africa to retain its independence,
the Ndebele kingdom became the focus of British, Portuguese
(q. v.), and Afrikaner diplomatic rivalries north of the Limpopo
River, even though the kingdom effectively controlled less than
half of what became Rhodesia. (Cf. GAZA KINGDOM.)

British interests prevailed through the vehicle of Cecil
Rhodes' BSAC (q. v.). By exaggerating the extent of Ndebele
dominance north of the Limpopo, while misrepresenting rights
granted by Lobengula (see MOFFAT TREATY; RUDD CONCES-
SION; LIPPERT CONCESSION), the BSAC occupied Mashonaland
(q. v.) in 1890. It then used that territory as a base for invading
the Ndebele in 1893 (see NDEBELE WAR). It has long been
argued that Lobengula's death in early 1894 brought the kingdom
to an end, but this view has recently been challenged by J. R.
Cobbing, who has demonstrated that the non-monarchical institutions of the state were only slightly disrupted; that the Ndebele
were far from "demilitarized"; and that British occupation of
Matabeleland was slight up to 1896. According to this view,
the Revolt (q. v.) of 1896 was the last gasp of the kingdom itself, and restoration of the monarchy was a main objective of
the rebels (see NYAMANDA). After the Revolt, BSAC occupation of Ndebele became effective for the first time. Communities were relocated into reserves (see TRIBAL TRUST LANDS),
and the kingdom became only a memory, despite continued Ndebele efforts to restore the monarchy (see MATABELE HOME
SOCIETY).

(2) Description. In contrast to the earlier, large Munhumutapa and Changamire state systems (qq. v.), the Ndebele
kingdom was highly centralized and capable of rapid and efficient military mobilization. However, these characteristics have
probably been exaggerated in the comparatively large literature
on the 19th century Ndebele kingdom. Family clans (see ISI-
BONGO) played a small part in Ndebele political organization,
but the kingdom was effectively a collection of hereditary chieftaincies (izigaba), whose members owed a common allegiance to
the kings (see INKOSI). Cutting across these chieftaincies were
a large number of male age-sets, or amabutho (see IBUTHO),
which the kings periodically raised to be trained as military and
police units. The amabutho are frequently described as "regiments," but they might more accurately be regarded as reserve
military units. The kings also appointed chiefs (see INDUNA)
over the amabutho, but over time the units tended to evolve into
chieftaincies whose leadership became effectively hereditary.
Tension between the kings and the chieftaincies increased over
time, particularly as outlying chiefs sought greater autonomy.
This was a problem experienced particularly by Lobengula, and
it partly explains Ndebele disunity in the 1893 Ndebele War and
the 1896 Revolt (qq. v.). (For examples of important chiefs, see
FAKU; GAMPU; MHLABA; MLUGULU; MPOTSHWANA; MTSHANI;
XUKUTWAYO; et al.)

Throughout the history of the kingdom raids were regularly mounted against other African communities. One purpose
of raids, particularly in the early decades, was to capture new
people to incorporate into the society, and cattle (q.v.). The
kings maintained their power partly by overseeing the distribution of booty. They also tended to monopolize the conduct of
foreign trade (see, e.g., IVORY; OSTRICHES; HORSES). The
19th-century Ndebele kingdom has typically been characterized
as economically parasitic, but the mainstays of the Ndebele diet
were grains which the Ndebele themselves grew (see AGRICUL-
TURE). Cattle were important as symbols of wealth and prestige, and as currency in social transactions, such as marriage
(see LOBOLO), but beef played a small role in diet.

A second purpose of raids was to reduce neighboring
communities to tributary status. Tributaries provided goods
and services, which the kings redistributed among the Ndebele,
and tributary communities stood as "buffers" against potential
foreign enemies. The notion that the Ndebele laid waste a
wide band of surrounding territory is a popular, but unfounded,
myth, as the Ndebele actually were surrounded by tributary
communities.

A third purpose of raiding was to punish tributaries
whose loyalty wavered. It was raids of this nature into Mashonaland in the early 1890s which gave L. S. Jameson (q.v.)
his immediate pretext for waging war on the Ndebele in 1893.

The core of the Ndebele kingdom was a c.10,000-sq. km.
area surrounding Bulawayo (q.v.), between the Matopo Hills on
the south, and the Somabula Forest (qq.v.) on the north. The
area of effective Ndebele domination over tributaries was considerably larger, but still only a large part of the territory later
designated as the province of Matabeleland (q.v.). People lived
in villages and towns of various sizes, up to several hundred
people each. Some of these towns were associated with the
amabutho, but few approached the enormous sizes popularly
ascribed to "regimental towns." Many adult males participated
in military campaigns for a few weeks during the dry seasons
(see CLIMATE). Otherwise, the day-to-day lives of the bulk
of the people were very similar to those of other, non-Ndebele
peoples in the country.

NDEBELE PEOPLE (Amandebele; on origin of name, see "MATA-
BELE"). The largest group of non-Shona-speaking people in the
country, the Ndebele live mostly in the southwestern districts,
particularly around Bulawayo (q.v.). Creation of an "Ndebele"
ethnic identity coincided with the formation of the Ndebele kingdom (q.v.) in the early 19th century. Along with the kingdom,
this sense of ethnic identity developed as increasing numbers
of Nguni, Sotho, Shona (qq.v.), and other peoples were incorporated into the society. However, while the kingdom ended in
the 1890s, concepts of Ndebele identity have continued to develop.

During the 19th century Ndebeleness was primarily a political concept, measured by allegiance to the kings. An individual might therefore have been regarded as an Ndebele before

adopting all aspects of the dominantly Nguni (q.v.) Ndebele culture.   The sudden abolition of the kingdom by the Europeans
made such former political allegiances largely irrelevant (though
many chieftaincies survived).   Unlike the case of the Gaza (q.v.),
whose kingdom was abolished in southern Mozambique, the identity of the Ndebele remained strong into the 20th century.   The
inchoate kingdom impressed its Sindebele language (q.v.) on most
of its subjects permanently.   Ndebele society subsequently grew
larger through both natural population growth and voluntary ac-
culturation by individuals eager to share the historical identity.
This latter phenomenon has compounded the problem of defining
who is an "Ndebele."   Language has become the most important
modern criterion.   Another is family name (see ISIBONGO).
Nineteenth-century Ndebele society was broadly inclusive (see,
e.g., WILLIAM THE GRIQUA; MZIZI, W.), but today only family
names brought to the country by the original immigrants from
South Africa guarantee recognition as an Ndebele to any individual.   This situation implies a certain contradiction, as the
majority of the people regarded as Ndebele by the late 19th
century were of local origin.

During the mid-19th century Europeans began to propound
the notion that Ndebele society was rigidly divided into three
"castes."   The aristocratic zansi (q.v.) were said to be at the
top politically and socially.   The enhla (q.v.) were in the middle,
and the majority holi (q.v.) were at the bottom, in an allegedly
servile capacity.   Intermarriage between these "castes" was said
to be forbidden, and is said still to be rare.   It should be
stressed that there is no evidence that the Ndebele ever practiced a caste system comparable to that found in Indian Hindu
society.   The terms zansi and enhla served mainly to identify
people on the basis of their geographical origins--a system more
analogous to eastern American "high society."   It remains to be
demonstrated to what extent these distinctions helped or hindered
Ndebele individuals' actual social and political opportunities.

Historically, estimates of the size of the Ndebele population have been crude because of primitive census-taking techniques and the problem of identifying who are Ndebele.   With
these limitations in mind, the following figures may be taken as
indicative of the orders of magnitude of the numbers of Ndebele
since the 1820s: c.1821--500 people; the 1830s--20,000; c.1840--
10,000; the 1890s--100,000; in 1948--300,000+; and in 1976--
1,000,000+.   (See also POPULATION; RELIGION--NDEBELE.)

NDEBELE REVOLT   see   REVOLTS OF 1896/7

NDEBELE RULERS.   Historians have generally only recognized two
Ndebele monarchs, but other leaders also played roles.   c.1821-
68 Mzilikazi, 1868-9 Mncumbathe (regent), 1870-94 Lobengula,
1894-6 (interregnum), 1896 Nyamanda (qq.v.).

NDEBELE WAR (1893) (a.k.a. Matabele or Anglo-Ndebele War).
Popular descriptions of the British occupation of the Ndebele
kingdom (q.v.) as a "war" are misleading.   There were few

military engagements, and most Ndebele were left largely unaffected by the occupation until the much larger-scale hostilities
of the 1896 Revolt (q. v.).

Historians have recently argued that the Ndebele War was
planned by Cecil Rhodes and the BSAC as early as 1889 because
of Lobengula's repudiation of the Rudd Concession (q. v.), with
which the Company had hoped to gain control of the country
peacefully.   The Ndebele themselves anticipated a direct British
invasion of their country the next year, when the Company's
Pioneer Column (q. v.) occupied neighboring Mashonaland (q. v.).
The Mashonaland occupation was carried out without violence,
but it left the Ndebele surrounded by hostile neighbors (see
BORDERS).   As British settlement of Mashonaland became more
extensive, tensions in the frontier zone increased.   Ndebele intentions to avert war with the British were manifested by Lobengula's repeated efforts to negotiate directly with the British
government (see MSHETE), but the Company built up an anti-
Ndebele propaganda campaign by cataloguing Ndebele raids on
the Shona and other "incidents."

On July 18, 1893, an Ndebele punitive raid against Shona
tributaries near Fort Victoria* was blown into a major incident
by the British administrator L. S. Jameson (q. v.), whose attitude towards the Ndebele was particularly bellicose.   Jameson
instructed P. W. Forbes (q. v.), then magistrate at Salisbury,
to prepare Company forces for war.   As late as October Lobengula sent three peace emissaries south with J. Dawson (q. v.).
Two of these men were killed by the Bechuanaland Border Police
(q. v.) at Tati* in a misunderstanding.   Meanwhile, the British
launched three separate columns against the Ndebele.   Those
setting out from Salisbury and Fort Victoria converged at Iron
Mine Hill* on October 15th.   From there they marched southwest towards Bulawayo (q. v.).   A third column of BBP troops
marched northeast from Tati.

On October 25th Forbes' northern column engaged Mtshani's
(q. v.) Ndebele forces at the headwaters of the Shangani River* in
a laager* action.   The Ndebele recaptured cattle collected by the
column, but retreated in the face of machine gun fire.   On November 1st the column engaged the Ndebele in a somewhat briefer
action by the headwaters of the Bembezi River*.   The Battles
of Shangani and Bembezi, as they came to be called, were the
largest actions of the "war."   Ndebele casualties in these battles are usually said to have been enormous, but contemporary
evidence suggests that only a few hundred Ndebele men were
actually killed.

After Lobengula learned of these setbacks, he burned
Bulawayo and fled north with a large retinue.   He continued
attempts to negotiate a truce, but his lines of communication
with British authorities were defective.   Forbes' column occupied Bulawayo on November 4th.   The BBP column under Goold-
Adams (q. v.) arrived a week later, after a brief skirmish with
Gampu's (q. v.) forces by the Mangwe Pass*.

The British saw the war as won when they occupied
Bulawayo.   Ndebele resistance continued in the west and south,

but the British soon abandoned attempts to deal with this opposition and instead concentrated on capturing Lobengula.   A
column under Forbes went north, but a detachment, now known
as the "Shangane Patrol," under Allan Wilson (qq.v.), was annihilated and the effort to capture Lobengula was abandoned.
The remainder of Forbes' column encountered heavy Ndebele
pressure during its retreat, and no further attempt was made
to pacify the northern Ndebele.   Reports of Lobengula's death
were later received, and the British declared the Ndebele kingdom at an end.
        Most literature on the Ndebele War suggests that the
British crushed the kingdom.   It is clear, however, that the
main British achievements were simply occupation of Bulawayo
and confiscation of large numbers of cattle (q.v.).   Except for
the looting of their cattle, most Ndebele settlements were little
affected by the British occupation over the next two and a half
years.   Some Ndebele supported the British presence (see
GAMPU; FAKU; MTSHANI), but few were disarmed.   The institutions of the kingdom continued, but without a monarch.   Restoration of the monarchy then became a central issue in the Revolt
of 1896 (q.v.).

NEAL, W. G. (d.1906/7).   South African prospector.   See under
RHODESIA ANCIENT RUINS, LTD.; HALL, R. N.

NEGOMO CHIRISAMHURU MUPUNZAGUTU (a.k.a. Sebastião) (c.1543-
c.1589).   First Christian Munhumutapa (q.v.).   Still a youth
when he succeeded his father Chivere Nyasoro (q.v.) as king in
c.1560, Negomo soon got himself into international difficulties.
Late in 1560 a Portuguese (q.v.) priest, Gonçalo da Silveira
(q.v.), arrived at Negomo's court in the Dande*.   Silveira's
selflessness contrasted sharply with the avarice of the Portuguese traders, making a deep impression on the young king.
Within a month Negomo accepted baptism, taking the name "Dom
Sebastião" in honor of the Portuguese king.   His mother was
also baptized.   Soon hundreds of other Shona sought similar
sanctification.   Local nganga and Muslims (qq.v.) apparently
convinced Negomo that Silveira was a dangerous spy, so he allowed Silveira to be killed in March 1561.   He quickly regretted
this murder, however, and had many of those responsible for it
executed.   Later the Portuguese government organized the Francisco Barreto (q.v.) expedition to avenge Silveira's death and to
seize the country's gold and silver mines.
        When the Barreto expedition finally arrived at the lower
Zambezi River in 1572, Negomo was having difficulties with rebellious Tonga (q.v.) tributaries in the area around Sena (q.v.).
Through intermediaries Negomo negotiated an agreement with
Barreto and the latter's successor, Vasco Honem (q.v.), where-
by the Portuguese put down the Tonga revolt in return for rights
to mines in Manicaland and Guruhuswa (qq.v.)--regions Negomo
did not even control.   The Portuguese thus secured Negomo's
eastern districts for him without gaining anything tangible in return.   Trade also increased in the Munhumutapa state as new

fairs (q.v.) were opened throughout the country. Negomo died
in c.1589 and was succeeded by Gatsi Rusere (q.v.), a member
of a collateral ruling family. Negomo's own son Mavura II
(q.v.) also later became Munhumutapa. (For Changamire Negomo, see under DOMBO.)

NEHANDA (variant: Nyanda). Name of a Shona "lion spirit," or
mhondoro (q.v.), which possessed female mediums in the Zezuru
(q.v.) region around the Mazoe Valley. (N.B.: the Korekore
have a mhondoro of the same name, said to be the spirit of the
consort-sister of the early Munhumutapa Matope, q.v.) By the
19th century the Zezuru Nehanda mediums were among the most
influential in central Shona territory, and were regarded as
equivalent in status with the famous Chaminuka (q.v.). During
the 1896-7 Revolt (q.v.) "Nehanda" played a leading role in
instigating the first killings of white settlers in the Mazoe area,
and in organizing resistance among the central Shona paramount
chiefs. She was popularly--but incorrectly--described by Europeans as a "witch." During the Revolt she allied with Kaguvi
(q.v.), another mhondoro leader. In contrast to Kaguvi, she
urged her own followers to repudiate European material goods
and to fight with traditional weapons. She was captured in December 1897, and was tried along with Kaguvi the following
March. On April 27, 1898 she and Kaguvi were hanged. A
new Nehanda medium emerged in 1906 and quickly re-established
the reputation enjoyed by her predecessor before the Revolt.

NEMAKONDE (variants: Lomagundi; Maconde). Dynastic title of
the rulers of a small but important Korekore (q.v.) chiefdom
in the south of the present Lomagundi District (q.v.). During
the 19th century the Nemakondes became tributaries of the
Ndebele kingdom. The Nemakondes themselves were said to
have made annual trips to Bulawayo to deliver tribute payments.
In 1889 Nemakonde Hodza sought to escape Ndebele domination
by accepting Portuguese "protection" from Manuel de Sousa and
J. C. P. d'Andrada (qq.v.). When the BSAC occupied Mashonaland the next year, Hodza shifted his allegiance to the British.
In 1891 the Ndebele king Lobengula (q.v.) sent him an ultimatum
to resume his former obligations. Hodza ignored the warning.
In November 1891 he was killed by Ndebele soldiers, who apparently had the support of his local political rivals. The British
protested the killing in what has been regarded as the first "incident" leading to the Ndebele War of 1893 (q.v.).
      The new Nemakonde, Mazimbaguba, acknowledged British
sovereignty, but soon came to resent forced labor levies on his
people. In late 1894 violent clashes over tax collection led to
deaths on both sides. The Nemakonde joined in the Revolt of
1896-7 (q.v.), but his territory lay outside the main theaters of
war throughout the conflict. The chiefdom is now in the Magondi
TTL (at 17° 45'S, 29° 50'E).

NESHANGWE MUNEMBIRE (d. c.1550). Early Munhumutapa (q.v.).
The son of a leper ineligible to rule (Munyore Karembera),

Neshangwe succeeded his uncle Chikuyo Chisamarengu (q.v.) as the Munhumutapa in c.1530. He established his headquarters west of the lower Hunyani River in the Dande (qq.v.). His reign was most notable for his success in expelling the Changamire (q.v.) from the Mbire region (q.v.) in c.1547. This feat earned him the praise-name "Munembire," "owner of Mbire." On his death in c.1550, the kingship was assumed by Chikuyo's son, Chivere Nyasoro (q.v.).

NEWSPAPERS see PRESS

NGANGA (variant: N'anga). Shona professional healers and diviners; sometimes described as "medicine men." Nganga have long played an important role in Shona everyday life. They treat mental and physical ailments, exorcise malevolent spirits, such as ngozi (q.v.), from unwilling hosts, divine causes of misfortune, and offer medicines and other forms of protection for all kinds of enterprises. Individual nganga may claim to be proficient in all skills, but most specialize. Many are, for example, proficient herbalists (see CHIREMBA). Though they have demonstrated considerable skill in treating illness, they do not necessarily compete with Western-type physicians, as patients often consult both. Some nganga are also practicing Christians. Most nganga are men, but many are women of equal reputation. Nganga either learn their techniques as apprentices, or obtain their skills through possession by spirits--typically shave (q.v.). Spirit-possession is usually regarded as a necessary condition for treating cases involving witchcraft or malevolent spirits. Diagnoses in such cases are often made by entranced nganga while throwing "divining dice" (see HAKATA). Nganga share many characteristics and functions of other spirit mediums, such as the mhondoro (q.v.), but differ in that they treat mainly individual or family cases, they work for fees, and they make great use of medicines and material devices. (See RELIGION--SHONA; HEALTH.)

NGANO, MARTHA (fl.1890s-1920s). An Mfengu (q.v.) immigrant from South Africa, Ngano came to Southern Rhodesia in 1897 and became an Apostolic Faith Mission teacher in Bulawayo. Perhaps one of the best educated local African women of her era, she was recruited into the RBVA (q.v.) as it was being formed in 1922-3. In 1924 she became secretary of the organization, remaining its leading spokesperson through the 1920s. She pushed hard for increased government registration of African voters. She particularly criticized the government for making English literacy a voter qualification while teaching only vernacular languages in African schools, and she demanded that communally-held property be counted in voter qualification requirements. A dynamic public speaker, she successfully established many rural branches of the RBVA throughout Matabeleland.

NGEZI (variants: Ingezi; Ngesi). The country has three rivers with this name, all of which rise near the crest of the Central Plateau

(q.v.). The southwestern-most Ngezi River rises near the
source of the Shangani River (q.v.), flowing southeast c.135 km.
before meeting the Lundi River (q.v.) by the village of Ingezi
(at 20° 34'S, 30° 24'E). The central Ngezi rises between the
towns of Lalapanzi and Umvuma (q.v.), flowing almost directly
south c.75 km. to feed the Tokwe River (q.v.). Just above
this confluence it is joined by the Shashe River (q.v.). The
northeastern-most Ngezi rises near the source of the Sabi River
(q.v.), flowing c.100 km. west to feed the Umniati River (q.v.)
just west of the Mashaba Mountains (q.v.). Ngezi Dam was
built in a gap in these mountains in 1945. The dam provides
local irrigation water, and is surrounded by a small national
park (q.v.).

NGONI (variants: Abangoni; Angoni; Mangoni; Wangoni). Itself a
variation of the name "Nguni" (q.v.), "Ngoni" has been loosely
applied to all the various Nguni-speaking migrant bands of the
Mfecane era (q.v.). In its narrower and more proper sense,
however, the name applies only to migrant bands led by Zwangendaba, Nyamazana, Maseko, and Nxaba (qq.v.)--all of whom
passed through present Rhodesia during the 1830s. These same
peoples are also frequently called "Swazi" (q.v.), the name of
a northern Nguni branch to which the original Ngoni leaders
were closely related. Other names by which the Ngoni were
known in central Africa during the 19th century include Landeen
and Dzviti (qq.v.). Modern Ngoni communities--like their Ndebele (q.v.) counterparts--contain descendants of numerous southern and central African societies. Distinct Ngoni communities
still exist in Zambia, Malawi, and Tanzania, but there are no
longer any in Rhodesia.

NGOZI. A class of Shona ancestor spirits characterized by their
malevolent or vengeful behavior. Victims of accidents, illness,
or other misfortunes frequently blame ngozi for their troubles
and seek means of appeasing or retaliating against them. The
word ngozi is nearly synonymous with "danger" or "harm" in
both Chishona and Sindebele (qq.v.). When used to describe a
Shona spirit, "ngozi" refers more to the spirit's malevolent behavior than to the type of spirit itself. (See RELIGION.)

NGUBOYENJA LOBENGULA (b. c.1880/1). Fifth son of Lobengula
(q.v.), by a wife named Sitshwapa Ndiweni. After his father's
death in 1894, Nguboyenja and his half-brothers Njube and
Mpezeni (qq.v.) were sent to the Cape Colony for European education. Nguboyenja proved an excellent student, so he was sent
to England for further studies in 1907. Had he been allowed to
pursue his own interests, he might have become the country's
first African lawyer (cf. CHITEPO, H.); however, the BSAC
wanted to keep him out of politics and instead encouraged him
to study veterinary medicine. The Company regarded him and
Njube as the only possible successors to King Lobengula, but
they had no intention of restoring the Ndebele monarchy, thus
adding to Nguboyenja's frustrations. He was permitted to visit

Bulawayo in 1908, but found his activities there so severely
circumscribed by the government that he soon voluntarily returned to South Africa. There he appears to have suffered a
complete nervous breakdown, for he soon became an uncommuni-
cative recluse. Nevertheless, as late as 1931 members of the
Matabele Home Society (q. v.) were collecting money to get him
medical treatment in the hope of returning him to Matabeleland.
F. W. T. Posselt (q. v.) reported that Nguboyenja was still "a
cripple" in 1945.

NGUNGUNYANA see GUNGUNYANE

NGUNI. Term for a cluster of southeast Bantu languages (q. v.)
originally spoken along the eastern coast of South Africa (q. v.).
The Nguni cluster is comparable to the Sotho cluster (q. v.),
spoken mainly in the highland areas north of the Orange River.
Nguni languages are further divided into southern and northern
branches. The former are spoken by the Pondo, Thembu,
Xhosa, and other peoples of southern Natal, the Transkei, and
the eastern Cape Province. The northern branch includes Swazi
and Zulu (qq. v.), spoken by peoples in northern Natal, Zululand,
and Swaziland. In contrast to Sotho, most Nguni languages contain many "click" sounds (q. v.) borrowed from Khoisan languages
(q. v.).
    The early 19th century was an era of rapid state-building
among the northern Nguni peoples. The wars of this era, known
as the Mfecane (q. v.), started wholesale migrations which brought
into present Rhodesia such northern Nguni-speaking peoples as
the Ndebele, Ngoni, and Gaza (qq. v.). Many additional northern
and southern Nguni peoples entered the country in the late 19th
and early 20th century as wagon-drivers and other kinds of European employees, military personnel, and missionary agents.
Prominent among these later Nguni immigrants were the Mfengu
(q. v.).

NGWATO (BAMANGWATO). Sotho (q. v.) speaking people of the
western, or Tswana (q. v.), branch. In the late 18th century
the Ngwato broke away from the Kwena and moved north to settle around Shoshong (at 22° 57'S, 26° 29'E) in what is now eastern
Botswana (q. v.). Another split occurred almost immediately,
as the Tawana (q. v.) separated and moved farther north. Under
the rule of Khama I and his successors, Kgari (q. v.) and Sekgoma, the Ngwato became the dominant people of eastern Botswana. Their settlements extended into the southwestern part
of present Rhodesia, where some Ngwato still live.
    During the late 1820s the Ndebele (q. v.) began occupying
the western Transvaal. The Ndebele then started raiding Ngwato
cattle and collecting tribute, but they never completely subdued
the Ngwato. In 1838 the Ndebele occupied Ngwato territory
briefly during their own migration to present Matabeleland.
Ndebele cattle raids against the Ngwato resumed in the early
1840s, when the Ndebele captured the future Ngwato ruler Macheng (q. v.). Through the rest of the 19th century the Ngwato

were perhaps the most formidable threat to Ndebele security.
The Ndebele and Ngwato raided each other's cattle frequently,
and both societies claimed overlapping territory around the Tati
River (q.v.). However, their conflicts never developed into a
major war. In early 1863 Mzilikazi's son Mangwane (q.v.) led
the last major Ndebele attack on the Ngwato at Shoshong. Under
the leadership of the future Ngwato ruler Khama III (q.v.), Ngwato
horsemen armed with guns repelled the assault easily.

From the 1860s Ngwato territory assumed increasing importance in Rhodesian affairs as the entry route to Matabeleland
(see HUNTERS' ROAD). The Ngwato gave refuge to many Ndebele political dissidents, including Mangwane and the pretender
"Nkulumane" (q.v.). In January 1872 Macheng lent these men
a military force to invade Matabeleland in the hope of overthrowing King Lobengula, but the Ngwato troops retreated before
reaching Matabeleland. After Khama III became Ngwato ruler
in 1875, he renounced "Nkulumane's" claims, and relations with
the Ndebele eased.

Declaration of the Bechuanaland Protectorate (q.v.) in
1885 created a new strain in Ngwato-Ndebele relations, but the
Ngwato now had the British as allies. In 1890 Khama provided
Ngwato men to help the BSAC's Pioneer Column (q.v.) cut a
road into Mashonaland. Ngwato mercenaries were recruited by
the British for the 1893 Ndebele War (q.v.), but Khama withdrew them before they saw any military action.

NHOWE (Vanhowe; variants: Wanoe; Nhohwe). A branch of the
Zezuru (q.v.) cluster of Shona-speaking peoples; now living
mainly in the Mrewa District (q.v.). Since the early 18th
century they have been ruled by the Mangwende dynasty (q.v.).

"NIBMAR." Acronymic slogan meaning "No Independence Before
Majority African Rule." British Prime Minister Harold Wilson
coined the expression in a declaration of British policy towards
Rhodesian constitutional negotiations in December 1966. (Cf.
"FIVE PRINCIPLES.")

NICKEL. Minor production of this mineral began at the Noel Mine
(at 21°18'S, 28°34'E) in the Gwanda District (q.v.) in 1928,
remaining small through the 1950s. In the late 1950s major
new discoveries were made at the Empress Mine near Gatooma
(q.v.), the Trojan Mine near Bindura (q.v.), and near Shamva
(q.v.). Thereafter production gradually increased until nickel
ranked as one of the country's most important mineral (q.v.)
products in the late 1960s. Nickel production appears to have
expanded very greatly since 1965, but the government has not
released precise statistics.

NIEKERK RUINS see VAN NIEKERK RUINS

NINI see MNCENGENCE

NJANJA (Vanjanja). A branch of the Zezuru (q.v.) cluster of Shona-

speaking peoples; now living mainly in the Charter District
(q. v.). During the 18th and 19th centuries the Njanja mined
iron at nearby Mount Wedza (q. v.) and became famous as
smiths. They maintained a widespread trade network in iron
tools and implements, such as the mbira (q. v.). (See also
HERA.)

NJELELE. Mwari (q. v.) cult oracular shrine in the Matopo Hills
(q. v.); located c. 50 km. south-southwest of Bulawayo. Its
origins remain controversial, but it is believed to have been
the most senior and influential Mwari shrine during the 19th
century--at least within the southwestern part of Matabeleland.
The shrine still operates today, but it has been described as
"partly defunct." (Cf. MATOJENI.)

NJUBE LOBENGULA (c.1879/80-June 10, 1910). Fourth son of the
Ndebele king Lobengula (q. v.), by a wife named Mpoliana Ndiweni. After the Ndebele War of 1893 (q. v.) the BSAC sent
Njube and his half-brothers Nguboyenja and Mpezeni (qq. v.) to
the Cape Colony to be educated. After the 1896 Revolt (q. v.)
Ndebele interest in restoring the monarchy centered on Njube
and Nguboyenja because they were the only sons of Lobengula
whom the Company considered eligible successors to the defunct
kingship (cf. NYAMANDA). However, Company officials had no
intention of restoring the monarchy. They frustrated Njube's
attempts to regain a foothold in Matabeleland, where Mlugulu
(q. v.) and other senior izinduna agitated for his return. Njube
was allowed to visit Bulawayo in late 1900, but his arrival there
created such a commotion among the Ndebele that the Company
soon returned him to the Cape. Thereafter he managed to ex-
tract increasingly large sums of money from the Company. He
is said to have lived "riotously" until dying of tuberculosis in
Grahamstown, where he is buried. He left two sons, Albert
and Rhodes Lobengula.

NKAI DISTRICT. A relatively recent creation, this district covers
4565 sq. km. of the east-central part of Matabeleland North
Province (q. v.). It was formed from the northeastern section
of the older Bubi District (q. v.). It is a little-developed region
made up almost entirely of Tribal Trust Land (q. v.). The almost exclusively African population numbered just over 65,000
in the 1969 census. The village of Nkai (at 19° S, 28° 54'E)
serves as administrative center. Nkai is bordered by the districts of Lupane on the west; Gokwe on the north; Que Que on
the east; and Bubi (qq. v.) on the south.

NKALIPI see KALIPHI

NKOMO, JOSHUA MQABUKO NYONGOLO (b.June 19, 1917). The
longest-established and best known of the country's nationalist
leaders, Nkomo was born in Matobo District near Bulawayo.
After he attended local mission schools and worked as a truck
driver, he went to South Africa in 1941, eventually to train as

a social worker in Johannesburg. He returned to Southern Rhodesia in 1947 and became the first African social worker employed by Rhodesia Railways (q.v.). From that position he
moved into trade unionism and became the general secretary of
the Rhodesia Railways African Employees Association. Meanwhile, he completed a bachelor's degree by correspondence from
the University of South Africa.

    Nkomo began his political career as an officer in the All-
African Convention (q.v.) in 1952. The same year he accompanied
Godfrey Huggins (q.v.) to London in order to represent African
opinions concerning Federation (q.v.). He denounced the Federation plans on his return home, but a year later he contested the
Matabeleland seat in the Federal Assembly, losing to M. M.
Hove (q.v.). He then became president of the Bulawayo branch
of the old African National Congress (q.v.). When the ANC was
reorganized in 1957, Nkomo was elected president. He was out
of the country when the government made sweeping arrests of
ANC leaders in 1959. The following year he was elected president in absentia of the new National Democratic Party (q.v.).

    Nkomo participated in the 1960-61 constitutional conference
in London (see CONSTITUTIONS). He initially accepted the
United (Federal) Party's (q.v.) proposals, but withdrew his en-
dorsement under pressure from fellow NDP officers. When the
NDP was banned in December 1961 Nkomo was again out of the
country. This time he was in Tanganyika (now Tanzania), where
he immediately formed ZAPU (q.v.) with the support of Ndabaningi
Sithole (q.v.). The following year Nkomo traveled widely, and
got the UN to recognize Southern Rhodesia as an international
problem. After his return to Southern Rhodesia the government
banned ZAPU in September 1962, arresting Nkomo in October.

    Nkomo was repeatedly arrested and released by the govern-
ment through 1963. Meanwhile, he and Sithole split over nationalist strategy. Sithole formed ZANU, and Nkomo formed the
People's Caretake Council (qq.v.) to hold together the remaining
ZAPU leadership. Immediately after Ian Smith (q.v.) came to
power in April 1964, Nkomo was again arrested. He then spent
most of the next decade in prisons and detention camps, emerging
occasionally to participate in talks with visiting British emissaries.

    Smith finally released Nkomo in December 1974 in order
for him to participate in Lusaka talks leading to a new constitutional conference. Nkomo was not rearrested on his return to
Salisbury on December 12th, when he made his first public appearance in the country since 1964. Through most of 1975 he
stayed out of the country, even while participating in the August
Victoria Falls Conference (q.v.). Nkomo had joined other nationalist leaders under the "umbrella" of the African National
Council (q.v.) in December 1974, but after the Victoria Falls
Conference collapsed, he denounced Sithole and James Chikerema
(q.v.), thereby re-establishing the old party rifts.

    At the end of 1975 Nkomo returned to Salisbury as the
head of the "internal" ANC. He was then recognized as a political moderate, in contrast to Abel Muzorewa (q.v.). From
mid-December to mid-March 1976 Nkomo and Ian Smith held a

series of informal weekly talks, but these produced no tangible
results and Nkomo was increasingly criticized by other nationalists.   In May 1976 he again left the country to consult
with leaders abroad.   He returned to Salisbury in late September 1976, announcing his willingness to participate in a new
round of constitutional talks based upon the proposals made by
U.S. Secretary of State Henry Kissinger.   Shortly before the
ensuing Geneva Conference (q.v.), Nkomo made a surprise move
by announcing formation of a "Patriotic Front" (q.v.) with Robert
Mugabe (q.v.), one of his longstanding political rivals.

When the Geneva Conference began in October 1976,
Nkomo and Mugabe stood out as the most intransigent critics
of the Kissinger proposals and of the Rhodesian government
delegation.   Nkomo then remained abroad through mid-1977, as
the world press openly speculated on the extent of his guerrilla
support in Zambia (see MILITARY FORCES).   In late July he
visited Cuba, where he was thought to be conferring with Fidel
Castro about Cuban arms support for the Zimbabwe liberation
movement.   By late 1977 Nkomo's rivals, Sithole and Muzorewa,
had returned to Salisbury and assumed the role of "moderates,"
while Nkomo was being regarded as a "hardliner."

NKOSI   see   INKOSI

NKULUMANE KHUMALO (variants: Unkulumane; Kuruman; a.k.a.
    "Kanda") (c. 1825-1839?).   An important, but enigmatic figure
    in Ndebele history, Nkulumane was the son of Mzilikazi (q.v.).
    by the latter's "royal" wife (see INKOSIKAZI), who is said to
    have been the daughter of the Ndwandwe king Zwide (q.v.).
    Whatever was Nkulumane's mother's exact identity, Nkulumane
    himself was clearly heir apparent to the Ndebele kingship.   He
    is said to have been named "Nkulumane" in honor of Robert
    Moffat's mission station at Kuruman (qq.v.), but he must have
    been born well before Mzilikazi met Moffat in 1829.

When the Ndebele migrated from the western Transvaal
    to present Matabeleland* in 1838-39, Nkulumane traveled with
    Kaliphi's division (q.v.), arriving there about a year before
    Mzilikazi himself did.   This first group of migrants seems to
    have made Nkulumane king in order to celebrate the inxwala
    (q.v.) in Mzilikazi's absence.   When Mzilikazi finally arrived
    in Matabeleland, he interpreted this action as treasonous and
    had many of the responsible izinduna executed (see NTABAZIN-
    DUNA).   Some traditions hold that Nkulumane escaped, or was
    sent, to Natal.   Others say that he was executed--a fate for
    which Mncumbathe (q.v.) later assumed personal responsibility.
    His fate remained a public secret for three decades.

When Mzilikazi died in 1868 Ndebele leaders still agreed
    that Nkulumane was rightful heir to the kingship, but they dis-
    agreed as to what had become of him.   Nkulumane was rumored
    to be living in Natal, so the first of three delegations went
    there to investigate in December.   Meanwhile, Lobengula (q.v.)
    was put forth as a candidate for the kingship by Mncumbathe.
    The embassy to Natal found an Ndebele man named Kanda in the

employ of Theophilus Shepstone (q.v.), a colonial official. Kanda
initially denied he was the missing heir, but later changed his
story. Shepstone evidently encouraged Kanda to claim that he
was Nkulumane in order to inject Natal's influence into Ndebele
politics. By the end of 1869 most Ndebele leaders concluded
that Kanda was not Nkulumane. Lobengula then became king.

Die-hard Nkulumane supporters, led by Mbigo (q.v.),
resisted Lobengula, but were suppressed in the battle at Zwangendaba (q.v.) in June 1870. Nevertheless, Shepstone provided
Kanda with a wagon and some men a year later, and sent him
to Ngwato (q.v.) country to organize a coup. Kanda was joined
by Mangwane (q.v.)--another disgruntled contender for the king-
ship--who took up the cause of "Nkulumane" to attract support.
In Shoshong the two men obtained military support from Maching
(q.v.), whose own political career contained striking parallels to
that of Kanda. In January 1872 Kanda and Mangwane's invasion
force approached Matabeleland, but the Ngwato pulled out at the
last minute. Mangwane led a handful of Ndebele dissidents into
Ndebele territory, sending out messengers to raise the cry of
revolt in the name of "Nkulumane." A few people responded,
but Lobengula's loyalists easily routed the invaders.

Kanda afterwards retired to Rustenburg in the Transvaal
(q.v.). There he continued to attract anti-Lobengula followers
until his own death in 1883. While it is almost certain that he
was not the true Nkulumane, it is possible that he was in fact
one of Mzilikazi's many sons. Whoever he was, his attempt to
become Ndebele king evidently inspired H. R. Haggard's (q.v.)
character "Umbopa" in King Solomon's Mines.

NKULUNKULU (variant: Unkulunkulu). Nguni* name for their high
god, meaning "greatest of the great." Nkulunkulu has stood at
the top of traditional Ndebele religious beliefs since Mzilikazi
left Zululand. He is a partly anthropomorphic sky god, regarded
as the creator and as the master of nature. Though he is om-
nipresent, he has otiose characteristics which make it necessary
for people to approach him through intermediary ancestor spirits
(see IDLOZI). To a great extent Ndebele concepts of Nkulunkulu
have fused with Sotho concepts of Mlimo (q.v.), for the two
names are now freely interchanged. (See RELIGION--NDEBELE.)

NOE (WANOE; variant: NOHWE) see NHOWE

NOGOMO see NEGOMO

NOMBATI see MNCUMBATHE

NORTHERN GOLDFIELDS. A 19th-century European nickname for
the region between the Gwelo and Hunyani rivers (qq.v.); now
known as the Hartley Goldfields (see GOLD). The name distinguished the region from the southern goldfields around Tati
(q.v.) after old Shona goldworkings were identified in both areas
by Henry Hartley and Karl Mauch (qq.v.) in 1866-67. (See
SOUTH AFRICAN GOLDFIELDS EXPLORATION CO.)

NORTHERN LIGHT GOLD AND EXPLORING COMPANY   see   TATI
    CONCESSION

NORTHERN OPTIMIST.   Original name of the Gwelo Times (q.v.).

NORTHERN RHODESIA.   Name by which Zambia (q.v.) was known
    as a British colony from 1911 to 1964.   From the early 1890s
    to 1911 the BSAC administered the territory as two separate
    units: Northwestern and Northeastern Rhodesia.   When written
    with capital "N's" neither of these terms properly applies to
    areas within present Rhodesia.

NORTON.   Small industrial town just west of Salisbury on the main
    road to Bulawayo (at 17° 53'S, 30° 42'E; alt. 1370 m.).   Norton's
    development has accelerated since the 1950s, when nearby Lake
    McIlwaine was created on the Hunyani River (q.v.).   After
    Kariba Dam (q.v.) was built, Norton became one of the main
    intake points for the country's electrical power (q.v.) network.
    Population in 1969 was 3380 (88% Africans).

NQABA   see NXABA

NSWATUGI CAVE.   Considered one of the finest rock painting (q.v.)
    sites in the country, Nswatugi is located in Matopos National
    Park (q.v.) about six km. southwest of World's View (q.v.).
    The paintings feature particularly fine polychrome pictures of
    giraffes.   Archaeological digs at the site by Neville Jones
    (q.v.) and others have also turned up important late Stone Age
    (q.v.) evidence.

NTABAZIKAMAMBO (variants: Taba Zika Mambo; Thabas-Zi-Ka-
    Mambo; etc.; a.k.a. Manyanga).   Ndebele name for the Changa-
    mire (q.v.) center known to the Rozvi (q.v.) as Manyanga; lo-
    cated in the Mambo Hills (19° 32'S, 29° 4'E), c.40 km. north-
    east of Inyati*, near the Shangani River*.   The site is a large,
    massive granite outcropping with a natural citadel.   It now
    contains some stone walls and the remains of huts, and is a
    National Monument on a private farm.
        Manyanga was one of several main Changamire centers
    (cf. DHLO DHLO; NALATALE) until the 1830s, when Zwangen-
    daba's Ngoni (qq.v.) sacked it and killed the reigning Changa-
    mire, Chirisamhuru (q.v.).   According to one tradition, Chirisa-
    mhuru hurled himself into the Ngoni throng from the citadel when
    his defeat appeared inevitable.   During the 1896 Ndebele Revolt
    (q.v.) the Mambo Hills served as an important refugee hiding
    place until it was overwhelmed by British forces in July.   It
    has been argued that Mkwati (q.v.) established a Mwari (q.v.)
    cult shrine there just before the Revolt, but this view has been
    recently challenged.

NTABAZINDUNA (variants: Thabas Induna; Intaba Yezinduna; etc.).
    The "Hill of the Indunas," Ntabazinduna is a prominent, flat-
    topped kopje (q.v.) near the source of the Bembezi River*,

northeast of modern Bulawayo (at 20° 2'S, 28° 51'E). It has apparently long been used as a lookout point, and was known to the Rozvi (q.v.) as Dombo ro Mambo ("Mambo's Rock"). Since the mid-19th century the hill has held an important, but unclear, place in Ndebele tradition. It is known that when Mzilikazi (q.v.) belatedly rejoined his people in Matabeleland after migrating from the Transvaal, he found his son Nkulumane (q.v.) installed as acting king in his place (c.1839). He responded to this situation by having many dissident izinduna (see INDUNA) executed. According to some traditions the izinduna were hurled off the hill which thus bears their name; however, the sides of the hill are insufficiently precipitous for such a method of execution. Other traditions hold merely that the izinduna were tried atop the hill, and that they were executed elsewhere. (See also MOFFAT MYTH.)

NTHUMBANE (variant: Entumbani). Kopje* on the northern fringe of the Matopo Hills* (at 20° 23'S, 28° 36'E) in which the body of Mzilikazi (q.v.) was interred in November 1868, several months after his death. During the midst of the 1896 Revolt (q.v.) Mzilikazi's grandson Nyamanda (q.v.) was made king there by fellow rebels. Later during the Revolt British soldiers desecrated the tomb, angering Cecil Rhodes, who had the site repaired and resanctified with oxen sacrifices. Nthumbane is now a National Monument (cf. MZILIKAZI MEMORIAL). Rhodes himself is said to have selected World's View (q.v.) for his own grave partly because of its nearness to Mzilikazi's tomb.

NUANETSI DISTRICT. A little-developed region in the Victoria Province (q.v.), covering 20,765 sq. km. between the Bubye and Lundi Rivers (qq.v.). The district was originally part of the once huge Chibi District (q.v.), which now touches Nuanetsi only at the latter's northern boundary. Nuanetsi also borders Chiredzi along the northeast; Mozambique along the southeast; Beitbridge on the southwest; and Gwanda and Belingwe (qq.v.) on the west. Most of the central part of the district is reserved for Europeans (see LAND TENURE ACT), while Gona-re-Zhou Game Reserve (q.v.) takes up most of the southeast. District headquarters are at Nuanetsi, located on the main road between Beitbridge and Ft. Victoria (at 21° 25'S, 30° 44'E). Just to the north of Nuanetsi is Rutenga (q.v.), another important center. Population of the district in 1969 was just under 79,000, all but 500 of whom were Africans.

NUANETSI RIVER (Shona variant: Munetsi). Rising on the Central Plateau* near Lancaster (20° 13'S, 29° 18'E), the Nuanetsi flows generally southeast through the district of the same name, joining the Limpopo in Mozambique. Nuanetsi village stands where the river is crossed by the main road between Beitbridge and Ft. Victoria.

NXABA MSANE (variants: Nqaba; Ngabe; a.k.a. Mpakana; Mpanka; Nyaba; Sikwanda) (fl.1820s-c.1840). Ngoni (q.v.) migration

leader. Originally a hereditary clan chief in northern Natal,
Nxaba became one of the many Nguni leaders to leave South
Africa during the Mfecane wars (q.v.). His career is imper-
fectly known. He appears to have led his followers through the
eastern Transvaal into southern Mozambique in c. 1822. He
possibly clashed with Mzilikazi's Ndebele along the way. He
later allied with the Maseko Ngoni (q.v.) while raiding Portuguese posts along the coast. In the early 1830s he seems to
have been defeated by the Gaza king Soshangane (q.v.) just before entering Mashonaland*. There he operated as a roving
predator among the Shona until 1835, when he clashed with
Zwangendaba's Ngoni (qq.v.), who then crossed the Zambezi
River. Nxaba appears then to have separated from the Maseko
and to have returned to the east coast, where he attacked Sofala*. By about 1840 he had again moved inland, this time as
far north as Barotseland in western Zambia. He arrived there
about the same time as Sebitwane's Kololo (qq.v.). His following was broken up by the Kololo, and he himself seems to have
been drowned by the Lozi (q.v.).

NXWALA. Spelling variant of inxwala (q.v.), whose proper radical
is -xwala, not -nxwala.

NYAI (variant plurals: Banyai; Manyai; Vanyai). A term used for
so many sub-groups of Shona throughout the country that it is
practically a synonym for "Shona" (q.v.). One more specific
application is, however, important. Shona chiefdoms of the
Karanga (q.v.) dialect cluster in the southeastern part of the
country came to be known as the Vanyai ("Banyai" to Europeans)
by the late 19th century. Their region thus came to be known
as "Banyailand" (see ADENDORFF TREK).

NYAMANDA LOBENGULA KHUMALO (c. 1873-1925). Son of the
Ndebele king Lobengula (q.v.) by the latter's wife Mbida Mk-
wanansi. Apparently Lobengula's favorite son, Nyamanda was
by the early 1890s the strongest candidate for succession to the
kingship in the absence of any sons by Lobengula's "great wife"
Xwalile (q.v.). Nyamanda's cause was championed by another,
and influential, wife of Lobengula, Lozigeyi (q.v.).
    During the 1896 Ndebele Revolt (q.v.) Nyamanda, his
younger brother Shakalisa, and Lozigeyi became the main
leaders of the northern rebels, establishing their headquarters
by the middle Bembezi River*. On June 15, 1896, Nyamanda
was installed as Ndebele king at Nthumbane (q.v.) by a group
of powerful izinduna including Babayane, Sikombo, Dhliso, Mlugulu, and others (qq.v.). After the Revolt collapsed, Nyamanda
surrendered to the British in December, and was made a government chief in January 1897. Later, however, the BSAC government deposed him, leaving him with neither a position nor land.
His presumptive status as Ndebele king was ignored by the
government, and other Ndebele leaders turned away from him
in favor of Njube and Nguboyenja (qq.v.) in the hope of finding
a more acceptable candidate for the kingship. Nyamanda

nevertheless started the Matabele (National) Home Movement
(q. v.) during the First World War to push for an Ndebele national homeland and for restoration of the kingship. He was
aided by South African political activists, including members
of AMEC, the South African ANC, and local Mfengu (qq. v.).
From 1919 to 1921 Nyamanda spearheaded an aggressive
campaign to secure British government recognition of Ndebele
grievances, but his efforts were futile in the face of local and
British concern with the larger questions of the constitutional
status of Southern Rhodesia after the demise of BSAC rule in
1923 (see RESPONSIBLE GOVERNMENT). In his last years
Nyamanda became an active member of RBVA (q. v.).

NYAMANDHLOVU DISTRICT. Western district, covering 12, 590
sq. km. in Matabeleland North Province (q. v.). The Nata
River* separates the district from Bulalima-Mangwe District--
from which it was divided in 1910--on the south. Bulawayo
and Bubi Districts border it on the east; Lupane and Wankie
(qq. v.) on the north. The district is little developed, with
agriculture, livestock, and timber its main industries. Its administrative center is the village of Nyamandhlovu (at 19° 52'S,
28° 16'E; alt. 1220 m.). Sawmills (q. v.) is another important
center. Under the Land Tenure Act (q. v.), the western part
of the district is Tribal Trust Land, and the east is reserved
for Europeans. Population of the district in 1969 was 78, 460.
The name of the district is taken from an Ndebele ibutho* (see
MPOTSHWANA).

NYAMAZANA (variant: Nyamabezana) (fl. 1830s-1890s). Ngoni
(q. v.) migration leader and wife of Mzilikazi (q. v.). According
to tradition, Nyamazana was the niece of the Ngoni king Zwangendaba (q. v.), from whom she separated with a small band of
followers when most of the Ngoni crossed the Zambezi River
into Zambia in 1835. She led her band from place to place in
Shona territory, until encountering an impi* of the recently-
arrived Ndebele in c. 1840. Nyamazana's people then were
absorbed into the Ndebele and she became one of Mzilikazi's
wives.
        Little is known about Nyamazana's subsequent life until
the 1896 Revolt (q. v.), in which her son Nyanda Khumalo was
an important leader. In August 1896 she met C. J. Rhodes
(q. v.) and helped to arrange his peace negotiations with the
Matopos rebels (see also "INDABA"; GROOTBOOM, J.). Rhodes
is said to have so greatly admired her that he afterwards kept
her photograph mounted in his bedroom.
        (N. B.: an unrelated man named Nyamazana was a promi-
nent vassal of Sikombo [q. v.] until he was killed by his master
around April 1896.)

NYAMBO KAPARARIDZE (c. 1580s-?1652). The son of Gatsi Rusere
(q. v.), Nyambo was the last member of the house of Neshangwe
(q. v.) to hold the Munhumutapa kingship (q. v.). He became the
Munhumutapa in 1623, devoting his brief reign to holding onto

his position. A year later he had to put down a revolt of his
own brothers. He then had to deal with rival claimants supported by the Portuguese (q.v.), who were dissatisfied with
Gatsi Rusere's cession of mines in 1607. In 1628 a general
war with the Portuguese broke out. In May 1629 a combined
Portuguese-African army ousted Nyambo from power and replaced him with Mavura II (q.v.). Nyambo spent the remainder
of his life trying to regain power.

NYANDA see NEHANDA and under NYAMAZANA

NYANDORO (a.k.a. Kunzwi, or Kunzwi-Nyandoro) (fl.c.1860s-1915).
It is not clear whether Nyandoro was the first ruler of his
chiefdom, or if "Nyandoro" was a dynastic title shared by a
predecessor. In any case, Nyandoro was a member of the
Pfumbe branch of the Korekore (q.v.) cluster of Shona from
northern Mrewa District* who moved into central Zezuru (q.v.)
territory and established a strong independent chiefdom in the
mid-19th century. His people became known as Tsunga. During
the 1860s he was repeatedly attacked by the Ndebele and forced
to move about frequently. By the 1870s his people were living
just west of the Mangwende's (q.v.) country in the southern
Mrewa District. There he established a stronghold on a naturally fortified hill and armed his men well with guns obtained
from dealings with Manuel de Sousa (q.v.) in the 1880s.
    When the British occupied Mashonaland in the 1890s,
Nyandoro maintained cordial relations with individual Europeans,
but refused to acknowledge British sovereignty. From October
1895 until the outbreak of the 1896 Revolt (q.v.) he successfully resisted British efforts to collect hut tax payments. His
defiance is regarded as the first signal of the impending Revolt,
in which he played a prominent part. During the Revolt he held
his position for an entire year until a massive British assault
on June 19, 1897, drove him into flight. He then lived as a
refugee, finally surrendering at the end of August. Afterwards
he retained both his chiefship and his prestige among neighboring
Shona. The British watched him suspiciously. Around 1907 his
people were moved to the Marandellas District*, where his successors are still called Nyandoro.

NYANDORO, GEORGE BODZO (b.Oct. 8, 1926). Nationalist leader.
Born in the Marandellas District*, Nyandoro is the grandson of
the famous 1896 Revolt leader, Chief Nyandoro (q.v.). His
family is noted for its tradition of resistance to European rule.
His father was deposed as government chief in 1946 for criti-
cizing the government. Nyandoro himself taught briefly in the
mid-1940s and then became active in both Charles Mzingeli's
and Benjamin Burombo's (qq.v.) quasi-political movements. In
1952 he became provisional secretary of the All-African Convention (q.v.), and he helped to found the Youth League (q.v.) three
years later. He played a leading role in organizing farmers for
both the Youth League and African National Congress (q.v.) until
he was imprisoned during the government sweep of ANC leaders

in February 1959. After his release in 1963 he joined Joshua
Nkomo in the PCC (qq. v.), and then based himself in Lusaka,
Zambia as a ZAPU official. He left ZAPU in 1970 and helped
James Chikerema to found FROLIZI (qq. v.) the following year.
In 1975 he became closely identified with Abel Muzorewa (q. v.)
in the ANC.

NYANGWE FORT. Most famous example of a class of massively-
    built stone enclosures characteristic of the Inyanga Ruins (q. v.).
    The structure stands atop Nyangwe Hill, beside the Mare River
    in the center of Inyanga National Park (at 18° 17'S, 32° 47'E;
    alt. 2025 m.). The ruin features crude, but massive stone
    work, many lintelled entrances, "loopholes," and parapets. In
    common with other such "forts," Nyangwe is believed to have
    been used as a look-out point and refuge from about the late 16th
    century.

NYASHANU. Dynastic title of the rulers of an important Hera (q. v.)
    chiefdom in the present Buhera District*.

NYATSIME COLLEGE. African secondary school and technical col-
    lege stressing business education; founded in 1960. Located at
    Seki, just south of Salisbury.

NYIKA. Chishona* term for "country" or "territory"; used particu-
    larly for the territory of a chiefdom, or for the chiefdom itself.
    For Nyika people, see MANYIKA.

NYORA. Cicatrization marks, or "tattoos," once commonly made
    on Shona youths.

                                - O -

OCCUPATION DAY. Former name of Pioneer Day (q. v.).

OCCUPATION (BRITISH) OF MASHONALAND see PIONEER
    COLUMN

OCCUPATION (BRITISH) OF MATABELELAND see NDEBELE WAR

ODZANI RIVER. Rises in the hills north of Umtali (q. v.), whence
    it flows west into the Odzi River (q. v.). A dam on the Odzani
    forms Lake Alexander (alt. 1615 m.), which supplies Umtali's
    municipal water. The lake is the largest stretch of bilharzia-
    free (q. v.) water in the country. Below the lake are the Od-
    zani Falls (18° 46'S, 32° 42'E).

ODZI. Town located 32 km. west of Umtali on the Salisbury road;
    the center of a tobacco and mixed agriculture region (at 18° 58'S,
    32° 23'E; alt. 960 m.).

ODZI RIVER. One of the main tributaries of the Sabi River (q. v.), the Odzi flows south from the Inyanga Mountains (q. v.).

OFFICER ADMINISTERING THE GOVERNMENT (OAG). Office
    created by the Rhodesian Front government shortly after UDI
    in 1965. In the revised 1965 Constitution (q. v.) the OAG was
    given virtually the same functions as the British governor
    (q. v.) had held under the 1961 Constitution. The OAG theo-
    retically represented the British Crown, but was not so ac-
    knowledged by the British government. In 1970 the OAG be-
    came the President (q. v.) under a republican constitution.
    Clifford Dupont (q. v.) was the only person to hold the office.

OLD UMTALI. Located just northwest of present Umtali (q. v.), to
    which its original European settlers were removed in 1896 when
    the Beira railway line (qq. v.) opened. In 1898 the BSAC ad-
    ministration granted the site of "Old Umtali" and its buildings
    to American missionaries of the Methodist Episcopal Church
    (see UNITED METHODIST CHURCH). The Methodists made the
    town their headquarters and established a lay theological training
    center there.

OMAY RIVER (variant: Ume) see BUMI RIVER

"OPERATION NOAH." Project undertaken to rescue animals from
    the Zambezi Valley when the waters of Lake Kariba (q. v.) began
    to rise in 1959. Thousands of animals were boated or forced
    to swim from newly-created islands to the mainland.

"OPERATION SUNRISE." Government code name for the arrest of
    about 500 African National Congress (q. v.) leaders on the morn-
    ing of February 26, 1959.

OPHIR. Ancient Biblical country said to be rich in gold and con-
    nected with Solomon and Sheba. Though Ophir is now thought
    to have been located in southwestern Arabia, its whereabouts
    were long the subject of intense speculation. Incredibly, the
    notion that Ophir lay within present Rhodesia has played a role
    in the country's history since the 16th century, when Muslim
    (q. v.) traders introduced the idea to the Portuguese (q. v.). The
    idea gained currency as more was learned about Shona stone
    ruins (q. v.) and the gold (q. v.) trade through Sofala (q. v.),
    which itself has been equated with "Ophir." When John Milton
    wrote Paradise Lost in the 1660s, he included a passage linking
    Sofala with Ophir. The idea was revived in the 1860s when the
    German missionary Alexander Merensky (q. v.) began circulating
    the first European reports of the Zimbabwe Ruins (q. v.). Me-
    rensky popularized the expression "King Solomon's Mines,"
    which was picked up by H. R. Haggard (q. v.). Early European
    investigations of Great Zimbabwe led to further speculations
    about the ruins' having ancient Near Eastern origins (see ZIM-
    BABWE CONTROVERSY). Cecil Rhodes accepted these inter-
    pretations, and his BSAC promoted the idea that Mashonaland*
    was indeed "Ophir" in order to attract prospectors and settlers.

Some Europeans thought that Mount Pfuru (see DARWIN) was Ophir itself. All subsequent scientific archaeological investigations discredited such ideas, however.

OSTRICHES. These giant flightless birds are now rarely seen outside of the country's national parks and game reserves (qq. v.), but they once pervaded the country's semi-arid savanna* regions. Early San (q. v.) inhabitants used ostrich egg shells as water containers and as painting surfaces (see ROCK PAINTINGS). They also made necklace beads from shell fragments--a practice adopted by later Bantu-speaking inhabitants. Early Shona states (q. v.) traded both ostrich shell fragments and ostrich feathers. In the 19th century the Ndebele made extensive use of ostrich plumes in their headdresses and robes. An export trade developed when ostrich plumes became fashionable in Europe. This trade peaked in the early 1880s, when European prices were at their highest.

OTTO BEIT BRIDGE. Spans the Zambezi River, just above the Kafue confluence, at the village of Chirundu (q. v.). Named after Otto Beit (1865-1930), a younger brother of Alfred Beit (q. v.), the bridge was opened in mid-1939. (Cf. BEITBRIDGE.)

OX-WAGONS (a. k. a. trek wagons). Principle transport vehicles used by European and Griqua traders, missionaries, and immigrants in the 19th century. These heavily-built wagons were developed in South Africa by Afrikaner (q. v.) farmers, and they cost from £80 to £300 new. Essentially tented-boxes on wheels --similar to American "covered wagons"--ox-wagons were typically pulled by spans of twelve oxen, requiring three-man crews. Carrying capacities were limited; locomotion was slow; routes were circumscribed by terrain, seasonal conditions, and availability of fodder; and oxen were highly vulnerable to local diseases (see HEALTH). Nevertheless, the wagons served as the main means of carriage in the country from the 1860s until the development of railways (q. v.) in the 1890s. The Ndebele kings owned some wagons from the 1830s, but these were mainly for their own personal use, and wheeled transportation played an insignificant role in African transportation generally. (See also HUNTERS' ROAD; TRANSPORT.)

- P -

PAGE, GERTRUDE (Mrs. Alexander Dobbin) (1873-April 1, 1922). English-born writer. Page came to Salisbury with her Irish husband around the turn of the century. There she wrote a series of popular novels dealing with local rural life which made the country better known in England. Her books included Love in the Wilderness (1907), Paddy-the-Next-Best-Thing (1908), Edge o' Beyond (1908), Jill's Rhodesian Philosophy (1910), and The Rhodesian (1912). In 1911 she was officially honored as the colony's best publicist in England, where her books sold

well. In other writings she condemned forced recruitment of
African labor, and supported women's suffrage. (See also
LITERATURE; WOMEN'S FRANCHISE ORDINANCE.)

PAGET, EDWARD FRANCIS (July 8, 1886-April 21, 1971). Anglican
(q. v.) cleric. Born in England, Paget came to South Africa in
1914. In 1925 he was made Bishop of the Church of England's
Diocese of Southern Rhodesia. When the Province of Central
Africa was created in 1955, he became its first archbishop.
Two years later he retired to Natal, where he later died.

PAINTINGS see ROCK PAINTINGS

PANDAMATENGA (variant: Panda-Ma-Tenga). Small post on the
Botswana border (qq. v.), located just west of the town of Wankie
(q. v.). It was established near the site of a trading station of
the same name founded by George Westbeech (q. v.) in 1871 (at
18° 30'S, 25° 40'E).

PARIRENYATWA, STEPHEN (b. 1925). A first cousin of Tichafa
Parirenyatwa (q. v.); has been an active member of ZAPU, PCC,
FROLIZI, and ANC since 1962.

PARIRENYATWA, TICHAFA SAMUEL ("Pari") (1927-Aug. 14, 1962).
Trained in medicine in Johannesburg, Parirenyatwa became
Southern Rhodesia's first African doctor in 1957. After working
briefly as a government medical officer at Antelope Mine (q. v.),
he entered private practice in Harare (q. v.). There he became
politically active. He was a close associate of Joshua Nkomo,
serving as the latter's deputy after the formation of ZAPU in
1962. A vastly popular leader, he was considered a prime contender for top political leadership in the nationalist movement
until he was killed in a car accident while driving from Salisbury
to Bulawayo to meet with Nkomo. An official government commission of inquiry ruled his death accidental, but many Africans
believed he had been murdered by whites. His funeral drew
enormous crowds. In death he became a figure of legendary
stature.

PARLIAMENT. The country's Legislative Assembly (q. v.) was
formally designated "Parliament" after UDI in 1965. Prior to
UDI the term "parliament" applied properly only in the generic
sense of a legislative session, although members of the Assembly styled themselves "Members of Parliament" as early as
1933. The Constitution of 1969 (q. v.) made Parliament bicameral. The main body became the House of Assembly, and the
Senate was created as an upper chamber (qq. v.), following the
South African system.

"PARTNERSHIP." Concept articulated by European politicians--es-
pecially Godfrey Huggins (q. v.)--during the 1950s as the goal of
Federation (q. v.). The term "partnership" was meant to imply
an equality of African and European responsibilities and benefits,

but to Africans it came to symbolize European hypocrisy because
real political and economic power lay almost entirely in European hands.

PASIPAMIRE.   Most famous of the Chaminuka mediums (q.v.).

PASS LAWS.   The BSAC administration issued the first pass law in
1892 to control African entry into Salisbury.   Over the next
decade similar laws were refined and extended throughout the
country.   Initially, the pass system was used to enable police
identification of suspects, to facilitate labor recruitment, and
to provide a means of checking on individual tax payments.
With the passage of time, however, the system was used increasingly as a means of maintaining racial segregation, particularly in the towns.   Adult males have been required to carry
an assortment of documents, of which the most important has
been the registration certificate, or book, known to Africans as
the "Situpa" (q.v.).   Men have been required to produce these
documents to any policemen demanding to see them.   Failure to
carry the correct documents has always been a criminal offense,
punishable by fines or imprisonment.   Reform or abolition of
the pass laws was a primary goal of the earliest African nationalist movements.   In 1936 Godfrey Huggins (q.v.) personally
introduced the Native Registration Act which required men in
towns to obtain additional documentation certifying they were
employed or seeking employment.   Later legislation modified
many rules, but the basic requirement that all adult African
males carry registration certificates at all times has not yet
been changed.

PATRICK, MOTHER   see   COSGRAVE, MARY ANN

"PATRIOTIC FRONT" (PF).   Political alliance between Joshua Nkomo
and Robert Mugabe (qq.v.), announced in mid-October 1976, on
the eve of the Geneva Conference (q.v.).   The PF, which excluded Ndabaningi Sithole and Abel Muzorewa (qq.v.), was denounced as a "Marxist-indoctrinated minority" by Ian Smith's
government, which has refused to negotiate with its leaders
through 1977.   In January 1977 the PF was endorsed as the
primary Zimbabwe nationalist body by the "Frontline Presidents" (q.v.) and by the Liberation Committee of the Organization of African Unity.   In July 1977 the general conference of
the OAU at Libreville, Gabon endorsed the PF as the sole legitimate Zimbabwe liberation organization.   PF leaders claimed
to control most of the nationalist guerrillas fighting from bases
in Mozambique and Zambia, but other nationalist leaders disputed this claim.   At the same time, the degree of cooperation
between the PF's main leaders remained unclear through 1977.

PATTERSON INCIDENT (1878).   In 1877 Captain R. Robert Patter-
son of the British army took a leave to hunt in South Africa.
He arrived in the Transvaal* shortly after its annexation by the
British Crown, and was there prevailed upon by Theophilus

Shepstone (q.v.) to investigate charges of Ndebele mistreatment
of British travelers in Matabeleland. Patterson's semi-official
embassy arrived in Bulawayo in late August 1878. There Patterson alarmed the Ndebele king Lobengula by hinting that the
British might support the cause of the royal pretender "Nkulumane" (q.v.). Lobengula nevertheless permitted Patterson to
continue north to hunt by the Victoria Falls, and provided him
with a 20-man escort.

About a month later Patterson, two European companions,
two African employees and five of the Ndebele guides perished
at the lower Gwaai River*. The returning Ndebele reported that
the others had died after drinking from a waterhole poisoned by
San (q.v.) hunters. Lobengula would not allow other Europeans
to investigate the scene of death, and he denied any personal
responsibility in the affair. British Transvaal authorities
claimed that Patterson's party had been murdered on Lobengula's orders, but the missionary T. M. Thomas (q.v.)--whose
own son was among the dead--supported Lobengula's claims.
H. R. Haggard (q.v.) and others agitated for British retribution
against the Ndebele, but the dispute was ignored when Afrikaners
arose to challenge British rule in the Transvaal a few years
later.

The Patterson Incident was the only instance in the history
of the Ndebele kingdom in which peaceful white travelers may
have been killed by the Ndebele. Historians now tend to accept
Ndebele responsibility for the deaths, but the question of Lobengula's part in the incident has remained a lively issue to the
present day.

PAULING, GEORGE (Sept. 1854-Feb. 10, 1919). British railroad
contractor. Pauling came to South Africa in 1875 and worked
on government railroads there until becoming an independent
contractor. After meeting Cecil Rhodes in 1891 he directed the
construction of most of present Rhodesia's early railway (q.v.)
lines. In the late 1890s he held several major posts in the
BSAC administration at Salisbury.

PAVER BROTHERS see under AFRICAN NEWSPAPERS, LTD.

PEARCE COMMISSION (1972). British government body commissioned to investigate the acceptability of Anglo-Rhodesian settlement proposals in early 1972. After the failed "Fearless Talks"
(q.v.) of October 1968, the governments of Britain and Rhodesia
did not attempt formally to resolve their constitutional dispute
over UDI (q.v.) until early 1971, when British officials began
holding secret talks with Rhodesian officials in Salisbury. By
September news of these talks was public, and Lord Goodman
was openly visiting Rhodesia as a special emissary. In mid-
November Alec Douglas Home, British Foreign Secretary and
former Prime Minister, met with Ian Smith in Salisbury. On
November 24 these two men signed an agreement which came
to be known as the Anglo-Rhodesian Settlement Proposals.

These new proposals were widely seen as a significant

British retreat from the "Five Principles" (q.v.) articulated six years earlier. The proposals called for immediately increased African representation in Parliament (q.v.), and they contained complex formulae which would theoretically bring majority rule to the country. Sceptics noted that even under the best of circumstances this transformation could not occur until well into the 21st century. In the meantime the Rhodesian government was to be recognized. In contrast to earlier British settlement proposals, the 1971 agreement was based upon modification of the Constitution (q.v.) of 1969, not that of 1961. The Rhodesian government promised to work to end racial discrimination, to review the cases of political prisoners, and to promote certain advances in African economic welfare, but it was required neither to abrogate existing discriminatory laws, nor to make guarantees against future retrogressive constitutional amendments. Britain did hold firm on one crucial principle--that the proposals undergo a "test of acceptability" by the people of Rhodesia as a whole before they would be implemented. The prevailing British mood was that the proposals represented the last chance for a graceful withdrawal from the country's responsibility for Rhodesia. The House of Commons approved the proposals by a 297 to 269 vote on December 1, 1971, and a commission was created to investigate the question of the proposals' acceptability in Rhodesia.

Lord Edward Pearce, a former High Court judge with no African experience, was named to head the 24-man commission. His deputies were Sir Maurice Dorman, ex-governor of Sierra Leone; Sir Glyn Jones, ex-governor of Nyasaland (Malawi); and Lord Harlech, former ambassador to the United States (a fourth deputy, Sir Frederick Pedler, withdrew before the commission began its work). The other commissioners were all Europeans with former African colonial backgrounds.

The Pearce Commission arrived in Rhodesia in the third week of January 1972. Since the Rhodesian government refused to allow a public referendum on the proposals, the Commission sampled public opinion through public and private meetings, and by correspondence. It canvassed the country for two months, completing its work on March 10, and issuing its formal report (Cmnd. 4964) in late May. The Commission reported wide acceptance of the proposals among European Rhodesians, mixed reactions among Asians and Coloureds, and 97% negative responses from the more than 100,000 Africans polled. Because of the overall numerical preponderance of Africans in the country's population (q.v.), the Commission concluded that the people of the country as a whole rejected the proposals, which were then officially abandoned by Britain.

Creation of the Commission set off a dramatic mobilization of African political activity. The African National Council (q.v.) was formed in December 1971 in order to organize opposition to the proposals. Although growth of the ANC was largely spontaneous, the ANC itself was generally credited with eliciting the successful African opposition. Spontaneous mass demonstrations occurred frequently in urban centers. These occasionally grew unruly, bringing down severe police reprisals. The police killed a few dozen demonstrators--mainly in Gwelo--and arrested more than a thousand political leaders, including the Chinamanos and Judith and Garfield Todd (qq. v.). The Rhodesian government charged that subversive elements were coercing Africans into rejecting the proposals, but African opposition appeared both natural and universal. Most African Members of Parliament and almost half of all government chiefs openly voiced opposition to the proposals, though both groups were noted for their support of the white government.

Charges and counter-charges continued long after the Commission published its report, but the unmistakable finding of the Commission was that almost all Africans deeply distrusted the existing Rhodesian government. The whole episode brought Rhodesia back to the center of world attention, and it started a new era in African nationalist political activity within the country. The ANC evolved into a permanent political body. Some of its leaders continued to conduct private consultations with Smith's government in order to bring about a constitutional change, but external bodies such as ZANU and ZAPU (qq.v.) instead committed themselves to violent overthrow of the regime. Late 1972 thus saw the launching of a long civil war (see MILITARY FORCES).

PENHALONGA. Town near the Mozambique border (at 18° 53'S, 32° 41'E), about 10 km. north of Umtali*. The town arose by the Penhalonga gold mine, which was named after a Portuguese count when it was started by British prospectors in 1889. The nearby Rezende Mine was also started at the same time. In mid-1891 Bishop Knight-Bruce (q. v.) founded the St. Augustine Mission in Penhalonga, thereby starting Anglican mission work in the country. The local gold mines were largely worked out early in the 20th century, and the area is now a diverse agricultural region. Population of the town in 1969 was 1870 (including 92% Africans).

PENNEFATHER, EDWARD GRAHAM (Feb. 12, 1850-April 29, 1928). British army officer, with experience in Zululand and Botswana during the 1880s. When the British South African Police (q. v.) were formed in 1890, Pennefather became their first commander, as a brevet lieutenant-colonel. He then assumed overall command of the Pioneer Column (q. v.) when it occupied Mashonaland. During the Column's march into the country he selected the sites of four forts which developed into the towns of Tuli, Ft. Victoria, Charter, and Salisbury (qq. v.). After the BSAP's manpower was sharply curtailed in late 1891, Pennefather resigned his command and returned to his South African regiment.

PEOPLE'S CARETAKER COUNCIL (PCC). Interim African political party formed by Joshua Nkomo's loyal ZAPU (qq. v.) supporters in August 1963, soon after the formation of the rival ZANU (q. v.). Nkomo was imprisoned in April 1964 and the PCC was banned by the government on August 26, 1964. PCC leaders then regrouped in Lusaka, Zambia, where they later reconstituted the Council as ZAPU.

PETROGLYPHS. Although there are vast numbers of rock paintings (q.v.) throughout the country, only about ten petroglyph, or rock engraving, sites have been found. The most sophisticated of these is a finely-carved representation of a giraffe, located just off the Bulawayo road about 32 km. north of Beitbridge*. Crudely engraved representations of animal spoor (q.v.) have been found at Bumbuzi (q.v.) in Wankie District. All of these petroglyphs are ascribed to Stone Age (q.v.) peoples of undetermined antiquity. In addition, pecked etchings, apparently of village plans, have been found near Melsetter*, but these are attributed to Iron Age (q.v.) peoples.

PFUMBI   see   MATIBI

PHILLIPS, GEORGE ARTHUR (c.1837-1896). English hunter and trader. Phillips arrived in Matabeleland in 1864, living there most of the time until his retirement in 1890. In 1868 he entered a trading partnership with George Westbeech (q.v.). Westbeech worked out of the Zambezi basin, while Phillips worked out of Matabeleland. Phillips became an intimate friend of the Ndebele king Lobengula, and is regarded as one of the latter's strongest Westernizing influences. A ruin at Zimbabwe (q.v.) was later named after Phillips.

"PIONEER." This term is used in two distinct senses. (1) European traders, hunters, missionaries, and explorers who entered the country before 1880. (2) Europeans who settled in the country during the 1890s.

PIONEER COLUMN (1890). Collective name for the British forces which occupied Mashonaland (q.v.) in late 1890. The Column was assembled in mid-1890, after L. S. Jameson (q.v.) persuaded the Ndebele king Lobengula to modify his repudiation of the Rudd Concession (q.v.). The Column comprised three main components: (1) The "Pioneer Corps" of 212 men (mainly South African whites), recruited and organized by Frank Johnson (q.v.), who acted as a private contractor for Cecil Rhodes. Most of these men were given military ranks and assigned to three "troops." F. C. Selous (q.v.) served as chief scout. Other civilians included L. S. Jameson and Archibald Colquhoun (q.v.). (2) Five hundred members of the British South African Police (q.v.) commanded by Lt.-Col. E. G. Pennefather (q.v.), who was also overall commander of the Column. This group was heavily armed in anticipation of attack by the Ndebele. (3) About 200 Ngwato (q.v.) mercenaries led by the brother of Khama III (q.v.).
        The Column entered present Rhodesia from eastern Botswana at the end of June 1890. It followed a gently curving route to the northeast, skirting the southeastern fringes of the Ndebele kingdom's domain. Along the way it built and garrisoned forts

at Tuli, Ft. Victoria, Charter, and Salisbury (qq.v.), where it halted on September 12, 1890. The Column was disbanded on September 30th, after a fort was completed at Salisbury. Most of its members dispersed to prospect for gold. In addition to daily wages, the members of the "Pioneer Corps" were rewarded with 1210-hectare (3000-acre) farms and 15 gold claims each; the police got 1640-hectare (4500-acre) farms.

So as not to compromise British claims of Ndebele sovereignty over Mashonaland--upon which the British right of occupation was allegedly based through the Rudd Concession--the occupation was carried out without reference to the rights of the Shona, with the exception of the Manyika ruler Mutasa (q.v.). While the Column was advancing into Mashonaland, the Ndebele prepared for war, but no armed conflict developed. The Shona, apparently unaware of the British intention to occupy their country permanently, did not forcibly resist until the Revolt of 1896 (q.v.).

PIONEER DAY. Rhodesian public holiday commemorating the Pioneer Column's (q.v.) occupation of Mashonaland on September 12. The holiday was created as "Occupation Day" in 1920, and was renamed in 1961. (See HOLIDAYS.)

PIT STRUCTURES (a.k.a. pit circles; pit dwellings; etc.) see STONE-LINED PITS

PLUMER, HERBERT CHARLES ONSLOW (March 13, 1857-July 16, 1932). British army officer of 20 years' experience and the rank of colonel when he was asked to recruit and to train the Matabeleland Relief Force (q.v.) in 1896. Under his command the MRF arrived at Bulawayo on May 14, 1896, becoming the first unit of British Imperial troops to fight in the Ndebele Revolt (q.v.). Plumer's arrival ended the first phase of the Revolt, shifting the Ndebele mainly to the defensive. Under F. Carrington's (q.v.) overall command Plumer engaged in considerable action during the war. Four years later he commanded the Rhodesia Regiment (q.v.) which relieved Baden-Powell (q.v.) at Mafeking in the South African War (q.v.). In 1919 Plumer was made viscount in recognition of his services as general of the British Second Army in France during the First World War.

PLUMTREE. Southwestern border town, established on the main railway line and road from Francistown* in Botswana (at 20° 29'S, 27° 49'E; alt. 1385 m.). The town is the administrative center for the Bulalima-Mangwe District (q.v.), as well as commercial center for an extensive cattle raising region. Population in 1969 was 2040 (68% Africans; 30% Europeans).

POLICE see BRITISH SOUTH AFRICA POLICE; see also MILITARY FORCES

POLITICAL PARTIES see under names of individual organizations

POMONGWE CAVE. An important Stone Age (q.v.) site, Pomongwe
Cave once contained the most easily accessible rock paintings
(q.v.) in the Matopo Hills* (at 20° 33'S, 28° 31'E). During the
early 1970s the paintings were mostly destroyed in an unsuccessful attempt at permanent preservation.

POPULATION/CENSUSES. Until recently European political and
economic dominance has given Rhodesia the misleading appearance of an ethnically well-mixed country. However, the country's most striking demographic fact is the overwhelming numerical preponderance of black Africans. More than 95% of the
population is black, and this figure is steadily rising. During
the 1970s the natural rate of African population increase has
been about 3.6% per annum, against about 1.1% for the Europeans, whose net migration is now negative. Rhodesia is thus
essentially a black African country, and is becoming ever more
so.

    The first government census was taken in 1901, but only
the settler population was counted (see EUROPEANS). The
African population was merely estimated, at 500,000. Formal
censuses of the European population were thereafter periodically
taken, and increasingly precise estimates of the African population were made. A sample formal census of Africans was
undertaken in 1948, but the first full African census was not
taken until 1962. The last full national census was taken in
1969. (The 1969 figures are used throughout this book, except
where authoritative, recent estimates are available for towns.)
According to government estimates and censuses, the African
population first exceeded one million in 1930; two million in
1950; and three million in the late 1950s. The 1969 census
enumerated 4,818,000 Africans, 228,044 Europeans, and 23,525
Asians and Coloured people (qq.v.) in a total population of
5,069,570. Government figures for the end of 1975 estimated
a total population of 6,418,900 people, including 6,100,000 Africans and 278,000 Europeans.

    Although the African population as a whole is much less
urbanized (see URBANIZATION) than is the European, Africans
greatly outnumber Europeans in all areas, including those reserved for Europeans by the Land Tenure Act (q.v.). The ratio
of Africans to Europeans in urban areas is about 3:1. In rural
areas this ratio averages about 80:1. According to the 1969
census, 60% of the total African population lived in Tribal Trust
Lands (q.v.), 2.7% in Purchase Areas (q.v.), 20.6% in European
rural areas, and 16.6% in urban areas.

    By the population figures of 1901, Africans outnumbered
Europeans 45 to 1. Rapid European immigration over the next
half century steadily lowered this ratio until the 1950s, when
the African/European ratio leveled off at 16:1. Thereafter the
combination of rapid African natural population growth and de-
clining European immigration reversed the trend towards parity.
In 1969 Africans outnumbered Europeans by 21 to 1. By the
late 1970s this ratio had risen to about 24:1.

PORTUGUESE.   The goldfields of present Rhodesia attracted Portuguese interest before Vasco da Gama even reached southeast Africa, or the Portuguese knew where the goldfields were. Through Arab writings the Portuguese knew about the rich gold (q.v.) trade conducted through the Muslim (q.v.) port of Sofala (q.v.), and they were quick to believe that the region was the Biblical land of "Ophir" (q.v.).   They occupied Sofala in 1505 hoping simply to tap the existing trade, but soon found themselves drawn deeper and deeper into the interior in search of the actual goldfields.

Antonio Fernandez (q.v.) became the first known European to enter present Rhodesia in c.1511.   He was soon followed by sertanejo traders (q.v.), who communicated news of the Munhumutapa state (q.v.) to the coast.   Portuguese officialdom then followed the traders up the Zambezi River, occupying Muslim trading fairs (q.v.) at Sena and Tete (qq.v.) in the 1530s.   In late 1560 the Jesuit priest Gonçalo da Silveira (q.v.) entered Mashonaland*, thus becoming the first missionary in the country (see MISSIONS).   Silveira also became the country's first Christian martyr when he was murdered by the Shona.   A decade later the Portuguese crown launched a major military expedition to avenge Silveira's death and to seize whatever goldfields that could be found.   Neither Francisco Barreto nor his successor Vasco Honem (qq.v.) successfully penetrated the country, but they obtained Munhumutapa Negomo's (q.v.) concession of trading privileges.   The Portuguese then tried to sweep the Muslims out of the Zambezi Valley.

Union of the Portuguese and Spanish crowns in 1580 retarded official Portuguese involvement in the southeast African interior, and it introduced new problems of competition with the Dutch and British on the Indian Ocean.   Private trading and military ventures nevertheless increased.   Trading fairs were opened in Manicaland* and northeastern Mashonaland, and Dominican missionaries opened numerous stations among the Shona. Traders like D. S. Madeira (q.v.) meddled in Shona politics and were meddling in Munhumutapa political successions by the early 17th century.

It is uncertain to what extent the Portuguese penetrated the vast southwestern section of the country during this early period.   S. D. Bayão (q.v.) intervened in a Changamire (q.v.) succession dispute in the 1640s, but the military posts he established were soon withdrawn.   Archaeologists have turned up Portuguese relics in present Matabeleland* sites.   These have often been interpreted as indications of direct Dominican mission activity at Dhlo Dhlo and Khami (qq.v.).   More likely, such relics were simply trade items or booty from Changamire wars in the northeast.   The Changamire state began expanding into the northeast in the 1680s, wiping out most Portuguese centers by the early 1690s.   Thereafter the Portuguese conducted trade with the Shona from peripheral bases in Manicaland and a new fair opened at Zumbo (q.v.) in c.1714.   Dominican and Jesuit missionary efforts left no lasting mark on the country, and Portuguese influence generally gradually diminished in the country

through the 1830s.   The Gaza (q.v.) invasion of the Eastern
Highlands* at that time drove the Portuguese back even farther
from the interior, and reduced many surviving Portuguese outposts to tributaries.
     Portuguese imperial influence in the interior underwent
a resurgence in the late 1880s when it became clear that British
and Afrikaners would compete with Portugal for political mastery
of Mashonaland.   J. C. P. d'Andrada and Manuel de Sousa
(qq.v.) moved through northern Shona territory trading firearms
and obtaining treaties from minor rulers.   By then it was too
late, however.   The BSAC occupied Mashonaland proper in 1890,
resulting in direct clashes between British and Portuguese agents.
Incidents at Macequece (q.v.) and Delagoa Bay nearly led to a
British-Portuguese war, but an amicable settlement was reached
in the Anglo-Portuguese Convention of 1891 (q.v.).   Thereafter
small-scale Portuguese immigration into Rhodesia continued
through the 20th century.   This increased greatly after the Portuguese revolution of 1974, when it became clear that Portugal's
neighboring colony, Mozambique (q.v.), was soon to become independent.

PORTUGUESE EAST AFRICA (PEA).   English name for colonial
     Mozambique (q.v.).   In a broader historical sense, the name
     has also been applied to most of the eastern African coast,
     whose port towns Portugal dominated during the 16th and 17th
     centuries.

POSSELT, FRIEDRICH WILHELM TRAUGOTT (d.1950).   Officer of
     wide experience in the Southern Rhodesian Native Affairs Depart-
     ment from 1908 to 1941.   An amateur ethnographer and historian,
     Posselt published numerous articles and books on both the Nde-
     bele and Shona peoples.   (See BIBLIOGRAPHY.)
          Note that the "Posselt Ruin" at Zimbabwe (q.v.) was
     named after an apparently unrelated hunter, Willie Posselt, who
     discovered the "Zimbabwe Birds" (q.v.).

POSTAL SYSTEM AND STAMPS.   Mail services of sorts from Mata-
     beleland to South Africa began in 1859, when newly-arrived LMS
     agents began using African runners to carry letters.   This in-
     formal system of runners continued through the 19th century,
     though runners were increasingly replaced by European riders
     and wagon drivers.   In 1892 the BSAC administration established
     the first formal post office at Salisbury, and it began issuing
     postage stamps carrying its own name.   In 1900 the territory
     entered the Universal Postal Union.   The name "Rhodesia" (q.v.)
     first appeared as an overprint on BSAC stamps in 1909, fully
     displacing the BSAC imprint the next year.   The name "Southern
     Rhodesia" appeared on stamps from 1924 to 1965--except during
     the years of Federation (q.v.).   Franking machines were first
     used in 1928, and air services began in 1932 (see AIR RHO-
     DESIA).   The first locally-printed stamps were not produced un-
     til 1961.   In 1966 the name "Rhodesia" reappeared on stamp
     issues and the traditional portrait of the British monarch was

dropped.   (Cf. CURRENCY; see also TRANSPORT AND COM-
MUNICATIONS.)

POTGIETER, ANDRIES HENDRIK (a. k. a. Ndaleka) (Dec. 19, 1792-
March 1853). Afrikaner (q. v.) leader during South Africa's
"Great Trek" of the 1830s. In mid-1836 Potgieter led a Voortrekker scouting party from the present Orange Free State
across the Limpopo River, reaching the upper Bubye River* in
what is believed to have been the first European penetration of
present Rhodesia since the early Portuguese (q. v.) days. The
following year he commanded two major Voortrekker assaults
on Ndebele settlements--then in the western Transvaal--thereby
contributing to the pressures which drove the Ndebele into what
became Matabeleland*. As Voortrekkers settled in the Transvaal during the 1840s, Potgieter strove to organize commando
raids against the Ndebele in their new home. He finally led a
commando against Ndebele towns in the Matopo Hills (q. v.) in
1847. This raid was repelled by the induna Mbigo (q. v.).
Potgieter afterwards ceased to trouble the Ndebele and he is
believed to have signed a peace treaty with Ndebele emissaries
shortly before his death.

PRESIDENT OF RHODESIA. Head of state under the republican
Constitution of 1969 (q. v.). This office superseded that of the
British governor (q. v.). The Constitution empowers the president to sign legislative bills, to appoint prime ministers and
judges, and to proclaim general elections. Clifford Dupont
(q. v.) became the first president on April 16, 1970, after appointment by the government's Executive Council (q. v.). J. J.
Wrathall (q. v.) became the second president on December 10,
1975.

PRESS. Newspaper publication began almost immediately after the
British occupation of Mashonaland in the early 1890s when
numerous small papers sprang up in most major European settlements. Most of these papers were short-lived, and all
catered strictly to the interests of settlers. Of the commercial
papers which survived into the 20th century, the most important
were absorbed by the South African-based Argus group (q. v.).
Argus now controls the Rhodesia Herald, Sunday Mail, Bulawayo
Chronicle, Umtali Post (qq. v.), and many other publications.
The independent papers are all small, local publications, notably
the Gwelo Times (q. v.), Fort Victoria News (1959-), Gatooma
Mail (1912-), and Midlands Observer (Que Que, 1952-). The
Argus papers generally supported the Southern Rhodesia and
Federation (q. v.) governments between 1923 and 1962. Since
1962 they have tended to oppose the Rhodesian Front (q. v.)
government and have consequently been faced with increasing
censorship (q. v.).
     There have been many newspapers for African readers,
but these have been mostly controlled by whites, and have been
politically impotent. African newspaper publication began with
the Bantu Mirror (q. v.) in the 1930s. It was most prolific

during the 1950s when African Newspapers, Ltd. (q.v.) was at
its peak. This group of papers died after the banning of its
African Daily News (q.v.) in 1964. The few attempts at independent African newspaper publication, such as Chapupu and the
Zimbabwe Sun (qq.v.), were also suppressed by the government.
In their place the government's Ministry of Information has
published a free propaganda paper, the African Times (q.v.),
since 1965. At present more than a hundred periodicals of all
types are published within the country, and externally-based
political organizations, notably ZANU and ZAPU, publish their
own newspapers dealing with national affairs. (See also RHO-
DESIA BROADCASTING CORP.)

PRESTAGE, PETER (Feb. 27, 1842-April 11, 1907). English
Jesuit missionary. Prestage came to South Africa in 1877 to
serve in the Jesuit college at Grahamstown. In 1882 he joined
the Zambezi Mission (q.v.) and spent two years at Tati* before moving on to Bulawayo. In 1887 he persuaded Lobengula
to grant the Jesuits land for a station at Empandeni (q.v.),
where he was joined by Andrew Hartmann (q.v.) a year later.
The two Jesuits closed this station down in 1889 and joined the
BSAC's Pioneer Column (q.v.) as chaplains the next year.
Prestage then helped Mary Cosgrave (q.v.) to establish a hospital, the country's first, in Salisbury in 1891. The following
year he joined Hartmann in founding the Chishawasha Mission
(q.v.) nearby. After the 1896-7 Revolts Prestage returned to
work at Empandeni. In 1902 he attempted to start yet another
station in Northern Rhodesia, but he abandoned the effort because of poor health.

PRIME MINISTERS. Since the achievement of Responsible Government (q.v.) in 1923, the head of the white government has been
the prime minister ("premier" until 1933). The British governors
(q.v.) held discretionary power over appointments of the prime
ministers, but in practice the office has always gone to the
recognized heads of the ruling parties in the Legislative Assembly (q.v.) The governors also consistently followed the advice
of the prime ministers in designating cabinet members (see
EXECUTIVE COUNCIL). The prime ministers have been:
1923-27 Charles Coghlan, 1927-33 H. U. Moffat, 1933 George
Mitchell, 1933-53 Godfrey Huggins, 1953-58 Garfield Todd,
1958-62 Edgar Whitehead, 1962-64 Winston Field, and 1964-
Ian Smith (qq.v.). (For Federal prime ministers, see under
FEDERATION.)

PRINCE EDWARD DAM   see under   HUNYANI RIVER

"PROTECTED VILLAGES." In 1974 the Rhodesian government responded to increasing infiltration of nationalist guerrillas--par-
ticularly in the northeast--by concentrating isolated African
farming communities in "protected villages." The program was
designed to sever communications between guerrillas and uncom-
mitted Africans. By mid-1977 an estimated 300,000 people were

living in such villages, with government plans for creation of
many more. The villages averaged about 2500 residents, living
within chain-link fence enclosures (unfenced settlements were
apparently known as "consolidated villages") illuminated by elec-
tric lights at night. Soldiers stationed at the villages had orders
to shoot dusk-to-dawn curfew violators without challenging them.
The government provided no food or supplies for the residents,
who typically had to walk long distances to work their farms.
Malnutrition became a serious problem in the villages, as farms
fell prey to neglect, untended livestock, and vermin.

PROVIDENTIAL PASS.   Defile in the Devuli Hills, just west of Kyle
Lake (q.v.), through which the Pioneer Column (q.v.) ascended
from low to high veld in early August 1890 (at 20° 11'S, 30° 47'E).
So named because its discovery was thought to have delivered the
Column from the last serious threat of Ndebele attack during its
advance into Mashonaland.

PROVINCES, ADMINISTRATIVE.   Between the 1890s and 1962 Southern
Rhodesia was administratively divided into two provinces of roughly
equal size: Mashonaland and Matabeleland (qq.v.).   Under the
General Administration Act of 1962, the country was redivided
into seven provinces, which also encompassed a total of 50 African administrative districts (q.v.).   Each province is now administered by a Provincial Commissioner within the Department
of Internal Affairs.   The provinces are also used for magisterial
territories within the Department of Justice.   The seven provinces
are Matabeleland North, Matabeleland South, Mashonaland North,
Mashonaland South, Manicaland, Midlands, and Victoria (qq.v.).

PUNGWE RIVER.   Rises in the Inyanga Mountains (q.v.), whence it
flows east, through Mozambique* to the Indian Ocean, between
Beira and Sofala (qq.v.).   The Pungwe is fed by the Honde River
(q.v.), and it forms a short stretch of the border (q.v.) between
Rhodesia and Mozambique.   In 1891 L. S. Jameson and Frank
Johnson (qq.v.) made an adventurous trip down the Pungwe in a
futile attempt to demonstrate its potential as a passageway into
the country.

PURCHASE AREAS (PA).   In 1930 the Land Apportionment Act (q.v.)
created "Native Purchase Areas" (later redesignated "African
Purchase Areas") in response to African demands for more land
expressed before the Morris Carter Commission (q.v.) five years
earlier.   Almost 8% of the country was originally set aside for
Purchase Areas, in which individual Africans were to be able to
buy or lease farms, but the designated areas were scattered,
isolated, unsurveyed, and mostly semi-arid.   African response
to the scheme was limited during the 1930s, with mostly Mfengu
(q.v.) and other foreign Africans acquiring the available farms.
Local African interest picked up greatly in the 1940s.   By 1968
there were about 7000 PA farms in operation, providing for about
2.7% of the country's resident African population (q.v.).
     Although there have been many exceptions, most PA

farmers have employed the same farming techniques used in
Tribal Trust Lands (q.v.), so few have achieved significant
commercial success. There are now about 85 blocs of PA
land, located mostly around the fringes of European reserved
lands. The largest blocs of PA land are in the central Charter
District, northeastern Gokwe, northwestern Gatooma, and southwest Mtoko Districts (qq.v.). Since 1933 most PA farmers
have been members of the African Farmers Union (q.v.).

- Q -

-Q-. In languages such as Sindebele (q.v.) which contain click
sounds (q.v.), the letter q represents the palatal click, as in
ukuqwaqwaza, "to make a clicking noise." The letter q is not
used in Chishona (q.v.) orthography.

QUE QUE. The country's fifth largest urban (q.v.) center, Que
Que is located midway between Bulawayo and Salisbury at the
very center of the country (18° 55'S, 29° 49'E; alt. 1205 m.).
The town takes its name from nearby Kwe Kwe River (q.v.).
It was established by settlers at the beginning of the century to
serve the needs of the adjacent Globe and Phoenix Mine (q.v.).
Que Que has remained an important mining center, and has also
developed into a commercial center for European ranches and
mixed farms in Que Que District (q.v.), for which the town
serves as administrative center. Large-scale manufacturing industries spill over into nearby Redcliff (q.v.). Que Que's population in late 1974 was estimated at 45,000, including c.40,000
Africans and 3900 Europeans.

QUE QUE DISTRICT. Covering 9120 sq. km. in central Midlands
Province (q.v.), Que Que District formerly was the northern
part of Gwelo District (q.v.). Other districts which Que Que
borders are Bubi and Nkai on the west ; Gokwe on the northwest; Gatooma on the northeast; and Chilimanzi (qq.v.) on the
east. District headquarters are at the town of Que Que. Other
important centers include Empress Mine and Redcliff (qq.v.).
Under the terms of the Land Tenure Act (q.v.), the eastern two-
thirds of the district are reserved for Europeans. Tribal Trust
Lands and some Purchase Areas (qq.v.) are scattered in the
west. District population in 1969 included 123,970 Africans and
5835 Europeans.

QUEENS' LOCATION (a.k.a. Queens' Kraal). Site by the Bembezi
River* where Lozigeyi (q.v.) and others of Lobengula's widows
settled after the Ndebele War of 1893 (q.v.). Queen's Mine and
Queen's Mountain (both at 19° 48'S, 28° 45'E) are nearby. Queen's
Mine takes its name from an abandoned gold mine pegged just
before the 1896 Revolt.

- R -

-R-   see under -L-

RABIES (hydrophobia). Nerve-destroying viral disease transmitted
  by animal saliva, mainly through dog bites. Rabies appears
  first to have entered the country from the north in 1902. It
  spread throughout the entire country within five years, but was
  virtually eliminated as an epidemic threat by 1913. (See
  HEALTH.)

RADIO AND TELEVISION   see   RHODESIAN BROADCASTING COR-
  PORATION

RAILWAYS. When the British South Africa Company (q.v.) occupied
  the country in the early 1890s, it had several reasons for rapid
  railway development. Its 1889 Charter (q.v.) required it to extend rail services to the Zambezi River; the 1891 Anglo-Portuguese Convention (q.v.) required that the BSAC connect Beira
  with Mashonaland (qq.v.); development of the new colony's mineral
  resources (q.v.) depended upon good transport facilities; and Cecil
  Rhodes, the BSAC's leader, was personally motivated to connect
  Cape Town with Cairo by rail. Only the fourth goal remains
  to be achieved.
      The first two rail lines were started almost simultaneously
  from Beira to Salisbury, through Umtali; and from Vryburg,
  South Africa to Salisbury, through Bulawayo. Most of the early
  construction was contracted by George Pauling (q.v.). In contrast to government-sponsored transport projects elsewhere in
  southern Africa, these construction projects were financed by a
  private company, Rhodesia Railways (q.v.), a BSAC subsidiary.
      The Beira line was begun in 1892, reaching Umtali in
  1898, and Salisbury a year later. To overcome engineering
  problems the line was built with narrow-gauge track, but this
  was later replaced with 3'6" (1.067 m.) gauge, which became
  standard throughout southern Africa and Zaïre. Malaria (q.v.)
  and dysentery killed more than 900 Indians and Europeans who
  worked on the line in Mozambique.
      The line originating in South Africa was begun in 1893.
  It ran through Francistown, Botswana (q.v.), reaching Bulawayo
  in 1897. The Salisbury link was completed only in 1902, because of the disruption of the South African War (q.v.). Gwelo,
  Que Que, and Gatooma (qq.v.) later developed into major urban
  centers along this line.
      Rhodes' plan to extend a line north from Salisbury through
  present Zambia received little support for economic reasons.
  The idea was permanently dropped after the discovery of coal at
  Wankie (qq.v.). A line between Bulawayo and Wankie was then
  completed in 1903, and extended to Victoria Falls (q.v.) the next
  year. After a bridge was built across the Zambezi by the Falls,
  the line was extended into Zambia, reaching the Copperbelt and
  connecting to southern Zaïre's mines a few years later.
      Branch lines, mainly to major mining centers, have been

added continuously since the main lines were finished. Important lines were opened to West Nicholson (q.v.) in 1905; Fort
Victoria (q.v.) in 1914; Shamva (q.v.) in 1913; and Sinoia (q.v.)
in 1902.   In 1955 a major new connection with Mozambique was
made by way of Vila Salazar (q.v.), linking the country to the
port of Lourenzo Marques (now Maputo).   An additional, and
direct, link with South Africa was extended off Rutenga (q.v.)
to Beitbridge (q.v.) in 1974.   By the mid-1970s more than 3250
km. of track were in use throughout the country.

Throughout the 20th century the country's railway network has greatly facilitated economic development by transporting
bulky export goods, moving coal for thermal electrical power
(q.v.) generation, and earning revenues from the trans-shipment
of Zambian exports (mainly copper).   By the 1970s the country's
trains were devoting more than 90% of their carrying capacity
to freight, which amounted to more than 12 million metric tons
annually.   Since the mid-1970s, however, closures of the Zambia
and Mozambique borders (q.v.) have altered trade patterns considerably, and reliable current data is unobtainable.   (See also
ROADS; TRANSPORT & COMMUNICATIONS.)

RAINFALL   see   CLIMATE; DAMS AND WATER SUPPLY; RIVERS;
LAKES

RAMAQUABANE RIVER.   Flows south from Plumtree (q.v.) for 130
km. before joining the Shashi River (q.v.).   The whole length
of the Ramaquabane forms part of the border (q.v.) with Botswana.

RANA.   Acronym for Rhodesia and Nyasaland Airways, a predecessor
of Air Rhodesia (q.v.) during the 1930s.   Since rana is also the
Latin word for "frog," the name came to symbolize the airline's
puddle-jumping reputation.

RANCHE HOUSE COLLEGE.   Private adult education college, founded
in Salisbury in the early 1960s with money from the Beit Trust
(q.v.) and other non-government funds.   As a non-racial institution it has served a uniquely diverse variety of southern African
communities.   During a typical year it enrolls as many as 3000
part-time students.   (See EDUCATION.)

RANDALL-MacIVER, DAVID (1873-1945).   British archaeologist.
From April to August 1905 Randall-MacIver investigated Iron
Age (q.v.) ruins with the support of the Rhodes Trust and the
British Association.   The first professionally-trained archaeologist to work in the country, he was invited specifically to investigate the claims of ancient and exotic origin of the stone ruins
(q.v.) made by J. T. Bent, R. N. Hall (qq.v.), and others.
After working briefly at several different sites, he made a major
dig in the main enclosure of the Zimbabwe Ruins (q.v.).   His
findings, published in Mediaeval Rhodesia (London, 1906) contained two startling conclusions: that the ruins were of purely
local African origin; and that Great Zimbabwe itself was

constructed only after about the A.D. 1300s--not in ancient
times.   Professional archaeologists immediately accepted his
findings, but local settlers were outraged.   Hall published a
tendentious rebuttal a few years later, and the Zimbabwe Controversy (q.v.) has raged ever since.   Although Randall-Mac-
Iver's findings are still regarded as essentially sound, his main
error was in ascribing somewhat too late a date to Zimbabwe's
construction.   In 1929 Gertrude Caton-Thompson (q.v.) was
called in to investigate this question.

THE RANGE.   Village just east of Enkeldoorn (q.v.) in the Charter
District* (at 19° S, 31° 2'E) serving as the local African ad-
ministrative center.   Charter District was formerly called the
Range-Charter District.   The Range Dam on the upper Sebakwe
River (q.v.), built in 1968, provides water for Enkeldoorn.

RANGER, TERENCE OSBORN (b.Nov. 29, 1929).   A British historian, Ranger came to Salisbury in 1957 to teach in the newly-
created University College (q.v.).   There he became interested
in African history and began researching and writing about African resistance to colonial rule.   An active supporter of African
nationalism, he became one of the few Europeans openly to join
ZAPU and he helped to lead the anti-color bar movement.   After
the government banned ZAPU in September 1962, it served
Ranger with a restriction order, deporting him the following
year.   He then went to Tanganyika (now Tanzania) to assume
the chair of history at the new University College of Dar es
Salaam.   In 1967 he published <u>Revolt in Southern Rhodesia</u>, a
major study of the 1896-7 Revolts (q.v.) which stimulated many
similar studies in other regions.   Ranger taught at UCLA from
1969 to 1974, and then accepted the chair of modern history at
the University of Manchester.   By constantly delving into fresh
fields in inquiry, such as religious history, by posing controversial historical models, and by vigorously organizing international conferences of Africanist scholars, Ranger has had a profound influence on current scholarship and he is regarded as a
leading authority on central African history.   (See BIBLIOG-
RAPHY.)

REDCLIFF.   Industrial town just south of Que Que (q.v.) at the
heart of the country (19° 2'S, 29° 47'E; alt. 1220 m.).   Redcliff
is virtually an adjunct of the Rhodesian Iron and Steel Company
(RISCO), which administers the town and employs most of its
adult residents.   RISCO was established as a government-owned
commission in 1942 in order to mine and process local iron ore
(q.v.) deposits to meet the country's internal needs.   Although
production increased steadily, limited national markets and other
problems caused the government to sell the company to a consortium of British industrialists in 1957.   Since 1961 RISCO has
maintained an annual production of over 360,000 metric tons of
heavy and light steel products.   Population of Redcliff in late
1974 was estimated at 13,000 (85% Africans).

REFERENDUMS.   The overwhelmingly white electorate has publicly
    voted in favor of Responsible Government (q. v.) over union
    with South Africa (Oct. 27, 1922); joining the Federation (q. v.;
    April 9, 1953); the Constitution (q. v.) of 1961 (July 26, 1961);
    independence (Nov. 5, 1964; see UDI); the Constitution of 1969
    and republican government (June 20, 1969).   Through 1977 the
    Rhodesian Front regime resisted all proposals to put the question
    of the country's constitutional future to a referendum of the
    people of the country as a whole.

REFORM PARTY.   Short-lived European political party formed by
    supporters of Godfrey Huggins (q. v.) in 1931.   Its members
    were mostly dissidents from the ruling Rhodesian Party (q. v.),
    from which it differed mainly in its fervor for territorial
    racial segregation.   The Reform Party won the 1933 general
    election, bringing Huggins to power as prime minister.   A
    party revolt against Huggins' leadership soon caused him to
    dissolve parliament in order to call a new election as the head
    of the newly-formed United Party (q. v.).   Only one member of
    the Reform Party retained his legislative seat, and the party
    faded into insignificance.

REFORMED INDUSTRIAL AND COMMERCIAL UNION (RICU).   Es-
    sentially an African protest organization, the RICU was formed
    early in 1946 by Charles Mzingeli (q. v.) and other African labor
    leaders in Salisbury.   The RICU revived the name of the defunct
    Industrial and Commercial Union (q. v.), but failed to re-estab-
    lish the earlier body's national impact.   Nevertheless, under
    Mzingeli's presidency the RICU became the dominant voice of
    African political and economic dissent in the Salisbury area,
    while Benjamin Burumbo (q. v.) inherited the ICU tradition in
    Bulawayo.   The RICU led local protests against the Native (Ur-
    ban Areas) Accommodation Act (q. v.), and it became the local
    center of the 1948 general strike.   In the mid-1950s, however,
    both Mzingeli's leadership and the RICU itself were eclipsed by
    the new Youth League and the African National Congress (qq. v.).

"REGIMENTS, " NDEBELE   see   IBUTHO

RELIGION, NDEBELE.   Traditional Ndebele (q. v.) beliefs have
    changed little since the 19th century.   In common with other
    Nguni (q. v.) peoples, the Ndebele believe in a remote high god,
    Nkulunkulu (q. v.), who must be approached indirectly, through
    ancestor spirits (see IDLOZI).   These beliefs were modified
    somewhat by absorption of Sotho (q. v.) concepts of mlimo (q. v.)
    adopted during the formative years of the Ndebele kingdom.
    When the Ndebele arrived in Matabeleland in c. 1839, they found
    a local cult system worshipping Mwari (q. v.) in the Matopo
    Hills.   Previously it has been thought that the Ndebele adopted
    Mwari worship so thoroughly that the Mwari cult leaders were
    influential in Ndebele politics by the end of the 19th century
    (see REVOLT).   It now appears, however, that the Mwari cult

system had only a small influence on Ndebele beliefs.   (See also MISSIONS.)

RELIGION, SHONA.   A large and complex body of beliefs have been described as making up "Shona religion, " but not all Shona (q. v.) groups accept all aspects of these beliefs, nor is belief in many important features confined to the Shona people. Nevertheless, it is possible to make some generalizations about Shona religion.   In simplified terms, the Shona venerate a complex hierarchy of spirits and a high god, Mwari (q. v.), who stands above the spirit hierarchy.   The spirits are either personal (see MUDZIMU; NGOZI; SHAVE), or communal (see MHONDORO; GOMBWE).   These spirits typically communicate with the living through mediums known as svikiro (q. v.)   The high god Mwari can be approached in either of two ways--a distinction which represents an apparently basic split between northern Shona and southern Shona and Venda (q. v.) religious observances.   In the north spirit mediums act as intermediaries in dealings with Mwari.   In the south and southwest Mwari can be approached directly through oracular shrines centered in the Matopo Hills (q. v.).   The Mwari cult is an elaborate and highly organized religious system with few indigenous parallels in southern Africa.
     Other aspects of Shona belief less directly concerned with the spirit world are the arts of healing and divination.   There are many male and female professional nganga (q. v.; see also CHIREMBA) who offer individuals cures and protection from every-day maladies and accidents, which are frequently attributed to witchcraft.   While many such practitioners have readily accom-modated to Christianity, Mwari priests and spirit mediums have remained antagonistic to Christianity in order to preserve the sacred veneration of ancestors.   (See also MISSIONS.)

REMBA   see   LEMBA

RENDER, ADAM (variant: Renders) (1822-1876?).   An enigmatic figure, Render is credited with having been the first European to visit the Zimbabwe Ruins (q. v.).   He was a German-born emigrant to America who later came to South Africa around 1842.   He became a hunter in the Transvaal and first visited Zimbabwe in 1867.   On his return trip to Zimbabwe the next year he was unable to get home, so he married a Shona woman and settled in her village.   In 1871 Render helped Karl Mauch (q. v.) to explore Zimbabwe.   His subsequent fate is unknown. "Renders Ruin" at Zimbabwe was later named after him by R. N. Hall (q. v.).

REPUBLIC.   Under the terms of the Constitution of 1969 (q. v.), the Rhodesian government declared itself a republic as of March 2, 1970, with a president (q. v.) as head of state.

REPUBLIC DAY.   Official Rhodesian holiday, falling on the second to last Monday of October.

REPUBLIC OF SOUTH AFRICA   see   SOUTH AFRICA

RESERVES, AFRICAN   see   TRIBAL TRUST LANDS

RESPONSIBLE GOVERNMENT MOVEMENT. By the time of the First World War it was generally acknowledged that BSAC rule would end within a decade. Two alternatives were seen for the country's constitutional future: union with South Africa (see UNIONIST MOVEMENT), or local responsible government. The latter effectively meant full self-government by the tiny European (q.v.) minority. As early as 1908 settlers had held the majority of seats on the territory's Legislative Council (q.v.), but their powers were severely limited, and the country's large capital interests doubted the economic feasibility of a fully responsible government regime. Despite such opposition, the majority of the European farmers, small-workers, and wage-earners supported the idea of responsible government as the only attractive alternative to either union with South Africa or continued BSAC rule.

     In 1917 the Responsible Government Association (later known as the Rhodesian Responsible Government Party) was formed. The Association received a major boost two years later when Charles Coghlan (q.v.) joined. As the leader of the elected members of Legco, Coghlan was made the Association's president and leading spokesman (cf. TAWSE-JOLLIE, E.). The movement placed increasing pressure on the British government to provide a responsible government constitution (q.v.), and its goals were supported by the reports of the Cave and Buxton commissions (qq.v.) in 1920-21. In the 1920 election the party won 12 of 13 legislative seats. There was virtually no organized African opposition to the movement--perhaps because the unionist alternative was even less attractive to Africans--and even missionaries such as A. S. Cripps and John White (qq.v.) lent the movement tacit support.

     On October 27, 1922, a referendum was held among the electorate. Responsible government was approved by 8774 voters, while 5989 people voted for union. At the most, about 60 Africans were then eligible to vote. The referendum settled the issue, leaving only the constitutional and fiscal arrangements to be worked out. Southern Rhodesia was declared a British Crown Colony in September 1923, and Coghlan was sworn in as first premier on October 1st. The Legislative Assembly (q.v.) replaced Legco, and a British governor (q.v.) replaced the office of BSAC administrator (q.v.). The new responsible government was required to pay £2 million to the Crown for public works and unalienated land, while the Crown in turn paid the BSAC £3.75 million for the same interests in both Southern and Northern Rhodesia together. The BSAC retained only its mineral rights (later sold to H. U. Moffat's administration) and its interests in the railways (q.v.). Day-to-day operation of the government changed little. Meanwhile, the Responsible Government Party was reorganized as the Rhodesian Party (q.v.) in late 1923.

REVOLTS OF 1896-97 (a.k.a. <u>chimurenga</u> or <u>chindunduma</u>, qq.v.). Between late March 1896 and October 1897 a large part of the

country's population rose in violent rebellion against white settlers and the BSAC administration. About 10% of the whites in
the country were killed; all development stopped as the government mobilized military forces; and the BSAC was brought
nearly to a point of collapse. No other tropical African colony
experienced an early rebellion of comparable scale or impact.
Although these revolts eventually failed, thus bringing a con-
clusive end to African independence, they are today regarded as
the country's dominant historical epic.

The Ndebele and Shona peoples and their allies waged essentially separate revolts, but they rose for much the same
reasons, and at roughly the same time. Their grievances
against the BSAC and settlers were many: land encroachments,
cattle (q.v.) seizures, forced labor recruitment, inept and bully-
ing police and administrators, and a general BSAC failure to
legitimize its presumed sovereignty. Further, in early 1896,
the country was devastated by drought, rinderpest (q.v.), and
locust invasions (q.v.). Africans tended to attribute these
natural disasters to the European occupation. Africans still
owned good supplies of firearms and ammunition, and the
Europeans in the country were entirely unprepared for war.

(1) The Ndebele Revolt can be seen as a continuation of
the 1893 Ndebele War (q.v.). The BSAC had occupied central
Matabeleland, seized many cattle, and seen the end of King
Lobengula, but it had not effectively disarmed or broken up the
quasi-military ibutho organization (q.v.). The Ndebele were
aggrieved by their humiliation, by the Company's refusal to
recognize their izinduna (see INDUNA) or a new king, and by
the Company's continuing seizures of cattle. The Jameson Raid
(q.v.) of late 1895, which took many troops out of the country,
has been seen as a trigger to the Revolt. Whether or not this
was true, it is evident that the rising was being planned at least
as early as February 1896. On March 20, 1896, the Ndebele
began to kill African policemen and Europeans around Filabusi*.
By the end of the month virtually the entire kingdom and
its former tributaries were in open revolt. The BSAC's
first response was to organize the Bulawayo Field Force
(q.v.).

Progress of the revolt was too complex to detail here,
but general observations can be made. Ndebele leaders co-
operated with each other until their lines of communication were
severed around August, but they had no unitary command structure. One major group coalesced around the Khumalo royal
family (q.v.) by the Bembezi River* in the north. Leaders of
this bloc included Lobengula's son Nyamanda, his wife Lozigeyi,
and Mpotshwana (qq.v.) and many other izinduna. A second and
more loosely united group operated in the Matopo Hills (q.v.)
under the leadership of Babayane, Dhliso Mathemu, Mlugulu,
Sikombo (q.v.), and others. A third group operated around the
Insiza River*, east of the Matopos. Among its leaders was
Somabulana (q.v.). Allied with these groups were such non-
Ndebele tributaries as the Lemba, Birwa, Rozvi, Kalanga, and
Dumbuseya (qq.v.). Religious authorities such as Mkwati and

Tenkela (qq. v.) played a small role as well. Not all Ndebele
rebelled. Some formerly powerful izinduna, notably Mtshane
(q. v.), remained neutral. Others, notably Gampu and Faku
(qq. v.), actively collaborated with the British. These collaborators helped the British especially to keep southwestern supply
routes open, and their fighting with the rebels had overtones of
an Ndebele civil war.

By the end of April 1896 the Ndebele had driven Europeans
out of outlying areas and had most survivors under siege in
laagers (q. v.) at Bulawayo, Belingwe, and elsewhere. This moment represented the height of Ndebele success. In mid-May
H. C. O. Plumer (q. v.) arrived with the Matabeleland Relief
Force (q. v.), and the Ndebele war against the BSAC became a
guerrilla war against British Imperial forces. On June 2nd
Frederick Carrington (q. v.) took command of British forces,
and the Ndebele soon found themselves fighting a defensive war.
Rebel forces got lifts when the Shona Revolt (see below) began
in mid-June, and when Nyamanda was proclaimed Ndebele king
on June 25, but by then many rebels were already surrendering.
The situation progressively deteriorated as rebels were driven
from their stores of grain and their ammunition ran short.

In August British forces began assaulting guerrilla positions in the Matopo Hills. This campaign proved so difficult that
Cecil Rhodes and other Company leaders decided to attempt a
negotiated peace for fear that the expenses of the Matopos fighting
would break the Company. On August 21st Rhodes conducted the
first "indaba" (q. v.) with southern rebel leaders. Northern
leadership was ignored, but the general situation had gotten so
bad for all rebels that virtually all major leaders surrendered
by December. Many rebel leaders were then made government-
salaried chiefs, but the Ndebele regained no lost land, and other
reforms were minor.

(2) Shona Revolt. Both the origins and course of the revolt in Mashonaland (q. v.) were more complex than those of the
Ndebele rising. It has been estimated that something under a
third of all Shona rebelled. Most of these were people in the
Hartley, Charter, Salisbury, Marandellas, Mrewa, Makoni, Mazoe, and eastern Lomagundi districts (qq. v.). Most Shona had
grievances against the BSAC, but the central and northern Shona
were perhaps those most intensely pressured by British occupation. Further, the rebels included many of the paramount chiefs
who had previously sought Portuguese (q. v.) arms and alliances
in the late 1880s in an effort to repel Ndebele raids and, occasionally, to fight each other. Their determination to rebel was
encouraged by religious authorities, notably the mediums of Kaguvi
and Nehanda (qq. v.) and the Mwari cult figure Bonda (q. v.).
These figures also actively helped to organize rebel communications. The main rebel leaders were mostly paramount chiefs,
or members of ruling families. These included Mashayamombe,
Mangwende and son Mchemwa, Makoni, Hwata, Nyandoro, Mutekedzi, Chinamora, Nemakonde (qq. v.), and others.

Many Shona groups living in a belt running south from the
Chilimanzi District* collaborated with the British--either against

other Shona, or against the Ndebele. All generalizations about
the revolts are risky, but collaborators such as Chirumanzu,
Chivi, and Matibi (qq. v.) tended to represent those Shona who
had borne grudges against the Ndebele, but who had not been
influenced by Portuguese attempts at alliance. Shona groups in
the extreme north, extreme east, and southeast mostly remained
neutral throughout the revolt.

The Shona revolt first erupted in the third week of June
1896, catching Europeans in Zezuru (q. v.) territory completely
by surprise. Whereas doubts had previously existed about the
endurance of Ndebele acquiesence to European rule, the Shona
had been regarded as passive, cowardly, and unlikely to fight.
After the revolt started, the ruthlessness, courage, and persistence of the Shona rebels soon dispelled all such notions.

The absence of European troops in Mashonaland and
problems of supply left the military initiative in the hands of
the rebels until August, when E. A. H. Alderson (q. v.) arrived
and organized the Mashonaland Field Force (q. v.). Alderson
directed a campaign of assaults against Shona strongholds, but
these were heavily fortified and well defended with firearms.
Strong defensive positions gave the Shona an advantage lacked
by most Ndebele rebels outside the Matopos. After the Ndebele
revolt was effectively suppressed in October, Carrington's Imperial troops arrived from Matabeleland. Little was accomplished
before December, however, when all Imperial forces were removed from the country to save the BSAC money. BSAC Police
(q. v.) then took over.

Hostilities generally ceased through the rainy season which
ensued, but attempts at negotiation in January 1897 proved fruitless. To an extent even greater than among the Ndebele rebels,
the Shona lacked a central command structure. The British were
thus hard pressed to know exactly whom to strike, or with whom
to deal, to achieve significant results. As hostilities again picked
up around March, more effective assaults were mounted against
Shona strongholds. Dynamite was used ruthlessly to blast de-
fenders out of caves. By October virtually all major rebel
leaders had either been killed or captured. Surrenders were
taken unconditionally, and many defeated rebels were executed.
Afterwards, Shona chiefdoms underwent profound changes as the
government began installing its own nominees as chiefs.

RHINOCEROS. Both white (Ceratotherium simum) and black (Diceros
bicornis) rhinos were fairly common in the country until the mid-
19th century. Both varieties, particularly the white, were easily
killed by hunters (q. v.) armed with firearms after that time, as
they were routinely shot for meat and hides (see SJAMBOK).
From the late 1860s rhinos were increasingly killed for their
horns, which were sold in South Africa for resale in east Asia.
By the end of the 19th century the white rhinoceros was virtually
extinct in the country. Some native black rhinos still inhabit the
Zambezi Valley, and a few whites have recently been reintro-
duced to national parks (q. v.) from Natal.

RHODES, CECIL JOHN (July 5, 1853-March 26, 1902). South African financier and politician. Born in Hertfordshire, England, Rhodes came to South Africa in 1870 to improve his health. Within a year he was at the Kimberley diamond fields, where he collected mining claims and began amassing a personal fortune. Later he invested successfully in the Rand gold fields. By 1888 he and his personal ally, Alfred Beit (q.v.), had either bought out or co-opted all their competitors on the diamond fields, so they formed De Beers Consolidated Mining, Ltd. As company chairman, Rhodes was able to marshal De Beers' financial power to help forward his developing imperial schemes.

Rhodes' first venture in imperialism came in the early 1880s, when he assisted the maneuverings leading to the creation of the Bechuanaland Protectorate (q.v.). He favored British/ Afrikaner cooperation in South Africa, but was opposed to further expansion of the existing Afrikaner (q.v.) republics. The British government was reluctant to compete directly with the Afrikaner republics in northward expansion, so Rhodes personally took the initiative. In 1888, he, C. D. Rudd, and F. R. Thompson (qq.v.) formed a syndicate to seek a mineral concession (q.v.) from the Ndebele king Lobengula (q.v.). The result was the Rudd Concession (q.v.). This in turn led to formation of the British South Africa Company (q.v.), of which Rhodes became a director. Thereafter Rhodes used the BSAC as his primary tool to extend British authority north of the Limpopo River. In late 1889 the BSAC was granted a royal Charter (q.v.) which gave it rights to govern central African territory. The Company organized the Pioneer Column (q.v.) the next year to exercise its Charter rights by occupying Mashonaland*. Through these proceedings L. S. Jameson (q.v.) acted as Rhodes' personal agent in the interior. The following year, 1891, Rhodes himself finally visited Mashonaland, where he listened to settlers' complaints. In 1893 BSAC forces occupied neighboring Matabeleland*, and the country soon to be called "Rhodesia" (q.v.) assumed nearly its present shape.

Meanwhile, Rhodes was active in the Cape Colony's parliament, to which he had first been elected in 1880. On July 17, 1890--just after the Pioneer Column crossed into present Rhodesian territory--Rhodes was sworn in as prime minister of the Cape. He pledged his government to the task of reconciling differences between Afrikaners and British settlers in South Africa, as he hoped to see the whole region united under the British flag. Unable to gain the cooperation of Paul Kruger's government in the Transvaal, Rhodes backed the disastrous Jameson Raid (q.v.) in late 1895. When his personal involvement was revealed, he had to resign both his premiership and his BSAC directorship. Several months later the Revolts (q.v.) began in Rhodesia. Rhodes salvaged some of his prestige by personally negotiating a truce with Ndebele rebel leaders in August 1896 (see "INDABA"), but his days of real power were over. He devoted his remaining years mostly to personal projects. After a prolonged illness, he died near Cape Town. A large railway

procession carried his body to the Matopo Hills, where it was
interred at World's View (q.v.).

RHODES DAY. The birthday of Cecil Rhodes, July 5th, was made
a public holiday in 1903, the year after his death. In 1910 the
holiday was moved to the second Monday in July so that it and
Founders Day (q.v.) would create an annual four-day weekend
for reserve military training. (See HOLIDAYS.)

RHODES INYANGA NATIONAL PARK see INYANGA MOUNTAINS

RHODES MATOPOS NATIONAL PARK see MATOPO HILLS

RHODESIA ... see also entries entitled RHODESIAN ...

"RHODESIA" [the name]. At the time the BSAC received its Charter
(q.v.) in 1889, the first name proposed for its prospective central African territories was "Zambezia" (q.v.). Other names
considered early included "Charterland" and "Cecilia," the latter
in honor of Cecil Rhodes. As the BSAC actually extended its
authority over territory on both sides of the Zambezi River, the
names "Northern" and "Southern Zambezia" came to refer to
present Zambia (a contraction of "Zambezia") and Rhodesia,
respectively. Meanwhile, it was apparently Rhodes' associate
L. S. Jameson (q.v.) who proposed "Rhodesia" as an alternative
name in 1890. This new name became popular after the BSAC
added Matabeleland to its domain in 1894, thereby rendering
"Mashonaland" (q.v.) an inadequate designation for the Company's entire southern Zambezia sphere. In May 1895 an Administrator's Proclamation made "Rhodesia" the official name
for both Zambia and Rhodesia. Two years later "Southern" and
"Northern Rhodesia" were designated separate entities, and the
name "Rhodesia" was formally recognized by the British Secretary
of State. These new names stuck until the mid-1960s, making
Rhodes perhaps the only figure in history to have two modern
countries named in his honor.
    When Northern Rhodesia became independent as "Zambia"
(q.v.) in 1964, Southern Rhodesia dropped the "Southern" in its
own name. This last change has never been officially recognized
by either the British government or the United Nations. Meanwhile, the African nationalist name "Zimbabwe" (q.v.) has gained
wider currency outside the country as the white government has
become increasingly unpopular around the world.

RHODESIA ANCIENT RUINS, LTD. (a.k.a. Ancient Ruins Company).
Organization granted exclusive concession by the British South
Africa Company administration in September 1895 to prospect
for treasure in the stone ruins (q.v.) of Matabeleland*. The
Ruins Company was organized by members of the Bechuanaland
Exploration Company and by W. G. Neal (d.1906/7), a South
African prospector. The company's prospectors soon started
work at the Dhlo Dhlo ruins (q.v.), where they extracted nearly
20 kg. of gold beads and other objects. Their work was inter-

rupted by the rinderpest epidemic (q.v.) and the Revolts (q.v.) until September 1897. From then until May 1900 an additional 50 sites were pillaged (not including the Zimbabwe Ruins, q.v.), but these failed to yield sufficient gold to make the operation profitable. After Hans Sauer (q.v.) called attention to the terrible damage the company's men were inflicting on historic sites, the company's work was halted by court order in May 1900. The following year the Legislative Council (q.v.) passed the country's first ordinance protecting ruins from treasure hunters. The Ancient Ruins Co. was then disbanded in 1903. Meanwhile, Neal tried to salvage the company's reputation by turning over its written records to R. N. Hall (q.v.), who published a massive descriptive account of the country's ruins. (See also HISTORICAL MONUMENTS COMMISSION; GOLD.)

RHODESIA FIELD FORCE (RFF). British Imperial military unit raised during the South African War (q.v.) to defend Southern Rhodesia from Afrikaners (q.v.) and to invade the Transvaal (q.v.) from the north. In 1900 the RFF advanced from Beira* to the Transvaal under the command of General Frederick Carrington (q.v.).

RHODESIA HERALD (RH). Published in Salisbury, the RH is the country's biggest daily newspaper, with a circulation in 1973 of 64,500. It began publication on June 17, 1891, as the Mashonaland Herald and Zambesian Times, a hand-written and crudely duplicated paper completely produced by W. E. Fairbridge (q.v.). It became the RH in October 1892, when its first printed copies were issued. Since its inception it has been a member of the "Argus Group" (q.v.) of newspapers. It and its co-publication, the Sunday Mail (q.v.), have been the country's most influential newspapers. Like their fellow Argus papers, they consistently supported the European governments, while maintaining a paternalistic attitude towards Africans through 1962. Since 1962 they have been outspoken in opposition to the Rhodesian Front (q.v.) government. They have consequently been subjected to considerable censorship (q.v.), much of it self-imposed. (United States libraries receiving the RH: Boston University; Hoover Institution; Howard University; Library of Congress; Northwestern University; UCLA; University of Wisconsin.)

RHODESIA PRINTING AND PUBLISHING COMPANY   see   "ARGUS GROUP"

RHODESIA RAILWAYS COMPANY. Government-owned statutory body, created in 1949 after purchase from the BSAC in 1947. The company was originally created as a subsidiary of the BSAC in 1893, under the name Bechuanaland Railway Company. In 1899 the name was changed to Rhodesia Railways Ltd. The company built and operated railway (q.v.) lines in present Rhodesia, Zambia, and Mozambique. Rhodesia Railways now only operates the lines in Rhodesia and Botswana.

RHODESIA REGIMENT.   The first unit with this name was raised
by Col. H. C. O. Plumer (q.v.) on the eve of the South African
War (q.v.) in 1899.   This regiment helped to relieve the siege
of Mafeking the next year and then was disbanded.   During the
First World War the 1st Rhodesia Regiment was raised among
European volunteers.   This unit saw limited military action
against Afrikaner (q.v.) rebels within South Africa and against
Germans in South West Africa (Namibia) before its disbandment
in 1915.   The same year the 2nd Rhodesia Regiment was raised
for the East African campaign.   After rigorous actions against
German forces in present Tanzania, this unit was disbanded in
April 1917.   In 1929 the Rhodesia Regiment was reconstituted,
and it was later expanded for service in the Second World War.
(See MILITARY FORCES.)

RHODESIA SCIENTIFIC ASSOCIATION (RSA).   Learned society
formed in Salisbury in 1899.   Its annual publication is Proceedings and Transactions of the RSA (originally, Proceedings
of the RSA).

RHODESIA UNIONIST ASSOCIATION.   Party formed in 1919 to support the movement for union with South Africa, in opposition to
the Responsible Government Movement (q.v.).   The Association
was headed by Herbert T. Longden, a Bulawayo lawyer.   It
received much of its support from the local mining industry.
(See UNIONIST MOVEMENT.)

RHODESIAN ...   see also entries beginning   RHODESIA ...

RHODESIAN ACTION PARTY (RAP).   Right-wing political party
formed in July 1977 by 12 European members of parliament
expelled from the Rhodesian Front (q.v.) by Ian Smith after
they failed to support his proposed legislation easing racial
discrimination.   Under the interim leadership of Ian Sandeman,
the Party called for a slower timetable in the move towards
majority rule, and for guarantees in any settlement achieved.
The Party won no parliamentary seats in the election of August
31, 1977.

RHODESIAN AFRICAN RIFLES (RAR).   All-black army unit, under
white officers.   The unit's origins go back to 1898, when an
African reserve company was incorporated into the British South
African Police (q.v.) as a standing unit.   This served against
the Germans in South West Africa (Namibia) in 1914, and then
became the nucleus of the Rhodesian Native Regiment raised in
1916 to fight in the East African campaign.   This regiment was
disbanded after the war, but many of its members reentered the
police askari (African) division.   The RAR itself was first raised
in June 1940, when the veteran askaris served as its first non-com-
missioned officers.   During the Second World War the RAR
served with distinction in Burma.   Afterwards the RAR was
nearly disbanded, but was kept together to serve along the Suez
Canal.   The RAR was maintained as a unit in the new Federation

(q. v.) army during the 1950s, and it played an active role in anti-guerrilla campaigns in Malaya in 1956-8.

After UDI in 1965 the RAR's strength was maintained at a little over a thousand men.   As the anti-nationalist fighting intensified in the early 1970s, the government reluctantly responded to white manpower shortages by announcing plans to double the size of the RAR in early 1974.   In common with most aspects of Rhodesia's security forces, little is known about the specific composition of the RAR, but it is believed that most of its recruits are Karanga (q. v.) from the Fort Victoria region. (See MILITARY FORCES.)

RHODESIAN BANTU VOTERS' ASSOCIATION (RBVA).   Now regarded as the first association to focus African attention on the national political center, the RBVA was essentially an elitist organization dominated by Ndebele, Mfengu (qq. v.), and other immigrant African leaders.   The movement was started in 1922 by Abraham Twala, a Zulu (q. v.) Anglican teacher from South Africa. Twala rejected violent protest movements, seeking instead to draw Africans into active participation in territorial electoral politics.   His followers held their first meeting at Gwelo* on January 20, 1923, when they formally launched the RBVA. Twala himself held no post in the organization.   Leadership posts went instead to Ernest Dube, an Ndebele teacher; Thomas Mazinyane, a Sotho (q. v.) immigrant; and Garner Sojini, a prosperous Mfengu farmer.   Martha Ngano (q.v.) became secretary the following year and was the RBVA's leading spokesperson through the balance of the decade.

A general meeting of the RBVA was held in July 1923 and a constitution was drafted.   This document asserted the organization's respectful intentions to cooperate with the government in a peaceful effort to uplift the condition of the country's African peoples.   Fewer than 30 Africans were then registered voters, so the RBVA sought a wider membership to demonstrate broader African support.   Nevertheless, the government dismissed the organization as an unrepresentative body dominated by foreigners bent on agitating local Africans.   When the Morris Carter Commission (q. v.) collected evidence on land allocation in 1925, RBVA leaders strove to be heard.   The Commission's report and the ensuing Land Apportionment Act (q. v.) were bitter disappointments.

Despite the RBVA's goal of becoming a territory-wide organization, its effective branches were limited to the Matabeleland*, and Mashonaland* was never penetrated.   In 1929 Ngano participated in a meeting with leaders of the ICU (q. v.) and other African organizations, but efforts to create a unified congress movement failed.   The Bantu Congress (q. v.) which arose five years later was completely unrelated to the organizations of the 1920s.

RHODESIAN BROADCASTING CORPORATION (RBC).   Radio broadcasting began experimentally during the early 1930s, drawing heavily upon British Broadcasting Corporation (BBC) programs

and recorded music.   By 1941 a regular studio was established
in Salisbury, where a fulltime professional broadcaster was employed.   During the 1940s the Salisbury studio concentrated on
English-language programming, while African listeners were
served by broadcasts originating in Lusaka, Northern Rhodesia.
The Federation (q.v.) government took over English broadcasts
in the 1950s, formally establishing the Federal Broadcasting
Corporation (FBC) in 1958.   The same year an African language
studio was opened in Harare (q.v.) for the development of more
relevant local broadcasts.   After the Federation's breakup in
late 1963, the Salisbury headquarters of the FBC was transformed into the Southern Rhodesian Broadcasting Corporation
(later called the RBC), which soon reached the entire country
from seven medium-wave stations.

Television broadcasting began as a private commercial
operation in 1960, initially serving only Salisbury.   In 1964 the
government-owned RBC bought out the Rhodesian Television company, making television broadcasting a government monopoly.
Additional stations were added in Bulawayo in 1961, Gwelo in
1970, and Umtali in 1972.   Each station transmits effectively
over a radius of only 160 km., but it is estimated that 80% of
the country's settler population was being reached by the early
1970s, with a growing number of African viewers in the main
urban centers.   Both radio and television sets require annual
licenses.

Technically, the RBC is constituted as an autonomous
authority, free from government control.   In practice, however,
the RBC has become a government propaganda arm since the
assumption of power by the Rhodesian Front (q.v.) in 1962.
When the government acquired RBC in 1964, it replaced the
corporation's board members and news service personnel with
RF supporters willing to practice self-censorship.   Ian Smith
openly stated his aim of using the broadcast media to counter
unfavorable criticism leveled by the country's independent press
(q.v.).   BBC programs, which previously dominated the air-
waves, were largely eliminated, and their place was taken by
South African Broadcasting Corporation and RBC-produced programs.   Some BBC-originated programs have, however, continued to reach the southwestern part of the country from a
station in Francistown, Botswana (q.v.).   (See also CENSOR-
SHIP; TRANSPORT AND COMMUNICATIONS.)

RHODESIAN COMMENTARY   see under   AFRICAN TIMES

RHODESIAN DOLLAR (R$)   see   CURRENCY

RHODESIAN FRONT (RF).   European political party founded in
March 1962 to succeed the Dominion Party (q.v.) and such
rightist allies as the Southern Rhodesian Association and the
United Group.   The RF campaigned against the country's
membership in the Federation (q.v.) with a policy of "Rhodesia
First," outlining a set of principles stressing the primacy of
European interests.   Under the leadership of party president

Winston Field, chairman Clifford Dupont, and deputy chairman
Ian Smith (qq. v.), the RF defeated the United (Federal) Party
(q. v.) in the following December's general elections.   Field
then became prime minister.

Since its creation the RF has consistently stood strongly
for the exclusion of external control over settler government.
Field's failure to get Britain to pledge Rhodesian independence
during the dissolution of Federation talks was a chief cause of
the RF's ousting him from the premiership in favor of Ian Smith
in April 1964 (see also LILFORD, D. C.).   Under Smith's leadership the party made independence its chief cause, and it intensified government harassment of African nationalist organizations,
such as the PCC and ZANU.   The party proved its strength in
August 1964, when Dupont defeated Roy Welensky (q.v.) in a
parliamentary by-election.   The following May it won all 50 reserved European seats in the Legislative Assembly (q.v.).   On
the strength of this election and a general referendum of the
previous November, the RF government issued its Unilateral
Declaration of Independence (q.v.) on November 11, 1965.

Under the post-UDI pressures of world criticism and
economic sanctions (q.v.), the country's European electorate has
drawn even more closely together, leaving the RF virtually without significant European opposition within the country.   Although
party leaders such as W. J. Harper (q.v.) have occasionally
withdrawn from the RF--usually to attempt formation of more
rightist parties--the general electorate's support of the RF has
never wavered.   The goal of maintaining the country's pre-
carious independence has ruled out serious public rifts in party
leadership, and the actual power politics within the party have
remained largely inscrutable to outsiders.

Aside from the party's international notoriety as the un-
abashed champion of minority government, the RF is significant
as the country's first European political party to develop into a
truly broad-based (among whites) and permanent organization.
This attribute contrasts with the tradition of earlier parties
which were little more than transient bodies mobilized by top
leadership before each election.   A large part of the country's
white electorate are dues-paying RF members, all of whom are
organized in an active hierarchy of branches and committees.
Regular party members have always played a real role in decision-making processes through the party organization, direct
personal influence on MP's, and annual conventions.   In return
for their share of real power, party regulars have faithfully
supported their government leaders through numerous crises
and in every election.   Despite occasional defections of party
leaders and party MP's, the RF won all 50 European parliamentary seats in the general elections of 1965, 1970, 1974, and
1977.

Since the visit of the Pearce Commission (q.v.) in early
1972, the party has gradually accepted the principle of greatly
increased African participation in government.   In April 1977 a
party convention attended by 471 delegates voted 422 to 35 to
support a resolution acknowledging the inevitability of African

majority rule, while calling for guarantees that whites would
retain a major share of power in any future African government. A second resolution authorized the government to continue negotiations which would bring about such a political transformation. Several months later 12 MP's bolted from the RF
to form the Rhodesia Action Party (q.v.) to resist the RF's apparent liberalization. In the general election of August 31, 1977,
the RF again swept the 50 reserved European parliamentary
seats. Through early 1978, however, the question of how the
party could reconcile its principles of white primacy with the
goal of majority African rule was still unsettled.

RHODESIAN HISTORY. Scholarly journal of the Central Africa His-
    torical Association; published annually by the University of Rho-
    desia's (q.v.) Department of History since 1970 (but actual pub-
    lication of each volume has been delayed by at least a year).
    Rhodesian History is the first professional journal to deal mainly
    with Rhodesian history. Despite the often hostile attitude of the
    government towards independent scholarship, it has attracted in-
    ternational contributors, and its articles have increasingly re-
    flected the trends of Africanist historical scholarship elsewhere.
    A useful bibliographical feature of the journal is its comprehen-
    sive list of books and articles published on Rhodesian history in
    each year. (Cf. NADA; RHODESIANA.)

RHODESIAN IRON AND STEEL COMPANY (RISCO) see under RED-
    CLIFF

RHODESIAN IRONWOOD see MOPANE

"RHODESIAN MAN." Popular name for an early human sub-species
    (Homo sapiens rhodesiensis) which occupied eastern and central
    Africa during the early middle Stone Age (q.v.). Some authori-
    ties describe this sub-species as an African equivalent of its
    European contemporary, the Neanderthal Man (Homo sapiens
    neanderthalensis). The name "Rhodesian Man" was coined in
    1921 when the first Rhodesioid skull fragments were discovered
    at Broken Hill, Northern Rhodesia (now Kabwe, Zambia).

RHODESIAN PARTY (a.k.a. Rhodesia Party). Name given to Southern
    Rhodesia's ruling Responsible Government Party (q.v.) by Charles
    Coghlan (q.v.) in late 1923. The party held power until 1933,
    when Godfrey Huggins (q.v.) led his breakaway Reform Party
    (q.v.) to victory. Two years later most of the Rhodesian Party
    members joined with Huggins' supporters to form the United
    (Rhodesian) Party (q.v.). Some conservative Rhodesian Party
    members under H. U. Moffat (q.v.) later attempted to revive the
    party, but they were decisively defeated in the 1939 election. By
    1946 no party members still held Legislative Assembly (q.v.)
    seats.

RHODESIAN RIDGEBACK DOG (a.k.a. Rhodesian lion dog). The only
    internationally recognized dog breed developed in southern Africa,

ridgebacks are large dogs with short, light hair, distinguished
by a forward-pointing ridge atop their backs. The breed originated in South Africa, where Europeans interbred European
hunting dogs with indigenous ridgebacked varieties. The missionary Charles Helm (q.v.) brought a pair of the dogs to Matabeleland in 1875. There the breed was standardized and given
its name, which was officially registered in 1922.

RHODESIANA. Journal of the Rhodesiana Society, an antiquarian
organization with branches throughout the country. Rhodesiana
articles deal mostly with early European activities in the country. Started as an annual in 1956, it became semi-annual in
1963. Early volumes are now being reprinted by Books of Rhodesia (q.v.).

RHODESIOIDS see "RHODESIAN MAN"

RINDERPEST EPIDEMIC (1896-8). Rinderpest, or "cattle plague,"
is a virulent, highly infectious disease affecting ruminant animals, especially cattle (q.v.). It causes fever, dysentery, in-
flammation of the mucous membranes, and speedy death. The
disease was unknown to southern Africa before the late 19th
century, though it had long been endemic in Asia, and had even
reached Western Europe as early as 1500 years ago. The virus
spreads both directly and indirectly among ruminants, and can
be carried for periods up to several months in hay, cloth, and
other articles, and in other animals and vermin.
        Rinderpest first appeared in sub-Saharan Africa after
being introduced into Somalia in 1889. From there it spread
quickly through eastern Africa, reaching Zambia* by late 1892.
The Zambezi River* appears to have halted the epidemic temporarily, for it was not reported in present Rhodesia until it
reached Bulawayo* in February 1896. There it quickly devastated
game, cattle, and draft oxen. The Ndebele people, who had recently lost most of their cattle to the British South Africa Company, were hit hardest. To add to their consternation, the Company administration began shooting cattle to halt the spread of
the disease. These calamities apparently contributed to the outbreak of the ensuing Revolt (q.v.). Meanwhile, the disease
spread rapidly into South Africa*, reaching Cape Town by late
1897.
        The impact of the rinderpest epidemic on Rhodesia was
great. It was estimated that up to 95% of the country's cattle
succumbed to the disease. The devastation of oxen severely
impaired transportation (q.v.), hindering European defenses
against the revolt, driving up import prices for some time, and
accelerating the building of the first railways (q.v.). The loss
of cattle also forced Africans to turn increasingly to agriculture
(q.v.) and to wage labor.
        Although rinderpest had hit Western Europe only two
decades earlier, the first medical advances against it were
made in southern Africa after 1896. With new immunizing
techniques developed in South Africa, inoculation of cattle began

in late 1897 in Matabeleland. By late 1898 the disease was
virtually eradicated, and no further major outbreaks have occurred since in the country. (See HEALTH.)

"RING KOPS." Nineteenth-century European nickname for Ndebele
(q.v.) men who wore headrings (q.v.). From Afrikaans (q.v.)
word kop for "head."

RIVERS. The almost uniformly high altitude of the country relative
to surrounding regions makes it a single great watershed, laced
with an immense number of rivers (see ALTITUDINAL ZONES).
However, the country's climate (q.v.) delivers too little rainfall to keep all these rivers flowing year-round, and there are
few natural catchments to collect the water (see LAKES; VLEIS).
Much of the rainfall drains off quickly in seasonal floods, leaving
most rivers either dry or mere trickles during the winter months.
None of the rivers--except parts of the Zambezi (q.v.)--is navigable. Water conservation is a crucial problem, resulting in the
building of weirs and dams (q.v.) throughout the country.
    The Central Plateau (q.v.), which runs from southwest to
northeast, forms the main watershed. Its rivers are grouped
into four separate drainage systems: (1) Between Plumtree* and
Shabani* a number of important rivers flow south or southeast
into the Limpopo (q.v.), which defines the border with South
Africa. (2) From Shabani to Marandellas* a somewhat larger
number of rivers flow southeast into the Sabi (q.v.), which is
also fed by rivers rising in the Eastern Highlands (q.v.). More
than half the country's water runoff drains through these two
river systems, which are now being exploited by the Sabi-Limpopo Authority (q.v.). (3) Across the entire width of the northern part of the country a large number of rivers flow generally
north into the Zambezi. The Limpopo, Sabi, and Zambezi all
empty into the Indian Ocean through Mozambique. (4) Of minor
significance are the Nata (q.v.) and a few other small rivers
which flow west, into Botswana's Markikari Basin. Yet another
group of rivers--unconnected with the Central Plateau--rise in
the Eastern Highlands, flowing east directly into the sea. The
Pungwe (q.v.) is the most notable of these. Their contribution
to the country's water resources is slight, as they enter Mozambique almost immediately after they rise.

ROADS. Before the arrival of Europeans in the country in the mid-
19th century, there were neither wheeled vehicles nor true roads.
The advent of ox wagon (q.v.) traffic led to development of the
"Hunters' Road" (q.v.) through Matabeleland, but this was little
more than a wagon track. The basis for the first true road was
the route cut by the 1890 Pioneer Column (q.v.) between Tati
and Salisbury (qq.v.). European occupation of the entire country
during the 1890s promoted development of a road network, with
the best roads linking the main European centers. Problems
created by heavy seasonal rains (see CLIMATE) were tackled
with a major bridge-building program after 1924, and with the
strip road (q.v.) program of the early 1930s. Full-width asphalt

roads were not started until just after the Second World War.
By the mid-1970s the country contained c. 6000 km. of major
paved roads, c. 25, 000 km. of unpaved rural roads, and
c. 40, 000 km. of municipal roads.   (See TRANSPORT AND
COMMUNICATIONS.)

ROCK PAINTINGS.   It is said that southern Africa contains more
specimens of ancient rock art than does the entire rest of the
world.   Most sites are found in South Africa, but Rhodesia itself has more than 1500 known rock art sites.   A handful of
these sites contain petroglyphs (q. v.).   The rest have only
paintings.   Rock art is therefore virtually synonymous with
rock paintings in Rhodesia.
    The ancient artists painted almost exclusively on granite
surfaces.   Exfoliation and other natural processes of decay
make granite surfaces impermanent.   The oldest extant paintings
therefore cannot be more than about 7000 years old.   If any
paintings were executed earlier, they have probably left no
trace.   The surviving paintings thus are associated with late
Stone Age (q. v.) cultures.   This association is further supported by the depiction of such late Stone Age culture features
as bow and arrow-carrying humans in most hunting paintings.
    Since the paintings appear on granite surfaces, it is not
surprising that the rocky Matopo Hills (q. v.) contain one of the
largest concentrations of paintings in Africa (see, e. g.,
BAM-BATA; BULUBAHWE; NSWATUGI; POMONGWE; and SILOZWANE
CAVES; and WHITE RHINO SHELTER).   There are also many
sites in the highland areas of Mashonaland* (see, e. g., DIANA'S
VOW; DOMBOSHAWA; EPWORTH; MAKUMBE; MREWA; RU-
CHERO; and ZOMBEPATA).   Isolated but important sites are
also scattered elsewhere, e. g., Mchela (q. v.).
    No technique has yet been devised to date the paintings.
Many occur in or near former occupation sites, notably caves,
which provide datable artifacts and bones, but these materials
cannot always be confidently associated with the paintings themselves.   It is generally agreed that San people (q. v.) executed
the best paintings of at least the most recent centuries, but it
is not certain that San were also the earliest artists.   Attempts
have been made to link southern African rock art with similar
forms elsewhere, but diffusionist theories are, by their nature,
highly speculative and unrewarding.
    The variety of subjects depicted in the paintings is vast.
While certain animals, such as antelope, elephants, and giraffes,
appear frequently, a bewildering array of other animals, including birds, reptiles, and even insects, also appear.   Human
figures are typically depicted as hunters.   Herders also occasionally appear, as do people in domestic and ceremonial scenes.
A difficulty in interpreting the paintings arises from a fundamental distinction in stylistic treatment.   Animal figures are
typically naturalistic, while human figures are highly stylized,
and therefore not amenable to positive ethnic identification.
Frequently-depicted steatopygic hunters were likely Khoisan
(q. v.) peoples.   Other human figures are believed to have been

Bantu-speakers (q.v.). In contrast to paintings in South Africa,
Rhodesia has no known examples of European figures in rock
paintings.
          C. K. Cooke, curator of national monuments, offers a
useful typology of painting styles with these numbers: (1) Simple
monochrome silhouettes without movement.   (2) Similar paintings
depicting movement.   (3) More realistic outline drawings, which
are rare.   (4) Realistic polychromes depicting complex interac-
tions among humans and animals.   This style is most common.
(5 & 6) Crude copies of presumably earlier styles, believed to
have been painted recently by Bantu-speakers.   Cooke suggests
a chronological framework corresponding to these numbered
styles; however, any such chronology remains speculative for
the reasons suggested above.   Further difficulties arise from
the universal problem of attempting to assign subjective art
forms to precise categories.   This difficulty is manifest in the
fact that paintings assigned to "early" styles are occasionally
found superimposed over "late" styles.   If such problems can
ever be resolved, the country's rock paintings may yet prove
to be as valuable a historical record as they are an esthetic
resource.

RODWELL, CECIL HUNTER (Dec. 29, 1874-Feb. 1953).   Second
     Governor (q.v.) of Southern Rhodesia (1928-34).   After serving
     in the South African War (q.v.), Rodwell joined the staff of
     British High Commissioner Lord Milner (1901-3), and served
     as Imperial Secretary in South Africa.   He then became governor
     of Fiji (1918-24) and of British Guiana (1925-8) before replacing
     J. R. Chancellor (q.v.) in Southern Rhodesia.   In contrast to
     his predecessor, Rodwell was reluctant to advise Godfrey Hug-
     gins (q.v.) on ministerial appointments.   He later returned to
     South Africa to work in the mining industry.   He was succeeded
     in Southern Rhodesia by H. J. Stanley (q.v.).

ROLI (variant: ROLE) see HOLI

ROTSE (BAROTSE) see LOZI

ROWORO (variant: ROORA).   Chishona* form of lobolo (q.v.).

ROZVI (variants: Rozwi; Barozwi; Varozvi; etc.).   Name of an im-
     portant but enigmatic section of the Shona people (q.v.).   Al-
     though the name "Rozvi" pervades the literature on Shona history,
     authorities differ greatly on who these people were and are, and
     on where they came from.   The Rozvi have been variously de-
     scribed as an intrusive alien group; an indigenous and ancient
     Shona "tribe"; a clan; a dynasty; and a dialect group (usually af-
     filiated with Kalanga, q.v.).   Today people calling themselves
     Rozvi are spread throughout the country.   Rozvi identification is
     prestigious, and the claims of some Rozvi are disputed by others.
     The only universally recognized Rozvi are those people whose
     mutupo (q.v.) is Moyo Ndizvo (or Mhondizvo).   Other Rozvi base
     their identification on historical political connections with what

were once Rozvi-ruled states.

According to the most convincing interpretations of Rozvi
identity, the original Rozvi were purely indigenous Shona associated with the rise of the Changamire state (q.v.) initiated by
Dombo (q.v.) in the late 17th century. Dombo's destructive conquests earned his followers the nickname varozvi, or "destroyers"
(cf. DZVITI). There is no uncontestable evidence that the name
Rozvi was applied to any Shona group before the time of Dombo,
though the Changamire state itself clearly had ties with the Togwa, Munhumutapa (qq.v.), and other Shona states (see SHONA
HISTORY). The rulers of the Changamire state apparently
adopted the name "Rozvi" during the 18th century. The name
later conveyed considerable political prestige because of this association.

The Nguni (q.v.) invasions of the early 19th century
Mfecane (q.v.) broke up the Changamire state, causing a rapid
dispersal of Rozvi people throughout the rest of the country,
particularly to the southeast. Since then many small chieftaincies
have claimed Rozvi connections, but it is likely that some such
claims are spurious. Confusion over Rozvi identity has been
magnified by alterations in traditional histories, which project
Rozvi population movements and conquests deep into the pre-
Dombo past.

Rozvi identity has also been perpetuated in the name
Abelozwi for Shona incorporated into the Ndebele state (see
HOLI). It should also be noted that while attempts have been
made to link the Rozvi with the Lozi (q.v.), or "Rotse," of
western Zambia, there is no evidence to connect these two
peoples. (See also UROZVI.)

RUCHERO CAVE (a.k.a. Mtoko Cave). Important rock painting
(q.v.) site located near Mtoko village (q.v.). The cave's main
frieze features figures interpreted as Khoi (q.v.) men herding
sheep.

RUDD, CHARLES DUNELL (Oct. 22, 1844-Nov. 1916). British
businessman. Rudd came to South Africa in 1865 and later became a partner of Cecil Rhodes in the Kimberley diamond fields.
With Rhodes he helped to found DeBeers Consolidated Mining
Company, of which he became a director, and he obtained a
major interest in the Rand gold mines in the 1880s. From
1883 to 1888 he represented Kimberley in the Cape Parliament.
In late 1888 he replaced Ivon Fry (q.v.) as Rhodes' agent at
Bulawayo*, where he got Lobengula to sign the "Rudd Concession" (q.v.). He retired to England in 1902.

RUDD CONCESSION (1888). Popular name for agreement signed on
October 30, 1888, by the Ndebele king Lobengula (q.v.), and by
C. D. Rudd, F. R. Thompson, and J. R. Maguire (qq.v.), as
agents for Cecil Rhodes (q.v.). Acquisition of the Concession by
a syndicate comprising Rhodes, Rudd, and Thompson led directly
to formation of the British South Africa Company (q.v.) and its
royal Charter (q.v.) the next year.

There were two versions of the Concession: one written
in English and fully accepted by the BSAC and the British government; the other an oral version communicated to the Ndebele by
the interpreter C. D. Helm (q.v.), who also signed the written
version as a witness. As the Ndebele soon learned to their
distress, the two versions differed greatly. This mattered little
to Rhodes and his associates, however, as their main purpose
in obtaining the Concession was not so much formation of an
agreement with the Ndebele kingdom, as the securing of a signed
document which could be used to exclude European imperial competitors from the territory north of the Limpopo River.

The Ndebele understood the agreement as a limited concession (q.v.) for a small number of Europeans to prospect
near the Ramaquabane River (q.v.). By contrast, the written
document granted Rhodes' group "exclusive charge over all metals
and minerals" in all of Lobengula's domain--the extent of which
the BSAC exaggerated in its representations to outsiders. Only
the Tati Concession (q.v.) area was specifically excluded. The
document also gave the grantees power to exclude--with Ndebele
assistance if necessary--other prospectors and concessionaires
from the region, and the right of veto over any future Ndebele
concessions.

The oral and written versions of the Concession seem to
have coincided only on the form of payment to the Ndebele.
Lobengula was to receive £100 each lunar month; 1000 rifles
and 100,000 rounds of ammunition; and an armed steamboat
placed on the Zambezi River, or £500 cash. The BSAC honored
all but the last of these provisions.

Rhodes' rivals in Bulawayo soon alerted the Ndebele to
the discrepancies between the oral and written versions of the
Concession. These revelations brought about a political crisis
in which the induna Lotshe (q.v.) was killed. King Lobengula
meanwhile sent Babayane and Mshete (qq.v.) to London to seek
advice, and then publicly repudiated the Concession in January
1889. In March Helm admitted to the Ndebele his deceptive
interpretation of the Concession, spurring further Ndebele re-
nunciations and refusals to accept shipments of the Concession
rifles. Although the BSAC continued to regard the Concession
as a valid agreement, Rhodes sent L. S. Jameson (q.v.) to
Bulawayo several times to renegotiate the agreement. Alarmed
at the prospect of armed British invasion, Lobengula modified
his previous oral agreement on a few points to gain time.
Jameson then distorted Lobengula's position in order to convince
the British government that Lobengula had in fact confirmed the
original written concession. After the BSAC occupied Mashonaland with its Pioneer Column (q.v.) in 1890, the validity of the
Rudd Concession became less important, as British occupation
was an accomplished fact. Nevertheless, Lobengula was persuaded to sign the Lippert Concession (q.v.) in 1891, thinking
he was dealing with a rival European party. He in fact was
dealing with agents of the BSAC, which used his various concessions to build a legal justification for the Ndebele War of
1893 (q.v.). Thereafter the BSAC claimed territorial authority
over Matabeleland by right of conquest.

RUENYA RIVER. One of the more important rivers in the northeast, the Ruenya itself flows northeast, separating the Mtoko
and Inyanga districts (q. v.). It is joined by the Gairezi River
(q. v.) as it enters Mozambique, where it is known as the
Luenha, finally feeding the Zambezi.

RUINS. Although the country's borders (q. v.) were artificially
created by Europeans during the 1890s, they have since been
found to encompass a nearly congruent region of stone ruins
unparalleled in tropical Africa. More than 400 stone building
sites are known within the country. Almost all of these represent purely indigenous building traditions. Two independent traditions have been identified; both share techniques of mortarless
granite block construction. Ruins are most common in, but by
no means exclusive to, the belt of granite outcroppings which
coincides roughly with the Central Plateau and central Eastern
Highlands (qq. v.).
    Rudimentary stone-walling was initiated by the late
Leopard's Kopje culture people (q. v.), but substantial building
in stone is believed to have originated at the site of the Zimbabwe Ruins (q. v.) only in about the 12th century. There techniques were developed which spread to more than 150 other sites
by the mid-15th century, when Zimbabwe itself was abandoned.
The early Munhumutapa (q. v.) rulers, who are believed to have
migrated into the northern Dande* region from Zimbabwe around
this time, continued the building tradition there, but only briefly.
The Dande is outside the granite area, so stone-building was
apparently given up to make use of more accessible construction
materials. The Togwa and Changamire (qq. v.) states continued
the stone-building tradition in the south, shifting the center west
to southern Matabeleland*. There the Khami Culture (q. v.)
arose as a Zimbabwe derivative. The Khami-type builders made
great use of retaining walls, in contrast to the Zimbabwe-type
emphasis on free-standing walls. This tradition, too, was
largely abandoned in the early 19th century, after the Mfecane
(q. v.) invasions disrupted Shona life.
    The second independent building tradition is found in the
Inyanga Ruins (q. v.) in the northeast. Stonework there was
cruder, with more emphasis on massive structures, and considerable work on retaining walls for cultivation terraces. The
Inyanga tradition started somewhat later than its southern counterparts, but also appears to have ended in the early 19th century.
    Many popular theories have been advanced for non-African
origins of the country's stone ruins, but none stands up against
scientific archaeological research. Portuguese (q. v.) traders and
missionaries did, however, leave many ruins in the northeastern
part of the country during the 16th and 17th centuries (see
FAIRS). There are no similarities between their ruins and those
of the purely indigenous traditions. (See also IRON AGE.)

RUKWADZANO RWE WADZIMAYI see RUWADZANO

RUSAPE (variant: Rusapi). Commercial and administrative center

established in the Makoni District (q. v.) in 1894.   Rusape
stands on the main road between Umtali and Salisbury (at 18°
32'S, 32° 7'E; alt. 1405 m.).   Population in 1969 was 5290
(85% Africans).   Nearby is Diana's Vow Cave (q. v.).

RUTENGA.   Village in southeastern low veld, at the junction of the
main road from Beitbridge to Fort Victoria, and the Somabula
to Vila Salazar railway line (qq. v.) (at 21° 15'S, 30° 44'E).   In
the mid-1970s the railway was extended from Rutenga to Beitbridge, giving the country its first direct rail link to South
Africa.

RUWADZANO (variant: Rukwadzano).   Chishona* term for "fellowship, " popularly applied to a Methodist (q. v.) women's movement
introduced to the country in 1919 from the Transvaal*, where
the movement was called Manyano.   Ruwadzano organizations
have historically mobilized African women to support Methodist
evangelism and to maintain high family spiritual and moral
principles.   Since the 1960s these organizations have become
more directly concerned with community and national problems,
and have occasionally been mobilized in political protests.
          Although the first ruwadzano arose among members of
the Wesleyan Methodist (q. v.) churches, the largest organization
is that affiliated with the United Methodist Church (q. v.)--the
Rukwadzano rwe Wadzimayi (literally, "Women's Fellowship").
This organization was founded in 1929 at the Old Umtali Mission
(q. v.), and has since developed into both the largest lay organization in the UMC and the largest African women's voluntary
organization in the country.   By 1971 it claimed nearly 8700
dues-paying members--43% of the UMC's total membership.   As
is the case with other ruwadzano, the members of the Rukwadzano rwe Wadzimayi wear distinctive uniforms and emblems at
gatherings, and they assemble for annual revivals during the
Easter week.   A major contribution of such organizations has
been their raising of women's self-esteem and social assertive-
ness.

- S -

SABI-LIMPOPO AUTHORITY (SLA).   Major government irrigation
project established in January 1965 to develop the southern low
veld region, covering a 65,000 sq. km. sector east of Beitbridge
and Shabani, and south of Fort Victoria and Melsetter (qq. v.).
A particular goal of the project has been to encourage European
settlement in the low veld (see ALTITUDINAL ZONES).   The
SLA was empowered to coordinate all aspects of governmental
economic and social planning in the region, but in practice it
has concentrated on building dams (q. v.) and developing irrigation for both private and SLA-owned estates.   The region has
fertile soils, well suited for sugar (q. v.), citrus, and other
crops, but its rainfall is sparse and irregular (see CLIMATE).
The SLA was created to take advantage of the fact that half of

the country's rainfall is drained by the Sabi, Lundi, and Limpopo (qq.v.) river systems which empty through the low veld.
The SLA started with a 25-year plan to bring under cultivation
more than 300,000 hectares (750,000 acres) of land, which
would eventually support more than two million Africans and
120,000 Europeans. The first irrigation projects enjoyed only
mixed successes, and the contraction of export markets due to
sanctions (q.v.) stifled investment. By 1975 an estimated
40,500 hectares were under cultivation. The administrative
and commercial center for the SLA is at Chiredzi (q.v.).

SABI RIVER. The largest river inside the country, the Sabi rises
at a point midway between Enkeldoorn and Marandellas on the
Central Plateau, flowing southeast more than 200 km. to its
junction with the Odzi River, west of Melsetter (qq.v.). From
there it flows south a somewhat greater distance, and then is
joined by the Lundi River (q.v.) at the country's lowest point,
where as the Save River it enters Mozambique* and then
empties into the Indian Ocean by Mambone. (See RIVERS.)

SADZA. A thick millet (q.v.) porridge which has traditionally been
the staple dish of the Shona people. The equivalent Ndebele
dish is isitshwala, a porridge made from maize (q.v.).

SAKUBVA. The largest African township in Umtali (q.v.).

SALISBURY. National capital; the largest city in the country; a
leading commercial, financial, and industrial center; and administrative center for both Salisbury District and the two
Mashonaland Provinces (qq.v.). Located on the northeastern
part of the Central Plateau* (at 17° 50'S, 31° 3'E; alt. 1500 m.).
The town was established as "Fort Salisbury" when the Pioneer
Column (q.v.) halted there on September 12, 1890. The BSAC
named the site in honor of the British Prime Minister Lord
Salisbury in order to build goodwill with the imperial government. The name became simply "Salisbury" in 1897, when the
town was declared a municipality.
      Salisbury's location was chosen somewhat arbitrarily, as
a practical high veld site suitably distant from the potentially
hostile Ndebele kingdom. Salisbury's growth experienced a brief
setback in 1894, after Bulawayo (q.v.) was occupied by the
British, but Cecil Rhodes quickly promised that Salisbury would
remain the country's capital, and its growth has since been continuous. It was linked with the Beira railway line in 1899, and
to the Bulawayo line in 1902 (qq.v.). In 1935 it was proclaimed
a "city." Between 1953 and 1963 it served as capital of the
Federation (q.v.).
      Salisbury has always been the predominant center of
European settlement. The 1969 census recorded 112,900 European residents, accounting for 42% of the country's entire European population. This figure rose an estimated 10% through
1974, but African population growth in Salisbury has been even
greater. Of the estimated 545,000 residents in late 1974, 75%

were Africans. Residential segregation is formalized. Virtually
the entire area north of the city center is reserved for Europeans, who live mostly in low density suburbs, such as Mount
Pleasant (q. v.), Highlands, Borrowdale, Greendale, and elsewhere. Townships in the southeastern sector are also mostly
European, while African townships are mostly in the southwestern
sector. Of the ten official African townships, the largest are
Harare, Highfield, and Mufakose (qq. v.). Marimba Park (q. v.)
is a small area for wealthy Africans. A large number of Africans live in European areas, mostly as servants, but Westwood
(q. v.) is the only township with racially mixed home owners.
   Salisbury draws most of its electrical power (q. v.) from
Lake Kariba (q. v.), but also has its own thermal plant. Its
water comes mainly from dams on the nearby Hunyani River
(q. v.).

SALISBURY DISTRICT. Shaped like a crude number "7," this district bisects Mashonaland South Province (q. v.). Goromanzi
District (q. v.), which once was part of Salisbury, borders the
district on the northeast. Salisbury also borders the districts
of Marandellas on the southeast; Charter on the south; Gatooma
on the southwest; Hartley on the west; Lomagundi on the northwest; and Mazoe (qq. v.) on the north. Except for two small
Purchase Areas (q. v.), the entire 4745-sq. km. district is reserved for Europeans by the Land Tenure Act (q. v.). Outside
its capital city of Salisbury (q. v.) the main industry is agriculture (q. v.). District population in 1969 (including the city)
comprised 456,000 Africans, 127,000 Europeans, and 14,120
other peoples.

"SALTED HORSES." Nineteenth-century term for horses (q. v.)
thought to be immune from horsesickness (q. v.) by virtue of
their having survived a bout with the disease. Such animals
commanded from five to ten times as much money as "unsalted"
horses, with prices ranging from £40 to £100 a head during
the late 19th century. Fraud was common among horse traders,
although guarantees of survival were a part of most deals.

SALUGAZANA see TENKELA

SAMKANGE, STANLAKE JOHN WILLIAM (b. March 11, 1922). Historian, novelist, and nationalist leader. The second son of T.
D. Samkange (q. v.), Stanlake Samkange was born in the Zwimba
Reserve of southern Lomagundi District*. Raised a Methodist,
he was educated at Waddilove Institution (q. v.)--which provides
the setting for his novel The Mourned One (London, 1975)--and
at Adams College and Ft. Hare University College in South
Africa. On his return to Southern Rhodesia in 1946, he briefly
taught at a government school, but quit this job to organize one
of the country's first independent African schools at Nyatsime,
just south of Salisbury. In 1951 he entered nationalist politics
as secretary-general of the old African National Congress (q. v.).
Always an advocate of African political unity, he helped to

organize the All-African Convention (q.v.) in 1952 and served as
its secretary-general. During the mid-1950s he worked as a
free-lance journalist. In January 1954 he made an unsuccessful
bid for one of the African seats in the Federal Assembly, losing
to Jasper Savanhu (q.v.).

Samkange went to the United States in 1957. There he
earned a master's degree from Syracuse University and married
an American woman. On his return home the following year he
joined Garfield Todd's (q.v.) United Rhodesian Party. He became an officer of that group's successor body, the Central
African Party (q.v.) in 1959, but resigned a year later. In
1966 he returned to the United States and earned, in 1968, a
Ph.D. in history from Indiana University. Later he taught at
Northwestern, Harvard, and elsewhere in the United States,
while starting to write history texts and novels with Rhodesian
historical settings (see BIBLIOGRAPHY). Since October 1976
he has served as an adviser to Abel Muzorewa (q.v.) and has
returned home.

SAMKANGE, THOMPSON DOUGLAS (1887-Aug. 27, 1956). Methodist
minister and nationalist leader. Samkange was born in the
Lomagundi District's* Zwimba Reserve, where he later declined
a government chiefship. He was educated at Waddilove Institution (q.v.) and afterwards was ordained a Methodist minister.
During his long and varied career he served as president of the
African division of the Southern Rhodesian Missionary Conference
(q.v.), and as president of the old African National Congress
(q.v.) from the mid-1940s. During his last years he developed
the Pakame Mission, 30 km. southeast of Selukwe*. His children
included Stanlake Samkange (q.v.), and Sketchley Samkange, the
latter an active ANC and NDP leader who accidentally drowned
in Lake Nyasa in 1961.

SAN (a.k.a. "Bushmen"; Twa; Sarwa*; etc.). "San" is a Khoi (q.v.)
word preferred as the collective name for the Khoisan (q.v.)
people popularly called "Bushmen." Once widespread in eastern
and southern Africa, there are now only a few tens of thousands
of San in southern Africa. Most live in Namibia (South West
Africa) and Botswana (q.v.); others reside in southern Angola.
A few bands also still live in the western fringes of present Rhodesia. The San are the descendants of the Stone Age (q.v.)
peoples who predominated in the country until the arrival of
Bantu-speakers (q.v.) in the early first millenium A.D. The
early San were mostly hunter-gatherers who lived in small,
nomadic bands. They are generally credited with production of
most of southern Africa's rock paintings (q.v.). The often-
stated assumption that the San were either "exterminated" or
driven out of the country by invading Bantu-speakers is insup-
portable. It is instead quite clear that the San in the better-
watered parts of the country were absorbed into Shona (q.v.)
society long before the 19th century, thereby contributing a considerable element of Shona physical ancestry. The Ndebele
(q.v.) continued the process of absorbing San after their own

arrival in the country in the mid-19th century. The current
number of independent San living in the country is difficult to
determine because the remaining bands move freely across the
Botswana border; nevertheless, it is clear that their numbers
are small.

SANCTIONS. (1) Imposition. Immediately after Ian Smith's Rhodesian Front government issued its Unilateral Declaration of
Independence (q. v.) in November 1965, the British government
made it clear it would not attempt to use military force to
bring down the rebel regime. Britain instead quickly imposed
various economic sanctions against Rhodesia which Prime Minister Harold Wilson predicted would cause Smith's speedy collapse.
Britain moved to block Rhodesian access to capital markets and
export credits in Britain, and banned British import of Rhodesian sugar and tobacco--soon adding chrome, iron, copper,
and asbestos (qq. v.) to the list. The United Nations Security
Council meanwhile resolved that no member nation should aid
or recognize the Rhodesian regime, and it instituted what has
been called "Phase One" of international economic sanctions.
These called for voluntary bans on imports of key Rhodesian
products, as well as an embargo on sales of petroleum to the
country. In March 1966 Britain began a naval blockade of ships
carrying Rhodesian-bound petroleum through the Mozambique
Channel of the Indian Ocean. The next month the UN Security
Council ruled that Britain could use force, if necessary, to stop
petroleum deliveries. Because of Rhodesia's total dependence
on imported petroleum, the effort to stop its delivery to the
country was, and still is, regarded as the key element of sanctions policies.
      The apparent failure of voluntary sanctions to weaken the
Rhodesian regime caused the UN General Assembly to urge the
Security Council to take tougher action. On December 16, 1966,
the Security Council initiated "Phase Two" by passing a resolution calling for mandatory sanctions against importation of selected Rhodesian goods. This phase lasted until May 1968, when
the Security Council established a "Phase Three" policy of comprehensive mandatory sanctions. Rhodesia's evident success in
combating sanctions caused the Security Council periodically to
pass more refined resolutions, closing loopholes and broadening
applications, but proposed resolutions against Rhodesia's trade
collaborators, South Africa (q. v.) and Portugal, failed to pass
on several occasions. By 1977 it was generally recognized that
no sanctions policy against Rhodesia would work without the active cooperation of South Africa, which had steadfastly ignored
sanctions. As a consequence there was increased international
pressure to invoke economic sanctions against South Africa itself. The strength of this threat lay largely in South Africa's
own dependence upon foreign suppliers of petroleum. South
Africa responded to the threat by intensifying its own efforts to
persuade the Rhodesian regime to find a constitutional settlement
with African nationalists, but by late 1978 the UN has not yet
passed sanctions against South Africa.

(2) <u>Responses to Sanctions</u>.   Efforts of the Rhodesian
regime to combat sanctions began at least a year before UDI,
and UDI itself was timed so as not to interfere with advance
sales of such products as tobacco and sugar to foreign markets.
In anticipation of sanctions, the Rhodesian government had
earlier instituted import controls, cultivated trade relations
with countries least likely to honor international sanctions, arranged for long-term trade agreements wherever possible, and
repudiated foreign debts for which Britain could be held responsible.   South Africa and Portugal then allowed transshipment of
Rhodesian exports through South Africa, Mozambique (q. v.), and
Angola under the pretext that Rhodesian goods were originating
in those countries so as to fool buyers otherwise honoring sanctions.   Some non-members of the UN such as Switzerland and
West Germany (which joined the UN in 1973) continued to trade
legally with Rhodesia, while many other countries, notably
Japan, traded covertly with Rhodesia.   By 1972 Rhodesia's
total foreign trade, much altered in composition, had reached
its pre-UDI levels in value, and the UN reported that from a
third to a half of all Rhodesian exports were reaching member
nations which nominally adhered to sanctions policies.   The subsequent independence of Angola and Mozambique soon added new
restrictions to Rhodesia's trade channels, but the main effect of
this political transformation was merely to make Rhodesia more
reliant on South Africa.   Meanwhile, the United States, through
its Byrd Amendment (q. v.), was the only other UN member
openly to flout UN sanctions, but the U.S. reversed its policy
in 1977.   Nevertheless, by then goods which clearly originated
in Rhodesia were still reaching many nations, including nominally hostile black African countries, and the UN was revealing
extensive sanctions violations by the Soviet Union and some of
its east European allies.   Neighboring Zambia (q. v.) remained
the most consistently rigorous adherent to sanctions policies, but
even that country was importing South Africa goods through Rhodesia, despite the official closure of its borders and the latent
state of war.

(3) <u>Impact of Sanctions</u>.   Rhodesian law forbids the reve-
lation of any economic data which do not demonstrate the country's success in beating sanctions.   In the absence of full data
it is impossible fully to assess the impact of sanctions on the
country, but certain trends are evident.   The psychological effect of being under a state of economic siege has drawn the
settler population more closely together in support of the Rhodesian Front (q. v.) regime, which has been able to attribute
most economic problems to outside forces.   The government itself has taken an increasingly active role in the economy, intensifying its historical trend towards full management.   It directly manages all foreign trade and currency transactions, it
stockpiles commodities, and it fosters mining and European
agricultural sectors with extensive price supports.   Whereas
external responses to sanctions have been indifferent or casual,
Rhodesian efforts to circumvent sanctions have been both vigorous and thorough.   Government trade agents, often traveling on

British passports, have arranged for complex transshipments
of exports and imports, mainly through South Africa, and have
dealt particularly with dummy corporations based in Switzerland.
Much of Rhodesia's success in overcoming the handicaps
intended by sanctions has been attributed to the large slack
existing in its industrial capacity at the time of UDI. Rapid
expansion and diversification of local manufacturing has substituted local goods for imports, making the country virtually self-
sufficient in most minerals, raw and processed foods, paper
products, iron and steel, cotton, leather, fertilizers, and other
goods. Refusal of other countries to recognize the Rhodesian
government freed local manufacturers from having to honor
patent rights and licensing controls, thereby enabling them to
manufacture copies of many vitally needed spare parts for
existing capital equipment and vehicles. Rhodesian imports
have meanwhile shifted mostly to capital goods and equipment,
and certain chemicals and metals. Such local shortages of goods
as have been observed through government secrecy have been
mostly non-essential consumer items.
European agriculture (q.v.) was the economic sector hit
hardest by the loss of export markets. Nevertheless, this
sector underwent sufficient diversification to remain strong,
while helping both to fill demand for formerly imported goods
and to produce many products which could still find export
markets. The mining (q.v.) sector also expanded and diversified, as minerals were found to be among the most easily exported goods. By 1977 Rhodesia's export earnings were apparently about equally divided between the agricultural, mineral,
and manufacturing sectors.
Despite sanctions Rhodesia generally ran only a small
annual balance of payments deficit from 1965 to 1973, and internal prices rose at an annual inflation rate of only about 3%.
This generally favorable situation began to shift around 1973,
as international commodity prices began to damage Rhodesia's
terms of trade, as long-term trade agreements ran out, and
as Mozambique's independence led to further restrictions on the
transport of trade goods. By early 1978 the long-term impact
of sanctions on Rhodesia was still not clear, however, and the
country's economic prospects appeared to rest largely on the
willingness of South Africa to continue its support.

SANYATI RIVER. Name once more commonly used for the stretch
of the Umniati River (q.v.) below its confluence with the Umfuli
(q.v.).

SARWA (Masarwa; variants: Maisiri; Amasili). Bantu* name for
San people (q.v.) living in Rhodesia and Botswana.

SAUER, HANS (June 11, 1857-Aug. 28, 1939). An Afrikaner (q.v.)
of German extraction, Sauer was born in the Orange Free State.
After qualifying as a medical doctor in Edinburgh in 1881, he
returned to South Africa and made a fortune on the diamond and
gold fields. He then qualified as a lawyer in London and came

to present Rhodesia to assist Cecil Rhodes in a mining venture.
During the Ndebele War (q.v.) he bought up mining claims and
land in Matabeleland* to augment his wealth.   He was later ar-
rested in the Transvaal because of his connections with the
Jameson Raid (q.v.), but was released without imprisonment.
He returned to Matabeleland during the Ndebele Revolt (q.v.)
and participated in Rhodes' "Indaba" (q.v.) with rebels.   In
April 1899 he was elected to the newly-formed territorial Legis-
lative Council (q.v.), but he moved to England the next year.
Over the next decade he spent half of each year managing his
Matabeleland holdings locally, and then retired permanently to
Europe.   He died in France, two years after publishing Ex
Africa, a colorful but not thoroughly reliable autobiography
which has helped to make him well known.

SAVANHU, JASPER ZENGEZA (b.1917).   Journalist and politician.
Born in the Goromanzi District* and educated at Waddilove
(q.v.) and Domboshawa Technical School, Savanhu emerged as
a radical labor organizer in Bulawayo during the Second World
War.   He was a vigorous critic of the government and was an
active leader of the old African National Congress (q.v.).
Forced by illness to turn to less physically demanding activities,
he joined the staff of the African Newspapers Ltd. group (q.v.),
becoming its editor-in-chief by the early 1950s.
        In 1952 Savanhu accompanied Joshua Nkomo and Godfrey
Huggins (qq.v.) to the London conference on Federation (q.v.).
Though he opposed creation of the Federation, he accepted its
inevitability and defeated Stanlake Samkange (q.v.) and others
in the first election for one of the two Federal Assembly seats
reserved for Africans (the other African elected was M. M.
Hove, q.v.).   He was re-elected twice, becoming the only Southern Rhodesian African to serve in the Federal Assembly for its
entire duration.   Throughout his tenure of office he generally
supported the policies of the ruling United (Federal) Party (q.v.)
to which he belonged, and he became popularly regarded as a
government "stooge" by Africans.   In 1958 Prime Minister Roy
Welensky (q.v.) appointed Savanhu parliamentary secretary to
the Minister of Home Affairs--a post which made him the
highest-ranking African member of government in 20th-century
Rhodesia.   In August 1962, however, he embarrassed UFP
leadership by resigning his ministerial post to protest the failure
of the government to make "partnership" (q.v.) meaningful.   After
dissolution of the Federation the next year he was treated as a
pariah by African nationalists.

SAVANNA.   An internationally used term for grassy plains with
scattered, scrubby trees, such as characterize most of Rhodesia
and the rest of the great African plateau.   This type of vegetation is the product of limited rainfall (see CLIMATE), which
inhibits larger tree growth (see FORESTS), while allowing tall
grasses to predominate.   It is well suited for extensive livestock
raising.   The Rhodesian savanna differs somewhat from that of
other African countries in that it is frequently broken up by

granite kopjes (q. v.), moist vleis (q. v.), and other kinds of
terrain. (See ALTITUDINAL ZONES.)

SAWMILLS. Village on the railway line in the central Nyamandhlovu
District* (at 19° 35'S, 28° 2'E). Appropriately named, the village is the center of the local hardwood industry (see FORESTS).

SCHREINER, OLIVE (March 24, 1855-Dec. 12, 1920). South African
author. A former governess in the Cape Colony who gained
fame with the novel The Story of an African Farm (London,
1883), Schreiner married a Cape politician, Samuel Cronwright,
in 1894, and then campaigned and pamphleteered with her husband for liberal causes. Both were especially suspicious of
BSAC activities in present Rhodesia. During the Ndebele/Shona
Revolt of 1896-7 (q. v.) Schreiner wrote a novel, Trooper Peter
Halket of Mashonaland (London, 1897), which presented a scathing
indictment of BSAC mistreatment of Africans and of Cecil
Rhodes' policies. In her later life she turned her pen to support radical feminist causes.

"SEA COWS" see HIPPOPOTAMUSES

SEASONS see CLIMATE

SEBAKWE RIVER. Rising on Mount Mtoro (18° 54'S, 31° 5'E), just
northeast of Enkeldoorn*, the Sebakwe River flows generally
west in a sweeping curve below the Umniati River (q. v.), which
it joins just west of the Que Que* to Gatooma* road. The
Sebakwe Dam, built in the Mashaba Mountains (q. v.) in 1957,
is one of the country's largest internal dams (q. v.). Its lake
covers 60% of the 2510-hectare Sebakwe National Park which
surrounds it. This dam, and the smaller Dutchman's Pool Dam,
built north of Que Que in 1954, supply Que Que and the surrounding farms with water.

SEBITWANE (d. 1851). Founder-king of the Kololo (q. v.).

SEBUNGWE DISTRICT. Former administrative district (q. v.)
covering 32,845 sq. km. in the northwest, between the Zambezi, Umniati, Kana, and Gwaai rivers. Sebungwe's successor
districts are Gokwe in the east, Binga in the west, and part
of Kariba in the northeast (qq. v.).

SEKGOMA (variant: Sekhome) (c. 1815-1883). Ruler of the Ngwato
(q. v.) and father of Khama III (q. v.).

SELOUS, FREDERICK COURTENEY (Dec. 31, 1851-Jan. 4, 1917).
Hunter and author. Born in London, Selous came to southern
Africa in 1871 to hunt elephants (q. v.). Over the next two
decades he traveled and hunted widely in Matabeleland and
Mashonaland, collecting animal specimens for British museums
and writing numerous magazine articles about his exploits. He
achieved some renown with the publication of two popular books,

A Hunter's Wanderings in Africa (1883) and Travel and Adventure in South-East Africa (1893), and his career is believed to have inspired H. R. Haggard's (q.v.) fictional character "Allen Quartermain." Selous's writings extolled Shona culture, but he used his unique knowledge of the Shona to help Cecil Rhodes and the BSAC to lay claim to Mashonaland. In 1890 he served as guide to the Pioneer Column (q.v.) which occupied Mashonaland. After the BSAC occupied Matabeleland three years later, Selous settled there with his family. During the Ndebele Revolt of 1896 (q.v.), he fought with the Bulawayo Field Force (q.v.), and then wrote Sunshine and Storm in Rhodesia (1896) describing the early stages of the revolt. Afterwards he hunted big game throughout the world until the First World War, in which he was killed by German forces in the East African campaign. (See HUNTERS; IVORY.)

SELOUS SCOUTS (SS). Elite Rhodesian army counter-insurgency unit, similar to the American army's Green Berets. The SS are credited with spearheading anti-guerrilla raids into Mozambique, and they have been often accused by African nationalists of committing many atrocities against civilians which the Rhodesian government blames on "terrorists." (See MILITARY FORCES.)

SELUKWE. Important mining town and administrative center of the district of the same name (at 19° 40'S, 30° E; alt. 1445 m.). The town was founded on goldfields in 1899, and has since developed into one of the country's major chrome (q.v.) producing centers. It is just southeast of Gwelo (q.v.), to which it is connected by a branch railway line. Population of the town and adjacent mines in 1969 was 10,200 (92% Africans).

SELUKWE DISTRICT. Covers 3550 sq. km. at the southern bend of Midlands Province (q.v.). It borders the districts of Chilimanzi on the east; Victoria and Chibi on the southeast; Shabani on the south; Insiza on the southwest; and Gwelo (qq.v.) on the west and north. A well-wooded and well-watered region, the district is about equally divided between European and African-reserved land (see LAND TENURE ACT), with European areas dominating the west and northeast. District population in 1969 included 54,770 Africans, 850 Europeans, and 262 other people.

SENA. Mozambique (q.v.) town on the right bank of the Zambezi River, about 260 km. up from the coast. Established as a Muslim (q.v.) trading post perhaps as early as the tenth century, Sena was occupied by the Portuguese (q.v.) in 1531. Thereafter it became a major base for trade routes to Shona country. The name "Sena" has also been applied to a local branch of Bantu (q.v.) languages.

SENATE. Upper chamber of the Rhodesian Parliament (q.v.), established in 1970 by the 1969 Constitution (q.v.). The body's 23 members included ten Europeans elected by the European members of the House of Assembly (q.v.); ten African chiefs selected by the Council of Chiefs (q. v.); and three members appointed by the President (q. v.). The Senate's main function is to approve bills amending the entrenched clauses of the constitution, such as those pertaining to land tenure. In this respect the body assumed the reserved powers once held by the British Crown.

SENGWA RIVER. Rises on the Mafungabusi Plateau (q. v.), whence it flows west, then north, entering Lake Kariba* at the latter's mid-point--a location which was once the Kansala Rapids on the Zambezi River.

SERTANEJO. Portuguese (q. v.) term for backwoodsman; applied to early traders and adventurers operating in the inland areas of the Zambezi Valley. (See, e.g., BAYÃO; MADEIRA.)

SHABANI. Mining, commercial, and administrative center in the district of the same name, just south of the country's center (at 20°20'S, 30°2'E; alt. 925 m.). Shabani Mine began exploiting asbestos (q.v.) deposits just before the First World War, and is now the country's largest producer of this product. The town has grown along with the mine. In late 1974 it ranked eighth among the country's urban centers with a population of about 17,000 (88% Africans).

SHABANI DISTRICT. Covering 2490 sq. km. in the northeastern corner of Matabeleland South Province (q. v.), Shabani District was formerly the northern part of Belingwe District (q. v.), the rest of which now borders Shabani on the south. Shabani also borders the districts of Chibi on the east; Insiza on the west; and Selukwe (qq. v.) on the north. The central part of the district is reserved for Europeans; the other parts are mostly Tribal Trust Lands (q. v.). District population in the 1969 census included 54,630 Africans and 1757 Europeans.

SHAKA (variants: Chaka, Tshaka) (c.1780s-1828). South African Zulu (q. v.) ruler credited with building the Zulu kingdom into a major military power during the 1820s. Mzilikazi (q. v.) served under him briefly before fleeing to the Transvaal in c.1821. The story of Mzilikazi's break from Shaka figures prominently in Ndebele historical traditions. (Cf. ZWIDE.)

SHAMUYARIRA, NATHAN (b.1929). Educationalist, journalist, and nationalist leader. Born into a Methodist family, Shamuyarira was educated at Waddilove Institution (q. v.) before teaching at a number of schools. In May 1953 he joined African Newspapers, Ltd. (q. v.), becoming the first editor of African Daily News (q. v.) in 1956, and then the whole group's editor-in-chief in 1959. In September 1962 he quit the newspapers and joined ZAPU under Joshua Nkomo (q.v.). The next year he broke from Nkomo, following Ndabaningi Sithole (q. v.) into ZANU. From 1964 to 1967 he studied at Princeton University. During this period he wrote Crisis in Rhodesia (London, 1965), a personal memoir with a historical survey of African nationalism in Rhodesia. From Princeton he went to the University of Dar es Salaam in Tanzania to lecture in political science. He also served as ZANU's secretary for external affairs until late 1971, when he became an officer in the newly-formed FROLIZI (q. v.) and resigned his lectureship. In mid-1973 he quit FROLIZI and returned to teaching in Dar es Salaam.

SHAMVA. Administrative and commercial center of the district of the same name. The town of Shamva, originally called Abercorn*, was formerly an important gold (q. v.) mining center. Shamva Gold Mine operated between 1908 and 1930, and was recently reopened. In the third week of September 1927 the mine was the site of a major African labor strike. About 3500 mine and contractor employees--almost all from eastern Zambia and Malawi--struck for better wages and improved accident compensation. Heavy government pressure caused the strike to collapse, but it nevertheless demonstrated to the country the ability of African workers to organize effectively on a large scale. Subsequent closure of the mine halted the town's development, and in 1969 its population was less than a thousand. The town stands at the terminus of a branch railway (q. v.) line from Salisbury (at 17° 19'S, 31° 34'E; alt. 970 m.).

SHAMVA DISTRICT. Recently carved out of Mazoe and Darwin districts (qq. v.), it covers 2665 sq. km. within Mashonaland North Province (q. v.). The Nyagui and Mazoe rivers separate Shamva from the Mrewa District on the east. The district also borders the districts of Darwin on the north, and Bindura on the west, and it touches Goromanzi (qq. v.) on the south. Except for some Tribal Trust Land (q. v.) in its center and northwest corner, the district's lands are reserved for Europeans. District population in 1969 was 19,000.

SHANGANE (Amashangane; variants: Shangaan; Changana). After Soshangane (q. v.) founded the Gaza kingdom (q. v.) in the early 19th century, his followers became known as Amashangane, "the people of Soshangane." In this narrow sense, "Shangane" is synonymous with "Gaza." Since the mid-19th century, however, the name Shangane has acquired a looser meaning. It is now frequently applied to Ndau, Hlengwe (qq. v.), and other peoples formerly associated with the Gaza. Most of the people now called "Shangane" do not speak the Nguni (q. v.) language of the original Gaza. In contemporary usage the name is best regarded as a regional, rather than ethnic, identification.

SHANGANI DISTRICT. Former 10,485 sq. km. district surrounding the Shangani River (q. v.) in the west. Originally the northern part of Bubi District (q. v.), Shangani itself was recently divided into the present Lupane and Nkai districts (qq. v.). Its former administrative center was at the village of Lupane. The village of Shangani is a small trading center on the main railway line (at 19° 47'S, 29° 22'E; alt. 1375 m.).

"SHANGANI PATROL" (a.k.a. "Wilson Patrol") (1893).   Perhaps
   the single most famous military confrontation between Europeans
   and Africans in the history of the country, the "Shangani Patrol" symbolizes to European settlers their blood sacrifice in
   their occupation of the country during the early 1890s.   After
   the BSAC had occupied the Ndebele capital, Bulawayo, during
   the Ndebele War (q.v.), L. S. Jameson dispatched Major P. W.
   Forbes with a column to pursue King Lobengula (qq.v.), who
   was fleeing north in November 1893.   Heavy rains allowed
   Forbes' column to advance only c.27 km. in 14 days, so Forbes
   sent back the wagons and most of his men on November 28th.
   On December 3rd the force camped on the south bank of the
   Shangani River (q.v.).   Forbes then sent Major Allan Wilson
   (q.v.) and a few dozen men across the river to reconnoiter.
   That evening Wilson reported he had found Lobengula and asked
   for reinforcements.   Forbes was reluctant to move at night, so
   he sent only a few more men.   The next day the river rose so
   high it was almost unfordable.   F. R. Burnham (q.v.) reported
   that Wilson's patrol was trapped by the Ndebele, who then killed
   all 34 of its members.   Months later the bodies were recovered
   below the river's confluence with the Gwelo*.   The bones were
   temporarily buried at the Zimbabwe Ruins*, and later reinterred
   with a shrine at World's View (q.v.) in the Matopo Hills.
        The undoubted courage of the fallen men has long been
   stressed in settler traditions.   Only recently has it been pointed
   out that this last action of the Ndebele War was an Ndebele
   victory, and that the event itself demonstrated the incomplete-
   ness of the British "conquest."

SHANGANI RIVER.   The main tributary of the Gwai River (q.v.), the
   Shangani rises near Dhlo Dhlo*, whence it flows generally northwest before meeting the Gwai near Lubimbi Hot Springs.   Along
   the way the Shangani is fed by the Vungu and Gwelo* rivers from
   the east.

SHANGWA.   Chishona* term for misery or famine; associated particularly with a widespread drought and famine which occurred
   just before the Mfecane invasions (q.v.) of the 1830s.

SHANGWE (Vashangwe; variants: Shankwe; Bashangwe).   Small Shona
   (q.v.) community speaking a sub-dialect of Korekore (q.v.).
   Since at least the early 19th century the Shangwe have lived in
   the tsetse*-infested region around the Bumi River* just southeast of central Lake Kariba*.   During the 19th century the
   Shangwe avoided Ndebele raids by paying tribute in salt obtained
   from the Bari Pan (at 17° 34'S, 28° 35'E).

SHASHANI RIVER.   Rising near the mid-point of the Plumtree to
   Bulawayo road, the Shashani flows south by southeast for c.160
   km. before joining the Shashi River (q.v.) at the Botswana border.

SHASHE RIVER (not to be confused with Shashi).   Rises on the
   Central Plateau* near Felixburg (at 19° 26'S, 30° 50'E).   The

Shashe initially flows north, but quickly turns west and then south to feed the Ngezi River (q.v.) just above the latter's confluence with the Tokwe. The Shashe defined part of the "boundary" between Mashonaland and Matabeleland declared by L. S. Jameson (q.v.) in 1893.

SHASHI RIVER (not to be confused with Shashe). One of the main tributaries of the Limpopo (q.v.), the Shashi rises in Botswana about 50 km. west of Plumtree*. It flows south, curving below Francistown*, then is joined by the Ramaquabane River (q.v.) at the Rhodesian border. From there it flows southeast 160 km. before meeting the Limpopo. This stretch defines the Botswana/Rhodesia border (q.v.), except at the "Tuli Circle" (q.v.). During the 19th century the Shashi was regarded as the boundary line between the Ndebele and Ngwato spheres of influence.

SHAVASHA (Vashavasha; variant: Shawasha). Branch of the Zezuru (q.v.) cluster of Shona-speaking peoples, living mainly in the present Salisbury District*, northeast of the capital city. The most important of the Shavasha royal dynasties was that of the Chinamoras (q.v.).

SHAVE (variants: shabe; shawe; shavi; pl., mashave). A variety of Shona spirits. In contrast to personal ancestor spirits (see MUDZIMU), and tutelary community spirits (see MHONDORO and GOMBWE), the mashave are nontutelary spirits of strangers. These strangers are usually people who die locally and are not buried properly. They may include neighboring Shona individuals, Europeans, animals--especially baboons--or even airplanes. The mashave are said to select the hosts whom they possess rather arbitrarily. They are usually benevolent, but they may be malevolent, in which case they are also classed as ngozi (q.v.), whom the unwilling mediums try to have exorcised. Mashave are often credited with giving their hosts special skills, such as hunting, iron-working, mbira (q.v.) playing, or healing and divining. Some nganga (q.v.) receive their healing and divining skills from mashave. Many mashave are thought to be very fond of dancing. They possess their hosts, particularly women, in lively dancing séances which frequently develop into popular social events. (See RELIGION--SHONA.)

SHEPSTONE, THEOPHILUS (Jan. 8, 1815-June 23, 1893). British official in charge of African affairs in Natal, and self-styled expert on African politics. Always anxious to extend British influence in southern Africa, Shepstone supported the claim of his gardener, Kanda, to be the missing Ndebele royal heir "Nkulumane" (q.v.). He supported Kanda in an invasion of Matabeleland in 1872, and persisted to taunt Lobengula (q.v.) with the Nkulumane threat afterwards. In 1877 Shepstone became British administrator of the Transvaal (q.v.). The next year he sent R. R. Patterson (q.v.) on his ill-fated mission to Matabeleland.

SHILOH.   Small, independent mission station founded by T. M.
Thomas (q. v.) in 1876.   Thomas's widow sold the station, located c. 50 km. west of Inyati (q. v.), to a farmer in 1889.

SHIMMIN, ISAAC (1860- Feb. 26, 1933).   British missionary.   Manx
by birth, Shimmin came to South Africa in the mid-1880s as
an agent of the Westleyan Methodist Missionary Society (q. v.).
While working in the Transvaal in 1891 he met Cecil Rhodes,
who agreed to contribute £100 a year to a Methodist mission
in Mashonaland.   That September Shimmin and Owen Watkins
(b. 1842), a fellow missionary, arrived in Salisbury.   There
they obtained a land grant from the BSAC on which they founded
Epworth Mission (q. v.).   Watkins returned to South Africa and
Shimmin remained to direct Wesleyan work in Mashonaland.   In
1907 Shimmin returned to England to work as a pastor.

SHONA HISTORY.   The problem of dating the earliest arrival of
Shona-speaking peoples (q. v.) in the country has long perplexed
historians.   On the basis of oral traditions, dates as late as
the 11th through 15th centuries have been variously assigned to
this event.   In view of the early first millenium dates which
archaeologists have established for the beginnings of the local
Iron Age (q. v.), a second millenium date for the Shona arrival
leaves the problem of identifying their immediate Iron Age
predecessors.   The introduction of the Iron Age is generally
attributed to the arrival of the first Bantu-speakers (q. v.).
The modern dominance of the country by Shona suggests that
they must have been among the first Bantu-speakers to arrive.
Indeed, recent linguistic research indicates that this was the
case.   The widespread distribution and diversification of Shona
dialects (see CHISHONA) point to an early first millenium Shona
presence in the country.   Linguistic research further suggests
that Chishona developed as a distinct language within the country, where it separated from a parent language which also gave
rise to other southeast Bantu languages which developed dif-
ferently after other early migrants moved farther south.
     The history of the country since the early first millenium
is, then, essentially the history of its Shona-speaking peoples,
who absorbed the original Khoisan (q. v.) and, possibly Central
Sudanic (a branch of Chari-Nile) speakers.   Most later arrivals
to the country became Shona-speakers as they too were absorbed
by the dominant group.
     Little is known about the political systems of the Shona
before about the 14th century.   By then the first large-scale
state system had arisen among the Karanga (q. v.) branch of
Shona.   This state was centered in the southeast at the site
now known as the Zimbabwe Ruins (q. v.).   The Zimbabwe state
declined suddenly in the 15th century.   At the same time an
apparently related state was established by the Munhumutapa
dynasty (q. v.) in the northern Dande (q. v.) region.   This state
briefly developed into an empire along the southern banks of the
Zambezi River.   It then went into a gradual decline as tributary

provinces broke away, forming autonomous states, and as other competing Shona states rose to prominence. The most important of these were the Togwa and Changamire states (qq.v.) in the south, and the Mutasa (q.v.), or, originally, Chikanga, dynasty in the east. Shona-derived dynasties were also established over such non-Shona peoples as the Barwe (q.v.) in the northeast.

In the late 17th century the Changamire state rapidly developed into an empire which dominated more of the country than did any other pre-colonial state system. The Changamire rulers became known as "Rozvi" (q.v.), a name which has caused considerable confusion in reconstructing Shona history generally. The Rozvi empire, like its predecessor states, was really more a confederation than a centralized polity. It comprised a collection of tribute-paying chiefdoms with their own dynasties. The tendency towards local autonomy was persistent, and by the late 18th century the "empire" was disintegrating. The Mfecane (q.v.) invasions of the 1830s accelerated this process. Afterwards there were more than a hundred independent Shona chiefdoms, many of which had to struggle for autonomy against the raids and tribute exactions of the newly-arrived Ndebele and Gaza kingdoms (qq.v.). Shona independence came to its decisive end only in 1897, however, after the failure of a large-scale Revolt (q.v.) against British occupation of the country. Since then Shona chiefdoms have survived merely as government-sanctioned administrative units in Tribal Trust Lands (q.v.), formerly called "reserves."

Even during the peak periods of the large-scale Shona states, Shona societies remained rooted in subsistence agriculture (q.v.) and limited animal husbandry. State systems emerged partly as a response to competition for control of ivory and gold trades (qq.v.) with the east coast, but these pursuits were essentially limited, part-time economic activities within the total Shona economic systems. Generalizations about Shona political structures are difficult to make, but their lack of uniform systems of political succession stands out clearly. Shona social structure is patrilineal, and family power blocs often developed quickly. Competition for political succession among rival families was--and still is--a major feature of Shona politics. Fission occurred frequently within dynasties and was a major cause of the proliferation of autonomous states. Rivalries among neighboring states were often intense, accounting for the relative ease with which the Ndebele dominated the western part of the country in the 19th century, as well as attributing to the failure of the Shona to mount an effective resistance against the British in the 1890s.

SHONA LANGUAGES see CHISHONA

SHONA PEOPLES (Mashona, or Vashona). Roughly three-quarters of the country's people are known as "Shona." Not all of these people recognize the name, however. Historically, Shona have tended to identify themselves as members of either dialect clusters, such as Karanga (q.v.), or smaller groupings, such as Shavasha (q.v.). The origin of the name "Shona" itself is obscure. The name was almost certainly coined by outsiders in the early 19th century (cf. SWINA; NYAI). Its invention is usually attributed to the Ndebele (q.v.), who are said to have used it as a term of abuse, but a European traveler, Andrew Smith, recorded the name "Mashoona" in 1835--three years before the Ndebele settled in the country. The country's later European rulers applied the name "Shona" to all the peoples belonging to the large cultural grouping now generally called Shona. The Shona themselves began accepting the name as increasing external pressures gave them a greater sense of commonality. Government-sponsored standardization of the Shona language, or Chishona (q.v.), in the 1930s and the spread of literacy enhanced the trend towards unification of Shona identity.

The country's borders (q.v.) correspond fairly closely to the perimeters of Shona distribution, except in the east, where Shona communities extend across part of Mozambique (q.v.). The term "Mashonaland" (q.v.) was applied by Europeans to the eastern parts of the country where few non-Shona peoples lived in the 19th century, but Shona-speakers also pervade Matabeleland (q.v.) in the west, and some spill over into Botswana*. The Ndebele are the most numerous single non-Shona people in the country, but most present Ndebele are physically descended, at least in part, from 19th-century Shona incorporated into the Ndebele state (see HOLI).

Despite many attempts to classify the Shona into component "ethnic groups" or "tribes," no satisfactory classification has been achieved. There are few simple correlations between dialect groups, ethnic groups, and historical political units. Individuals, families, ruling dynasties and even whole communities have historically moved about the country frequently. Almost every modern Shona community is a complex ethnic amalgam. Nevertheless, a number of distinct dialect clusters are generally recognized as meaningful division. These correspond, at least broadly, to recognized ethnic divisions. Korekore-speakers live in the north; Zezuru live around Salisbury; Manyika are in the east; Ndau in the southeast; Karanga in the south; and Kalanga (qq.v.) in the far west. A seventh recognized branch, the Rozvi (q.v.), are found throughout the country, confounding attempts at neat regional classifications.

SHONA RELIGION   see   RELIGION--SHONA

SHONA REVOLT (1896-7)   see   REVOLTS OF 1896-7

SIBAMBAMU.   (1) Name of one of Lobengula's (q.v.) brothers.
(2) Variant of Shona name Chibambamu, also known as Tohwe-chipi (q.v.).

SIKOMBO MGUNI (fl. 1860s-1890s).   Ndebele induna*, closely associated with Xukutwayo (q.v.), under whom he served in the

northeastern part of the kingdom. From at least the early
1860s Sikombo accompanied Xukutwayo on many military campaigns. He later married a daughter of Lobengula and became
influential at Bulawayo. In 1889 he was associated with Lotshe
(q. v.) in the group accused of selling out the kingdom to Europeans, but he emerged unscathed to become one of Lobengula's
main advisers. In early 1895 Sikombo was one of the major
planners of the Revolt (q.v.) which began the next year. During
the revolt he was a top leader in the eastern Matopo Hills.
Afterwards he participated in the peace negotiations with Cecil
Rhodes and was made a salaried chief in the Umzingwane District*.

SILINDA, MOUNT (variant: Selinda). Located near the Mozambique* border at 20° 25'S latitude, where a post leads to Espungabera. The hill rises to 1065 m., with the Chirinda
Forest (q.v.) covering its slopes. During the 19th century
the Gaza kingdom (q.v.) maintained its Manhlagazi (q. v.) headquarters nearby. In 1893 the BSAC granted the land around
the hill to the American Board of Commissioners for Foreign
Missions (q.v.), which established its Mount Silinda Mission
there (see also ALVORD, E. D.).

SILKAATS (variant: Zelkaats). Afrikaans (q.v.) form of Mzilikazi
(q. v.).

SILOZWANE CAVE. Important rock painting (q.v.) site, located
on the southern edge of the Matopo Hills (q.v.) in the Khumalo
Tribal Trust Land (at 20° 38'S, 28° 35'E). Its paintings feature
unusually large representations of animals and humans, the
latter evidently depicting Bantu-speaking agriculturalists.

SILVEIRA, GONÇALO DA (Feb. 26, 1526-March 16, 1561). First
Christian missionary in the country. Born into a Portuguese
(q.v.) noble family, Silveira joined the Society of Jesus in 1543
and was sent to the Jesuit mission in Goa in 1556. After
hearing of the interest of the Shona Munhumutapa (q.v.) in
Christianity, he hurried off to Mozambique in 1560, and then
went up the Zambezi River to the court of Munhumutapa Negomo
Chirisamhuru (q.v.). He arrived there around Christmas.
Silveira apparently impressed Negomo with his piety, for he
baptized the Munhumutapa and his mother within a month. Over
the next several months he baptized another 300 or so Shona.
It is usually said that Muslim (q.v.) traders in the country
conspired against Silveira, telling Negomo that the priest was
a spy. It appears, however, that it was actually Shona nganga
(q. v.) who recommended his murder after they had cast hakata
(q.v.) divining bones to determine his intentions. In any case,
Negomo had Silveira strangled on the night of 15/16 March.
His body was thrown into the Musengedzi River*. A decade
later the Portuguese government used Silveira's martyrdom as
a justification for launching Francisco Barreto's (q.v.) punitive
expedition against Negomo. (On Jesuits, see also ZAMBEZI
MISSION.)

SILVER. Significant extraction of this metal in the country began
only with modern European gold mining (q. v.), which separates silver as a by-product. Through 1964 total production
of silver was valued at £1,462,267--a figure equivalent to one-
half of 1% of the value of gold produced through the same
period.

SINDEBELE (variant: Isindebele). The language of the Ndebele
people (q. v.). Sindebele is closely related to Zulu (q. v.), an
Nguni (q. v.) language from which it separated when Mzilikazi
began his migrations in c. 1821. Sindebele differs from Zulu
largely in its accretion of foreign Bantu (q. v.) words, drawn
mostly from Sotho and Shona languages (qq. v.). Until recently
Rhodesian schools used mostly Zulu texts for Ndebele pupils,
but these have caused confusion because of somewhat different
orthographies. Sindebele, for example, makes less use of the
aspirative -h- after consonants, as in dlozi/dhlozi. Like other
Nguni languages, Sindebele contains many click consonants (q. v.).
In common with all Bantu languages, Sindebele nouns employ a
complex system of noun prefixes, such as aba-, ama-, i-, isi-,
and izi- (qq. v.). Since the fall of the Ndebele kingdom in the
1890s, speaking Sindebele has become the single most important
criterion for individuals claiming "Ndebele" identity.

SINOIA. Administrative and commercial center of the large Lomagundi District (q. v.) in the north (at 17° 22'S, 30° 12'E; alt.
1390 m.). Sinoia, founded in 1895, and nearby Eldorado (q. v.)
are now important centers of tobacco and copper production
(qq. v.). Sinoia is c. 115 km. northwest of Salisbury near the
terminus of a major branch railway line. Its population in 1969
was 13,360 (87% Africans).

SINOIA CAVES. Subterranean limestone caverns, located eight km.
west of Sinoia town (at 17° 21'S, 30° 8'E). The caves include
stalactite formations and an impressive deep water pool. A
major tourist attraction, the caves were made a national park
(q. v.) in 1955.
    The name "Sinoia" derives from a Zezuru* chief, Chinoyi.
During the 19th century Chinoyi and his people barricaded themselves inside the cave complex for protection against occasional
Ndebele raids and against the British in the 1896-7 Revolt (q. v.).
The name "Sinoia" has also been applied to an Iron Age (q. v.)
culture sequence.

SIPOLILO DISTRICT. Northern border district, covering 8830 sq.
km. of what was once the northeastern corner of the original
Lomagundi District (q. v.). Administrative center is the village
of Sipolilo, located just northwest of the Umvukwe Mountains*
(at 16° 40'S, 30° 42'E; alt. 1180 m.). The district's northern
panhandle just touches the Zambia border. The district also
borders Mozambique on the north, and the districts of Darwin
on the east, Mazoe on the southeast, Lomagundi on the south,
and Urungwe (qq. v.) on the west. The sparsely populated

northern two-thirds of the district is Tribal Trust Land (q. v.);
the south is reserved mostly for Europeans. District population
in 1969 was just under 60,000, including only 300 Europeans.
The name "Sipolilo" is taken from Chipuriro (q. v.), a local
Shona dynasty.

SIRI CHENA CHURCH (a. k. a. Church of the White Bird) see under
    ZWIMBA, MATTHEW

SITHOLE, EDSON FURATIDZAYI CHISINGAITWI (b. June 5, 1935).
    Attorney and nationalist leader. Politically active from 1951,
    Sithole helped to found the Youth League (q. v.) in 1955, the
    reorganized African National Congress (q. v.) in 1957, and the
    Zimbabwe National Party (q. v.) in 1961. After the collapse
    of the ZNP, he became a leader in ZANU (q. v.), but he spent
    most of the 1960s in prisons and detention camps. Through
    this period he continued his education by correspondence and
    became the country's second African attorney in 1963. After
    one of his releases from detention in late 1971 he became pub-
    licity chairman of the new African National Council (q. v.),
    which he helped to found. He was again imprisoned in 1972.
    After his release in December 1974 he went to Lusaka, Zambia,
    where he created an international stir in July 1975 by claiming
    to have been poisoned by the Rhodesian government. He par-
    ticipated in the Victoria Falls Conference (q. v.) the following
    month as an ANC representative, and then mysteriously disap-
    peared from the streets of Salisbury in October. Widely be-
    lieved to have been the victim of a government kidnapping, by
    1977 he was generally thought to be dead. (N. B.: Edson Si-
    thole is not related to Ndabaningi Sithole, q. v.)

SITHOLE, NDABANINGI (b. July 21, 1920). Congregationalist minis-
    ter and nationalist leader. Born at Nyamandhlovu*, Sithole was
    educated at Garfield Todd's (q. v.) Dadaya mission school and
    at Waddilove (q. v.) during the late 1930s. During the 1940s
    and early 1950s he taught at mission schools and obtained a
    degree by correspondence from the University of South Africa.
    He then studied divinity in New Hampshire from 1955 to 1958,
    returning home to be ordained a minister at the ABC's Mount
    Silinda Mission (q. v.). During this period he also published
    some fiction in both Sindebele* and English, and attracted inter-
    national attention with the publication of African Nationalism
    (Cape Town, 1959), a now classic, political treatise calling for
    an end to racialism in Africa. He soon abandoned his teaching
    career and became an officer in the new National Democratic
    Party (q. v.).
        After the government banned the NDP, Sithole worked
    with Joshua Nkomo (q. v.) to found ZAPU (q. v.). ZAPU was
    banned in 1962, and Sithole and Nkomo found themselves dis-
    agreeing increasingly about what strategy the nationalist move-
    ment should employ. Sithole advocated working within the
    country, while Nkomo proposed forming a government in exile--
    positions on which both men have since shifted many times. In

July 1963 the two leaders split permanently. The following
month Sithole formed ZANU (q.v.) while Nkomo formed the
PCC. When ZANU was banned by the government a year later,
Sithole was arrested. He was in and out of prison until early
1969, when he was sentenced to six years in prison on a charge
of having plotted to kill Prime Minister Ian Smith.

In December 1974 Sithole was released from prison to
participate in constitutional talks to be held in Lusaka. He was
rearrested in Salisbury the following March on charges of plotting
to assassinate fellow nationalists, but the government soon released him under the urgings of South African Prime Minister
John Vorster. Later in 1975 Sithole participated in the abortive
Victoria Falls Conference (q.v.), during which he was loosely
allied with Abel Muzurewa (q.v.). Through this period he claimed
to be the leader of a section of the old ZANU organization, but
he appeared to have lost control of all ZANU external forces to
Robert Mugabe (q.v.), his former lieutenant, and other ZANU
leaders refuted his claims of leadership. By the time of the
Geneva Conference (q.v.) of October 1976 Sithole was based in
Tanzania and had broken from Muzorewa. On July 10, 1977,
he returned to Salisbury after receiving assurances he would not
be rearrested, and announced his desire to become "head of
state." There he joined Muzorewa in denouncing the Organization of African Unity's support of the "Patriotic Front" (q.v.),
and signified his support of the then current Anglo-American
settlement initiative. In early 1978 he was participating in constitutional talks between Smith's government and other local nationalists.

SITI KAZURUKUMUSAPA (d. 1663). In May 1652 Siti succeeded his
father, Mavura II (q.v.), as Munhumutapa (q.v.). Usually described as weak and vacillating, Siti was beset by an ambitious
younger brother, and by unruly Portuguese (q.v.) residents in
the kingdom. In 1663 an army of Portuguese land owners
(prazeros) organized against him, but he was suddenly assassinated by his own noblemen. His brother Kamharapasu Mukombwe
(q.v.) then became Munhumutapa.

SITUPA. Widely-used African term for registration certificates,
from the Nguni* term for thumb, or thumb-print. The Chishona*
form is chitupa. (See PASS LAWS.)

SJAMBOK. Whip, about two meters long, made of tough animal
hides, and used for driving livestock. Not to be confused with
the much longer cracking whips used on teams of oxen. From
a Malay word introduced into South Africa.

SKERM. Temporary fence of thorn trees and branches made to protect travelers at night; derives from the Dutch word scherm for
"fence" or "screen." Frequently used in 19th-century travel accounts.

SKOKIAAN. Alcoholic beverage made from fermented cereals spiked

with typically toxic ingredients such as tobacco, methylated
spirits, or carbonates.   Though illegal and often physically
harmful or even fatal to drinkers, skokiaan has been a popular
drink in African townships, particularly during the late 1940s.
Prostitutes and other women, known as "Skokiaan Queens, "
have made small fortunes from its sale.   It was introduced to
the country from Johannesburg.   The term apparently derives
from the Afrikaans* word skok, for "shock" or "jolt. "

"SLAVE PITS"   see   STONE-LINED PITS

SLAVE TRADE.   The region which is now Rhodesia was almost untouched by the external slave trade which took many people from
Zambia, Malawi, and Mozambique through the 19th century.
The early Shona states traded extensively with Indian Ocean ports
over a long period, but there is no evidence of their having dealt
in slaves.   Likewise, coastal-based slavers appear not to have
penetrated the country significantly, although slavers were operating far up the Zambezi River by the mid-19th century.   By
contrast, the mainly Shona-speaking peoples of the country were
hit fairly hard by 19th-century Mfecane (q. v.) migrants from
South Africa.   Among these migrants were the Ndebele (q. v.),
who occupied part of Matabeleland.   The Ndebele took many
people as captives in raids.   These people (see HOLI) are often
described as "slaves. "   There were unquestionably aspects of
involuntary servitude in such captives' status, but they were not
slaves any more than were Africans forced into labor by the
early British settlers and BSAC.   Ndebele captives were normally absorbed into Ndebele society and their former status
eventually forgotten.   The Ndebele captured other peoples solely
to build up their own numbers, and were actively hostile to the
commercial slave trade connected to the coast.

SLEEPING SICKNESS (trypanosomiasis).   Human variety of a parasitic disease transmitted by certain varieties of tsetse flies
(q. v.).   Though less severe than the equivalent animal disease,
nagana (q. v.), sleeping sickness can cause death.   The first
case recorded in the country occurred in 1912, after the disease
had entered the country from the north.   Since then the disease
has been combatted mainly by eliminating tsetse-fly breeding
grounds.   The disease now occurs only along the northern borders, especially in and around the lower Hunyani River (q. v.).
(See HEALTH.)

SMALLPOX.   This serious infectious viral disease is now eliminated
from the country, and it has not been a major health threat
since 1909, when an epidemic occurred in the northern districts.
The first recorded epidemic occurred in 1862, when the disease
entered Matabeleland* from South Africa.   Accompanied by
measles, smallpox killed many Ndebele people.   In 1893 members of an Ndebele impi* contracted the disease during a campaign into the Zambezi Valley.   The Ndebele soldiers remained
in quarantine through the ensuing Ndebele War*.   King Lobengula

(q. v.) is believed to have died from smallpox during his northward flight early the next year.   (See HEALTH.)

SMALL-WORKERS.   Term for European miners--particularly gold
(q. v.) miners--running small-scale operations, typically those
producing less than 28 kilograms (1000 ounces) of gold per year.
The number of such miners increased rapidly after 1904, when
the BSAC administration began allowing individual prospectors
and small syndicates to work claims without having to float
capitalized companies.   In 1933 755 "small" mines produced
127, 459 oz. of gold.   By contrast, the country's ten "big" mines
(over 10, 000 ounces a year) produced 333, 243 oz.; and 71 "medium" mines produced 154, 566 oz.   In more recent times small-
workers have taken over most of the country's gemstone (q. v.)
production.

SMITH, IAN DOUGLAS (b. April 8, 1919).   Eighth Prime Minister
(q. v.) of Rhodesia (1964-).   The son of a Scot who immigrated
to Southern Rhodesia in 1898, Smith was born in the Selukwe
District*--making him the country's first native-born prime
minister.   He joined the British Royal Air Force in 1939 and
became a fighter pilot.   After being shot down in North Africa,
he underwent massive facial surgery before returning to action.
The Germans shot him down a second time over Italy, where
he spent five months working with anti-Nazi partisans behind
enemy lines.   After the war he attended Rhodes University in
Grahamstown, South Africa, graduating with a commerce degree.
     When Smith returned to Southern Rhodesia he acquired a
large cattle ranch in Selukwe which he still owns.   In 1948 he
was elected to the Legislative Assembly (q. v.) as a member of
the Liberal Party (q. v.).   Five years later he switched to the
United (Federal) Party (q. v.) and was elected to the new Federal
Assembly.   In that body he rose to the post of chief government
whip under Prime Minister Roy Welensky (q. v.).   Smith broke
from the UFP in 1961 in order to help form a party less amenable to political concessions to Africans.   As a member of the
new Rhodesian Front (q. v.) he was elected to the territorial assembly in December 1962.   He then served as deputy prime
minister under Winston Field (q. v.) until April 1964, when he
joined a right-wing revolt which ousted Field and made Smith
himself prime minister.
     Smith took office on April 13, 1964, pledging to secure
Rhodesia's independence under white rule.   Within a few days he
ordered the arrests of Joshua Nkomo (q. v.) and other nationalist
leaders.   In September he went to London for constitutional talks
with British Prime Minister Alec Douglas-Home.   In order to
impress Britain with Rhodesia's support for independence, he
organized the "Domboshawa Indaba" (q. v.) of African chiefs in
October, and held a referendum on the issue among the white
electorate in November.   To strengthen his hand in the government, he ordered a new general election for May 7, 1965, in
which the RF swept the 50 reserved European seats.   Further
negotiations with Britain broke down in October, so on November

11, 1965, he led the signing of the Unilateral Declaration of Independence (q. v.).

Smith's survival in office for 14 years (through early 1978) would be remarkable in any parliamentary democracy. His achievement is especially remarkable in the context of the perpetual crises through which he has governed since UDI. He has had to combat international economic sanctions (q. v.), fight a growing civil war (see MILITARY FORCES), and participate at the center of a bewildering succession of international and internal constitutional conferences. Because of the secrecy in which his party and government operate, it is presently very difficult to determine the extent to which Smith has been a shaper of government policies, and not just a mouthpiece for others. During the first post-UDI negotiations he held with British Prime Minister Harold Wilson, the 1966 "Tiger Talks" (q. v.), Smith appeared to have reached an agreement with Wilson, only to be overruled by his own cabinet when he returned home. In the subsequent "Fearless Talks, " pre-Pearce Commission negotiations, Victoria Falls and Geneva conferences (qq. v.), and other negotiations, he has not been similarly embarrassed in public. This could indicate either that he was working more efficiently with behind-the-scenes party powers, or that his personal leadership was growing stronger. In any case, his position as head of the RF party and the government has not yet been seriously challenged within the framework of public European politics.

Since UDI Smith has undergone a remarkable reversal in his public statements concerning African political rights. He entered office vowing never to allow majority African rule during his lifetime. After the Pearce Commission visit of early 1972 he increasingly softened his stance on the maintenance of white political monopoly. His first major shift came in March 1976, when he announced he was willing to reconsider the whole issue of Rhodesian independence. Increased pressure from the government of South Africa (q. v.) clearly helped to change Smith's position. In September 1976 he met with American Secretary of State Henry Kissinger and South African Prime Minister John Vorster, who apparently persuaded him that Rhodesia could no longer count on Western support in any all-out war with Africans. On September 24th he stunned the world by announcing his willingness to negotiate a transition to African majority rule within two years. He quickly withdrew from the ensuing Geneva Conference because of fundamental disagreements with nationalist negotiators over the form of the necessary transition period government, but he continued to assert his intention to negotiate a transition to African rule with nationalist leaders based within Rhodesia.

In early 1977 Smith led parliamentary efforts to alleviate some laws pertaining to racial segregation and discrimination. He encountered a potentially dangerous right-wing revolt within the RF party's members of parliament, but in April he got a special general party convention to endorse his moves towards African rule. In July he dissolved parliament. Under his leadership the RF again swept the general election on August 31st, thereby eliminating his parliamentary opposition. He then met with

American UN Ambassador Andrew Young and British Foreign
Secretary David Owen to hear a new Anglo-American plan for
bringing about majority rule.   Later in September he went to
Zambia (q.v.) to confer with President Kenneth Kaunda about
Rhodesia's future, despite the long-hostile relations between the
two countries.
      On November 24, 1977, Smith removed one more obsta-
cle to political change by announcing his acceptance of the principle of universal adult suffrage for Rhodesia.   The following
month he began a series of new negotiations with Abel Muzorewa,
Ndabaningi Sithole (qq.v.), and ZUPO (q.v.) leader and government chief Jeremiah Chirau to bring about a purely internal settlement.   By early 1978 the most outstanding obstacle to reaching a settlement among these parties appeared to be Smith's insistence upon generous special representation of Europeans in
any new African government.   However, despite all Smith's
verbal concessions by this time, he had still not yet handed
over any real power to Africans, and his efforts were dismissed
as "irrelevant" by such external nationalist leaders as Joshua
Nkomo and Robert Mugabe (qq.v.).

SOCIETY FOR PROPAGATION OF GOSPEL (SPG)   see   ANGLICANS

SOFALA.   Former Mozambique (q.v.) coastal port, once located
      just south of the Pungwe River (q.v.).   Sofala was the southern-
      most Muslim (q.v.) town on the eastern coast at least as early
      as the 10th century, when it was noted by the Arab writer al-
      Masudi.   By 1300 it was the main outlet for Shona gold (q.v.)
      exports, which were then funneled through Kilwa in present Tan-
      zania.   The Portuguese (q.v.) occupied Sofala in September
      1505, severing this trade link.   Thereafter the town declined
      into insignificance.   (See also YUFI; OPHIR.)

SOMABULA FOREST.   Region just northwest of Gwelo*; now the
      center of the country's gemstone (q.v.) production.   During the
      early 19th century the forest was considerably more extensive
      than it now is.   The region was infested with tsetse flies (q.v.)
      which limited the northern extent of Ndebele cattle grazing, but
      by the end of the century the Ndebele had cut the forest back
      considerably for fuel and building materials.
            Somabula River is a minor tributary of the Gwelo River
      (q.v.).   The village of Somabula is located 27 km. southwest of
      Gwelo, on the main road to Bulawayo (at 19° 42'S, 29° 40'E; alt.
      1415 m.).   Population in 1969 was 290.

SOMABULANA DHLODHLO (fl. 1880s-1890s).   Ndebele induna*.   By
      the 1890s Somabulana was serving as regent of the Insinga
      chieftaincy, whose head town was located about 50 km. east of
      Bulawayo.   During the 1896 Revolt (q.v.) he became one of the
      main military leaders in the region between the Insiza River*
      and the Matopo Hills*.   In the first "indaba" (q.v.) with Cecil
      Rhodes he emerged as a leading Ndebele spokesman.   After the

revolt, he was made a salaried chief, but was deposed by the Native Department within a year.

SOSHANGANE NXUMALO (variants: Shoshangane; Sotshangane; a.k.a. Manikusa) (c.1790s-c.1859). Founder-king of the Gaza state (q.v.). Born in what is now Zululand, Soshangane became a leading military commander in Zwide's (q.v.) Ndwandwe confederation during the 1810s. After Shaka's Zulu (qq.v.) broke up the Ndwandwe in c.1819, Soshangane led a group of kinsmen north into southern Mozambique*. There he began building up a kingdom through conquests and voluntary submissions. His subsequent migrations are complex and are intertwined with those of other major Mfecane (q.v.) leaders, including Zwangendaba, Nxaba, and Maseko (qq.v.). By the 1830s Soshangane was operating within present Rhodesia, near Mount Silinda (q.v.). There he defeated Nxaba and established his headquarters. Within a few years he returned to the lower Limpopo* basin in Mozambique. His successors later re-established Gaza headquarters inside Rhodesia.

SOSWE   see SVOSVE

SOTHO (Basotho; variant: Basutu). Sotho languages constitute one of the most important divisions of southern Bantu (q.v.). Sotho-speakers have long been numerically dominant in Botswana, Lesotho, and South Africa north of the Orange River. These peoples are linguistically divided into three clusters, each containing distinct ethnic and political groups. The peoples of the western cluster are commonly known as Tswana (q.v.). Scattered small Sotho communities have long been established in the southwestern parts of present Rhodesia. Many additional Sotho entered the country in 1838-9 as part of the Ndebele (q.v.) migration into Matabeleland* from the Transvaal*. These Sotho, who had become attached to the Ndebele kingdom during its formative decades, were eventually absorbed into the kingdom's predominantly Nguni (q.v.) culture, in which they were known as enhla (q.v.).

SOUSA, MANUEL ANTÓNIO de (a.k.a. Gouveia; variants: Guveya; Kuvheya) (Nov. 10, 1835-Jan. 1, 1892). Portuguese (q.v.) warlord of Goanese extraction (whence his nickname, "Gouveia"); first came to Mozambique (q.v.) to administer family estates in the early 1850s. Based south of the lower Zambezi River, he built up his power by assembling a private army and by marrying into many African royal families, while simultaneously gaining Portuguese recognition as Capitão-Mor over Manicaland (q.v.). In the mid-1870s Sousa allied with the Manyika ruler Mutasa (q.v.) against the Makoni and Makombe chiefdoms (qq.v.), and then sought to claim the Makombe title for himself. By the 1880s he was the most powerful ruler between the Zambezi and Pungwe* rivers.

    In 1886 Sousa occupied the northeastern part of Mashonaland (q.v.). The next year he achieved a temporary military

success against the Mtoko chiefdom (q.v.). Anxious to buttress
its own territorial claims against the northward surge of the
British, the Portuguese government brought Sousa to Lisbon in
1888 with J. C. P. d'Andrada (q.v.). There Sousa was feted
and made a "colonel" in the Portuguese army. In 1889 he and
Andrada secured treaties for Portugal from northern Shona
rulers. After the BSAC (q.v.) occupied Mashonaland in 1890,
Sousa and Andrada went to Manicaland to secure the Mutasa's cooperation. In November a small force of British troops under
P. W. Forbes (q.v.) "arrested" the two Portuguese representatives, who were sent to the Cape. Both were released the next
year, and Sousa returned to his own territory in May. He found
that during his absence his personal empire had begun to disinte-
grate. While fighting to restore his authority the following year,
he was badly wounded. Unable to walk, he was killed by a child.

SOUTH AFRICA, REPUBLIC OF (formerly: Union of South Africa).
With an area just over three times greater than that of Rhodesia,
and with a population more than four times as large, South
Africa is separated from Rhodesia by a stretch of the Limpopo
River (q.v.). Historical connections between the two regions
stretch deep into the remote past, when Rhodesia served as a
corridor for southward population movements into South Africa.
After Khoisan (q.v.) peoples had passed through, Rhodesia appears to have been the area in which the early southern Bantu-
speaking (q.v.) peoples broke into separate groups, giving rise
to South Africa's Sotho and Nguni (qq.v.) peoples and others.
    The long period of mainly southward population movements
was reversed in the early 19th century, when South Africa's
Mfecane wars (q.v.) sent powerful Nguni states north into Rhodesia and its neighbors. The Nguni were soon followed by an
influx of South African hunters, missionaries (qq.v.), and traders.
In the late 19th century competition for regional dominance between the British Empire and the newly-formed Afrikaner (q.v.)
republics made present Botswana (q.v.) and Rhodesia the potential prizes of expansionism. Britain made Botswana into the
Bechuanaland Protectorate (q.v.) in 1885, but then hesitated to
take on more colonies. Cecil Rhodes (q.v.) then took the initiative within South Africa in order to prevent the Transvaal Republic (q.v.) from occupying Rhodesia. The consequence was
formation of the British South Africa Company (q.v.), which occupied Rhodesia as a private operation during the 1890s.
    A large part of the first European (q.v.) settlers in Rho-
desia were born in South Africa, and many of the rest, though
born elsewhere, were South African residents before going to
Rhodesia. As late as 1969 more than a fifth of the Rhodesian
settler population were South African-born.
    When the administration of Southern Rhodesia, as it was
then called, was firmly organized in 1898, it was modeled after
that of the Cape Colony, in whose administration the first governor, W. H. Milton (q.v.), had served. Southern Rhodesia
adopted the Cape's currency (q.v.), and after the South African
War (q.v.) joined the South African Customs Union. Although

the new colony was strongly tied to South Africa through its
transportation and communications (q. v.) network, trade, civil
service, settlers, and other links, its leaders rejected incorporation into the Union of South Africa when it was being formed
in 1908-10. As the BSAC administration was about to end in
the early 1920s, the issue of union with South Africa again arose.
South African Prime Minister Jan Smuts, Southern Rhodesia's
powerful mining interests, and its local Unionist Movement (q.v.)
favored union, but most settlers wanted autonomy. The settlers
voted for Responsible Government (q. v.) over union in a 1922
referendum.

Thereafter Southern Rhodesia's interests in expanding its
external ties were directed towards amalgamation (q. v.) with
Northern Rhodesia (now Zambia, q. v.). Creation of the Federation of Rhodesia and Nyasaland (q. v.) in 1953 heralded a further
major shift of Southern Rhodesia's orientation from the south to
the north. The country's African population generally opposed
the Federation, supporting it only to the extent that it helped to
shift Southern Rhodesia away from the forms of racial oppression being developed in South Africa. Collapse of the Federation
in 1963 and the subsequent independence of Malawi and Zambia
destroyed Rhodesia's northward orientation, driving its white
government back into an informal, but strong, alliance with
South Africa. When Rhodesia declared its independence (see
UDI) in late 1965, it effectively declared its intention to continue
building the country on South African lines.

It has long been a popular commonplace that Rhodesia's
political and racial laws lag about ten years behind those of
South Africa. This assertion is broadly accurate. The Land
Apportionment Act of 1930 (q. v.) was similar to South Africa's
1913 Land Act. Southern Rhodesia passed its Industrial Conciliation Act (q. v.) in 1934, exactly ten years after South Africa's
own such act. Southern Rhodesia's Unlawful Organisations Act of
1959 (q. v.) is similar to South Africa's Suppression of Commu-
nism Act of 1950, and the Rhodesian Land Tenure Act of 1969
(q. v.) parallels South Africa's Group Areas Act of 1950 and 1966.
Further, the Rhodesian Front's (q. v.) assumption of power in
1962 has been likened to the Nationalist Party's rise to power in
South Africa in 1948. Finally, Rhodesia became a republic
(q. v.) in 1969, eight years after South Africa had become one.

Rhodesia's ties with South Africa have extended into many
different fields. During the early 1960s the top military leaders
of South Africa, Rhodesia, and Portugal began conferring regularly as the prelude to an unofficial military alliance in the
growing struggle against African liberation movements in southern
Africa (see MILITARY FORCES). In August 1967 South African
troops began entering Rhodesia to help defend the Zambezi Valley
against guerrilla incursions from Zambia. By 1970 South Africans accounted for about half--three or four thousand--of the
government military forces deployed inside Rhodesia. South
Africa claimed these troops were merely "paramilitary police,"
but they were clearly operating as combat soldiers. Under
mounting international criticism, and in order to improve its

own relations with black-ruled African nations, South Africa withdrew all these troops by August 1975, but it evidently continued to assist Rhodesia with locally produced and imported weaponry. In the meantime, Rhodesia continued to recruit individual white South Africans directly into its own military forces.

The world's attempt to cripple Rhodesia with economic sanctions (q.v.) since UDI has virtually made Rhodesia into a South African colony. Even before UDI South Africa ranked behind only Britain as a Rhodesian trading partner. In 1965 it supplied 23% of Rhodesia's imports and bought 9% of Rhodesia's exports. Both countries have subsequently kept secret trade statistics, but it is clear that their mutual trade has risen greatly, and that without South African support Rhodesia's economy would quickly collapse. South Africa has openly ignored UN sanctions in order both to bolster Rhodesia's regime as a bastion against black nationalism, and to take advantage of Rhodesia's plight. With its immensely larger economic base and its free access to the world's markets, South Africa has had an enormous advantage in all economic and financial transactions with Rhodesia. Its ports have handled virtually all of Rhodesia's external trade--especially since Mozambique (q.v.) closed its borders to Rhodesia. This situation has put South Africa in the position of controlling all of Rhodesia's crucial petroleum imports. Its own industries have provided Rhodesia with a wide range of vital goods, including military arms. Its investors have controlling interests in many major Rhodesian corporations, and its people account for most of Rhodesia's dwindling foreign tourist trade.

By mid-1975 South Africa's support for Rhodesia was beginning to wane as the ability of the latter's regime to survive much longer became doubtful. The South African government apparently resigned itself to accepting a black regime in Rhodesia, and decided to set about to help insure an orderly transition to a non-radical government. To this end Prime Minister John Vorster participated in the Victoria Falls Conference (q.v.). Over the next two years he was reported to be putting increasing pressure on the Rhodesian regime to find a settlement with black nationalists. By late 1977 South Africa itself was being threatened with UN economic sanctions because of its support for Rhodesia, and Vorster was reportedly ready to cut off petroleum and arms shipments to Rhodesia.

SOUTH AFRICAN GOLD FIELDS EXPLORATION COMPANY. Prospecting company formed as a subsidiary of the Natal Land and Colonization Company to seek gold mining (q.v.) concessions in Matabeleland. The Company hired Thomas Baines (q.v.) to lead its first expedition. Baines enlisted the aid of Henry Hartley and J. L. Lee, and then obtained the support of the Ndebele regent Mncumbathe (qq.v.) in mid-1869. This company competed for the right to prospect in the "Northern Goldfields" (q.v.) with the London and Limpopo Mining Company (q.v.), which was supported by the missionary T. M. Thomas and the induna Mbigo (qq.v.). In July 1869 Baines led a party of

prospectors to the Hartley Hills*, which he named, but then all
Europeans had to leave the country because of the Ndebele succession dispute. The following April Baines obtained a verbal
concession* to the Northern Goldfields from the new king Lobengula (q.v.). Lobengula reconfirmed the "Baines Concession" in
writing on August 29, 1871, but the Company was meanwhile
collapsing. After Baines' death the concession passed through
several parties' hands until it was bought by the British South
Africa Company (q.v.) around 1890. (See also TATI CONCES-
SION.)

SOUTH AFRICAN REPUBLIC (19th century) see TRANSVAAL

SOUTH AFRICAN WAR (a.k.a. Boer War; Second Boer War; Anglo-
    Boer War) (Oct. 1899-May 1902). The largest military conflict
    ever fought in southern Africa, it was waged between Afrikaners
    (q.v.) of the Transvaal (q.v.) and Orange Free State Republics
    and the British Imperial Government. The war was the climax
    of British and Afrikaner competition for mastery of southern
    Africa. It was, in part, aggravated by tensions arising from
    the British South Africa Company's (q.v.) efforts to block Afri-
    kaner expansion north of the Limpopo River* (see ADENDORFF
    TREK). By 1896 any hopes for a peaceful reconciliation of
    British and Afrikaner differences were shattered when Cecil
    Rhodes supported the abortive Jameson Raid (q.v.) on Paul
    Kruger's government. Although the Afrikaners eventually lost
    the war, they obtained a settlement which paved the way for
    their later political domination of South Africa.
        Except for brief Afrikaner raids north of the Limpopo at
    the onset of hostilities, the South African War did not affect
    Southern Rhodesia directly. Its indirect impact was, however,
    great. During the first few months of the war Afrikaners be-
    sieged Kimberley, Mafeking, and other South African centers,
    effectively cutting off railway (q.v.) transport into Southern Rho-
    desia and driving up prices of the colony's imported goods.
    British settlers there enthusiastically supported the war. It is
    estimated that about 1700 men--from a total white population of
    only 11,000--saw military service in South Africa. The inter-
    ruption of supplies and the severe drain on settler manpower
    closed down the colony's mines and halted construction of the
    railways. Existing railway lines in the colony were clogged with
    British troops and supplies brought in through Beira (q.v.). The
    colony's limited manufacturing capacity contributed to British
    armament production, and the BSAC administration was once
    again nearly broken by increased war time expenses (cf. RE-
    VOLTS).
        The colony's African population was not militarily in-
    volved in the war, but it too suffered from higher prices, and
    from the temporary halt in labor migration to South Africa.
    With the exception of Mapondera (q.v.), Africans did not take
    advantage of the general disruption to rebel.
        After the war ended Southern Rhodesia recovered fairly
    quickly. It had escaped the devastation experienced within South

Africa, and it received a new influx of Europeans from the south
for this reason. Railway construction, especially, was accelerated. (See also RHODESIA FIELD FORCE; RHODESIA REGI-
MENT; BSAP; SOUTHERN RHODESIAN VOLUNTEERS.)

"SOUTHERN AFRICA." Application of this geographical term has
varied. Some authorities apply it to the great bulge of the continent south of the equator--an area roughly congruent with the
distribution of Bantu*-speaking peoples. More commonly the
term is restricted to the area south of the Zambezi River (q.v.).
This usage is employed in this dictionary. It should be noted
that "southern Africa" and "central Africa" (q.v.) overlap in
Rhodesia.

"SOUTHERN RHODESIA." Name given to the country in 1897 to dif-
ferentiate it from Northern Rhodesia*. The white government
changed the name to "Rhodesia" (q.v.) in 1964 when Northern
Rhodesia became independent as Zambia (q.v.), but Britain, the
United Nations, and other governments have never officially recognized this change.

SOUTHERN RHODESIAN AFRICAN NATIONAL CONGRESS   see
AFRICAN NATIONAL CONGRESS

SOUTHERN RHODESIAN MISSIONARY CONFERENCE (SRMC). Interdenominational body formed in 1906 to coordinate the work of missions (q.v.) and to represent their interests before the government. Initially founded as a Protestant organization, the SRMC
represented all the major missions in the country, including
those of the Roman Catholics, by the 1920s. By this time the
SRMC was one of the most powerful lobbying bodies in the country. The government regarded it as a valid representative of
African interests, and government officials regularly attended
the SRMC's biennial meetings. Under the leadership of John
White (q.v.), SRMC chairman from 1924 to 1928, the SRMC
particularly championed the improvement of African education
(q.v.), stimulating the government to form the Department of
Native Education in 1927. A subordinate body comprising African clerics, the Native Christian Conference, was formed in
1926. This body's resolutions were communicated to the government through the SRMC, making it the only African organization
to have anything like an official voice in the government.
        After reaching its peak influence in the early 1930s, the
SRMC swiftly declined as a lobbying body. The missionaries
lost H. U. Moffat (q.v.) and other allies in the government, and
the balance of influence in African affairs passed back to the Native Affairs Department, which favored preservation of traditional
African life. Interdenominational squabbles disrupted the SRMC,
and the Roman Catholics and other denominations began dropping
out.

SOUTHERN RHODESIAN VOLUNTEERS (SRV). Reserve territorial
military force, formed in 1898 out of the heterogeneous white

volunteer forces which had served in the Revolts of 1896-7
(q. v.). The SRV provided the nucleus of the Rhodesia Regiments (q. v.) formed during the South African War (q. v.) and
the First World War, and it has been described as the nucleus
of the modern Rhodesian army. (See MILITARY FORCES.)

SPRUIT. Small stream, or dry watercourse; from the Afrikaans*
word for "sprout" or "stream."

STANLEY, HERBERT JAMES (July 25, 1872-June 5, 1955). Third
Governor (q. v.) of Southern Rhodesia (1935-42). A career
British civil servant, Stanley was resident commissioner in
Northern and Southern Rhodesia (1915-8) and Governor of Northern Rhodesia (1924-7) before replacing C. H. Rodwell (q. v.) as
Governor of Southern Rhodesia in 1935. He was strongly committed to the idea of central African amalgamation (q. v.) and
is credited with helping to formulate Godfrey Huggins' (q. v.)
ideas on this goal. He was succeeded by Evelyn Baring (q. v.)
in 1942.

STILLBAY CULTURE. Stone Age (q. v.) culture of the middle
period; also known as Bambata* culture within Rhodesia. It is
characterized by pressure-flaked stone implements, and is associated with the period of "Rhodesian Man" (q. v.).

STONE AGE. Modern man (Homo sapiens) has occupied the country
for at least 100, 000 years, and his hominid antecedents there
go back perhaps a further million years. The country is rich
in Stone Age sites of early man, and these have been investigated more intensively than in most tropical African countries.
The country's Stone Age culture sequence corresponds with that
developed for the rest of eastern and southern Africa. Authorities generally divide the Stone Age into Early, Middle, and Late
periods, with two intermediate periods, each representing a
major shift in tool-making techniques. Many "cultures," or
"industries," are assigned to each period. The terminology for
these is complex, changing constantly as archaeologists make
new finds and reclassify old ones. Dates are based upon carbon-
14 and other tests, but it should be understood that different cultures often overlapped in both time and space.
    The Early Stone Age (ESA) extended from the very earliest
pebble and flaked-stone tool users of the pre-Homo sapiens era
to the first fire users in about 40, 000 or 30, 000 B. C. The last
thirty millenia of the ESA are also known as the First Intermediate Stone Age.
    The Middle Stone Age (MSA) heralded the mastery of fire
and refinements in pressure-flaked stone implements. The MSA
ended in roughly 9000 B. C., with the previous ten millenia also
known as the Second Intermediate Stone Age. The most important local MSA industries are Stillbay and Magosian (qq. v.).
    The Late Stone Age (LSA) extended from the end of the
MSA into the first millenium A. D., when it was displaced by
intrusive Iron Age (q. v.) cultures. There was no "Bronze Age"

(cf. TIN). The LSA saw the refinement of small stone implements, or microliths, bored stones, polished axes, and hollow
scrapers. It is believed that the bow and arrow were introduced
early in the LSA. The dominant LSA industry within present
Rhodesia is generally known as Wilton (q.v.), the culture associated with the country's prolific rock paintings (q.v.). Khoisan
(q.v.) peoples are generally regarded as the modern descendants
of LSA peoples. Isolated pockets of San (q.v.) have maintained
an advanced form of LSA culture into modern times.

STONE-LINED PITS (a.k.a. pit structures; "slave pits"; etc.).
General term for a class of ruins (q.v.) characteristic of the
Eastern Highlands*, particularly within the Inyanga Ruins complex (q.v.), where thousands of such structures have been found.
Remarkably uniform in their dimensions, the pits are typically
circular, with stone-lined floors about six meters in diameter,
and stone walls two to three meters in height. They are partly
dug into hillsides, with narrow entrances on their upper sides,
and small drain holes on their lower sides. They are usually
surrounded by platforms which once supported dwelling structures. Most pit sites were abandoned by the 19th century.
Many odd theories have since been advanced to account for their
. functions. It is said, for example, that Cecil Rhodes coined
the term "slave pits" on the assumption that the pits were used
to imprison slave laborers. The most widely accepted theory--
supported by local traditions--holds that the pits were used to
house small livestock, probably pigs and goats. (See SLAVE
TRADE.)

STONE RUINS see RUINS; IRON AGE; and names of individual sites

STRIP ROADS. Single-land roads comprising parallel strips of asphalt pavement. Government engineers invented the strip road
technique in 1930 as a means of building durable all-weather
roads (q.v.) cheaply. During the world depression a major strip
road building program was begun, partly to provide employment
for European workers. The program ended in 1945, by which
time about 3600 km. of strip roads crisscrossed the country.
Thereafter only full-width paved roads were built.

SUGAR. Commercial production of this crop began at the Triangle
Estate (q.v.) in the southeastern low veld during the 1920s.
Successful irrigation schemes led to greatly increased production
during the mid-1950s, when the Hippo Valley Estate (q.v.) was
started nearby. By 1965 production was expected to reach
300,000 tons, most of which was slated for export to Commonwealth countries. Post-UDI sanctions (q.v.) reportedly hit the
sugar industry hard, causing production to fall off sharply.
However, at the end of 1977 Hippo Valley sugar production was
said to be flourishing, and Rhodesian sugar was still reaching
even black African countries. (See SABI-LIMPOPO AUTHORITY;
AGRICULTURE.)

SUMMERS, ROGER F. H. (b. 1907). British-born archaeologist.
Summers came to the country in 1947 to serve as Keeper of An-
tiquities in the National Museum in Bulawayo. He also served
on the Historical Monuments Commission (q. v.) from 1950 to
1967 (as chairman, 1954-9). During the 1950s he conducted major archaeological digs at Inyanga, Zimbabwe, Dhlo Dhlo (qq. v.)
and other Iron Age (q. v.) sites. He has published extensively
on the Iron Age sequence, and has written on Ndebele history
(q. v.), stressing a militaristic interpretation of the Ndebele
state. In 1970 he left the National Museum for the South African Museum in Cape Town. (See BIBLIOGRAPHY.)

SUNDAY MAIL. Salisbury-based affiliate of the daily Rhodesia
Herald (q. v.). The Mail's circulation of c. 80, 000 makes it the
largest commercial newspaper in the country (see PRESS). It
was founded as the Weekly Review and later renamed Sunday
Mail when it was acquired by the Argus Group (q. v.) of newspapers in the mid-1930s. The paper has a national circulation,
in contrast to the Bulawayo-based Sunday News, which has had
about a third of the Mail's circulation. (American libraries receiving the Mail: Howard University; Library of Congress.)

SVIKIRO (variant: tswikiro). Mediums possessed by Shona spirits,
such as the mhondoro (q. v.). Not to be confused with the
spirits themselves. (See RELIGION--SHONA.)

SVOSVE (variants: Soswe; Swoswe). Dynastic title of the rulers of
an Mbire (q. v.) chiefdom of the Zezuru (q. v.) cluster of Shona.
The chiefdom was established around the early 18th century in
the southeastern part of the present Marandellas and Wedza
districts (qq. v.). The Mbire suffered greatly during the 1830s,
when the region was occupied by Zwangendaba's Ngoni (qq. v.).
Sometime later Svosve Gusha was killed during a Gaza (q. v.)
raid. In 1896-7 Svosve Chikosha participated in the Revolt
(q. v.) against the British. He was captured by the British and
died soon afterwards. Since then the Svosves have been government chiefs, and the Mbire have lived mostly in the Wedza Tribal Trust Land.

SW- . Many Chishona (q. v.) words spelled with sw- should properly
have sv-, which consonant cluster is an unvoiced alveolar la-
bialized sibilant fricative.

SWAZI (Amaswazi). The Swazi constitute one of the major branches
of Nguni-speaking peoples (q. v.) in southern Africa. The modern
country of Swaziland, which lies about 360 km. south of Rhodesia,
derives from the Swazi kingdom which arose in the early 19th
century, at the same time the neighboring Zulu (q. v.) kingdom
was developing. When the Mfecane (q. v.) wars affected Swaziland, many Swazi clans and individuals joined the various Nguni
bands which migrated north. There were so many Swazi among
the Ngoni (q. v.) that the name "Swazi" has frequently been used
as a synonym for Ngoni in central Africa. Other Swazi were

absorbed by the Ndebele, but still retained their Swazi identity. The Ngoni of Nyamazana (q.v.), who joined the Ndebele around 1840, are perhaps the best known "Swazi" in Rhodesian history.

SWINA (variant: Svina; pl., Amaswina, or Maswina). Alternative name for the Shona (q.v.), usually regarded as derogatory. It is often suggested that the Ndebele (q.v.) were the first to call the Shona "Swina," but the word itself appears to derive from Chishona* svina (or tsvina) for "dirt."

SWINBURNE, JOHN (1831-July 15, 1914). A British naval officer of worldwide experience, Swinburne was the first chairman of the London and Limpopo Mining Company (q.v.). While on inactive duty, between 1868 and 1870, he led an expedition to Matabeleland* to seek a gold mining concession (q.v.) from the Ndebele, relying heavily on the assistance of the missionary T. M. Thomas (q.v.). Swinburne later sat in the British Parliament (1885-92).

SYKES, WILLIAM (March 13, 1829-July 22, 1887). English agent of the London Missionary Society (q.v.). Together with J. S. Moffat and T. M. Thomas (qq.v.), Sykes opened the first permanent mission station in the country at Inyati (q.v.) in 1860. His personal conflicts with Thomas led to the latter's being recalled, but he himself remained at Inyati until his death. In nearly 27 years of proselytizing, he failed to obtain a single Ndebele convert.

- T -

TABA. Variant of Sindebele* word intaba, for "hill"; usually rendered ntaba (q.v.) in place names.

TABLER, EDWARD C. (b. Dec. 30, 1916). American amateur historian of 19th-century exploration in southern Africa. A chemical engineer by profession, Tabler began publishing articles on Rhodesian history during the 1940s. Publication of two standard books, The Far Interior (Cape Town, 1955) and Pioneers of Rhodesia (Cape Town, 1966), and many editions of early travelers' accounts has made him the leading authority within his field.

TAIT, W. E. CAMPBELL (Aug. 12, 1886-July 17, 1946). Fifth Governor (q.v.) of Southern Rhodesia (1945-6). A career naval officer, Tait resigned from his post as commander-in-chief of British southern Atlantic forces at Simonstown, South Africa, to become governor of Southern Rhodesia in 1945. He died in office and was succeeded by J. N. Kennedy (q.v.).

TAKAWIRA, LEOPOLD (1916-June 15, 1970). Nationalist leader. Born at Chilimanzi*, and educated at Kutama* and in Natal, Takawira became a government schoolmaster in Highfield* in the

late 1930s. By the early 1950s he was a leading member of
the African Teachers' Association. Attracted by the ideals of
the Federal "partnership" (q.v.) policy, he left teaching to join
the Capricorn Africa Society (q.v.), in which he became an
executive officer. When he became disillusioned by "partnership," he turned to African nationalist politics, joining the new
African National Congress and then helping to found the National
Democratic Party (qq.v.) in the late 1950s. In September 1960
he became acting president of the NDP after Michael Mawema
(q.v.) was forced to resign, but he soon lost this post to Joshua
Nkomo (q.v.) in a party election. He followed Nkomo into
ZAPU, but then broke from him and joined Ndabaningi Sithole
(q.v.) in ZANU. After being arrested in late 1964, he spent
most of the late 1960s in detention. He died in Salisbury
Prison in mysterious circumstances, possibly related to his af-
fliction with diabetes.

TALOWTA (Batalowta; variant: Talaota). Small branch of Sotho-
speaking people (q.v.) who apparently broke away from the
Ngwato (q.v.) in the early 19th century, when they settled in
the region just west of the Matopo Hills* in southwestern Rhodesia. After the arrival of the Ndebele in the country, a Talowta chief named Mahuku (q.v.) submitted to Mzilikazi's rule.

TANGWENA LAND DISPUTE. The Tangwena people are a small
branch of Shona (q.v.) who have lived in what is now the border
region of the Inyanga Mountains* for at least eight generations.
In 1902 their chief, Dzeka Chigumira (d.1928), got government
permission to move about 70 Tangwena families to the Southern
Rhodesian side of the border in order to avoid the conflict between Makombe (q.v.) and the Portuguese in Mozambique*. Un-
beknownst to the Tangwena, their ancestral land was sold to a
private company by the BSAC in 1905, and it was later declared
European land by the 1930 Land Apportionment Act (q.v.). Most
Tangwena land was later sold to the Gaeresi Ranch Company
(centered at 18° 15'S, 32° 52'E), which left them alone until the
Rhodesian Front (q.v.) came to power. Under government pressure the Ranch Company tried to evict the Tangwena in 1963.
This effort began a decade-long struggle between the government
and the Tangwena, who steadfastly refused to move to the nearby Holdenby Tribal Trust Land (18° 25'S, 32° 55'S). The government lost a legal battle in the courts with the Tangwena in 1968,
and then issued a special proclamation in order to evict them
legally. From 1969 to 1972 the government attracted international indignation by burning and bulldozing Tangwena homes and
impounding their cattle in efforts to drive them out of Gaeresi
Ranch. Under their new, and officially non-recognized chief,
Rekayi Tangwena (b., c.1900), the son of Dzeka, the Tangwena
persistently resisted, while enduring many sacrifices and hardships.

TATI CONCESSION. District of 5355 sq. km. in eastern Botswana
(q.v.) which surrounds the Tati River (q.v.) and contains

Francistown (q.v.). During the 19th century the Ndebele (q.v.) regarded the area as part of their domain, but this claim was disputed by the Ngwato (q.v.). European interest in the region grew rapidly after gold was discovered there in 1866. The first serious effort to mine in the area was made by the London and Limpopo Mining Company (q.v.), which obtained an Ndebele concession* in 1870. Work was soon abandoned, however. In 1880 S. H. Edwards (q.v.) and several other men formed a new syndicate, the Northern Light Gold and Exploring Company, which obtained a fresh Ndebele concession in return for an annual rent. Over the next seven years King Lobengula (q.v.) reconfirmed and elaborated on this company's exclusive mining rights at Tati. In 1888 the company was effectively transformed into the Tati Concession Mining and Exploration Company, Ltd., in which Alfred Beit (q.v.) was a major shareholder, and Lobengula granted it further monopolies over grazing, timber, and settlement. Later that year the Tati Concession was specifically excluded from the Rudd Concession (q.v.) granted to Cecil Rhodes' group. In 1892 British High Commissioner Henry Loch brought the area under the administration of the new Bechuanaland Protectorate (q.v.), but the British government later recognized the Company's ownership of the land.

When Bechuanaland was about to become independent as Botswana during the 1960s, white settlers in the Tati district petitioned either to become independent, or to be affiliated with South Africa or Rhodesia, but the district's land was eventually incorporated into Botswana.

TATI RIVER. A tributary of the Shashi River (q.v.) which flows entirely within Botswana, but which was regarded as part of Matabeleland* in the 19th century.

TAVARA (variant: Tawara). Shona (q.v.) group occupying the area between northern Darwin District* and the Zambezi River, mostly within Mozambique (q.v.). The Tavara language, or Chitavara, is usually classified as a subdialect of Korekore (q.v.), but Tavara culture is so distinct from that of the Korekore that the Tavara are often described as a separate ethnic group.

TAWANA (Batawana). Branch of western Sotho-, or Tswana-speaking (qq.v.) people in central Botswana (q.v.). The Tawana separated from the Ngwato (q.v.) in the late 18th century, when they moved to the region around Lake Ngami. During the 19th century the Ndebele (q.v.) launched several long-distance raids against them. The biggest were in the 1880s. In April 1883 Gampu (q.v.) and Manyeu commanded an Ndebele attack which was initially repelled by the Tawana, but which ended in success. In April 1885 Lotshe (q.v.) commanded an Ndebele campaign against the Tawana which proved a major disaster. This set-back has often been cited as evidence of a presumed Ndebele military decline in the late 19th century.

TAWARA   see   TAVARA

TAWSE-JOLLIE, ETHEL MAUDE (née Cookson) (March 8, 1878-
Sept. 21, 1950). Politician. Born in England, Ethel Cookson
married A. R. Colquhoun (q. v.) in 1900 and visited Southern
Rhodesia with him in 1904. After his death ten years later,
she returned to the colony and soon married John Tawse-Jollie,
a local farmer. She quickly got involved in politics as a leader
in the Responsible Government Movement (q. v.), and as an advocate of women's suffrage (see WOMEN'S FRANCHISE ORDI-
NANCE). In 1920 she was elected to the Legislative Council
(q. v.). After Responsible Government was attained, she represented Umtali* in the Legislative Assembly (1923-7), thereby
becoming the first female parliamentarian in the British Empire.
A strong supporter of the Empire, she opposed union with South
Africa and the local movement to make Afrikaans (q. v.) a second
official language. She presented these views and an account of
the Responsible Government Movement in her book, The Real
Rhodesia (1924). During the Second World War she served as
the country's women's employment officer.

TEBELE. Short form of Matabele (q. v.). See also NDEBELE;
SINDEBELE.

TELEGRAPHS. In June 1889 the BSAC built the country's first telegraph line from Mafeking, South Africa, to Tati (q. v.). The
line was extended to Fort Victoria* in October 1891, and to
Salisbury* in 1892. Shortly after the 1893 Ndebele War*, the
South African connection reached Bulawayo*, from which it too
was extended to Salisbury. In 1895 Salisbury was connected
with Beira*, through Umtali*. The South African War (q. v.)
interrupted communications with the south, requiring that mes-
sages be conveyed by sea from Beira. After the war most of
the rest of the country was gradually brought into the telegraphic
network. (See TRANSPORT AND COMMUNICATIONS; POSTAL
SYSTEM.)

TELEPHONES. During the 1896 Ndebele Revolt* jerry-built telephones were introduced at Bulawayo in order to connect British
military command with outlying forts. A formal telephone exchange was first established in Salisbury in 1898, with other
major urban centers soon following. By 1930 there were 4200
telephone sets in operation throughout the country. This number
increased to 21,000 in 1950, and to c. 156,000 in 1975, by which
time fully automatic equipment linked the main centers.

TELEVISION   see   RHODESIAN BROADCASTING COMPANY

TENKELA (a. k. a. Salugazana; Wamponga) (fl. 1870s-1900s). Either
a mhondoro (q. v.) or a Mwari (q. v.) cult figure, Tenkela worked
closely with Mkwati (q. v.) during the 1896-7 Revolts (q. v.).
After Mkwati's death in Mashonaland in September or October

1897, Tenkela withdrew into the northern part of the country, where she was captured by the British the next year. She was taken to Bulawayo and tried for insurrection, but was freed because of insufficient evidence.

TERRITORIAL FORCE (TF). Official name of the reserve corps of the Rhodesian army. The TF is composed of men assigned to reserve battalions for periods of three years after completing their active military service. Size of the force in early 1974 was estimated at 10,000 Europeans, but the government announced its intention to increase its manpower five-fold. (See MILITARY FORCES.)

TETE. Mozambique (q.v.) town on the south bank of the Zambezi River (at 16° 11'S, 33° 34'E). Originally a Muslim (q.v.) trading fair (q.v.), Tete was occupied by the Portuguese (q.v.) in the 1530s. It continued to serve as an important inland base for coastal trade with Mashonaland (q.v.), and it developed into the largest inland Portuguese town. The name Tete was later also given to the Mozambican province between Rhodesia and Malawi.

THABA. Variant of Sindebele* intaba for "hill"; usually rendered ntaba (q.v.) in place names.

"THIRD FORCE." Term apparently coined by Tanzanian President Julius Nyerere (see "FRONTLINE PRESIDENTS") to refer to the nationalist guerrilla army operating out of Mozambique independent of either ZAPU or ZANU leadership. This seems to have been the same force variously identified as the Zimbabwe People's Army (ZIPA) or the Zimbabwe Liberation Army (ZLA) (qq.v.). (See MILITARY FORCES.)

THOMAS, THOMAS MORGAN (March 13, 1828-Jan. 8, 1884). Pioneer missionary. A Welshman, Thomas came to Matabeleland* with the first London Missionary Society (q.v.) party in 1859. He soon mastered the Sindebele* language and became one of King Mzilikazi's (q.v.) European confidants. Thomas's fellow missionaries resented his intimacy with the Ndebele and his trading activities, and they quibbled with him over spelling rules for Sindebele, into which they were translating religious texts. After Mzilikazi's death in 1868, Thomas meddled in the Ndebele succession dispute (see NKULUMANE), and attempted to control European miners seeking concessions* (see e.g., J. SWINBURNE). His colleagues charged him with improper political and commercial conduct, so he was recalled to England and expelled from the LMS. While in Britain Thomas hastily wrote Welsh and English versions of a long book, Eleven Years in Central South Africa. This book proved a small popular success, particularly in Wales, where Thomas also collected contributions to start a new mission. The book, despite many flaws, still stands as the most valuable single description of Ndebele life in the mid-19th century.

In 1875 Thomas returned to Matabeleland as an independent missionary, founding a new station at Shiloh (q.v.). There he later baptized the first handful of Ndebele converts to Christianity (cf. SYKES, WILLIAM).

One of Thomas's sons, Evan Morgan Thomas, died in the Patterson incident (q.v.) in 1878. Another son, Thomas Morgan Thomas, Jr. (1875-1949), later became a Native Commissioner in Matabeleland.

THOMPSON, FRANCIS ROBERT (a.k.a. "Matabele Thompson") (1857-May 5, 1927). South African concessionarie. While working as an African labor organizer at the Kimberley diamond mines, Thompson met Cecil Rhodes. Because of his presumed knowledge of Africans and their languages, he was asked to accompany C. H. Rudd (q.v.) to Bulawayo in 1888. He participated in the negotiations leading to the Rudd Concession (q.v.), and then remained in the country briefly after Rudd had left. Fearful for his personal safety, he suddenly bolted from the country, thereby increasing Ndebele anxieties about the Concession. He later served in the Cape Parliament (1895-1903) and lived briefly in Southern Rhodesia. His daughter published his "autobiography" posthumously.

THOMSON, JOHN BODEN (1841-Sept. 1878). Scottish London Missionary Society (q.v.) agent. In 1870 Thomson replaced T. M. Thomas (q.v.) at Inyati (q.v.) mission station, but he soon got King Lobengula's permission to found a new station, Hope Fountain (q.v.), closer to Bulawayo (q.v.). In 1876 the LMS recalled him from the country to help start a mission at Lake Tanganyika, where fever killed him two years later.

THONGA. Variant of Tsonga. See HLENGWE.

"TIGER TALKS" (1966). About five months after UDI (q.v.), British officials began visiting Salisbury to discuss a reopening of formal constitutional negotiations. On December 2-4, 1966 Prime Minister Ian Smith (q.v.) and British Prime Minister Harold Wilson negotiated an agreement aboard the British cruiser HMS Tiger, just off Gibraltar. Their agreement called for a temporary suspension of Rhodesian independence while the 1961 Constitution (q.v.) was modified to conform to Britain's "Five Principles" (q.v.). Although Wilson was widely criticized for having virtually conceded independence to Smith's government, his own cabinet quickly approved his agreement with Smith. Smith's cabinet, however, rejected the plan on December 5th, citing the dangers posed by allowing re-establishment of a British presence in the country, and what they regarded as an offensive call to return to "legality." Wilson then immediately called upon the UN to impose mandatory economic sanctions (q.v.) against Rhodesia. The next official round of negotiations was called the "Fearless Talks" (q.v.).

TILCOR. Acronym for Tribal Trust Land Development Corporation (q.v.).

TIME.   The country is bisected by its standard meridian at 30° east
longitude.   Along with the rest of southern Africa, it lies entirely within a time zone two hours ahead of Greenwich Mean
Time, and seven hours ahead of Eastern Standard Time in the
United States.

TIN.   This metal has been found at sites scattered throughout the
country.   Alluvial tin occurs, but the metal is extracted mostly
from cassiterite (SnO_2), the most common tin ore.   There is
no direct archaeological evidence of pre-20th-century tin mining
in the country, but bronze objects containing 8% to 12% tin have
been found at Khami, Zimbabwe (qq.v.) and elsewhere.   It is
possible that such bronze was made from local copper (q.v.) and
tin imported from the Transvaal*, where old workings have been
found.   Modern production of tin began in 1908 at mines mainly
in eastern Mashonaland.   Production increased greatly after 1936,
when a major mine was started at Kamativi (q.v.), near Wankie*.
Since the mid-1950s the country has been self-sufficient in tin
production.   (See MINERALS/MINING.)

TOBACCO.   The date of tobacco's introduction to the country is uncertain, but it appears to have been introduced by early Portuguese (q.v.), since many Chishona (q.v.) terms for tobacco are
clearly borrowed from Portuguese.   By at least the 19th century
the Shona themselves were growing fine grades of tobacco in
Mashonaland*.   Commercial production of the crop by European
settlers began at Umtali* in the 1890s.   Production developed
slowly over the next three decades, rising rapidly only in the
late 1920s.   However, the sudden spurt in production of 1927 and
1928 glutted the market, depressing prices and producing a slump
from which the industry took another decade to recover.   Production again rose quickly during the Second World War, when British
dollar shortages turned British markets away from American
sources of tobacco.   Between 1945 and 1956 production tripled
in quantity and quadrupled in value, and tobacco displaced maize
(q.v.) as the country's most important crop (see AGRICULTURE).
Further expansion of export markets, improved strains of Virginia flue-cured leaf, and careful government regulation of the
industry led to more dramatic production increases over the next
decade.   By 1965 the country was producing 112 million kg. of
tobacco annually, accounting for nearly half the value of the
country's total agricultural production.   The country then ranked
as the world's second leading producer of tobacco, after the
United States, and it supplied more than a quarter of the world
trade in Virginia flue-cured leaf.

   Tobacco prices reached their all-time high in 1963, but
slumped greatly in 1964.   Post-UDI sanctions (q.v.) dealt the
industry an even harder blow.   Compared to many other primary
export goods, notably minerals (q.v.), tobacco is easy to identify
by origin, making enforcement of sanctions more efficient.   Production thus fell off rapidly after 1965, with the government imposing limits of just over half the pre-UDI levels by 1968.   Public tobacco auctions were terminated, with export sales conducted

through more clandestine methods.   By 1972 Rhodesia's contribution to the world tobacco trade was estimated to be about 10%
of the total value.   This share appears to have increased subsequently, but precise data are not available.

Government restrictions on African production of tobacco
have made commercial production of Virginia leaf virtually a
European monopoly.   Most production is in the modern Mashonaland provinces (q. v.), where soil conditions are most ideal.
Since UDI many tobacco farmers have turned to other crops and
beef cattle (q. v.) with government encouragement.

TODD, REGINALD STEPHEN GARFIELD (b. July 13, 1908).   Fifth
Prime Minister (q. v.) of Southern Rhodesia (1953-8).   Born in
New Zealand, Todd came to the country in 1934 and worked as
a missionary at the Dadaya Mission near Bannockburn* until
1946.   He gave up mission work for politics, and was elected
to the Legislative Assembly (q. v.) on the United Party (q. v.)
ticket in 1946.   When Godfrey Huggins (q. v.) assumed leadership of the new Federation government in 1953, Todd replaced
him as territorial premier.   During his administration he helped
to promote African education and African participation in electoral politics, but also supported increasingly draconian measures
to break up labor strikes.   His most notably liberal action was
appointment of Robert Tredgold (q. v.) as head of a commission
to investigate widening the franchise in 1956.

In January 1958 Todd's cabinet resigned to protest his
leadership.   He bucked tradition by attempting to form a new
government instead of stepping down, but he was voted out of
office by a special party congress in February.   His liberal
image and support of enfranchising more Africans are usually
cited as the reasons for his ouster, but some authorities now
argue that these issues were less relevant to his dismissal than
his personality clashes with the top leaders of the United (Federal) Party.   Assessments of Todd's administration have no doubt
been colored by the demonstrably more liberal stance he took on
African rights in later years.

After his dismissal as prime minister, Todd briefly served
in the cabinet of his successor, Edgar Whitehead (q. v.).   He
broke from Whitehead in order to contest the general election of
June 1958 as the head of a reconstituted United Rhodesian Party.
The complete defeat of this party at the polls effectively ended
Todd's career in electoral politics, though he then formed the
short-lived Central African Party (q. v.).

During the 1960s Todd became increasingly outspoken
against the Rhodesian Front (q. v.) government.   In 1965-6 Ian
Smith (q. v.) had him restricted to the huge farm he had acquired during his missionary days.   When the Pearce Commission (q. v.) arrived in early 1972, Todd was imprisoned, attracting considerable international attention.   Smith released him from
prison, but kept him under restriction at his farm until May 1976.
Todd later served as one of Joshua Nkomo's (q. v.) consultants
during the abortive Geneva Conference (q. v.).   In mid-1977 he
visited the United States in an effort to persuade the American

government to tighten its economic sanctions (q.v.) against Rhodesia.

TOGWA (variants: Torwa; Toloa).   Name of a little understood but possibly historically pivotal Shona (q.v.) dynasty.   The eponymous Togwa is claimed, possibly speciously, by Munhumutapa (q.v.) tradition to have been a relative of Munhumutapa Matope (q.v.), and to have been appointed to administer a southern district of the Munhumutapa state in the late 15th century.   During the early 1490s this Togwa and another ruler, Changa (q.v.), are said by the same traditions to have rebelled against Matope's successor, with Changa briefly becoming Munhumutapa.   When Changa was overthrown, Togwa appears to have retreated to the south, establishing an independent state in the Guruhuswa region (q.v.).   Little is known about Togwa's successors, except that they used "Togwa" either as their dynastic title or as the name of their kingdom.   Recent research has indicated that the Togwa state may have been responsible for introducing Khami Culture (q.v.) to the region now known as Matabeleland*, and that Khami (q.v.) itself was built as a Togwa center.   The Changamire dynasty (q.v.) appears to have displaced the Togwa dynasty in the late 16th century, after Munhumutapa Neshangwe (q.v.) expelled the Changamire people from the Mbire region (q.v.) in the northeast.

TOHWECHIPI (variant: Towechipi; a.k.a. Chibambamu, variant: Sibambamu) (d.c.1873).   Changamire (q.v.) ruler and leader of resistance against Ndebele (q.v.).   Tohwechipi was apparently installed as Changamire at Dhlo Dhlo (q.v.) after his father, Changamire Chirisamhuru (q.v.), was killed by Ngoni (q.v.) invaders in the early 1830s.   When Mzilikazi's Ndebele arrived in present Matabeleland* in the late 1830s, Tohwechipi and many other Rozvi people (q.v.) fled east.   Although a split had previously developed within the Changamire dynasty, Tohwechipi was recognized as mambo (q.v.), or ruler, by the rival Mutinhima faction during the 1850s.   By then he was living near the Zimbabwe Ruins*, and was leading Rozvi raids against Ndebele cattle posts.   Around the early 1850s Tohwechipi used firearms to defeat the Ndebele in a battle, earning himself the onomatopoeic nickname "Chibambamu," after the sound of gunfire. Despite his use of firearms, Tohwechipi was soon driven even farther east by the Ndebele.   In late 1866 the Ndebele captured him in the Mavange Hills of the upper Sabi* Valley.   He was taken before Mzilikazi, but was soon released.   Described as "old" in 1866, he died around 1873.   His title of mambo passed to a son of his former rival, Mutinhima, but the Changamire dynasty was finished as a significant political entity.

TOKWE RIVER.   Rises on the Central Plateau* near Lalapanzi (at 19°20'S, 30°11'E), flowing south, then southeast, to join the Lundi River (q.v.) above its confluence with the Mtilikwe*. West of Fort Victoria*, the Tokwe is fed by the Mushandike River (q.v.).

TONGA (BATONGA). Many Bantu-speaking (q.v.) peoples between
Malawi and South Africa are known by this name. Two Tonga
groups are part of the Tsonga cluster of peoples (see HLENGWE).
Another Tonga group, associated with the Barwe (q.v.), occupies
part of the Inyanga District (q.v.) along the border with Mozambique*. The western-most branch of the Shona-speaking Ndau
(q.v.) are also called Tonga.

The most important Tonga group in present Rhodesia has
long occupied both sides of the Zambezi River, between the Victoria Falls and Kariba*. They are also known as Batonka, or
Batoka (as in "Batoka Gorge," q.v.). About 20,000 of these
people were forcibly removed from the Zambezi Valley when
Lake Kariba (q.v.) was filling in the late 1950s. These Zambezi, or "river," Tonga are related to the Ila and other Zambian peoples. Tsetse flies (q.v.) have prevented them from
keeping significant numbers of livestock, so they have been
mainly cultivators and fishermen (see FISHING). During the
19th century they were noted as great boatmen, playing a major
role in ferrying combatants in the Ndebele-Kololo (qq.v.) wars
of the 1840s. During the late 19th century they were forced to
pay tribute to both the Ndebele and the Lozi (q.v.), and were
hard pressed by raids from both sides of the river, particularly
during the 1880s. In 1893 the Tonga were hit by smallpox
(q.v.), which they transmitted to an Ndebele raiding party on
the eve of the Ndebele War*.

TORWA. (1) Shona dynasty: see TOGWA. (2) Chishona term for
"stranger"; see MUTORWA.

TRACHOMA. Viral eye infection, transmitted by ordinary flies and
unhygienic wash towels. The disease inflames the eyes and can
cause partial or full blindness. It is a major problem in rural
areas, particularly among children. (See HEALTH.)

TRANSPORT AND COMMUNICATIONS. The country's transport and
communications networks are among the best in tropical Africa.
An impetus for rapid development of these networks lay in the
British South Africa Company's (q.v.) early need to make the
country economically profitable. Telegraph (q.v.) lines were
built as fast as the Company occupied the country. Railway
(q.v.) lines and a formal postal system (q.v.) followed quickly.
Bridge and road (q.v.) building programs have also been extensive. Newspapers began appearing immediately after British
occupation. Telephone (q.v.) services began in the late 1890s.
Radio broadcasting commenced in the 1930s, followed by television in the early 1960s (see RHODESIAN BROADCASTING
CORP.). Since July 1, 1970, all postal, telephone, and telegraph services have been in the hands of the government-owned
Telecommunications Corporation. (See map on p. 326.)

TRANSPORT DRIVER. Term used for drivers of ox-wagons (q.v.)
in the 19th century, and for truck drivers in the 20th century.

TRANSVAAL. Now a province of the Republic of South Africa (q.v.),
the Transvaal covers a 286,070 sq. km. area between the Vaal

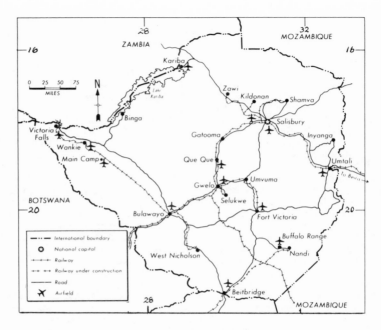

Map 5.   Transportation System

and Limpopo* rivers.   It is the only part of South Africa which
borders present Rhodesia.   Its peoples, mostly Sotho and Venda
(qq.v.), have historically moved freely back and forth across
the easily fordable Limpopo.   During the 1820s and 1830s Mzilikazi's Ndebele kingdom (q.v.) occupied a series of settlements
in the Transvaal before permanently settling in present Matabeleland*.   After the Ndebele left, Afrikaner (q.v.) emigrants from
the Cape Colony (now the Cape Province) began occupying the
Transvaal, establishing the South African Republic in 1852.
Thereafter the Limpopo was increasingly recognized as a boundary line.   Transvaal Afrikaners, such as Jan Viljoen (q.v.),
hunted and traded north of the Limpopo, but they restricted
firearm trade to the north, forcing the Ndebele rulers to use
Ngwato (q.v.) territory in Botswana* as the main southern approach to their domain.
        From 1877 to 1881 the British government occupied the
Transvaal, with Theophilus Shepstone (q.v.) serving as administra-
trator.   The Afrikaners regained their independence after the
"First Boer War," and Paul Kruger became their president in
1883.   During the late 1880s Afrikaner interest in further northward expansion elicited strong British responses.   The Bechuanaland Protectorate (q.v.) was declared over Botswana in 1885,
and the British South Africa company (q.v.) occupied Mashonaland* in 1890 (see also GROBLER, P.; ADENDORFF TREK).
Discovery of vast gold fields in the central Transvaal's Rand
region led to an influx of British prospectors, giving Cecil
Rhodes (q.v.) an excuse to meddle in Transvaal politics.   At
Rhodes' instigation the abortive Jameson Raid (q.v.) was launched

from Rhodesia in late 1895. This affair helped to touch off the
Ndebele and Shona Revolts (q.v.), and led directly to the South
African War of 1899-1902 (q.v.).

The Union of South Africa was created in 1910, with
Pretoria--a former Ndebele occupation site--as the national
capital. Beitbridge (q.v.) was completed in 1929, and has
since remained as the main link between Rhodesia and the
Transvaal. In 1974 the first direct railway* link between the
two regions was established through Beitbridge.

TRANSVAAL NDEBELE. Collective name for several remotely related African communities in the Transvaal (q.v.). These groups
were founded by pre-19th-century Nguni (q.v.) settlers from the
east coast, but all had become largely Sotho (q.v.) in culture
and language by the 19th century. These communities are frequently said to have been created by stragglers from Mzilikazi's
Ndebele (qq.v.) 19th-century migrations, but they clearly existed
long before his arrival. Some of Mzilikazi's Ndebele did remain
in the Transvaal after his departure, and others, such as Mangwane and "Nkulumane" (qq.v.), resettled there later, but these
people have nothing to do with the "Transvaal Ndebele" proper.
(On name, see MATABELE.)

TREDGOLD, ROBERT CLARKSON (b.June 2, 1899). Judge. Tredgold's mother was a daughter of J. S. Moffat (q.v.); his father,
Clarkson Henry Tredgold (1865-1938) was an immigrant from
South Africa who became a Southern Rhodesian justice. R. C.
Tredgold himself was born in Bulawayo. He studied at Oxford
on a Rhodes Scholarship and returned to central Africa to practice law. In 1934 he was elected to the Legislative Assembly
(q.v.) as a United Party (q.v.) member. From 1936 to 1943 he
served as Godfrey Huggins' (q.v.) Minister of Justice and Defence. In 1943 he became a High Court Justice, rising to Chief
Justice in 1950. In 1955 he became Chief Justice of the Federation (q.v.). He resigned in 1960 in protest against Southern
Rhodesia's proposed Law and Order (Maintenance) Bill (q.v.).
Highly regarded for his judicial integrity, Tredgold is generally
regarded as having had a liberal but paternalistic attitude towards
Africans. In 1956 he headed a commission to study franchise
reform in Southern Rhodesia. His report, only partly adopted,
advocated a double roll system which would exclude most Africans
from the top roll, while giving many more Africans a lower roll
vote which would count less. He published his autobiography,
The Rhodesia That Was My Life, in 1968.

TREK. Term for journey or migration, from Dutch/Afrikaans*.
Also used as a verb.

TRIANGLE. Center of a major sugar (q.v.) estate in the southeastern low veld, just north of the Lundi/Mtilikwe (qq.v.) confluence (at 21° 2'S, 32° 27'E; alt. 420 m.). During the 1920s
Thomas Murray MacDougall (1881-1964), a Scottish immigrant,
began a large-scale private irrigation scheme at the Triangle Estate, while pioneering the country's sugar industry. The govern-

ment bought him out in 1944, but later allowed the Estate to re-
vert to private ownership, while assisting in irrigation development.   By the early 1960s Triangle and neighboring Hippo Valley
(q. v.) were the country's only major sugar producers.   Post-
UDI sanctions (q. v.) reduced sugar export markets sharply, so
agricultural production was greatly diversified to serve local
markets.   Population in Triangle village in 1969 was 5050 (87%
Africans).   (See also SABI-LIMPOPO AUTHORITY.)

TRIBAL TRUST LAND DEVELOPMENT CORPORATION (TILCOR).
Body established by the Rhodesian government in 1968 to promote industrial development of African rural areas.   Despite
ambitious plans, Tilcor had initiated only two manufacturing industries and a few irrigation schemes by the early 1970s.

TRIBAL TRUST LANDS (TTL).   Official name for rural areas formerly known as "Native Reserves."   After the conclusion of the
Ndebele War (q. v.) in 1894 a land commission was formed to
investigate the problem of relocating the Ndebele people.   This
commission created two large reserves in Matabeleland*, establishing the principle that African needs had to be met before
land could be alienated to Europeans.   A British order-in-council in 1898 reiterated this principle and made the BSAC administration responsible for assigning land to Africans.   However,
no guidelines for determining African land needs were established,
so the administration simply passed its responsibility on to its
District Commissioners to enforce (see DISTRICTS).   The result
was piecemeal allocation of African reserves, based on situations
pertaining in individual districts.   By 1913 more than a hundred
separate reserves of vastly different sizes had been designated
throughout the country.   These were consolidated somewhat over
the next decade, and the basic pattern of land allocation was
firmly set by the early 1920s.   The 1923 Constitution (q. v.)
formalized the existing reserves.   The Land Apportionment Act
of 1930 (q. v.) enlarged the reserves slightly, so they accounted
for 22.4% of the whole country.
   Since 1930 perhaps the single most important economic
issue in the country has been the inadequacy of reserve lands in
the face of rapidly growing African population (q. v.).   Increased
human and livestock pressure on the reserves has depleted their
productive capacity, while essentially subsistence methods of
communal agriculture (q. v.) have failed to keep pace with population growth.
   During the early 1960s the United (Federal) Party (q. v.)
government began a policy of combining reserves with recently
created "Special Native Areas" to form newly designated "Tribal
Trust Lands," but this policy was abandoned by the Rhodesian
Front (q. v.) after it came to power in 1962.   The RF government articulated a policy of achieving "parity" between European
and African lands, formalized in the Land Tenure Act of 1969
(q. v.).   Under this Act total European and African areas were
equalized, with TTL areas fixed at 16,151,520 hectares, or
41.4% of the total land in the country.   Most of the remaining

African land was divided into non-communally owned Purchase
Areas (q.v.). The President (q.v.) of the country was empowered to transfer pieces of land among categories, while retaining the basic overall proportions. By the early 1970s TTL's
were fragmented into more than 160 units.

TTL units are scattered throughout the country, but most
are in the middle and low veld areas (see ALTITUDINAL ZONES).
Districts which are totally, or predominantly, made up of TTL
include Buhera, Ndanga, Gokwe, Nkai, Chibi, Belingwe, Mrewa,
and Mtoko (qq.v.). Districts with little or no TTL include Bindura, Salisbury, Lomagundi, Gatooma, Hartley, Gwelo, Bubi,
Insiza, Chiredzi, Wankie, Mazoe, and Shamva (qq.v.). (See
also NATIVE LAND HUSBANDRY ACT.)

TROJAN MINE   see   BINDURA

TROOPIES. Nickname for Rhodesian government soldiers.

TRUEY THE GRIQUA (Truey David)   see under   WILLIAM THE
   GRIQUA

TRYPANOSOMIASIS   see   SLEEPING SICKNESS; NAGANA

TSETSE FLY (Diptera glossina). Blood-feeding insect, several varieties of which transmit trypanosome parasites which give the
   disease trypanosomiasis to animals (see NAGANA) and humans
   (see SLEEPING SICKNESS). The insect is found only in tropical
   Africa. It thrives in shady, dry places near the game on which
   it feeds. It is rarely found above altitudes of 1000 meters, and
   tends to live by water, which attracts game. Since the insect
   tends not to migrate, destruction of its habitat is an effective
   means of combating the very serious diseases it carries.

   Before the 19th century tsetse flies covered most of the
   country's lowland areas. Ndebele settlement in Matabeleland*
   in the 1840s began a process of tsetse fly retreat, as the Ndebele cut back the Somabula Forest (q.v.). Increasingly intensive
   big game hunting (q.v.) accelerated the retreat of tsetse by diminishing the flies' natural food supplies. The rinderpest epidemic of 1896 (q.v.) destroyed huge numbers of cattle (q.v.),
   pushing the tsetse fly "belt" even farther north. After these
   setbacks the flies began recovering their former territories at
   a rate of about 2500 sq. km./year. During the present century
   the government has combated tsetse flies by clearing indigenous
   forests (q.v.) and shooting game. The intensification of guerrilla warfare in the mid-1970s has inhibited tsetse fly abatement
   work, allowing the flies to begin a new recovery of territory.

TSH-. Chishona (q.v.) words starting with this digraph, which is
   sounded as ch- in "church," are now generally spelled with ch-.
   Tsh- also appears frequently as a variant of the sh- sound in
   Sindebele and other Nguni languages (qq.v.).

TSONGA (variant: Thonga)   see   HLENGWE

TSORO. Chishona* name for the widespread African board game
played with pebbles or pips in rows of holes. The game is
played throughout the country, as well as much of Africa.

TSWANA (Batswana; variants: Bechuana; Bechwana). Common name
for the western branch of Sotho-speaking (q.v.) peoples. Tswana groups have long been the majority population in present
Botswana (q.v.) and the western Transvaal (q.v.). Some of
these peoples, notably the Ngwato and Talowta (qq.v.), occupied
parts of southwestern Rhodesia as late as the 19th century.
The arrival of the Ndebele (q.v.) in Matabeleland* after 1838
led to a retreat of some Tswana communities towards the west
and southwest. Other Tswana groups were absorbed into Ndebele
culture, both in Matabeleland, and during the kingdom's formation earlier in the Transvaal. (See also TAWANA.)

TULI. The Tuli River rises in the Matopo Hills (q.v.), whence it
flows south c.160 km. before joining the Shashi River (q.v.) at
the Botswana border. Just below this confluence the boundary
line leaves the Shashi, curving into Botswana (q.v.) in an arc
known as the "Tuli Circle," a Rhodesian region now designated
a "Controlled Hunting Area." The small town of Tuli stands by
the Shashi, at a point near the center of the Tuli Circle. The
town was founded when the Pioneer Column (q.v.) established
Fort Tuli (at 21° 56'S, 29° 11'E) just before it crossed the Shashi
River in July 1890. The town appeared destined to develop into
a major stop along the main road to Salisbury, but its development was arrested when British occupation of Matabeleland* in
early 1894 led to the opening of another route through Bulawayo*.

TURK MINE. Village between Inyati* and the Bembezi River*, adjacent to the Turk Gold Mine (19° 43'S, 28° 47'E), long one of
the country's major gold (q.v.) producers.

TWALA, ABRAHAM see under RHODESIAN BANTU VOTERS' AS-
SOCIATION

"TWO PYRAMID POLICY." Concept articulated by Godfrey Huggins'
(q.v.) government in the late 1930s in order to express the goal
of completely separate European and African development. The
concept was largely abandoned by the late 1940s, when the frag-
mentation of land and the growing economic interdependence of
African and Europeans were seen to point up the impracticality
of total territorial segregation. (Cf. "PARTNERSHIP"; APART-
HEID.)

TYPHOID FEVER (a.k.a. enteric fever). This infectious bacterial
disease is widespread in the country, and is one of the country's
most serious health (q.v.) problems.

- U -

U-.. (1) In Chishona (q.v.) u- is a noun prefix (Class 14) for a wide variety of nouns, including those pertaining to states of being and places, as in Urozvi (q.v.), "the country of the Rozvi." It is sometimes rendered as hu- (or hw- before vowels) or as bw-.

(2) The initial u- of many Ndebele and other Nguni (qq.v.) proper names is usually dropped in English usage. Thus, for Umzilikazi and Umzila, for example, see Mzilikazi and Mzila, etc. By contrast, the initial u- of many Nguni-derived place names, such as Umzingwani River, is usually retained. Convention, rather than logic, dictates these usages, and consistency is difficult to attain.

ULOPENGULA see LOBENGULA

UME RIVER (variant: Omay) see BUMI RIVER

UMFULI RIVER (variant: Mumvuri). One of the Umniati River's (q.v.) main tributaries, the Umfuli rises about 35 km. southwest of Marandellas*, flowing c.200 km. northwest before it joins the Umniati's course to the Zambezi. Numerous small dams on the river supply regional water needs.

UMGUSA RIVER (variant: Umguza). Rises near Ntabazinduna*, flowing northwest to feed the Gwai River (q.v.). Several dams built on the Umgusa in 1936 and 1947 provide irrigation water to the region just north of Bulawayo*.

UMNIATI RIVER (variant: Munyati). One of the country's most reliable Zambezi affluents, the Umniati rises north of Enkeldoorn* on the Central Plateau*, whence it follows a long, winding course before entering the east end of Lake Kariba*. Most important of its own tributaries are the Sebakwe, Umsweswe, and Umfuli rivers (qq.v.). The stretch of the Umniati below the Umfuli confluence was once more commonly called the Sanyati River.

UMTALI. The fourth largest urban center in the country, with a population over 59,000 at the end of 1974, Umtali is an important industrial center, as well as commercial and administrative centers of both Umtali District and Manicaland Province (qq.v.). It is situated on the Mozambique border at 18° 57' South latitude, at an altitude of 1190 meters. Across the border stands Villa de Manica, formerly known as Maçequeçe (q.v.).

Umtali is entirely a colonial creation. Soon after Salisbury (q.v.) was founded in 1890, a small party of Europeans entered Manicaland, where they obtained a treaty from the Manyika ruler Mutasa (q.v.). They then founded Ft. Umtali near the Mutari River (which Nguni-speakers* rendered Mtali). A year later the settlement was shifted to a higher and healthier site, now known as "Old Umtali" (q.v.). This location also proved unsuitable when it was realized that the projected railway (q. v.) between Beira (q. v.) and Salisbury could pass only through a gap in the Eastern Highlands (q. v.) 15 km. to the south. So, the settlement was again moved in 1896, this time to its present site on the railway line. The several hundred European settlers forced to move were paid £50,000 by the BSAC.

During the 20th century Umtali has grown steadily as a center for tobacco, maize (qq. v.), tea, and other agricultural production, as well as gold (q. v.) mining and mixed manufacturing. Africans account for 80% of the city's population, and about two-thirds of them live in Sakubva township.

UMTALI DISTRICT. Eastern border district, covering 7160 sq. km. in the center of Manicaland Province (q. v.). Umtali borders the districts of Melsetter on the south; Buhera on the southwest; Makoni on the northwest; and Inyanga (qq. v.) on the north. Administrative headquarters are at Umtali (q. v.). Other centers include Penhalonga and Old Umtali (qq. v.). The southwestern corner of the district is mostly Tribal Trust Land (q. v.); most of the rest of the well-watered and mountainous district is reserved for Europeans, with a few pockets of Purchase Areas (q. v.). District population in 1969 included 200,980 Africans, 9985 Europeans, and 985 Asians and Coloureds.

UMTALI POST. Founded in December 1893 as the Umtali Advertiser, this newspaper was absorbed by the "Argus Group" (q. v.) in 1895. It started as a weekly, and is now a daily. (See PRESS.)

UMTASA. Nguni* form of Mutasa (q. v.), the dynastic title of Manyika rulers.

UMVUKWE HILLS. Mountain range running astride the northern part of the Great Dyke (q. v.), along the boundary between the Lomagundi and Mazoe Districts (qq. v.), north from a point about 50 km. northwest of Salisbury. Most of the range exceeds 1500 meters in elevation, with Mount Umvukwe (at 17° 12' S, 30° 41'E) being the highest point at 1748 meters. The hills are rich in chrome ore (q. v.), which is mined intensively. Umvukwes Village (at 17° 2'S, 30° 51'E) is the administrative and commercial center for an important tobacco (q. v.) producing region. Its population in 1969 was 1500.

UMVUMA (variant: Mumvumi). Administrative center of the Chilimanzi District (q. v.); located about halfway between Fort Victoria and Gwelo (qq. v.) on the former's branch railway (q. v.) line (at 19° 17'S, 30° 32'E; alt. 1395 m.). The town was founded in 1902 to serve the Falcon Mine, which was the country's leading gold and copper (qq. v.) producer between 1912 and 1924. The mine was started over minor pre-colonial African workings, and it has retained its position as the country's leading copper producer. Population of Umvuma in 1969 was 1520 (91% Africans).

UMVUTSHA (variants: Umvutchwa; Umvutja). Small, late 19th-
century Ndebele village, located just north of Bulawayo (q.v.)
on the right bank of the Umgusa River (q.v.). It was one of
several private kraals (q.v.) in which Lobengula (q.v.) frequently resided and conducted Ndebele state business. It was
here that he signed the Rudd Concession (q.v.) in 1888.

UMZINGWANE DISTRICT (former variants: Mzingwana; Mzingwane).
District covering 2760 sq. km. of Matabeleland South Province
(q.v.), just southeast of Bulawayo (q.v.). The district was
separated from Bulawayo District in 1897, but was later reab-
sorbed into Bulawayo and neighboring districts before being recreated in its present shape. It now borders the districts of
Bulawayo on the northwest; Bubi on the north; Insiza on the east;
Gwanda on the south; and Matobo (qq.v.) on the southwest. The
southwestern corner of the district is Tribal Trust Land (q.v.);
the rest is reserved for Europeans. District headquarters are
at Essexvale (q.v.). District population in 1969 included 46,098
Africans and 1143 Europeans.

UMZINGWANE RIVER (variants: Umzingwani; Mudzingwani). Rising
in the Matopo Hills*, just south of Bulawayo*, the Umzingwane
first flows east, then turns south, following a course roughly
parallel to that of the Tuli River (q.v.), located c. 50 km. to
its west. The Umzingwane meets the Limpopo (q.v.) just above
Beitbridge*. Its largest affluent is the Insiza (q.v.). Umzingwane Dam was built just south of Essexvale (q.v.) in 1958 to
contribute to Bulawayo's water supply.

UNCOMBATA see MNCUMBATHE

UNILATERAL DECLARATION OF INDEPENDENCE (UDI) (1965).
Colloquial name for proclamation issued by the Rhodesian government on November 11, 1965, declaring Rhodesia to be an independent monarchy under Queen Elizabeth II.
    The proclamation was the culmination of British-Rhodesian
constitutional negotiations begun during the creation of the Southern
Rhodesian Constitution of 1961 (q.v.). The Rhodesian Front party
(q.v.) came to power in December 1962 pledged to achievement
of independence under white rule. When Prime Minister Winston
Field (q.v.) failed to press Britain hard enough on this issue, he
was replaced by Ian Smith (q.v.) in April 1964. Smith's government soon attempted to demonstrate popular support for independence by getting African chiefs to endorse the idea in the "Domboshawa Indaba" (q.v.) during October, and by having the predominantly European electorate vote overwhelmingly for independence in a November referendum (58,091 "yes," 6906 "no").
Negotiations with Britain continued through October 1965, when
Prime Minister Harold Wilson visited Salisbury for the last time.
On November 11th Smith publicly proclaimed Rhodesia's independence from Britain, and the action has since been known almost
universally as "UDI."
    The UDI proclamation was signed by Smith and all 15

members of his cabinet, including C. W. Dupont, W. J. Harper, P. K. F. V. van der Byl, and J. J. Wrathall (qq.v.). Except for the proclamation's expressions of loyalty to the British monarch, its wording deliberately recalled that of the American Declaration of Independence. Especially similar is the preamble, which begins: "Whereas in the course of human affairs history has shown that it may become necessary for a people to resolve...." The proclamation continues in this vein, pointing out that the government has exercised self-government for 42 years; that the country has always been loyal to the British Crown; that the country represents a rare bastion of civilized democracy in the region; that the country's people enthusiastically endorse independence; and that Britain has failed to negotiate Rhodesia's future in good faith.

International reaction to UDI was both swift and negative, and no country, including South Africa (q.v.), has ever formally recognized Rhodesia's independence. Britain declared the regime to be "illegal," but it had previously disavowed the use of military force. It instead instituted unilateral economic sanctions (q.v.), which were soon internationalized by the UN. Despite the ostensibly rigid positions taken by both the Rhodesian and British governments, they continued to pursue a negotiated settlement which would legitimize Rhodesia's separation from Britain. The first formal negotiations held after UDI were the December 1966 "Tiger Talks" (q.v.).

UNION PARTY. Avowedly Afrikaner (q.v.) nationalist party which emerged briefly to field two unsuccessful candidates in the 1939 general election.

UNIONIST MOVEMENT. The idea of joining Southern Rhodesia to South Africa (q.v.) first arose when the unification of South Africa's four colonies was being planned. In 1908 Charles Coghlan (q.v.) attended the national convention in South Africa as a non-voting delegate with this possibility in mind. Coghlan and other Southern Rhodesian politicians thought that union with South Africa was probably inevitable, but they decided to wait until a more propitious moment because of the disadvantageous position Southern Rhodesia's small European (q.v.) community would give the country in the context of South Africa's emerging constitution.

The union idea was revived a decade later as an alternative for the country's future after the termination of BSAC rule. By then, however, Coghlan and most other settlers opposed union, instead favoring autonomous Responsible Government (q.v.). The BSAC and local industrials favored union with South Africa, and the Rhodesia Unionist Association (q.v.) was formed by a faction of settlers. Major capitalist interests within the country feared bankruptcy under a responsible government, seeing union as their salvation. Opponents of union feared South African--and particularly Afrikaner (q.v.)--domination, a loss of African laborers to the south, an influx of poor South African whites (bywoners), higher taxes, and trouble with South African

labor unions.   In the absence of a realistic third alternative to
union and responsible government, missionary and non-white
opinion tended to favor the latter.

Prime Minister Jan Smuts of South Africa pushed hard
for Southern Rhodesia's entry into the Union of South Africa.
He is said to have bribed Coghlan with an offer of a cabinet
post to this end.   In 1922 Smuts published a definite offer to
Southern Rhodesia, promising provincial status, a generous
number of parliamentary seats, substantial local autonomy, development funds, expansion of the port of Beira (q.v.), and
preservation of existing civil servant jobs.   The unionist movement was backed by the Argus Group (q.v.) of newspapers, but
unionist organization did not match that of Coghlan's Responsible
Government Movement.   In October 1922 the settlers voted
three to two in favor of responsible government, thereby killing
the unionist movement.   (Cf. AMALGAMATION MOVEMENT.)

UNITED AFRICAN NATIONAL COUNCIL (UANC).   Designation for
Abęl Muzorewa's (q.v.) branch of the African National Council
(q.v.).

UNITED FEDERAL PARTY   see   UNITED PARTY

UNITED METHODIST CHURCH (UMC) (formerly: Methodist Episcopal Church).   Missionaries of the American-based Methodist
Episcopal Church followed their British Wesleyan (q.v.) counterparts into Southern Rhodesia in 1898.   Under the leadership of
Joseph Hartzell they established their headquarters at Old Umtali (q.v.), which was granted to them by the BSAC.   Throughout the early 20th century the Americans concentrated their
work in the eastern and northeastern parts of the country, while
the Wesleyans and other Methodist (q.v.) societies operated elsewhere.   David Mandisodza was the first African ordained a
minister in 1924.   In 1968 Abel Muzorewa (q.v.) became bishop
of the national church.   The same year the worldwide church
became known as the United Methodist Church after a series of
mergers among various American Methodist bodies.   By the
early 1970s the UMC claimed over 20,000 African members in
all parts of Rhodesia.

In 1959 the American and British Methodists began shar-
ing theological training facilities, with the Epworth (q.v.) Theological College concentrating on ministerial training, and the
Old Umtali Biblical Institute training lay workers.   Women
members have developed an influential lay organization known
as Ruwadzano (q.v.).   (Cf. AFRICAN METHODIST EPISCOPAL
CHURCH.)

UNITED PARTY (UP; a.k.a. United Federal Party).   The country's
governing party for three decades, the UP was formed by Godfrey Huggins (q.v.) in 1934 out of a merger of the main leader-
ships of the Reform Party and the originally ruling Rhodesian
Party (qq.v.).   The UP won majorities in every general election
from 1934 to 1958, except that of 1946, when Huggins nevertheless

retained control of the government.   When the Federation (q.v.)
was being formed in 1953, the UP was reorganized as the United
Rhodesia Party (URP), incorporating former supporters of the
Liberal and Labour parties (qq.v.).   Huggins also formed a
separate Federal Party out of UP leadership.   In 1958 the URP
merged with the Federal Party to become the United Federal
Party (UFP).   The party leadership's ouster of Garfield Todd
(q.v.) from the territorial premiership early that year created
a split, with Todd contesting the June election as head of a reconstituted URP.   The new URP won no Legislative Assembly
(q.v.) seats, while the UFP held off a strong challenge from
the Dominion Party (q.v.) to retain control of the government.
In late 1962 the UFP lost the general election to the DP's successor, the Rhodesian Front (q.v.).   Afterwards it was reorganized as the Rhodesian Party, which faded away when the RF
swept the 1965 election.

UNITED PEOPLE'S PARTY (UPP).   African political party announced
on May 31, 1965, by ten African members of parliament who had
originally been elected to "B" roll seats as representatives of
the United (Federal) Party's (q.v.) successor, the Rhodesia
Party.   The UPP was recognized as the official opposition by
the Rhodesian Front (q.v.) government, becoming the first African body so recognized.   The UPP sought majority rule through
constitutional change, but was wracked by leadership quarrels
over the most efficacious means to be employed.   Tolerated by
the RF because of their ultimate political impotence, the UPP
leaders were regarded as government "stooges" by leaders of
extra-parliamentary nationalist parties.   A splinter group under
Chad Chipunza (b. 1923), an uncle of Abel Muzorewa (q.v.),
formed a breakaway Democratic Party (q.v.) in August 1968,
but the two bodies reunited as the National People's Union (q.v.)
in June 1969.

UNITED RHODESIA PARTY   see   UNITED PARTY

UNIVERSITY OF RHODESIA (UR).   Moves to found a local university
for European students began in 1945.   The coming of the Federation (q.v.) in 1953 transformed the original concept into a multi-
racial university college for all central Africans under the aegis
of the new Federal Government.   The Salisbury city government
donated land in the white suburb of Mount Pleasant (q.v.), where
Queen Elizabeth II laid the first foundation stone in July 1953.
In September the British government capitalized the project with
a one-time grant of £1.25 million and construction began in
earnest.   In February 1955 the University College of Rhodesia
and Nyasaland (UCRN) was incorporated as an autonomous institution by royal charter.   A special relationship was established
with the University of London, which later awarded UCRN degrees.   When a medical school was begun in 1963, a similar
arrangement was established between it and the University of
Birmingham.

UCRN opened to its first 70 full-time students in March

1957. Enrollments rose to over 550 in 1964, when it was re-constituted as the University College of Rhodesia (UCR) and separate institutions were begun in Zambia and Malawi. After the breakup of the Federation, the Rhodesian government assumed responsibility for the university college's financing. On January 1, 1971, the special ties with the University of London were terminated, and the UCR assumed full autonomy as the University of Rhodesia, awarding its own degrees for the first time. At the beginning of the 1972 academic year there were 967 full-time students (53% Europeans, 40% Africans, and 7% Asians and Coloureds, qq. v.). By 1975 full-time enrollments had risen to 1361.

Founded as an expression of the federal principle of "partnership" (q. v.), the university has become a social and political anomaly within the white-ruled country since the dissolution of the Federation. Despite its continued dependence upon the Rhodesian Front (q. v.) government for funding, the university has largely retained its academic autonomy under the terms of its original charter, and it has stood out as a unique enclave of racial integration in the center of an increasingly hostile environment. Nevertheless, many people outside the country have continued to regard the university as merely an arm of the internationally unpopular government.

UNLAWFUL ORGANISATIONS ACT (1959). Law passed by the government of Edgar Whitehead (q. v.) after the banning of the African National Congress (q. v.), giving the police wide powers of search and seizure, and enabling the government to arrest any person in any way associated with a banned organization. In July 1960 sections of the Act were invoked to arrest leaders of the National Democratic Party (q. v.) for their presumed membership in the banned ANC. Subsequent amendments to the Act further increased government controls over political organizations, and the Act was later invoked to ban ZAPU, ZANU, PCC, and FROLIZI (qq. v.).

UPENGULA   see   LOBENGULA

URBANIZATION. The country's major towns are essentially 20th-century creations, although some of them were built on the sites of 19th-century African settlements. The first European towns were established mainly along the route of the 1890 Pioneer Column (q. v.), whose terminal camp became the present capital of Salisbury (q. v.). Occupation of Matabeleland* in 1894 led quickly to the establishment of modern Bulawayo (q. v.). The new high veld route between Bulawayo and Salisbury soon displaced the original Pioneer Column route to the east as the nexus of urban centers, giving rise to Gwelo, Que Que, and Gatooma (qq. v.). The only comparably large urban center which arose elsewhere is Umtali (q. v.), established at the eastern border where the Beira railway (q. v.) line enters the country. With the exceptions of Marandellas and Fort Victoria (qq. v.), the country's only other major towns are mostly

specialized mining centers, such as Wankie and Shabani (qq.v.).
Although the country's population (q.v.) as a whole remains essentially rural, Rhodesia ranks as one of the most
highly urbanized countries in tropical Africa, along with neighboring Zambia (q.v.). By the early 1960s an estimated 15% of
the country's population resided in centers of more than 20,000
people. The European (q.v.) population is especially highly
urbanized. More than two-thirds of the settlers lived in large
towns during the early 1950s, and this figure rose to an estimated 82% in 1975. (See also LAND APPORTIONMENT and
LAND TENURE ACTS; PASS LAWS; NATIVE (URBAN AREAS)
ACCOMMODATION ACT; and under names of individual districts
for major urban centers.)

UROZVI (variant: Vurozvi). Literally, "the country of the Rozvi"
(q.v.); used mainly to refer to the traditional domain of the
Changamire state (q.v.).

URUNGWE DISTRICT. Northernmost district, covering 18,235 sq.
km. which once were the western half of the original Lomagundi District (q.v.). The district borders Zambia (q.v.) along
almost the entire stretch of the Zambezi River between Lake
Kariba and Mozambique. The district of Sipolilo (q.v.) borders
it on the northeast. The Angwa River (q.v.) separates it from
the Lomagundi District on the southeast, and the Umniati River
(q.v.) separates it from the Gokwe District (q.v.) on the southwest. Urungwe also borders Kariba District (q.v.) on the west.
It is mostly a low veld area, and is relatively undeveloped, except around Karoi (q.v.). To an extent far greater than in most
districts, the Land Tenure Act (q.v.) divides Urungwe into a
complex patchwork of Tribal Trust Lands, Purchase Areas,
European areas, unreserved lands, and national areas. Administrative headquarters are at Miami (q.v.). District population in
1969 included 116,230 Africans and 1859 Europeans.

USHER, WILLIAM FILMER (1850-Sept. 22, 1916). A British trader,
Usher came to Bulawayo* in 1883 and became an advisor and
letter-writer for King Lobengula (q.v.). During the 1893 Ndebele
War (q.v.) he and J. Fairbairn (q.v.) were left unharmed in
Bulawayo when Lobengula fled the British invasion. Their treatment at the hands of the Ndebele is frequently cited as evidence
of Lobengula's good-will towards Europeans.

UXWITI see ZWIDE

- V -

VA-. Chishona (q.v.) noun prefix (Class 2), normally used for
plural forms of Class 1 mu- prefix nouns for people. In the
cases of proper names, such prefixes are dropped in this dictionary; thus for "Vakaranga," for example, see KARANGA.

For ordinary nouns, see under <u>mu</u>-; e.g., for <u>vadzimu</u>, see
MUDZIMU. (Cf. MA-.)

VAMBE, LAWRENCE (b.1917). Journalist. Born at Chishawasha
(q.v.), Vambe was educated at the mission station there and in
South Africa. He trained for the Roman Catholic priesthood and
teaching, but instead became a journalist. In 1953 he assumed
the chief editorship of African Newspapers, Ltd. (q.v.). After
a study and speaking tour of the United States in 1957, he received a British MBE as a reward for his journalistic support
of the Federation (q.v.). He left Southern Rhodesia in 1959,
after the African National Congress (q.v.) was banned. He returned in 1962 and became public relations officer for the Anglo-
American Corporation. Later he went into voluntary self-exile
in England, where he began writing a series of books. His
first, An Ill-Fated People (1972), recounts the history of the
country up to the 1920s through the eyes of the Shavasha people
(q.v.). From Rhodesia to Zimbabwe (1976) carries the story
through 1962, while injecting Vambe's own memoirs.

VAN DER BYL, PIETER K. F. V. (b.Nov. 11, 1923). Politician.
Born in South Africa, van der Byl became a tobacco (q.v.)
farmer in Southern Rhodesia after World War II. In 1962 he
was first elected to the Legislative Assembly (q.v.) for Hartley*. He became Deputy Minister of Information in 1964,
rising to the head of the ministry in September 1968. He later
became Minister of Defence, but was dismissed in September
1976. As Foreign Minister he served as Ian Smith's (q.v.)
deputy at the Geneva Conference (q.v.) later in 1976. A noted
hardliner, he clashed verbally with African representatives,
thereby helping to scuttle the conference.

VAN NIEKERK RUINS. Major lowland complex of the Inyanga Ruins
group (q.v.), covering more than 50 sq. km. north of the Inyanga National Park* (at 18° 8'S, 32° 40'E). The complex extends along about 8 km. of the Nyangombe River; a 36 sq. km.
section of the ruins east of the river was declared a National
Monument* in 1946. The ruins were first examined in 1905
by David Randall-MacIver (q.v.), who named them after a local
farmer who had found them some years earlier. The ruins include numerous examples of walled enclosures, "forts," stone-
lined pits (q.v.), and agricultural terraces. They appear to
have been built and occupied during the 18th and early 19th
centuries. Mt. Ziwa (q.v.) is located within the complex.

VELANI   see   WILLIAM THE GRIQUA

VELD. From the Dutch/Afrikaans word for field; a term for open
grassland country, such as characterizes much of southern
Africa. The terms "low veld," "middle veld," and "high veld"
refer to altitudinal zones (q.v.).

VENDA (BAVENDA). Branch of Bantu-speaking (q.v.) people

occupying an apparently distinct intermediate linguistic position
between Shona and Sotho-speakers (qq. v.). The Venda appear
to have lived in the Matabeleland* region until about the late
17th century, when most of them crossed the Limpopo River*
into northwestern Transvaal (q. v.). Venda royal clans are
connected to those of the southern Shona. During the 19th
century many Venda recrossed the Limpopo into present Rhodesia, where they became noted as iron (q. v.) workers and
gunsmiths. They traded firearms to the Shona and occasionally
served as mercenaries in Shona wars. The Venda also became closely associated with the Mwari (q. v.) cult centers in
the Matopo Hills*. One historian has recently argued that it
was the Venda themselves who founded these cult centers, but
this thesis has not yet been widely supported. (See also
LEMBA.)

VICTORIA DISTRICT. Located on a transitional zone between the
Central Plateau* and the southeastern low veld*, the Victoria
District covers 4635 sq. km. of the west-central part of Victoria Province (q. v.). The southern part of the district once
extended into what is now the Chiredzi District (q. v.). Other
districts which border Victoria include Chibi on the southwest;
Selukwe on the northwest; Chilimanzi and Gutu on the north;
and Ndanga (qq. v.) on the east. District headquarters are at
Fort Victoria (q. v.). Other district centers and places of
interest are Mashaba, Zimbabwe Ruins, and Lake Kyle (qq. v.).
Under the Land Tenure Act (q. v.), the central belt which encompasses these centers, and the southern tip of the district
are reserved for Europeans. The remaining parts of the district are about equally divided between Purchase Areas and
Tribal Trust Lands (qq. v.). District population in 1969 included 91, 300 Africans and 4165 Europeans.

VICTORIA FALLS (a. k. a. Musi O Tunya, q. v.). One of the world's
most spectacular natural scenic attractions, the Victoria Falls
are easily the country's top tourist draw. They lower the mile-
wide Zambezi River (q. v.) an average of 93 meters at a point
roughly in the middle of the river's long course. The relatively
straight crest of the Falls is divided into separately-named individual falls, all of which are visible from the Rhodesian bank,
which lies across the first of a series of gorges formed by
earlier recessions of the crest. Water flows across the Falls
at a mean annual rate of about 57 million liters (c. 15 million
gallons) per minute. This rate increases by a factor of eight
during the peak flood season (see CLIMATE).
     The Falls were first brought to the attention of the out-
side world by David Livingstone (q. v.), who named them during
his first visit in November 1855. Seven years later Thomas
Baines (q. v.) depicted them in the first oil paintings.

VICTORIA FALLS BRIDGE. Towering about 90 meters over the
Zambezi River (q. v.) just below the Victoria Falls (q. v.), this
202-meter bridge was opened in 1905. It was built to carry two

railway (q.v.) tracks linking Southern and Northern Rhodesia at a site offering a spectacular view of the Falls to passengers. In 1930 the structure was strengthened and modified to handle automobile traffic (see ROADS). The bridge has always been a major link between Rhodesia and Zambia, but in early 1973 Zambia (q.v.) closed its side to travelers, who have since had to enter through Kazungula (q.v.) upriver. The bridge has nevertheless continued to carry trade goods between white-ruled southern Africa and Zambia and Zaïre. Cargoes have been openly moved across the bridge in unmanned railroad cars, which have been pushed across the center of the bridge and re-connected to locomotives on the opposite sides (see SANCTIONS). The border (q.v.) between Rhodesia and Zambia runs through the center of the bridge. When the Victoria Falls Conference (q.v.) was held on the bridge in August 1975, delegates sat with-in a single railroad car, but on opposite sides of the border.

VICTORIA FALLS CONFERENCE (1975). In December 1974 Rho-desian government officials met with African National Council (q.v.) leaders in Lusaka, Zambia, to arrange for a constitu-tional conference. Ian Smith's (q.v.) government abandoned its previously rigid position in regard to recognition of African na-tionalist groups only after considerable joint pressure from the governments of Zambia and South Africa (qq.v.), and in the face of dangers posed by imminent Mozambican (q.v.) independence. On December 11, 1974, Smith announced, from Salisbury, his intention to release political prisoners in return for a cease-fire in the guerrilla war (see MILITARY FORCES), and agreement to participate in a constitutional conference at a then undetermined site.

　　After prolonged disagreement over the site of the con-ference, Smith and his top aides met with Abel Muzorewa, Nda-baningi Sithole, Joshua Nkomo, James Chikerema (qq.v.), and other nationalist leaders in a railroad dining car atop the Vic-toria Falls Bridge (q.v.) on August 25, 1975. The car straddled the international boundary line, allowing Smith's delegation to sit on the Rhodesia side, while the Africans sat on the Zambia side. South African Prime Minister John Vorster and Zambian Presi-dent Kenneth Kaunda attended the first session of talks, in which optimism prevailed. The conference broke down the very next day, however, when Smith refused to consider allowing nation-alists wanted by the Rhodesian police for "terrorist" activities to participate freely in politics within Rhodesia, where the final constitutional settlement was to be worked out. Smith and Nkomo conducted a series of fruitless negotiations early the next year, but the next major attempt at a general settlement was the Geneva Conference (q.v.) at the end of 1976.

VICTORIA FALLS NATIONAL PARK. Forming a 595-sq. km. tri-angle west of the Victoria Falls-Bulawayo road and south of the Zambezi River, the Victoria Falls National Park has been one of the country's most popular tourist centers. It comprises the Falls themselves, a large game reserve, and a reproduction of

a 19th-century African village. In the mid-1970s foreign tourism began dropping off as anti-Rhodesia guerrillas and, apparently, some Zambian soldiers began firing guns and rockets
from across the river. White Rhodesian tourist patronage of
the park's hotels reportedly remained heavy through 1977, however.

VICTORIA FALLS TOWNSHIP. Founded during the construction of
Victoria Falls Bridge (q.v.), this town has served as a major
tourist center, a border (q.v.) post, and the commercial and
administrative center for the northwest corner of Wankie District (q.v.). It is connected to Bulawayo* by a 441-km. road
and railway (qq.v.), and it has an international airport (see
AIR RHODESIA). Its permanent population was counted at 3450
(83% Africans) in 1969, but this figure has usually been greatly
enlarged by influxes of mainly white tourists. Location:
17° 56'S, 25° 50'E; alt. 910 m.

VICTORIA PROVINCE. One of seven administrative provinces
(q.v.), Victoria separates Matabeleland South on the west from
Manicaland on the east, and it also borders Midlands on the
north (qq.v.). On the southeast, Victoria borders Mozambique
between the Sabi and Limpopo Rivers (qq.v.). The province
comprises the districts of Bikita, Chibi, Chiredzi, Gutu, Ndanga,
Nuanetsi, and Victoria (qq.v.).

VIEW OF THE WORLD see WORLD'S VIEW

VILA SALAZAR. Village established as a railway (q.v.) station
near the Mozambique border in 1955, when the railway link to
Lourenzo Marques (now Maputo) was opened (at 22° 3'S, 31° 42'E).
The post was named after the ruling Portuguese dictator António
de Oliveira Salazar. The Mozambique post on the opposite side
of the border was named Malvernia, after the Federation* Prime
Minister Lord Malvern (Godfrey Huggins, q.v.). After Mozambique closed its borders to Rhodesia in March 1976, Vila Salazar
became a frequent target of nationalist guerrillas operating from
within Mozambique. In late May 1977 Rhodesian forces used the
post to launch a foray deep into Mozambican territory.

VILJOEN, JAN WILLEM (1811-1891). Transvaal* hunter, trader,
and government agent. After unsuccessfully attempting to hunt
in Matabeleland* during the mid-1850s, Viljoen paid his first
visit to King Mzilikazi (q.v.) there in 1861. Over the next two
decades he hunted regularly north of the Limpopo River*, becoming one of the first Afrikaners (q.v.) to enter Mashonaland*
in 1865. In 1868 he was sent by the Transvaal republican
government to try to persuade Mzilikazi and the Ngwato ruler
Macheng (q.v.) to accept Afrikaner protectorates, but this mission failed.

VLEI. Afrikaans*-derived term (from Dutch vallei) for a shallow
depression in the earth which collects water just below the

surface level. Vleis are found throughout the country, and they have often been important water sources for people during the dry winter months. (Cf. DONGA.)

VUMBA MOUNTAINS. Region just southeast of Umtali*, along the Mozambique border. The minuscule Vumba National Park, covering only 200 hectares (494 acres), is essentially a botanical garden. It was known as "Manchester Gardens" until purchased by the Federation* government in 1957. A well known feature of the region is Leopard Rock Hotel, an attractive stone edifice built by Italian prisoners of war during the Second World War. The park also includes Bunga Forest.

- W -

WA-. Common Bantu (q.v.) noun prefix for plural forms of names of peoples; frequently written in place of va- (q.v.) in Shona names. Such prefixes are dropped for proper names in this dictionary. For example, for "Wanhowe" (or Wanoe), see NHOWE. (Cf. AMA-, BA-, MA-.)

WADDILOVE INSTITUTION. One of the most important African educational facilities in the country, Waddilove was originally founded by Wesleyan (q.v.) missionaries as the Nenguwo Mission in the early 1890s. It became "Waddilove" in 1915. John White (q.v.) developed the station into a training center after 1910. The Wesleyans later shifted theological training to their Epworth Mission (q.v.), making Waddilove a teacher training center. It is located about 20 km. southeast of Marandellas*, at 18°15'S, 31°23'E.

WANKIE. Largest urban center in the western part of the country, serving as headquarters of the district of the same name (at 18°22'S, 26°29'E; alt. 760 m.). The town takes its name from the title of the local Nanzwa (q.v.) rulers, the Zanke. It was founded early in the 20th century as an adjunct of the Wankie Colliery, which taps the region's vast coal (q.v.) reserves. The colliery administers most of the town and provides employment for the majority of the adult population. Total population was estimated at 26,000 in late 1974.

WANKIE DISTRICT. Westernmost district in the country, Wankie covers 27,835 sq. km. in Matabeleland North Province (q.v.). The district was formerly somewhat larger, but gave up its northeastern corner to help form Binga District (q.v.). Wankie also borders the districts of Lupane on the east, and Nyamandhlovu on the southeast (qq.v.), as well as Zambia on the north, and Botswana (qq.v.) on the west. The southern half of the district comprises Wankie National Park (q.v.). Under the Land Tenure Act (q.v.), the northern part of the district is a patchwork of unreserved land, national land, European Land and a large block of Tribal Trust Land (q.v.) along the Zambezi

River.   District headquarters are at Wankie (q.v.).   Other
centers include Victoria Falls and Kamativi (qq.v.).   District
population in 1969 included 60,810 Africans and 3787 whites.

WANKIE NATIONAL PARK.   Located on the Botswana border, this
national park (q.v.) covers 13,470 sq. km. between Pandamatenga and the Nata River, accounting for half the Wankie District (qq.v.).   Most of the present park became the country's
first protected game reserve (q.v.) in 1928.   In 1949 the area
was augmented and made one of the first national parks.   The
park is noted for its vast herds of large game.   Though little
developed, it has become a major tourist attraction, often
visited in conjunction with Victoria Falls (q.v.).   The northern
edge of the park is designated a Controlled Hunting Area, and
it contains the Bumbuzi Ruins (q.v.).

WARREN, CHARLES (1840-1927).   British soldier.   After service
in South Africa's Griqualand West from 1876 to 1878, Warren
returned to southern Africa in 1884 as a major-general to head
an expedition into present Botswana (q.v.).   He commanded a
force of 5000 men which pushed Afrikaners (q.v.) out of Tswana
(q.v.) border areas and secured treaties from leading rulers,
including Khama III (q.v.).   In 1885 he declared Botswana to be
the Bechuanaland Protectorate (q.v.).   He later served as a
lieutenant-general in the South African War (q.v.).

WARS.   Entries discussing the earliest recorded warfare in the
country fall under the general headings of SHONA HISTORY and
PORTUGUESE.   Early 19th-century warfare is best approached
through the entry on the MFECANE.   The brief Ndebele civil
war of 1870 is treated under ZWANGENDABA.   The wars of
British occupation are treated under the headings of NDEBELE
WAR and REVOLTS OF 1896/7.   Southern Rhodesia's role in
the "Boer War" is treated under SOUTH AFRICAN WAR.   Twen-
tieth-century warfare, including recent guerrilla fighting, is
treated under the collective heading, MILITARY FORCES.   Each
of the above entries offers more specific cross-references.

WATA   see   HWATA

WATER SUPPLIES   see   DAMS; LAKES; RIVERS; CLIMATE

WEDENGA (variant: Nyadenga).   Chishona* term for "supreme
spirit," or "god of heaven"; variously used as a synonym for,
or description of, the high god Mwari (q.v.).   Some early
translations of Christian scriptures also used "Wedenga" for
God.

WEDZA.   The Chishona* word hwedza means "tomorrow," or "the
day after tomorrow."   Spelled "Wedza," it appears in many
place names, perhaps because non-Shona travelers were sometimes confused by Shona who answered "Hwedza!" when asked
for directions.   Wedza was also the name of a 19th-century

Dumbuseya (q.v.) ruler. The best known places called Wedza
are in the present Wedza District (q.v.). They include the
Wedza Mountains (18° 45'S, 31° 35'E). Within this range Wedza
Mountain (a.k.a. Dangamwire Mountain; alt. 1800 m.) has long
been famous as a rich iron (q.v.) bearing area, exploited by
the Njanja and Hera peoples (qq.v.). Just north of this peak
is Wedza village, the district headquarters. Another well-known
Wedza Mountain is in the Belingwe District* (at 20° 15'S, 29°
32'E).

WEDZA DISTRICT. Once the southeastern section of Marandellas
District (q.v.), Wedza now covers 2570 sq. km. in Mashonaland South Province (q.v.). It borders the districts of Makoni
on the east; Buhera on the south; Charter on the west; and
Marandellas (qq.v.) on the north. The northern part of the
district is reserved for Europeans; a broad central belt is all
Tribal Trust Land (q.v.); and the southeastern tip is Purchase
Area (q.v.). District population in 1969 included 45, 940 Africans and only 182 Europeans.

WEEKLY REVIEW. Original name of the Sunday Mail (q.v.).

WELENSKY, ROY (RAPHAEL) (b.Jan. 20, 1907). Second and last
Prime Minister of the Federation* (1956-63). Born in Salisbury
to poor white immigrant parents, Welensky had little formal
education before joining Rhodesia Railways (q.v.) as a fireman
in 1924. Like Uganda's Idi Amin, he became a national heavy-
weight boxing champion (1925-7). In 1933 he moved to Broken
Hill, Northern Rhodesia (now Kabwe, Zambia), where he soon
became a powerful trade union leader. He was elected to
Northern Rhodesia's Legislative Council in 1938, rising to
leadership of the Council's unofficial members in 1947. After
the war he joined Godfrey Huggins (q.v.) in leading the fight,
first for amalgamation (q.v.) of the Rhodesias, and then for
Federation.
        When Federation was achieved in 1953, Welensky took a
seat in the Federal Assembly and joined Huggins' government
first as a cabinet minister, later as deputy premier. Welensky
assumed the premiership when Huggins retired in November
1956. Under his tutelage the United Federal Party (q.v.) was
formed out of the Federal and United Rhodesian parties.
        During the remaining years of the Federation Welensky
grew alarmed with Britain's apparently increasing support of
African majority rule, so he began advocating dominion status
for the Federation in order to preserve white rule. He threatened to declare the Federation independent, thereby alienating
his African supporters and establishing the European mood which
later condoned Ian Smith's Unilateral Declaration of Independence
(q.v.). Unable to prevent the Federation's dissolution in late
1963, Welensky later detailed his grievances against what he saw
as British perfidy in Welensky's 4000 Days (London, 1964). Although he had advocated independence for the Federation, he opposed it for Southern Rhodesia by challenging a Rhodesian Front

candidate for a Legislative Assembly seat in a Salisbury by-
election in October 1964.   His decisive loss to Clifford Dupont
(q. v.) in this election effectively retired him from politics.

WESLEYAN METHODIST MISSIONARY SOCIETY (WMMS).   Agents
of the London-based WMMS were among the first missionaries
to work north of South Africa's Vaal River in the 1820s.   In
1829 one of these missionaries, James Archbell, tried to start
a mission among Mzilikazi's Ndebele, who then lived near
present Pretoria.   In 1891 the WMMS entered Mashonaland*
and Isaac Shimmin (q. v.) founded Epworth Mission (q. v.) near
Salisbury.   Early efforts were concentrated in northern Mashonaland, but stations also were established in Matabeleland*
after the 1893 Ndebele War*.   The Wesleyans produced one of
the country's most influential European missionaries, John
White (q. v.), who founded the Waddilove Institution (q. v.).
They also had the distinction of training the first Shona teacher
to break away from a mission church to form an independent
Christian church--Matthew Zwimba (q. v.).   By 1959 the Wesleyans claimed more than 24, 000 African members throughout
the country.   Their local church has since become known as
the Methodist Church in Rhodesia.   (See also UNITED METHO-
DIST CHURCH; METHODISTS.)

WEST NICHOLSON.   Town in the Gwanda District (q. v.), just south
of the tip of the Insiza District*, where the Bulawayo to Beitbridge road meets the Umzingwane River* (at 21° 4'S, 29° 22'E;
alt. 850 m.).   The town was founded in the late 1890s near the
Nicholson Gold Mine, and is now the center of an important
beef producing region.   Since 1905 it has been the terminus of
a branch railway (q. v.) line from Bulawayo, by way of Heany
Junction (q. v.).   Population in 1969 was 1930 (95% Africans).

WESTBEECH, GEORGE (d. July 1888).   British trader.   In the mid-
1860s Westbeech came to Matabeleland* to trade.   There he
formed a commercial partnership with G. A. Phillips (q. v.) in
1868.   Operating from his own base at Pandamatenga (q. v.) in
the north, he became an intimate friend of both the Ndebele
king Lobengula (q. v.) and the Lozi (q. v.) rulers of western
Zambia.   He used his unique dual influence to help mitigate
disputes between the two nations, and to introduce British influence into Lozi country.

"WESTBEECH ROAD. "   A 19th-century track which branched off
from the "Hunters' Road" (q. v.) at Tati (q. v.), extending north
to the Zambezi River by way of Pandamatenga (q. v.).

WESTWOOD.   Small, racially-mixed township located eight km.
west of Salisbury's (q. v.) city center.

WHA WHA DETENTION CENTER.   Located northeast of Gwelo* (at
19° 22'S, 30° 1'E), Wha Wha has been the main government
detention center for political prisoners since the closing of

Gonakudzingwa (q.v.) in 1974.   In 1976 more than 500 Africans
were thought to be held at Wha Wha.

WHITE, JOHN (Jan. 6, 1866-Aug. 7, 1933).   English missionary.
An agent of the Wesleyan Methodist Missionary Society (q.v.),
White came to the Transvaal* in 1888, and transferred to
Mashonaland* in 1894.   There he founded Nengubo Mission,
which he later developed into Waddilove Institution (q.v.), and
he began a farm project at Epworth (q.v.).   From the time he
started his work he was an outspoken critic of government
treatment of Africans, and he was one of the first Europeans
to point out the abuses which led to the Shona Revolt of 1896-7
(q.v.).   In 1901 he was made chairman of the Methodist mission district, and he later became principal at Waddilove.
Criticized by Europeans for his "negrophilia," he was a leading
voice in the Southern Rhodesia Missionary Conference (q.v.),
which he and his Anglican ally A. S. Cripps (q.v.) tried to
transform into a strong lobbying body for African rights.
Through the 1920s he fought relentlessly for extensions of African land rights.   Frustrated in his attempts to win significant
government concessions, he reluctantly advocated territorial
segregation--on the condition that African areas first be enlarged.   His advocacy of segregation lent support to the government's Land Apportionment Act of 1930 (q.v.).   Ill health later
forced White's return to England, where he died.

WHITE BIRD, CHURCH OF   see under   ZWIMBA, MATTHEW

WHITE RHINO SHELTER.   Important rock painting (q.v.) site, located about one kilometer east of World's View (q.v.) in the
Matopo Hills (q.v.).   Its pictures include what are regarded as
some of the country's finest monochrome outline drawings.   The
main figures are large wildebeests, but the cave takes its modern name from smaller representations of black and white rhinoceroses (q.v.).

WHITE RHODESIA COUNCIL.   Settler organization founded in 1949
to campaign for the principle of white supremacy in the country.
Under the leadership of Charles Olley, a Salisbury politician,
the Council advocated dominion status, white job reservation,
territorial segregation of the races, and exclusion of Africans
from elected offices.

WHITEHEAD, EDGAR CUTHBERT FREMANTLE (Feb. 8, 1905-1971).
Sixth Prime Minister (q.v.) of Southern Rhodesia (1958-62).
Born in Berlin of British parents, Whitehead came to Southern
Rhodesia in 1928 to enter the civil service after an Oxford education.   In 1939 he was elected to the Legislative Assembly
(q.v.).   He resigned the next year to join the British army.
After the war he served as Southern Rhodesia's High Commissioner in London (1945-6).   On his return home, he was re-
elected to the Assembly for Umtali* (1946-53).   Through this
period he also served as Godfrey Huggins' (q.v.) Minister of

Finance, Posts and Telegraphs, until retiring because of his poor health.

Whitehead came out of retirement in 1957 to become the Federation's (q.v.) minister in Washington, D.C. He returned home early in 1958 to head the government, after a special United Federal Party (q.v.) congress ousted Garfield Todd (q.v.) from the premiership. Whitehead stood for his own Assembly seat in a Bulawayo by-election in April, but was surprisingly defeated by a Dominion Party (q.v.) candidate. He then dissolved the Assembly, calling a general election for June which was the last his party won. His government was a transitional period for both white and black political movements. Early in 1959 he declared a state of emergency and banned the African National Congress (q.v.). Two years later he banned the ANC's successor, the National Democratic Party (q.v.). Although Whitehead encouraged greater African participation in electoral politics under the terms of the Constitution of 1961 (q.v.; see also "BUILD A NATION"), he succeeded only in alienating Africans from established politics. In December 1962 his party lost the general election to the Rhodesian Front (q.v.) and Winston Field (q.v.) became prime minister. Afterwards Whitehead retired to England, where he died.

WILLIAM THE GRIQUA (a.k.a. WILLEM; VELANI) (c.1820s-1859). Ndebele induna*. Born a Griqua (q.v.) in South Africa, William and his younger cousin Truey David were captured by the Ndebele (q.v.) during a raid on Griqua hunters by the Vaal River in 1834. William soon mastered the Sindebele* language and Sesotho (the language of the Sotho), and became a personal interpreter for Mzilikazi (q.v.). After the Ndebele moved to Matabeleland*, William became a soldier and was eventually honored with the head-ring of an indoda (qq.v.). He served in at least one of the campaigns against the Kololo*, during which he was badly wounded. By the 1850s he had an Ndebele family, he commanded at least 100 men as an induna, and he was said to be well trusted by the king. His cousin Truey returned to South Africa with Robert Moffat* in 1854, but William elected to remain with the Ndebele. Five years later, however, he was executed, apparently in connection with some kind of cattle dispute. Although his end was tragic, his career demonstrated the pan-ethnic inclusiveness of 19th-century Ndebele (q.v.) society.

WILLIAM-POWLETT, P. B. R. W. (b. March 5, 1898). Seventh Governor (q.v.) of Southern Rhodesia (1954-9). After a career in the British navy, William-Powlett succeeded J. N. Kennedy (q.v.) as governor of Southern Rhodesia. He was in turn succeeded by H. V. Gibbs (q.v.).

WILLOUGHBY, JOHN CHRISTOPHER (Feb. 20, 1859-April 16, 1918). British army officer and financier. After seeing military service in Egypt and the Sudan, Willoughby came to South Africa, where he became second-in-command, under Lt. Col. Pennefather (q.v.), in the Pioneer Column (q.v.) which occupied Mashonaland*

in 1890.   In March 1891 Cecil Rhodes sent him to Beira* to
negotiate with Portuguese officials who had closed the eastern
approaches to Mashonaland.   The next year he recklessly exca-
vated the Zimbabwe Ruins (q.v.).   During the 1893 Ndebele
War (q.v.) Willoughby served as L. S. Jameson's (q.v.) military adviser in the march against Bulawayo.   The next year he
formed the first of several development companies to exploit
huge grants of land and vast herds of looted Ndebele cattle
(q.v.) in Matabeleland*.   He next served as military commander in the abortive Jameson Raid (q.v.) of late 1895, and then
spent 15 months in an English jail as a punishment.   Willoughby
also later served in the South African War (q.v.) and in the
East African campaign of the First World War.

WILMOT, ALEXANDER (April 9, 1836-April 3, 1923).   Scottish-born
author and member of the Cape Colony Legislative Assembly
(1889-1910), where he became an avid supporter of Cecil Rhodes
(q.v.).   Rhodes commissioned Wilmot to study the origins of the
Zimbabwe Ruins culture (q.v.).   He did most of his research in
European archives, where he collected arcane evidence intended
to support J. T. Bent's (q.v.) theory that Zimbabwe was built
by ancient Phoenicians.   He published his findings in Monomotopa
(Rhodesia) (London, 1896), a book which also served to debunk
Portuguese (q.v.) claims to having had priority in the Shona
(q.v.) territories claimed by Rhodes' British South Africa Com-
pany (q.v.).   The book also contains a laudatory preface by H.
R. Haggard (q.v.).   (See ZIMBABWE CONTROVERSY.)

WILSON, ALLAN (1856-Dec. 4, 1893).   Scottish-born soldier.   Wilson came to South Africa in 1878 and served in several local
British military units.   After prospecting in Mashonaland* during
the early 1890s, he was commissioned a major in the army
formed by L. S. Jameson (q.v.) to fight the Ndebele in July
1893.   Wilson commanded the Victoria Column which joined P.
W. Forbes' (q.v.) column at Iron Hill Mine, whence the combined forces marched on Bulawayo* to end the Ndebele War
(q.v.).   After occupying Bulawayo, Wilson led the famous "Shangani Patrol" (q.v.) which was wiped out.

WILSON, BENJAMIN "MATABELE" (1861-March 28, 1960).   English
concessionaire and early settler.   Wilson went to Bulawayo to
seek a mining concession (q.v.) in 1888, but instead joined with
Cecil Rhodes' (q.v.) group and remained there while the latter's
Pioneer Column (q.v.) entered Mashonaland*.   Wilson fought
against the Ndebele in both the 1893 War and the 1896 Revolt
(qq.v.).   He later served as a ranch manager in Mashonaland
before retiring to the Cape in 1922.

WILTON CULTURE.   Name, taken from a South African site, for a
late Stone Age (q.v.) industry found throughout eastern and southern Africa.   It is the dominant LSA industry within present Rhodesia, where it has also been known as Matopo Industry.   It is
characterized by small, finely crafted stone tools and weapons,

polished axes, bored stones, and associations with rock painting (q. v.) sites. One major phase of the Wilton Culture is named after Pomongwe Cave (q. v.). Wilton Culture contrasts with the large stone implements characteristic of the Smithfield Industry, which predominated south of the Limpopo River*.

WOMEN'S FRANCHISE ORDINANCE (1919). When the Legislative Council (q. v.) was created in 1898, voting was open only to males over 21 years old who met certain income and property qualifications. In 1919 C. P. Coghlan (q. v.) put through Legco the Women's Franchise Ordinance at the last session before a general election. This was an apparent political maneuver, sanctioned by the enhanced respect European women in the country had garnered through their wartime services. The Ordinance allowed women to qualify for the vote on the basis of their husbands' financial means, provided they were not married polygamously. This stipulation effectively debarred the few African women who might otherwise have become eligible to vote. (American women got the vote a year later; South African white women 11 years later.) Ethel Tawse-Jollie (q. v.) was elected to Legco in 1920, and she later became the first female parliamentarian in the British Empire.

WOOD, JOSEPH GARBETT (Jan. 4, 1833-Sept. 25, 1894). South African concession-hunter. After serving as a member of the Cape Colony's Legislative Assembly (1879-87), Wood formed a syndicate with two other men and went to Matabeleland* to seek a mineral concession (q. v.) from King Lobengula (q. v.). In November 1887 Lobengula granted them a concession by the Shashi River (q. v.). This region was claimed by both the Ndebele and the Ngwato (qq. v.), and the latter had given mining rights there to another party already. A dispute over land ownership thus quickly arose. While attempting to straighten out the matter the next year, Wood was arrested in Ngwato territory by British officials of the Bechuanaland Protectorate (q.v.). In 1891 the matter was settled when Wood's group, the Ngwato concession party, and the BSAC amalgamated their different interests. Wood's account of his experiences, <u>Through Matabeleland</u>, was published shortly after he died.

WORLD'S VIEW. Two well-known lookout points in the country were given this name by Cecil Rhodes (q. v.). One is on the western edge of the Inyanga Mountains (q. v.), overlooking scenic plains. The second, more properly known as "View of the World," is a prominent granite <u>kopje</u> (q. v.) in the middle of the spectacular Matopo Hills (q. v.). This latter site contains the graves of Rhodes, L. S. Jameson, Charles Coghlan, and the members of the "Shangani Patrol" (qq. v.). It was previously known to the Ndebele as <u>Malindidzimu</u>, "the dwelling place of spirits." (Cf. NTHUMBANE.)

WRATHALL, JOHN JAMES (Aug. 28, 1913-Aug. 31, 1978). Second President (q. v.) of Rhodesia (1975-1978). Born and educated in

England, Wrathall emigrated to Southern Rhodesia in 1936. He
worked there in the government Tax Department until becoming
a chartered accountant in 1946, and he was later elected to the
Legislative Assembly (q.v.). When the Rhodesian Front (q.v.)
took power in December 1962, he entered Winston Field's (q.v.)
cabinet. After Ian Smith (q.v.) became prime minister in April
1964, Wrathall became Minister of Finance. In this capacity
he has been credited with much of the country's success in overcoming the effects of economic sanctions (q.v.) since UDI. He
was rewarded with the additional post of deputy prime minister
in September 1966. On December 10, 1975, he left the cabinet
to succeed Clifford Dupont (q.v.) as president of the country
until his sudden death in mid-1978.

- X -

-X-. In languages such as Sindebele (q.v.) which contain click
    sounds (q.v.), the letter x represents a consonant made with a
    lateral click, as in Xukutwayo*. This sound can be modified,
    as in inxwala*, wherein the nx represents a nasalized lateral
    click.

XUKUTWAYO MLOTSHA (d. Nov. 1890). Ndebele induna*, described
    as one of the most powerful men in the kingdom during the
    1860s. Xukutwayo was chief of the cluster of towns around the
    Intemba and Izinkondo amabutho (see IBUTHO), located by the
    upper Bubi River*. Sikombo Mguni (q.v.) was his head sub-
    chief and successor as chief. Xukutwayo commanded an impi*
    against Chibi (q.v.) in 1861, and directed the capture of Tohwe-
    chipi (q.v.) in 1866. In 1870 he moved his towns south to an
    area about 25 km. east of present Bulawayo. In 1879 he and
    Lotshe (q.v.) went to Gazaland* to fetch Lobengula's royal bride
    Xwalile (q.v.). During the 1880s he returned to Gazaland to
    deliver the balance of cattle owed for lobolo (q.v.), but was re-
    fused entry to the country.

XWALILE (variant: Cwalili) (fl. 1870s-1900s). Lobengula's (q.v.)
    "royal wife" (or "great wife") (see INKOSIKAZI). In 1871 Lo-
    bengula sent oxen to the Gaza king Mzila (q.v.) to open nego-
    tiations for an exchange of royal wives. Lobengula preferred
    Mzila's eldest daughter, Dombole, but Mzila thought her too
    old to be suitable. Instead he offered a younger daughter,
    Xwalile. In August 1879 the Ndebele izinduna Lotshe and Xuku-
    twayo (qq.v.) fetched Xwalile and her large retinue from Gaza-
    land to Bulawayo. The next month Lobengula married Xwalile
    and seven of her "sisters" in a three-week ceremony. These
    wives became popularly known as the "Gaza Queens." The mar-
    riage got off to a poor start, with the new wives insulting Lo-
    bengula publicly. There was also a dispute with the Gaza king-
    dom over the lobolo (q.v.) payment which was never fully re-
    solved, and Lobengula never sent any Ndebele wives to the Gaza
    king. Worse, Xwalile was expected to bear Lobengula's heir in

her capacity as royal wife, but she proved infertile. Lobengula's sister Mncengence (q.v.) was accused of bewitching her.
Xwalile's childlessness left open the question of Lobengula's
successor. Xwalile herself was soon banished to the town of
the Mzinyathi ibutho*, where she became the subject of many
adultery rumors during the 1880s. After the 1896 Revolt (q.v.)
the British South Africa Company (q.v.) provided Xwalile and
the other Gaza "queens" with small pensions, but she and her
kinswomen were unhappy among the Ndebele, so they returned
to Gazaland.

- Y -

YAVE. Chishona* word for the Judaeo-Christian god; from Hebrew
    Yahweh (Jehovah). (Cf. MWARI; MLIMO.)

YOUNG, HILTON see HILTON YOUNG COMMISSION

YOUTH LEAGUE (a.k.a. City Youth League; Southern Rhodesian
    African National Youth League) (YL). Now regarded as the
    country's first truly modern nationalist movement, the YL was
    founded as a civic organization, the Harare* Youth Club, in
    Salisbury in August 1955. Under the leadership of James Chi-
    kerema, George Nyandoro (qq.v.), and Dunduzu Chisiza (1930-
    62)--a Nyasaland immigrant who was later deported--the YL
    quickly developed into a mass political movement active in both
    towns and rural areas. The YL successfully contested the po-
    litical influence of Charles Mzingeli (q.v.), ignoring purely
    trade union issues while challenging the very authority of the
    government to rule over Africans. In August 1956 the YL
    organized a successful bus boycott in Salisbury. A year later
    the League merged with the Bulawayo branch of the old African
    National Congress (q.v.) to launch a revitalized and more ag-
    gressive ANC.

YUFI. When the famous Arab traveler Ibn Battuta (1304-1377)
    visited Kilwa Kisiwani on Tanzania's coast in 1331, he described
    the source of Sofala's gold (qq.v.) as "Yufi, in the country of
    the Limiin," a month's march inland from Sofala. Assuming
    that his "Sofala" was then at its later, known location, it is
    likely that Ibn Battuta's "Yufi" referred to the kingdom which
    built the Zimbabwe Ruins (q.v.). If so, this may be the earliest
    explicit documentary reference to a place within present Rhodesia.

- Z -

ZAKA. Village located on the Chiredzi River* (at 20° 21'S, 31° 27'E;
    alt. 760 m.). Established in 1923 as the administrative center
    of the Ndanga District (q.v.).

ZAMBEZI ESCARPMENT. Steep ridge running from east to west along

approximately 16° 30' south latitude. The escarpment separates
the Zambezi Valley from the Central Plateau (q. v.). The scarp
drops as much as 1500 meters in the Mavuradonha Mountains
(q. v.). (See also DANDE; MANA POOLS.)

ZAMBEZI MISSION. In the late 1870s the Roman Catholic Society
of Jesus began to organize a major missionary thrust into central Africa. This effort was known as the Zambezi Mission.
Under the leadership of Henri Depelchin (q. v.) the first party
of Jesuits reached Tati* in August 1879. Several men remained
there while the rest advanced to Bulawayo, where they were
hospitably received by King Lobengula (q. v.). The Jesuits per-
formed many small services for the Ndebele, but like their
Protestant predecessors of the London Missionary Society (q. v.),
they had almost no success in attracting converts. Their attempts to build a substantial station were ruined when Lobengula
removed the town of Bulawayo (q. v.) to a new location in mid-
1881. Six years later the Jesuits relocated their own station at
Empandeni (q. v.). Meanwhile, the Zambezi Mission segmented
in an ambitious effort to open new stations elsewhere. In 1880
Augustus Law and Frans DeSadeleer (qq. v.) made a disastrous
trip to Gazaland*. Other Jesuits traveled north in several unsuccessful attempts to start missions at Pandamatenga (q. v.)
and in Lozi (q. v.) country. It was only after the 1896-7 Revolts (q. v.) that the Jesuits put their work within Southern Rhodesia on a sound footing. (See PRESTAGE, P.; HARTMANN, A.)

ZAMBEZI RIVER (variant: Zambesi). The fourth largest river in
Africa, the Zambezi is also the continent's only major river to
empty into the Indian Ocean. It rises in the extreme northwest
corner of Zambia (q. v.), near the sources of the Congo River
(a. k. a. Zaïre River), whence it turns south, flowing through
eastern Angola and western Zambia before meeting Rhodesia at
Kazungula (q. v.). From there the river flows in a generally
northeasterly direction, defining the entire 715 km. border (q.v.)
between Rhodesia and Zambia. It enters Mozambique (q. v.)
just west of Zumbo (q. v.), where it is fed by the large Luangwa
River from the north. About 65 km. east of Kazungula, the
Zambezi dramatically plunges over Victoria Falls (q. v.). From
there it enters the Batoka Gorge (q. v.), which now meets the
calm waters of artificially made Lake Kariba (q. v.), whose
great dam taps the river's enormous hydroelectric potential.
     The Zambezi draws most of its waters from its northern
affluents. Rhodesia contributes a smaller share through rivers
which drain the Central Plateau (q. v.). The most important of
these affluents are--from west to east--the Gwai, Sengwa,
Bumi, Umniati, Hunyani, and Mazoe rivers (qq. v.). The last
two of these rivers meet the Zambezi inside Mozambique. The
broad, flat Zambezi Valley is a hot, sultry region, containing
some of the country's wildest and least-populated terrain. (See
ALTITUDINAL ZONES; CLIMATE.)
     Stretches of the Zambezi are navigable, but the river
has never afforded a practical transportation link to the sea.

Between Victoria Falls and the coast, the river drops more
than 900 meters, thereby creating impassable falls and rapids
along the way.   Further, the mouth of the river is a shallow,
muddy system of deltas, navigable only by small boats.   Early
Portuguese (q. v.) explorers attempted to penetrate the interior
by way of the Zambezi Valley, but they never transformed it
into a significant avenue of commerce.   Since the 1890s the
country's main access route to the sea has been overland, from
Umtali to Beira (qq. v.).

Historically, the Zambezi has tended to separate cultural
regions; however, its many stretches of comparatively shallow
and sluggish water have been far from unfordable.   In 1835, for
example, Zwangendaba (q. v.) led his entire Ngoni nation across
the river at a point near Zumbo.   Later in the 19th century the
Ndebele (q. v.) met with disaster on at least one occasion while
campaigning against the Kololo (q. v.), but they later waged many
successful campaigns against other peoples on the northern side.
During the present century major crossing points have been established at Kazungula, Victoria Falls, Kariba, and Chirundu
(qq. v.).   (See RIVERS.)

"ZAMBEZIA. "   Long a popular European term for the region around
the Zambezi River (q. v.), "Zambezia" was unofficially adopted
as the name of the British South Africa Company's (q. v.) central African territories until the name "Rhodesia" (q. v.) was
adopted in 1895.   Present Rhodesia was, until then, called
"Southern Zambezia, " and Zambia (q. v.), "Northern Zambezia. "
When Northern Rhodesia became independent in 1964, "Zambezia" was contracted to form the country's new name, "Zambia. "   Zambezia has also been the name of a province in Mozambique (q. v.).

ZAMBIA.   With a slightly smaller population and almost twice the
land area of Rhodesia, Zambia is separated from the latter by
about 715 km. of the Zambezi River (q. v.) between Kazungula
and Zumbo (qq. v.).   From very early times Zambia was a corridor for population movements into Rhodesia and beyond, but
more recent movements across the Zambezi have generally been
less fluid than has been the case along Rhodesia's other borders
(q. v.).   The only major African peoples living in both Zambia
and Rhodesia are the river Tonga (q. v.).   During the early 19th
century Mfecane (q. v.), such migrant groups as the Kololo and
Ngoni (qq. v.) crossed the Zambezi into Zambia, but the river
appears to have been one of the obstacles to further northward
migration by the Ndebele (q. v.), who settled in Matabeleland*.
Nevertheless, the Ndebele often raided into Zambia later in the
19th century (see also LOZI; NANZWA).

During the late 19th century the same northward imperialist thrust that took the British South Africa Company (q. v.)
into present Rhodesia took the Company into Zambia, where it
established two colonies, North-Eastern and North-Western Rhodesia, in the 1890s.   In 1911 the BSAC brought these two territories under a single administration as Northern Rhodesia.

When Southern Rhodesia gained Responsible Government (q. v.)
as a British Crown Colony in 1923, the BSAC also quit Northern
Rhodesia, which became a British Protectorate.

From the early 20th century Northern Rhodesia's economy,
built around copper mining, was tied in to that of Southern Rhodesia.   A railway (q.v.) link between the two countries was established through Victoria Falls* in 1904-5.   Thereafter most of
Northern Rhodesia's export trade was carried through Southern
Rhodesia.   As Southern Rhodesia itself turned away from closer
ties with South Africa (q.v.), increased attention was given to
amalgamation (q.v.) of Southern and Northern Rhodesia.   This
was achieved in 1953, when the two countries, along with Nyasaland (now Malawi), were joined in the Federation of Rhodesia
and Nyasaland (q.v.).   Under the aegis of the Federation, Kariba
Dam (q.v.) was built in the late 1950s, supplying both Rhodesias
with most of their electrical power.   From the start of Federation, however, African opinion in the northern territories strongly
opposed Southern Rhodesian settler domination, one manifestation
of which was placement of Kariba's hydroelectric plant on the
southern side of the dam.

African political activities in the northern territories
focused upon opposition to the Federation, from which both territories were allowed to secede at the end of 1963.   On October
24, 1964, Northern Rhodesia became independent as "Zambia"
(a contraction of "Zambezia," q.v.), with Kenneth Kaunda as first
prime minister (later, first president).

When Rhodesia, as that country was now known, declared
its own independence a year later, the Zambian government became perhaps the strongest and most consistent foe of UDI.
Zambia's support of economic sanctions (q.v.) against Rhodesia
has always been strong, but never total because of its need for
Rhodesian coal (q.v.) and foods.   Zambia's heavy dependence
upon Rhodesian transport facilities for its own international trade
created special hardships, as efforts were made to switch to
alternative supply routes, which were both more expensive and
less efficient.   In early 1973 Rhodesia closed its border with
Zambia.   It quickly relented, but Zambia has since kept its side
of the border closed.   Later in 1973 a new trans-Tanzania truck
route was opened to handle Zambian trade.   In 1974 the Chinese-
built "Tanzam" railroad across Tanzania was finished.   By this
time Zambia's economic losses due to Rhodesian independence
were estimated to have exceeded $600 million, and Zambia was
believed to have suffered more from sanctions than had Rhodesia.

Even before UDI Zambia served as a sanctuary for Rhodesian African nationalists seeking to avoid detention at home.
Since UDI the number of Rhodesian blacks living in Zambia has
increased greatly, and the capital city, Lusaka, has been the
external headquarters for such bodies as ZAPU, PCC, and
FROLIZI (qq.v.).   There is little available hard data on the
extent of guerrilla training and fighting bases inside Zambia, but
ZANU and ZAPU launched raids from Zambia into Rhodesia as
early as 1966 (see MILITARY FORCES).   These early Zambian-
based incursions soon petered out, and Mozambique instead

developed into the major staging ground for guerrilla raids in
the early 1970s.   In the meantime President Kaunda worked to
unify Rhodesian nationalist leadership, while especially favoring
ZAPU's Joshua Nkomo (q.v.).

   In December 1974 Kaunda joined the new "Frontline
Presidents" group (q.v.), which appeared to have united Rhodesian nationalist leaders in Lusaka.   In the hope of promoting
a negotiated settlement within Rhodesia, Kaunda cosponsored
the Victoria Falls Conference (q.v.) of August 1975.   After the
failure of this conference and the subsequent quarreling among
rival Rhodesian nationalists, Zambia's stance towards Rhodesia
became more belligerent.   In late May 1976 Kaunda announced
his willingness to allow guerrillas to use Zambia as a base
against Rhodesia.   A year later he announced that Zambia was
"in a state of war" with Rhodesia.   No major fighting developed,
but Zambian forces occasionally fired at people on the Rhodesian
side of the Zambezi.   Despite Zambia's hostility towards Rhodesia, Kaunda allowed Ian Smith (q.v.) to consult with him in
Lusaka in late September 1977, but nothing came of this meeting
publicly.   By early 1978 Kaunda was generally regarded to be
throwing most of his support behind Nkomo and the "Patriotic
Front" (q.v.).

ZANKE (variants: Hwange; Wankie, q.v.).   Dynastic title of the
   Nanzwa (q.v.) rulers.

ZANSI.   Sindebele* term from word for "south," applied to members of Ndebele society (q.v.) who came from the south, i.e.,
   Nguni (q.v.) country in South Africa (properly, sing., izansi;
   pl., abezansi).   These people are descendents mostly of Mzilikazi's original northern Nguni followers and of other Nguni who
   joined him in the Transvaal*.   The term was apparently first
   used in this context during the 1820s and 1830s.   At that time
   Ndebele society was absorbing many Sotho-speaking (q.v.) peoples who became known as enhla (q.v.), or "those from the
   north."   The zansi were soon a minority within the growing society, and they constituted an even smaller part of the whole
   population after the holi were added north of the Limpopo River*.
   Because the zansi occupied most hereditary offices within the
   Ndebele kingdom, they were a dominant and highly visible minority by the mid-19th century.   Europeans described the zansi
   as a closed aristocracy, giving rise to the exaggerated notion
   that the Ndebele were divided into a rigid, three-tier "caste"
   system.

ZAWI.   Village located c.125 km. due northwest of Salisbury,
   serving as the terminus of the branch railway line into Lomagundi District* (at 17° 13'S, 30° 2'E).

ZEEDERBERG COACHES.   Mule-drawn carriages, similar to stage
   coaches of the United States, from which country many Zeederberg Coaches were imported in the late 19th century.   Mail and
   passenger services on such coaches were introduced into present

Rhodesia during the 1890s by the South African Zeederberg
family. During the early 20th century these coaches were soon
displaced by expanding railway (q.v.) services.

ZEZURU (a.k.a. "Central Shona"). Linguistic and ethnic name for
the central-most cluster of Shona-speaking peoples (q.v.). The
Zezuru (or Vazezuru) constitute about a quarter of the country's
Shona peoples. They live mainly in the region between Sinoia
in the northwest, Umvukwes in the north, Mtoko in the northeast, Wedza in the east, Bikita in the southeast, and Que Que
(qq.v.) in the southwest. As the central Shona dialect, Zezuru
(or Chizezuru) contains the largest number of typically Shona
language features. For this reason, and because the Zezuru
people surround the highly-developed Salisbury* region, Chizezuru forms the basis of standardized Chishona (q.v.). Among
the important ethnic sub-groups of the Zezuru are the Shavasha,
Hera, Gova, Njanja, and Mbire (qq.v.).

"ZHUWAWO." Symbolic name for mythical common man (analogous
to, e.g., the German Jedermann) popularized by the African
National Congress (q.v.) during the late 1950s to express the
movement's non-elitist ideals. From Chishona* word for ordinary laborer.

ZIMBA (a.k.a. Zumba; Mumba). Famous, but historically poorly
understood, migrant bands which ravaged the entire eastern
African coast during the late 16th century, while earning a
reputation as cannibals. The Zimba people apparently derived
from the Marave, just north of the lower Zambezi River. In
1597 two groups of "Zimba" entered present Rhodesia during the
reign of Munhumutapa Gatsi Rusere (q.v.). One group was
forcibly expelled, the other was apparently peacefully absorbed
by the Shona (q.v.).

ZIMBABWE [the word] (variants: dzimbabwe; dzimbahwe). Generic
Chishona* term for stone dwelling (pl., madzimbabwe). Both
the etymology of the word and its precise applications are controversial. It is usually interpreted as a contraction either of
the phrase dzimba ("large house") dza ("of") mabwe ("stones"),
or of dzimba woye ("venerated house"). Dzimbabwe is also
translated as "walled grave" or "royal court." Some authorities
argue that these different translations actually derive from
several similar, but distinct, Chishona words, but in practice
the term "zimbabwe" is applied in English to different kinds of
stone structures. It should be understood that "Great Zimbabwe"
of the Zimbabwe Ruins (q.v.) is merely the largest and most
famous of many ruins (q.v.) known as "zimbabwes."
Since at least the formation of the Zimbabwe National
Party (q.v.) in 1961, "Zimbabwe" has increasingly gained currency among African nationalists as the name which will be used
to replace "Rhodesia" (q.v.) when the country is ruled by Africans. The process by which this name was adopted is already
obscure, but it is clear that the name was chosen to evoke

memories of an old African civilization.

ZIMBABWE AFRICAN NATIONAL LIBERATION ARMY (ZANLA).
Name for the military wing of Zimbabwe African Nationalist
Union (ZANU, q.v.). Precise composition of ZANLA and its
direct connection with ZANU's political leadership have never
been clear to outsiders. Since early 1976 the name has generally been superseded by either Zimbabwe Peoples' Army or
Zimbabwe Liberation Army (qq.v.).

ZIMBABWE AFRICAN NATIONAL UNION (ZANU). African nationalist political party founded on August 8, 1963, under the
leadership of Ndabaningi Sithole (q.v.). ZANU was formed by
dissident members of the Zimbabwe African People's Union
(ZAPU, q.v.) who rejected Joshua Nkomo's (q.v.) leadership.
The immediate issue leading to the split between ZANU and
ZAPU was disagreement over Nkomo's proposed strategy of
forming a government in exile instead of working within Southern
Rhodesia. In practice, however, no substantive ideological or
strategic principles separated the two parties.
    In May 1964 ZANU held its first general meeting in
Gwelo*, where Sithole, Leopold Takawira, and Robert Mugabe
(qq.v.) were elected to the party's top offices. On August 26,
1964, the government banned ZANU and ZAPU's front organization, PCC (q.v.). Thereafter the ZANU leadership joined their
ZAPU rivals in voluntary exile, with both parties making Lusaka, Zambia their headquarters. ZANU's subsequent history
is similar to that of ZAPU in that both parties struggled to
muster external support and recruits from within Rhodesia,
while engaging in bitter denunciations of each other and occasional violent conflicts. In contrast to Nkomo, whose identification with ZAPU has never been in doubt, Sithole lost control
of most ZANU supporters to Mugabe, who has been based in
Mozambique (q.v.) during the 1970s. Mugabe joined with Nkomo
to form the "Patriotic Front" (q.v.) in late 1976, but this move
appears to have been more a personal alliance than a substantive
merger of their respective organizations. As with ZAPU, ZANU's
ties with such guerrilla bodies as the Zimbabwe African National
Liberation Army (q.v.) are not clear to outsiders.

ZIMBABWE AFRICAN PEOPLE'S UNION (ZAPU). African nationalist
political party founded on December 18, 1961, nine days after
the government banned the National Democratic Party (q.v.).
With Joshua Nkomo (q.v.) as its president, ZAPU adopted virtually the entire organization, leadership, and goals of the National Democratic Party. In September 1962 the government
banned ZAPU and arrested all its officers except Nkomo, who
was out of the country. During the next year many nationalist
leaders regrouped in Dar es Salaam, Tanganyika (now Tanzania),
where they discussed future strategy. Criticism of Nkomo's
leadership and especially his tendency to spend long periods outside of Southern Rhodesia created a sharp rift in the nationalist
leadership, which until then had generally been united. In a

surprise move, Nkomo returned to Salisbury, where he denounced Ndabaningi Sithole, Leopold Takawira, Robert Mugabe (qq.v.), and others as dissidents and "expelled" them from the party. The dissidents then returned home and announced formation of a rival party, the Zimbabwe African Nationalist Union (ZANU, q.v.), under Sithole's leadership on August 8, 1963. Nkomo quickly countered by announcing formation of the People's Caretaker Council (PCC, q.v.), with himself as head. The PCC was merely a front organization for the banned ZAPU, whose name resurfaced after the banning of the PCC in August 1964.

Although the split between ZANU and ZAPU had no real ideological basis, it persisted because of strong personal differences between Nkomo and his rivals. A further element which exacerbated this split has been the de facto ethnic division of popular support. The Ndebele (q.v.) have tended to support mainly ZAPU, and the Shona (q.v.) have mainly supported ZANU --a cleavage exploited by the government. During the late 1960s both parties maintained their headquarters in Lusaka, Zambia, where rival party members frequently clashed. Although the government of Zambia (q.v.) strove to reunite the two parties, it tended to favor ZAPU, thereby contributing to the shift of ZANU headquarters to Mozambique (q.v.) in the 1970s. Periodic attempts to reunify the parties, such as formation of the Front for the Liberation of Zimbabwe (FROLIZI, q.v.) in 1971, and a coalition of parties under the African National Council (q.v.) in December 1974 had no lasting results. However, on the eve of the late 1976 Geneva Conference (q.v.) Nkomo and ZANU's Robert Mugabe allied in the "Patriotic Front" (q.v.).

The degree to which ZAPU has continued to function as a tangible political organization since the mid-1960s and the nature of its ties with such guerrilla bodies as the Zimbabwe Peoples' Revolutionary Army (q.v.) have been unclear to outsiders. Until more substantive evidence emerges, it is perhaps best to view ZAPU primarily as a label for Nkomo's personal political following.

ZIMBABWE "BIRDS." The only sizeable representational carvings yet found in a pre-colonial archaeological site so far are eight soapstone "bird" figures taken from the Zimbabwe Ruins (q.v.) between 1889 and the early 1900s. Though more reptilian than avian in overall appearance, these figures are called "birds" because they are winged (but without tails) and bipedal. Each specimen is about 36 cm. in height, carved atop a meter-long monolith. Except for numerous monoliths with only geometric incisions, nothing similar has been found anywhere else in the country. Seven of the bird figures were taken from the Hill Ruin at Zimbabwe; the eighth was found in the valley Phillips Ruin. Since their original locations were not accurately recorded when they were collected, their placement and function have inspired considerable controversy. Some authorities speculate that each figure symbolized the ancestral spirit of a former ruler. During the 20th century the "birds" have come to symbolize the Zimbabwe Ruins themselves, and they are frequently depicted in illustrative materials, including Rhodesian currency (q.v.) and the government's official coat of arms.

ZIMBABWE CONTROVERSY. An expression generally applied to the still-active debate over the origins of the Zimbabwe Ruins (q.v.). The "controversy" has its roots in early Muslim and Portuguese (qq.v.) myths about Ophir (q.v.) and "King Solomon's Mines." The Solomonic myth of Zimbabwe's origins was adopted by Karl Mauch, the first European to describe Zimbabwe, and was later elaborated by J. T. Bent, R. N. Hall, A. Wilmot (qq.v.), and other antiquarian investigators of the ruins. On the basis of this myth, racialist assumptions of African creative incapacity, popular diffusionist theories, superficial similarities between features of the Zimbabwe Ruins and Near Eastern structures, and the apparent absence of local African traditions about the origins of the ruins, Bent and Hall published elaborate arguments that the ruins had been built by ancient Near Easterners, such as Phoenicians or Sabean Arabs. Such theories went unchallenged until scientific archaeological investigation was initiated by David Randall-MacIver (q.v.) in 1905.

Publication of Randall-MacIver's findings turned the theories of ancient and exotic Zimbabwe origins inside-out. Randall-MacIver demonstrated that the ruins were purely African in origin and of comparatively recent ("medieval") date. Randall-MacIver's strong attack on Hall's work embarrassed the latter, who--unlike Randall-MacIver--was a local settler with aspirations for further employment at the ruins sites. Hall responded with a vigorous rebuttal, thus keeping alive in the local public mind a debate which was, for all trained scholars, already closed.

All archaeological and historical research undertaken since 1905 has solidly reconfirmed and refined Randall-MacIver's essential findings. Yet, the "controversy" has remained a lively issue among white southern Africans. In recent years new books have been published with such titles as The Arab Builders of Zimbabwe, and some elements of the Rhodesian government have worked to suppress archaeological interpretations incompatible with the "ancient" Zimbabwe myth. Aside from the government's longstanding interest in promoting local tourism by making Zimbabwe seem "mysterious, " motives for promoting belief in non-African origins of the ruins are essentially political. African nationalists have selected the name "Zimbabwe" (q.v., above) for the country to reinforce African historical pride. Attempts to undermine acceptance of the true origins and history of the ruins civilization are therefore attempts to undermine African support for the nationalist movement.

ZIMBABWE LIBERATION ARMY (ZLA). This name first appeared in the country in September 1962, when an otherwise anonymous call to form a revolutionary army was made publicly in Salisbury. More recently the name ZLA has been associated with the guerrilla forces operating out of Mozambique (q.v.) under the apparent leadership of Robert Mugabe (q.v.). Connections between

ZLA and the established nationalist parties, Zimbabwe African Nationalist Union and Zimbabwe African People's Union (qq. v.), have not been clear, however, and for this reason ZLA has sometimes been described as a "Third Force" (q. v.) in the anti-Rhodesian struggle. The size and composition of ZLA are also unknown. Between mid-1976 and mid-1977 it was variously estimated to contain between 12,000 and 22,000 men, most of whom were in Mozambique at any given moment. (See MILITARY FORCES; cf. ZIMBABWE PEOPLE'S ARMY.)

ZIMBABWE NATIONAL PARK. A 723-hectare (1786-acre) area surrounding the Zimbabwe Ruins (q. v.) was declared a national park (q. v.) in 1951. In addition to the ruins, the park includes a museum maintained by the Historical Monuments Commission (q. v.), a golf course, and limited tourist lodgings. Just to the north is Lake Kyle (q. v.).

ZIMBABWE NATIONAL PARTY (ZNP). Short-lived nationalist political party founded in June 1961 to oppose the National Democratic Party (q. v.), which had initially endorsed the terms of the Constitution of 1961 (q. v.). Among the ZNP leaders were Patrick Matimba, Michale Mawema (q. v.), and Edson Sithole (q. v.). Never able to attract a significant following, the ZNP faded quickly after the emergence of the Zimbabwe African People's Union (q. v.) later the same year.

ZIMBABWE PEOPLE'S ARMY (ZIPA). Name for the main African nationalist guerrilla forces; apparently first publicized around May 1976. ZIPA was said to be run by a high command comprising 18 former members of the Zimbabwe African Nationalist Union and Zimbabwe African People's Union forces who had united under the banner of the African National Council (q. v.). This seems to be the same force also identified as the Zimbabwe Liberation Army, or ZLA (q. v.).

ZIMBABWE PEOPLE'S REVOLUTIONARY ARMY (ZIPRA). Name for the purported military wing of the Zimbabwe African People's Union (q. v.). Like its ZANU counterpart, Zimbabwe African National Liberation Army (ZANLA, q. v.), ZIPRA is little understood by outsiders. It is believed to have operated mainly out of Zambia (q. v.) since 1967, and to have been much smaller than ZANLA. Its connections, if any, with the Zimbabwe People's Army and Zimbabwe Liberation Army (qq. v.) are also unclear.

ZIMBABWE RUINS (a. k. a. Great Zimbabwe). Justly famous as the site of the largest stone edifice built in early sub-Saharan Africa, Zimbabwe played a seminal role in the country's history. It was the original center of monumental stone buildings (see RUINS); the center of the earliest known large-scale state system (see SHONA HISTORY); and probably the earliest local center of international trade (see GOLD; YUFI; MUSLIMS).
     Description. The ruins are located in the Mtilikwe*

basin, on the southern scarp of the Central Plateau*, about
29 km. southeast of Fort Victoria* (at 20° 17'S, 30° 56'E; alt.
1100 m.). Their surroundings are perennially moist, well
wooded, and filled with granite outcroppings, whose natural exfoliation provides easily-dressed building stones. The ruins
complex comprises three main groups. On the north is the
Hill Ruin (a.k.a. "Acropolis," q.v.), built atop a kopje* which
rises about 100 meters above the rest of the complex. The
Hill contains a complicated network of enclosures separated by
free-standing walls and natural rock formations. One enclosure
contains a natural cave which efficiently resonates voices into
the lower valley, giving rise to speculation that this cave was
an early oracular shrine which may have provided an original,
religious basis for the whole complex (see RELIGION--SHONA).

About 600 meters due south of the Hill's "Western Enclosure" is the famous Elliptical Building on the valley floor.
This structure has also been popularly called "The Temple,"
"The Great Enclosure," and other names which reflect modern
confusion over the structure's original purpose. Though built
later than the Hill Ruin, the Elliptical Building clearly became
the complex's most important structure. The overall enclosure
is shaped like an irregular ellipse more than 250 m. in circum-
ference. The great "outer wall" rises to nearly ten meters
in height, and expands to more than five meters in thickness in
places. This wall alone is said to be the largest single pre-
colonial African structure in sub-Saharan Africa. It contains a
greater volume of stones than the entire rest of the complex.
Inside the main enclosure are smaller enclosures, a smaller
and older wall separated from the eastern outer wall by the
narrow "parallel passage," and the famed "conical tower" (q.v.)
at the southern end of the parallel passage.

Between the Hill Ruin and the Elliptical Building is the
"Valley of Ruins." The valley contains ten distinct ruins, half
of which were named after 19th-century Europeans (Kark Mauch,
George Phillips, E. A. Maund, Adam Renders, and Willie Posselt, qq.v.) by R. N. Hall (q.v.). These ruins contain most
of the architectural features of the Elliptical Building, but each
is built on a much smaller scale.

Three wall styles have been discerned in the complex.
The earliest (style "P") features undressed facing blocks arranged in uneven and undulating courses. Most of the Hill Ruin
is built in this style. A later style ("Q") represents the finest
stonework found in the complex, and is that which was later
employed in the best Khami Culture (q.v.) buildings in the west.
This style features dressed and carefully matched stone blocks,
arranged in closely fitting, even courses, as in the Elliptical
Building's outer wall and conical tower. The third style ("R")
is regarded as a degenerate form of the intermediate style.
Its walls are built with ill-matched and loosely fitted stones in
uncoursed rows. An even later period of building has left many
walls which are little more than crude piles of stones.

Other notable features of the complex include numerous
sandstone monoliths, including the famous Zimbabwe "birds"

(q. v.), lintelled doorways, stairways, turrets, and a particularly fine chevron frieze atop the Elliptical Building's southeastern outer wall. Most of the enclosures formerly contained
daga (q. v.) huts, and it is believed that most interior stone
walls and dirt floors were once thoroughly plastered with daga.
Many walls--all of which are unmortared--have collapsed, and
others have been badly damaged by overgrown vegetation and
treasure hunters. Considerable rebuilding by late occupants of
the site and by early 20th-century government workers, the
disappearance of almost all daga-work, and damage done by
untrained archaeologists have all greatly altered the original
appearance of the ruins.

    History. Attempts have been made to periodize the
ruins' occupation sequences, but these have not yet achieved a
consensus among archaeologists and historians. Such periodizations as have been produced have been frequently, and sometimes greatly, revised, adding to the bewildering terminology
applied to the country's Iron Age (q. v.) culture history. The
general trend in modern scholarship, however, has been to
contract the length of the whole stone-building era to within the
first half of the present millenium. It is now generally agreed
that Zimbabwe was abandoned as a major culture and political
center during the 15th century. Nevertheless, the site still
ranks both as the longest-occupied center in the country, and
as the original stone-building complex.

    After a few centuries of very early Iron Age occupation,
Zimbabwe seems to have been unpopulated until about the A. D.
800s, when a Leopard's Kopje-type culture (q. v.) occupied Zimbabwe Hill, the site of the present Hill Ruin. Stone-building
began in about the 12th century, and the 13th century saw major refinements in metal-working, spinning and weaving, and
stone carving. An elite minority among the local Karanga
people (q. v.) was emerging in the region. By the 14th century
these people were clearly engaging in a profitable gold trade
with the east coast, apparently through the port of Sofala (q. v.).
Little is known about the nature of this state system, but its
rulers were almost certainly receiving tribute payments and
laborers from a large area, as the immediate region had insufficient resources to support the estimated 2000 people who
resided at Zimbabwe during its peak period.

    The Elliptical Building is now generally believed to have
contained the chief ruler's residence and court. The valley
ruins probably housed lesser officials and royal family members,
while the bulk of the population lived in surrounding, non-stone
dwellings. The "Zimbabwe Culture" was spread throughout the
southern part of the country by the construction of more than a
hundred similar, but smaller, stone complexes. These were
probably residences of provincial administrators or local tributary chiefs.

    The elaborate and permanent nature of Zimbabwe's
buildings was incompatible with the essentially subsistence agriculture (q. v.) on which the society was based, making its rulers
heavily dependent upon tribute and external trade. In the early

or mid-15th century the site was suddenly abandoned, perhaps as a response to changing political or commercial circumstances. Furthermore, local forests appear to have been largely depleted as a result of heavy use of firewood burned to accelerate granite exfoliation for the collection of building stones. It appears possible that the establishment of the Munhumutapa state (q.v.) in the north around this time represented a shift of the Zimbabwe state's power center. A direct connection between these two state systems remains to be proven, however.

After the 15th century Zimbabwe was cut off from foreign trade and no new building was undertaken by its remaining inhabitants. It is unclear who occupied the site over the next several centuries, but by the early 19th century the minor Mugabe chiefdom was centered near Zimbabwe. This chiefdom had nothing to do with the earlier Zimbabwe rulers, and its people's ignorance of the buildings' origins later contributed to European theories about ancient non-African builders. Zimbabwe is frequently said to have been sacked by Mfecane (q.v.) invaders during the 1830s, but there is no evidence that this really happened. By the time Europeans arrived in Zimbabwe in the 1870s, Zimbabwe's buildings were heavily overgrown with vegetation and in a state of advanced dereliction.

Archaeological investigations. Karl Mauch (q.v.) became the first European to study Zimbabwe in 1871. He produced the first drawings of the ruins, and introduced the first explicit theories about their early non-African origins. After the BSAC occupied Mashonaland in 1890, Europeans recklessly pillaged the ruins, despite administrative efforts to protect them. J. T. Bent (q.v.) was commissioned to investigate the site in 1891, but his work was careless and destructive of stratigraphical evidence. The next authorized excavator, R. N. Hall (q.v.), did even more damage. The first professional archaeologists to excavate were David Randall-MacIver and Gertrude Caton-Thompson (qq.v.). The only other major excavations were undertaken in 1958 by Roger Summers (q.v.) and K. R. Robinson. When their work was completed, the government issued a 25-year moratorium on excavations at Zimbabwe. (See also ZIMBABWE CONTROVERSY, above.)

ZIMBABWE SUN. Newspaper briefly published in Salisbury by the Zimbabwe African Nationalist Union (ZANU) and the People's Caretaker Council (qq.v.) in 1964. Like Chapupu (q.v.) and other African nationalist publications, the Sun was quickly banned by the white government. Since 1964 most nationalist papers, such as the Zimbabwe African People's Union's Zimbabwe Review and ZANU's Zimbabwe News, have been irregularly issued from external cities, especially Lusaka, Zambia. (See PRESS; CENSORSHIP.)

ZIMBABWE UNITED PEOPLE'S ORGANISATION (ZUPO). Conservative African political party formed on December 29, 1976, by government chiefs. The party has been headed by Jeremiah S. Chirau (b.,c.1924), a chief in the Lomagundi District* since

1961, and president of the Council of Chiefs (q.v.) since 1973.
From December 1977 into early 1978 Chirau represented ZUPO
in constitutional negotiations with Ian Smith, Abel Muzorewa,
and Ndabaningi Sithole (qq.v.). ZUPO has aligned with the
government on most substantive political issues, and is believed
to have little popular support.

ZIWA (variant: Zewa). Archaeological term for an early Iron Age
(q.v.) culture, or industry, named after a site on the slopes of
Mount Ziwa, a 1745-meter-high mountain in the Inyanga District*
(at 18° 8'S, 32° 40'E). The Ziwa cultural complex covered the
extreme northeastern part of the country, and has been dated to
as early as A.D. 300s. Roughly contemporary with the Gokomere culture (q.v.) to the southwest, Ziwa is now regarded as
a variant of Gokomere, and not an independent tradition. Within the Inyanga region there appears to have been a hiatus of
several centuries between the end of Ziwa occupation and the
beginning of the terrace-building culture of the Inyanga Ruins
complex (q.v.) in about the 15th century.

ZIZI, WILLIAM see MZIZI, WILLIAM

ZOMBEPATA CAVE. Important Stone Age (q.v.) archaeological site
in the Sipolilo District* (at 16° 51'S, 30° 34'E). The cave also
contains rock paintings (q.v.) which incorporate several features
rarely observed elsewhere in the country. These include in-
frequently painted animal figures, and geometric figures resem-
bling active beehives.

ZULU (Amazulu; variant: Zooloo). Large group of Nguni-speaking
(q.v.) peoples inhabiting what is now the northern Natal Province
and KwaZulu "bantustan" of South Africa (q.v.)--a region known
historically as Zululand. During the early 19th century King
Shaka (q.v.) molded the Zulu into a powerful and aggressive
state whose wars spawned a diaspora of Nguni-speaking bands
into northern countries (see MFECANE). Many of these peoples,
including the Ndebele (q.v.), were also known colloquially as
"Zulu." Indeed, both Mzilikazi and Lobengula (qq.v.) called
their own Ndebele people "Amazulu." During the late 19th and
early 20th centuries many South African Zulu played important
roles as employees or agents of European missionaries, traders,
concession-hunters, and military forces occupying present Rhodesia. A particularly famous Rhodesian-born Zulu was Albert
Luthuli (q.v.). The Zulu language, or Sizulu, is now the standard northern Nguni dialect and it is very similar to Sindebele
(q.v.), which separated from it in the 1820s.

ZUMBO. Mozambique (q.v.) town just northeast of the confluence
of the Luangwa and Zambezi* rivers, where the present borders
of Rhodesia, Mozambique, and Zambia meet. The town was
founded around 1714 as a trading fair (q.v.), situated so as to
take advantage of the gold (q.v.) trade from the Changamire
state (q.v.), from which direct Portuguese (q.v.) trade was

debarred. Through the 18th century Zumbo served as the most important Shona trading link with the outside world, while simultaneously connecting Portuguese trade with Zambian peoples to the north. The present Zambian town of Feira was established as a fair on the opposite side of the Luangwa River in c. 1788.

ZVI-. Chishona (q.v.) prefix (Class 8), normally used for plural forms of chi- prefix (q.v.) nouns.

ZWANGENDABA. Ndebele ibutho (q.v.) raised by King Mzilikazi in the early 1840s. Its town was situated by the upper Bembezi River, near the present site of Turk Mine (q.v.). Under the leadership of induna Mbigo Masuku (q.v.), the men of Zwangendaba played a key role in turning back A. H. Potgieter's (q.v.) invasion of the Matopo Hills* in 1847. The members of the ibutho were said to be "pure" zansi (q.v.). Partly for this reason Zwangendaba led the opposition to Lobengula's (q.v.) accession to the kingship in 1870 in the belief that Lobengula's mother was of non-zansi origin. Mbigo was a leading advocate of locating the presumably missing royal heir, Nkulumane (q.v.), even after Lobengula was made king in January 1870. By the middle of that year the Zwangendaba, Induba, Inqobo, and Nyamayendhlovu amabutho still refused to acknowledge Lobengula's authority. In June Lobengula assembled a force of around 5000-6000 loyal men to subordinate the dissidents. The other rebel amabutho fell into line, but the Zwangendaba refused even to negotiate. On June 5th the loyalists crushed the Zwangendaba at their town in a bloody battle in which Mbigo and about 300 or 400 of his men died. Their town was razed, and the name of Zwangendaba became anathema within the Ndebele kingdom. Lobengula treated the Zwangendaba survivors leniently, but many fled south, joining Mangwane (q.v.) and the pretender "Nkulumane" in the Transvaal*. The men who stayed in Matabeleland were dispersed throughout other amabutho, in which they kept alive the spirit of resistance to Lobengula through the rest of his reign.

ZWANGENDABA JERE (c. 1780s-c. 1845). Most important of the Ngoni (q.v.) migration leaders and father of Mpezeni Jere (q.v.). Zwangendaba was hereditary chief of the Jere clan in South Africa's northern Nguni (q.v.) country. During the 1810s he became a leading military commander in Zwide's (q.v.) Ndwandwe state. After the Ndwandwe were defeated by Shaka's Zulu (q.v.) around 1819, Zwangendaba fled north with a band of followers. Through conquests and voluntary submissions he built up his following in southern Mozambique during the 1820s. Late in this decade he appears to have allied with the Gaza king Soshangane (q.v.) at Delagoa Bay. The two leaders clashed around 1830, so Zwangendaba led his people into Shona country in present Rhodesia. There his Ngoni disrupted the Changamire state (q.v.), killing the reigning king, Chirisamhuru (q.v.). Early in 1835 Zwangendaba appears to have been defeated near the Mazoe River* by the Ngoni of Nxaba and Maseko (qq.v.). Towards the end of

the year Zwangendaba crossed the Zambezi River* into present
Zambia* near Zumbo*. According to tradition the crossing
took place on the day of a solar eclipse, which must have been
that of November 20, 1835.

Part of Zwangendaba's following remained in Mashonaland* under the leadership of his kinswoman Nyamazana (q.v.).
Zwangendaba continued north with the bulk of his Ngoni, including many new Shona recruits who were eventually absorbed
into Ngoni society. Zwangendaba himself traveled as far north
as the Zambia/Tanzania border region, where he died in the
mid-1840s. His kingdom then divided into five major groups
which later settled in Tanzania, Zambia, and Malawi. The
modern Songea District of southern Tanzania is named after
Songea Mbano (c.1836-1906), a Zambian-born Ngoni whose
Shona parents were captured by Zwangendaba in Mashonaland.

ZWIDE (variants: Uzwide; Zwiti; Zidze; Uxwiti) (d.1825). South
African Ndwandwe king. A somewhat older contemporary of
the Zulu king Shaka (q.v.), Zwide built a powerful northern
Nguni (q.v.) state around his Ndwandwe clan during the first
decades of the 19th century. He was the maternal grandfather
of Mzilikazi (q.v.), who served under him during his youth.
When Zwide's state was broken up by the Zulu in c.1819, Zwide
fled to just north of Swaziland. Two of his military commanders,
Soshangane and Zwangendaba (qq.v.), led other bands farther
north. Because of his close association with these Mfecane
(q.v.) bands, Zwide's own name was later used to identify ma-
rauding Nguni groups (see DZVITI).

ZWIMBA, MATTHEW (fl.1880s-1930s). Independent church founder.
Zwimba's father, Chigaga, was made a government-salaried
chief in the Zwimba Reserve (now Tribal Trust Land, q.v.) of
the southern Lomagundi District* after the 1896-7 Revolts*.
Matthew Zwimba was thus raised in a family loyal to European
rule. He converted to Christianity at a local Wesleyan mission
(q.v.) and became a teacher and lay evangelist. After starting
the first school in the Zwimba Reserve, he got into disciplinary
conflicts with mission authorities, who transferred him to Gatooma*. Outraged by this arbitrary action, Zwimba got into
further difficulties with his superiors until he was dismissed
from all his positions in 1907. Now fiercely opposed to white
authority, he returned to Zwimba Reserve, where he clashed
with government authorities and was briefly imprisoned.

In 1915 Zwimba started his own church just outside the
reserve at Kanyemba. He soon re-entered the reserve and took
over his former mission school. He called his new church Siri
Chena, the "Original Church of the White Bird." Drawing upon
Christian and Shona symbols, he described "white bird" as the
dove of the Holy Ghost and the messenger of the Shona High God
Mwari (q.v.). He made "saints" of Shona killed by Europeans
in the Revolts. Alarmed government officials suspected sedition
and quickly moved to suppress his church by proscribing him
and his brother from preaching or teaching. Persistent govern-

ment harassment discouraged people from joining Zwimba's church, which languished from lack of support. Despite Zwimba's failure, his church--the first such independent body founded by Shona--became an important symbol of African resistance to white rule, and Zwimba's personal prestige remained great. In 1925 he testified before the Morris Carter Commission (q. v.) in behalf of local chiefs.

ZWITI (Mazwiti)   see   DZVITI

THE BIBLIOGRAPHY

- CONTENTS -

Introduction   372

Abbreviations Used in Bibliography   382

1. GENERAL

        Bibliographies and Research Guides   383
        General Information: Encyclopedias, Handbooks,
            Guides   384
        Travel and Modern Description   385

2. BIOGRAPHY

        Collections of Biographies   386
        Pre-20th-Century Figures   386
        20th-Century Figures   388

3. CULTURE

        Art: Ancient and Modern   389
        Languages and Linguistics   390
        Literature
            African Languages   391
            English Language   391
            Novels in English   392
        Media: Broadcasting, Publishing, and the Press 393
        Music and Drama   394
        Philately: Postage Stamps   394

4. ECONOMICS

        General   395
        Agriculture and Animal Husbandry   396
        Commerce and International Sanctions   397
        Industry   398
        Labor and Unions   399
        Land and Land Policy   401
        Mining   402
        Transport and Communications   403

369

5. HISTORY

General Histories and Historiography   404
Local and District Histories   405
Stone Age   406
Iron Age
    General   407
    Zimbabwe Ruins and "Zimbabwe Controversy"   408
Shona History (Early and General)   409
Early Portuguese Activities   411
The 19th Century (Contemporary and Modern Works)   412
Ndebele Kingdom   413
Mfecane Invasions   414
European Contact Era, 1880s-1890s   415
African Armed Resistance to European Occupation   417
Era of BSAC Rule, 1890-1923   418
British Crown Colony Period, 1923-1965   419
Federation, 1953-1963   420
UDI, 1965+   421

6. POLITICS AND GOVERNMENT

General   422
African Nationalism and Nationalist Movements   423
Constitutions and Law   424
Government African Policy and Administration   425
International Relations   426
Military and Police
    Government Forces   427
    Modern African Liberation Movement   428

7. RELIGION

General   428
African Religions and Beliefs   429
Independent Christian Churches   430
Missions and Missionary Churches   430

8. SCIENCES

Geography
    General   432
    Kariba Dam and Region   433
Geology   433
Medicine and Health   434
Natural History
    Fauna   434
    Flora   435

9. SOCIAL

General   436
African Societies (General)   436

Demography   437
Education   437
Immigrant Societies   438
Inter-ethnic Relations   439
Urban Studies   440

10. SERIAL PUBLICATIONS   441

Newspapers and General Interest   441
Scholarly, Specialized and Professional   442

BIBLIOGRAPHY: INTRODUCTION

Although it is only a modestly-sized country, Rhodesia--or
Zimbabwe, as it is to be renamed--has attracted a great deal of attention since the mid-19th century.   As a result, there is an abun-
dance of published material on almost every aspect of Rhodesian
studies.   Happily for American and British students of the country,
most of this material is written in English, and much of the rest
has been translated.

The present bibliography is only a carefully selected sam-
pling of what is available in Rhodesian studies.   More than 10, 000
additional sources can be found in Oliver and Karen Pollak's nearly
exhaustive Rhodesia/Zimbabwe: An International Bibliography (1977).
Many other specialized bibliographies are also available, and the
Pollaks are now completing a book-length annotated bibliography of
500 important sources on Rhodesia/Zimbabwe for the World Bibliography Series of Clio Press (Oxford, scheduled for 1979).

The Pollaks' big bibliography covers works published through
mid-1975, so the present bibliography gives special attention to works
published since that date, as well as earlier works overlooked by the
Pollaks.   This bibliography also corrects minor mistakes found in
Pollak and Pollak; it adds many details, particularly on reprint editions; and it offers a shorter but more detailed list of serial publications than that found in Pollak and Pollak.

In general, this bibliography gives priority to books over
articles; recent publications over older publications; specialized
studies of Rhodesia over general studies of larger regions; and materials reasonably accessible to American and British students over
more difficult-to-find materials.   The bibliography includes a number
of recent doctoral dissertations to help indicate current trends in

scholarship and to call attention to new scholars who have not yet published extensively.   The British theses are hard to get hold of, even in Britain, but xerographic or microfilm copies of most American dissertations can be purchased directly from Xerox University Microfilms, 300 North Zeeb Road, Ann Arbor, Michigan   48106.

This bibliography also lists some "forthcoming" publications, although not all of these titles will necessarily ever appear.   The prospective dates of publication of forthcoming works are qualified with either "c." or "?," depending upon the firmness of information available in March 1978.

In order to conserve space, this bibliography omits all articles contained in edited books, such as Stokes and Brown, The Zambesian Past, which are listed under their editors' names.

Government publications are a special problem, as always, because their bibliographical details are typically chaotic and they are generally difficult to get hold of.   American holdings of Rhodesian government publications have been in particular disorder since UDI, so few are listed here.   For pre-1965 government publications, see Audrey A. Walker, The Rhodesias and Nyasaland: A Guide to the Official Publications (1965).   For post-1965 Rhodesian publications, see the annual Rhodesia National Bibliography, which can be obtained free by writing to the National Archives of Rhodesia, Private Bag 7720, Causeway, Salisbury, Rhodesia.

Note that asterisked (*) items in the bibliography indicate that entries on these authors, institutions, or titles can be found in the dictionary.

GENERAL WORKS

Compilation of this dictionary was made easier by the existence of a number of encyclopedias and handbooks on Rhodesia and Southern Africa, but none of these treats African peoples and history in any depth.   Mary Akers (ed.), Encyclopaedia Rhodesia (1973), for example, is most useful for geography, natural history, and European history and government institutions.   W. V. Brelsford (ed.), Handbook to the Federation (1960), contains a wealth of

information on a broad range of subjects, but much of its material
is now out of date, and the book's utility is limited by its lack of
an index. Harold Nelson, et al., Area Handbook for Southern Rhodesia (1975), is particularly useful on recent political and economic
history, and is well indexed.

BIOGRAPHY

Biographical data on Europeans in Rhodesian history is relatively easy to find. Edward Tabler, Pioneers of Rhodesia (1966),
contains detailed biographies of more than 400 people who visited
Rhodesia between 1836 and 1880. T. W. Baxter and E. E. Burke,
Guide to the Historical Manuscripts in the National Archives of Rhodesia (1970), contains useful brief biographies of individuals (and institutions) whose papers are in the National Archives. The various
Central and Southern African Who's Who annuals (see 10. SERIAL
PUBLICATIONS) contain numerous biographies, but these are mostly
of European businessmen and government figures.

Several recent books are very useful for modern African
political leaders. Robert Cary and Diana Mitchell, African Nationalist Leaders in Rhodesia: Who's Who (1977) has detailed biographies of more than 60 figures, including some who are deceased,
and briefer notes on dozens more. John Dickie and Alan Rake,
Who's Who in Africa (1973) covers 35 Rhodesians, including some
white politicians and business leaders.

There are many short biographical studies of individual Africans and Europeans, but unfortunately there are few full-length biographies of any merit. Even Cecil Rhodes awaits a definitive biography. J. G. Lockhart and C. M. Woodhouse, Rhodes (1963), is
probably the most satisfactory study, but it should be read in conjunction with T. O. Ranger, "The Last Word on Rhodes?" (1964).
Of biographies of other figures, perhaps L. H. Gann and Michael
Gelfand, Huggins of Rhodesia (1964), is most outstanding.

CULTURE

There is a significant body of literature on prehistoric rock paintings, but most of this is merely descriptive. C. K. Cooke, Guide to the Rock Art of Rhodesia (1974), and Roger Summers (ed.), Prehistoric Rock Art of the Federation (1959), are both well-illustrated volumes. Modern Shona art is attracting increased attention, and has been treated several times in African Arts, an illustrated magazine published by UCLA's African Studies Center.

Literature is discussed within the dictionary. Here it need only be added that S. M. Mutswairo (ed.), Zimbabwe Prose and Poetry (1974), is a useful anthology in English of African literature published in Shona and English over the past two decades.

Among the studies of the media, perhaps the most useful are the books published by former newspaper editors and publishers: W. D. Gale, B. G. Paver, John Parker, Nathan Shamuyarira, and Lawrence Vambe. (See also SERIAL PUBLICATIONS, p. 381, below.)

ECONOMICS

Duncan Clarke's essay on economic bibliography (see 1. GENERAL--Bibliographies) is the best introduction to works on economics published before 1973. Major works published since include Ian Phimister and Charles van Onselen's seminal studies of mining and African labor, and Robin Palmer's books on land and rural economics. The Rhodesian Journal of Economics (1967+) has been an important forum for a wide spectrum of economic views.

HISTORY

Students of Rhodesian history can do no better than to start with the historiographical essays of George Shepperson and T. O. Ranger. From there efforts should be made to acquire Rhodesian History (1970+) and Mbire (1972+) to keep abreast of current research.

Surprisingly, there is still no satisfactory one-volume history of the country. Most of the histories published before 1965 are apologiae for white rule of varying degrees of sophistication. L. H. Gann, A History of Southern Rhodesia (1965), is the first professionally-written history of the country, but it, too, has a strong Eurocentrism and it carries the story only up to 1934. Gann's

Central Africa: The Former British States (1971) is more sensitive
to African history and it carries the story past UDI, but the book's
attention to Rhodesia is much briefer.   Other useful regional histories are Donald Denoon, Southern Africa Since 1800 (1972); T. O.
Ranger (ed.), Aspects of Central African History (1968); and A. J.
Wills, An Introduction to the History of Central Africa (3rd ed.,
1973).   The volumes edited by Eric Stokes and Richard Brown and
by L. M. Thompson contain important contributions to Rhodesian
history, but they make no attempt at complete coverage of their
regions' histories.

Iron Age archaeology and history are very well served.
Useful introductions to the subject can be found in the articles and
books by P. S. Garlake, T. N. Huffman, K. R. Robinson, and
Roger Summers.   See also the dictionary entry on the ZIMBABWE
CONTROVERSY.

Early Shona history was pioneered by D. P. Abraham, but
his articles are difficult for nonspecialists to interpret.   One should
therefore start with the various articles by David Beach, and supplement these with the writings of H. H. K. Bhila and S. I. Mudenge.
The antiquarian journal Nada is loaded with articles on Shona history,
but these are of such mixed value that only the most important and
most recent are listed here.

The books by Eric Axelson and M. D. D. Newitt are the
best introduction to early Portuguese involvement in central Africa.
Original Portuguese documents are available in English translation,
thanks to the Records of South-Eastern Africa (1898-1903), edited by
G. M. Theal, and the Documentos Sobre os Portugueses (1962+),
now being published by the Rhodesian and Portuguese archives.

The 19th century is naturally the best known pre-colonial
era.   There are numerous firsthand accounts written by travelers
and missionaries, and most of these have been reprinted--sometimes
more than once--by Books of Rhodesia (Bulawayo), Negro Universi-
ties Press (New York), and Frank Cass (London).   Many previously
unpublished documents are also available in book form in volumes
edited by E. C. Tabler, J. P. R. Wallis and others.   The biographical entries in this dictionary should help to serve as guides to the

content of many of these works.

Ndebele history has long attracted considerable attention, but solid scholarship is a recent development. Richard Brown has contributed important articles to the volumes edited by Stokes and Brown and by L. M. Thompson. R. K. Rasmussen, Migrant Kingdom (1978), treats the early history of the Ndebele, and Julian Cobbing's doctoral thesis covers the later years of the Ndebele kingdom very thoroughly. Some of Cobbing's findings are published in the Journal of African History and in Rhodesian History.

J. D. Omer-Cooper, The Zulu Aftermath (1966), is now somewhat outdated, but it remains the single most useful guide to the Mfecane era as a whole. In addition to the Ndebele studies cited, Omer-Cooper is usefully supplemented by Gerhard Liesegang's articles.

In common with historical scholarship elsewhere in Africa, the late-19th-century era of European occupation and African resistance has inspired an immense body of literature. H. M. Hole's books are perhaps the most useful statements of a British participant in the occupation era. Philip Mason, The Birth of a Dilemma (1958), turned attention to the African perspective, which has since been more thoroughly articulated in T. O. Ranger's various works and in Stanlake Samkange, Origins of Rhodesia (1968). Ranger's now classic Revolt in Southern Rhodesia (1967) has inspired an important debate on African resistance to European rule.

The era of British South Africa Company rule is well covered in Gann's History of Southern Rhodesia, which is usefully supplemented by Ranger's African Voice in Southern Rhodesia, 1898-1930 (1970). J. S. Galbraith, Crown and Charter (1974), is an analysis of the Company's early days.

For the era of "Responsible Government," which started in 1923, one might start with Elaine Windrich, The Rhodesian Problem, 1923-1973 (1975), a documentary history. Richard Gray, The Two Nations (1960) treats Southern Rhodesia within the context of British central Africa, but it is nevertheless the most thorough history of the country's African political and labor movements through 1953. Gray is richly supplemented by Lawrence Vambe, From Rhodesia to

Zimbabwe (1976), which is at once a personal memoir and a history
of African politics into the 1960s.   Colin Leys, European Politics in
Southern Rhodesia (1958) remains the best account of purely European
politics through the late 1950s.

The Federation era inspired an enormous contemporary body
of commentaries and speculations, most of which are now of little
interest.   Among the works listed here, the most accessible are
Herbert Spiro's long article in Five African States (1963) and Patrick
Keatley's contribution to the Penguin African Library, The Politics
of Partnership (1963).

Literature on the post-UDI history of the country merges
into the contemporary studies of politics and government.   For background to UDI, the studies of James Barber, Martin Loney, B. V.
Mtshali, and R. W. Peterson are all useful.

POLITICS AND GOVERNMENT

Post-UDI Rhodesia has been treated in innumerable books
and articles, most of which will have little lasting value.   Objective
studies are rare, but D. J. Murray, The Governmental System in
Southern Rhodesia (1970), and Larry Bowman, Politics in Rhodesia
(1973), provide solid starting points.   More recent developments can
be followed in such periodicals as African Report (New York) and
Africa Today (Denver), and in Africa Contemporary Record, an annual edited by Colin Legum and published by Rex Collings (London).

Articulation of African nationalist viewpoints began with
Ndabaningi Sithole's classic African Nationalism (2nd ed., 1968).
Other important contributions have been made by Enoch Dumbutshena,
Leonard Kapungu, Eshmael Mlambo, Nathan Shamuyarira, and others.

The works on African policy and administration are quite a
mixed bag, with useful articles going back to the early years of
Nada (1923+).   Among the important recent overviews are the works
of J. F. Holleman, A. K. H. Weinrich (a.k.a. Sister Mary Aquina),
and Murray Steele.

Claire Palley, Constitutional History and Law of Southern
Rhodesia (1966), is a nearly definitive treatment of the country's

legal history.   It is well supplemented by the works of Gloria Passmore and others.

Most of what has been published on Rhodesia's military forces is pretty standard military history.   This subject is best approached through R. S. Roberts' review article in Rhodesian History (1974).   The modern liberation movement has naturally spawned strongly polarized views of the conduct of recent warfare.   R. W. Baldock's review article in Rhodesian History (1974) is the best introduction to this subject, while Kees Maxey, The Fight for Zimbabwe (1975), is perhaps the best book-length overview of the fighting itself.

RELIGION

Religious studies have attracted an unusual amount of attention in Rhodesia, with many studies available on the history and practice of African traditional religions, mission churches, and African independent churches.   Anthony Dachs (ed.), Christianity South of the Zambezi (1973), and T. O. Ranger and John Weller (eds.), Themes in the Christian History of Central Africa (1975), both deal with a broader range of religious topics than their titles imply, making each a useful introduction to religion in Rhodesia. Michael Bourdillon and Michael Gelfand have both published many studies of traditional religious beliefs.   M. L. Daneel's monumental study of Shona independent churches is setting a new standard for the study of Christian independency in Africa.

The history of mission churches is well covered in both primary and secondary published sources.   Paul King (ed.), Missions in Southern Rhodesia (1959) is a handy, but perhaps hard to find, overview of this subject.

SCIENCES

George Kay, Rhodesia: A Human Geography (1970), is easily the best introduction to Rhodesian geography, and it contains considerable material on history, peoples, and economic development.   M. O. Collins, Rhodesia: Its Natural Resources and Economic

Development (1965), is a valuable large-format atlas, but much of its economic data is out of date, and government secrecy has made publication of a revised edition impractical. Specialized geological publications are numerous, as is attested by C. C. Smith and H. E. van der Heyde's large bibliography (see p. 384).

Medical studies are best approached through the books by Michael Gelfand, and in the Central African Journal of Medicine, which Gelfand edits. Since the traditional African arts of healing are also tied into religious beliefs, some attention should also be paid to the literature on religion.

The natural history of the country is well covered, particularly in the "Bundu Books" published by Longman Rhodesia.

SOCIAL

The starting point for any study of the African peoples of the country is still Hilda Kuper, A. J. B. Hughes, and J. van Velsen, The Shona and Ndebele of Southern Rhodesia (1954), in the International Africa Institute's Ethnographic Survey of Africa. Michael Bourdillon, The Shona Peoples (1976), is perhaps the most valuable general study recently published, but many specialized studies have been published, including many articles in Nada, Africa, and elsewhere.

The study of immigrant societies is best approached through the works of L. H. Gann and Peter Duignan, and through the more recent studies by B. A. Kosmin and Barry Schutz. Inter-ethnic, or "race," relations is obviously a well covered field. D. K. Davies (comp.), Race Relations in Rhodesia: A Survey for 1972-73 (1975), covers those years and includes considerable background material. It is as yet uncertain whether additional annual surveys will ever appear.

The literature on education is diverse. It is perhaps best approached through Marshall Murphree (ed.), Education, Race and Employment in Rhodesia (1975).

Urban studies are also a mixed bag. Clive Kileff and W. C. Pendleton (eds.), Urban Man in Southern Africa (1975), is useful general approach. A. K. H. Weinrich, Mucheke: Race, Status, and Politics (1976), surveys a Fort Victoria township.

SERIAL PUBLICATIONS

This bibliography lists most past and present Rhodesian newspapers, excluding political publications (which are typically short-lived and difficult to acquire). The most important of these newspapers are discussed in the dictionary, and general discussions of newspapers can be found under the headings PRESS, AFRICAN NEWSPAPERS LTD., and ARGUS GROUP.

This bibliography also lists a selection of specialized serial publications published within Rhodesia, as well as a few specialized journals on southern Africa published elsewhere. For a more complete listing, see Alison Thomas and Dorothea Rowse (comps.), Current Rhodesian Periodicals (1974), available free from the National Archives of Rhodesia. Reference can also be made to Ulrich's International Periodicals Directory, 17th ed. (New York: R. R. Bowker, 1977) and Sub-Saharan Africa: A Guide to Serials (Washington, D.C.: Library of Congress, 1970).

ABBREVIATIONS USED
IN BIBLIOGRAPHY

*	(cross reference to dictionary entry)
+	(indicates continuous publication since the date shown)
Afr.	Africa(n)
Arch.	Archive(s); Archaeology
BOR	Books of Rhodesia
comp.	compiler
Econ.	Economics
ed.	editor; edited; edition
Fed.	Federation
Hist.	history; historical
Instit.	Institute
Internat.	International
Jnl.	Journal
Lib.	Library
Nat.	National
NUP	Negro Universities Press
OUP	Oxford University Press
rep.	reprint edition
rev.	revised
Proc.	proceedings
pseud.	pseudonym
Pub.	published; Publishing
rev. art.	review article
Rhod.	Rhodesia(n)
S. Afr.	South Africa(n)
So. Afr.	Southern Africa(n)
Soc.	Society
Trans.	translated; Transactions
Univ.	University
UP	University Press

BIBLIOGRAPHY: 1. GENERAL*

BIBLIOGRAPHIES AND RESEARCH GUIDES

Ansari, S. (ed.). Liberation Struggle in Southern Africa: A Bibliography of source material. Gurgaon, India: Indian Documentation Service, 1972. 118p.

Baxter, T. W. (ed.). Guide to the Public Archives of Rhodesia. Vol. 1: 1890-1923. Salisbury: Nat. Arch. Rhod., 1969. 262p.

_____ & E. E. Burke. Guide to the Historical Manuscripts in the National Archives of Rhodesia. Salisbury: Nat. Arch. Rhod., 1970. 527p.

Bennett, T. W. & Sally Phillips. A Bibliography of African Law, with Special Reference to Rhodesia. Salisbury: Univ. Rhod., 1975. 324p.

Burke, Eric Edward. A Bibliography of Cecil John Rhodes (1853-1902). Salisbury: Central Afr. Arch., 1952. Rep. in The Story of Cecil Rhodes (Salisbury: Central Afr. Arch., 1953), 115-92.

_____. "Rhodesia in books," Rhodesiana, 24 (1971), 11-20.

Clarke, Duncan G. "The economics of underdevelopment in Rhodesia: an essay on selected bibliography," Current Bibliography on Afr. Affairs, VI, 3 (1973), 293-332.

Coggin, C. "Rhodesian bibliography: a survey," Rhod. Librarian, II, 4 (1970), 81-98.

Cooke, Cranmer Kenrick. A Bibliography of Rhodesian Archaeology from 1874. Salisbury: Nat. Museums and Monuments of Rhod., Arnoldia, VI, 38 (1974), 56p.

Doro, Marion E. "A bibliographical essay on the November 1971 Rhodesian settlement proposals," Current Bibliog. on Afr. Affairs, VI, 4 (1973), 411-30.

_____

*An asterisk indicates that an entry on the indicated person, institution or title may be found in the dictionary.

383

Pollak, Oliver Burt & Karen Pollak. An International Bibliography of Theses and Dissertations on Southern Africa. Boston: G. K. Hall, 1976. 236p.

_____ & _____ . Rhodesia/Zimbabwe: An International Bibliography. Boston: G. K. Hall, 1977. 621p.

Rhodesia National Bibliography (formerly, List of Publications Deposited in the Library of the National Archives). Salisbury: Nat. Arch. Rhod., 1961+. Annual.

Smith, Craig C. & H. E. van der Heyde. Rhodesian Geology: A Bibliography and Brief Index to 1968. Salisbury: Trustees of the Nat. Museums of Rhod., 1971. 252p.

Thompson, Leonard, Richard Elphick, & Inez Jarrick. Southern African History Before 1900: A Select Bibliography of Articles. Stanford, Calif.: Hoover Instit. Press, 1971. 102p.

Walker, Audrey A. (comp.). The Rhodesias and Nyasaland: A Guide to the Official Publications. Washington: Lib. Congress, 1965. 285p.

Wilding, Norman W. (comp.). Catalogue of the Parliamentary Papers of Southern Rhodesia and Rhodesia, 1954-1970 and the Federation of Rhodesia and Nyasaland, 1954-1963. Salisbury: Univ. Coll. of Rhodesia, 1970. 161p.

Willson, Francis Michael Glenn & Gloria C. Passmore (comps.). Catalogue of the Parliamentary Papers of Southern Rhodesia, 1899-1953. Salisbury: Univ. of Rhodesia, 1965. 484p.

GENERAL INFORMATION:
ENCYCLOPEDIAS, HANDBOOKS, GUIDES

Akers, Mary (gen. ed.). Encyclopaedia Rhodesia. Salisbury: College Press, 1973. 445p.

Blake, Wilfrid Theodore. Central African Survey: Facts and Figures on Rhodesia and Nyasaland. London: A. Redman, 1961. 133p.

Brelsford, W. V. (ed.). Handbook to the Federation of Rhodesia and Nyasaland. London: Cassell; Salisbury: Govt. Printer, 1960. 803p.

Joelson, F. S. (ed.). Rhodesia and East Africa. London: East Africa & Rhodesia, 1958. 432p.

Levin, L. S. (ed.). Rhodesia and Nyasaland. Salisbury: Central Afr. Airways, 1961. 662p.

Macmillan, Allister. Rhodesia and Eastern Africa: Historical Descriptive, Commercial and Industrial Facts, Figures, and Resources. London: W. H. & L. Collingridge, 1931. 414p.

Nelson, Harold D., et al. Area Handbook for Southern Rhodesia.
Washington: U. S. Gov. Printing Office, 1975. 392p.

Official Yearbook of (the Colony of) Southern Rhodesia. Salisbury:
Rhod. Printing & Pub. Co., 1924, 1930, 1932, 1952.

Rosenthal, Eric (comp.). Encyclopedia of Southern Africa. 6th
ed., London: Frederick Warne, 1973 (first publ., 1961).
662p.

Southern Rhodesia Department of Statistics. Statistical Yearbook of
Southern Rhodesia. Salisbury, 1924, 1938, 1947.

Standard Encyclopedia of Southern Africa. 12 vols. Cape Town:
Nasou, Ltd., 1970-76. D. J. Potgieter, Ed.-in-chief.

United States Board on Geographic Names. Southern Rhodesia: Official Standard Names [Gazetteer]. Washington: Defense Mapping
Agency Topographic Center, 1973. 362p.

TRAVEL AND MODERN DESCRIPTION

Berlyn, Phillippa. This Is Rhodesia. Salisbury: College Press,
1969. 184p.

Cooke, Cranmer Kenrick. A Guide to the Historic and Pre-Historic
Monuments of Rhodesia. Bulawayo: Hist. Monuments Commiss.,
1972. 84p.

Edwards, S. J. Zambezi Odyssey. Cape Town: T. V. Bulpin,
1974. 230p.

Fisher, Allan C., Jr. "Rhodesia, a house divided, " National Geographic (May 1975), 641-71.

Hills, Denis. Rebel People. London: Allen & Unwin, 1978.

Hoare, Rawdon. Rhodesian Mosaic. London: J. Murray, 1934.
259p.

Jumbo Guide to Rhodesia. Salisbury: Wilrey Publications, 1972.
252p.

Ransford, Oliver & Peter Steyn. Historic Rhodesia. Salisbury:
Longman Rhodesia, 1975. 70p.

Tanser, George Henry (ed.). The Guide to Rhodesia. Salisbury:
Winchester Press, 1975. 337p.

Tanser, Tony & Phillippa Berlyn. Rhodesian Panorama. Salisbury: Mardon, 1967. 242p.

Wadia, Ardaser Sorabjee N. The Romance of Rhodesia: Being Impressions of a Sightseeing Tour of Southern and Northern Rhodesia. London: J. M. Dent, 1947. 146p.

Waugh, Evelyn. "The Rhodesias," in E. Waugh, A Tourist in Africa (London: Chapman & Hall, 1960), 114-60.

2. BIOGRAPHY

COLLECTIONS OF BIOGRAPHIES

Cary, Robert & Dianna Mitchell. African Nationalist Leaders in Rhodesia: Who's Who. Johannesburg: Africana Book Soc.; London: Rex Collings; Bulawayo: BOR, 1977. 310p.

Dickie, John & Alan Rake. Who's Who in Africa. London: African Development, 1973. 602p. (Rhodesians: pp. 357-86).

Dictionary of South African Biography. 5 vols. (projected). Cape Town & Johannesburg: Tafelberg-Uitgewers, Ltd., 1968+. Vol. I: ed., W. J. de Kock; Vol. II: ed., D. W. Kruger.

Lipschutz, Mark R. & R. Kent Rasmussen. A Dictionary of African Historical Biography. London: Heinemann; Chicago: Aldine, 1978. 292p.

Lloyd, Jessie M. (comp.). Rhodesia's Pioneer Women (1859-1896). Rev. & enlarged by Constance Parry. Bulawayo: Rhodesian Pioneers & Early Settlers' Soc., 1974 (first publ., 1960). 105p.

Profiles of Rhodesia's Women. Salisbury: Nat. Fed. of Business & Professional Women of Rhod., 1976. 176p.

Segal, Ronald. Political Africa. London: Stevens & Sons, 1961. 475p.

*Tabler, Edward C. Pioneers of Rhodesia. Cape Town: C. Struik, 1966. 185p.

PRE-20TH-CENTURY FIGURES

Becker, Peter. Path of Blood: The Rise and Conquests of Mzilikazi. London: Longmans, 1962. 289p.

Bhebe, Ngwabi. Lobengula of Zimbabwe. London: Heinemann, 1977. 48p.

387   --Biography

Blair, R. "Selous: a reassessment," Rhodesiana, 17 (1967), 1-26.

Bulpin, Thomas Victor. The White Whirlwind [J. W. Colenbrander].
    London: Nelson, 1961. 343p.

*Colquhoun, Archibald R. Dan to Beersheba: Work and Travel in
    Four Continents. London: W. Heinemann, 1908. 348p.

Colvin, Ian D. The Life of Jameson. 2 vols. London: E. Arnold,
    1923. 314, 352p.

Cooke, Cranmer Kenrick. "Lobengula: second and last king of the
    Amandebele--his final resting place and treasure," Rhodesiana,
    23 (1970), 3-53.

Farrant, Jean. Mashonaland Martyr: Bernard Mizeki and the
    Pioneer Church. Cape Town: OUP, 1966. 258p.

Flint, John. Cecil Rhodes. Boston: Little, Brown, 1974. 268p.

Hassing, Per. "Lobengula," in Norman R. Bennett (ed.), Leader-
    ship in Eastern Africa (Boston: Boston UP, 1968), 221-60.

Henderson, Ian. "Lobengula: achievement and tragedy," Tarikh,
    2, 2 (1968), 53-68.

*Johnson, Frank. Great Days: The Autobiography of an Empire
    Builder. London: G. Bell, 1940. 366p. (Rep., BOR, 1972).

Langham-Carter, R. R. Knight Bruce: First Bishop and Founder
    of the Anglican Church in Rhodesia. Salisbury: Christ-Church,
    Borrowdale, 1975. 72p.

Lockhart, John Gilbert & Alfred Beit. The Will and the Way; Being
    an Account of Alfred Beit and the Trust Which He Founded,
    1906-1956. London: Longmans, Green, 1958. 106p.

_____ & C. M. Woodhouse. Rhodes. London: Hodder & Stough-
    ton, 1963. 511p.

Mauch, Karl. Karl Mauch: African Explorer. Ed. & trans. by
    F. O. Bernard. Cape Town: C. Struick, 1971. 247p.

Millais, J. G. A Life of Frederick Courteney Selous, D.S.O.
    London: Longmans, Green, 1919. 387p. (Rep., Salisbury:
    Pioneer Head, 1975).

Moffat, Robert U. John Smith Moffat, Missionary; A Memoir.
    London: John Murray, 1921. 388p. (Rep., NUP).

Newton, Gwenda. "The go-between--John Grootboom," Rhodesiana,
    29 (1973), 68-75.

Northcott, Cecil. Robert Moffat. London: Lutterworth, 1961. 357p.

Preller, Gustav S. Lobengula: The Tragedy of a Matabele King. Johannesburg: Afrikaanse Pers-Boekhandel, 1963. 318p.

*Ranger, Terence. "The last word on Rhodes?", Past and Present, 28 (July 1964), 116-27.

Rasmussen, R. Kent. "A lost man in southern African history: Kaliphi/Gundwane of the Ndebele," Internat. Jnl. Afr. Hist. Studies, X, 1 (1977), 96-110.

_____. Mzilikazi of the Ndebele. London: Heinemann, 1977. 48p.

Rea, W. F. ["The life of Gonçalo da Silveira, 1526-1560"], Rhodesiana, 6 (1961), 1-40.

_____. "Livingstone's Rhodesian legacy," History Today, 23 (1973), 633-9.

Rouillard, Nancy (ed.). Matabele Thompson: His Autobiography. Rev. ed., South Africa: Central News Agency, Dassie Books, 1957. 160p. (First pub., London: Faber & Faber, 1936. 293p.).

Wallis, John Peter Richard. Thomas Baines of King's Lynn. London: J. Cape, 1941. 351p. (New ed., Cape Town, 1976).

Woollacott, R. C. "Pasipamire--spirit medium of Chaminuka, the 'Wizard' of Chitungwiza," Nada, XI, 2 (1975), 154-67.

20TH-CENTURY FIGURES

Andrews, C. F. John White of Mashonaland. London, 1935. 316p. (Rep., NUP).

*Gann, Lewis H. & Michael Gelfand. Huggins of Rhodesia; The Man and His Country. London: G. Allen & Unwin, 1964. 285p.

Gibbon, Geoffrey. Paget of Rhodesia. Bulawayo: BOR, 1973. 164p.

Joyce, Peter. Anatomy of a Rebel; Smith of Rhodesia. Salisbury: Graham Pub. Co., 1974. 480p.

*Lamont, Donal. Speech from the Dock. London: Kevin Mayhew, 1977. 143p.

Long, B. K. Drummond Chaplin: His Life and Times in Africa. London: OUP, 1941. 373p.

Moyo, Temba. The Organizer: Story of Temba Moyo. Recorded
& ed., by Ole Gjerstad. Richmond, Brit. Col.: Liberat. Support Movement Press, 1974. 85p.

Ndansi Kumalo. "The story of Ndansi Kumalo of the Matabele Tribe,
Southern Rhodesia," recorded by J. W. Posselt & Margery Per-
ham, in M. Perham (ed.), Ten Africans (London: Faber &
Faber, 1936), 63-79.

*Lessing, Doris. Going Home. New York: Popular Library, 1968.
253p. (First pub., London: M. Joseph, 1957).

*Sauer, Hans. Ex Africa. London: Geoffrey Bles, 1937. 336p.
(Rep., BOR, 1973).

*Sithole, Ndabaningi. Letters from Salisbury Prison. Nairobi:
Transafrica, 1976. 186p.

_____. Obed Mutezo: The Mudzimu Christian Nationalist. Intro.
by T. O. Ranger. Nairobi: OUP, 1970. 210p.

Steere, D. V. God's Irregular; Arthur Shearly Cripps. London:
Soc. for the Propagation of Christian Knowledge, 1973. 158p.

Taylor, Don. The Rhodesian: Life of Sir Roy Welensky. London:
Museum Press, 1955. 191p.

*Tredgold, Robert C. The Rhodesia That Was My Life. London:
G. Allen & Unwin, 1968. 271p.

Wallis, John Peter Richard. One Man's Hand: The Story of Sir
Charles Coghlan. London, 1950. (Rep., Bulawayo: BOR,
1972. 254p.).

3.   CULTURE

ART: ANCIENT AND MODERN

Cooke, Cranmer Kenrick. A Guide to the Rock Art of Rhodesia.
Salisbury: Nat. Museums & Monuments, 1974. 64p. illus.

_____. Rock Art of Southern Africa. Cape Town: Books of
Africa, 1969. 166p.

Johnston, I. F. "New Shona sculpture," African Arts, VII, 1
(1973), 87-8.

McEwen, Frank. "Shona art today," African Arts, V, 4 (1972),
8-11.

Polakoff, C. "Contemporary Shona sculpture at the Musée Rodin, Paris," _African Arts_, V, 3 (1972), 57-9.

*Summers, Roger F. H. (ed.). _Prehistoric Rock Art of the Federation of Rhodesia and Nyasaland_. Illus. by Elizabeth Goodall. Salisbury: Nat. Pub. Trust, 1959. 267p.

Woodhouse, H. C. "Rock paintings of southern Africa," _African Arts_, II, 3 (1969), 44-9.

LANGUAGES AND LINGUISTICS

Beeton, D. R. & Helen Dorner. _A Dictionary of English Usage in Southern Africa_. Cape Town: OUP, 1975. 196p.

Bhila, H. H. K. "Munhumutapa: the history and mis-spelling of a Shona term," _Rhod. Hist._, 5 (1974), 79-80.

Cade, S. E. Altken. _Kitchen Kaffir Dictionary_. Salisbury: Central Afr. Press, n.d. 48p.

Dale, D. _A Basic English-Shona Dictionary_. Gwelo: Mambo, 1975. 212p.

_____. _Shona Companion_. Gwelo: Mambo, 1968. 192p.

Doke, Clement Martyn. _A Comparative Study in Shona Phonetics_. Johannesburg: Univ. of Witwatersrand Press, 1931. 298p.

_____. _Report on the Unification of the Shona Dialects_. Hertford, England: Stephen Austin, 1931. 156p.

Fivaz, Derek & Jeannette Ratzlaff. _Shona Language Lessons_. Salisbury: Word of Life Pubs. & Rhod. Literature Bureau, 1969. 169p.

Fortune, George. _Elements of Shona (Zezuru dialect)_. 2nd ed. Salisbury: Longmans, 1967. 286p. (First pub., 1957).

_____. _A Guide to Shona Spelling_. Salisbury: Longman Rhodesia, 1972. 64p.

Hannan, M. _Standard Shona Dictionary_. 2nd ed. Salisbury: Marden, 1972. 996p.

Pelling, James. _A Practical Ndebele Dictionary_. Bulawayo: Daystar Pubs., 1966. 148p.

_____ & Pamela Pelling. _Lessons in Ndebele_. Salisbury: Longman Rhodesia, 1974. 210p.

Rasmussen, R. Kent. "From Cillicaats to Zelkaats: the orthographic odyssey of Mzilikazi," Rhodesiana, 33 (1975), 52-61.

Shenk, J. R. A New Ndebele Grammar. Bulawayo: Brethren in Christ Church, 1971. 229p.

Stevick, Earl W. Shona: Basic Course. Washington: Foreign Service Institute, 1965. 633p.

von Sicard, Harald. "The derivation of the name Mashona," African Studies, 9, 3 (1950), 138-43.

LITERATURE: AFRICAN LANGUAGES

*Chitepo, Herbert W. Soko Risina Musoro. Trans. & ed. by Hazel Carter. London: OUP, 1958. 63p. (Rep. in S. M. Mutswairo, ed., below).

Fortune, George. "75 years of writing in Shona," Zambezia, 1, 1 (1969), 55-67.

_____. "Shona traditional poetry," Zambezia, 2, 1 (1971), 41-60.

_____. "Variety in Shona literature," Nada, X, 4 (1972), 69-76.

Hamutyinei, M. A. & A. B. Plangger (eds.). Tsumo-Shumo: Shona Proverbial Lore and Wisdom. Gwelo: Mambo, 1974. 500p.

Kahari, George P. The Novels of Patrick Chakaipa. Salisbury: Longman Rhodesia, 1972. 110p.

_____. "Tradition and innovation in Shona literature," Zambezia, 2, 2 (1971), 47-54.

_____. "Tradition and innovation in the Shona novel," Nada, XI, 3 (1976), 309-20.

Krog, E. W. African Literature in Rhodesia. Gwelo: Mambo, 1966. 236p.

Lamplough, R. W. Matabele Folk Tales. Cape Town: OUP, 1968. 48p.

*Mutswairo, Solomon M. (ed.). Zimbabwe Prose and Poetry. Washington: Three Continents Press, 1974. 276p.

LITERATURE: ENGLISH LANGUAGE

Brewster, Dorothy. Doris Lessing. New York: Twayne, 1965. 173p.

Brown, G. R., et al. (comps.). Arthur Shearly Cripps: A

Selection of His Prose and Verse. Gwelo: Mambo, 1976.
308p.

*Fairbridge, Kingsley. Kingsley Fairbridge: His Life and Verse.
Bulawayo: BOR, 1974. 246, 118p. (Includes The Life of
Kingsley Fairbridge, first pub., London, 1927).

Finn, D. E. Poetry in Rhodesia: 75 Years. Salisbury: College
Press, 1968. 80p.

*Gouldsbury, Cullen. Rhodesian Rhymes. Bulawayo: BOR, 1969.
264p. (First pub., 1932).

*Lessing, Doris. African Stories. New York: Ballantine, 1966.

Schleuter, Paul. The Novels of Doris Lessing. London & Amster-
dam: Feffer & Simons, 1973.

Snelling, John. A New Anthology of Rhodesian Verse. Oxford:
Blackwell, 1950. 104p.

Steele, Murray C. "Children of Violence" and Rhodesia: A Study
of Doris Lessing as Historical Observer. Salisbury: Cent.
Afr. Hist. Assoc., 1974?

LITERATURE: NOVELS IN ENGLISH

Chalmers, J. Fighting the Matabele. London: Blackie, 1898.
288p.

*Cripps, Arthur Shearly. Africans All. London, 1928.

*Haggard, Henry Rider. Doom of Zimbabwe. London: Hodder &
Stoughton, 1917. 320p.

_____. King Solomon's Mines. London: Cassell, 1885. 320p.

*Hole, Hugh Marshall. Lobengula. London: Philip Allan, 1929.
211p.

Katiyo, Wilson. Going to Heaven. London: Rex Collings, 1978?
c.160p.

*Lessing, Doris. The Grass Is Singing. New York: Balantine,
1964. (First pub., London, 1950).

Mitford, Bertram. John Ames, Native Commissioner; A Romance
of the Matabele Rising. London: F. V. White, 1900. 312p.

Mungoshi, Charles. Waiting for the Rain. London: Heinemann,
1975. 180p.

*Page, Gertrude. Jill's Rhodesian Philosophy. London: Hurst & Blackett, 1910. 230p.

_____. The Rhodesian. London: Hurst & Blackett, 1912. 360p.

Partridge, Nan. Not Alone: A Story for the Future of Rhodesia. Gwelo: Mambo, 1972. 142p.

Rorke, Melina. Melina Rorke--Told by Herself. London: G. G. Harrap, 1939. 284p. (Rep., Bulawayo: BOR, 1971; South Africa: Dassie Books, n.d.).

*Samkange, Stanlake. The Chief's Daughter Who Would Not Laugh. London: Longmans, Green, 1964.

_____. The Mourned One. London: Heinemann, 1975. 150p.

_____. On Trial for My Country. London: Heinemann, 1966. 160p.

_____. The Year of the Uprising. London: Heinemann, 1977. 144p.

*Schreiner, Olive. Trooper Peter Halket of Mashonaland. London: T. Fisher Unwin, 1897. 264p.

*Sithole, Ndabaningi. The Polygamist. London: Hodder & Stoughton, 1972. 178p.

_____. Roots of a Revolution: Scenes from Zimbabwe's Struggle. London: OUP, 1977?

Walker, Ken. The Barrier. Salisbury: Galaxie, 1972. 399p.

MEDIA: BROADCASTING,
PUBLISHING, AND THE PRESS

Dellar, Geoffrey. "The changing pattern of Rhodesian publishing," Rhod. Librarian, I, 3 (1969), 71-6.

Fraenkel, Peter. Wayaleshi: Radio in Central Africa. London: Weidenfeld & Nicholson, 1959. 224p.

Gale, W. D. The Rhodesian Press: The History of the Rhodesian Printing and Publishing Company, Ltd. Salisbury: Rhod. Printing & Pub. Co., 1962. 225p.

Kinloch, Graham C. Flame or Lily: Rhodesian Values as Defined by the Press. Durban: Alpha Graphic, 1970. 134p.

Parker, John. Rhodesia: Little White Island. London: Pitman, 1972. 166p.

*Paver, B. G. His Own Oppressor. London: Peter Davies, 1958.
     235p.

Powell, Jon T. "South-central Africa," in Sydney Head (ed.),
     Broadcasting in Africa (Philadelphia: Temple UP, 1974), 125-
     33.

Smith, M. "Censorship in Rhodesia: the experience of a Salisbury
     editor," Round Table, 59 (London, 1969), 60-7.

Wason, E. Banned: African Daily News, Southern Rhodesia 1964.
     London: H. Hamilton, 1976. 161p.

MUSIC AND DRAMA

Berliner, Paul. "The soul of mbira: an ethnography of the mbira
     among the Shona people of Rhodesia." Ph.D. thesis, Wesleyan
     Univ., Middleton, Conn., 1974. 447p.

Cary, Robert. The Story of Reps: The History of the Salisbury
     Repertory Players. Salisbury: Galaxie, 1975. 240p.

Kauffman, Robert. "Multipart relationships in the Shona music of
     Rhodesia." Ph.D. thesis, Univ. California, Los Angeles, 1970.
     346p.

_____. "Some aspects of aesthetics in the Shona music of Rho-
     desia," Ethnomusicology, XIII, 3 (Middleton, Conn., 1969),
     507-11.

Maraire, Dumisani. The Mbira Music of Rhodesia (booklet with
     record). Seattle: Univ. of Washington Press, 1970.

Taylor, C. T. C. The History of Rhodesian Entertainment, 1890-
     1930. Salisbury: M. O. Collins, 1968. 186p.

Tracey, Andrew. "The Matepe mbira music of Rhodesia," African
     Music, II, 4 (Johannesburg, 1961), 44-63.

Tracey, Hugh T. "The mbira class of African instruments in Rho-
     desia (1932)," African Music, IV, 3 (1969), 78-95.

Wortham, C. J. "The state of the theatre in Rhodesia," Zambezia,
     I, 1 (1969), 47-53.

PHILATELY: POSTAGE STAMPS

Mashonaland Philatelic Society. A Guide to the Postage Stamps of
     the Rhodesias and Nyasaland, 1888-1963. Salisbury: The Soc.,
     1965. 149p.

Smith, Robert C. Rhodesia: A Postal History; Its Stamps, Posts, and Telegraphs. Salisbury: Mardon, 1967. 454p.

_____. A Supplement to Rhodesia: A Postal History. Salisbury: Mardon, 1970. 62p.

4. ECONOMICS

GENERAL

Arrighi, Giovanni. The Political Economy of Rhodesia. The Hague: Mouton, 1967. 60p.

Barber, William J. The Economy of British Central Africa: A Case Study of Economic Development in a Dualistic Society. London: OUP; Stanford, Calif.: Stanford UP, 1961. 271p.

Beach, David N. "Second thoughts on the Shona economy: suggestions for further research," Rhod. Hist., 7 (1976), 1-11.

Clarke, Duncan G. "Public sector economics in Rhodesia: the growth and impact of the public sector," Rhod. Jnl. Econ., VI (1972), 48-60.

Cole, R. L. "Commercial banking in Rhodesia," Rhod. Jnl. Econ., VIII (1974), 55-65.

Davies, C. S. "Tribalism and economic development," Nada, X, 2 (1970), 78-83.

Erbmann, C. A. & J. R. Sheen, "Some reasons for the low rate of inflation in Rhodesia since the UDI," American Economist, XVIII (1974), 99-107.

Le Roux, A. A. "African contribution to the Rhodesian GNP," Rhod. Jnl. Econ., IV (1970), 8-16.

Palmer, Robin & Neil Parsons (eds.). The Roots of Rural Poverty in Central and Southern Africa. London: Heinemann, 1977. c. 320p.

Ramsay, D. I. "Capital and productivity in Rhodesia," Rhod. Jnl. Econ., VIII, 2 (1974), 67-82.

Thompson, Cecil H. & Harry W. Woodruff. Economic Development in Rhodesia and Nyasaland. London: D. Dobson, 1954. 205p.

United States Bureau of Foreign Commerce. Investment in Federation of Rhodesia and Nyasaland; Basic Information for United

States Businessmen.   Washington: U.S. Gov. Printing Office, 1956.   158p.

Walker, R. S.   "The essentials of Rhodesian economic policy," Rhod. Jnl. Econ., V (1971), 25-31.

AGRICULTURE AND ANIMAL HUSBANDRY

*Alvord, Emory D.   "Agricultural life of Rhodesian natives," Nada, 7 (1929), 9-16.

Clements, Frank & Edward Harben.   Leaf of Gold: The Story of Rhodesian Tobacco.   London: Methuen, 1962.

Danckwerts, J. P.   "Technology and economic development of African agriculture in Rhodesia," Rhod. Jnl. Econ., IV, 4 (1970), 17-30.

Duncan, B. H. G.,   "The wages and supply position in European agriculture," Rhod. Jnl. Econ., VII, 1 (1973), 1-13.

Dunlop, Harry.   The Development of European Agriculture in Rhodesia, 1945-1965.   Salisbury: Univ. of Rhod., 1971.   71p.

Le Roux, A. A.   "African agriculture in Rhodesia," Rhod. Agric. Jnl., LXVI (1969), 146-52.

Massell, Benton F. & R. W. M. Johnson.   African Agriculture in Rhodesia: An Econometric Study.   Santa Monica, Calif.:   Rand Corp., 1966.   138p.

Metcalfe, C. B.   A Guide to Farming in Rhodesia.   Salisbury: Rhod. Farmer Pubs., 1971.   166p.

Nobbs, E. A.   "The native cattle of Southern Rhodesia," S. Afr. Jnl. Science, 24 (Dec. 1927), 328-42.

Oliver, J.   Introduction to Dairying in Rhodesia.   Salisbury: Univ. of Rhod., 1971.   152p.

Phillips, John, et al.   The Development of the Economic Resources of Southern Rhodesia with Particular Reference to the Role of African Agriculture.   Salisbury: Gov. Printer, 1962.   484p.

Phimister, Ian R.   "Peasant production and underdevelopment in Southern Rhodesia, 1890-1914," Afr. Affairs, LXXIII (Apr. 1974), 217-28.

Pollak, Oliver B.   "Black farmers and white politics in Rhodesia, 1930-1972," Afr. Affairs, LXXIV (1975), 263-77.

Stocking, M. A.   "Aspects of the role of man in erosion in Rhodesia,"

Zambezia, 2, 2 (1972), 1-10.

Tracey, L. T. Approach to Farming in Southern Rhodesia. London: Univ. of London Press, 1953. 428p.

Weinmann, H. Agricultural Research and Development in Southern Rhodesia, 1890-1923. Salisbury: Univ. of Rhod., 1972. 166p.

_____. Agricultural Research and Development in Rhodesia, 1924-1970. Salisbury: Univ. of Rhod., 1975. 240p.

Weinrich, Anna Katherine Hildegaard. African Farmers in Rhodesia: Old and New Peasant Communities in Karangaland. London: OUP for Internat. Afr. Inst., 1975. 342p.

Yudelman, Montague. Africans on the Land: Economic Problems of African Agricultural Development ... with Special Reference to Southern Rhodesia. Cambridge, Mass.: Harvard UP, 1964. 288p.

COMMERCE AND INTERNATIONAL SANCTIONS

Arnold, Guy. Sanctions Against Rhodesia, 1965-1972. London: Africa Bureau, 1972.

Cole, R. L. "The tariff policy of Rhodesia, 1899-1963, " Rhod. Jnl. Econ., II (1968), 28-47.

Davies, R. J. "Aspects of trade policy in the Federation of Rhodesia and Nyasaland, " Rhod. Jnl. Econ., VII, 3 (1973), 165-72.

Doxey, Margaret P. Economic Sanctions and International Enforcement. London: OUP, 1971. 162p.

Gibson, C. A. "Export development: the mining industry as an exporter, " Rhod. Jnl. Econ., VI (1972), 72-80.

Girdlestone, J. A. C., "The foreign exchange costs of Rhodesian economic development, " Rhod. Jnl. Econ., IV (1970), 31-45.

_____. "A policy for import control, " Rhod. Jnl. Econ., II (1968), 59-69.

Handford, John F. Portrait of an Economy: Rhodesia Under Sanctions. Salisbury, Mercury, 1976. 208p.

Hawkins, R. T. R. "Export development: transport for exports, " Rhod. Jnl. Econ., VI (1972), 49-57.

Irvine, Alexander G. The Balance of Payments of Rhodesia and Nyasaland, 1945-1954. London: OUP, 1959. 643p.

Kapungu, Leonard. The United Nations and Economic Sanctions Against Rhodesia. Lexington, Mass.: D. C. Heath, 1973. 155p.

Le Roux, A. A. "British sanctions legislation," Rhod. Law Jnl., IX (1969), 40-81.

McKinnell, Robert. "Sanctions and the Rhodesian economy," Jnl. Modern Afr. Studies., VII, 4 (1969), 559-81.

Margoles, W. "Export development: agriculture as an exporter," Rhod. Jnl. Econ., VI (1972), 81-7.

Ngwa, Collins Esau Njinta. "The Rhodesian imperial genesis, colonial recalcitrance and sanctions experiment," Ph. D. thesis, Univ. of Massachusetts, Amherst, 1973. 179p.

Park, Stephen & Anthony Lake. Business as Usual; Transactions violating Rhodesian Sanctions. New York: Carnegie Endowment for Internat. Peace, 1973. 54p.

Strack, H. R. Sanctions: The Case of Rhodesia. Syracuse, N. Y.: Syracuse UP, 1977. c.256p.

Wilson, Ewen Maclellan. "An elasticity analysis of the Rhodesian trade embargo." Ph. D. thesis, North Carolina State Univ., Raleigh, 1973. 107p.

INDUSTRY

Abrahamson, A. E. "Industrialisation and employment in Rhodesia," Rhod. Jnl. Econ., III (1969), 24-30.

Association of Rhodesian Industries. The ARNI Register of Manufacturers, 1965-66. Salisbury: Assoc. Rhod. Industries, 1965. 212p.

Cameron, J. D., "Industrial growth and the subsistence economy," Rhod. Jnl. Econ., III (1969), 16-23.

Del's Directory: Who's Who and What's What in Rhodesian Business. Bulawayo: Delwin Pubs., 1969. 302p.

Federation of Rhodesian Industries. Survey of Rhodesian Industry. Salisbury, 1954. 139p.

Graylin, J. C. "Industrial development in Rhodesia," Rhod. Jnl. Econ., III (1969), 38-43.

Harris, Peter S. "Industrial relations in Rhodesia," S. Afr. Jnl. Econ., XLII (1974), 65-84.

McCrystal, L. P. "Dispersal of economic activity and industrial development," Rhod. Jnl. Econ., III (1969), 31-41.

Mussett, B. H. "Rhodesia's industrial policy," Rhod. Jnl. Econ., III (1969), 7-14.

Nowacek, Charles G. "Manpower development and utilization policies and practices in the Rhodesian private sector and their inter-relationships with public policy and the management system," Ph.D. thesis, New York Univ., New York, 1966. 306p.

Resources and Opportunities in the Rhodesias and Nyasaland: A Guide to Commerce and Industry in the Territories. Nairobi & Salisbury: Guides and Handbooks of Africa Pub. Co., 1963. 198p.

Stringer, Brian. "Trade and industry," Rhod. Jnl. Econ., IV (1970), 23-8.

Tow, Leonard. The Manufacturing Economy of Southern Rhodesia: Problems and Prospects. Washington: Nat. Acad. of Sciences, 1960. 141p.

LABOR AND UNIONS

Arrighi, Giovanni. "Labour supplies in historical perspective: a study of the proletarianization of African peasantry in Rhodesia," Jnl. of Development Studies, 6 (1970), 197-234.

Brand, C. M. "Politics and African trade unionism in Rhodesia since Federation," Rhod. Hist., 2 (1974), 88-109.

Chavunduka, G. L. "Farm labourers in Rhodesia," Rhod. Jnl. Econ., VI, 4 (1972), 18-25.

_____. "Labour problems in Rhodesia: farm labourers in Rhodesia," Rhod. Jnl. Econ., VI, 4 (1972), 18-25.

Clarke, Duncan G. Domestic Workers in Rhodesia: The Economics of Masters and Servants. Gwelo: Mambo, 1974. 88p.

Crookes, K. B. "Labour problems in Rhodesia: an employer's viewpoint," Rhod. Jnl. Econ., VI (1972), 1-8.

Dawson, R. "The Rhodesian employment problem: three views; towards a better understanding of manpower supply in Rhodesia," Rhod. Jnl. Econ., VI (1972), 1-20.

Gelfand, Michael. "Migration of African labourers in Rhodesia and Nyasaland, 1890-1914," Cent. Afr. Jnl. Medicine, VII (Aug. 1961), 233-300.

Gussman, B. "Industrial efficiency and the urban African: a study of conditions in Southern Rhodesia," Africa, XXIII, 2 (1953), 135-44.

Harris, Peter S. Black Industrial Workers in Rhodesia. Gwelo: Mambo, 1974. 71p.

_____. "Government policy and African wages in Rhodesia," Zambezia, 2, 2 (1972), 39-45.

_____. "Industrial workers in Rhodesia, 1946-1972," Jnl. So. Afr. Studies, I, 2 (Apr. 1975), 139-61.

_____. "Ten popular myths concerning the employment of labour in Rhodesia," Rhod. Jnl. Econ., VIII (1974), 38-48.

Hooker, J. R. "The African worker in Southern Rhodesia: black aspirations in a white economy, 1927-36," Race, VI, 2 (1964), 142-51.

Mackenzie, J. M. "African labour in the Chartered Company period," Rhod. Hist., 1 (1970), 43-58.

Mitchell, J. C. "Structural plurality, urbanisation and labour circulation in Rhodesia," in J. A. Jackson (ed.), Migrations (Cambridge, England: Cambridge UP, 1969), 156-80.

Mswaka, T. E. "African unemployment and the rural areas of Rhodesia," Rural Africana, 24 (East Lansing, Mich., 1974), 59-73.

Murphree, Marshall W. Employment Opportunities and Race in Rhodesia. Denver: Univ. of Denver, Center on Internat. Race Relations, 1973. 39p.

Phimister, Ian R. "The Shamva mine strike of 1927: an emerging African proletariat," Rhod. Hist., 2 (1971), 65-88.

Pollak, Oliver B. "The impact of the Second World War on African labour organisation in Rhodesia," Rhod. Jnl. Econ., VII, 3 (1973), 121-38.

Riddell, Roger C. "The Salisbury Municipal Worker's Union--a case study," Rhod. Jnl. Econ., VII, 1 (1973), 25-40.

Scott, Peter. "Migrant labour in Southern Rhodesia," Geog. Review, 44, 1 (New York, 1954), 29-48.

*Sithole, Edson. "The African worker in Southern Rhodesia," World Trade Union Movement, X (Paris, Oct. 1958), 17-20.

Steele, Murray C. "White working-class disunity: the Southern Rhodesia Labour Party," Rhod. Hist., 1 (1970), 59-81.

van Onselen, Charles. Chibaro: African Mine Labour in Southern
    Rhodesia, 1900-1933. London: Pluto Press, 1976. 326p.

_____. "The 1912 Wankie colliery strike, " Jnl. Afr. Hist., XV,
    2 (1974), 275-89.

_____. "Worker consciousness in black mines: Southern Rho-
    desia, 1900-1920, " Jnl. Afr. Hist., XIV, 2 (1973), 237-55.

Warhurst, Philip R. "The Tete Agreement, " Rhod. Hist., 1 (1970),
    31-41.

LAND AND LAND POLICY

Bulman, Mary Elizabeth. The Native Land Husbandry Act of
    Southern Rhodesia: A Failure in Land Reform. Salisbury:
    Tribal Areas of Rhod. Research Foundation, 1973. 45p.

Christopher, A. J. "Land tenure in Rhodesia, " S. Afr. Geog.
    Jnl., 13 (1971), 39-52.

Clutton-Brock, Guy. Rekayi Tangwena: Let Tangwena Be. Gwelo:
    Mambo, 1969. 25p.

*Cripps, Arthur Shearly. An African for Africans: A Plea on Be-
    half of Territorial Segregation Areas and of Their Freedom in
    a South African Colony. London: Longmans, Green, 1927.
    203p.

Dunlop, Harry. "Land and economic opportunity in Rhodesia, "
    Rhod. Jnl. Econ., VI, 1 (1972), 1-19.

Fleming, C. J. W. "Systems of land tenure, " Nada, XI, 1 (1974),
    53-63.

Floyd, B. N. "Changing patterns of African land use in Southern
    Rhodesia, " Rhodes-Livingston Jnl., 25 (1959), 20-39.

_____. "Land apportionment in Southern Rhodesia, " Geog. Re-
    view, 12 (New York: Oct. 1962), 566-88.

Garbett, G. K. "The Land Husbandry Act of Southern Rhodesia, "
    in Daniel Biebuyck (ed.), African Agrarian Systems (London:
    OUP, 1961), 185-202.

Hamilton, P. "The changing pattern of African land use in Rho-
    desia, " in J. B. Whitton & P. D. Wood (eds.), Essays in
    Geography for Austin Miller (Reading, England: Reading UP,
    1965), 247-71.

*International Defence and Aid Fund. Rhodesia: The Ousting of the
    Tangwena. London: Christian Action, 1972. 51p.

Johnson, R. W. M.   "Human problems in Central Africa.   Four
    papers on the social and economic problems of the reserves of
    Southern Rhodesia, " Rhodes-Livingstone Jnl. , 36 (1965), 1-108.

Mackenzie, J. M.   "Red soils in Mashonaland: a re-assessment, "
    Rhod. Hist. , 5 (1974), 81-8.

Palmer, Robin H.   Land and Racial Domination in Rhodesia.   Lon-
    don: Heinemann, 1977.   c. 352p.

_____ . "War and land in Rhodesia, " Trans-Afr. Jnl. Hist. , I,
    2 (1971), 43-62.

Rifkind, M. L.   "Land apportionment in perspective, " Rhod. Hist. ,
    3 (1972), 53-62.

Roder, Wolf.   "The division of land resources in Southern Rho-
    desia, " Annals of Assoc. of American Geog. , 54, 1 (1964),
    41-58.

*Samkange, Stanlake John T.   "The establishment of African reserves
    in Matabeleland, 1893-1898."   Ph. D. thesis, Indiana Univ. ,
    1968.   306p.

Weinrich, Anna K. H.   Black and White Elites in Rural Rhodesia.
    Manchester, England: Manchester UP; Totowa, NJ: Rowman
    & Littlefield, 1973.   244p.

*Wrathall, J. J.   "The Tribal Trust Lands: their need for develop-
    ment, " Nada, X (1969), 92-9.

MINING

*Baines, Thomas.   The Gold Regions of South Eastern Africa.   Lon-
    don: E. Stanford, 1968.   187p.   (Rep., Bulawayo: BOR, 1968).

Carlylle-Gall, C.   Mines of Rhodesia.   London: Afr. and Rhod.
    Mines Pub. Co. , 1937.   735p.

Hedley, R. J.   "Industrial growth and the mining industry, " Rhod.
    Jnl. Econ. , III (1969), 29-37.

Huffman, T. N.   "Ancient mining and Zimbabwe, " Jnl. S. Afr.
    Instit. Mining & Metallurgy, LXXIV, 6 (1974), 238-42.

Johnson, James Paul.   The Mineral Industry of Rhodesia.   London:
    Longmans, Green, 1911.   90p.

Nicoll, I. M.   Mining and Industry.   Salisbury: M. O. Collins,
    1973.   35p.

Phimister, Ian R.   "Alluvial gold mining and trade in nineteenth century south central Africa, " Jnl. Afr. Hist., XV, 3 (1974), 445-56.

_____. "Ancient mining near Great Zimbabwe, " Jnl. S. Afr. Instit. Mining & Metallurgy, LXXIV, 6 (1974), 233-7.

_____. "The reconstruction of the Southern Rhodesian gold mining industry, 1903-19, " Econ. Hist. Review, XXIX, 3 (1976), 465-81.

_____. "White mines in historical perspective: Southern Rhodesia, 1890-1953, " Jnl. So. Afr. Studies, III, 2 (1977), 187-206.

*Summers, Roger. Ancient Mining in Rhodesia. Salisbury: Nat. Museums of Rhod., 1969. 236p.

van Onselen, Charles. "The role of collaborators in the Rhodesian mining industry, 1900-1935, " Afr. Affairs, 72 (1973), 401-18.

Wilson, N. D. (comp.). Notes on the Mining Industry of Southern Rhodesia. Salisbury: Gov. Printer, c.1933. 94p.

TRANSPORT AND COMMUNICATIONS

Croxton, Anthony H. Railways of Rhodesia: The Story of the Beira, Mashonaland and Rhodesia Railways. Newton Abbot, England: David & Charles, 1973. 315p.

Hyatt, Stanley Portal. The Old Transport Road. London: A. Melrose, 1914. 301p. (Rep., Bulawayo: BOR, 1969).

Letcher, Owen. When Life Was Rusted Through. New ed., Bulawayo: BOR, 1973. 54p. (First pub., 1934).

McAdam, J. "The birth of an airline: the establishment of Rhodesia and Nyasaland Airways, " Rhodesiana, 21 (1969), 36-50.

*Pauling, George. The Chronicles of a Contractor. Rep. ed., Bulawayo: BOR, 1969. 264p. (First pub., 1926).

Smith, R. Cherer. "The Africa trans-continental telegraph line, " Rhodesiana, 33 (Sept. 1975), 1-18.

Varian, H. F. Some African Milestones. Oxford: Ronald, 1953. 272p. (Rep., Bulawayo: BOR, 1973).

West, John H. "Railway economics in Rhodesia, " Rhod. Jnl. Econ., II (1968), 48-57.

5. HISTORY

GENERAL HISTORIES AND HISTORIOGRAPHY

Baxter, T. W. & R. W. S. Turner. Rhodesian Epic. 3rd ed.,
Cape Town: H. Timmins, 1973. c. 240p. (First pub., 1966).

Beach, David N. "The historiography of the people of Zimbabwe
in the 1960s," Rhod. Hist., 4 (1973), 21-30.

Blake, Robert. A History of Rhodesia. New York: Knopf, 1977.
430p.

Bulpin, Thomas Victor. To the Banks of the Zambezi. London:
Nelson, 1965. 441p.

Cooke, Cranmer Kenrick. "The Commission for the Preservation
of Natural and Historical Monuments and Relics: a history,"
Rhodesiana, 24 (1971), 32-54.

Denoon, Donald, with Balam Nyeko. Southern Africa Since 1800.
London: Longman; New York: Praeger, 1972. 242p.

*Gann, Lewis H. Central Africa: The Former British States.
Englewood Cliffs, NJ: Prentice-Hall, 1971. 180p.

_____. A History of Southern Rhodesia: Early Days to 1934.
London: Chatto & Windus, 1965. 354p.

_____ & Peter Duignan. Burden of Empire: An Appraisal of
Western Colonialism in Africa South of the Sahara. New York:
Praeger, 1967. 435p. (Special ref. to Rhodesia.)

Hanna, Alexander John. The Story of the Rhodesias and Nyasaland.
2nd ed., London: Faber & Faber, 1965 (first pub., 1960).
331p.

Historians in Tropical Africa: Proceedings of the Leverhulme Inter-
Collegiate History Conference Held at the University College of
Rhodesia and Nyasaland, September 1960. Salisbury: Univ.
Coll. of Rhod. & Nyasa., 1962. (Chapters are individually
paginated).

Illustrated Life Rhodesia. All Our Yesterdays, 1890-1970: A Pictorial Review of Rhodesia's Story from the Best of "Illustrated
Life Rhodesia." Salisbury: Graham Pub. Co., 1970. 201p.

Kane, Nora S. The World's View: The Story of Southern Rhodesia.
London: Cassell, 1954. 294p.

*Ranger, Terence O. (ed.). Aspects of Central African History.
London: Heinemann, 1968. 291p.

_____. "The historiography of Southern Rhodesia," Trans-Afr. Jnl. Hist., I, 2 (1971), 63-76.

Ransford, Oliver. The Rulers of Rhodesia: From Earliest Times to the Referendum. London: J. Murray, 1968. 345p.

Rayner, William. The Tribe and Its Successors; An Account of African Traditional Life and European Settlement in Southern Rhodesia. London: Faber & Faber; New York: Praeger, 1962. 239p.

*Rhodesiana Society. "Bulawayo lectures on aspects of Rhodesian history," Rhodesiana, 29 (Dec. 1973), 1-87.

_____. Occasional Paper I: A Record of the Proceedings at a Series of 5 Lectures on Rhodesia, 1896 to 1923. Salisbury: Mashonaland Branch, Rhod. Soc., 1976. 95p.

Shepperson, George. "British Central Africa," in Robin Winks (ed.), The Historiography of the British Empire-Commonwealth (Durham, NC: Duke UP, 1966), 237-47.

Standing, T. G. A Short History of Rhodesia and Her Neighbors. London: Longmans, 1935. 210p.

Stokes, Eric & Richard Brown (eds.). The Zambesian Past: Studies in Central African History. Manchester, England: Manchester UP, 1966. 427p.

Thompson, Leonard M. (ed.). African Societies in Southern Africa: Historical Studies. London: Heinemann, 1969. 336p.

Tindall, P. E. N. A History of Central Africa. New York: Praeger, 1968. 348p.

*Vambe, Lawrence. An Ill-Fated People: Zimbabwe Before and After Rhodes. London: Heinemann, 1972. 254p.

Walker, Eric A. A History of Southern Africa. 3rd ed., London: Longmans, 1957. 973p. (First pub., 1928).

Wills, A. J. An Introduction to the History of Central Africa. 3rd ed., London: OUP, 1973. 450p. (First pub., 1964).

Wright, Harrison M. The Burden of the Present: The Liberal-Radical Controversy over Southern African History. Cape Town: D. Philip; London: R. Collings, 1977. 137p.

LOCAL AND DISTRICT HISTORIES

Beach, David N. "Afrikaner and Shona settlement in the Enkeldoorn area, 1890-1900," Zambezia, 1,2 (1970), 25-34.

Blick, G. A. B. The History of Shamva. Shamva: Rural Council, 1972. 50p.

Bourdillon, Michael F. C. "Peoples of Darwin," Nada, X, 2 (1970), 103-14.

Edwards, J. A. "The Lomagundi District: an historical sketch," Rhodesiana, 7 (1962), 1-21.

Meredith, L. C. "Melsetter District--history of native tribes and chiefs," Nada, XI, 3 (1976), 338-44.

Morris, E. W. "'Marondella's district'--history of native tribes and chiefs," Nada, XI, 4 (1977), 436-42.

Ransford, Oliver. Bulawayo: Historic Battleground of Rhodesia. Cape Town: A. A. Balkema, 1968. 182p.

Robinson, K. R. "A history of the Bikita District," Nada, 34 (1957), 75-87.

Sinclair, Shirley. The Story of Melsetter. Salisbury: M. O. Collins, 1971. 197p.

Tanser, George Henry. A Scantling of Time: The Story of Salisbury, Rhodesia (1890 to 1900). Salisbury: Stuart Manning, 1965. 276p. (Rep., 1975).

_____. A Sequence of Time: The Story of Salisbury, Rhodesia, 1900 to 1914. Salisbury: Pioneer Head, 1974. 299p.

von Sicard, Harald. "The origin of some of the tribes in the Belingwe Reserve," Nada, 25 (1948), 93-104; 27 (1950), 7-19; 28 (1951), 5-25; 29 (1952), 43-64; 30 (1953), 64-71; 32 (1955), 77-92.

White, J. D. "Some notes on the history and customs of the Urungwe District," Nada, X, 3 (1971), 33-72.

Wild, N. C. "A question of succession: Maribeha T. T. L.: Matobo District," Nada, XI, 4 (1977), 415-27.

STONE AGE

Clark, John Desmond. The Prehistory of Southern Africa. Harmondsworth, England: Penquin, 1959. 341p.

Cooke, Cranmer Kenrick. "Evidence of human migrations from the rock art of Southern Rhodesia," Africa, XXXV, 3 (1965), 263-85.

Cooke, Herbert Basil Sutton, Roger Summers, & K. R. Robinson,

"Rhodesian prehistory re-examined," pt. I: "The Stone Age,"
Arnoldia, II, 12 (1966).

Inskeep, R. R. "The late Stone Age in Southern Africa," in W. W.
Bishop & J. D. Clark (eds.), Background to Evolution in Africa
(Chicago, 1967), 557-82.

*Jones, Neville. The Prehistory of Southern Rhodesia: An Account
of the Progress of the Research from 1900 to 1946. Cambridge, England: Cambridge UP, 1949. 77p.

_____. The Stone Age in Rhodesia. London: OUP, 1926. 120p.
(Rep., New York: NUP, 1969).

Sampson, C. Garth. The Stone Age Archaeology of Southern Africa.
New York: Academic Press, 1974. 518p.

IRON AGE: GENERAL

*Bent, James Theodore. The Ruined Cities of Mashonaland: Being
a Record of Excavation and Exploration in 1891. London: Longmans, Green, 1892. 427p. (Reps. of 3rd ed., 1895; Bulawayo:
BOR, 1969; London: Cass, 1975).

Bernhard, F. O. "Notes on the pre-ruin Ziwa culture of Inyanga,"
Rhodesiana, 11 (Dec. 1964), 22-30.

Cooke, Cranmer Kenrick, Roger Summers, & K. R. Robinson.
"Rhodesian prehistory re-examined," pt. II: "The Iron Age,"
Arnoldia, II, 17 (Feb. 1966), 11p.

Crawford, J. R. "The Monk's Kop ossuary," Jnl. Afr. Hist., VIII,
3 (1967), 373-82.

Fagan, Brian M. Southern Africa During the Iron Age. New York:
Praeger, 1965. 222p.

Garlake, Peter S. "Rhodesian ruins--a preliminary assessment of
their styles and chronology," Jnl. Afr. Hist., XI, 4 (1970),
495-513.

_____. "The value of imported ceramics in the dating and inter-
pretation of the Rhodesian Iron Age," Jnl. Afr. Hist., IX, 1
(1968), 13-33.

*Hall, Richard N. Prehistoric Rhodesia: An Examination of the
Historical, Ethnological and Archaeological Evidences as to the
Origin and Age of the Rock Mines and Stone Buildings....
London: Unwin, 1909. 488p.

_____ & W. G. Neal. The Ancient Ruins of Rhodesia (Monomotopae

Imperium). London: Methuen, 1902. 396p. (Reps., 2nd ed., 1904; Bulawayo: BOR, 1972; New York: NUP).

Huffman, Thomas N. The Leopard's Kopje Tradition. Salisbury: Nat. Museums and Monuments of Rhod., 1975. 155p.

_____. "The linguistic affinities of the Iron Age in Rhodesia," Arnoldia, VII, 7 (1974), 1-11.

Jaffey, A. J. E. "A reappraisal of the history of the Rhodesian Iron Age up to the fifteenth century," Jnl. Afr. Hist., VII, 2 (1966), 189-95.

Lancaster, C. S. & A. Pohorilenko, "Ingombe Ilede and the Zimbabwe culture," Internat. Jnl. Afr. Hist. Studies, X, 1 (1977), 1-30.

*Randall-MacIver, David. Mediaeval Rhodesia. London: Macmillan, 1906. 106p. (Reps., New York: NUP, 1969; London: Cass).

Robinson, Keith Radcliffe. "The Leopard's Kopje culture; its position in the Iron Age of Southern Rhodesia," S. Afr. Arch. Bullet. XXI, pt. I, 81 (March 1966), 5-51.

_____, et al. Khami Ruins: Report on Excavations ... 1947-1955. Cambridge: Cambridge UP, 1959. 192p.

*Summers, Roger F. H. Ancient Ruins and Vanished Civilizations of Southern Africa. Cape Town: T. V. Bulpin, 1971. 246p.

_____. Inyanga: Prehistoric Settlements in Southern Rhodesia. Cambridge: Cambridge UP, 1958. 336p.

*Wilmot, Alexander. Monomotopa (Rhodesia); Its Monuments, and Its History from the most Ancient Times to the Present Century. London: T. Fisher Unwin, 1896. 259p. (Rep., New York: NUP, 1969).

IRON AGE: ZIMBABWE RUINS
AND "ZIMBABWE CONTROVERSY"

*Caton-Thompson, Gertrude. The Zimbabwe Culture: Ruins and Reactions. Oxford: Clarendon, 1931. 299p. (Rep., New York: NUP; 2nd ed. with new intro. by author, London: Cass, 1971. 304p.).

_____. "Zimbabwe, all things considered," Antiquity, XXXVIII, 150 (June 1964), 99-102.

Chanaiwa, David. The Zimbabwe Controversy: A Case of Colonial Historiography. Syracuse, N.Y.: Syracuse Univ. Eastern Afr. Studies Program, 1973. 142p.

Fagan, Brian M. "Zimbabwe--a century of discovery, " Afr. Arts,
    II, 3 (1969), 20-4.

Garlake, Peter S. Great Zimbabwe. New York: Stein & Day,
    1973. 224p.

_____. The Ruins of Zimbabwe. Lusaka: Hist. Assoc. Zambia,
    1974. 46p. (Synopsis of his Great Zimbabwe.)

_____. "The Zimbabwe ruins re-examined, " Rhod. Hist., 1
    (1970), 17-29.

*Hall, Richard N. Great Zimbabwe, Mashonaland, Rhodesia; An Ac-
    count of Two Years' Examination Work in 1902-4.... London:
    Methuen, 1905. 459p. (Reps., New York: NUP; London:
    Cass).

Huffman, Thomas N. "Great Zimbabwe: a review article, " Rho-
    desiana, 29 (Dec. 1973), 88-92.

_____. "The rise and fall of Zimbabwe, " Jnl. Afr. Hist., XIII,
    3 (1972), 253-66.

*Summers, Roger. Zimbabwe: A Rhodesian Mystery. London:
    Nelson, 1963. 120p.

_____, K. R. Robinson, & A. Whitty. "Zimbabwe excavations,
    1958, " Occ. Papers Nat. Museum S. Rhod., 23A (Dec. 1961),
    157-332.

Tindall, P. E. N. "Great Zimbabwe in recent literature, " Rhod.
    Hist., 4 (1973), 93-104.

Wieschhoff, Heinrich A. The Zimbabwe-Monomotapa Culture in
    South-East Africa. Menasha, Wisc.: G. Banta Pub. Co.,
    1941. 115p.

*Willoughby, John Christopher. A Narrative of Further Excavations
    at Zimbabwe (Mashonaland). London: Philip & Son, 1893.
    43p.

SHONA HISTORY (Early and General)

*Abraham, Donald P. "Ethno-history of the empire of Mutapa, " in
    Jan Vansina, et al. (eds.), The Historian in Tropical Africa
    (London: OUP, 1964), 104-26.

_____. "Maramuca: an exercise in the combined use of Portu-
    guese records and oral tradition, " Jnl. Afr. Hist., II, 2 (1961),
    211-25.

_____. "The Monomotapa dynasty, " Nada, 36 (1959), 58-84.

_____. "The principality of Maungwe: its history and traditions,"
Nada, 28 (1951), 56-83.

Alpers, Edward A. "Dynasties of the Mutapa-Rozwi complex," Jnl.
Afr. Hist., XI, 2 (1970), 203-20.

Beach, David N. "Mutapa: an alternative approach to the study of
titles in Shona history," Rhod. Hist., 6 (1975), 97-9.

_____. "The Mutapa dynasty: a comparison of traditional and
documentary evidence," Hist. in Africa, 3 (1976), 1-17.

Bhila, Hoyini H. K. "The Manyika and the Portuguese, 1575-1863."
Ph.D. thesis, Univ. of London, 1971. 278p.

_____. "Trade and the survival of an African polity: the ex-
ternal relations of Manyika from the 16th to the early 19th
century," Rhod. Hist., III (1972), 11-28.

Chanaiwa, David. "A history of the Nhowe before 1900." Ph.D.
thesis, Univ. of Calif., Los Angeles, 1971. 286p.

_____. "Politics and long-distance trade in the Mwene Mutapa
empire during the 16th century," Internat. Jnl. Afr. Hist.
Studies, V, 3 (1972), 424-35.

Chidziwa, Joshua. "History of the Vashawasha," Nada, IX, 1 (1964),
16-33.

Edwards, William. "The Wanoe: a short historical sketch," Nada,
4 (1926), 13-28.

Hughes, A. J. B. (ed.). Duma Texts: Report on the Mukanganwi
People.... Compiled & trans. by J. O. Gandari. 2nd ed.,
Salisbury: Tribal Areas of Rhod. Research Foundat., 1975.
77p.

Latham, C. J. K. "Munhumutapa: oral traditions," Nada, X, 4
(1972), 77-82.

Machiwanyika, Jason. "Extracts from 'A History and customs of the
Manyika People,'" trans. by R. E. Reid, Nada, XI, 3 (1976),
300-8.

Mudenge, S. I. "An identification of the Rozvi and its implications
for the history of the Karanga," Rhod. Hist., 5 (1974), 19-31.

_____. "The role of foreign trade in the Rozvi empire: a re-
appraisal," Jnl. Afr. Hist., XV, 3 (1974), 373-91.

Mutunhu, Tendai. "The rise of the Mwenemutapa empire from 450-
1696: a politico-military history of its founding by the Mbire,"
Jnl. So. Afr. Affairs, II, 2 (1977), 183-215.

Randles, W. G. L. L'Empire du Monomotapa du XVe au XIXe
    Siècle. Paris: Mouton, 1975. 167p.

Storry, J. G. "The settlement and territorial expansion of the
    Mutasa dynasty," Rhod. Hist., 7 (1976), 13-30.

Sutherland-Harris, Nicola. "Trade and the Rozwi mambo," in
    Richard Gray & David Birmingham (eds.), Pre-Colonial African
    Trade (London: OUP, 1970), 243-64.

von Sicard, Harald. "The Dumbuseya," Nada, IX, 5 (1968), 22-38.

_____. "The Jawunda," Nada, 36 (1959), 103-28.

EARLY PORTUGUESE ACTIVITIES

Axelson, Eric. Portuguese in South-East Africa, 1488-1600. Cape
    Town: C. Struik, 1973. 276p.

_____. The Portuguese in South-East Africa, 1600-1700. Johan-
    nesburg: Witwatersrand UP, 1960. 226p.

Chirenje, J. Mutero. "Portuguese priests and soldiers in Zimbabwe,
    1560-1572," Internat. Jnl. Afr. Hist. Studies, VI, 1 (1973),
    36-48.

Devlin, Christopher. "The Mashona and the Portuguese," Month,
    XXV, 3 (London, March 1961), 140-51.

Dickinson, R. W. "Antonio Fernandes--a reassessment," Rhodesiana,
    25 (1971), 45-53.

Documentos Sobre os Portugueses em Moçambique e na Africa
    Central/Documents on the Portuguese in Mozambique and Cen-
    tral Africa, 1497-1840. Lisboa: Centro de Estudos Hist. Ul-
    tramarinos; Salisbury: Nat. Arch. Rhod., 1962+. (8 vols.
    pub. through 1975).

Garlake, Peter S. "Excavations at the 17th century Portuguese
    site at Dambarare," Proc. Rhod. Scien. Assoc., 54 (1969),
    23-61.

_____. "Seventeenth century Portuguese earthworks in Rhodesia,"
    S. Afr. Arch. Bullet., XXI, pt. 4, 84 (Jan. 1967), 157-70.

Godlonton, W. A. "The journeys of António Fernandes...," Proc.
    & Trans. Rhod. Scien. Assoc., 40 (April 1945), 71-103; 48
    (Aug. 1960), 44-8.

Mudenge, S. I. "Eighteenth century Portuguese settlements on the
    Zambezi and the dating of the Rhodesian ruins...," Internat.
    Jnl. Afr. Hist. Studies (1976?).

Newitt, M. D. D. Portuguese Settlement on the Zambesi. New
    York: Africana Pub. Co., 1973. 434p.

Theal, George McCall (ed.). Records of South-Eastern Africa.
    9 vols. London: Printed for the Govt. of the Cape Colony,
    1898-1903.

THE 19TH CENTURY (Contemporary and Modern Works)

*Baines, Thomas. The Northern Goldfields Diaries of Thomas
    Baines. Ed. by J. P. R. Wallis. London: Chatto & Windus,
    1946. 3 vols.

Beach, D. N. "Ndebele raiders and Shona power," Jnl. Afr. Hist.,
    XV, 4 (1974), 633-51.

Bhebe, N. M. B. "Some aspects of Ndebele relations with the
    Shona in the 19th century," Rhod. Hist., 4 (1973), 31-8.

Bhila, H. H. K. "Manyika's relationship with the Portuguese and
    the Gaza-Nguni from 1832-1890," Rhod. Hist., 7 (1976), 31-7.

Burke, E. E. "The southern approach to the 'Far Interior,'"
    Rhodesiana, 33 (Sept. 1975), 19-31.

Cairns, H. Alan C. Prelude to Imperialism: British Reactions to
    Central African Society, 1840-1890. London: Routledge &
    Kegan Paul, 1965. 330p.

*Coillard, François. On the Threshold of Central Africa. London:
    Hodder & Stoughton, 1896. 646p. (Rep. of 3rd ed., London:
    Cass).

*Finaughty, William. The Recollections of an Elephant Hunter, 1864-
    1875. 2nd ed. with new material, ed. by E. C. Tabler. Cape
    Town: A. A. Balkema, 1957. 244p. (First pub., Philadel-
    phia, 1916; rep. of 2nd ed., Bulawayo: BOR, 1973).

*Leask, Thomas. The Southern African Diaries of Thomas Leask,
    1865-1870. Ed. by J. P. R. Wallis. London: Chatto &
    Windus, 1954. 253p.

*Mackenzie, John. Ten Years North of the Orange River ... 1859-
    1869. Edinburgh: Edmonston & Douglas, 1871. 523p. (Rep.
    of 3rd ed., London: Cass. Abridged as Day-Dawn in Dark
    Places. London: 1883; rep., New York: NUP, 1969).

*Mauch, Karl. The Journals of Carl Mauch, 1869-1872. Trans. by
    F. O. Bernhard; ed. by E. E. Burke. Salisbury: Nat. Arch.
    Rhod., 1969. 314p.

*Moffat, Robert. The Matabele Journals of Robert Moffat, 1829-1860.

Ed. by J. P. R. Wallis. London: Chatto & Windus, 1945. 2 vols. 382, 295p. (Rep., 1977).

Mohr, Eduard. To the Victoria Falls of the Zambesi. Trans. by N. D'Anvers. London: Sampson, Low, 1876. 462p. (Rep., Bulawayo: BOR, 1973).

Oates, Frank. Matabele Land and the Victoria Falls. Ed. by C. G. Oates. London: C. Kegan Paul, 1881. 383p. (Rep., Salisbury: Pioneer Head, 1971).

*Selous, Frederick Courteney. A Hunter's Wanderings in Africa. London: R. Bentley, 1881. 455p. (Rep., Bulawayo: BOR, 1971).

_____. Travel and Adventure in South-East Africa. London: R. Ward, 1893. 503p. (Reps., Bulawayo: BOR, 1972; Salisbury: Pioneer Head).

Stabb, Henry. To the Victoria Falls via Matabeleland: The Diary of Major Henry Stabb, 1875. Ed. by E. C. Tabler. Cape Town: C. Struik, 1967. 268p.

*Tabler, Edward C. The Far Interior: Chronicles of Pioneering in the Matabele and Mashona Countries, 1847-1879. Cape Town: A. A. Balkema, 1955. 443p.

_____ (ed.). Zambezia and Matabeleland in the Seventies: The Narrative of Frederick Hugh Barber, 1875 and 1877-1878; and the Journal of Richard Frewen, 1877-1878. London: Chatto & Windus, 1960. 212p.

*Thomas, Thomas Morgan. Eleven Years in Central South Africa. London: John Snow, 418p. (Reps., Bulawayo: BOR, 1970; London: Cass, 1971).

NDEBELE KINGDOM

Beach, D. N. "Ndebele history in 1971 [rev. art.], Rhod. Hist., 1 (1970), 87-94.

Bhebe, Ngwabi M. B. "Ndebele trade in the 19th century," Jnl. Afr. Studies, I, 1 (Los Angeles, 1974), 87-100.

Brown, Richard. The Ndebele Succession Crisis, 1868-1877. Salisbury: Cent. Afr. Hist. Assoc., 1966. 18p. (First pub. in Historians in Tropical Africa, 1962).

*Carnegie, David. Among the Matabele. London: Relig. Tract Soc., 1894. 128p. (Rep., New York: NUP).

Chanaiwa, David. "The army and politics in pre-industrial Africa:

the Ndebele nation, 1822-1893," Afr. Studies Rev., XIX, 2 (Sept. 1976), 49-68.

Cobbing, Julian. "The evolution of Ndebele Amabutho," Jnl. Afr. Hist., XV, 4 (1974), 607-31.

_____. "The Ndebele under the Khumalos, 1820-1896." Ph.D. thesis, Univ. of Lancaster, 1976. 504p.

*Elliott, William A. Gold From the Quartz. London: London Miss. Soc., 1910. 223p.

Lye, William F. "The Ndebele kingdom south of the Limpopo River," Jnl. Afr. Hist., X, 1 (1969), 87-104.

Mhlagazanhlansi [pseud., Neville Jones*]. My Friend Kumalo. Bulawayo: Rhod. Printing & Pub. Co., c.1945. 54p. (Rep., Bulawayo: BOR, 1972).

Mutunhu, Tendai. "The Matabele nation: the dynamic socio-political & military development of an African state, 1840-1893," Jnl. Afr. Studies, III, 2 (1976), 165-82.

'Mziki [pseud. for A. A. Campbell*]. 'Mlimo: The Rise and Fall of the Matabele. Pietermaritzburg: The Natal Witness, 1926 (New ed., Bulawayo: BOR, 1972. 193p).

Ndlovu, Callistus Phios. "Missionaries and traders in the Ndebele kingdom: an African response to colonialism, a case study, 1859-1890." Ph.D. thesis, State Univ. of New York, Stony Brook, 1973. 316p.

*Posselt, F. W. T. Upengula the Scatterer; or, Lobengula and the Amandebele. Bulawayo: Rhod. Printing & Pub. Co., 1945. 140p.

Rasmussen, R. Kent. Migrant Kingdom: Mzilikazi's Ndebele in South Africa. London: R. Collings; Cape Town: D. Philip; Totowa, N.J.: Rowman & Littlefield, 1978. 262p.

_____. "Mzilikazi's migrations south of the Limpopo, c.1821-1827: a re-assessment," Trans-Afr. Jnl. Hist., V, 1 (1976), 52-74.

Storry, J. G. The Shattered Nation. Cape Town: H. Timmins, 1974. 175p.

*Summers, Roger & C. W. Pagden. The Warriors. Cape Town: Books of Africa, 1970. 181p.

MFECANE INVASIONS

Bryant, A. T. Olden Times in Zululand and Natal. London: Longmans, 1929. 710p. (Rep., Cape Town: C. Struik, 1965).

Fleming, C. J. W. "The Swazi in Rhodesia," Nada, X, 3 (1971), 3-7.

Liesegang, Gerhard J. "Aspects of Gaza Nguni history, 1821-1897," Rhod. Hist., 6 (1975), 1-14.

_____. "Nguni migrations between Delagoa Bay and the Zambezi, 1821-1839," Afr. Hist. Studies, III, 2 (1970), 317-37.

Omer-Cooper, J. D. The Zulu Aftermath: A Nineteenth Century Revolution in Bantu Africa. London: Longmans; Evanston, Ill.: Northwestern UP, 1966. 208p.

EUROPEAN CONTACT ERA, 1880s-1890s

Beach, D. N. "The Adendorff Trek in Shona history," S. Afr. Hist. Jnl., 3 (Nov. 1971).

Blennerhassett, Rose & Lucy Sleeman. Adventures in Mashonaland. New York: Macmillan, 1893. 340p. (Rep., Bulawayo: BOR, 1969).

*Brown, William Harvey. On the South African Frontier. London: Sampson, Low, 1899. 430p. (Reps., Bulawayo: BOR, 1970; New York: NUP).

Cary, Robert. Charter Royal. Cape Town: H. Timmins, 1970. 192p.

_____. A Time to Die. Cape Town: H. Timmins, 1968. 179p.

Cobbing, J. R. D. "Lobengula, Jameson and the occupation of Mashonaland, 1890," Rhod. Hist., 4 (1973), 39-56.

_____. "The unknown fate of the Rudd Concession rifles," Rhod. Hist., 3 (1972), 77-81.

Cooper-Chadwick, J. Three Years with Lobengula, and Experiences in South Africa. London: Cassell, 1894. 160p. (Rep., Bulawayo: BOR, 1975).

Darter, Adrian. The Pioneers of Mashonaland. London: Simpkin, Marshall, Hamilton, Kent, 1914. 213p. (Rep., Bulawayo: BOR, 1977).

Devlin, Christopher. "The Mashona and the British," Month, XXV, 1 (London, April 1961), 197-208.

De Waal, D. C. With Rhodes in Mashonaland. Trans. by J. H. H.

De Waal.   Cape Town: Juta, 1896.   351p.   (Rep., Bulawayo: BOR, 1974).

Frippe, C. E. & V. W. Hiller (eds.).   Gold and the Gospel in Mashonaland, 1888 [the jnls. of C. D. Rudd & G. W. H. Knight-Bruce].   London: Chatto & Windus, 1949.   246p.

Gibbs, Peter.   A Flag for the Matabele.   London: F. Muller, 1955.   192p.

Hensman, Howard.   A History of Rhodesia, Compiled From Official Sources.   London: Blackwood, 1900.   381p.   (Rep., New York: NUP).

*Hole, Hugh Marshall.   The Jameson Raid.   London: P. Allan, 1930.   306p.   (Rep., Bulawayo: BOR, 1973).

_____.   The Making of Rhodesia.   London: Macmillan, 1926. 415p.   (Reps., New York: Barnes & Noble, 1967; London: Cass, 1967).

_____.   Old Rhodesian Days.   London: Macmillan, 1928.   140p. (Rep., London: Cass, 1968).

Knight, Edward Frederick.   Rhodesia of Today: A Description of the Prospects of Matabeleland and Mashonaland.   London, 1895. 151p.   (Reps., Bulawayo: BOR, 1975; New York, NUP).

Mason, Philip.   The Birth of a Dilemma: The Conquest and Settlement of Rhodesia.   London: OUP, 1958.   366p.

Mathers, Edward Peter.   Zambesia, England's El Dorado in Africa....   London: King, Sell, & Railton; Cape Town: Juta, 1891.   480p.   (Rep., Bulawayo: BOR, 1977).

Phimister, Ian R.   "Rhodes, Rhodesia, and the Rand," Jnl. So. Afr. Studies, I, 1 (1974), 74-90.

*Ranger, Terence O.   "The rewriting of African history during the Scramble: the Matabele dominance in Mashonaland," Afr. Soc. Research, IV (Dec. 1967), 271-82.

*Samkange, Stanlake.   Origins of Rhodesia.   London: Heinemann; New York: Praeger, 1969.   304p.

Vaughan-Williams, Herbert Wynne.   A Visit to Lobengula in 1889. Pietermaritzburg: Shuter & Shooter, 1947.   192p.

Warhurst, Philip R.   Anglo-Portuguese Relations in South-Central Africa, 1890-1900.   London: Longmans, 1962.   169p.

*Wood, Joseph Garbett.   Through Matabeleland: The Record of a Ten Months' Trip in an Ox-Wagon.   London: Richards, Glan-

ville; Grahamstown: Grocott & Sherry, 1893. 198p. (Rep.,
Bulawayo: BOR, 1974).

AFRICAN ARMED RESISTANCE
TO EUROPEAN OCCUPATION

*Alderson, E. A. H. With the Mounted Infantry and the Mashonaland
Field Force, 1896. London: Methuen, 1898. 308p. (Rep.,
Bulawayo: BOR, 1971. 295p.).

*Baden-Powell, R. S. S. The Matabele Campaign, 1896. London:
Methuen, 1897. 500p. (Rep., New York: NUP, 1970).

Beach, David N. "The rising in south-western Mashonaland, 1896-
7." Ph.D. thesis, Univ. of London, 1971. 476p.

Bond, Geoffrey. Remember Mazoe. The Reconstruction of an Incident. Salisbury: Pioneer Head, 1973. 164p.

*British South Africa Company. Reports on the Native Disturbances
in Rhodesia, 1896-7. Printed for the information of shareholders. London: BSAC, 1898. 160p. (Rep. as The '96 Rebellions. Bulawayo: BOR, 1975).

*Burnham, Frederick Russell. Scouting on Two Continents. Garden
City, NY: Garden City Pub. Co., 1926. 370p. (Rep., Bulawayo: BOR, 1975).

Cobbing, Julian. "The absent priesthood: another look at the Rhodesian risings of 1896-1897," Jnl. Afr. Hist., XVIII, 1 (1977),
61-84.

Dachs, Anthony J. "The course of African resistance in Southern
Rhodesia" [rev. art.], Rhod. Hist., 1 (1970), 95-101.

Glass, Stafford. The Matabele War. London: Longmans, 1968. 308p.

Green, Elsa Goodwin. Raiders and Rebels in South Africa. London:
G. Newnes, 1898. 208p. (Rep., Bulawayo: BOR, 1976).

Laing, D. Tyrie. The Matabele Rebellion, 1896; With the Belingwe
Field Force. London: Dean, 1897. 327p.

Leonard, Arthur Glyn. How We Made Rhodesia. London: Kegan
Paul, 1896. 364p. (Rep., Bulawayo: BOR, 1973. 356p.).

Norris-Newman, Charles L. Matabeleland and How We Got It; With
Notes on the Occupation of Mashunaland. London: Unwin, 1895.
243p.

O'Reilly, John. Pursuit of the King: An Evaluation of the Shangani
Patrol. Bulawayo: BOR, 1970. 218p.

*Plumer, Herbert Charles. An Irregular Corps in Matabeleland. London: Kegan Paul, 1897. 250p.

*Ranger, Terence O. "African reactions to the imposition of colonial rule in east and central Africa," in L. H. Gann & Peter Duignan (eds.), The History and Politics of Colonialism, 1870-1914 (Cambridge, England: Cambridge UP, 1969), 293-324.

_____. Revolt in Southern Rhodesia, 1896-7. London: Heinemann; Evanston: Northwestern UP, 1967. 403p.

*Selous, Frederick Courteney. Sunshine and Storm in Rhodesia ... A Narrative of Events in Matabeleland. London: R. Ward, 1896. 290p. (Reps., Bulawayo: BOR, 1968; New York: NUP).

Stigger, P. "Volunteers and the profit motive in the Anglo-Ndebele War, 1893," Rhod. Hist., 2 (1971), 11-23.

Sykes, Frank William. With Plumer in Matabeleland. London: A. Constable, 1897. 296p. (Reps., Bulawayo: BOR, 1972; New York: NUP).

Tsomondo, Madziwanyika. "Shona reaction and resistance to the European colonization of Zimbabwe, 1890-1898," Jnl. So. Afr. Affairs, II, 1 (1977), 11-32.

Wills, William Arthur & Leonard Thomas Collingridge (eds.). The Downfall of Lobengula: The Cause, History, and Effect of the Matabeli War. London: The African Review, 1894. 335p. (Reps., Bulawayo: BOR, 1971, 347p. New York: NUP).

ERA OF BSAC RULE, 1890-1923

Chanock, Martin. Unconsummated Union: Britain, Rhodesia and South Africa, 1900-1945. Manchester, England, 1977. c.320p.

Di Perna, Anthony Paul. "The struggle for self-government and the roots of white nationalism in Rhodesia, 1890-1922." Ph.D. thesis, St. John's Univ., Jamaica, NY, 1972. 410p.

Ferguson, Fergus W. Southern Rhodesia: An Account of Its Past History, Present Development, Natural Riches, and Future Prospects. With Special Particulars for Intending Settlers. London: W. H. & L. Collingridge, 1907. 327p.

Galbraith, John S. Crown and Charter: The Early Years of the British South Africa Company. Berkeley: Univ. of Calif. Press, 1974. 354p.

Harris, John Hobbis. The Chartered Millions: Rhodesia and the Challenge to the British Commonwealth. London: Swarthmore, 1920. 320p.

Hodder-Williams, R.   "The British South Africa Company in Marandellas: some extra-institutional constraints, " Rhod. Hist., 2
(1971), 39-63.

Hone, Percy Frederick.   Southern Rhodesia.   London: G. Bell,
1909.   406p.   (Rep., New York: NUP, 1969).

Lee, M. Elaine.   "The origins of the Rhodesian Responsible Government Movement, " Rhod. Hist., 6 (1975), 33-52.

_____.   "Politics and pressure groups in Southern Rhodesia,
1898-1923."   Ph.D. thesis, Univ. of London, 1974.

*Maguire, James Rochfort.   The Pioneers of Empire.   Being a Vin-
dication of the Principle, and a Short Sketch of the History of
Chartered Companies, with Special Reference to the British
South Africa Company.   London: Methuen, 1896.   139p.

Malcolm, Dougal O.   The British South Africa Company, 1889-1939.
London: BSAC, 1939.   73p.

Palmer, Robin H.   "Johnston and Jameson: a comparative study in
the imposition of colonial rule, " in Bridglal Pachai (ed.), The
Early History of Malawi (London: Longmans, 1972), 293-322.

*Ranger, Terence O.   The African Voice in Southern Rhodesia, 1898-
1930.   London: Heinemann; Nairobi: East Afr. Pub. House,
1970.   252p.

*Tawse-Jollie, Ethel.   The Real Rhodesia.   London: Hutchinson,
1924.   304p.   (Rep., Bulawayo: BOR, 1971).

Warhurst, Philip R.   "Rhodesian-South African relations, 1900-23, "
S. Afr. Hist. Jnl., III (Nov. 1971), 92-108.

BRITISH CROWN COLONY PERIOD, 1923-1965

Baldock, R. W.   "Sir John Chancellor and the Moffat succession, "
Rhod. Hist., 3 (1972), 41-52.

Chanaiwa, David.   "The premiership of Garfield Todd in Rhodesia:
racial partnership vs. colonial interests, 1953-1958, " Jnl. So.
Afr. Affairs, I (Oct. 1976), 83-94.

Clements, Frank.   Rhodesia: A Study of the Deterioration of a
White Society.   New York: Praeger, 1969.   286p.

Day, John.   "Southern Rhodesian African nationalists and the 1961
constitution, " Jnl. Mod. Afr. Studies, VII, 2 (1969), 221-47.

Gale, William Daniel.   The Years Between.   1923-1973.   Half a

Century of Responsible Government in Rhodesia. Salisbury: H. C. P. Andersen, 1973. 92p.

Gibbs, Peter. Landlocked Island: A Commentary on Southern Rhodesia. Bulawayo: Philpott & Collins, 1947. 120p.

Gray, Richard. The Two Nations: Aspects of the Development of Race Relations in the Rhodesias and Nyasaland. London: OUP, 1960. 373p.

Hancock, I. R. "Sane and pragmatic liberalism: the Action Group in Bulawayo, 1955-1965," Rhod. Hist., 7 (1976), 65-83.

Leys, Colin. European Politics in Southern Rhodesia. Oxford: Clarendon, 1959. 323p.

Tsomondo, Micah S. "Major factors in the making of Rhodesia," Ufahamu, V, 3 (Los Angeles, 1975), 119-34.

*Vambe, Lawrence. From Rhodesia to Zimbabwe. London: Heinemann, 1976. 290p.

Wetherell, H. I. "N. H. Wilson: populism in Rhodesian politics," Rhod. Hist., 6 (1975), 53-76.

Windrich, Elaine. The Rhodesian Problem: A Documentary Record, 1923-1973. London: Routledge & Kegan Paul, 1975. 312p.

Zvobgo, Chengetai J. M. "Southern Rhodesia under Edgar Whitehead: 1958-1962," Jnl. So. Afr. Affairs, II, 4 (1977), 481-92.

FEDERATION, 1953-1963

Clegg, Edward M. Race and Politics; Partnership in the Federation of Rhodesia and Nyasaland. London & New York: OUP, 1960. 280p.

Creighton, Thomas R. M. The Anatomy of Partnership; Southern Rhodesia and the Central African Federation. London: Faber & Faber, 1960. 257p.

Dunn, Cyril. Central African Witness. London: V. Gollancz, 1959. 254p.

Franck, Thomas M. The Struggle for Power in Rhodesia-Nyasaland. New York: Fordham UP, 1960. 369p.

Franklin, Harry. Unholy Wedlock; The Failure of the Central African Federation. London: G. Allen & Unwin, 1963. 239p.

Gibbs, Peter. Avalanche in Central Africa. London: Barker, 1961. 169p.

Gray, James Andrew (ed.). Rhodesia & Nyasaland: A Survey of the Central African Federation. London: Marshall, 1957. 80p.

Keatley, Patrick. The Politics of Partnership. Baltimore: Penguin, 1963. 528p.

Leys, Colin & Cranford Pratt (eds.). A New Deal in Central Africa. New York: Praeger, 1960. 226p.

Mason, Philip. Year of Decision; Rhodesia and Nyasaland in 1960. London: OUP, 1960. 282p.

Phillips, Cecil E. Lucas. The Vision Splendid. London: Heinemann, 1960. 384p.

Sanger, Clyde. Central African Emergency. London: Heinemann, 1960. 342p.

Spiro, Herbert J. "The Rhodesias & Nyasaland," in Gwendolen M. Carter (ed.), Five African States (Ithaca, N.Y.: Cornell UP, 1963), 361-470.

*Welensky, Roy. Welensky's 4,000 Days. London: Collins, 1964. 383p.

UDI, 1965+ [see also 6. POLITICS]

Barber, James. Rhodesia: The Road to Rebellion. London: OUP, 1967. 338p.

Callinicos, Alex & John Rogers. Southern Africa After Soweto. London: Pluto Press, 1977. 229p.

Hirsch, Morris I. A Decade of Crisis: Ten Years of Rhodesian Front Rule (1963-1972). Salisbury: Peter Dearlove, 1973. 186p.

Loney, Martin. Rhodesia: White Racism and Imperial Response. Baltimore: Penguin, 1975. 235p.

Mtshali, B. Vulindlela. Rhodesia: Background to Conflict. London: Leslie Frewin, 1968. 255p.

Peterson, Robert W. (ed.). Rhodesian Independence. New York: Facts on File, 1971. 142p.

*Smith, Ian Douglas. "Southern Rhodesia and its future," Afr. Affairs, LXIII (1964), 13-22.

6.   POLITICS AND GOVERNMENT

GENERAL

Bowman, Larry Wells. Politics in Rhodesia: White Power in an
    African State. Cambridge, Mass.: Harvard UP, 1973. 206p.

Clutton-Brock, Guy & Molly Clutton-Brock. Cold Comfort Confronted.
    London: Mowbrays, 1972. 201p.

Ellis, B. S. In Search of Meaning. Salisbury: Kingstons, 1973.
    111p.

Good, Robert C. "Rhodesia: more of the same with a difference,"
    Afr. Today, 23, 3 (1976), 37-45.

Harrigan, Anthony. One Against the Mob. With Questions Answered
    by Prime Minister Ian Smith. Arlington, Va.: Crestwood Books,
    1966. 169p.

Henderson, I. "White populism in Southern Rhodesia," Compar.
    Studies in Soc. & Hist., XIV, 4 (1972), 387-99.

Hull, R. W. "The conflict in Rhodesia," Current Hist., (Nov. 1976),
    149-52, 185.

Ilsley, Lucretia L. Rhodesia's Independence Struggle: The Role of
    Immigrants and Investors. New York: Andronicus Pub. Co.,
    1976. 384p.

Mufuka, Kenneth N. "Reflections on Southern Rhodesia: an African
    viewpoint," Afr. Today, 24, 2 (1977), 51-63.

Murray, David J. The Governmental System in Southern Rhodesia.
    Oxford: Clarendon, 1970. 393p.

O'Meara, Patrick. Rhodesia: Racial Conflict or Coexistence?
    Ithaca, N.Y.: Cornell UP, 1975. 217p.

Peck, A. J. A. Rhodesia Accuses. Boston: Western Islands, 1966.
    175p.

Plangger, Albert (ed.). Rhodesia--The Moral Issue: Pastoral Let-
    ters of the Catholic Bishops. Gwelo: Mambo, 1968. 108p.

Rea, F. B. (ed.). Southern Rhodesia--The Price of Freedom: A
    Series of Essays by Nine Rhodesians on the Present Political
    Impasse. Bulawayo: Stuart Manning, 1964. 141p.

Todd, Judith. Rhodesia. London: Panther Books, 1967. 189p.

Young, Kenneth. Rhodesia and Independence: A Study in British

<u>Colonial Policy</u>. London: J. M. Dent, 1969. 684p.

Zelniker, Shimshon. "Settlers and settlement: the Rhodesian crisis, 1974-5," <u>Afr. Today</u>, 22, 2 (1975), 23-44.

AFRICAN NATIONALISM
AND NATIONALIST MOVEMENTS

Daniels, George M. (ed.). <u>Drums of War: The Continuing Crisis
in Rhodesia</u>. New York: Third Press, 1974. 190p.

Day, John. "The creation of political myths: African nationalism in
Southern Rhodesia," <u>Jnl. So. Afr. Studies</u>, II, 1 (1975), 52-65.

_____. <u>International Nationalism: The Extraterritorial Relations
of Southern Rhodesian African Nationalists</u>. London: Routledge
& Kegan Paul, 1967. 141p.

Dumbutshena, Enoch. <u>Zimbabwe Tragedy</u>. Nairobi: East Afr. Pub.
House, 1975. 138p.

Kapungu, Leonard T. <u>Rhodesia: The Struggle for Freedom</u>. New
York: Orbis Books, 1974. 177p.

Khapoya, Vincent. "African political factors in post-UDI Rhodesia:
resistance or accommodation," <u>Ufahamu</u>, IV (1973), 127-44.

Kornegay, Francis A., Jr. "Zimbabwe nationalism in Southern Rhodesia," <u>Current Bibliog. on African Affairs</u>, II, 2 (1969), 5-11.

Malandu, D. Enos. "African political organizations in Rhodesia,"
<u>Genève-Afrique</u>, VII, 2 (1968), 60-77.

Mlambo, Eshmael. <u>No Future Without Us: The Story of the African
National Council in Zimbabwe</u>. London: ANC, 1973. 48p.

_____. <u>Rhodesia: The Struggle for a Birthright</u>. London: C.
Hurst, 1972. 333p.

Mubako, Simbi. "The quest for unity in the Zimbabwe liberation
movement," <u>Issue</u>, V, 1 (Waltham, Mass., 1975), 1-17.

Mutambirwa, James A. Chamunorwa. "The impact of Christianity
on nationalism in Zimbabwe: a critique of the Sithole thesis,"
<u>Jnl. So. Afr. Affairs</u>, I (Oct. 1976), 69-81.

Mutasa, Didymus. <u>Rhodesian Black Behind Bars</u>. London: Mow-
brays, 1974. 150p.

Ngwenyama, Niko M. "Rhodesia approaches collapse: a study of
settler resistance to African nationalism," <u>Ufahamu</u>, V, 3 (1975),
11-61.

*Nkomo, Joshua. "Southern Rhodesia: apartheid country," in James Duffy & Robert A. Manners (eds.), Africa Speaks (Princeton, N.J.: Princeton UP, 1961), 130-43.

————— & Julius Nyerere. Rhodesia: The Case for Majority Rule. New Delhi: Indian Council for Afr., 1966. 60p.

Nyangoni, Christopher & Gideon Nyandoro (eds.). Zimbabwe Independence Movements: Select Documents. London: Rex Collings, c.1978.

Roder, Wolf (ed.). Voices of Liberation in Southern Africa. Waltham, Mass.: Afr. Studies Assoc., 1972. 95p.

*Shamuyarira, Nathan M. Crisis in Rhodesia. London: Andre Deutsch; Nairobi: East Afr. Pub. House, 1967. 240p.

————— (ed.). Essays on the Liberation of Southern Africa. Dar es Salaam: Tanzania Pub. House, 1975. 95p.

*Sithole, Ndabaningi. African Nationalism. 2nd ed., London: OUP, 1968. 196p. (First pub., Cape Town: OUP, 1959).

Todd, Judith. The Right to Say No. London: Sidgwick & Jackson, 1972. 200p.

Weinrich, A. K. H. "The African National Council: past performance and present prospects in Rhodesia," Afr. Today, 22, 1 (1975), 5-29.

Wilmer, S. E., et al. Zimbabwe Now. London: Rex Collings, 1973. 141p.

CONSTITUTIONS AND LAW

Bourdillon, M. F. C. "Is 'customary law' customary?," Nada, XI, 2 (1975), 140-9.

Child, H. F. The History and Extent of Recognition of Tribal Law in Rhodesia. Salisbury: Ministry of Internal Affairs, 1965. 147p.

Evans, Morgan O. The Statute Law of Southern Rhodesia from the Charter to December 31, 1898. Salisbury: Argus Print. & Pub. Co., 1899. 804p.

Fox, H. Wilson. Memorandum on Constitutional, Political, and Financial and Other Questions Concerning Rhodesia. London: BSAC, 1912. 337p.

Howman, Roger. "Trial by jury in Southern Rhodesia: an historical and sociological analysis of an institution, " Rhodes-Livingstone Jnl., 7 (1949), 41-67.

International Commission of Jurists. Racial Discrimination and Repression in Southern Rhodesia. London: Catholic Inst. for Internat. Relat.; Geneva: Internat. Comm. of Jurists, 1976. 119p.

*International Defence and Aid Fund. Ian Smith's Hostages: Political Prisoners in Rhodesia. London: IDAF for Southern Africa, 1976. 38p.

Mittlebeeler, Emmet V. African Custom and Western Law: The Development of the Rhodesian Criminal Law for Africans. New York: Afr. Pub. Corp., 1975. 256p.

Niesewand, Peter. In Camera: Secret Justice in Rhodesia. London: Weidenfeld & Nicolson, 1973. 209p.

Palley, Claire. The Constitutional History and Law of Southern Rhodesia, 1888-1965, with Special Reference to Imperial Control. Oxford: Clarendon, 1966. 872p.

Passmore, Gloria C. Local Government Legislation in Southern Rhodesia up to 30th September, 1963. Salisbury: Univ. of Rhod., 1966. 75p.

_____ & M. T. Mitchell. Source Book of Parliamentary Elections and Referenda in Southern Rhodesia, 1898-1962. Salisbury: Univ. of Rhod., 1966. 255p.

St. Leger, F. Y. "Crime in Southern Rhodesia, " Rhodes-Livingstone Jnl., 38 (1966), 11-4.

Seymour, Lindsay F. The Law and You; An Introduction to the Legal System of Rhodesia. Gwelo: Mambo, 1965. 88p.

Weinberg, S. An Outline of Constitutional Law of Rhodesia and Nyasaland. Salisbury: Gov. Printer, 1959. 150p.

Willson, Francis Michael Glenn & Gloria C. Passmore. Holders of Administrative and Ministerial Office, 1894-1964 and Members of the Legislative Council, 1889-1923 and the Legislative Assembly, 1924-1964. Salisbury: Univ. of Rhod., 1966. 77p.

GOVERNMENT AFRICAN POLICY
AND ADMINISTRATION

Evans, Ifor Leslie. Native Policy in Southern Africa: An Outline. Cambridge, England: Cambridge UP, 1934. 177p.

Hemans, Herbert Nassau. The Log of a Native Commissioner.
  Rep., Bulawayo: BOR, 1971. 224p. (First pub., 1935).

Holleman, John Frederick. Chief, Council, and Commissioner:
  Some Problems of Government in Rhodesia. Assen, the Nether-
  lands: Royal van Gorcum Ltd., 1968. 391p.

Howman, Roger H. G. "African local government in Southern Rhodesia," Jnl. Afr. Administ., XI (London, July 1959), 132-8.

_____. "The Native Affairs Department and the African," Nada,
  31 (1945), 42-9.

Maclean, Joy. The Guardians: A Story of Rhodesia's Outposts.
  Bulawayo: BOR, 1974. 305p.

Masterson, Mrs. G. M. "Memories of a native commissioner's
  wife," (part 1), Nada, XI, 4 (1977), 397-406.

*Mnyanda, B. J. In Search of Truth: A Commentary on Certain
  Aspects of Southern Rhodesia's Native Policy. Bombay: Hind
  Kitabs, 1954. 173p.

Passmore, Gloria C. The National Policy of Community Development in Rhodesia, with Special Reference to Local Government
  of the African Rural Areas. Salisbury: Univ. of Rhod., 1972.
  360p.

Steele, Murray C. "Community development in Rhodesia" [rev.
  art.], Rhod. Hist., 4 (1973), 105-12.

_____. "The foundation of a 'Native' policy: Southern Rhodesia,
  1923-1933." Ph.D. thesis, Simon Fraser Univ., Burnaby, Brit.
  Col., 1972.

Stigger, P. "The emergence of the Native Department in Matabeleland, 1893-1899," Rhod. Hist., 7 (1976), 38-64.

*Tawse-Jollie, Ethel. "Native administration in Southern Rhodesia,"
  Jnl. Royal Soc. Arts, 83 (Aug. 30, 1935), 973-85.

Weinrich, A. K. H. [Sister Mary Aquina]. Chiefs and Councils in
  Rhodesia. London: Heinemann, 1971. 272p.

INTERNATIONAL RELATIONS

Beza, S. Jabulani. "The Organization of African Unity and Rhodesia." Ph.D. thesis, Southern Illinois Univ., Carbondale,
  1971. 202p.

Carter, Gwendolen & Patrick O'Meara (eds.). Southern Africa in
  Crisis. Bloomington: Indiana UP, 1977. 279p.

Good, Robert C. U.D.I.: The International Politics of the Rhodesian Rebellion. London: Faber & Faber, 1973. 368p.

Grundy, Kenneth W. Confrontation and Accommodation in Southern Africa. Berkeley: Univ. Calif. Press, 1974. 385p.

Lake, Anthony. The "Tar Baby" Option: American Policy Toward Southern Rhodesia. New York: Columbia UP, 1976. 316p.

Potholm, C. P. & R. Dale (eds.). Southern Africa in Perspective: Essays in Regional Politics. New York: Free Press, 1972. 418p.

Sprack, John. Rhodesia: South Africa's Sixth Province: An Analysis of the Links Between South Africa and Rhodesia. London: IDAF, 1974. 87p.

MILITARY AND POLICE: GOVERNMENT FORCES

Black, C. Fighting Forces of Rhodesia. 2 vols., Salisbury: H. C. P. Andersen, 1974-5. 95, 70p.

Capell, A. E. The 2nd Rhodesia Regiment in East Africa. London: Simson, 1923. 132p.

Fothergill, E. R. Gunners: A Narrative of the Gunners of Southern Rhodesia During the Second World War. Salisbury: So. Rhod. Artillery Assoc., 1947. 383p.

*Gann, Lewis H. "The development of Southern Rhodesia's military system, 1890-1953," Nat. Arch. Rhod. Occas. Papers, No. 1 (1965), 60-79.

_____. "From ox waggon to armoured car in Rhodesia," Military Rev. (Ft. Leavenworth, Kansas, 1968), 63-72.

Gibbs, Peter. The History of the British South African Police. Vol. 1: 1889-1903; Vol. 2: 1903-1939. Salisbury: Kingstons, 1972, 1974. 266, 244p.

Hamley, R. The Regiment: An Outline of the History and Uniforms of the British South African Police. Cape Town: T. V. Bulpin, 1971. 120p.

Harding, Colin. Frontier Patrols: A History of the British South African Police and Other Rhodesian Forces. London: G. Bell, 1937. 372p.

Hickman, A. S. Men Who Made Rhodesia: A Register of Those Who Served in the British South Africa Company's Police. Salisbury: BSAC, 1960. 462p.

Bibliography-- 428

_____. Rhodesia Served the Queen: Rhodesian Forces in the
Boer War, 1899-1902. 2 vols., Salisbury: Gov. Printer, 1970,
c.1976.

Macdonald, J. F. The War History of Southern Rhodesia, 1939-45.
2 vols., Salisbury: Gov. Printer, 1947, 1950. 353, 319p.
(Rep., Bulawayo, 1976).

Owen, Christopher. The Rhodesian African Rifles. London: Leo
Cooper, 1970. 75p.

R[oberts], R. S. "Towards a history of Rhodesia's armed forces"
[rev. art.], Rhod. Hist., 5 (1974), 103-10.

MILITARY...: MODERN AFRICAN LIBERATION MOVEMENT

Baldock, R. W. "Towards a history of insurgency in Rhodesia"
[rev. art.], Rhod. Hist., 5 (1974), 97-102.

*Gann, Lewis H. "Rhodesia and the prophets," Afr. Affairs, 71
(April 1972), 125-43.

Kirk, Tony. "Politics and violence in Rhodesia," Afr. Affairs, 74
(1975), 3-38.

Maxey, Kees. The Fight for Zimbabwe. London: Rex Collings,
1975. 196p.

Morris, Michael. Armed Conflict in Southern Africa. Cape Town:
Jeremy Spence, 1974.

Venter, Al J. The Zambesi Salient: Conflict in Southern Africa.
Cape Town: H. Timmins, 1974. 395p.

Waldman, Selma. "Armed struggle in Zimbabwe: a brief chronology
of guerrilla warfare, 1966-74," Ufahamu, V, 3 (Los Angeles,
1975), 4-10.

Weinrich, A. K. H. "Strategic resettlement in Rhodesia," Jnl. So.
Afr. Studies, III, 2 (1977), 207-29.

Wilkinson, A. R. Insurgency in Rhodesia, 1957-1973: An Account
and Assessment. London: Internat. Instit. for Strategic Studies,
1973. 47p.

7. RELIGION

GENERAL

Aquina, Mary [A. K. H. Weinrich]. "Christianity in a Rhodesian tribal trust land, " Afr. Soc. Research, 1 (1966), 1-40.

Dachs, Anthony J. (ed.). Christianity South of the Zambezi. Gwelo:
    Mambo, 1973. 213p.

Murray, Jocelyn & Terence Ranger (eds.). [Report on the Confer-
    ence on the History of Central African Religious Systems, Univ.
    of Zambia, Aug. 31-Sept. 8, 1972], African Relig. Research,
    II, 2 (Los Angeles, Nov. 1972). 34p.

*Ranger, Terence O. State and Church in Southern Rhodesia, 1919-
    1939. Salisbury: Hist. Assoc. of Rhod. & Nyasa., 1961. 28p.

_____ & John Weller (eds.). Themes in the Christian History
    of Central Africa. Berkeley: Univ. of Calif. Press; London:
    Heinemann, 1975. 285p.

Thomas, Norman E. "Christianity, politics and the Manyika: a
    study of the influence of religious attitudes and loyalties on po-
    litical values and activities of Africans in Rhodesia." Ph.D.
    thesis, Boston Univ., 1968. 396p.

AFRICAN RELIGIONS AND BELIEFS

Beach, David N. "Great Zimbabwe as a Mwari-cult centre, " Rhod.
    Prehistory, 11 (1973).

Bourdillon, Michael F. C. "The manipulation of myth in a Tavara
    chiefdom, Africa, XLII, 2 (1972), 112-21.

_____. "Spirit mediums in Shona belief and practice, " Nada, XI,
    1 (1974), 30-7.

Crawford, J. R. Witchcraft and Sorcery in Rhodesia. London:
    OUP, 1967. 312p.

Daneel, M. L. The God of the Matopo Hills: An Essay on the
    Mwari Cult in Rhodesia. The Hague: Mouton, 1970. 95p.

Fortune, George. "Who was Mwari?, " Rhod. Hist., 4 (1973), 1-20.

Fry, P. "Zezuru mediums: a study of the legitimacy and authority
    of Shona spirit mediums." Ph.D. thesis, Univ. of London, 1969.

Garbett, G. Kingsley. "Spirit mediums as mediators in Korekore
    society, " in John Beattie & John Middleton (eds.), Spirit Medium-
    ship and Society in Africa (New York: Africana Pub. Co., 1969),
    104-27.

Gelfand, Michael. "The Mhondoro cult among the Manyika peoples
    of the eastern region of Mashonaland, " Nada, XI, 1 (1974),
    64-93.

_____ . Shona Religion (with Special Reference to the Makore-kore). Cape Town: Juta, 1962. 184p.

_____ . Shona Ritual, with Special Reference to the Chaminuka Cult. Cape Town: Juta, 1959. 217p.

Lancaster, C. S. "The Zambezi Goba [northern Shona] ancestral cult, " Africa, 47, 3 (1977), 229-41.

Mtetwa, Richard M. G. "The relationship between the Gutu dynasty and the Mwari cult in the 19th century, " Rhod. Hist., 6 (1975), 89-95.

*Ranger, Terence O. "The meaning of Mwari, " Rhod. Hist., 5 (1974), 5-17.

Werbner, Richard P. "Atonement ritual and guardian-spirit posession among Kalanga, " Africa, XXXIV (July 1964), 206-23.

INDEPENDENT CHRISTIAN CHURCHES

Daneel, Marthinus Louis. Old and New in Southern Shona Independent Churches. Vol. 1: Background and Rise of the Major Movements; Vol. 2: Church Growth--Causative Factors and Recruitment Techniques. The Hague: Mouton, 1971, 1974. 557, 373p. (More vols. projected).

_____ . Zionism and Faith Healing in Rhodesia: Aspects of African Independent Churches. Trans. by V. A. February. The Hague: Mouton, 1970. 64p.

Martin, Marie-Louise. "The Mai Chaza Church in Rhodesia, " in D. B. Barrett (ed.), African Initiatives in Religion (Nairobi: East Afr. Pub. House, 1971), 109-21.

Murphree, M. W. "Indigenous independency and the church in Rhodesia" [rev. art.], Rhod. Hist., 3 (1972), 83-7.

_____ . "Religious interdependence among the Budjga Vapostori, " in D. B. Barrett (ed.), African Initiatives in Religion (Nairobi: East Afr. Pub. House, 1971), 171-80.

*Ranger, T. O. "The early history of independency in Southern Rhodesia, " in W. M. Watt (ed.), Religion in Africa (Edinburgh: Edinburgh Univ., 1964), 52-74.

MISSIONS AND MISSIONARY CHURCHES

Bhebe, Ngwabi M. B. "Christian missions in Matabeleland, 1859-1923. " Ph.D. thesis, Univ. of London, 1972. 338p.

431   --Religion

Clinton, Iris. Hope Fountain Story. Gwelo: Mambo, 1969. 101p.

_____. "These Vessels...": The Story of Inyati, 1859-1959.
Bulawayo: S. Manning, 1959. 96p.

Gelfand, Michael (ed.). Gubulawayo and Beyond: Letters and
Journals of the Early Jesuit Missionaries to Zambesia (1879-
1887). London: G. Chapman, 1968. 496p.

King, Paul S. (comp.). Missions in Southern Rhodesia. Inyati:
Inyati Centenary Trust, 1959. 80p.

*Knight-Bruce, G. W. H. Memories of Mashonaland. London &
New York: E. Arnold, 1895. 242p. (Rep., Bulawayo: BOR,
1970).

Kwidini, D. J. "The missionary factor in Rhodesian native policy,
1910-1939." Ph.D. thesis, Cambridge Univ., 1970-1.

Mashingaidze, E. K. "Christian missions in Mashonaland, Southern
Rhodesia, 1890 to 1930." D.Phil. thesis, Univ. of York, 1973.

*Moffat, John S., et al. The Matabele Mission: A Selection from
the Correspondence of John and Emily Moffat, David Livingstone,
and others, 1858-1878. Ed. by J. P. R. Wallis. London:
Chatto & Windus, 1945. 268p.

Murphree, Marshall W. Christianity and the Shona. London: Ath-
lone; New York: Humanities Press, 1969. 200p.

Peaden, W. R. Missionary Attitudes to Shona Culture, 1890-1923.
Salisbury: Cent. Afr. Hist. Assoc., 1970. 41p.

Rea, W. F. "Agony on the Zambezi: the first Christian mission to
southern Africa and its failure, 1580-1759," Zambezia, 1, 2
(1970), 46-53.

_____. "Christian missions in central Africa, 1560-1890 and
modern missiology," Rhod. Hist., 3 (1972), 1-10.

_____. "The missions as an economic factor on the Zambezi,
1580-1759." Ph.D. thesis, Univ. of London, 1974.

Rennie, John Keith. "Christianity, colonialism and the origins of
nationalism among the Ndau of Southern Rhodesia, 1890-1935."
Ph.D. thesis, Northwestern Univ., 1973. 659p.

Smith, Edwin W. The Way of the White Fields in Rhodesia; A
Survey of Christian Enterprise in Northern and Southern Rhodesia. London: World Dominion Press, 1928. 172 + 20p.

Zvobgo, Chengetai J. M. "Christian missionaries and the establishment of colonial rule in Zimbabwe, 1888-1898, " Jnl. So. Afr. Affairs, II, 2 (1977), 217-34.

_____. "The Revd. E. T. J. Nemapare and the African Methodist Church in Southern Rhodesia, 1930-1950, " Rhod. Hist., 6 (1975), 83-7.

_____. "The Wesleyan Methodist missions in Southern Rhodesia, 1891-1945." Ph. D. thesis, Univ. of Edinburgh, 1974. 423p.

8. SCIENCES

GEOGRAPHY: GENERAL

Andrews, B. The Lowveld: An Economic Survey. Salisbury: Ramsay Parker Pubs., 1965. 84p.

Brain, C. K. "New evidence for climatic change during the middle and late Stone Age times in Rhodesia, " S. Afr. Arch. Bullet., XXIV, 3 & 4 (1969), 95-6, 127-43.

Collins, Michael Owen (ed.). Rhodesia: Its Natural Resources and Economic Development. Salisbury: M. O. Collins, 1965. 52p. (Atlas with gazetteer.)

Hussey, D. E. "The Rhodesian lowveld, " Geog. Mag., XXXVIII, (London, 1965), 249-62.

Kay, George. Rhodesia: A Human Geography. London: Univ. of London Press, 1970. 192p.

Macdonald, John Forest. Zambesi River. London: Macmillan, 1955. 239p.

Phillipson, D. W. (ed.). Mosi-oa-Tunya: A Handbook to the Victoria Falls Region. 3rd ed., Salisbury: Longman Rhodesia, 1975. 222p. (Earlier eds. edited by J. D. Clark and Brian M. Fagan under title, The Victoria Falls: A Handbook...).

*Summers, Roger F. H. "Environment and culture in Southern Rhodesia: a study in the 'personality' of a land-locked country, " Proc. Amer. Philosoph. Soc., CIV (June 1960), 266-92.

Wellington, John H. Southern Africa; A Geographical Study. Vol. 1: Physical Geography; Vol. 2: Economic and Human Geography. Cambridge: Cambridge UP, 1955. 528, 283p.

GEOGRAPHY: KARIBA DAM AND REGION

Clements, Frank. Kariba: The Struggle with the River God. New
    York: Putnam, 1960. 223p.

Colson, Elizabeth. "Land rights and land use among the Valley
    Tonga of the Rhodesian Federation: the background to the
    Kariba resettlement programme," in Daniel Biebuyck (ed.),
    African Agrarian Systems (London: OUP, 1963), 137-56.

Deare, A. G. & A. R. Brownlee Walker. "Kariba," Nada, XI, 3
    (1976), 271-82.

De Blij, Harm Jan. "Some aspects of the Kariba hydroelectric
    project," Jnl. of Geog., LVI, 9 (Lancaster, Pa., 1957), 413-28.

Howarth, David Armine. The Shadow of the Dam. New York:
    Macmillan, 1961. 175p.

Lagus, Charles. Operation Noah. London: Kimber, 1959. 176p.

Robbins, Eric & Ronald Legge. Animal Dunkirk: The Story of Lake
    Kariba and "Operation Noah." London: H. Jenkins, 1959. 188p.

Scudder, Thayer. "The ecological hazards of making a lake,"
    Natural Hist. (Feb. 1969), 68-72.

GEOLOGY

Anderson, R. B. A Handbook of Useful Information Regarding Base Min-
    erals. Salisbury: Dept. of Mines, Lands & Surveys, 1957. 184p.

Lightfoot, B. "The geological map of Southern Rhodesia," Proc.
    Rhod. Scien. Assoc., 41 (April 1946), 13-21.

McAdam, J. "The flying mapmakers: some notes on the early
    development of air survey in central and southern Africa,"
    Rhodesiana, 30 (June 1974), 44-64.

Pelletier, Rene A. Mineral Resources in South-Central Africa.
    New York: OUP, 1964. 277p.

Swift, W. H. "An outline of the geology of Southern Rhodesia," S.
    Rhod. Geol. Survey Bullet., 50 (Salisbury, 1961), 73p.

Tyndale-Biscoe, Ronald McIver. The Rhodesia Geological Survey:
    The First Half-Century, 1910-1960. Salisbury: Rhodesia Geol.
    Survey, 1972. 73p.

Worst, B. G. "The Great Dyke of Southern Rhodesia," S. Rhod.
    Geol. Survey Bullet., 47 (1960), 234p.

MEDICINE AND HEALTH

Blair, D. M. "Human trypanosomiasis in Southern Rhodesia, 1911-1938," Trans. Royal Soc. Tropical Med. & Hygiene, XXXII (1939), 720-42.

Carr, W. R. & Michael Gelfand. "The biochemistry of the African in Southern Rhodesia," Trans. Roy. Soc. Trop. Med. & Hyg., LIV (1960), 474-92.

Chavunduka, G. L. "Interaction of folk and scientific beliefs in Shona medical practice." Ph.D. thesis, Univ. of London, 1972.

Gelfand, Michael. Diet and Tradition in an African Culture. Edinburgh: E. & S. Livingstone, 1970. 248p.

_____. Medicine and Magic of the Mashona. Cape Town: Juta, 1956. 266p.

_____. A Service to the Sick: A History of the Health Services for Africans in Southern Rhodesia, 1890-1953. Gwelo: Mambo, 1976. 187p.

_____. "Suicide and attempted suicide among the Shona," Zambezia, 2, 2 (1972), 73-8.

_____. Tropical Victory: An Account of the Influence of Medicine on the History of Southern Rhodesia, 1890-1923. Cape Town: Juta, 1953. 256p.

_____. Witch Doctor: Traditional Medicine Man of Rhodesia. Don Mills, Ontario: Collins, 1964. 191p.

Mozley, Alan. The Control of Bilharzia in Southern Rhodesia. Salisbury, 1944. 307p.

Phimister, Ian R. "The 'Spanish' influenza pandemic of 1918 and its impact on the Southern Rhodesian mining industry," Cent. Afr. Jnl. of Med., XIX, 7 (1973).

Watson, Malcolm. African Highway; The Battle for Health in Central Africa. London: Murray, 1953. 294p.

NATURAL HISTORY: FAUNA

Alston, Madeline. Sunbirds and Jacarandas, a Bird-Lover in Rhodesia. Cape Town: Juta, 1951. 253p.

Astley Maberly, Charles Thomas. Animals of Rhodesia. Cape Town: H. Timmins, 1959. 211p.

Balneaves, Elizabeth. Elephant Valley: The Adventures of J.

McGregor Brooks, Game and Tsetse Officer, Kariba. London:
Lutterworth, 1962. 179p.

Cooper, Richard. Butterflies of Rhodesia. Salisbury: Longman
Rhodesia, 1973. 138p.

Davison, Ted. Wankie: The Story of a Great Game Reserve.
Cape Town: Books of Africa, 1967. 211p.

Ginn, Peter. Birds of the Highveld. Salisbury: Longman Rhodesia, 1972. 124p.

Jubb, Rex A. An Illustrated Guide to the Freshwater Fishes of the
Zambezi River, Lake Kariba, Pungwe, Sabi, Lundi, and Limpopo Rivers. Bulawayo: S. Manning, 1961. 171p.

Priest, Cecil Damer. A Guide to the Birds of Southern Rhodesia
and a Record of Their Nesting Habits. London: W. Clowes,
1929. 233p.

*Selous, Frederick Courteney. African Nature Notes and Reminis-
cences. London: Macmillan, 1908. 356p. (Rep., Salisbury:
Pioneer Head, 1968).

*Summers, Roger. "Archaeological distribution and a tentative his-
tory of tsetse infestation in Rhodesia and the northern Transvaal," Arnoldia (Aug. 1967), 18p.

NATURAL HISTORY: FLORA

Boughey, A. S. "The vegetation types of Southern Rhodesia," Proc.
Rhod. Sci. Assoc., 49 (1961), 54-98.

Coates Palgrave, Olive H. Trees of Central Africa. Salisbury:
Nat. Pubs. Trust., 1956. 466p.

Drummond, R. B. & Keith Coates Palgrave. Common Trees of the
Highveld. Salisbury: Longman Rhodesia, 1973. 99p.

Guy, Graham L. & B. D. Elkington. The Bundu Book of Flowers,
Trees and Grasses. Salisbury: Longmans, 1965. 97p.

Huntly, Jeff. Veld Sketchbook. Bulawayo: Mardon, 1974. 168p.

Lightfoot, Christopher. Common Veld Grasses of Rhodesia. Salisbury: Nat. Resources Board, 1971. 131p.

Linley, Kay & Bryan Baker. Flowers of the Veld. Salisbury:
Longman Rhodesia, 1972. 120p.

Wild, H., H. M. Biegel, & S. Mavi. A Rhodesian Botanical Dictionary of African and English Plant Names. Salisbury: Gov.
Printer, 1973. 281p.

9. SOCIAL

GENERAL

Dixon, Hilde. "Urgent research in Rhodesia," Bullet. Internat.
Committ. on Urgent Anthrop. & Ethnol. Research, 10 (Vienna,
1968), 79-88.

Goldin, Bennie. Unhappy Marriage and Divorce: The Problem in
Rhodesia. Salisbury: Kingstons, 1971. 120p.

Weinrich, A. K. H. Black and White Elites in Rural Rhodesia.
Manchester: Manchester UP, 1973. 256p.

AFRICAN SOCIETIES (General)

Bourdillon, Michael F. C. Myths About Africans, Myth-Making in
Rhodesia. Gwelo: Mambo, 1976. 35p.

_____. The Shona Peoples: An Ethnography of the Contemporary
Shona, with Special Reference to Their Religion. Gwelo: Mambo, 1976. 399p.

*Bullock, Charles. The Mashona and the Matabele. Cape Town:
Juta, 1950. 310p.

Garbett, G. Kingsley. "Prestige, status, and power in a modern
valley Korekore chiefdom, Rhodesia," Africa, XXXVII, 3 (1967),
307-26.

Gelfand, Michael. The Genuine Shona: Survival Values of an African Culture. Gwelo: Mambo, 1973. 205p.

_____. "The Shona woman," Nada, X, 5 (1973), 41-50.

Hayes, M. E. "The Nambiya [Nanzwa] people of Wange," Nada,
XI, 4 (1977), 385-93.

Holleman, John F. African Interlude. Cape Town: Nasionale
Boekhandel, 1958. 269p.

_____. "Some 'Shona' tribes of Southern Rhodesia," in Elizabeth
Colson & Max Gluckman (eds.), Seven Tribes of British Central
Africa (London: OUP, 1951), 354-95.

Hughes, A. J. B. Kin, Caste and Nation Among the Rhodesian
Ndebele. Manchester, England: Manchester UP for Rhodes-
Livingstone Instit., 1956. 86p.

*Jones, Neville. Early Days and Native Ways in Southern Rhodesia.
Bulawayo, 1945.

Kuper, Hilda, A. J. B. Hughes, & Jap van Velsen. The Shona and
Ndebele of Southern Rhodesia. London: Internat. Afr. Instit.,
1954. 129p.

Lancaster, C. S. "Brideservice, residence, and authority among
the Goba (N. Shona) of the Zambezi valley," Africa, XLIV, 1
(1974), 46-64.

Latham, C. J. K. "The social organization of the Mashona," Nada,
X, 5 (1973), 35-40; XI, 1 (1974), 96-108.

*Posselt, F. W. T. Fact and Fiction: A Short Account of the Na-
tives of Southern Rhodesia. Bulawayo: Rhod. Print. & Pub.
Co., 1935. 210p.

_____. A Survey of the Native Tribes of Southern Rhodesia.
Salisbury: Gov. Printer, 1927. 31p.

DEMOGRAPHY

Clarke, D. "Population and family planning in the economic development of Rhodesia," Zambezia, 2, 1 (1971), 11-22.

_____. "Problems of family planning amongst Africans in Rho-
desia," Rhod. Jnl. Econ., VI (1972), 35-47.

Johnson, R. W. M. "African population estimates--myth or reality?,"
Rhod. Jnl. Econ., III (1969), 5-16.

Kay, George. Distribution and Density of African Population in Rhodesia. Hull, England: Univ. of Hull, 1972. 28p.

_____. "Population problems and development strategy in Rho-
desia," Scottish Geog. Mag. (Dec. 1976), 148-60.

EDUCATION

Atkinson, Norman Joseph. Teaching Rhodesians: A History of Educational Policy in Rhodesia. London: Longman, 1972. 244p.

Bone, R. C. "Educational development in Rhodesia," Rhod. Jnl.
Econ., II (1968), 5-27.

Carruthers-Smith, E. E. "African education in Bulawayo from 1893,"
Nada, X, 3 (1971), 81-93.

Challiss, R. J. "The origins of the educational system of Southern
Rhodesia," Rhod. Hist., 4 (1973), 57-77.

Davies, C. S. "African education in Rhodesia," Nada, X, 1 (1969),
23-37.

Flood, D. "Industrial school at Inyati, 1919-1933," Nada, X, 2
(1970), 69-77.

Hirsch, Morris I. "Trends in African education," Rhod. Jnl.
Econ., I (1967), 52-7.

Mashingaidze, E. K. "Government-mission co-operation in African
education in Southern Rhodesia up to the late 1920's," Kenya
Hist. Rev., 4, 2 (1976), 265-81.

*Mnyanda, B. J. "Native education," Nada, 10 (1932), 108-11.

Murphree, Betty Jo. "The acculturative effects of schooling on
African attitudes and values," Zambezia, 2, 2 (1972), 11-21.

Murphree, Marshall W. "A village school and community development in a Rhodesian Tribal Trust Land," Zambezia, 1, 2
(1970), 13-23.

_____ (ed.). Education, Race and Employment in Rhodesia.
Salisbury: Assoc. of Round Tables in Central Afr., 1975.
478p.

Ndlovu, Saul. "Student protest in Salisbury," Afr. Today, 21, 2
(1974), 39-42.

Parker, Franklin. African Development and Education in Southern
Rhodesia. Columbus: Ohio State UP, 1960. 165p.

*Ranger, Terence O. "African attempts to control education in east
and central Africa, 1900-1939," Past & Present, XXXII (1965),
57-85.

Reader, D. H. "African education and the Rhodesian employer,"
Rhod. Jnl. Econ., VI (1972), 1-8.

Rich, F. "The economics of African education," Rhod. Jnl. Econ.,
I (1967), 3-12.

IMMIGRANT SOCIETIES

Boggie, Jeannie M. Experiences of Rhodesia's Pioneer Women:
Being a True Account of the Adventures of the Early White Wom-
en Settlers in Southern Rhodesia from 1890. Bulawayo: Philpott & Collins, 1938. 264p.

Dotson, Floyd & Lillian Dotson. The Indian Minority of Zambia,
Rhodesia, and Malawi. New Haven, Conn.: Yale UP, 1968.
444p.

*Gann, Lewis H. & Peter Duignan. "Changing patterns of a white
elite: Rhodesia and other settlers," in Gann & Duignan (eds.),

The History and Politics of Colonialism, 1914-1960 (Cambridge, England: Cambridge UP, 1970), 92-170.

_____ & _____. White Settlers in Tropical Africa. Harmondsworth, England: Penguin, 1962. 170p.

Garstin, Crosbie. The Sunshine Settlers. London: P. Allan, 1935. 240p. (Rep., Bulawayo: BOR, 1971).

Good, Kenneth. "Settler colonialism in Rhodesia," Afr. Affairs (Jan. 1964), 10-36.

Hodder-Williams, R. H. "Afrikaners in Rhodesia," Afr. Soc. Research, 18 (1974).

Kosmin, Barry A. "'Freedom, justice and commerce': some factors affecting Asian trading patterns in Southern Rhodesia, 1897-1942," Rhod. Hist., 6 (1975), 15-32.

_____. "A note on Southern Rhodesian Jewry, 1890-1936," Jewish Jnl. of Sociology, 15 (1973), 205-12.

_____. "On the imperial frontier: the pioneer community of Salisbury in November 1897," Rhod. Hist., 2 (1971), 25-37.

Macdonald, Sheila. Sally in Rhodesia. Rep., Bulawayo: BOR, 1970. 207p. (First pub., 1927).

Patel, H. H. Indians in Uganda and Rhodesia: Some Comparative Perspectives on a Minority in Africa. Denver: Univ. of Denver, 1973. 38p.

Schutz, Barry M. "European population patterns, cultural persistence, and political change in Rhodesia," Canadian Jnl. Afr. Studies, VII, 1 (1973), 3-25.

Shinn, Allison. "The early European settlement of the southwestern districts of Rhodesia" (Part 1), Rhodesiana, 30 (June 1974), 13-33.

Stigger, P. "Asians in Rhodesia and Kenya: a comparative political history," Rhod. Hist., 1 (1970), 1-8.

White Migration to Southern Africa. Geneva: Centre Europe Tiers Monde, 1975. 260p.

INTER-ETHNIC RELATIONS

Austin, Reginald. Racism and Apartheid in Southern Africa: Rhodesia. Paris: UNESCO Press, 1975. 122p.

Bull, Theodore (ed.). Rhodesian Perspective. London: M. Joseph, 1967. 184p.

Davies, Dorothy Keyworth (comp.). Race Relations in Rhodesia:
A Survey for 1972-73. London: Rex Collings, 1975. 458p.

Kinloch, G. C. "Changing black reaction to white domination,"
Rhod. Hist., 5 (1974), 67-78.

_____. "Social types and race relations in the colonial setting:
a case study of Rhodesia," Phylon, XXXIII, 3 (Atlanta, 1972),
276-89.

Mazobere, Crispin Christopher Godzo. "Racial conflict in Rhodesia." Ph.D. thesis, Boston Univ., 1973. 322p.

*Muzorewa, Abel T. "Black vs. white in Rhodesia," Crisis, LXXIX
(London, May 1972), 151-5.

Rogers, Cyril A. & C. Frantz. Racial Themes in Southern Rhodesia: The Attitudes and Behavior of the White Population.
New Haven, Conn.: Yale UP, 1962. 427p.

URBAN STUDIES

Barber, William J. "Urbanisation and economic growth: the cases
of two white settler territories," in Horace Miner (ed.), The
City in Modern Africa (New York: Praeger, 1967), 91-125.

Cubbitt, V. S. & R. C. Riddell. The Urban Poverty Datum Line
in Rhodesia. Salisbury: Univ. of Rhod., 1974. 139p.

Davenport, T. R. H. "Rhodesian and South African policies for
urban Africans: some historical similarities and contrasts,"
Rhod. Hist., 3 (1972), 63-76.

Gussman, B. W. African Life in an Urban Area: A Study of the
African Population of Bulawayo. Bulawayo: Fed. of Afr. Welfare Societies, 1952-3. 2 vols.

Hartley, G. H. "The development of an African urban community,"
Nada, 35 (1958), 87-98.

Ibbotson, Percy. "Urbanization in Southern Rhodesia," Africa, XVI
(April 1946), 73-82.

Kay, George & Michael Smout (eds.). Salisbury: A Geographical
Survey of the Capital of Rhodesia. New York: Afr. Pub. Co.,
1977. 119p.

Kileff, Clive. "Black suburbanites: adaptation to Western culture
in Salisbury, Rhodesia." Ph.D. thesis, Rice Univ., Houston,
1970. 192p.

_____ & Wade C. Pendleton (eds.). Urban Man in Southern

Africa. Gwelo: Mambo, 1975. 254p.

Lukhero, M. B. "The social characteristics of an emergent elite
    in Harare, " in P. C. Lloyd (ed.), The New Elites of Tropical
    Africa (London: OUP, 1966), 126-38.

McEwan, P. J. M. "The urban African population of Southern Rho-
    desia, " Civilisations, 13, 3 (1963), 267-90.

Schwab, W. B. "Social stratification in Gwelo," in Aidan Southall
    (ed.), Social Change in Modern Africa (London: OUP, 1961),
    126-44.

Weinrich, Anna Katherina H. Mucheke: Race, Status, and Politics
    in a Rhodesian Community. London: UNESCO, 1976. c.250p.

                    10. SERIAL PUBLICATIONS

        Wherever possible, the following pieces of information
        are given for each serial: full title, former or variant
        titles, place of publication, publisher or sponsor, origi-
        nal and terminal dates of publication, frequency of pub-
        lication.

NEWSPAPERS AND GENERAL INTEREST

*African Daily News (a.k.a. Central Afr. Daily News). Salisbury:
        Afr. Newspapers Ltd., 1956-64. Daily.

*African Times. Salisbury: Ministry of Information, 1965+. Fort-
        nightly.

*African Weekly. Salisbury: Afr. Newspapers Ltd., 1944-62 (ab-
        sorbed by African Daily News, q.v.).

*Bantu Mirror (orig., Native Mirror). Bulawayo, c.1934-44; Salis-
        bury: Afr. Newspapers Ltd., 1944-62. Weekly (absorbed by
        African Daily News, q.v.).

*Bulawayo Chronicle (a.k.a. The Chronicle). Bulawayo: Rhod. Print.
        & Pub. Co., 1894+. Daily since 1897.

*Central African Examiner. Salisbury, 1957-65. Fortnightly.

Citizen. Umtali (independent). Weekly.

Evening Standard. Salisbury, 1958-62. Daily, Monday-Friday.

Federal Government Gazette. Salisbury: Fed. Gov., 1953-63.
        Weekly.

Focus on Rhodesia. Salisbury: Ministry of Information, March
    1976+. Fortnightly? (successor to Rhod. Commentary, q.v.).

Fort Victoria Advertiser. Fort Victoria (independent). Weekly.

Gatooma Mail (& Mining Gazette). Gatooma, c.1910?+. Weekly.

*Gwelo Times. Gwelo (independent), 1897+. Weekly.

Illustrated Life Rhodesia. Salisbury: Graham Pub. Co., 1968+.
    Fortnightly.

Midlands Observer. Gwelo (independent). Weekly.

*Moto. Gwelo: Mambo Press, 1959-74. Weekly.

National Observer. Salisbury: Independent Newspapers. Weekly.

Rhodesia & Eastern Africa (a.k.a. East Africa & Rhodesia). Lon-
    don: 1924-67. Weekly.

Rhodesia Calls (formerly, Africa Calls--From Rhodesia). Salisbury:
    Nat. Tourist Board, c.1960+. Bimonthly.

*Rhodesia Herald (orig., Mashonaland Herald & Zambesian Times).
    Salisbury: Rhod. Print. & Pub. Co., 1891+. Daily.

Rhodesian Commentary. Salisbury: Ministry of Information, Immi-
    gration & Tourism, 1966-76. Fortnightly. (Superseded by
    Focus on Rhodesia, q.v.)

Rhodesian Government Gazette. Salisbury: Gov. Printer, 1965+.
    Weekly. (Supersedes Southern Rhodesian Government Gazette,
    1923-64, and BSAC Government Gazette, c.1894-1923.)

Rhodesian Monthly Review. Salisbury, 1939-64. Monthly.

*Sunday Mail. Salisbury: Rhod. Print. & Pub. Co., c.1932+.
    Weekly.

Sunday News. Bulawayo: Rhod. Print. & Pub. Co., c.1932+.
    Weekly.

Umbowo. Umtali: United Methodist Church. Monthly.

*Umtali Post. Umtali: Rhod. Print. & Pub. Co., 1893+. Daily.

Weekly Express. Bulawayo. Weekly.

SCHOLARLY, SPECIALIZED, AND PROFESSIONAL

Arnoldia. Salisbury: Nat. Museums of Rhod., 1964+. Irregular.

443 --Serials

Central African Journal of Medicine. Salisbury, 1955+. Monthly.

Central African Who's Who [title varies]. Salisbury, 1953-6.
Annual. (Absorbed by Who's Who in Southern Africa, q.v.)

Chamber of Mines Journal. Salisbury: Thomson Newspapers,
1959+. Monthly.

Geological Survey Bulletin. Salisbury: Dept. of Geol. Survey,
1951+. Irregular.

Journal of Southern African Affairs: An Interdisciplinary Research
Quarterly. College Park: Univ. of Maryland, 1976+. Quarterly.

Journal of Southern African Studies. Oxford: OUP, 1974+ Semi-
annual.

Mapolisa: The Magazine of African Members of the BSAP. Salisbury: BSAP, 1938-63. Monthly. (Absorbed by Outpost, q.v.)

Mbire; Historical Research South of the Zambezi. Salisbury: David
Beach, 1971; Cent. Afr. Hist. Assoc., 1972+. Irregular annual.

Mining in Rhodesia. Salisbury: Thomson Newspapers, 1950+. Annual.

Modern Farming (formerly, Modern Farming in Central Africa).
Salisbury: Rhod. Farmer Pubs., 1964?+. Quarterly.

Mohlomi: Journal of Southern African Historical Studies. Roma,
Lesotho: Nat. Univ. of Lesotho, 1976+.

Monthly Digest of Statistics. Salisbury: Central Statistical Office,
1964-7. Monthly. (Superseded by Quarterly Statistical Summary, q.v.)

Murimi. Gwelo: African Farmers Union, ? -c.1977. Monthly.

*Nada (a.k.a. N.A.D.A.); The Southern Rhodesia Native Affairs
Department Annual. Salisbury: Dept. of Native Affairs, 1923-
63; Ministry of Internal Affairs, 1964+. Annual.

Occasional Papers of the National Archives of Rhodesia (& Nyasaland). Salisbury: Gov. Printer, 1963+. Irregular.

Occasional Papers of the National Museums and Monuments of Rhodesia. Bulawayo, 1932+. Irregular.

The Outpost. Salisbury: BSAP, 1911+. Monthly.

The Pioneer: Journal of the Rhodesia Pioneers' & Early Settlers'

Society. Bulawayo, 1968+. Irregular.

Proceedings of the Geographical Association of Rhodesia. Salisbury: Univ. of Rhod., Dept. of Geog., 1968+. Annual.

Proceedings & Transactions of the Rhodesia Scientific Association. Salisbury: Rhod. Scient. Assoc., 1899+. Annual. (The phrase "& Transactions" added to title in 1933.)

Proceedings of the Rhodesian Economic Society. Salisbury: Rhod. Econ. Soc., 1959-66. Semi-annual, 1959, 1961-2; annual, 1960, 1963-6. (Superseded by Rhodesian Journal of Economics, q.v.)

Quarterly Statistical Summary. Salisbury: Central Stat. Off., 1967+. Quarterly.

Rhodesia Railways Magazine. Bulawayo: Rhod. Railways, 1952+. Monthly.

Rhodesia Research Index: Register of Current Research in Rhodesia. Salisbury: Dept. of the Prime Minister, Scientific Liaison Off. & Univ. of Rhod., Library Ref. Dept., 1971+. Annual.

Rhodesia Science News. Salisbury: Assoc. of Scien. Socs. in Rhod., 1967+. Monthly.

Rhodesia(n) Agricultural Journal. Salisbury: Ministry of Agriculture, 1903+. Bimonthly.

Rhodesian Farmer. Salisbury: Nat. Farmers Union, 1930+. Weekly.

*Rhodesian History. Salisbury: Cent. Afr. Hist. Assoc., 1970+. Annual.

Rhodesian Journal of Agricultural Research. Salisbury: Ministry of Agriculture, 1963+. Semiannual.

Rhodesian Journal of Economics. Salisbury: Rhod. Econ. Soc., 1967+. Quarterly. (Supersedes Proceedings of the Rhodesian Economic Society, q.v.)

Rhodesian Law Journal (orig., Rhodesian-Nyasaland Law Journal). Salisbury: Univ. (College) of Rhod. (& Nyasa.), Dept. of Law, 1961+. Semiannual.

Rhodesian Librarian. Salisbury: Rhod. Lib. Assoc., 1969+. Quarterly. (Supersedes Rhodesian & Nyasaland Library Association Newsletter).

Rhodesian Mining (& Engineering) Review. Salisbury, 1936-63. (Absorbed by Chamber of Mines Journal, q.v.)

Rhodesian Prehistory. Salisbury: Mashonaland Prehistory Soc.,
 1969+. Irregular quarterly?

Rhodesian Property & Finance. Salisbury, 1956-c.1976. Monthly.

Rhodesian Tobacco Journal. Salisbury: Thomson Newspapers,
 1949+. Monthly.

*Rhodesiana. Salisbury: Rhodesiana Soc., 1956+. Annual, 1956-
 62; semi-annual, 1963+.

Sitima. Bulawayo: Rhodesia Railways, 1948+. Monthly.

Who's Who in Southern Africa (title varies). Johannesburg, 1907+.
 Annual. (Absorbed Central African Who's Who, q.v., in 1959).

Zambezia: A Journal of Social Studies in Southern and Central
 Africa. Salisbury: Univ. of Rhod., 1969+. Semiannual.